经典原版书库

数据库系统实现

（英文版·第2版）

Database System Implementation

(Second Edition)

（美）

Hector Garcia-Molina
斯坦福大学
Jeffrey D. Ullman
斯坦福大学
Jennifer Widom
斯坦福大学

著

机械工业出版社
China Machine Press

本书英文影印版由 Pearson Education Asia Ltd. 授权机械工业出版社独家出版。未经出版者书面许可，不得以任何方式复制或抄袭本书内容。

仅限于中华人民共和国境内（不包括中国香港、澳门特别行政区和中国台湾地区）销售发行。

本书封面贴有 Pearson Education（培生教育出版集团）激光防伪标签，无标签者不得销售。

版权所有，侵权必究

本书法律顾问　北京市展达律师事务所

本书版权登记号：图字：01-2009-5643

图书在版编目（CIP）数据

数据库系统实现（英文版·第 2 版）/（美）加西亚 – 莫利纳（Garcia-Molina，H.）等著. —北京：机械工业出版社，2010.1

（经典原版书库）

书名原文：Database System Implementation，Second Edition

ISBN 978-7-111-28860-2

Ⅰ. 数… Ⅱ. 加… Ⅲ. 数据库系统 – 英文 Ⅳ. TP311. 13

中国版本图书馆 CIP 数据核字（2009）第 195847 号

机械工业出版社（北京市西城区百万庄大街 22 号　邮政编码　100037）
责任编辑：迟振春
北京京师印务有限公司印刷
2011 年 12 月第 1 版第 2 次印刷
150mm×214mm·20. 75 印张
标准书号：ISBN 978-7-111-28860-2
定价：55. 00 元

凡购本书，如有缺页、倒页、脱页，由本社发行部调换
客服热线：（010）88378991；88361066
购书热线：（010）68326294；88379649；68995259
投稿热线：（010）88379604
读者信箱：hzjsj@ hzbook. com

出版者的话

文艺复兴以降,源远流长的科学精神和逐步形成的学术规范,使西方国家在自然科学的各个领域取得了垄断性的优势;也正是这样的传统,使美国在信息技术发展的六十多年间名家辈出、独领风骚。在商业化的进程中,美国的产业界与教育界越来越紧密地结合,计算机学科中的许多泰山北斗同时身处科研和教学的最前线,由此而产生的经典科学著作,不仅擘划了研究的范畴,还揭示了学术的源变,既遵循学术规范,又自有学者个性,其价值并不会因年月的流逝而减退。

近年,在全球信息化大潮的推动下,我国的计算机产业发展迅猛,对专业人才的需求日益迫切。这对计算机教育界和出版界都既是机遇,也是挑战;而专业教材的建设在教育战略上显得举足轻重。在我国信息技术发展时间较短的现状下,美国等发达国家在其计算机科学发展的几十年间积淀和发展的经典教材仍有许多值得借鉴之处。因此,引进一批国外优秀计算机教材将对我国计算机教育事业的发展起到积极的推动作用,也是与世界接轨、建设真正的世界一流大学的必由之路。

机械工业出版社华章分社较早意识到“出版要为教育服务”。自1998年开始,华章分社就将工作重点放在了遴选、移译国外优秀教材上。经过多年的不懈努力,我们与 Pearson, McGraw-Hill, Elsevier, MIT, John Wiley & Sons, Cengage 等世界著名出版公司建立了良好的合作关系,从他们现有的数百种教材中甄选出 Andrew S. Tanenbaum, Bjarne Stroustrup, Brain W. Kernighan, Dennis Ritchie, Jim Gray, Afred V. Aho, John E. Hopcroft, Jeffrey D. Ullman, Abraham Silberschatz, William Stallings, Donald E. Knuth, John L. Hennessy, Larry L. Peterson 等大师名家的一批经典作品,以“计算机科学丛书”为总称出版,供读者学习、研究及珍藏。大理石纹理的封面,也正体现了这套丛书的品位和格调。

"计算机科学丛书"的出版工作得到了国内外学者的鼎力襄助,国内的专家不仅提供了中肯的选题指导,还不辞劳苦地担任了翻译和审校的工作;而原书的作者也相当关注其作品在中国的传播,有的还专程为其书的中译本作序。迄今,"计算机科学丛书"已经出版了近两百个品种,这些书籍在读者中树立了良好的口碑,并被许多高校采用为正式教材和参考书籍。其影印版"经典原版书库"作为姊妹篇也被越来越多实施双语教学的学校所采用。

权威的作者、经典的教材、一流的译者、严格的审校、精细的编辑,这些因素使我们的图书有了质量的保证。随着计算机科学与技术专业学科建设的不断完善和教材改革的逐渐深化,教育界对国外计算机教材的需求和应用都将步入一个新的阶段,我们的目标是尽善尽美,而反馈的意见正是我们达到这一终极目标的重要帮助。华章分社欢迎老师和读者对我们的工作提出建议或给予指正,我们的联系方法如下:

华章网站:www. hzbook. com

电子邮件:hzjsj@ hzbook. com

联系电话:(010)88379604

联系地址:北京市西城区百万庄南街1号

邮政编码:100037

华章教育

华章科技图书出版中心

Preface⊖

This book covers the core of the material taught in the database sequence at Stanford. The introductory course, CS145, uses the first twelve chapters, and is designed for all students — those who want to use database systems as well as those who want to get involved in database implementation. The second course, CS245 on database implementation, covers most of the rest of the book. However, some material is covered in more detail in special topics courses. These include CS346 (implementation project), which concentrates on query optimization as in Chapters 15 and 16. Also, CS345A, on data mining and Web mining, covers the material in the last two chapters.

What's New in the Second Edition

After a brief introduction in Chapter 1, we cover relational modeling in Chapters 2–4. Chapter 4 is devoted to high-level modeling. There, in addition to the E/R model, we now cover UML (Unified Modeling Language). We also have moved to Chapter 4 a shorter version of the material on ODL, treating it as a design language for relational database schemas.

The material on functional and multivalued dependencies has been modified and remains in Chapter 3. We have changed our viewpoint, so that a functional dependency is assumed to have a set of attributes on the right. We have also given explicitly certain algorithms, including the "chase," that allow us to manipulate dependencies. We have augmented our discussion of third normal form to include the 3NF synthesis algorithm and to make clear what the tradeoff between 3NF and BCNF is.

Chapter 5 contains the coverage of relational algebra from the previous edition, and is joined by (part of) the treatment of Datalog from the old Chapter 10. The discussion of recursion in Datalog is either moved to the book's Web site or combined with the treatment of recursive SQL in Chapter 10 of this edition.

Chapters 6–10 are devoted to aspects of SQL programming, and they represent a reorganization and augmentation of the earlier book's Chapters 6, 7, 8, and parts of 10. The material on views and indexes has been moved to its own chapter, number 8, and this material has been augmented with a discussion of

⊖ 本书分两部分出版，第 1~12 章为《数据库系统基础教程》，第 13~23 章为《数据库系统实现》。前半部分已由机械工业出版社出版（书号： 978-7-111-24733-3），本书为后半部分。——编辑注

important new topics, including materialized views, and automatic selection of indexes.

The new Chapter 9 is based on the old Chapter 8 (embedded SQL). It is introduced by a new section on 3-tier architecture. It also includes an expanded discussion of JDBC and new coverage of PHP.

Chapter 10 collects a number of advanced SQL topics. The discussion of authorization from the old Chapter 8 has been moved here, as has the discussion of recursive SQL from the old Chapter 10. Data cubes, from the old Chapter 20, are now covered here. The rest of the chapter is devoted to the nested-relation model (from the old Chapter 4) and object-relational features of SQL (from the old Chapter 9).

Then, Chapters 11 and 12 cover XML and systems based on XML. Except for material at the end of the old Chapter 4, which has been moved to Chapter 11, this material is all new. Chapter 11 covers modeling; it includes expanded coverage of DTD's, along with new material on XML Schema. Chapter 12 is devoted to programming, and it includes sections on XPath, XQuery, and XSLT.

Chapter 13 begins the study of database implementation. It covers disk storage and the file structures that are built on disks. This chapter is a condensation of material that, in the first edition, occupied Chapters 11 and 12.

Chapter 14 covers index structures, including B-trees, hashing, and structures for multidimensional indexes. This material also condenses two chapters, 13 and 14, from the first edition.

Chapters 15 and 16 cover query execution and query optimization, respectively. They are similar to the old chapters of the same numbers. Chapter 17 covers logging, and Chapter 18 covers concurrency control; these chapters are also similar to the old chapters with the same numbers. Chapter 19 contains additional topics on concurrency: recovery, deadlocks, and long transactions. This material is a subset of the old Chapter 19.

Chapter 20 is on parallel and distributed databases. In addition to material on parallel query execution from the old Chapter 15 and material on distributed locking and commitment from the old Chapter 19, there are several new sections on distributed query execution: the map-reduce framework for parallel computation, peer-to-peer databases and their implementation of distributed hash tables.

Chapter 21 covers information integration. In addition to material on this subject from the old Chapter 20, we have added a section on local-as-view mediators and a section on entity resolution (finding records from several databases that refer to the same entity, e.g., a person).

Chapter 22 is on data mining. Although there was some material on the subject in the old Chapter 20, almost all of this chapter is new. It covers association rules and frequent itemset mining, including both the famous A-Priori Algorithm and certain efficiency improvements. Chapter 22 includes the key techniques of shingling, minhashing, and locality-sensitive hashing for finding similar items in massive databases, e.g., Web pages that quote substantially from other Web pages. The chapter concludes with a study of clustering, especially for massive datasets.

Chapter 23, all new, addresses two important ways in which the Internet has impacted database technology. First is search engines, where we discuss algorithms for crawling the Web, the well-known PageRank algorithm for evaluating the importance of Web pages, and its extensions. This chapter also covers data-stream-management systems. We discuss the stream data model and SQL language extensions, and conclude with several interesting algorithms for executing queries on streams.

Prerequisites

We have used the book at the "mezzanine" level, in a sequence of courses taken both by undergraduates and by beginning graduate students. The formal prerequisites for the course are Sophomore-level treatments of:

1. Data structures, algorithms, and discrete math, and

2. Software systems, software engineering, and programming languages.

Of this material, it is important that students have at least a rudimentary understanding of such topics as: algebraic expressions and laws, logic, basic data structures, object-oriented programming concepts, and programming environments. However, we believe that adequate background is acquired by the Junior year of a typical computer science program.

Exercises

The book contains extensive exercises, with some for almost every section. We indicate harder exercises or parts of exercises with an exclamation point. The hardest exercises have a double exclamation point.

Support on the World Wide Web

The book's home page is

    http://infolab.stanford.edu/~ullman/dscb.html

You will find errata as we learn of them, and backup materials, including homeworks, projects, and exams. We shall also make available there the sections from the first edition that have been removed from the second.

In addition, there is an accompanying set of on-line homeworks and programming labs using a technology developed by Gradiance Corp. See the section following the Preface for details about the GOAL system. GOAL service can be purchased at http://www.prenhall.com/goal. Instructors who want to use the system in their classes should contact their Prentice-Hall representative or request instructor authorization through the above Web site.

There is a solutions manual for instructors available at

http://www.prenhall.com/ullman

This page also gives you access to GOAL and all book materials.

Acknowledgements

We would like to thank Donald Kossmann for helpful discussions, especially concerning XML and its associated programming systems. Also, Bobbie Cochrane assisted us in understanding trigger semantics for a earlier edition.

A large number of people have helped us, either with the development of this book or its predecessors, or by contacting us with errata in the books and/or other Web-based materials. It is our pleasure to acknowledge them all here.

Marc Abromowitz, Joseph H. Adamski, Brad Adelberg, Gleb Ashimov, Donald Aingworth, Teresa Almeida, Brian Babcock, Bruce Baker, Yunfan Bao, Jonathan Becker, Margaret Benitez, Eberhard Bertsch, Larry Bonham, Phillip Bonnet, David Brokaw, Ed Burns, Alex Butler, Karen Butler, Mike Carey, Christopher Chan, Sudarshan Chawathe.

Also Per Christensen, Ed Chang, Surajit Chaudhuri, Ken Chen, Rada Chirkova, Nitin Chopra, Lewis Church, Jr., Bobbie Cochrane, Michael Cole, Alissa Cooper, Arturo Crespo, Linda DeMichiel, Matthew F. Dennis, Tom Dienstbier, Pearl D'Souza, Oliver Duschka, Xavier Faz, Greg Fichtenholtz, Bart Fisher, Simon Frettloeh, Jarl Friis.

Also John Fry, Chiping Fu, Tracy Fujieda, Prasanna Ganesan, Suzanne Garcia, Mark Gjol, Manish Godara, Seth Goldberg, Jeff Goldblat, Meredith Goldsmith, Luis Gravano, Gerard Guillemette, Himanshu Gupta, Petri Gynther, Zoltan Gyongyi, Jon Heggland, Rafael Hernandez, Masanori Higashihara, Antti Hjelt, Ben Holtzman, Steve Huntsberry.

Also Sajid Hussain, Leonard Jacobson, Thulasiraman Jeyaraman, Dwight Joe, Brian Jorgensen, Mathew P. Johnson, Sameh Kamel, Jawed Karim, Seth Katz, Pedram Keyani, Victor Kimeli, Ed Knorr, Yeong-Ping Koh, David Koller, Gyorgy Kovacs, Phillip Koza, Brian Kulman, Bill Labiosa, Sang Ho Lee, Younghan Lee, Miguel Licona.

Also Olivier Lobry, Chao-Jun Lu, Waynn Lue, John Manz, Arun Marathe, Philip Minami, Le-Wei Mo, Fabian Modoux, Peter Mork, Mark Mortensen, Ramprakash Narayanaswami, Hankyung Na, Mor Naaman, Mayur Naik, Marie Nilsson, Torbjorn Norbye, Chang-Min Oh, Mehul Patel, Soren Peen, Jian Pei.

Also Xiaobo Peng, Bert Porter, Limbek Reka, Prahash Ramanan, Nisheeth Ranjan, Suzanne Rivoire, Ken Ross, Tim Roughgarten, Mema Roussopoulos, Richard Scherl, Loren Shevitz, Shrikrishna Shrin, June Yoshiko Sison,

Man Cho A. So, Elizabeth Stinson, Qi Su, Ed Swierk, Catherine Tornabene, Anders Uhl, Jonathan Ullman, Mayank Upadhyay.

Also Anatoly Varakin, Vassilis Vassalos, Krishna Venuturimilli, Vikram Vijayaraghavan, Terje Viken, Qiang Wang, Steven Whang, Mike Wiacek, Kristian Widjaja, Janet Wu, Sundar Yamunachari, Takeshi Yokukawa, Bing Yu, Min-Sig Yun, Torben Zahle, Sandy Zhang.

The remaining errors are ours, of course.

H. G.-M.
J. D. U.
J. W.
Stanford, CA
March, 2008

About the Authors

HECTOR GARCIA-MOLINA is the L. Bosack and S. Lerner Professor of Computer Science and Electrical Engineering at Stanford University. His research interests include digital libraries, information integration, and database application on the Internet. He was a recipient of the SIGMOD Innovations Award and a member of PITAC (President's Information-Technology Advisory Council). He currently serves on the Board of Directors of Oracle Corp.

JEFFREY D. ULLMAN is the Stanford W. Ascherman Professor of Computer Science (emeritus) at Stanford University. He is the author or co-author of 16 books, including *Elements of ML Programming* (Prentice Hall 1998). His research interests include data mining, information integration, and electronic education. He is a member of the National Academy of Engineering, and recipient of a Guggenheim Fellowship, the Karl V. Karlstrom Outstanding Educator Award, the SIGMOD Contributions and Edgar F. Codd Innovations Awards, and the Knuth Prize.

JENNIFER WIDOM is Professor of Computer Science and Electrical Engineering at Stanford University. Her research interests span many aspects of nontraditional data management. She is an ACM Fellow and a member of the National Academy of Engineering, she received the ACM SIGMOD Edgar F. Codd Innovations Award in 2007 and was a Guggenheim Fellow in 2000, and she has served on a variety of program committees, advisory boards, and editorial boards.

Table of Contents⊖

⊖ 第 1~12 章是《数据库系统基础教程（英文版 · 第 3 版）》的内容，这里将其列入目录
是为了保持完整性。——编辑注

II Relational Database Programming 203

5 Algebraic and Logical Query Languages 205

III   Modeling and Programming for Semistructured Data   481

11 The Semistructured-Data Model   483

Part IV

Database System Implementation

Part IV

Database System
Implementation

Chapter 13

Secondary Storage Management

Database systems always involve secondary storage — the disks and other devices that store large amounts of data that persists over time. This chapter summarizes what we need to know about how a typical computer system manages storage. We review the memory hierarchy of devices with progressively slower access but larger capacity. We examine disks in particular and see how the speed of data access is affected by how we organize our data on the disk. We also study mechanisms for making disks more reliable.

Then, we turn to how data is represented. We discuss the way tuples of a relation or similar records or objects are stored. Efficiency, as always, is the key issue. We cover ways to find records quickly, and how to manage insertions and deletions of records, as well as records whose sizes grow and shrink.

13.1 The Memory Hierarchy

We begin this section by examining the memory hierarchy of a computer system. We then focus on disks, by far the most common device at the "secondary-storage" level of the hierarchy. We give the rough parameters that determine the speed of access and look at the transfer of data from disks to the lower levels of the memory hierarchy.

13.1.1 The Memory Hierarchy

A typical computer system has several different components in which data may be stored. These components have data capacities ranging over at least seven orders of magnitude and also have access speeds ranging over seven or more orders of magnitude. The cost per byte of these components also varies, but more slowly, with perhaps three orders of magnitude between the cheapest and most expensive forms of storage. Not surprisingly, the devices with smallest capacity also offer the fastest access speed and have the highest cost per byte. A schematic of the memory hierarchy is shown in Fig. 13.1.

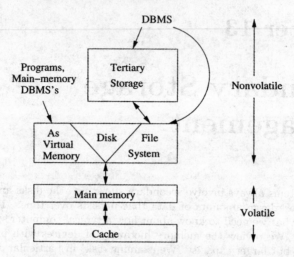

Figure 13.1: The memory hierarchy

Here are brief descriptions of the levels, from the lowest, or fastest-smallest level, up.

1. *Cache.* A typical machine has a megabyte or more of cache storage. *On-board cache* is found on the same chip as the microprocessor itself, and additional *level-2 cache* is found on another chip. Data and instructions are moved to cache from main memory when they are needed by the processor. Cached data can be accessed by the processor in a few nanoseconds.

2. *Main Memory.* In the center of the action is the computer's *main memory*. We may think of everything that happens in the computer — instruction executions and data manipulations — as working on information that is resident in main memory (although in practice, it is normal for what is used to migrate to the cache). A typical machine in 2008 is configured with about a gigabyte of main memory, although much larger main memories are possible. Typical times to move data from main memory to the processor or cache are in the 10–100 nanosecond range.

3. *Secondary Storage.* Secondary storage is typically magnetic disk, a device we shall consider in detail in Section 13.2. In 2008, single disk units have capacities of up to a terabyte, and one machine can have several disk units. The time to transfer a single byte between disk and main

Computer Quantities are Powers of 2

It is conventional to talk of sizes or capacities of computer components as if they were powers of 10: megabytes, gigabytes, and so on. In reality, since it is most efficient to design components such as memory chips to hold a number of bits that is a power of 2, all these numbers are really shorthands for nearby powers of 2. Since $2^{10} = 1024$ is very close to a thousand, we often maintain the fiction that $2^{10} = 1000$, and talk about 2^{10} with the prefix "kilo," 2^{20} as "mega," 2^{30} as "giga," 2^{40} as "tera," and 2^{50} as "peta," even though these prefixes in scientific parlance refer to 10^3, 10^6, 10^9, 10^{12} and 10^{15}, respectively. The discrepancy grows as we talk of larger numbers. A "gigabyte" is really 1.074×10^9 bytes.

We use the standard abbreviations for these numbers: K, M, G, T, and P for kilo, mega, giga, tera, and peta, respectively. Thus, 16Gb is sixteen gigabytes, or strictly speaking 2^{34} bytes. Since we sometimes want to talk about numbers that are the conventional powers of 10, we shall reserve for these the traditional numbers, without the prefixes "kilo," "mega," and so on. For example, "one million bytes" is 1,000,000 bytes, while "one megabyte" is 1,048,576 bytes.

A recent trend is to use "kilobyte," "megabyte," and so on for exact powers of ten, and to replace the third and fourth letters by "bi" to represent the similar powers of two. Thus, "kibibyte" is 1024 bytes, "mebibyte" is 1,048,576 bytes, and so on. We shall not use this convention.

---

memory is around 10 miliseconds. However, large numbers of bytes can be transferred at one time, so the matter of how fast data moves from and to disk is somewhat complex.

4. *Tertiary Storage.* As capacious as a collection of disk units can be, there are databases much larger than what can be stored on the disk(s) of a single machine, or even several machines. To serve such needs, *tertiary storage* devices have been developed to hold data volumes measured in terabytes. Tertiary storage is characterized by significantly higher read/write times than secondary storage, but also by much larger capacities and smaller cost per byte than is available from magnetic disks. Many tertiary devices involve robotic arms or conveyors that bring storage media such as magnetic tape or optical disks (e.g., DVD's) to a reading device. Retrieval takes seconds or minutes, but capacities in the petabyte range are possible.

13.1.2 Transfer of Data Between Levels

Normally, data moves between adjacent levels of the hierarchy. At the secondary and tertiary levels, accessing the desired data or finding the desired place to store data takes a great deal of time, so each level is organized to transfer large amounts of data to or from the level below, whenever any data at all is needed. Especially important for understanding the operation of a database system is the fact that the disk is organized into *disk blocks* (or just *blocks*, or as in operating systems, *pages*) of perhaps 4–64 kilobytes. Entire blocks are moved to or from a continuous section of main memory called a *buffer*. Thus, a key technique for speeding up database operations is to arrange data so that when one piece of a disk block is needed, it is likely that other data on the same block will also be needed at about the same time.

The same idea applies to other hierarchy levels. If we use tertiary storage, we try to arrange so that when we select a unit such as a DVD to read, we need much of what is on that DVD. At a lower level, movement between main memory and cache is by units of *cache lines*, typically 32 consecutive bytes. The hope is that entire cache lines will be used together. For example, if a cache line stores consecutive instructions of a program, we hope that when the first instruction is needed, the next few instructions will also be executed immediately thereafter.

13.1.3 Volatile and Nonvolatile Storage

An additional distinction among storage devices is whether they are *volatile* or *nonvolatile*. A volatile device "forgets" what is stored in it when the power goes off. A nonvolatile device, on the other hand, is expected to keep its contents intact even for long periods when the device is turned off or there is a power failure. The question of volatility is important, because one of the characteristic capabilities of a DBMS is the ability to retain its data even in the presence of errors such as power failures.

Magnetic and optical materials hold their data in the absence of power. Thus, essentially all secondary and tertiary storage devices are nonvolatile. On the other hand, main memory is generally volatile (although certain types of more expensive memory chips, such as flash memory, can hold their data after a power failure). A significant part of the complexity in a DBMS comes from the requirement that no change to the database can be considered final until it has migrated to nonvolatile, secondary storage.

13.1.4 Virtual Memory

Typical software executes in *virtual-memory*, an address space that is typically 32 bits; i.e., there are 2^{32} bytes, or 4 gigabytes, in a virtual memory. The operating system manages virtual memory, keeping some of it in main memory and the rest on disk. Transfer between memory and disk is in units of disk

Moore's Law

Gordon Moore observed many years ago that integrated circuits were improving in many ways, following an exponential curve that doubles about every 18 months. Some of these parameters that follow "Moore's law" are:

1. The number of instructions per second that can be executed for unit cost. Until about 2005, the improvement was achieved by making processor chips faster, while keeping the cost fixed. After that year, the improvement has been maintained by putting progressively more processors on a single, fixed-cost chip.

2. The number of memory bits that can be bought for unit cost and the number of bits that can be put on one chip.

3. The number of bytes per unit cost on a disk and the capacity of the largest disks.

On the other hand, there are some other important parameters that do not follow Moore's law; they grow slowly if at all. Among these slowly growing parameters are the speed of accessing data in main memory and the speed at which disks rotate. Because they grow slowly, "latency" becomes progressively larger. That is, the time to move data between levels of the memory hierarchy appears enormous today, and will only get worse.

blocks (pages). Virtual memory is an artifact of the operating system and its use of the machine's hardware, and it is not a level of the memory hierarchy.

The path in Fig. 13.1 involving virtual memory represents the treatment of conventional programs and applications. It does *not* represent the typical way data in a database is managed, since a DBMS manages the data itself. However, there is increasing interest in *main-memory database systems*, which do indeed manage their data through virtual memory, relying on the operating system to bring needed data into main memory through the paging mechanism. Main-memory database systems, like most applications, are most useful when the data is small enough to remain in main memory without being swapped out by the operating system.

13.1.5 Exercises for Section 13.1

Exercise 13.1.1: Suppose that in 2008 the typical computer has a processor chip with two processors ("cores") that each run at 3 gigahertz, has a disk of 250 gigabytes, and a main memory of 1 gigabyte. Assume that Moore's law (these factors double every 18 months) holds into the indefinite future.

a) When will terabyte main memories be common?

b) When will terahertz processor chips be common (i.e., the total number of cycles per second of all the cores on a chip will be approximately 10^{12}?

c) When will petabyte disks be common?

d) What will be a typical configuration (processor, disk, memory) in the year 2012?

! **Exercise 13.1.2:** Commander Data, the android from the 24th century on *Star Trek: The Next Generation* once proudly announced that his processor runs at "100 teraops." While an operation and a cycle may not be the same, let us suppose they are, and that Moore's law continues to hold for the next 300 years. If so, what would Data's true processor speed be?

13.2   Disks

The use of secondary storage is one of the important characteristics of a DBMS, and secondary storage is almost exclusively based on magnetic disks. Thus, to motivate many of the ideas used in DBMS implementation, we must examine the operation of disks in detail.

13.2.1   Mechanics of Disks

The two principal moving pieces of a disk drive are shown in Fig. 13.2; they are a *disk assembly* and a *head assembly*. The disk assembly consists of one or more circular *platters* that rotate around a central spindle. The upper and lower surfaces of the platters are covered with a thin layer of magnetic material, on which bits are stored. 0's and 1's are represented by different patterns in the magnetic material. A common diameter for disk platters is 3.5 inches, although disks with diameters from an inch to several feet have been built.

The disk is organized into *tracks*, which are concentric circles on a single platter. The tracks that are at a fixed radius from the center, among all the surfaces, form one *cylinder*. Tracks occupy most of a surface, except for the region closest to the spindle, as can be seen in the top view of Fig. 13.3. The density of data is much greater along a track than radially. In 2008, a typical disk has about 100,000 tracks per inch but stores about a million bits per inch along the tracks.

Tracks are organized into *sectors*, which are segments of the circle separated by *gaps* that are not magnetized to represent either 0's or 1's.[1] The sector is an indivisible unit, as far as reading and writing the disk is concerned. It is also indivisible as far as errors are concerned. Should a portion of the magnetic layer

---

[1] We show each track with the same number of sectors in Fig. 13.3. However, the number of sectors per track normally varies, with the outer tracks having more sectors than inner tracks.

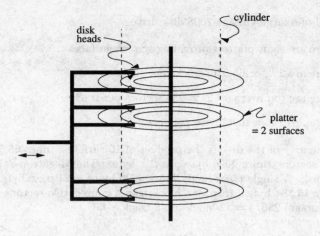

Figure 13.2: A typical disk

be corrupted in some way, so that it cannot store information, then the entire sector containing this portion cannot be used. Gaps often represent about 10% of the total track and are used to help identify the beginnings of sectors. As we mentioned in Section 13.1.2, blocks are logical units of data that are transferred between disk and main memory; blocks consist of one or more sectors.

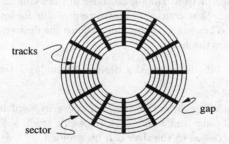

Figure 13.3: Top view of a disk surface

The second movable piece shown in Fig. 13.2, the head assembly, holds the *disk heads*. For each surface there is one head, riding extremely close to the surface but never touching it (or else a "head crash" occurs and the disk is destroyed). A head reads the magnetism passing under it, and can also alter the magnetism to write information on the disk. The heads are each attached to an arm, and the arms for all the surfaces move in and out together, being part of the rigid head assembly.

Example 13.1 : The *Megatron 747* disk has the following characteristics, which are typical of a large vintage-2008 disk drive.

- There are eight platters providing sixteen surfaces.

- There are 2^{16}, or 65,536, tracks per surface.

- There are (on average) $2^8 = 256$ sectors per track.

- There are $2^{12} = 4096$ bytes per sector.

The capacity of the disk is the product of 16 surfaces, times 65,536 tracks, times 256 sectors, times 4096 bytes, or 2^{40} bytes. The Megatron 747 is thus a terabyte disk. A single track holds 256×4096 bytes, or 1 megabyte. If blocks are 2^{14}, or 16,384 bytes, then one block uses 4 consecutive sectors, and there are (on average) $256/4 = 32$ blocks on a track. $\square$

13.2.2   The Disk Controller

One or more disk drives are controlled by a *disk controller*, which is a small processor capable of:

1. Controlling the mechanical actuator that moves the head assembly, to position the heads at a particular radius, i.e., so that any track of one particular cylinder can be read or written.

2. Selecting a sector from among all those in the cylinder at which the heads are positioned. The controller is also responsible for knowing when the rotating spindle has reached the point where the desired sector is beginning to move under the head.

3. Transferring bits between the desired sector and the computer's main memory.

4. Possibly, buffering an entire track or more in local memory of the disk controller, hoping that many sectors of this track will be read soon, and additional accesses to the disk can be avoided.

Figure 13.4 shows a simple, single-processor computer. The processor communicates via a data bus with the main memory and the disk controller. A disk controller can control several disks; we show three disks in this example.

13.2.3   Disk Access Characteristics

Accessing (reading or writing) a block requires three steps, and each step has an associated delay.

1. The disk controller positions the head assembly at the cylinder containing the track on which the block is located. The time to do so is the *seek time*.

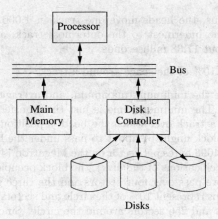

Figure 13.4: Schematic of a simple computer system

2. The disk controller waits while the first sector of the block moves under the head. This time is called the *rotational latency*.

3. All the sectors and the gaps between them pass under the head, while the disk controller reads or writes data in these sectors. This delay is called the *transfer time*.

The sum of the seek time, rotational latency, and transfer time is the *latency* of the disk.

The seek time for a typical disk depends on the distance the heads have to travel from where they are currently located. If they are already at the desired cylinder, the seek time is 0. However, it takes roughly a millisecond to start the disk heads moving, and perhaps 10 milliseconds to move them across all the tracks.

A typical disk rotates once in roughly 10 milliseconds. Thus, rotational latency ranges from 0 to 10 milliseconds, and the average is 5. Transfer times tend to be much smaller, since there are often many blocks on a track. Thus, transfer times are in the sub-millisecond range. When you add all three delays, the typical average latency is about 10 milliseconds, and the maximum latency about twice that.

Example 13.2: Let us examine the time it takes to read a 16,384-byte block from the Megatron 747 disk. First, we need to know some timing properties of the disk:

- The disk rotates at 7200 rpm; i.e., it makes one rotation in 8.33 milliseconds.

- To move the head assembly between cylinders takes one millisecond to start and stop, plus one additional millisecond for every 4000 cylinders traveled. Thus, the heads move one track in 1.00025 milliseconds and move from the innermost to the outermost track, a distance of 65,536 tracks, in about 17.38 milliseconds.

- Gaps occupy 10% of the space around a track.

Let us calculate the minimum, maximum, and average times to read that 16,384-byte block. The minimum time is just the transfer time. That is, the block might be on a track over which the head is positioned already, and the first sector of the block might be about to pass under the head.

Since there are 4096 bytes per sector on the Megatron 747 (see Example 13.1 for the physical specifications of the disk), the block occupies four sectors. The heads must therefore pass over four sectors and the three gaps between them. We assume that gaps represent 10% of the circle and sectors the remaining 90%. There are 256 gaps and 256 sectors around the circle. Since the gaps together cover 36 degrees of arc and sectors the remaining 324 degrees, the total degrees of arc covered by 3 gaps and 4 sectors is $36 \times 3/256 + 324 \times 4/256 = 5.48$ degrees. The transfer time is thus $(5.48/360) \times 0.00833 = .00013$ seconds. That is, 5.48/360 is the fraction of a rotation needed to read the entire block, and .00833 seconds is the amount of time for a 360-degree rotation.

Now, let us look at the maximum possible time to read the block. In the worst case, the heads are positioned at the innermost cylinder, and the block we want to read is on the outermost cylinder (or vice versa). Thus, the first thing the controller must do is move the heads. As we observed above, the time it takes to move the Megatron 747 heads across all cylinders is about 17.38 milliseconds. This quantity is the seek time for the read.

The worst thing that can happen when the heads arrive at the correct cylinder is that the beginning of the desired block has just passed under the head. Assuming we must read the block starting at the beginning, we have to wait essentially a full rotation, or 8.33 milliseconds, for the beginning of the block to reach the head again. Once that happens, we have only to wait an amount equal to the transfer time, 0.13 milliseconds, to read the entire block. Thus, the worst-case latency is $17.38 + 8.33 + 0.13 = 25.84$ milliseconds.

Last, let us compute the average latency. Two of the components of the latency are easy to compute: the transfer time is always 0.13 milliseconds, and the average rotational latency is the time to rotate the disk half way around, or 4.17 milliseconds. We might suppose that the average seek time is just the time to move across half the tracks. However, that is not quite right, since typically, the heads are initially somewhere near the middle and therefore will have to move less than half the distance, on average, to the desired cylinder. We leave it as an exercise to show that the average distance traveled is 1/3 of the way across the disk.

The time it takes the Megatron 747 to move 1/3 of the way across the disk is $1 + (65536/3)/4000 = 6.46$ milliseconds. Our estimate of the average latency is thus $6.46 + 4.17 + 0.13 = 10.76$ milliseconds; the three terms represent average seek time, average rotational latency, and transfer time, respectively.   □

13.2.4 Exercises for Section 13.2

Exercise 13.2.1: The *Megatron 777* disk has the following characteristics:

1. There are eight surfaces, with 100,000 tracks each.

2. Tracks hold an average of 2000 sectors of 1024 bytes each.

3. 10% of each track is used for gaps.

4. The disk rotates at 6,000 rpm.

5. The time it takes the head to move n tracks is $1 + 0.0003n$ milliseconds.

Answer the following questions about the Megatron 777.

a) What is the capacity of the disk?

b) What is the maximum seek time?

c) What is the maximum rotational latency?

d) If a block is 65,546 bytes (i.e., 64 sectors), what is the transfer time of a block?

! e) What is the average seek time?

f) What is the average rotational latency?

g) If tracks are located on the outer inch of a 3.5-inch-diameter surface, what is the average density of bits in the sectors of a track?

!! **Exercise 13.2.2:** Prove that if we move the head from a random cylinder to another random cylinder, the average distance we move is 1/3 of the way across the disk (neglecting edge effects due to the fact that the number of cylinders is finite).

!! **Exercise 13.2.3:** Exercise 13.2.2 assumes that we move from a random track to another random track. Suppose, however, that the number of sectors per track is proportional to the length (or radius) of the track, so the bit density is the same for all tracks. Suppose also that we need to move the head from a random *sector* to another random sector. Since the sectors tend to congregate at the outside of the disk, we might expect that the average head move would be less than 1/3 of the way across the tracks. Assuming that tracks occupy radii from 0.75 inches to 1.75 inches, calculate the average number of tracks the head travels when moving between two random sectors.

! **Exercise 13.2.4:** Suppose the Megatron 747 disk head is at cylinder 4096, i.e., 1/16th of the way across the cylinders. Suppose that the next request is for a block on a random cylinder. Calculate the average time to read this block.

568 CHAPTER 13. SECONDARY STORAGE MANAGEMENT

! **Exercise 13.2.5 :** To modify a block on disk, we must read it into main memory, perform the modification, and write it back. Assume that the modification in main memory takes less time than it does for the disk to rotate, and that the disk controller postpones other requests for disk access until the block is ready to be written back to the disk. For the Megatron 747 disk, what is the time to modify a block?

13.3 Accelerating Access to Secondary Storage

Just because a disk takes an average of, say, 10 milliseconds to access a block, it does not follow that an application such as a database system will get the data it requests 10 milliseconds after the request is sent to the disk controller. If there is only one disk, the disk may be busy with another access for the same process or another process. In the worst case, a request for a disk access arrives more than once every 10 milliseconds, and these requests back up indefinitely. In that case, the *scheduling latency* becomes infinite.

There are several things we can do to decrease the average time a disk access takes, and thus improve the *throughput* (number of disk accesses per second that the system can accomodate). We begin this section by arguing that the "I/O model" is the right one for measuring the time database operations take. Then, we consider a number of techniques for speeding up typical database accesses to disk:

1. Place blocks that are accessed together on the same cylinder, so we can often avoid seek time, and possibly rotational latency as well.

2. Divide the data among several smaller disks rather than one large one. Having more head assemblies that can go after blocks independently can increase the number of block accesses per unit time.

3. "Mirror" a disk: making two or more copies of the data on different disks. In addition to saving the data in case one of the disks fails, this strategy, like dividing the data among several disks, lets us access several blocks at once.

4. Use a disk-scheduling algorithm, either in the operating system, in the DBMS, or in the disk controller, to select the order in which several requested blocks will be read or written.

5. Prefetch blocks to main memory in anticipation of their later use.

13.3.1 The I/O Model of Computation

Let us imagine a simple computer running a DBMS and trying to serve a number of users who are performing queries and database modifications. For the moment, assume our computer has one processor, one disk controller, and one disk. The database itself is much too large to fit in main memory. Key parts of the database may be buffered in main memory, but generally, each piece of the database that one of the users accesses will have to be retrieved initially from disk. The following rule, which defines the *I/O model of computation*, can thus be assumed.

> **Dominance of I/O cost**: The time taken to perform a disk access is much larger than the time likely to be used manipulating that data in main memory. Thus, the number of block accesses (*Disk I/O's*) is a good approximation to the time needed by the algorithm and should be minimized.

Example 13.3 : Suppose our database has a relation R and a query asks for the tuple of R that has a certain key value k. It is quite desirable to have an index on R to identify the disk block on which the tuple with key value k appears. However it is generally unimportant whether the index tells us where on the block this tuple appears.

For instance, if we assume a Megatron 747 disk, it will take on the order of 11 milliseconds to read a 16K-byte block. In 11 milliseconds, a modern microprocessor can execute millions of instructions. However, searching for the key value k once the block is in main memory will only take thousands of instructions, even if the dumbest possible linear search is used. The additional time to perform the search in main memory will therefore be less than 1% of the block access time and can be neglected safely. □

13.3.2 Organizing Data by Cylinders

Since seek time represents about half the time it takes to access a block, it makes sense to store data that is likely to be accessed together, such as relations, on a single cylinder, or on as many adjacent cylinders as are needed. In fact, if we choose to read all the blocks on a single track or on a cylinder consecutively, then we can neglect all but the first seek time (to move to the cylinder) and the first rotational latency (to wait until the first of the blocks moves under the head). In that case, we can approach the theoretical transfer rate for moving data on or off the disk.

Example 13.4 : Suppose relation R requires 1024 blocks of a Megatron 747 disk to hold its tuples. Suppose also that we need to access all the tuples of R; for example we may be doing a search without an index or computing a sum of the values of a particular attribute of R. If the blocks holding R are distributed around the disk at random, then we shall need an average latency (10.76 milliseconds — see Example 13.2) to access each, for a total of 11 seconds.

However, 1024 blocks are exactly one cylinder of the Megatron 747. We can access them all by performing one average seek (6.46 milliseconds), after which we can read the blocks in some order, one right after another. We can read all the blocks on a cylinder in 16 rotations of the disk, since there are 16 tracks.

Sixteen rotations take $16 \times 8.33 = 133$ milliseconds. The total time to access R is thus about 139 milliseconds, and we speed up the operation on R by a factor of about 80.   □

13.3.3   Using Multiple Disks

We can often improve the performance of our system if we replace one disk, with many heads locked together, by several disks with their independent heads. The arrangement was suggested in Fig. 13.4, where we showed three disks connected to a single controller. As long as the disk controller, bus, and main memory can handle n times the data-transfer rate, then n disks will have approximately the performance of one disk that operates n times as fast.

Thus, using several disks can increase the ability of a database system to handle heavy loads of disk-access requests. However, as long as the system is not overloaded (when requests will queue up and are delayed for a long time or ignored), there is no change in how long it takes to perform any single block access. If we have several disks, then the technique known as *striping* (described in the next example) will speed up access to large database objects — those that occupy a large number of blocks.

Example 13.5 : Suppose we have four Megatron 747 disks and want to access the relation R of Example 13.4 faster than the 139-millisecond time that was suggested for storing R on one cylinder of one disk. We can "stripe" R by dividing it among the four disks. The first disk can receive blocks $1, 5, 9, \ldots$ of R, the second disk holds blocks $2, 6, 10, \ldots$, the third holds blocks $3, 7, 11, \ldots$, and the last disk holds blocks $4, 8, 12, \ldots$, as suggested by Fig. 13.5. Let us contrive that on each of the disks, all the blocks of R are on four tracks of a single cylinder.

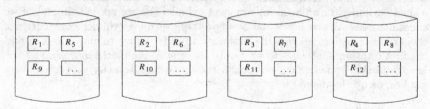

Figure 13.5: Striping a relation across four disks

Then to retrieve the 256 blocks of R on one of the disks requires an average seek time (6.46 milliseconds) plus four rotations of the disk, one rotation for each track. That is $6.46 + 4 \times 8.33 = 39.8$ milliseconds. Of course we have to wait for the last of the four disks to finish, and there is a high probability that one will take substantially more seek time than average. However, we should get a speedup in the time to access R by about a factor of three on the average, when there are four disks.   □

13.3.4 Mirroring Disks

There are situations where it makes sense to have two or more disks hold identical copies of data. The disks are said to be *mirrors* of each other. One important motivation is that the data will survive a head crash by either disk, since it is still readable on a mirror of the disk that crashed. Systems designed to enhance reliability often use pairs of disks as mirrors of each other.

If we have n disks, each holding the same data, then the rate at which we can read blocks goes up by a factor of n, since the disk controller can assign a read request to any of the n disks. In fact, the speedup could be even greater than n, if a clever controller chooses to read a block from the disk whose head is currently closest to that block. Unfortunately, the writing of disk blocks does not speed up at all. The reason is that the new block must be written to each of the n disks.

13.3.5 Disk Scheduling and the Elevator Algorithm

Another effective way to improve the throughput of a disk system is to have the disk controller choose which of several requests to execute first. This approach cannot be used if accesses have to be made in a certain sequence, but if the requests are from independent processes, they can all benefit, on the average, from allowing the scheduler to choose among them judiciously.

A simple and effective way to schedule large numbers of block requests is known as the *elevator algorithm*. We think of the disk head as making sweeps across the disk, from innermost to outermost cylinder and then back again, just as an elevator makes vertical sweeps from the bottom to top of a building and back again. As heads pass a cylinder, they stop if there are one or more requests for blocks on that cylinder. All these blocks are read or written, as requested. The heads then proceed in the same direction they were traveling until the next cylinder with blocks to access is encountered. When the heads reach a position where there are no requests ahead of them in their direction of travel, they reverse direction.

Example 13.6: Suppose we are scheduling a Megatron 747 disk, which we recall has average seek, rotational latency, and transfer times of 6.46, 4.17, and 0.13, respectively (in this example, all times are in milliseconds). Suppose that at some time there are pending requests for block accesses at cylinders 8000, 24,000, and 56,000. The heads are located at cylinder 8000. In addition, there are three more requests for block accesses that come in at later times, as summarized in Fig. 13.6. For instance, the request for a block from cylinder 16,000 is made at time 10 milliseconds.

We shall assume that each block access incurs time 0.13 for transfer and 4.17 for average rotational latency, i.e., we need 4.3 milliseconds plus whatever the seek time is for each block access. The seek time can be calculated by the rule for the Megatron 747 given in Example 13.2: 1 plus the number of tracks divided by 4000. Let us see what happens if we schedule disk accesses using

Cylinder of request	First time available
8000	0
24000	0
56000	0
16000	10
64000	20
40000	30

Figure 13.6: Arrival times for four block-access requests

the elevator algorithm. The first request, at cylinder 8000, requires no seek, since the heads are already there. Thus, at time 4.3 the first access will be complete. The request for cylinder 16,000 has not arrived at this point, so we move the heads to cylinder 24,000, the next requested "stop" on our sweep to the highest-numbered tracks. The seek from cylinder 8000 to 24,000 takes 5 milliseconds, so we arrive at time 9.3 and complete the access in another 4.3. Thus, the second access is complete at time 13.6. By this time, the request for cylinder 16,000 has arrived, but we passed that cylinder at time 7.3 and will not come back to it until the next pass.

We thus move next to cylinder 56,000, taking time 9 to seek and 4.3 for rotation and transfer. The third access is thus complete at time 26.9. Now, the request for cylinder 64,000 has arrived, so we continue outward. We require 3 milliseconds for seek time, so this access is complete at time 26.9+3+4.3 = 34.2.

At this time, the request for cylinder 40,000 has been made, so it and the request at cylinder 16,000 remain. We thus sweep inward, honoring these two requests. Figure 13.7 summarizes the times at which requests are honored.

Cylinder of request	Time completed
8000	4.3
24000	13.6
56000	26.9
64000	34.2
40000	45.5
16000	56.8

Figure 13.7: Finishing times for block accesses using the elevator algorithm

Let us compare the performance of the elevator algorithm with a more naive approach such as first-come-first-served. The first three requests are satisfied in exactly the same manner, assuming that the order of the first three requests was 8000, 24,000, and 56,000. However, at that point, we go to cylinder 16,000, because that was the fourth request to arrive. The seek time is 11 for this request, since we travel from cylinder 56,000 to 16,000, more than half way across the disk. The fifth request, at cylinder 64,000, requires a seek time of 13, and the last, at 40,000, uses seek time 7. Figure 13.8 summarizes the activity caused by first-come-first-served scheduling. The difference between the two algorithms — 14 milliseconds — may not appear significant, but recall that the number of requests in this simple example is small and the algorithms were assumed not to deviate until the fourth of the six requests. □

Cylinder of request	Time completed
8000	4.3
24000	13.6
56000	26.9
16000	42.2
64000	59.5
40000	70.8

Figure 13.8: Finishing times for block accesses using the first-come-first-served algorithm

13.3.6   Prefetching and Large-Scale Buffering

Our final suggestion for speeding up some secondary-memory algorithms is called *prefetching* or sometimes *double buffering*. In some applications we can predict the order in which blocks will be requested from disk. If so, then we can load them into main memory buffers before they are needed. One advantage to doing so is that we are thus better able to schedule the disk, such as by using the elevator algorithm, to reduce the average time needed to access a block. In the extreme case, where there are many access requests waiting at all times, we can make the seek time per request be very close to the minimum seek time, rather than the average seek time.

13.3.7   Exercises for Section 13.3

Exercise 13.3.1: Suppose we are scheduling I/O requests for a Megatron 747 disk, and the requests in Fig. 13.9 are made, with the head initially at track 16,000. At what time is each request serviced fully if:

a) We use the elevator algorithm (it is permissible to start moving in either direction at first).

b) We use first-come-first-served scheduling.

Cylinder of Request	First time available
8000	0
48000	1
4000	10
40000	20

Figure 13.9: Arrival times for four block-access requests

! Exercise 13.3.2: Suppose we use two Megatron 747 disks as mirrors of one another. However, instead of allowing reads of any block from either disk, we keep the head of the first disk in the inner half of the cylinders, and the head of the second disk in the outer half of the cylinders. Assuming read requests are on random tracks, and we never have to write:

a) What is the average rate at which this system can read blocks?

b) How does this rate compare with the average rate for mirrored Megatron 747 disks with no restriction?

c) What disadvantages do you foresee for this system?

! Exercise 13.3.3: Let us explore the relationship between the arrival rate of requests, the throughput of the elevator algorithm, and the average delay of requests. To simplify the problem, we shall make the following assumptions:

1. A pass of the elevator algorithm always proceeds from the innermost to outermost track, or vice-versa, even if there are no requests at the extreme cylinders.

2. When a pass starts, only those requests that are already pending will be honored, not requests that come in while the pass is in progress, even if the head passes their cylinder.[2]

3. There will never be two requests for blocks on the same cylinder waiting on one pass.

Let A be the interarrival rate, that is the time between requests for block accesses. Assume that the system is in steady state, that is, it has been accepting and answering requests for a long time. For a Megatron 747 disk, compute as a function of A:

---

[2]The purpose of this assumption is to avoid having to deal with the fact that a typical pass of the elevator algorithm goes fast at first, as there will be few waiting requests where the head has recently been, and slows down as it moves into an area of the disk where it has not recently been. The analysis of the way request density varies during a pass is an interesting exercise in its own right.

a) The number of requests serviced on one pass.

b) The average time taken to perform one pass.

c) The average time a request waits for service.

! **Exercise 13.3.4 :** If we read k randomly chosen blocks from one cylinder, on the average how far around the cylinder must we go before we pass all of the blocks?

!! **Exercise 13.3.5 :** In Example 13.5, we saw how dividing the data to be sorted among four disks could allow more than one block to be read at a time. Suppose our data is divided randomly among n disks, and requests for data are also random. Requests must be executed in the order in which they are received because there are dependencies among them that must be respected (see Chapter 18, for example, for motivation for this constraint). What is the average throughput for such a system?

13.4 Disk Failures

In this section we shall consider the ways in which disks can fail and what can be done to mitigate these failures.

1. The most common form of failure is an *intermittent failure*, where an attempt to read or write a sector is unsuccessful, but with repeated tries we are able to read or write successfully.

2. A more serious form of failure is one in which a bit or bits are permanently corrupted, and it becomes impossible to read a sector correctly no matter how many times we try. This form of error is called *media decay*.

3. A related type of error is a *write failure*, where we attempt to write a sector, but we can neither write successfully nor can we retrieve the previously written sector. A possible cause is that there was a power outage during the writing of the sector.

4. The most serious form of disk failure is a *disk crash*, where the entire disk becomes unreadable, suddenly and permanently.

We shall discuss parity checks as a way to detect intermittent failures. We also discuss "stable storage," a technique for organizing a disk so that media decays or failed writes do not result in permanent loss. Finally, we examine techniques collectively known as "RAID" for coping with disk crashes.

13.4.1   Intermittent Failures

An intermittent failure occurs if we try to read a sector, but the correct content of that sector is not delivered to the disk controller. If the controller has a way to tell that the sector is good or bad (as we shall discuss in Section 13.4.2), then the controller can reissue the read request when bad data is read, until the sector is returned correctly, or some preset limit, like 100 tries, is reached.

Similarly, the controller may attempt to write a sector, but the contents of the sector are not what was intended. The only way to check that the write was correct is to let the disk go around again and read the sector. A straightforward way to perform the check is to read the sector and compare it with the sector we intended to write. However, instead of performing the complete comparison at the disk controller, it is simpler to read the sector and see if a good sector was read. If so, we assume the write was correct, and if the sector read is bad, then the write was apparently unsuccessful and must be repeated.

13.4.2   Checksums

How a reading operation can determine the good/bad status of a sector may appear mysterious at first. Yet the technique used in modern disk drives is quite simple: each sector has some additional bits, called the *checksum*, that are set depending on the values of the data bits stored in that sector. If, on reading, we find that the checksum is not proper for the data bits, then we know there is an error in reading. If the checkum is proper, there is still a small chance that the block was not read correctly, but by using many checksum bits we can make the probability of missing a bad read arbitrarily small.

A simple form of checksum is based on the *parity* of all the bits in the sector. If there is an odd number of 1's among a collection of bits, we say the bits have *odd* parity and add a parity bit that is 1. Similarly, if there is an even number of 1's among the bits, then we say the bits have *even* parity and add parity bit 0. As a result:

- The number of 1's among a collection of bits and their parity bit is always even.

When we write a sector, the disk controller can compute the parity bit and append it to the sequence of bits written in the sector. Thus, every sector will have even parity.

Example 13.7: If the sequence of bits in a sector were 01101000, then there is an odd number of 1's, so the parity bit is 1. If we follow this sequence by its parity bit we have 011010001. If the given sequence of bits were 11101110, we have an even number of 1's, and the parity bit is 0. The sequence followed by its parity bit is 111011100. Note that each of the nine-bit sequences constructed by adding a parity bit has even parity.   □

Any one-bit error in reading or writing the bits and their parity bit results in a sequence of bits that has *odd parity*; i.e., the number of 1's is odd. It is easy for the disk controller to count the number of 1's and to determine the presence of an error if a sector has odd parity.

Of course, more than one bit of the sector may be corrupted. If so, the probability is 50% that the number of 1-bits will be even, and the error will not be detected. We can increase our chances of detecting errors if we keep several parity bits. For example, we could keep eight parity bits, one for the first bit of every byte, one for the second bit of every byte, and so on, up to the eighth and last bit of every byte. Then, on a massive error, the probability is 50% that any one parity bit will detect an error, and the chance that none of the eight do so is only one in 2^8, or $1/256$. In general, if we use n independent bits as a checksum, then the chance of missing an error is only $1/2^n$. For instance, if we devote 4 bytes to a checksum, then there is only one chance in about four billion that the error will go undetected.

13.4.3 Stable Storage

While checksums will almost certainly detect the existence of a media failure or a failure to read or write correctly, it does not help us correct the error. Moreover, when writing we could find ourselves in a position where we overwrite the previous contents of a sector and yet cannot read the new contents correctly. That situation could be serious if, say, we were adding a small increment to an account balance and now have lost both the original balance and the new balance. If we could be assured that the contents of the sector contained either the new or old balance, then we would only have to determine whether the write was successful or not.

To deal with the problems above, we can implement a policy known as *stable storage* on a disk or on several disks. The general idea is that sectors are paired, and each pair represents one sector-contents X. We shall refer to the pair of sectors representing X as the "left" and "right" copies, X_L and X_R. We continue to assume that the copies are written with a sufficient number of parity-check bits so that we can rule out the possibility that a bad sector looks good when the parity checks are considered. Thus, we shall assume that if the read function returns a good value w for either X_L or X_R, then w is the true value of X. The stable-storage writing policy is:

1. Write the value of X into X_L. Check that the value has status "good"; i.e., the parity-check bits are correct in the written copy. If not, repeat the write. If after a set number of write attempts, we have not successfully written X into X_L, assume that there is a media failure in this sector. A fix-up such as substituting a spare sector for X_L must be adopted.

2. Repeat (1) for X_R.

The stable-storage reading policy is to alternate trying to read X_L and X_R, until a good value is returned. Only if no good value is returned after some large, prechosen number of tries, is X truly unreadable.

13.4.4   Error-Handling Capabilities of Stable Storage

The policies described in Section 13.4.3 are capable of compensating for several different kinds of errors. We shall outline them here.

1. *Media failures.* If, after storing X in sectors X_L and X_R, one of them undergoes a media failure and becomes permanently unreadable, we can always read X from the other. If both X_L and X_R have failed, then we cannot read X, but the probability of both failing is extremely small.

2. *Write failure.* Suppose that as we write X, there is a system failure — e.g., a power outage. It is possible that X will be lost in main memory, and also the copy of X being written at the time will be garbled. For example, half the sector may be written with part of the new value of X, while the other half remains as it was. When the system becomes available and we examine X_L and X_R, we are sure to be able to determine either the old or new value of X. The possible cases are:

   (a) The failure occurred as we were writing X_L. Then we shall find that the status of X_L is "bad." However, since we never got to write X_R, its status will be "good" (unless there is a coincident media failure at X_R, which is extremely unlikely). Thus, we can obtain the old value of X. We may also copy X_R into X_L to repair the damage to X_L.

   (b) The failure occurred after we wrote X_L. Then we expect that X_L will have status "good," and we may read the new value of X from X_L. Since X_R may or may not have the correct value of X, we should also copy X_L into X_R.

13.4.5   Recovery from Disk Crashes

The most serious mode of failure for disks is the "disk crash" or "head crash," where data is permanently destroyed. If the data was not backed up on another medium, such as a tape backup system, or on a mirror disk as we discussed in Section 13.3.4, then there is nothing we can do to recover the data. This situation represents a disaster for many DBMS applications, such as banking and other financial applications.

   Several schemes have been developed to reduce the risk of data loss by disk crashes. They generally involve redundancy, extending the idea of parity checks from Section 13.4.2 or duplicated sectors, as in Section 13.4.3. The common term for this class of strategies is RAID, or *Redundant Arrays of Independent Disks.*

The rate at which disk crashes occur is generally measured by the *mean time to failure*, the time after which 50% of a population of disks can be expected to fail and be unrecoverable. For modern disks, the mean time to failure is about 10 years. We shall make the convenient assumption that if the mean time to failure is n years, then in any given year, $1/n$th of the surviving disks fail. In reality, there is a tendency for disks, like most electronic equipment, to fail early or fail late. That is, a small percentage have manufacturing defects that lead to their early demise, while those without such defects will survive for many years, until wear-and-tear causes a failure.

However, the mean time to a disk crash does not have to be the same as the mean time to data loss. The reason is that there are a number of schemes available for assuring that if one disk fails, there are others to help recover the data of the failed disk. In the remainder of this section, we shall study the most common schemes.

Each of these schemes starts with one or more disks that hold the data (we'll call these the *data disks*) and adding one or more disks that hold information that is completely determined by the contents of the data disks. The latter are called *redundant disks*. When there is a disk crash of either a data disk or a redundant disk, the other disks can be used to restore the failed disk, and there is no permanent information loss.

13.4.6 Mirroring as a Redundancy Technique

The simplest scheme is to mirror each disk, as discussed in Section 13.3.4. We shall call one of the disks the *data disk*, while the other is the *redundant disk*; which is which doesn't matter in this scheme. Mirroring, as a protection against data loss, is often referred to as *RAID level 1*. It gives a mean time to memory loss that is much greater than the mean time to disk failure, as the following example illustrates. Essentially, with mirroring and the other redundancy schemes we discuss, the only way data can be lost is if there is a second disk crash while the first crash is being repaired.

Example 13.8: Suppose each disk has a 10-year mean time to failure, which we shall take to mean that the probability of failure in any given year is 10%. If disks are mirrored, then when a disk fails, we have only to replace it with a good disk and copy the mirror disk to the new one. At the end, we have two disks that are mirrors of each other, and the system is restored to its former state.

The only thing that could go wrong is that during the copying the mirror disk fails. Now, both copies of at least part of the data have been lost, and there is no way to recover.

But how often will this sequence of events occur? Suppose that the process of replacing the failed disk takes 3 hours, which is 1/8 of a day, or 1/2920 of a year. Since we assume the average disk lasts 10 years, the probability that the mirror disk will fail during copying is $(1/10) \times (1/2920)$, or one in 29,200. If one disk fails every 10 years, then one of the two disks will fail once in 5 years on the average. One in every 29,200 of these failures results in data loss. Put another way, the mean time to a failure involving data loss is $5 \times 29{,}200 = 146{,}000$ years.   □

13.4.7   Parity Blocks

While mirroring disks is an effective way to reduce the probability of a disk crash involving data loss, it uses as many redundant disks as there are data disks. Another approach, often called *RAID level 4*, uses only one redundant disk, no matter how many data disks there are. We assume the disks are identical, so we can number the blocks on each disk from 1 to some number n. Of course, all the blocks on all the disks have the same number of bits; for instance, the 16,384-byte blocks of the Megatron 747 have $8 \times 16{,}384 = 131{,}072$ bits. In the redundant disk, the ith block consists of parity checks for the ith blocks of all the data disks. That is, the jth bits of all the ith blocks, including both the data disks and the redundant disk, must have an even number of 1's among them, and we always choose the bit of the redundant disk to make this condition true.

We saw in Example 13.7 how to force the condition to be true. In the redundant disk, we choose bit j to be 1 if an odd number of the data disks have 1 in that bit, and we choose bit j of the redundant disk to be 0 if there are an even number of 1's in that bit among the data disks. The term for this calculation is the *modulo-2 sum*. That is, the modulo-2 sum of bits is 0 if there are an even number of 1's among those bits, and 1 if there are an odd number of 1's.

Example 13.9 : Suppose for sake of an extremely simple example that blocks consist of only one byte — eight bits. Let there be three data disks, called 1, 2, and 3, and one redundant disk, called disk 4. Focus on the first block of all these disks. If the data disks have in their first blocks the following bit sequences:

$$\text{disk 1: } 11110000$$
$$\text{disk 2: } 10101010$$
$$\text{disk 3: } 00111000$$

then the redundant disk will have in block 1 the parity check bits:

$$\text{disk 4: } 01100010$$

Notice how in each position, an even number of the four 8-bit sequences have 1's. There are two 1's in positions 1, 2, 4, 5, and 7, four 1's in position 3, and zero 1's in positions 6 and 8.   □

Reading

Reading blocks from a data disk is no different from reading blocks from any disk. There is generally no reason to read from the redundant disk, but we could.

Writing

When we write a new block of a data disk, we need not only to change that block, but we need to change the corresponding block of the redundant disk so it continues to hold the parity checks for the corresponding blocks of all the data disks. A naive approach would read the corresponding blocks of the n data disks, take their modulo-2 sum, and rewrite the block of the redundant disk. That approach requires a write of the data block that is rewritten, the reading of the $n - 1$ other data blocks, and a write of the block of the redundant disk. The total is thus $n + 1$ disk I/O's.

A better approach is to look only at the old and new versions of the data block i being rewritten. If we take their modulo-2 sum, we know in which positions there is a change in the number of 1's among the blocks numbered i on all the disks. Since these changes are always by one, any even number of 1's changes to an odd number. If we change the same positions of the redundant block, then the number of 1's in each position becomes even again. We can perform these calculations using four disk I/O's:

1. Read the old value of the data block being changed.

2. Read the corresponding block of the redundant disk.

3. Write the new data block.

4. Recalculate and write the block of the redundant disk.

Example 13.10: Suppose the three first blocks of the data disks are as in Example 13.9:

$$\text{disk 1: } 11110000$$
$$\text{disk 2: } 10101010$$
$$\text{disk 3: } 00111000$$

Suppose also that the block on the second disk changes from 10101010 to 11001100. We take the modulo-2 sum of the old and new values of the block on disk 2, to get 01100110. That tells us we must change positions 2, 3, 6, and 7 of the first block of the redundant disk. We read that block: 01100010. We replace this block by a new block that we get by changing the appropriate positions; in effect we replace the redundant block by the modulo-2 sum of itself and 01100110, to get 00000100. Another way to express the new redundant block is that it is the modulo-2 sum of the old and new versions of the block

---

The Algebra of Modulo-2 Sums

It may be helpful for understanding some of the tricks used with parity checks to know the algebraic rules involving the modulo-2 sum operation on bit vectors. We shall denote this operation $\oplus$. As an example, $1100 \oplus 1010 = 0110$. Here are some useful rules about $\oplus$:

- The *commutative law*: $x \oplus y = y \oplus x$.

- The *associative law*: $x \oplus (y \oplus z) = (x \oplus y) \oplus z$.

- The all-0 vector of the appropriate length, which we denote $\bar{0}$, is the *identity* for $\oplus$; that is, $x \oplus \bar{0} = \bar{0} \oplus x = x$.

- $\oplus$ is its own inverse: $x \oplus x = \bar{0}$. As a useful consequence, if $x \oplus y = z$, then we can "add" x to both sides and get $y = x \oplus z$.

---

being rewritten and the old value of the redundant block. In our example, the first blocks of the four disks — three data disks and one redundant — have become:

$$\text{disk 1: } 11110000$$
$$\text{disk 2: } 11001100$$
$$\text{disk 3: } 00111000$$
$$\text{disk 4: } 00000100$$

after the write to the block on the second disk and the necessary recomputation of the redundant block. Notice that in the blocks above, each column continues to have an even number of 1's. □

Failure Recovery

Now, let us consider what we would do if one of the disks crashed. If it is the redundant disk, we swap in a new disk, and recompute the redundant blocks. If the failed disk is one of the data disks, then we need to swap in a good disk and recompute its data from the other disks. The rule for recomputing any missing data is actually simple, and doesn't depend on which disk, data or redundant, is failed. Since we know that the number of 1's among corresponding bits of all disks is even, it follows that:

- The bit in any position is the modulo-2 sum of all the bits in the corresponding positions of all the other disks.

If one doubts the above rule, one has only to consider the two cases. If the bit in question is 1, then the number of corresponding bits in the other disks that are 1 must be odd, so their modulo-2 sum is 1. If the bit in question is 0, then there are an even number of 1's among the corresponding bits of the other disks, and their modulo-2 sum is 0.

Example 13.11: Suppose that disk 2 fails. We need to recompute each block of the replacement disk. Following Example 13.9, let us see how to recompute the first block of the second disk. We are given the corresponding blocks of the first and third data disks and the redundant disk, so the situation looks like:

> disk 1: 11110000
> disk 2: ????????
> disk 3: 00111000
> disk 4: 01100010

If we take the modulo-2 sum of each column, we deduce that the missing block is 10101010, as was initially the case in Example 13.9. □

13.4.8 An Improvement: RAID 5

The RAID level 4 strategy described in Section 13.4.7 effectively preserves data unless there are two almost simultaneous disk crashes. However, it suffers from a bottleneck defect that we can see when we re-examine the process of writing a new data block. Whatever scheme we use for updating the disks, we need to read and write the redundant disk's block. If there are n data disks, then the number of disk writes to the redundant disk will be n times the average number of writes to any one data disk.

However, as we observed in Example 13.11, the rule for recovery is the same as for the data disks and redundant disks: take the modulo-2 sum of corresponding bits of the other disks. Thus, we do not have to treat one disk as the redundant disk and the others as data disks. Rather, we could treat each disk as the redundant disk for some of the blocks. This improvement is often called *RAID level 5*.

For instance, if there are $n + 1$ disks numbered 0 through n, we could treat the ith cylinder of disk j as redundant if j is the remainder when i is divided by $n + 1$.

Example 13.12: In our running example, $n = 3$ so there are 4 disks. The first disk, numbered 0, is redundant for its cylinders numbered 4, 8, 12, and so on, because these are the numbers that leave remainder 0 when divided by 4. The disk numbered 1 is redundant for blocks numbered 1, 5, 9, and so on; disk 2 is redundant for blocks 2, 6, 10, ..., and disk 3 is redundant for 3, 7, 11, ...

As a result, the reading and writing load for each disk is the same. If all blocks are equally likely to be written, then for one write, each disk has a 1/4 chance that the block is on that disk. If not, then it has a 1/3 chance that it will be the redundant disk for that block. Thus, each of the four disks is involved in $1/4 + (3/4) \times (1/3) = 1/2$ of the writes. □

13.4.9 Coping With Multiple Disk Crashes

There is a theory of error-correcting codes that allows us to deal with any number of disk crashes — data or redundant — if we use enough redundant disks. This strategy leads to the highest RAID "level," *RAID level 6*. We shall give only a simple example here, where two simultaneous crashes are correctable, and the strategy is based on the simplest error-correcting code, known as a *Hamming code*.

In our description we focus on a system with seven disks, numbered 1 through 7. The first four are data disks, and disks 5 through 7 are redundant. The relationship between data and redundant disks is summarized by the 3×7 matrix of 0's and 1's in Fig. 13.10. Notice that:

a) Every possible column of three 0's and 1's, except for the all-0 column, appears in the matrix of Fig. 13.10.

b) The columns for the redundant disks have a single 1.

c) The columns for the data disks each have at least two 1's.

	Data				Redundant		
Disk number	1	2	3	4	5	6	7
	1	1	1	0	1	0	0
	1	1	0	1	0	1	0
	1	0	1	1	0	0	1

Figure 13.10: Redundancy pattern for a system that can recover from two simultaneous disk crashes

The meaning of each of the three rows of 0's and 1's is that if we look at the corresponding bits from all seven disks, and restrict our attention to those disks that have 1 in that row, then the modulo-2 sum of these bits must be 0. Put another way, the disks with 1 in a given row of the matrix are treated as if they were the entire set of disks in a RAID level 4 scheme. Thus, we can compute the bits of one of the redundant disks by finding the row in which that disk has 1, and taking the modulo-2 sum of the corresponding bits of the other disks that have 1 in the same row.

For the matrix of Fig. 13.10, this rule implies:

1. The bits of disk 5 are the modulo-2 sum of the corresponding bits of disks 1, 2, and 3.

2. The bits of disk 6 are the modulo-2 sum of the corresponding bits of disks 1, 2, and 4.

3. The bits of disk 7 are the modulo-2 sum of the corresponding bits of disks 1, 3, and 4.

We shall see shortly that the particular choice of bits in this matrix gives us a simple rule by which we can recover from two simultaneous disk crashes.

Reading

We may read data from any data disk normally. The redundant disks can be ignored.

Writing

The idea is similar to the writing strategy outlined in Section 13.4.8, but now several redundant disks may be involved. To write a block of some data disk, we compute the modulo-2 sum of the new and old versions of that block. These bits are then added, in a modulo-2 sum, to the corresponding blocks of all those redundant disks that have 1 in a row in which the written disk also has 1.

Example 13.13: Let us again assume that blocks are only eight bits long, and focus on the first blocks of the seven disks involved in our RAID level 6 example. First, suppose the data and redundant first blocks are as given in Fig. 13.11. Notice that the block for disk 5 is the modulo-2 sum of the blocks for the first three disks, the sixth row is the modulo-2 sum of rows 1, 2, and 4, and the last row is the modulo-2 sum of rows 1, 3, and 4.

Disk	Contents
1)	11110000
2)	10101010
3)	00111000
4)	01000001
5)	01100010
6)	00011011
7)	10001001

Figure 13.11: First blocks of all disks

Suppose we rewrite the first block of disk 2 to be 00001111. If we sum this sequence of bits modulo-2 with the sequence 10101010 that is the old value of this block, we get 10100101. If we look at the column for disk 2 in Fig. 13.10, we find that this disk has 1's in the first two rows, but not the third. Since redundant disks 5 and 6 have 1 in rows 1 and 2, respectively, we must perform the sum modulo-2 operation on the current contents of their first blocks and the sequence 10100101 just calculated. That is, we flip the values of positions 1, 3, 6, and 8 of these two blocks. The resulting contents of the first blocks of all disks is shown in Fig. 13.12. Notice that the new contents continue to satisfy the constraints implied by Fig. 13.10: the modulo-2 sum of corresponding blocks that have 1 in a particular row of the matrix of Fig. 13.10 is still all 0's.   □

Disk	Contents
1)	11110000
2)	00001111
3)	00111000
4)	01000001
5)	11000111
6)	10111110
7)	10001001

Figure 13.12: First blocks of all disks after rewriting disk 2 and changing the redundant disks

Failure Recovery

Now, let us see how the redundancy scheme outlined above can be used to correct up to two simultaneous disk crashes. Let the failed disks be a and b. Since all columns of the matrix of Fig. 13.10 are different, we must be able to find some row r in which the columns for a and b are different. Suppose that a has 0 in row r, while b has 1 there.

Then we can compute the correct b by taking the modulo-2 sum of corresponding bits from all the disks other than b that have 1 in row r. Note that a is not among these, so none of these disks have failed. Having recomputed b, we must recompute a, with all other disks available. Since every column of the matrix of Fig. 13.10 has a 1 in some row, we can use this row to recompute disk a by taking the modulo-2 sum of bits of those other disks with a 1 in this row.

Disk	Contents
1)	11110000
2)	????????
3)	00111000
4)	01000001
5)	????????
6)	10111110
7)	10001001

Figure 13.13: Situation after disks 2 and 5 fail

Example 13.14: Suppose that disks 2 and 5 fail at about the same time. Consulting the matrix of Fig. 13.10, we find that the columns for these two disks differ in row 2, where disk 2 has 1 but disk 5 has 0. We may thus reconstruct disk 2 by taking the modulo-2 sum of corresponding bits of disks 1, 4, and 6, the other three disks with 1 in row 2. Notice that none of these three disks has failed. For instance, following from the situation regarding the first blocks in Fig. 13.12, we would initially have the data of Fig. 13.13 available after disks 2 and 5 failed.

If we take the modulo-2 sum of the contents of the blocks of disks 1, 4, and 6, we find that the block for disk 2 is 00001111. This block is correct as can be verified from Fig. 13.12. The situation is now as in Fig. 13.14.

Disk	Contents
1)	11110000
2)	00001111
3)	00111000
4)	01000001
5)	????????
6)	10111110
7)	10001001

Figure 13.14: After recovering disk 2

Now, we see that disk 5's column in Fig. 13.10 has a 1 in the first row. We can therefore recompute disk 5 by taking the modulo-2 sum of corresponding bits from disks 1, 2, and 3, the other three disks that have 1 in the first row. For block 1, this sum is 11000111. Again, the correctness of this calculation can be confirmed by Fig. 13.12. □

13.4.10 Exercises for Section 13.4

Exercise 13.4.1: Compute the parity bit for the following bit sequences:

a) 00111010.

b) 00000001.

c) 10101100.

Exercise 13.4.2: We can have two parity bits associated with a string if we follow the string by one bit that is a parity bit for the odd positions and a second that is the parity bit for the even positions. For each of the strings in Exercise 13.4.1, find the two bits that serve in this way.

Additional Observations About RAID Level 6

1. We can combine the ideas of RAID levels 5 and 6, by varying the choice of redundant disks according to the block or cylinder number. Doing so will avoid bottlenecks when writing; the scheme described in Section 13.4.9 will cause bottlenecks at the redundant disks.

2. The scheme described in Section 13.4.9 is not restricted to four data disks. The number of disks can be one less than any power of 2, say $2^k - 1$. Of these disks, k are redundant, and the remaining $2^k - k - 1$ are data disks, so the redundancy grows roughly as the logarithm of the number of data disks. For any k, we can construct the matrix corresponding to Fig. 13.10 by writing all possible columns of k 0's and 1's, except the all-0's column. The columns with a single 1 correspond to the redundant disks, and the columns with more than one 1 are the data disks.

Exercise 13.4.3: Suppose we use mirrored disks as in Example 13.8, the failure rate is 5% per year, and it takes 10 hours to replace a disk. What is the mean time to a disk failure involving loss of data?

!! Exercise 13.4.4: Suppose we use three disks as a mirrored group; i.e., all three hold identical data. If the yearly probability of failure for one disk is F, and it takes H hours to restore a disk, what is the mean time to data loss?

Exercise 13.4.5: Suppose we are using a RAID level 4 scheme with four data disks and one redundant disk. As in Example 13.9 assume blocks are a single byte. Give the block of the redundant disk if the corresponding blocks of the data disks are:

a) 01010110, 11000000, 00101011, and 10111011.

b) 11110000, 11111000, 00111100, and 01000001.

! Exercise 13.4.6: Suppose that a disk has probability F of failing in a given year, and it takes H hours to replace a disk.

a) If we use mirrored disks, what is the mean time to data loss, as a function of F and H?

b) If we use a RAID level 4 or 5 scheme, with N disks, what is the mean time to data loss?

Error-Correcting Codes and RAID Level 6

There is a theory that guides our selection of a suitable matrix, like that of Fig. 13.10, to determine the content of redundant disks. A *code* of length n is a set of bit-vectors (called *code words*) of length n. The *Hamming distance* between two code words is the number of positions in which they differ, and the *minimum distance* of a code is the smallest Hamming distance of any two different code words.

If C is any code of length n, we can require that the corresponding bits on n disks have one of the sequences that are members of the code. As a very simple example, if we are using a disk and its mirror, then $n = 2$, and we can use the code $C = \{00, 11\}$. That is, the corresponding bits of the two disks must be the same. For another example, the matrix of Fig. 13.10 defines the code consisting of the 16 bit-vectors of length 7 that have arbitrary values for the first four bits and have the remaining three bits determined by the rules for the three redundant disks.

If the minimum distance of a code is d, then disks whose corresponding bits are required to be a vector in the code will be able to tolerate $d - 1$ simultaneous disk crashes. The reason is that, should we obscure $d - 1$ positions of a code word, and there were two different ways these positions could be filled in to make a code word, then the two code words would have to differ in at most the $d - 1$ positions. Thus, the code could not have minimum distance d. As an example, the matrix of Fig. 13.10 actually defines the well-known *Hamming code*, which has minimum distance 3. Thus, it can handle two disk crashes.

Exercise 13.4.7: Using the same RAID level 4 scheme as in Exercise 13.4.5, suppose that data disk 1 has failed. Recover the block of that disk under the following circumstances:

a) The contents of disks 2 through 4 are 01110110, 11000000, and 00101011, while the redundant disk holds 11110011.

b) The contents of disks 2 through 4 are 11110000, 11111000, and 00110011, while the redundant disk holds 10000001.

Exercise 13.4.8: Suppose the block on the first disk in Exercise 13.4.5 is changed to 01010101. What changes to the corresponding blocks on the other disks must be made?

Exercise 13.4.9: Suppose we have the RAID level 6 scheme of Example 13.13, and the blocks of the four data disks are 00110100, 11100111, 01010101, and 10000100, respectively.

a) What are the corresponding blocks of the redundant disks?

b) If the third disk's block is rewritten to be 01111111, what steps must be taken to change other disks?

Exercise 13.4.10: Describe the steps taken to recover from the following failures using the RAID level 6 scheme with seven disks: (a) disks 1 and 4, (b) disks 1 and 7, (c) disks 2 and 5.

13.5   Arranging Data on Disk

We now turn to the matter of how disks are used store databases. A data element such as a tuple or object is represented by a *record*, which consists of consecutive bytes in some disk block. Collections such as relations are usually represented by placing the records that represent their data elements in one or more blocks. It is normal for a disk block to hold only elements of one relation, although there are organizations where blocks hold tuples of several relations. In this section, we shall cover the basic layout techniques for both records and blocks.

13.5.1   Fixed-Length Records

The simplest sort of record consists of fixed-length *fields*, one for each attribute of the represented tuple. Many machines allow more efficient reading and writing of main memory when data begins at an address that is a multiple of 4 or 8; some even require us to do so. Thus, it is common to begin all fields at a multiple of 4 or 8, as appropriate. Space not used by the previous field is wasted. Note that, even though records are kept in secondary, not main, memory, they are manipulated in main memory. Thus it is necessary to lay out the record so it can be moved to main memory and accessed efficiently there.

   Often, the record begins with a *header*, a fixed-length region where information about the record itself is kept. For example, we may want to keep in the record:

1. A pointer to the schema for the data stored in the record. For example, a tuple's record could point to the schema for the relation to which the tuple belongs. This information helps us find the fields of the record.

2. The length of the record. This information helps us skip over records without consulting the schema.

3. Timestamps indicating the time the record was last modified, or last read. This information may be useful for implementing database transactions as will be discussed in Chapter 18.

4. Pointers to the fields of the record. This information can substitute for schema information, and it will be seen to be important when we consider variable-length fields in Section 13.7.

```
CREATE TABLE MovieStar(
    name CHAR(30) PRIMARY KEY,
    address VARCHAR(255),
    gender CHAR(1),
    birthdate DATE
);
```

Figure 13.15: A SQL table declaration

Example 13.15: Figure 13.15 repeats our running MovieStar schema. Let us assume all fields must start at a byte that is a multiple of four. Tuples of this relation have a header and the following four fields:

1. The first field is for name, and this field requires 30 bytes. If we assume that all fields begin at a multiple of 4, then we allocate 32 bytes for the name.

2. The next attribute is address. A VARCHAR attribute requires a fixed-length segment of bytes, with one more byte than the maximum length (for the string's endmarker). Thus, we need 256 bytes for address.

3. Attribute gender is a single byte, holding either the character 'M' or 'F'. We allocate 4 bytes, so the next field can start at a multiple of 4.

4. Attribute birthdate is a SQL DATE value, which is a 10-byte string. We shall allocate 12 bytes to its field, to keep subsequent records in the block aligned at multiples of 4.

. The header of the record will hold:

a) A pointer to the record schema.

b) The record length.

c) A timestamp indicating when the record was created.

We shall assume each of these items is 4 bytes long. Figure 13.16 shows the layout of a record for a MovieStar tuple. The length of the record is 316 bytes. □

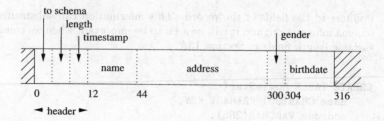

Figure 13.16: Layout of records for tuples of the MovieStar relation

13.5.2 Packing Fixed-Length Records into Blocks

Records representing tuples of a relation are stored in blocks of the disk and moved into main memory (along with their entire block) when we need to access or update them. The layout of a block that holds records is suggested in Fig. 13.17.

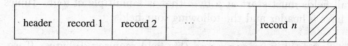

Figure 13.17: A typical block holding records

In addition to the records, there is a *block header* holding information such as:

1. Links to one or more other blocks that are part of a network of blocks such as those that will be described in Chapter 14 for creating indexes to the tuples of a relation.

2. Information about the role played by this block in such a network.

3. Information about which relation the tuples of this block belong to.

4. A "directory" giving the offset of each record in the block.

5. Timestamp(s) indicating the time of the block's last modification and/or access.

By far the simplest case is when the block holds tuples from one relation, and the records for those tuples have a fixed format. In that case, following the header, we pack as many records as we can into the block and leave the remaining space unused.

Example 13.16: Suppose we are storing records with the layout developed in Example 13.15. These records are 316 bytes long. Suppose also that we use 4096-byte blocks. Of these bytes, say 12 will be used for a block header, leaving 4084 bytes for data. In this space we can fit twelve records of the given 316-byte format, and 292 bytes of each block are wasted space. □

13.5.3   Exercises for Section 13.5

Exercise 13.5.1: Suppose a record has the following fields in this order: A character string of length 23, an integer of 2 bytes, a SQL date, and a SQL time (no decimal point). How many bytes does the record take if:

a) Fields can start at any byte.

b) Fields must start at a byte that is a multiple of 8.

c) Fields must start at a byte that is a multiple of 4.

Exercise 13.5.2: Assume fields are as in Exercise 13.5.1, but records also have a record header consisting of two 4-byte pointers and a character. Calculate the record length for the three situations regarding field alignment (a) through (c) in Exercise 13.5.1.

Exercise 13.5.3: Repeat Exercise 13.5.1 for the list of fields: a real of 8 bytes, a character string of length 25, a single byte, and a SQL date.

Exercise 13.5.4: Repeat Exercise 13.5.3 if the records also include a header consisting of an 8-byte pointer, and ten 2-byte integers.

13.6   Representing Block and Record Addresses

When in main memory, the address of a block is the virtual-memory address of its first byte, and the address of a record within that block is the virtual-memory address of the first byte of that record. However, in secondary storage, the block is not part of the application's virtual-memory address space. Rather, a sequence of bytes describes the location of the block within the overall system of data accessible to the DBMS: the device ID for the disk, the cylinder number, and so on. A record can be identified by giving its block address and the offset of the first byte of the record within the block.

In this section, we shall begin with a discussion of address spaces, especially as they pertain to the common "client-server" architecture for DBMS's (see Section 9.2.4). We then discuss the options for representing addresses, and finally look at "pointer swizzling," the ways in which we can convert addresses in the data server's world to the world of the client application programs.

13.6.1   Addresses in Client-Server Systems

Commonly, a database system consists of a *server* process that provides data from secondary storage to one or more *client* processes that are applications using the data. The server and client processes may be on one machine, or the server and the various clients can be distributed over many machines.

The client application uses a conventional "virtual" address space, typically 32 bits, or about 4 billion different addresses. The operating system or DBMS decides which parts of the address space are currently located in main memory, and hardware maps the virtual address space to physical locations in main memory. We shall not think further of this virtual-to-physical translation, and shall think of the client address space as if it were main memory itself.

The server's data lives in a *database address space*. The addresses of this space refer to blocks, and possibly to offsets within the block. There are several ways that addresses in this address space can be represented:

1. *Physical Addresses.* These are byte strings that let us determine the place within the secondary storage system where the block or record can be found. One or more bytes of the physical address are used to indicate each of:

   (a) The host to which the storage is attached (if the database is stored across more than one machine),

   (b) An identifier for the disk or other device on which the block is located,

   (c) The number of the cylinder of the disk,

   (d) The number of the track within the cylinder,

   (e) The number of the block within the track, and

   (f) (In some cases) the offset of the beginning of the record within the block.

2. *Logical Addresses.* Each block or record has a "logical address," which is an arbitrary string of bytes of some fixed length. A *map table*, stored on disk in a known location, relates logical to physical addresses, as suggested in Fig. 13.18.

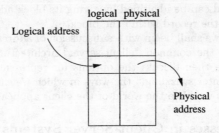

Figure 13.18: A map table translates logical to physical addresses

Notice that physical addresses are long. Eight bytes is about the minimum we could use if we incorporate all the listed elements, and some systems use many more bytes. For example, imagine a database of objects that is designed to last for 100 years. In the future, the database may grow to encompass one million machines, and each machine might be fast enough to create one object every nanosecond. This system would create around 2^{77} objects, which requires a minimum of ten bytes to represent addresses. Since we would probably prefer to reserve some bytes to represent the host, others to represent the storage unit, and so on, a rational address notation would use considerably more than 10 bytes for a system of this scale.

13.6.2 Logical and Structured Addresses

One might wonder what the purpose of logical addresses could be. All the information needed for a physical address is found in the map table, and following logical pointers to records requires consulting the map table and then going to the physical address. However, the level of indirection involved in the map table allows us considerable flexibility. For example, many data organizations require us to move records around, either within a block or from block to block. If we use a map table, then all pointers to the record refer to this map table, and all we have to do when we move or delete the record is to change the entry for that record in the table.

Many combinations of logical and physical addresses are possible as well, yielding *structured* address schemes. For instance, one could use a physical address for the block (but not the offset within the block), and add the key value for the record being referred to. Then, to find a record given this structured address, we use the physical part to reach the block containing that record, and we examine the records of the block to find the one with the proper key.

A similar, and very useful, combination of physical and logical addresses is to keep in each block an *offset table* that holds the offsets of the records within the block, as suggested in Fig. 13.19. Notice that the table grows from the front end of the block, while the records are placed starting at the end of the block. This strategy useful when the records need not be of equal length. Then, we do not know in advance how many records the block will hold, and we do not have to allocate a fixed amount of the block header to the table initially.

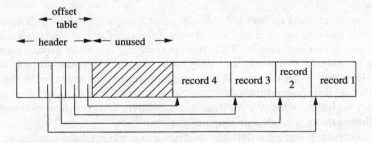

Figure 13.19: A block with a table of offsets telling us the position of each record within the block

The address of a record is now the physical address of its block plus the offset of the entry in the block's offset table for that record. This level of indirection within the block offers many of the advantages of logical addresses, without the need for a global map table.

- We can move the record around within the block, and all we have to do is change the record's entry in the offset table; pointers to the record will still be able to find it.

- We can even allow the record to move to another block, if the offset table entries are large enough to hold a *forwarding address* for the record, giving its new location.

- Finally, we have an option, should the record be deleted, of leaving in its offset-table entry a *tombstone*, a special value that indicates the record has been deleted. Prior to its deletion, pointers to this record may have been stored at various places in the database. After record deletion, following a pointer to this record leads to the tombstone, whereupon the pointer can either be replaced by a null pointer, or the data structure otherwise modified to reflect the deletion of the record. Had we not left the tombstone, the pointer might lead to some new record, with surprising, and erroneous, results.

13.6.3 Pointer Swizzling

Often, pointers or addresses are part of records. This situation is not typical for records that represent tuples of a relation, but it is common for tuples that represent objects. Also, modern object-relational database systems allow attributes of pointer type (called references), so even relational systems need the ability to represent pointers in tuples. Finally, index structures are composed of blocks that usually have pointers within them. Thus, we need to study the management of pointers as blocks are moved between main and secondary memory.

As we mentioned earlier, every block, record, object, or other referenceable data item has two forms of address: its *database address* in the server's address space, and a *memory address* if the item is currently copied in virtual memory. When in secondary storage, we surely must use the database address of the item. However, when the item is in the main memory, we can refer to the item by either its database address or its memory address. It is more efficient to put memory addresses wherever an item has a pointer, because these pointers can be followed using a single machine instruction.

In contrast, following a database address is much more time-consuming. We need a table that translates from all those database addresses that are currently in virtual memory to their current memory address. Such a *translation table* is suggested in Fig. 13.20. It may look like the map table of Fig. 13.18 that translates between logical and physical addresses. However:

a) Logical and physical addresses are both representations for the database address. In contrast, memory addresses in the translation table are for copies of the corresponding object in memory.

b) All addressable items in the database have entries in the map table, while only those items currently in memory are mentioned in the translation table.

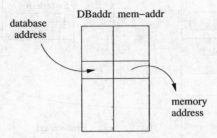

Figure 13.20: The translation table turns database addresses into their equivalents in memory

To avoid the cost of translating repeatedly from database addresses to memory addresses, several techniques have been developed that are collectively known as *pointer swizzling*. The general idea is that when we move a block from secondary to main memory, pointers within the block may be "swizzled," that is, translated from the database address space to the virtual address space. Thus, a pointer actually consists of:

1. A bit indicating whether the pointer is currently a database address or a (swizzled) memory address.

2. The database or memory pointer, as appropriate. The same space is used for whichever address form is present at the moment. Of course, not all the space may be used when the memory address is present, because it is typically shorter than the database address.

Example 13.17: Figure 13.21 shows a simple situation in which the Block 1 has a record with pointers to a second record on the same block and to a record on another block. The figure also shows what might happen when Block 1 is copied to memory. The first pointer, which points within Block 1, can be swizzled so it points directly to the memory address of the target record.

However, if Block 2 is not in memory at this time, then we cannot swizzle the second pointer; it must remain unswizzled, pointing to the database address of its target. Should Block 2 be brought to memory later, it becomes theoretically possible to swizzle the second pointer of Block 1. Depending on the swizzling strategy used, there may or may not be a list of such pointers that are in memory, referring to Block 2; if so, then we have the option of swizzling the pointer at that time.   □

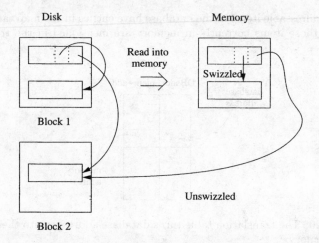

Figure 13.21: Structure of a pointer when swizzling is used

Automatic Swizzling

There are several strategies we can use to determine when to swizzle pointers. If we use *automatic swizzling*, then as soon as a block is brought into memory, we locate all its pointers and addresses and enter them into the translation table if they are not already there. These pointers include both the pointers *from* records in the block to elsewhere and the addresses of the block itself and/or its records, if these are addressable items. We need some mechanism to locate the pointers within the block. For example:

1. If the block holds records with a known schema, the schema will tell us where in the records the pointers are found.

2. If the block is used for one of the index structures we shall discuss in Chapter 14, then the block will hold pointers at known locations.

3. We may keep within the block header a list of where the pointers are.

When we enter into the translation table the addresses for the block just moved into memory, and/or its records, we know where in memory the block has been buffered. We may thus create the translation-table entry for these database addresses straightforwardly. When we insert one of these database addresses A into the translation table, we may find it in the table already, because its block is currently in memory. In this case, we replace A in the block just moved to memory by the corresponding memory address, and we set the "swizzled" bit to true. On the other hand, if A is not yet in the translation table, then its block has not been copied into main memory. We therefore cannot swizzle this pointer and leave it in the block as a database pointer.

Suppose that during the use of this data, we follow a pointer P and we find that P is still unswizzled, i.e., in the form of a database pointer. We consult the translation table to see if database address P currently has a memory equivalent. If not, block B must be copied into a memory buffer. Once B is in memory, we can "swizzle" P by replacing its database form by the equivalent memory form.

Swizzling on Demand

Another approach is to leave all pointers unswizzled when the block is first brought into memory. We enter its address, and the addresses of its pointers, into the translation table, along with their memory equivalents. If we follow a pointer P that is inside some block of memory, we swizzle it, using the same strategy that we followed when we found an unswizzled pointer using automatic swizzling.

The difference between on-demand and automatic swizzling is that the latter tries to get all the pointers swizzled quickly and efficiently when the block is loaded into memory. The possible time saved by swizzling all of a block's pointers at one time must be weighed against the possibility that some swizzled pointers will never be followed. In that case, any time spent swizzling and unswizzling the pointer will be wasted.

An interesting option is to arrange that database pointers look like invalid memory addresses. If so, then we can allow the computer to follow any pointer as if it were in its memory form. If the pointer happens to be unswizzled, then the memory reference will cause a hardware trap. If the DBMS provides a function that is invoked by the trap, and this function "swizzles" the pointer in the manner described above, then we can follow swizzled pointers in single instructions, and only need to do something more time consuming when the pointer is unswizzled.

No Swizzling

Of course it is possible never to swizzle pointers. We still need the translation table, so the pointers may be followed in their unswizzled form. This approach does offer the advantage that records cannot be pinned in memory, as discussed in Section 13.6.5, and decisions about which form of pointer is present need not be made.

Programmer Control of Swizzling

In some applications, it may be known by the application programmer whether the pointers in a block are likely to be followed. This programmer may be able to specify explicitly that a block loaded into memory is to have its pointers swizzled, or the programmer may call for the pointers to be swizzled only as needed. For example, if a programmer knows that a block is likely to be accessed heavily, such as the root block of a B-tree (discussed in Section 14.2), then the pointers would be swizzled. However, blocks that are loaded into memory, used once, and then likely dropped from memory, would not be swizzled.

13.6.4   Returning Blocks to Disk

When a block is moved from memory back to disk, any pointers within that block must be "unswizzled"; that is, their memory addresses must be replaced by the corresponding database addresses. The translation table can be used to associate addresses of the two types in either direction, so in principle it is possible to find, given a memory address, the database address to which the memory address is assigned.

However, we do not want each unswizzling operation to require a search of the entire translation table. While we have not discussed the implementation of this table, we might imagine that the table of Fig. 13.20 has appropriate indexes. If we think of the translation table as a relation, then the problem of finding the memory address associated with a database address x can be expressed as the query:

```
SELECT memAddr
FROM TranslationTable
WHERE dbAddr = x;
```

For instance, a hash table using the database address as the key might be appropriate for an index on the dbAddr attribute; Chapter 14 suggests possible data structures.

If we want to support the reverse query,

```
SELECT dbAddr
FROM TranslationTable
WHERE memAddr = y;
```

then we need to have an index on attribute memAddr as well. Again, Chapter 14 suggests data structures suitable for such an index. Also, Section 13.6.5 talks about linked-list structures that in some circumstances can be used to go from a memory address to all main-memory pointers to that address.

13.6.5   Pinned Records and Blocks

A block in memory is said to be *pinned* if it cannot at the moment be written back to disk safely. A bit telling whether or not a block is pinned can be located in the header of the block. There are many reasons why a block could be pinned, including requirements of a recovery system as discussed in Chapter 17. Pointer swizzling introduces an important reason why certain blocks must be pinned.

If a block B_1 has within it a swizzled pointer to some data item in block B_2, then we must be very careful about moving block B_2 back to disk and reusing its main-memory buffer. The reason is that, should we follow the pointer in B_1, it will lead us to the buffer, which no longer holds B_2; in effect, the pointer has become dangling. A block, like B_2, that is referred to by a swizzled pointer from somewhere else is therefore pinned.

When we write a block back to disk, we not only need to "unswizzle" any pointers in that block. We also need to make sure it is not pinned. If it is pinned, we must either unpin it, or let the block remain in memory, occupying space that could otherwise be used for some other block. To unpin a block that is pinned because of swizzled pointers from outside, we must "unswizzle" any pointers to it. Consequently, the translation table must record, for each database address whose data item is in memory, the places in memory where swizzled pointers to that item exist. Two possible approaches are:

1. Keep the list of references to a memory address as a linked list attached to the entry for that address in the translation table.

2. If memory addresses are significantly shorter than database addresses, we can create the linked list in the space used for the pointers themselves. That is, each space used for a database pointer is replaced by

   (a) The swizzled pointer, and

   (b) Another pointer that forms part of a linked list of all occurrences of this pointer.

Figure 13.22 suggests how two occurrences of a memory pointer y could be linked, starting at the entry in the translation table for database address x and its corresponding memory address y.

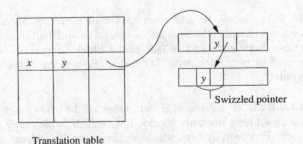

Figure 13.22: A linked list of occurrences of a swizzled pointer

13.6.6   Exercises for Section 13.6

Exercise 13.6.1: If we represent physical addresses for the Megatron 747 disk by allocating a separate byte or bytes to each of the cylinder, track within a cylinder, and block within a track, how many bytes do we need? Make a reasonable assumption about the maximum number of blocks on each track; recall that the Megatron 747 has a variable number of sectors/track.

Exercise 13.6.2: Repeat Exercise 13.6.1 for the Megatron 777 disk described in Exercise 13.2.1

Exercise 13.6.3: If we wish to represent record addresses as well as block addresses, we need additional bytes. Assuming we want addresses for a single Megatron 747 disk as in Exercise 13.6.1, how many bytes would we need for record addresses if we:

a) Included the number of the byte within a block as part of the physical address.

b) Used structured addresses for records. Assume that the stored records have a 4-byte integer as a key.

! **Exercise 13.6.4:** Suppose we wish to represent the addresses of blocks on a Megatron 747 disk logically, i.e., using identifiers of k bytes for some k. We also need to store on the disk itself a map table, as in Fig. 13.18, consisting of pairs of logical and physical addresses. The blocks used for the map table itself are not part of the database, and therefore do not have their own logical addresses in the map table. Assuming that physical addresses use the minimum possible number of bytes for physical addresses (as calculated in Exercise 13.6.1), and logical addresses likewise use the minimum possible number of bytes for logical addresses, how many blocks of 4096 bytes does the map table for the disk occupy?

Exercise 13.6.5: Today, IP addresses have four bytes. Suppose that block addresses for a world-wide address system consist of an IP address for the host, a device number between 1 and 10,000, and a block address on an individual device (assumed to be a Megatron 747 disk). How many bytes would block addresses require?

Exercise 13.6.6: In IP version 6, IP addresses are 16 bytes long. In addition, we may want to address not only blocks, but records, which may start at any byte of a block. However, devices will have their own IP address, so there will be no need to represent a device within a host, as we suggested was necessary in Exercise 13.6.5. How many bytes would be needed to represent addresses in these circumstances, again assuming devices were Megatron 747 disks?

Exercise 13.6.7: Suppose that if we swizzle all pointers automatically, we can perform the swizzling in half the time it would take to swizzle each one separately. If the probability that a pointer in main memory will be followed at least once is p, for what values of p is it more efficient to swizzle automatically than on demand?

! Exercise 13.6.8: Generalize Exercise 13.6.7 to include the possibility that we never swizzle pointers. Suppose that the important actions take the following times, in some arbitrary time units:

    i. On-demand swizzling of a pointer: 50.

    ii. Automatic swizzling of pointers: 15 per pointer.

    iii. Following a swizzled pointer: 1.

    iv. Following an unswizzled pointer: 10.

Suppose that in-memory pointers are either not followed (probability $1 - p$) or are followed k times (probability p). For what values of k and p do no-swizzling, automatic-swizzling, and on-demand-swizzling each offer the best average performance?

! Exercise 13.6.9: Suppose that we have 4096-byte blocks in which we store records of 200 bytes. The block header consists of an offset table, as in Fig. 13.19, using 2-byte pointers to records within the block. On an average day, two records per block are inserted, and one record is deleted. A deleted record must have its pointer replaced by a "tombstone," because there may be dangling pointers to it. For specificity, assume the deletion on any day always occurs before the insertions. If the block is initially empty, after how many days will there be no room to insert any more records?

13.7   Variable-Length Data and Records

Until now, we have made the simplifying assumptions that records have a fixed schema, and that the schema is a list of fixed-length fields. However, in practice, we also may wish to represent:

1. *Data items whose size varies.* For instance, in Fig. 13.15 we considered a MovieStar relation that had an address field of up to 255 bytes. While there might be some addresses that long, the vast majority of them will probably be 50 bytes or less. We could save more than half the space used for storing MovieStar tuples if we used only as much space as the actual address needed.

2. *Repeating fields.* If we try to represent a many-many relationship in a record representing an object, we shall have to store references to as many objects as are related to the given object.

3. *Variable-format records.* Sometimes we do not know in advance what the fields of a record will be, or how many occurrences of each field there will be. An important example is a record that represents an XML element, which might have no constraints at all, or might be allowed to have repeating subelements, optional attributes, and so on.

4. *Enormous fields.* Modern DBMS's support attributes whose values are very large. For instance, a movie record might have a field that is a 2-gigabyte MPEG encoding of the movie itself, as well as more mundane fields such as the title of the movie.

13.7.1   Records With Variable-Length Fields

If one or more fields of a record have variable length, then the record must contain enough information to let us find any field of the record. A simple but effective scheme is to put all fixed-length fields ahead of the variable-length fields. We then place in the record header:

1. The length of the record.

2. Pointers to (i.e., offsets of) the beginnings of all the variable-length fields other than the first (which we know must immediately follow the fixed-length fields).

Example 13.18: Suppose we have movie-star records with name, address, gender, and birthdate. We shall assume that the gender and birthdate are fixed-length fields, taking 4 and 12 bytes, respectively. However, both name and address will be represented by character strings of whatever length is appropriate. Figure 13.23 suggests what a typical movie-star record would look like. Note that no pointer to the beginning of the name is needed; that field begins right after the fixed-length portion of the record.   □

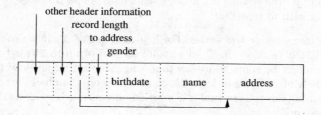

Figure 13.23: A MovieStar record with name and address implemented as variable-length character strings

---

Representing Null Values

Tuples often have fields that may be NULL. The record format of Fig. 13.23 offers a convenient way to represent NULL values. If a field such as address is null, then we put a null pointer in the place where the pointer to an address goes. Then, we need no space for an address, except the place for the pointer. This arrangement can save space on average, even if address is a fixed-length field but frequently has the value NULL.

13.7.2 Records With Repeating Fields

A similar situation occurs if a record contains a variable number of occurrences of a field F, but the field itself is of fixed length. It is sufficient to group all occurrences of field F together and put in the record header a pointer to the first. We can locate all the occurrences of the field F as follows. Let the number of bytes devoted to one instance of field F be L. We then add to the offset for the field F all integer multiples of L, starting at 0, then L, $2L$, $3L$, and so on. Eventually, we reach the offset of the field following F or the end of the record, whereupon we stop.

Example 13.19: Suppose we redesign our movie-star records to hold only the name and address (which are variable-length strings) and pointers to all the movies of the star. Figure 13.24 shows how this type of record could be represented. The header contains pointers to the beginning of the address field (we assume the name field always begins right after the header) and to the first of the movie pointers. The length of the record tells us how many movie pointers there are. □

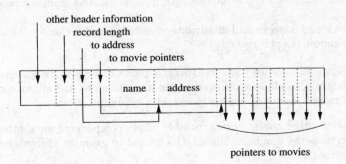

Figure 13.24: A record with a repeating group of references to movies

An alternative representation is to keep the record of fixed length, and put the variable-length portion — be it fields of variable length or fields that repeat an indefinite number of times — on a separate block. In the record itself we keep:

1. Pointers to the place where each repeating field begins, and

2. Either how many repetitions there are, or where the repetitions end.

Figure 13.25 shows the layout of a record for the problem of Example 13.19, but with the variable-length fields `name` and `address`, and the repeating field `starredIn` (a set of movie references) kept on a separate block or blocks.

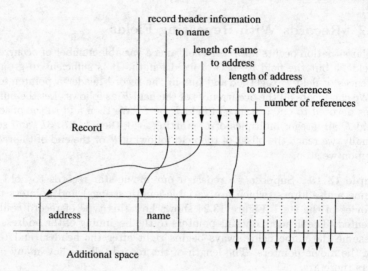

Figure 13.25: Storing variable-length fields separately from the record

There are advantages and disadvantages to using indirection for the variable-length components of a record:

- Keeping the record itself fixed-length allows records to be searched more efficiently, minimizes the overhead in block headers, and allows records to be moved within or among blocks with minimum effort.

- On the other hand, storing variable-length components on another block increases the number of disk I/O's needed to examine all components of a record.

A compromise strategy is to keep in the fixed-length portion of the record enough space for:

1. Some reasonable number of occurrences of the repeating fields,

2. A pointer to a place where additional occurrences could be found, and

3. A count of how many additional occurrences there are.

If there are fewer than this number, some of the space would be unused. If there are more than can fit in the fixed-length portion, then the pointer to additional space will be nonnull, and we can find the additional occurrences by following this pointer.

13.7.3 Variable-Format Records

An even more complex situation occurs when records do not have a fixed schema. We mentioned an example: records that represent XML elements. For another example, medical records may contain information about many tests, but there are thousands of possible tests, and each patient has results for relatively few of them. If the outcome of each test is an attribute, we would prefer that the record for each tuple hold only the attributes for which the outcome is nonnull.

The simplest representation of variable-format records is a sequence of *tagged fields*, each of which consists of the value of the field preceded by information about the role of this field, such as:

1. The attribute or field name,

2. The type of the field, if it is not apparent from the field name and some readily available schema information, and

3. The length of the field, if it is not apparent from the type.

Example 13.20: Suppose movie stars may have additional attributes such as movies directed, former spouses, restaurants owned, and a number of other known but unusual pieces of information. In Fig. 13.26 we see the beginning of a hypothetical movie-star record using tagged fields. We suppose that single-byte codes are used for the various possible field names and types. Appropriate codes are indicated on the figure, along with lengths for the two fields shown, both of which happen to be of type string. □

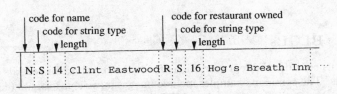

Figure 13.26: A record with tagged fields

13.7.4   Records That Do Not Fit in a Block

Today, DBMS's frequently are used to manage datatypes with large values; often values do not fit in one block. Typical examples are video or audio "clips." Often, these large values have a variable length, but even if the length is fixed for all values of the type, we need special techniques to represent values that are larger than blocks. In this section we shall consider a technique called "spanned records." The management of extremely large values (megabytes or gigabytes) is addressed in Section 13.7.5.

Spanned records also are useful in situations where records are smaller than blocks, but packing whole records into blocks wastes significant amounts of space. For instance, the wasted space in Example 13.16 was only 7%, but if records are just slightly larger than half a block, the wasted space can approach 50%. The reason is that then we can pack only one record per block.

The portion of a record that appears in one block is called a *record fragment*. A record with two or more fragments is called *spanned*, and records that do not cross a block boundary are *unspanned*.

If records can be spanned, then every record and record fragment requires some extra header information:

1. Each record or fragment header must contain a bit telling whether or not it is a fragment.

2. If it is a fragment, then it needs bits telling whether it is the first or last fragment for its record.

3. If there is a next and/or previous fragment for the same record, then the fragment needs pointers to these other fragments.

Example 13.21: Figure 13.27 suggests how records that were about 60% of a block in size could be stored with three records for every two blocks. The header for record fragment 2a contains an indicator that it is a fragment, an indicator that it is the first fragment for its record, and a pointer to next fragment, 2b. Similarly, the header for 2b indicates it is the last fragment for its record and holds a back-pointer to the previous fragment 2a.   □

13.7.5   BLOBs

Now, let us consider the representation of truly large values for records or fields of records. The common examples include images in various formats (e.g., GIF, or JPEG), movies in formats such as MPEG, or signals of all sorts: audio, radar, and so on. Such values are often called *binary, large objects*, or BLOBs. When a field has a BLOB as value, we must rethink at least two issues.

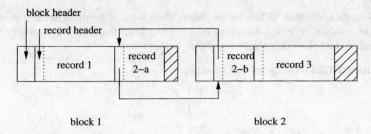

Figure 13.27: Storing spanned records across blocks

Storage of BLOBs

A BLOB must be stored on a sequence of blocks. Often we prefer that these blocks are allocated consecutively on a cylinder or cylinders of the disk, so the BLOB may be retrieved efficiently. However, it is also possible to store the BLOB on a linked list of blocks.

Moreover, it is possible that the BLOB needs to be retrieved so quickly (e.g., a movie that must be played in real time), that storing it on one disk does not allow us to retrieve it fast enough. Then, it is necessary to *stripe* the BLOB across several disks, that is, to alternate blocks of the BLOB among these disks. Thus, several blocks of the BLOB can be retrieved simultaneously, increasing the retrieval rate by a factor approximately equal to the number of disks involved in the striping.

Retrieval of BLOBs

Our assumption that when a client wants a record, the block containing the record is passed from the database server to the client in its entirety may not hold. We may want to pass only the "small" fields of the record, and allow the client to request blocks of the BLOB one at a time, independently of the rest of the record. For instance, if the BLOB is a 2-hour movie, and the client requests that the movie be played, the BLOB could be shipped several blocks at a time to the client, at just the rate necessary to play the movie.

In many applications, it is also important that the client be able to request interior portions of the BLOB without having to receive the entire BLOB. Examples would be a request to see the 45th minute of a movie, or the ending of an audio clip. If the DBMS is to support such operations, then it requires a suitable index structure, e.g., an index by seconds on a movie BLOB.

13.7.6 Column Stores

An alternative to storing tuples as records is to store each column as a record. Since an entire column of a relation may occupy far more than a single block, these records may span many blocks, much as long files do. If we keep the values in each column in the same order, then we can reconstruct the relation from the column records. Alternatively, we can keep tuple ID's or integers with each value, to tell which tuple the value belongs to.

Example 13.22: Consider the relation

X	Y
a	b
c	d
e	f

The column for X can be represented by the record (a, c, e) and the column for Y can be represented by the record (b, d, f). If we want to indicate the tuple to which each value belongs, then we can represent the two columns by the records $((1, a), (2, c), (3, e))$ and $((1, b), (2, d), (3, f))$, respectively. No matter how many tuples the relation above had, the columns would be represented by variable-length records of values or repeating groups of tuple ID's and values. □

If we store relations by columns, it is often possible to compress data, the the values all have a known type. For example, an attribute gender in a relation might have type CHAR(1), but we would use four bytes in a tuple-based record, because it is more convenient to have all components of a tuple begin at word boundaries. However, if all we are storing is a sequence of gender values, then it would make sense to store the column by a sequence of bits. If we did so, we would compress the data by a factor of 32.

However, in order for column-based storage to make sense, it must be the case that most queries call for examination of all, or a large fraction of the values in each of several columns. Recall our discussion in Section 10.6 of "analytic" queries, which are the common kind of queries with the desired characteristic. These "OLAP" queries may benefit from organizing the data by columns.

13.7.7 Exercises for Section 13.7

Exercise 13.7.1: A patient record consists of the following fixed-length fields: the patient's date of birth, social-security number, and patient ID, each 9 bytes long. It also has the following variable-length fields: name, address, and patient history. If pointers within a record require 8 bytes, and the record length is a 2-byte integer, how many bytes, exclusive of the space needed for the variable-length fields, are needed for the record? You may assume that no alignment of fields is required.

Exercise 13.7.2: Suppose records are as in Exercise 13.7.1, and the variable-length fields name, address, and history each have a length that is uniformly distributed. For the name, the range is 20–60 bytes; for address it is 40–80 bytes, and for history it is 0–2000 bytes. What is the average length of a patient record?

The Merits of Data Compression

One might think that with storage so cheap, there is little advantage to compressing data. However, storing data in fewer disk blocks enables us to read and write the data faster, since we use fewer disk I/O's. When we need to read entire columns, then storage by compressed columns can result in significant speedups. However, if we want to read or write only a single tuple, then column-based storage can lose. The reason is that in order to decompress and find the value for the one tuple we want, we need to read the entire column. In contrast, tuple-based storage allows us to read only the block containing the tuple. An even more extreme case is when the data is not only compressed, but encrypted.

In order to make access of single values efficient, we must both compress and encrypt on a block-by-block basis. The most efficient compression methods generally perform better when they are allowed to compress large amounts of data as a group, and they do not lend themselves to block-based decompression. However, in special cases such as the compression of a **gender** column discussed in Section 13.7.6, we can in fact do block-by-block compression that is as good as possible.

Exercise 13.7.3: Suppose that the patient records of Exercise 13.7.1 are augmented by an additional repeating field that represents cholesterol tests. Each cholesterol test requires 24 bytes for a date and an integer result of the test. Show the layout of patient records if:

a) The repeating tests are kept with the record itself.

b) The tests are stored on a separate block, with pointers to them in the record.

Exercise 13.7.4: Starting with the patient records of Exercise 13.7.1, suppose we add fields for tests and their results. Each test consists of a test name, a date, and a test result. Assume that each such test requires 100 bytes. Also, suppose that for each patient and each test a result is stored with probability p.

a) Assuming pointers and integers each require 8 bytes, what is the average number of bytes devoted to test results in a patient record, assuming that all test results are kept within the record itself, as a variable-length field?

b) Repeat (a), if test results are represented by pointers within the record to test-result fields kept elsewhere.

! c) Suppose we use a hybrid scheme, where room for k test results are kept within the record, and additional test results are found by following a pointer to another block (or chain of blocks) where those results are kept. As a function of p, what value of k minimizes the amount of storage used for test results?

!! d) The amount of space used by the repeating test-result fields is not the only issue. Let us suppose that the figure of merit we wish to minimize is the number of bytes used, plus a penalty of 5000 if we have to store some results on another block (and therefore will require a disk I/O for many of the test-result accesses we need to do. Under this assumption, what is the best value of k as a function of p?

!! **Exercise 13.7.5:** An MPEG movie uses about one gigabyte per hour of play. If we carefully organized several movies on a Megatron 747 disk, how many could we deliver with only small delay (say 100 milliseconds) from one disk. Use the timing estimates of Example 13.2, but remember that you can choose how the movies are laid out on the disk.

!! **Exercise 13.7.6:** Suppose blocks have 1000 bytes available for the storage of records, and we wish to store on them fixed-length records of length r, where $500 < r \leq 1000$. The value of r includes the record header, but a record fragment requires an additional 32 bytes for the fragment header. For what values of r can we improve space utilization by spanning records?

13.8   Record Modifications

Insertions, deletions, and updates of records often create special problems. These problems are most severe when the records change their length, but they come up even when records and fields are all of fixed length.

13.8.1   Insertion

First, let us consider insertion of new records into a relation. If the records of a relation are kept in no particular order, we can just find a block with some empty space, or get a new block if there is none, and put the record there.

There is more of a problem when the tuples must be kept in some fixed order, such as sorted by their primary key (e.g., see Section 14.1.1). If we need to insert a new record, we first locate the appropriate block for that record. Suppose first that there is space in the block to put the new record. Since records must be kept in order, we may have to slide records around in the block to make space available at the proper point. If we need to slide records, then the block organization that we showed in Fig. 13.19, which we reproduce here as Fig. 13.28, is useful. Recall from our discussion in Section 13.6.2 that we may create an "offset table" in the header of each block, with pointers to the location of each record in the block. A pointer to a record from outside the block is a "structured address," that is, the block address and the location of the entry for the record in the offset table.

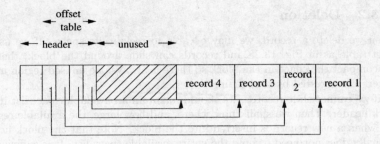

Figure 13.28: An offset table lets us slide records within a block to make room for new records

If we can find room for the inserted record in the block at hand, then we simply slide the records within the block and adjust the pointers in the offset table. The new record is inserted into the block, and a new pointer to the record is added to the offset table for the block. However, there may be no room in the block for the new record, in which case we have to find room outside the block. There are two major approaches to solving this problem, as well as combinations of these approaches.

1. *Find space on a "nearby" block.* For example, if block B_1 has no available space for a record that needs to be inserted in sorted order into that block, then look at the following block B_2 in the sorted order of the blocks. If there is room in B_2, move the highest record(s) of B_1 to B_2, leave forwarding addresses (recall Section 13.6.2) and slide the records around on both blocks.

2. *Create an overflow block.* In this scheme, each block B has in its header a place for a pointer to an *overflow* block where additional records that theoretically belong in B can be placed. The overflow block for B can point to a second overflow block, and so on. Figure 13.29 suggests the structure. We show the pointer for overflow blocks as a nub on the block, although it is in fact part of the block header.

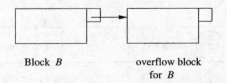

Block B overflow block
for B

Figure 13.29: A block and its first overflow block

13.8.2   Deletion

When we delete a record, we may be able to reclaim its space. If we use an offset table as in Fig. 13.28 and records can slide around the block, then we can compact the space in the block so there is always one unused region in the center, as suggested by that figure.

If we cannot slide records, we should maintain an available-space list in the block header. Then we shall know where, and how large, the available regions are, when a new record is inserted into the block. Note that the block header normally does not need to hold the entire available space list. It is sufficient to put the list head in the block header, and use the available regions themselves to hold the links in the list, much as we did in Fig. 13.22.

There is one additional complication involved in deletion, which we must remember regardless of what scheme we use for reorganizing blocks. There may be pointers to the deleted record, and if so, we don't want these pointers to dangle or wind up pointing to a new record that is put in the place of the deleted record. The usual technique, which we pointed out in Section 13.6.2, is to place a *tombstone* in place of the record. This tombstone is permanent; it must exist until the entire database is reconstructed.

Where the tombstone is placed depends on the nature of record pointers. If pointers go to fixed locations from which the location of the record is found, then we put the tombstone in that fixed location. Here are two examples:

1. We suggested in Section 13.6.2 that if the offset-table scheme of Fig. 13.28 were used, then the tombstone could be a null pointer in the offset table, since pointers to the record were really pointers to the offset table entries.

2. If we are using a map table, as in Fig. 13.18, to translate logical record addresses to physical addresses, then the tombstone can be a null pointer in place of the physical address.

If we need to replace records by tombstones, we should place the bit that serves as a tombstone at the very beginning of the record. Then, only this bit must remain where the record used to begin, and subsequent bytes can be reused for another record, as suggested by Fig. 13.30.

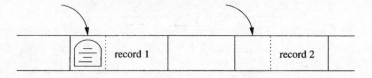

Figure 13.30: Record 1 can be replaced, but the tombstone remains; record 2 has no tombstone and can be seen when we follow a pointer to it

13.8.3 Update

When a fixed-length record is updated, there is no effect on the storage system, because we know it can occupy exactly the same space it did before the update. However, when a variable-length record is updated, we have all the problems associated with both insertion and deletion, except that it is never necessary to create a tombstone for the old version of the record.

If the updated record is longer than the old version, then we may need to create more space on its block. This process may involve sliding records or even the creation of an overflow block. If variable-length portions of the record are stored on another block, as in Fig. 13.25, then we may need to move elements around that block or create a new block for storing variable-length fields. Conversely, if the record shrinks because of the update, we have the same opportunities as with a deletion to recover or consolidate space.

13.8.4 Exercises for Section 13.8

Exercise 13.8.1: Relational database systems have always preferred to use fixed-length tuples if possible. Give two reasons for this preference.

13.9 Summary of Chapter 13

+ *Memory Hierarchy*: A computer system uses storage components ranging over many orders of magnitude in speed, capacity, and cost per bit. From the smallest/most expensive to largest/cheapest, they are: cache, main memory, secondary memory (disk), and tertiary memory.

+ *Disks/Secondary Storage*: Secondary storage devices are principally magnetic disks with multigigabyte capacities. Disk units have several circular platters of magnetic material, with concentric tracks to store bits. Platters rotate around a central spindle. The tracks at a given radius from the center of a platter form a cylinder.

+ *Blocks and Sectors*: Tracks are divided into sectors, which are separated by unmagnetized gaps. Sectors are the unit of reading and writing from the disk. Blocks are logical units of storage used by an application such as a DBMS. Blocks typically consist of several sectors.

+ *Disk Controller*: The disk controller is a processor that controls one or more disk units. It is responsible for moving the disk heads to the proper cylinder to read or write a requested track. It also may schedule competing requests for disk access and buffers the blocks to be read or written.

+ *Disk Access Time*: The latency of a disk is the time between a request to read or write a block, and the time the access is completed. Latency is caused principally by three factors: the seek time to move the heads to the proper cylinder, the rotational latency during which the desired block rotates under the head, and the transfer time, while the block moves under the head and is read or written.

✦ *Speeding Up Disk Access*: There are several techniques for accessing disk blocks faster for some applications. They include dividing the data among several disks (striping), mirroring disks (maintaining several copies of the data, also to allow parallel access), and organizing data that will be accessed together by tracks or cylinders.

✦ *Elevator Algorithm*: We can also speed accesses by queueing access requests and handling them in an order that allows the heads to make one sweep across the disk. The heads stop to handle a request each time it reaches a cylinder containing one or more blocks with pending access requests.

✦ *Disk Failure Modes*: To avoid loss of data, systems must be able to handle errors. The principal types of disk failure are intermittent (a read or write error that will not reoccur if repeated), permanent (data on the disk is corrupted and cannot be properly read), and the disk crash, where the entire disk becomes unreadable.

✦ *Checksums*: By adding a parity check (extra bit to make the number of 1's in a bit string even), intermittent failures and permanent failures can be detected, although not corrected.

✦ *Stable Storage*: By making two copies of all data and being careful about the order in which those copies are written, a single disk can be used to protect against almost all permanent failures of a single sector.

✦ *RAID*: These schemes allow data to survive a disk crash. RAID level 4 adds a disk whose contents are a parity check on corresponding bits of all other disks, level 5 varies the disk holding the parity bit to avoid making the parity disk a writing bottleneck. Level 6 involves the use of error-correcting codes and may allow survival after several simultaneous disk crashes.

✦ *Records*: Records are composed of several fields plus a record header. The header contains information about the record, possibly including such matters as a timestamp, schema information, and a record length. If the record has varying-length fields, the header may also help locate those fields.

✦ *Blocks*: Records are generally stored within blocks. A block header, with information about that block, consumes some of the space in the block, with the remainder occupied by one or more records. To support insertions, deletions and modifications of records, we can put in the block header an offset table that has pointers to each of the records in the block.

✦ *Spanned Records*: Generally, a record exists within one block. However, if records are longer than blocks, or we wish to make use of leftover space within blocks, then we can break records into two or more fragments, one on each block. A fragment header is then needed to link the fragments of a record.

✦ *BLOBs*: Very large values, such as images and videos, are called BLOBs (binary, large objects). These values must be stored across many blocks and may require specialized storage techniques such as reserving a cylinder or striping the blocks of the BLOB.

✦ *Database Addresses*: Data managed by a DBMS is found among several storage devices, typically disks. To locate blocks and records in this storage system, we can use physical addresses, which are a description of the device number, cylinder, track, sector(s), and possibly byte within a sector. We can also use logical addresses, which are arbitrary character strings that are translated into physical addresses by a map table.

✦ *Pointer Swizzling*: When disk blocks are brought to main memory, the database addresses need to be translated to memory addresses, if pointers are to be followed. The translation is called swizzling, and can either be done automatically, when blocks are brought to memory, or on-demand, when a pointer is first followed.

✦ *Tombstones*: When a record is deleted, pointers to it will dangle. A tombstone in place of (part of) the deleted record warns the system that the record is no longer there.

✦ *Pinned Blocks*: For various reasons, including the fact that a block may contain swizzled pointers, it may be unacceptable to copy a block from memory back to its place on disk. Such a block is said to be pinned. If the pinning is due to swizzled pointers, then they must be unswizzled before returning the block to disk.

13.10 References for Chapter 13

The RAID idea can be traced back to [8] on disk striping. The name and error-correcting capability is from [7]. The model of disk failures in Section 13.4 appears in unpublished work of Lampson and Sturgis [5].

There are several useful surveys of disk-related material. A study of RAID systems is in [2]. [10] surveys algorithms suitable for the secondary storage model (block model) of computation. [3] is an important study of how one optimizes a system involving processor, memory, and disk, to perform specific tasks.

References [4] and [11] have more information on record and block structures. [9] discusses column stores as an alternative to the conventional record structures. Tombstones as a technique for dealing with deletion is from [6]. [1] covers data representation issues, such as addresses and swizzling in the context of object-oriented DBMS's.

1. R. G. G. Cattell, *Object Data Management*, Addison-Wesley, Reading MA, 1994.

2. P. M. Chen et al., "RAID: high-performance, reliable secondary storage," *Computing Surveys* **26**:2 (1994), pp. 145–186.

3. J. N. Gray and F. Putzolo, "The five minute rule for trading memory for disk accesses and the 10 byte rule for trading memory for CPU time," *Proc. ACM SIGMOD Intl. Conf. on Management of Data*, pp. 395–398, 1987.

4. D. E. Knuth, *The Art of Computer Programming, Vol. I, Fundamental Algorithms, Third Edition*, Addison-Wesley, Reading MA, 1997.

5. B. Lampson and H. Sturgis, "Crash recovery in a distributed data storage system," Technical report, Xerox Palo Alto Research Center, 1976.

6. D. Lomet, "Scheme for invalidating free references," *IBM J. Research and Development* **19**:1 (1975), pp. 26–35.

7. D. A. Patterson, G. A. Gibson, and R. H. Katz, "A case for redundant arrays of inexpensive disks," *Proc. ACM SIGMOD Intl. Conf. on Management of Data*, pp. 109–116, 1988.

8. K. Salem and H. Garcia-Molina, "Disk striping," *Proc. Second Intl. Conf. on Data Engineering*, pp. 336–342, 1986.

9. M. Stonebraker et al., "C-Store: a column-oriented DBMS," *Proc. Thirty-first Intl. Conf. on Very Large Database Systems*" (2005).

10. J. S. Vitter, "External memory algorithms," *Proc. Seventeenth Annual ACM Symposium on Principles of Database Systems*, pp. 119–128, 1998.

11. G. Wiederhold, *File Organization for Database Design*, McGraw-Hill, New York, 1987.

Chapter 14

Index Structures

It is not sufficient simply to scatter the records that represent tuples of a relation among various blocks. To see why, think how we would answer the simple query SELECT * FROM R. We would have to examine every block in the storage system to find the tuples of R. A better idea is to reserve some blocks, perhaps several whole cylinders, for R. Now, at least we can find the tuples of R without scanning the entire data store.

However, this organization offers little help for a query like

```
SELECT * FROM R WHERE a=10;
```

Section 8.4 introduced us to the importance of creating *indexes* to speed up queries that specify values for one or more attributes. As suggested in Fig. 14.1, an index is any data structure that takes the value of one or more fields and finds the records with that value "quickly." In particular, an index lets us find a record without having to look at more than a small fraction of all possible records. The field(s) on whose values the index is based is called the *search key*, or just "key" if the index is understood.

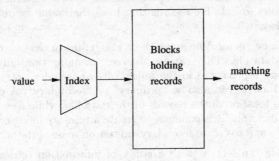

Figure 14.1: An index takes a value for some field(s) and finds records with the matching value

> ## Different Kinds of "Keys"
>
> There are many meanings of the term "key." We used it in Section 2.3.6 to mean the primary key of a relation. We shall also speak of "sort keys," the attribute(s) on which a file of records is sorted. We just introduced "search keys," the attribute(s) for which we are given values and asked to search, through an index, for tuples with matching values. We try to use the appropriate adjective — "primary," "sort," or "search" — when the meaning of "key" is unclear. However, in many cases, the three kinds of keys are one and the same.

In this chapter, we shall introduce the most common form of index in database systems: the B-tree. We shall also discuss hash tables in secondary storage, which is another important index structure. Finally, we consider other index structures that are designed to handle multidimensional data. These structures support queries that specify values or ranges for several attributes at once.

14.1   Index-Structure Basics

In this section, we introduce concepts that apply to all index structures. Storage structures consist of *files*, which are similar to the files used by operating systems. A *data file* may be used to store a relation, for example. The data file may have one or more *index files*. Each index file associates values of the search key with pointers to data-file records that have that value for the attribute(s) of the search key.

Indexes can be "dense," meaning there is an entry in the index file for every record of the data file. They can be "sparse," meaning that only some of the data records are represented in the index, often one index entry per block of the data file. Indexes can also be "primary" or "secondary." A primary index determines the location of the records of the data file, while a secondary index does not. For example, it is common to create a primary index on the primary key of a relation and to create secondary indexes on some of the other attributes.

We conclude the section with a study of information retrieval from documents. The ideas of the section are combined to yield "inverted indexes," which enable efficient retrieval of documents that contain one or more given keywords. This technique is essential for answering search queries on the Web, for instance.

14.1.1 Sequential Files

A *sequential file* is created by sorting the tuples of a relation by their primary key. The tuples are then distributed among blocks, in this order.

Example 14.1: Fig 14.2 shows a sequential file on the right. We imagine that keys are integers; we show only the key field, and we make the atypical assumption that there is room for only two records in one block. For instance, the first block of the file holds the records with keys 10 and 20. In this and several other examples, we use integers that are sequential multiples of 10 as keys, although there is surely no requirement that keys form an arithmetic sequence. □

Although in Example 14.1 we supposed that records were packed as tightly as possible into blocks, it is common to leave some space initially in each block to accomodate new tuples that may be added to a relation. Alternatively, we may accomodate new tuples with overflow blocks, as we suggested in Section 13.8.1.

14.1.2 Dense Indexes

If records are sorted, we can build on them a *dense index*, which is a sequence of blocks holding only the keys of the records and pointers to the records themselves; the pointers are addresses in the sense discussed in Section 13.6. The index blocks of the dense index maintain these keys in the same sorted order as in the file itself. Since keys and pointers presumably take much less space than complete records, we expect to use many fewer blocks for the index than for the file itself. The index is especially advantageous when it, but not the data file, can fit in main memory. Then, by using the index, we can find any record given its search key, with only one disk I/O per lookup.

Example 14.2: Figure 14.2 suggests a dense index on a sorted file. The first index block contains pointers to the first four records (an atypically small number of pointers for one block), the second block has pointers to the next four, and so on. □

The dense index supports queries that ask for records with a given search-key value. Given key value K, we search the index blocks for K, and when we find it, we follow the associated pointer to the record with key K. It might appear that we need to examine every block of the index, or half the blocks of the index, on average, before we find K. However, there are several factors that make the index-based search more efficient than it seems.

1. The number of index blocks is usually small compared with the number of data blocks.

2. Since keys are sorted, we can use binary search to find K. If there are n blocks of the index, we only look at $\log_2 n$ of them.

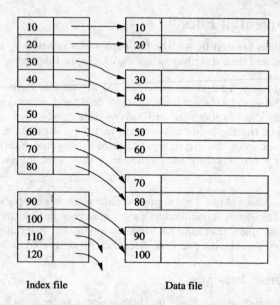

Figure 14.2: A dense index (left) on a sequential data file (right)

3. The index may be small enough to be kept permanently in main memory buffers. If so, the search for key K involves only main-memory accesses, and there are no expensive disk I/O's to be performed.

14.1.3 Sparse Indexes

A sparse index typically has only one key-pointer pair per block of the data file. It thus uses less space than a dense index, at the expense of somewhat more time to find a record given its key. You can only use a sparse index if the data file is sorted by the search key, while a dense index can be used for any search key. Figure 14.3 shows a sparse index with one key-pointer per data block. The keys are for the first records on each data block.

Example 14.3: As in Example 14.2, we assume that the data file is sorted, and keys are all the integers divisible by 10, up to some large number. We also continue to assume that four key-pointer pairs fit on an index block. Thus, the first sparse-index block has entries for the first keys on the first four blocks, which are 10, 30, 50, and 70. Continuing the assumed pattern of keys, the second index block has the first keys of the fifth through eighth blocks, which we assume are 90, 110, 130, and 150. We also show a third index block with first keys from the hypothetical ninth through twelfth data blocks. □

To find the record with search-key value K, we search the sparse index for the largest key less than or equal to K. Since the index file is sorted by key, a

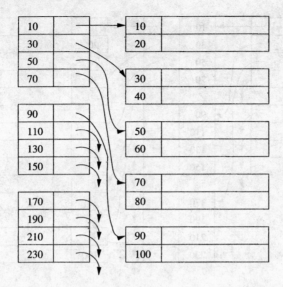

Figure 14.3: A sparse index on a sequential file

binary search can locate this entry. We follow the associated pointer to a data block. Now, we must search this block for the record with key K. Of course the block must have enough format information that the records and their contents can be identified. Any of the techniques from Sections 13.5 and 13.7 can be used.

14.1.4 Multiple Levels of Index

An index file can cover many blocks. Even if we use binary search to find the desired index entry, we still may need to do many disk I/O's to get to the record we want. By putting an index on the index, we can make the use of the first level of index more efficient.

Figure 14.4 extends Fig. 14.3 by adding a second index level (as before, we assume keys are every multiple of 10). The same idea would let us place a third-level index on the second level, and so on. However, this idea has its limits, and we prefer the B-tree structure described in Section 14.2 over building many levels of index.

In this example, the first-level index is sparse, although we could have chosen a dense index for the first level. However, the second and higher levels must be sparse. The reason is that a dense index on an index would have exactly as many key-pointer pairs as the first-level index, and therefore would take exactly as much space as the first-level index.

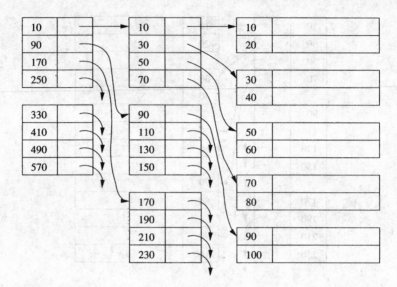

Figure 14.4: Adding a second level of sparse index

14.1.5 Secondary Indexes

A secondary index serves the purpose of any index: it is a data structure that
facilitates finding records given a value for one or more fields. However, the
secondary index is distinguished from the primary index in that a secondary
index does not determine the placement of records in the data file. Rather, the
secondary index tells us the current locations of records; that location may have
been decided by a primary index on some other field. An important consequence
of the distinction between primary and secondary indexes is that:

- Secondary indexes are always dense. It makes no sense to talk of a sparse,
  secondary index. Since the secondary index does not influence location,
  we could not use it to predict the location of any record whose key was
  not mentioned in the index file explicitly.

Example 14.4 : Figure 14.5 shows a typical secondary index. The data file
is shown with two records per block, as has been our standard for illustration.
The records have only their search key shown; this attribute is integer valued,
and as before we have taken the values to be multiples of 10. Notice that, unlike
the data file in Fig. 14.2, here the data is not sorted by the search key.

However, the keys in the index file *are* sorted. The result is that the pointers
in one index block can go to many different data blocks, instead of one or a few
consecutive blocks. For example, to retrieve all the records with search key 20,
we not only have to look at two index blocks, but we are sent by their pointers
to three different data blocks. Thus, using a secondary index may result in

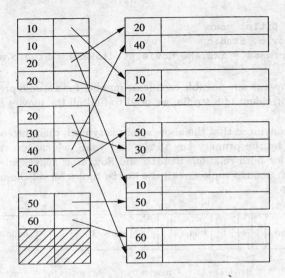

Figure 14.5: A secondary index

many more disk I/O's than if we get the same number of records via a primary index. However, there is no help for this problem; we cannot control the order of tuples in the data block, because they are presumably ordered according to some other attribute(s). □

14.1.6 Applications of Secondary Indexes

Besides supporting additional indexes on relations that are organized as sequential files, there are some data structures where secondary indexes are needed for even the primary key. One of these is the "heap" structure, where the records of the relation are kept in no particular order.

A second common structure needing secondary indexes is the *clustered file*. Suppose there are relations R and S, with a many-one relationship from the tuples of R to tuples of S. It may make sense to store each tuple of R with the tuple of S to which it is related, rather than according to the primary key of R. An example will illustrate why this organization makes good sense in special situations.

Example 14.5: Consider our standard movie and studio relations:

```
Movie(title, year, length, genre, studioName, producerC#)
Studio(name, address, presC#)
```

Suppose further that the most common form of query is:

```
SELECT title, year
FROM Movie, Studio
WHERE presC# = zzz AND Movie.studioName = Studio.name;
```

Here, *zzz* represents any possible certificate number for a studio president. That is, given the president of a studio, we need to find all the movies made by that studio.

If we are convinced that the above query is typical, then instead of ordering Movie tuples by the primary key title and year, we can create a *clustered file structure* for both relations Studio and Movie, as suggested by Fig. 14.6. Following each Studio tuple are all the Movie tuples for all the movies owned by that studio.

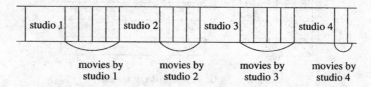

Figure 14.6: A clustered file with each studio clustered with the movies made by that studio

If we create an index for Studio with search key presC#, then whatever the value of *zzz* is, we can quickly find the tuple for the proper studio. Moreover, all the Movie tuples whose value of attribute studioName matches the value of name for that studio will follow the studio's tuple in the clustered file. As a result, we can find the movies for this studio by making almost as few disk I/O's as possible. The reason is that the desired Movie tuples are packed almost as densely as possible onto the following blocks. However, an index on any attribute(s) of Movie would have to be a secondary index.   □

14.1.7   Indirection in Secondary Indexes

There is some wasted space, perhaps a significant amount of wastage, in the structure suggested by Fig. 14.5. If a search-key value appears n times in the data file, then the value is written n times in the index file. It would be better if we could write the key value once for all the pointers to data records with that value.

A convenient way to avoid repeating values is to use a level of indirection, called *buckets*, between the secondary index file and the data file. As shown in Fig. 14.7, there is one pair for each search key K. The pointer of this pair goes to a position in a "bucket file," which holds the "bucket" for K. Following this position, until the next position pointed to by the index, are pointers to all the records with search-key value K.

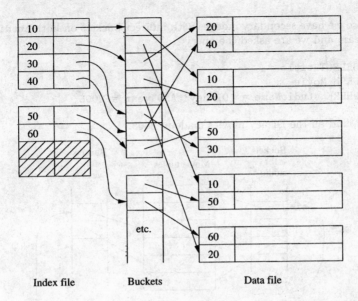

Figure 14.7: Saving space by using indirection in a secondary index

Example 14.6: For instance, let us follow the pointer from search key 50 in the index file of Fig. 14.7 to the intermediate "bucket" file. This pointer happens to take us to the last pointer of one block of the bucket file. We search forward, to the first pointer of the next block. We stop at that point, because the next pointer of the index file, associated with search key 60, points to the next record in the bucket file. □

The scheme of Fig. 14.7 saves space as long as search-key values are larger than pointers, and the average key appears at least twice. However, even if not, there is an important advantage to using indirection with secondary indexes: often, we can use the pointers in the buckets to help answer queries without ever looking at most of the records in the data file. Specifically, when there are several conditions to a query, and each condition has a secondary index to help it, we can find the bucket pointers that satisfy all the conditions by intersecting sets of pointers in memory, and retrieving only the records pointed to by the surviving pointers. We thus save the I/O cost of retrieving records that satisfy some, but not all, of the conditions.[1]

Example 14.7: Consider the usual Movie relation:

```
Movie(title, year, length, genre, studioName, producerC#)
```

---

[1] We also could use this pointer-intersection trick if we got the pointers directly from the index, rather than from buckets.

Suppose we have secondary indexes with indirect buckets on both `studioName` and year, and we are asked the query

```
SELECT title
FROM Movie
WHERE studioName = 'Disney' AND year = 2005;
```

that is, find all the Disney movies made in 2005.

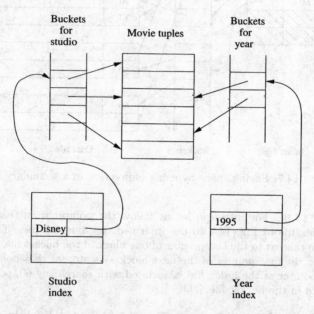

Figure 14.8: Intersecting buckets in main memory

Figure 14.8 shows how we can answer this query using the indexes. Using the index on `studioName`, we find the pointers to all records for Disney movies, but we do not yet bring any of those records from disk to memory. Instead, using the index on year, we find the pointers to all the movies of 2005. We then intersect the two sets of pointers, getting exactly the movies that were made by Disney in 2005. Finally, we retrieve from disk all data blocks holding one or more of these movies, thus retrieving the minimum possible number of blocks. □

14.1.8   Document Retrieval and Inverted Indexes

For many years, the information-retrieval community has dealt with the storage of documents and the efficient retrieval of documents with a given set of keywords. With the advent of the World-Wide Web and the feasibility of keeping all documents on-line, the retrieval of documents given keywords has become one of the largest database problems. While there are many kinds of queries that one can use to find relevant documents, the simplest and most common form can be seen in relational terms as follows:

- A document may be thought of as a tuple in a relation Doc. This relation has very many attributes, one corresponding to each possible word in a document. Each attribute is boolean — either the word is present in the document, or it is not. Thus, the relation schema may be thought of as

    Doc(hasCat, hasDog, ...)

    where hasCat is true if and only if the document has the word "cat" at least once.

- There is a secondary index on each of the attributes of Doc. However, we save the trouble of indexing those tuples for which the value of the attribute is FALSE; instead, the index leads us to only the documents for which the word is present. That is, the index has entries only for the search-key value TRUE.

- Instead of creating a separate index for each attribute (i.e., for each word), the indexes are combined into one, called an *inverted index*. This index uses indirect buckets for space efficiency, as was discussed in Section 14.1.7.

Example 14.8 : An inverted index is illustrated in Fig. 14.9. In place of a data file of records is a collection of documents, each of which may be stored on one or more disk blocks. The inverted index itself consists of a set of word-pointer pairs; the words are in effect the search key for the index. The inverted index is kept in a sequence of blocks, just like any of the indexes discussed so far.

The pointers refer to positions in a "bucket" file. For instance, we have shown in Fig. 14.9 the word "cat" with a pointer to the bucket file. That pointer leads us to the beginning of a list of pointers to all the documents that contain the word "cat." We have shown some of these in the figure. Similarly, the word "dog" is shown leading to a list of pointers to all the documents with "dog." □

Pointers in the bucket file can be:

1. Pointers to the document itself.

2. Pointers to an occurrence of the word. In this case, the pointer might be a pair consisting of the first block for the document and an integer indicating the number of the word in the document.

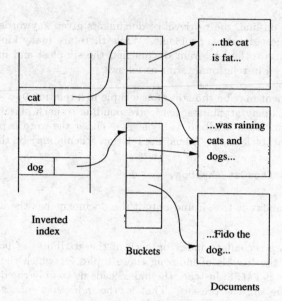

Figure 14.9: An inverted index on documents

When we use "buckets" of pointers to occurrences of each word, we may extend the idea to include in the bucket array some information about each occurrence. Now, the bucket file itself becomes a collection of records with important structure. Early uses of the idea distinguished occurrences of a word in the title of a document, the abstract, and the body of text. With the growth of documents on the Web, especially documents using HTML, XML, or another markup language, we can also indicate the markings associated with words. For instance, we can distinguish words appearing in titles, headers, tables, or anchors, as well as words appearing in different fonts or sizes.

Example 14.9: Figure 14.10 illustrates a bucket file that has been used to indicate occurrences of words in HTML documents. The first column indicates the type of occurrence, i.e., its marking, if any. The second and third columns are together the pointer to the occurrence. The third column indicates the document, and the second column gives the number of the word in the document.

We can use this data structure to answer various queries about documents without having to examine the documents in detail. For instance, suppose we want to find documents about dogs that compare them with cats. Without a deep understanding of the meaning of the text, we cannot answer this query precisely. However, we could get a good hint if we searched for documents that

a) Mention dogs in the title, and

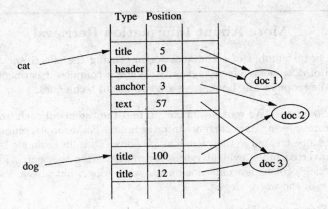

Figure 14.10: Storing more information in the inverted index

Insertion and Deletion From Buckets

We show buckets in figures such as Fig. 14.9 as compacted arrays of appropriate size. In practice, they are records with a single field (the pointer) and are stored in blocks like any other collection of records. Thus, when we insert or delete pointers, we may use any of the techniques seen so far, such as leaving extra space in blocks for expansion of the file, overflow blocks, and possibly moving records within or among blocks. In the latter case, we must be careful to change the pointer from the inverted index to the bucket file, as we move the records it points to.

---

b) Mention cats in an anchor — presumably a link to a document about cats.

We can answer this query by intersecting pointers. That is, we follow the pointer associated with "cat" to find the occurrences of this word. We select from the bucket file the pointers to documents associated with occurrences of "cat" where the type is "anchor." We then find the bucket entries for "dog" and select from them the document pointers associated with the type "title." If we intersect these two sets of pointers, we have the documents that meet the conditions: they mention "dog" in the title and "cat" in an anchor. □

14.1.9 Exercises for Section 14.1

Exercise 14.1.1: Suppose blocks hold either five records, or 20 key-pointer pairs. As a function of n, the number of records, how many blocks do we need to hold a data file and: (a) A dense index (b) A sparse index?

More About Information Retrieval

There are a number of techniques for improving the effectiveness of retrieval of documents given keywords. While a complete treatment is beyond the scope of this book, here are two useful techniques:

1. *Stemming.* We remove suffixes to find the "stem" of each word, before entering its occurrence into the index. For example, plural nouns can be treated as their singular versions. Thus, in Example 14.8, the inverted index evidently uses stemming, since the search for word "dog" got us not only documents with "dog," but also a document with the word "dogs."

2. *Stop words.* The most common words, such as "the" or "and," are called *stop words* and often are excluded from the inverted index. The reason is that the several hundred most common words appear in too many documents to make them useful as a way to find documents about specific subjects. Eliminating stop words also reduces the size of the inverted index significantly.

Exercise 14.1.2: Repeat Exercise 14.1.1 if blocks can hold up to 50 records or 500 key-pointer pairs, but neither data- nor index-blocks are allowed to be more than 80% full.

! Exercise 14.1.3: Repeat Exercise 14.1.1 if we use as many levels of index as is appropriate, until the final level of index has only one block.

! Exercise 14.1.4: Consider a clustered file organization like Fig. 14.6, and suppose that 5 records, either studio or movie records, will fit on one block. Also assume that the number of movies per studio is uniformly distributed between 1 and m. As a function of m, what is the average number of disk I/O's needed to retrieve a studio and all its movies? What would the number be if movies were randomly distributed over a large number of blocks?

Exercise 14.1.5: Suppose that blocks can hold either five records, twenty key-pointer pairs, or 100 pointers. Using the indirect-buckets scheme of Fig. 14.7:

a) If the average search-key value appears in 10 records, how many blocks do we need to hold 5000 records and its secondary index structure? How many blocks would be needed if we did *not* use buckets?

! b) If there are no constraints on the number of records that can have a given search-key value, what are the minimum and maximum number of blocks needed?

! Exercise 14.1.6: On the assumptions of Exercise 14.1.5(a), what is the average number of disk I/O's to find and retrieve the twelve records with a given search-key value, both with and without the bucket structure? Assume nothing is in memory to begin, but it is possible to locate index or bucket blocks without incurring additional I/O's beyond what is needed to retrieve these blocks into memory.

Exercise 14.1.7: If we use an augmented inverted index, such as in Fig. 14.10, we can perform a number of other kinds of searches. Suggest how this index could be used to find:

a) Documents in which "cat" and "dog" appeared within five positions of each other in the same type of element (e.g., title, text, or anchor).

b) Documents in which "dog" followed "cat" separated by exactly one position.

c) Documents in which "dog" and "cat" both appear in the title.

Exercise 14.1.8: Suppose we have a repository of 2000 documents, and we wish to build an inverted index with 10,000 words. A block can hold ten word-pointer pairs or 50 pointers to either a document or a position within a document. The distribution of words is Zipfian (see the box on "The Zipfian Distribution" in Section 16.4.3); the number of occurrences of the ith most frequent word is $100000/\sqrt{i}$, for $i = 1, 2, \ldots, 10000$.

a) Suppose our inverted index only records for each word all the documents that have that word. What is the maximum number of blocks we could need to hold the inverted index?

b) Repeat (a) if the 400 most common words ("stop" words) are *not* included in the index.

c) Suppose our inverted index holds pointers to each occurrence of each word. How many blocks do we need to hold the inverted index?

d) Repeat (c) if the 400 most common words are not included in the index.

e) What is the averge number of words per document?

14.2 B-Trees

While one or two levels of index are often very helpful in speeding up queries, there is a more general structure that is commonly used in commercial systems. This family of data structures is called *B-trees*, and the particular variant that is most often used is known as a *B+ tree*. In essence:

- B-trees automatically maintain as many levels of index as is appropriate for the size of the file being indexed.

- B-trees manage the space on the blocks they use so that every block is between half used and completely full.

In the following discussion, we shall talk about "B-trees," but the details will all be for the B+ tree variant. Other types of B-tree are discussed in exercises.

14.2.1   The Structure of B-trees

A B-tree organizes its blocks into a tree that is *balanced*, meaning that all paths from the root to a leaf have the same length. Typically, there are three layers in a B-tree: the root, an intermediate layer, and leaves, but any number of layers is possible. To help visualize B-trees, you may wish to look ahead at Figs. 14.11 and 14.12, which show nodes of a B-tree, and Fig. 14.13, which shows an entire B-tree.

There is a parameter n associated with each B-tree index, and this parameter determines the layout of all blocks of the B-tree. Each block will have space for n search-key values and $n + 1$ pointers. In a sense, a B-tree block is similar to the index blocks introduced in Section 14.1.2, except that the B-tree block has an extra pointer, along with n key-pointer pairs. We pick n to be as large as will allow $n + 1$ pointers and n keys to fit in one block.

Example 14.10: Suppose our blocks are 4096 bytes. Also let keys be integers of 4 bytes and let pointers be 8 bytes. If there is no header information kept on the blocks, then we want to find the largest integer value of n such that $4n + 8(n + 1) \leq 4096$. That value is $n = 340$. $\Box$

There are several important rules about what can appear in the blocks of a B-tree:

- The keys in leaf nodes are copies of keys from the data file. These keys are distributed among the leaves in sorted order, from left to right.

- At the root, there are at least two used pointers.[2] All pointers point to B-tree blocks at the level below.

- At a leaf, the last pointer points to the next leaf block to the right, i.e., to the block with the next higher keys. Among the other n pointers in a leaf block, at least $\lfloor (n + 1)/2 \rfloor$ of these pointers are used and point to data records; unused pointers are null and do not point anywhere. The ith pointer, if it is used, points to a record with the ith key.

---

[2]Technically, there is a possibility that the entire B-tree has only one pointer because it is an index into a data file with only one record. In this case, the entire tree is a root block that is also a leaf, and this block has only one key and one pointer. We shall ignore this trivial case in the descriptions that follow.

- At an interior node, all $n + 1$ pointers can be used to point to B-tree blocks at the next lower level. At least $\lceil (n + 1)/2 \rceil$ of them are actually used (but if the node is the root, then we require only that at least 2 be used, regardless of how large n is). If j pointers are used, then there will be $j - 1$ keys, say $K_1, K_2, \ldots, K_{j-1}$. The first pointer points to a part of the B-tree where some of the records with keys less than K_1 will be found. The second pointer goes to that part of the tree where all records with keys that are at least K_1, but less than K_2 will be found, and so on. Finally, the jth pointer gets us to the part of the B-tree where some of the records with keys greater than or equal to K_{j-1} are found. Note that some records with keys far below K_1 or far above K_{j-1} may not be reachable from this block at all, but will be reached via another block at the same level.

- All used pointers and their keys appear at the beginning of the block, with the exception of the $(n + 1)$st pointer in a leaf, which points to the next leaf.

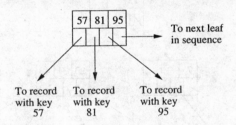

Figure 14.11: A typical leaf of a B-tree

Example 14.11: Our running example of B-trees will use $n = 3$. That is, blocks have room for three keys and four pointers, which are atypically small numbers. Keys are integers. Figure 14.11 shows a leaf that is completely used. There are three keys, 57, 81, and 95. The first three pointers go to records with these keys. The last pointer, as is always the case with leaves, points to the next leaf to the right in the order of keys; it would be null if this leaf were the last in sequence.

A leaf is not necessarily full, but in our example with $n = 3$, there must be at least two key-pointer pairs. That is, the key 95 in Fig. 14.11 might be missing, and if so, the third pointer would be null.

Figure 14.12 shows a typical interior node. There are three keys, 14, 52, and 78. There are also four pointers in this node. The first points to a part of the B-tree from which we can reach only records with keys less than 14 — the first of the keys. The second pointer leads to all records with keys between the first and second keys of the B-tree block; the third pointer is for those records

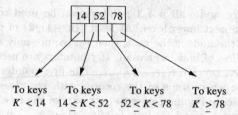

$$
\begin{array}{|c|c|c|}
\hline
14 & 52 & 78 \\
\hline
\end{array}
$$

To keys   To keys   To keys   To keys
$K < 14$ $14 < K < 52$ $52 < K < 78$ $K > 78$

Figure 14.12: A typical interior node of a B-tree

between the second and third keys of the block, and the fourth pointer lets us reach some of the records with keys equal to or above the third key of the block.

As with our example leaf, it is not necessarily the case that all slots for keys and pointers are occupied. However, with $n = 3$, at least the first key and the first two pointers must be present in an interior node. □

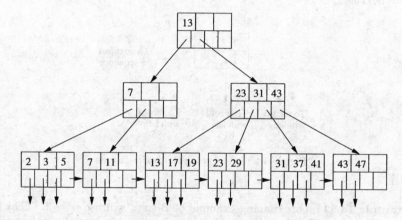

Figure 14.13: A B-tree

Example 14.12: Figure 14.13 shows an entire three-level B-tree, with $n = 3$, as in Example 14.11. We have assumed that the data file consists of records whose keys are all the primes from 2 to 47. Notice that at the leaves, each of these keys appears once, in order. All leaf blocks have two or three key-pointer pairs, plus a pointer to the next leaf in sequence. The keys are in sorted order as we look across the leaves from left to right.

The root has only two pointers, the minimum possible number, although it could have up to four. The one key at the root separates those keys reachable via the first pointer from those reachable via the second. That is, keys up to 12 could be found in the first subtree of the root, and keys 13 and up are in the second subtree.

If we look at the first child of the root, with key 7, we again find two pointers, one to keys less than 7 and the other to keys 7 and above. Note that the second pointer in this node gets us only to keys 7 and 11, not to *all* keys ≥ 7, such as 13.

Finally, the second child of the root has all four pointer slots in use. The first gets us to some of the keys less than 23, namely 13, 17, and 19. The second pointer gets us to all keys K such that $23 \leq K < 31$; the third pointer lets us reach all keys K such that $31 \leq K < 43$, and the fourth pointer gets us to some of the keys ≥ 43 (in this case, to all of them). $\square$

14.2.2 Applications of B-trees

The B-tree is a powerful tool for building indexes. The sequence of pointers at the leaves of a B-tree can play the role of any of the pointer sequences coming out of an index file that we learned about in Section 14.1. Here are some examples:

1. The search key of the B-tree is the primary key for the data file, and the index is dense. That is, there is one key-pointer pair in a leaf for every record of the data file. The data file may or may not be sorted by primary key.

2. The data file is sorted by its primary key, and the B-tree is a sparse index with one key-pointer pair at a leaf for each block of the data file.

3. The data file is sorted by an attribute that is not a key, and this attribute is the search key for the B-tree. For each key value K that appears in the data file there is one key-pointer pair at a leaf. That pointer goes to the first of the records that have K as their sort-key value.

There are additional applications of B-tree variants that allow multiple occurrences of the search key[3] at the leaves. Figure 14.14 suggests what such a B-tree might look like.

If we do allow duplicate occurrences of a search key, then we need to change slightly the definition of what the keys at interior nodes mean, which we discussed in Section 14.2.1. Now, suppose there are keys $K_1, K_2, \ldots, K_n$ at an interior node. Then K_i will be the smallest new key that appears in the part of the subtree accessible from the $(i + 1)$st pointer. By "new," we mean that there are no occurrences of K_i in the portion of the tree to the left of the $(i + 1)$st subtree, but at least one occurrence of K_i in that subtree. Note that in some situations, there will be no such key, in which case K_i can be taken to be null. Its associated pointer is still necessary, as it points to a significant portion of the tree that happens to have only one key value within it.

---

[3]Remember that a "search key" is not necessarily a "key" in the sense of being unique.

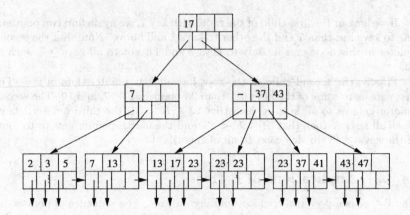

Figure 14.14: A B-tree with duplicate keys

Example 14.13 : Figure 14.14 shows a B-tree similar to Fig. 14.13, but with duplicate values. In particular, key 11 has been replaced by 13, and keys 19, 29, and 31 have all been replaced by 23. As a result, the key at the root is 17, not 13. The reason is that, although 13 is the lowest key in the second subtree of the root, it is not a *new* key for that subtree, since it also appears in the first subtree.

We also had to make some changes to the second child of the root. The second key is changed to 37, since that is the first new key of the third child (fifth leaf from the left). Most interestingly, the first key is now null. The reason is that the second child (fourth leaf) has no new keys at all. Put another way, if we were searching for any key and reached the second child of the root, we would never want to start at its second child. If we are searching for 23 or anything lower, we want to start at its first child, where we will either find what we are looking for (if it is 17), or find the first of what we are looking for (if it is 23). Note that:

- We would not reach the second child of the root searching for 13; we would be directed at the root to its first child instead.

- If we are looking for any key between 24 and 36, we are directed to the third leaf, but when we don't find even one occurrence of what we are looking for, we know not to search further right. For example, if there were a key 24 among the leaves, it would either be on the 4th leaf, in which case the null key in the second child of the root would be 24 instead, or it would be in the 5th leaf, in which case the key 37 at the second child of the root would be 24.

□

14.2.3 Lookup in B-Trees

We now revert to our original assumption that there are no duplicate keys at the leaves. We also suppose that the B-tree is a dense index, so every search-key value that appears in the data file will also appear at a leaf. These assumptions make the discussion of B-tree operations simpler, but is not essential for these operations. In particular, modifications for sparse indexes are similar to the changes we introduced in Section 14.1.3 for indexes on sequential files.

Suppose we have a B-tree index and we want to find a record with search-key value K. We search for K recursively, starting at the root and ending at a leaf. The search procedure is:

BASIS: If we are at a leaf, look among the keys there. If the ith key is K, then the ith pointer will take us to the desired record.

INDUCTION: If we are at an interior node with keys $K_1, K_2, \ldots, K_n$, follow the rules given in Section 14.2.1 to decide which of the children of this node should next be examined. That is, there is only one child that could lead to a leaf with key K. If $K < K_1$, then it is the first child, if $K_1 \leq K < K_2$, it is the second child, and so on. Recursively apply the search procedure at this child.

Example 14.14: Suppose we have the B-tree of Fig. 14.13, and we want to find a record with search key 40. We start at the root, where there is one key, 13. Since $13 \leq 40$, we follow the second pointer, which leads us to the second-level node with keys 23, 31, and 43.

At that node, we find $31 \leq 40 < 43$, so we follow the third pointer. We are thus led to the leaf with keys 31, 37, and 41. If there had been a record in the data file with key 40, we would have found key 40 at this leaf. Since we do not find 40, we conclude that there is no record with key 40 in the underlying data.

Note that had we been looking for a record with key 37, we would have taken exactly the same decisions, but when we got to the leaf we would find key 37. Since it is the second key in the leaf, we follow the second pointer, which will lead us to the data record with key 37. □

14.2.4 Range Queries

B-trees are useful not only for queries in which a single value of the search key is sought, but for queries in which a range of values are asked for. Typically, *range queries* have a term in the WHERE-clause that compares the search key with a value or values, using one of the comparison operators other than = or <>. Examples of range queries using a search-key attribute k are:

```
SELECT * FROM R    SELECT * FROM R
WHERE R.k > 40;    WHERE R.k >= 10 AND R.k <= 25;
```

If we want to find all keys in the range $[a, b]$ at the leaves of a B-tree, we do a lookup to find the key a. Whether or not it exists, we are led to a leaf where

a could be, and we search the leaf for keys that are a or greater. Each such key we find has an associated pointer to one of the records whose key is in the desired range. As long as we do not find a key greater than b in the current block, we follow the pointer to the next leaf and repeat our search for keys in the range $[a, b]$.

The above search algorithm also works if b is infinite; i.e., there is only a lower bound and no upper bound. In that case, we search all the leaves from the one that would hold key a to the end of the chain of leaves. If a is $-\infty$ (that is, there is an upper bound on the range but no lower bound), then the search for "minus infinity" as a search key will always take us to the first leaf. The search then proceeds as above, stopping only when we pass the key b.

Example 14.15: Suppose we have the B-tree of Fig. 14.13, and we are given the range $(10, 25)$ to search for. We look for key 10, which leads us to the second leaf. The first key is less than 10, but the second, 11, is at least 10. We follow its associated pointer to get the record with key 11.

Since there are no more keys in the second leaf, we follow the chain to the third leaf, where we find keys 13, 17, and 19. All are less than or equal to 25, so we follow their associated pointers and retrieve the records with these keys. Finally, we move to the fourth leaf, where we find key 23. But the next key of that leaf, 29, exceeds 25, so we are done with our search. Thus, we have retrieved the five records with keys 11 through 23.   □

14.2.5 Insertion Into B-Trees

We see some of the advantages of B-trees over simpler multilevel indexes when we consider how to insert a new key into a B-tree. The corresponding record will be inserted into the file being indexed by the B-tree, using any of the methods discussed in Section 14.1; here we consider how the B-tree changes. The insertion is, in principle, recursive:

- We try to find a place for the new key in the appropriate leaf, and we put it there if there is room.

- If there is no room in the proper leaf, we split the leaf into two and divide the keys between the two new nodes, so each is half full or just over half full.

- The splitting of nodes at one level appears to the level above as if a new key-pointer pair needs to be inserted at that higher level. We may thus recursively apply this strategy to insert at the next level: if there is room, insert it; if not, split the parent node and continue up the tree.

- As an exception, if we try to insert into the root, and there is no room, then we split the root into two nodes and create a new root at the next higher level; the new root has the two nodes resulting from the split as its children. Recall that no matter how large n (the number of slots for keys at a node) is, it is always permissible for the root to have only one key and two children.

When we split a node and insert it into its parent, we need to be careful how the keys are managed. First, suppose N is a leaf whose capacity is n keys. Also suppose we are trying to insert an $(n+1)$st key and its associated pointer. We create a new node M, which will be the sibling of N, immediately to its right. The first $\lceil (n+1)/2 \rceil$ key-pointer pairs, in sorted order of the keys, remain with N, while the other key-pointer pairs move to M. Note that both nodes N and M are left with a sufficient number of key-pointer pairs — at least $\lfloor (n+1)/2 \rfloor$ pairs.

Now, suppose N is an interior node whose capacity is n keys and $n+1$ pointers, and N has just been assigned $n+2$ pointers because of a node splitting below. We do the following:

1. Create a new node M, which will be the sibling of N, immediately to its right.

2. Leave at N the first $\lceil (n+2)/2 \rceil$ pointers, in sorted order, and move to M the remaining $\lfloor (n+2)/2 \rfloor$ pointers.

3. The first $\lceil n/2 \rceil$ keys stay with N, while the last $\lfloor n/2 \rfloor$ keys move to M. Note that there is always one key in the middle left over; it goes with neither N nor M. The leftover key K indicates the smallest key reachable via the first of M's children. Although this key doesn't appear in N or M, it is associated with M, in the sense that it represents the smallest key reachable via M. Therefore K will be inserted into the parent of N and M to divide searches between those two nodes.

Example 14.16: Let us insert key 40 into the B-tree of Fig. 14.13. We find the proper leaf for the insertion by the lookup procedure of Section 14.2.3. As found in Example 14.14, the insertion goes into the fifth leaf. Since this leaf now has four key-pointer pairs — 31, 37, 40, and 41 — we need to split the leaf. Our first step is to create a new node and move the highest two keys, 40 and 41, along with their pointers, to that node. Figure 14.15 shows this split.

Notice that although we now show the nodes on four ranks to save space, there are still only three levels to the tree. The seven leaves are linked by their last pointers, which still form a chain from left to right.

We must now insert a pointer to the new leaf (the one with keys 40 and 41) into the node above it (the node with keys 23, 31, and 43). We must also associate with this pointer the key 40, which is the least key reachable through the new leaf. Unfortunately, the parent of the split node is already full; it has no room for another key or pointer. Thus, it too must be split.

We start with pointers to the last five leaves and the list of keys representing the least keys of the last four of these leaves. That is, we have pointers P_1, P_2, P_3, P_4, P_5 to the leaves whose least keys are 13, 23, 31, 40, and 43, and

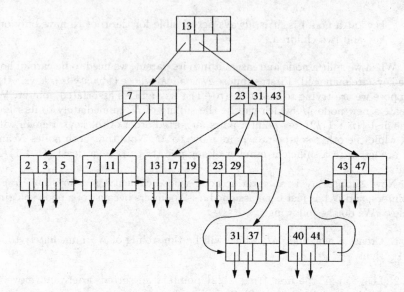

Figure 14.15: Beginning the insertion of key 40

we have the key sequence 23, 31, 40, 43 to separate these pointers. The first three pointers and first two keys remain with the split interior node, while the last two pointers and last key go to the new node. The remaining key, 40, represents the least key accessible via the new node.

Figure 14.16 shows the completion of the insert of key 40. The root now has three children; the last two are the split interior node. Notice that the key 40, which marks the lowest of the keys reachable via the second of the split nodes, has been installed in the root to separate the keys of the root's second and third children. □

14.2.6   Deletion From B-Trees

If we are to delete a record with a given key K, we must first locate that record and its key-pointer pair in a leaf of the B-tree. This part of the deletion process is essentially a lookup, as in Section 14.2.3. We then delete the record itself from the data file, and we delete the key-pointer pair from the B-tree.

If the B-tree node from which a deletion occurred still has at least the minimum number of keys and pointers, then there is nothing more to be done.[4] However, it is possible that the node was right at the minimum occupancy before the deletion, so after deletion the constraint on the number of keys is

---

[4]If the data record with the least key at a leaf is deleted, then we have the option of raising the appropriate key at one of the ancestors of that leaf, but there is no requirement that we do so; all searches will still go to the appropriate leaf.

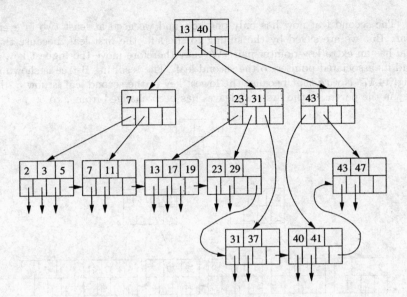

Figure 14.16: Completing the insertion of key 40

violated. We then need to do one of two things for a node N whose contents are subminimum; one case requires a recursive deletion up the tree:

1. If one of the adjacent siblings of node N has more than the minimum number of keys and pointers, then one key-pointer pair can be moved to N, keeping the order of keys intact. Possibly, the keys at the parent of N must be adjusted to reflect the new situation. For instance, if the right sibling of N, say node M, provides an extra key and pointer, then it must be the smallest key that is moved from M to N. At the parent of M and N, there is a key that represents the smallest key accessible via M; that key must be increased to reflect the new M.

2. The hard case is when neither adjacent sibling can be used to provide an extra key for N. However, in that case, we have two adjacent nodes, N and a sibling M; the latter has the minimum number of keys and the former has fewer than the minimum. Therefore, together they have no more keys and pointers than are allowed in a single node. We merge these two nodes, effectively deleting one of them. We need to adjust the keys at the parent, and then delete a key and pointer at the parent. If the parent is still full enough, then we are done. If not, then we recursively apply the deletion algorithm at the parent.

Example 14.17: Let us begin with the original B-tree of Fig. 14.13, before the insertion of key 40. Suppose we delete key 7. This key is found in the second leaf. We delete it, its associated pointer, and the record that pointer points to.

The second leaf now has only one key, and we need at least two in every leaf. But we are saved by the sibling to the left, the first leaf, because that leaf has an extra key-pointer pair. We may therefore move the highest key, 5, and its associated pointer to the second leaf. The resulting B-tree is shown in Fig. 14.17. Notice that because the lowest key in the second leaf is now 5, the key in the parent of the first two leaves has been changed from 7 to 5.

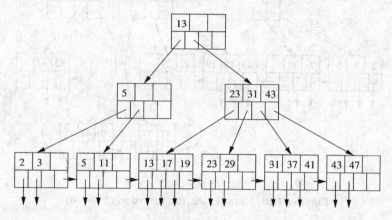

Figure 14.17: Deletion of key 7

Next, suppose we delete key 11. This deletion has the same effect on the second leaf; it again reduces the number of its keys below the minimum. This time, however, we cannot take a key from the first leaf, because the latter is down to the minimum number of keys. Additionally, there is no sibling to the right from which to take a key.[5] Thus, we need to merge the second leaf with a sibling, namely the first leaf.

The three remaining key-pointer pairs from the first two leaves fit in one leaf, so we move 5 to the first leaf and delete the second leaf. The pointers and keys in the parent are adjusted to reflect the new situation at its children; specifically, the two pointers are replaced by one (to the remaining leaf) and the key 5 is no longer relevant and is deleted. The situation is now as shown in Fig. 14.18.

The deletion of a leaf has adversely affected the parent, which is the left child of the root. That node, as we see in Fig. 14.18, now has no keys and only one pointer. Thus, we try to obtain an extra key and pointer from an adjacent sibling. This time we have the easy case, since the other child of the root can afford to give up its smallest key and a pointer.

The change is shown in Fig. 14.19. The pointer to the leaf with keys 13, 17,

---

[5]Notice that the leaf to the right, with keys 13, 17, and 19, is not a sibling, because it has a different parent. We could take a key from that node anyway, but then the algorithm for adjusting keys throughout the tree becomes more complex. We leave this enhancement as an exercise.

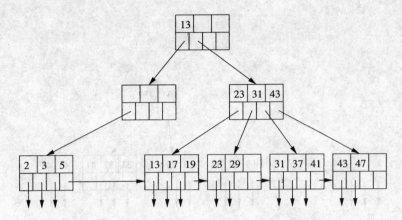

Figure 14.18: Beginning the deletion of key 11

and 19 has been moved from the second child of the root to the first child. We have also changed some keys at the interior nodes. The key 13, which used to reside at the root and represented the smallest key accessible via the pointer that was transferred, is now needed at the first child of the root. On the other hand, the key 23, which used to separate the first and second children of the second child of the root now represents the smallest key accessible from the second child of the root. It therefore is placed at the root itself. □

14.2.7 Efficiency of B-Trees

B-trees allow lookup, insertion, and deletion of records using very few disk I/O's per file operation. First, we should observe that if n, the number of keys per block, is reasonably large, then splitting and merging of blocks will be rare events. Further, when such an operation is needed, it almost always is limited to the leaves, so only two leaves and their parent are affected. Thus, we can essentially neglect the disk-I/O cost of B-tree reorganizations.

However, every search for the record(s) with a given search key requires us to go from the root down to a leaf, to find a pointer to the record. Since we are only reading B-tree blocks, the number of disk I/O's will be the number of levels the B-tree has, plus the one (for lookup) or two (for insert or delete) disk I/O's needed for manipulation of the record itself. We must thus ask: how many levels does a B-tree have? For the typical sizes of keys, pointers, and blocks, three levels are sufficient for all but the largest databases. Thus, we shall generally take 3 as the number of levels of a B-tree. The following example illustrates why.

Example 14.18: Recall our analysis in Example 14.10, where we determined that 340 key-pointer pairs could fit in one block for our example data. Suppose

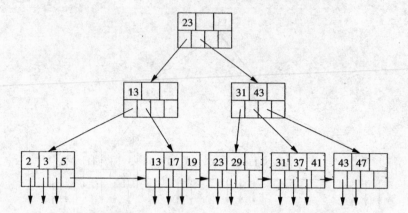

Figure 14.19: Completing the deletion of key 11

that the average block has an occupancy midway between the minimum and maximum, i.e., a typical block has 255 pointers. With a root, 255 children, and $255^2 = 65025$ leaves, we shall have among those leaves 255^3, or about 16.6 million pointers to records. That is, files with up to 16.6 million records can be accommodated by a 3-level B-tree.   □

However, we can use even fewer than three disk I/O's per search through the B-tree. The root block of a B-tree is an excellent choice to keep permanently buffered in main memory. If so, then every search through a 3-level B-tree requires only two disk reads. In fact, under some circumstances it may make sense to keep second-level nodes of the B-tree buffered in main memory as well, reducing the B-tree search to a single disk I/O, plus whatever is necessary to manipulate the blocks of the data file itself.

14.2.8   Exercises for Section 14.2

Exercise 14.2.1: Suppose that blocks can hold either ten records or 99 keys and 100 pointers. Also assume that the average B-tree node is 70% full; i.e., it will have 69 keys and 70 pointers. We can use B-trees as part of several different structures. For each structure described below, determine (*i*) the total number of blocks needed for a 100,000-record file, and (*ii*) the average number of disk I/O's to retrieve a record given its search key. You may assume nothing is in memory initially, and the search key is the primary key for the records.

a) The data file is a sequential file, sorted on the search key, with 20 records per block. The B-tree is a dense index.

b) The same as (a), but the data file consists of records in no particular order, packed 20 to a block.

Should We Delete From B-Trees?

There are B-tree implementations that don't fix up deletions at all. If a leaf has too few keys and pointers, it is allowed to remain as it is. The rationale is that most files grow on balance, and while there might be an occasional deletion that makes a leaf become subminimum, the leaf will probably soon grow again and attain the minimum number of key-pointer pairs once again.

Further, if records have pointers from outside the B-tree index, then we need to replace the record by a "tombstone," and we don't want to delete its pointer from the B-tree anyway. In certain circumstances, when it can be guaranteed that all accesses to the deleted record will go through the B-tree, we can even leave the tombstone in place of the pointer to the record at a leaf of the B-tree. Then, space for the record can be reused.

---

   c) The same as (a), but the B-tree is a sparse index.

   d) The data file is a sequential file, and the B-tree is a sparse index, but each primary block of the data file has one overflow block. On average, the primary block is full, and the overflow block is half full. However, records are in no particular order within a primary block and its overflow block.

! e) Instead of the B-tree leaves having pointers to data records, the B-tree leaves hold the records themselves. A block can hold ten records, but on average, a leaf block is 70% full; i.e., there are seven records per leaf block.

Exercise 14.2.2: Repeat Exercise 14.2.1 in the case that the query is a range query that is matched by 200 records.

Exercise 14.2.3: Suppose pointers are 4 bytes long, and keys are 20 bytes long. How many keys and pointers will a block of 16,384 bytes have?

Exercise 14.2.4: What are the minimum numbers of keys and pointers in B-tree (i) interior nodes and (ii) leaves, when:

   a) $n = 11$; i.e., a block holds 11 keys and 12 pointers.

   b) $n = 12$; i.e., a block holds 12 keys and 13 pointers.

Exercise 14.2.5: Execute the following operations on Fig. 14.13. Describe the changes for operations that modify the tree.

   a) Lookup the record with key 40.

   b) Lookup the record with key 41.

   c) Lookup all records with keys less than 30.

   d) Lookup all records with keys greater than 30.

   e) Lookup all records in the range 20 to 30.

   f) Insert a record with key 1.

   g) Delete the record with key 23.

   h) Insert records with keys 14 through 16.

   i) Delete all the records with keys 23 and higher.

! **Exercise 14.2.6:** In Example 14.17 we suggested that it would be possible to borrow keys from a nonsibling to the right (or left) if we used a more complicated algorithm for maintaining keys at interior nodes. Describe a suitable algorithm that rebalances by borrowing from adjacent nodes at a level, regardless of whether they are siblings of the node that has too many or too few key-pointer pairs.

! **Exercise 14.2.7:** If we use the 3-key, 4-pointer nodes of our examples in this section, how many different B-trees are there when the data file has the following numbers of records: (a) 6 (b) 10 !! (c) 15.

! **Exercise 14.2.8:** Suppose we have B-tree nodes with room for three keys and four pointers, as in the examples of this section. Suppose also that when we split a leaf, we divide the pointers 2 and 2, while when we split an interior node, the first 3 pointers go with the first (left) node, and the last 2 pointers go with the second (right) node. We start with a leaf containing pointers to records with keys 1, 2, and 3. We then add in order, records with keys 4, 5, 6, and so on. At the insertion of what key will the B-tree first reach four levels?

Exercise 14.2.9: When duplicate keys are allowed in a B-tree, there are some necessary modifications to the algorithms for lookup, insertion, and deletion that we described in this section. Give the changes for: (a) lookup (b) insertion (c) deletion.

14.3 Hash Tables

There are a number of data structures involving a hash table that are useful as indexes. We assume the reader has seen the hash table used as a main-memory data structure. In such a structure there is a *hash function* h that takes a search key (the *hash key*) as an argument and computes from it an integer in the range 0 to $B - 1$, where B is the number of *buckets*. A *bucket array*, which is an array indexed from 0 to $B - 1$, holds the headers of B linked lists, one for each bucket of the array. If a record has search key K, then we store the record by linking it to the bucket list for the bucket numbered $h(K)$.

14.3.1 Secondary-Storage Hash Tables

A hash table that holds a very large number of records, so many that they must be kept mainly in secondary storage, differs from the main-memory version in small but important ways. First, the bucket array consists of blocks, rather than pointers to the headers of lists. Records that are hashed by the hash function h to a certain bucket are put in the block for that bucket. If a bucket has too many records, a chain of overflow blocks can be added to the bucket to hold more records.

We shall assume that the location of the first block for any bucket i can be found given i. For example, there might be a main-memory array of pointers to blocks, indexed by the bucket number. Another possibility is to put the first block for each bucket in fixed, consecutive disk locations, so we can compute the location of bucket i from the integer i.

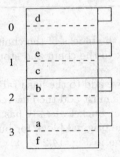

Figure 14.20: A hash table

Example 14.19: Figure 14.20 shows a hash table. To keep our illustrations manageable, we assume that a block can hold only two records, and that $B = 4$; i.e., the hash function h returns values from 0 to 3. We show certain records populating the hash table. Keys are letters a through f in Fig. 14.20. We assume that $h(d) = 0$, $h(c) = h(e) = 1$, $h(b) = 2$, and $h(a) = h(f) = 3$. Thus, the six records are distributed into blocks as shown. $\Box$

Note that we show each block in Fig. 14.20 with a "nub" at the right end. This nub represents additional information in the block's header. We shall use it to chain overflow blocks together, and starting in Section 14.3.5, we shall use it to keep other critical information about the block.

14.3.2 Insertion Into a Hash Table

When a new record with search key K must be inserted, we compute $h(K)$. If the bucket numbered $h(K)$ has space, then we insert the record into the block for this bucket, or into one of the overflow blocks on its chain if there is no room

---

Choice of Hash Function

The hash function should "hash" the key so the resulting integer is a seemingly random function of the key. Thus, buckets will tend to have equal numbers of records, which improves the average time to access a record, as we shall discuss in Section 14.3.4. Also, the hash function should be easy to compute, since we shall compute it many times.

A common choice of hash function when keys are integers is to compute the remainder of K/B, where K is the key value and B is the number of buckets. Often, B is chosen to be a prime, although there are reasons to make B a power of 2, as we discuss starting in Section 14.3.5. For character-string search keys, we may treat each character as an integer, sum these integers, and take the remainder when the sum is divided by B.

---

in the first block. If none of the blocks of the chain for bucket $h(K)$ has room, we add a new overflow block to the chain and store the new record there.

Example 14.20: Suppose we add to the hash table of Fig. 14.20 a record with key g, and $h(g) = 1$. Then we must add the new record to the bucket numbered 1. However, the block for that bucket already has two records. Thus, we add a new block and chain it to the original block for bucket 1. The record with key g goes in that block, as shown in Fig. 14.21. □

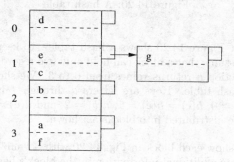

Figure 14.21: Adding an additional block to a hash-table bucket

14.3.3 Hash-Table Deletion

Deletion of the record (or records) with search key K follows the same pattern as insertion. We go to the bucket numbered $h(K)$ and search for records with that search key. Any that we find are deleted. If we are able to move records around among blocks, then after deletion we may optionally consolidate the blocks of a bucket into one fewer block.[6]

Example 14.21: Figure 14.22 shows the result of deleting the record with key c from the hash table of Fig. 14.21. Recall $h(c) = 1$, so we go to the bucket numbered 1 (i.e., the second bucket) and search all its blocks to find a record (or records if the search key were not the primary key) with key c. We find it in the first block of the chain for bucket 1. Since there is now room to move the record with key g from the second block of the chain to the first, we can do so and remove the second block.

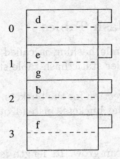

Figure 14.22: Result of deletions from a hash table

We also show the deletion of the record with key a. For this key, we found our way to bucket 3, deleted it, and "consolidated" the remaining record at the beginning of the block. □

14.3.4 Efficiency of Hash Table Indexes

Ideally, there are enough buckets that most of them fit on one block. If so, then the typical lookup takes only one disk I/O, and insertion or deletion from the file takes only two disk I/O's. That number is significantly better than straightforward sparse or dense indexes, or B-tree indexes (although hash tables do not support range queries as B-trees do; see Section 14.2.4).

However, if the file grows, then we shall eventually reach a situation where there are many blocks in the chain for a typical bucket. If so, then we need to search long lists of blocks, taking at least one disk I/O per block. Thus, there is a good reason to try to keep the number of blocks per bucket low.

The hash tables we have examined so far are called *static hash tables*, because B, the number of buckets, never changes. However, there are several kinds of *dynamic hash tables*, where B is allowed to vary so it approximates the number

---

[6]A risk of consolidating blocks of a chain whenever possible is that an oscillation, where we alternately insert and delete records from a bucket, will cause a block to be created or destroyed at each step.

of records divided by the number of records that can fit on a block; i.e., there is about one block per bucket. We shall discuss two such methods:

1. Extensible hashing in Section 14.3.5, and

2. Linear hashing in Section 14.3.7.

The first grows B by doubling it whenever it is deemed too small, and the second grows B by 1 each time statistics of the file suggest some growth is needed.

14.3.5 Extensible Hash Tables

Our first approach to dynamic hashing is called *extensible hash tables*. The major additions to the simpler static hash table structure are:

1. There is a level of indirection for the buckets. That is, an array of pointers to blocks represents the buckets, instead of the array holding the data blocks themselves.

2. The array of pointers can grow. Its length is always a power of 2, so in a growing step the number of buckets doubles.

3. However, there does not have to be a data block for each bucket; certain buckets can share a block if the total number of records in those buckets can fit in the block.

4. The hash function h computes for each key a sequence of k bits for some large k, say 32. However, the bucket numbers will at all times use some smaller number of bits, say i bits, from the beginning or end of this sequence. The bucket array will have 2^i entries when i is the number of bits used.

Example 14.22: Figure 14.23 shows a small extensible hash table. We suppose, for simplicity of the example, that $k = 4$; i.e., the hash function produces a sequence of only four bits. At the moment, only one of these bits is used, as indicated by $i = 1$ in the box above the bucket array. The bucket array therefore has only two entries, one for 0 and one for 1.

The bucket array entries point to two blocks. The first holds all the current records whose search keys hash to a bit sequence that begins with 0, and the second holds all those whose search keys hash to a sequence beginning with 1. For convenience, we show the keys of records as if they were the entire bit sequence to which the hash function converts them. Thus, the first block holds a record whose key hashes to 0001, and the second holds records whose keys hash to 1001 and 1100. □

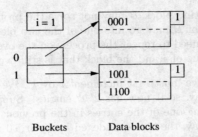

Figure 14.23: An extensible hash table

We should notice the number 1 appearing in the "nub" of each of the blocks in Fig. 14.23. This number, which would actually appear in the block header, indicates how many bits of the hash function's sequence is used to determine membership of records in this block. In the situation of Example 14.22, there is only one bit considered for all blocks and records, but as we shall see, the number of bits considered for various blocks can differ as the hash table grows. That is, the bucket array size is determined by the maximum number of bits we are now using, but some blocks may use fewer.

14.3.6 Insertion Into Extensible Hash Tables

Insertion into an extensible hash table begins like insertion into a static hash table. To insert a record with search key K, we compute $h(K)$, take the first i bits of this bit sequence, and go to the entry of the bucket array indexed by these i bits. Note that we can determine i because it is kept as part of the data structure.

We follow the pointer in this entry of the bucket array and arrive at a block B. If there is room to put the new record in block B, we do so and we are done. If there is no room, then there are two possibilities, depending on the number j, which indicates how many bits of the hash value are used to determine membership in block B (recall the value of j is found in the "nub" of each block in figures).

1. If $j < i$, then nothing needs to be done to the bucket array. We:

   (a) Split block B into two.

   (b) Distribute records in B to the two blocks, based on the value of their $(j + 1)$st bit — records whose key has 0 in that bit stay in B and those with 1 there go to the new block.

   (c) Put $j + 1$ in each block's "nub" (header) to indicate the number of bits used to determine membership.

   (d) Adjust the pointers in the bucket array so entries that formerly pointed to B now point either to B or the new block, depending on their $(j + 1)$st bit.

Note that splitting block B may not solve the problem, since by chance all the records of B may go into one of the two blocks into which it was split. If so, we need to repeat the process on the overfull block, using the next higher value of j and the block that is still overfull.

2. If $j = i$, then we must first increment i by 1. We double the length of the bucket array, so it now has 2^{i+1} entries. Suppose w is a sequence of i bits indexing one of the entries in the previous bucket array. In the new bucket array, the entries indexed by both $w0$ and $w1$ (i.e., the two numbers derived from w by extending it with 0 or 1) each point to the same block that the w entry used to point to. That is, the two new entries share the block, and the block itself does not change. Membership in the block is still determined by whatever number of bits was previously used. Finally, we proceed to split block B as in case 1. Since i is now greater than j, that case applies.

Example 14.23 : Suppose we insert into the table of Fig. 14.23 a record whose key hashes to the sequence 1010. Since the first bit is 1, this record belongs in the second block. However, that block is already full, so it needs to be split. We find that $j = i = 1$ in this case, so we first need to double the bucket array, as shown in Fig. 14.24. We have also set $i = 2$ in this figure.

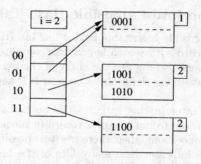

Figure 14.24: Now, two bits of the hash function are used

Notice that the two entries beginning with 0 each point to the block for records whose hashed keys begin with 0, and that block still has the integer 1 in its "nub" to indicate that only the first bit determines membership in the block. However, the block for records beginning with 1 needs to be split, so we partition its records into those beginning 10 and those beginning 11. A 2 in each of these blocks indicates that two bits are used to determine membership. Fortunately, the split is successful; since each of the two new blocks gets at least one record, we do not have to split recursively.

Now suppose we insert records whose keys hash to 0000 and 0111. These both go in the first block of Fig. 14.24, which then overflows. Since only one bit is used to determine membership in this block, while $i = 2$, we do not have to adjust the bucket array. We simply split the block, with 0000 and 0001 staying, and 0111 going to the new block. The entry for 01 in the bucket array is made to point to the new block. Again, we have been fortunate that the records did not all go in one of the new blocks, so we have no need to split recursively.

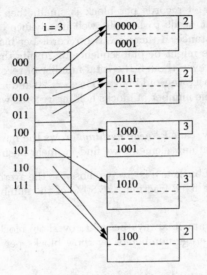

Figure 14.25: The hash table now uses three bits of the hash function

Now suppose a record whose key hashes to 1000 is inserted. The block for 10 overflows. Since it already uses two bits to determine membership, it is time to split the bucket array again and set $i = 3$. Figure 14.25 shows the data structure at this point. Notice that the block for 10 has been split into blocks for 100 and 101, while the other blocks continue to use only two bits to determine membership. □

14.3.7 Linear Hash Tables

Extensible hash tables have some important advantages. Most significant is the fact that when looking for a record, we never need to search more than one data block. We also have to examine an entry of the bucket array, but if the bucket array is small enough to be kept in main memory, then there is no disk I/O needed to access the bucket array. However, extensible hash tables also suffer from some defects:

1. When the bucket array needs to be doubled in size, there is a substantial amount of work to be done (when i is large). This work interrupts access to the data file, or makes certain insertions appear to take a long time.

2. When the bucket array is doubled in size, it may no longer fit in main memory, or may crowd out other data that we would like to hold in main memory. As a result, a system that was performing well might suddenly start using many more disk I/O's per operation.

3. If the number of records per block is small, then there is likely to be one block that needs to be split well in advance of the logical time to do so. For instance, if there are two records per block as in our running example, there might be one sequence of 20 bits that begins the keys of three records, even though the total number of records is much less than 2^{20}. In that case, we would have to use $i = 20$ and a million-bucket array, even though the number of blocks holding records was much smaller than a million.

Another strategy, called *linear hashing*, grows the number of buckets more slowly. The principal new elements we find in linear hashing are:

- The number of buckets n is always chosen so the average number of records per bucket is a fixed fraction, say 80%, of the number of records that fill one block.

- Since blocks cannot always be split, overflow blocks are permitted, although the average number of overflow blocks per bucket will be much less than 1.

- The number of bits used to number the entries of the bucket array is $\lceil \log_2 n \rceil$, where n is the current number of buckets. These bits are always taken from the *right* (low-order) end of the bit sequence that is produced by the hash function.

- Suppose i bits of the hash function are being used to number array entries, and a record with key K is intended for bucket $a_1 a_2 \cdots a_i$; that is, $a_1 a_2 \cdots a_i$ are the last i bits of $h(K)$. Then let $a_1 a_2 \cdots a_i$ be m, treated as an i-bit binary integer. If $m < n$, then the bucket numbered m exists, and we place the record in that bucket. If $n \leq m < 2^i$, then the bucket m does not yet exist, so we place the record in bucket $m - 2^{i-1}$, that is, the bucket we would get if we changed a_1 (which must be 1) to 0.

Example 14.24: Figure 14.26 shows a linear hash table with $n = 2$. We currently are using only one bit of the hash value to determine the buckets of records. Following the pattern established in Example 14.22, we assume the hash function h produces 4 bits, and we represent records by the value produced by h when applied to the search key of the record.

We see in Fig. 14.26 the two buckets, each consisting of one block. The buckets are numbered 0 and 1. All records whose hash value ends in 0 go in the first bucket, and those whose hash value ends in 1 go in the second.

Also part of the structure are the parameters i (the number of bits of the hash function that currently are used), n (the current number of buckets), and r

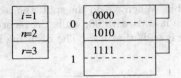

Figure 14.26: A linear hash table

(the current number of records in the hash table). The ratio r/n will be limited so that the typical bucket will need about one disk block. We shall adopt the policy of choosing n, the number of buckets, so that there are no more than $1.7n$ records in the file; i.e., $r \leq 1.7n$. That is, since blocks hold two records, the average occupancy of a bucket does not exceed 85% of the capacity of a block. □

14.3.8 Insertion Into Linear Hash Tables

When we insert a new record, we determine its bucket by the algorithm outlined in Section 14.3.7. We compute $h(K)$, where K is the key of the record, and we use the i bits at the end of bit sequence $h(K)$ as the bucket number, m. If $m < n$, we put the record in bucket m, and if $m \geq n$, we put the record in bucket $m - 2^{i-1}$. If there is no room in the designated bucket, then we create an overflow block, add it to the chain for that bucket, and put the record there.

Each time we insert, we compare the current number of records r with the threshold ratio of r/n, and if the ratio is too high, we add the next bucket to the table. Note that the bucket we add bears no relationship to the bucket into which the insertion occurs! If the binary representation of the number of the bucket we add is $1a_2 \cdots a_i$, then we split the bucket numbered $0a_2 \cdots a_i$, putting records into one or the other bucket, depending on their last i bits. Note that all these records will have hash values that end in $a_2 \cdots a_i$, and only the ith bit from the right end will vary.

The last important detail is what happens when n exceeds 2^i. Then, i is incremented by 1. Technically, all the bucket numbers get an additional 0 in front of their bit sequences, but there is no need to make any physical change, since these bit sequences, interpreted as integers, remain the same.

Example 14.25: We shall continue with Example 14.24 and consider what happens when a record whose key hashes to 0101 is inserted. Since this bit sequence ends in 1, the record goes into the second bucket of Fig. 14.26. There is room for the record, so no overflow block is created.

However, since there are now 4 records in 2 buckets, we exceed the ratio 1.7, and we must therefore raise n to 3. Since $\lceil \log_2 3 \rceil = 2$, we should begin to think of buckets 0 and 1 as 00 and 01, but no change to the data structure is necessary. We add to the table the next bucket, which would have number 10. Then, we split the bucket 00, that bucket whose number differs from the added bucket only in the first bit. When we do the split, the record whose key hashes to 0000 stays in 00, since it ends with 00, while the record whose key hashes to 1010 goes to 10 because it ends that way. The resulting hash table is shown in Fig. 14.27.

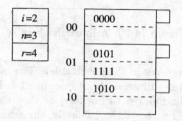

Figure 14.27: Adding a third bucket

Next, let us suppose we add a record whose search key hashes to 0001. The last two bits are 01, so we put it in this bucket, which currently exists. Unfortunately, the bucket's block is full, so we add an overflow block. The three records are distributed among the two blocks of the bucket; we chose to keep them in numerical order of their hashed keys, but order is not important. Since the ratio of records to buckets for the table as a whole is 5/3, and this ratio is less than 1.7, we do not create a new bucket. The result is seen in Fig. 14.28.

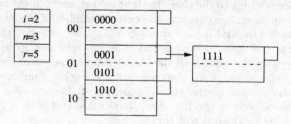

Figure 14.28: Overflow blocks are used if necessary

Finally, consider the insertion of a record whose search key hashes to 0111. The last two bits are 11, but bucket 11 does not yet exist. We therefore redirect this record to bucket 01, whose number differs by having a 0 in the first bit. The new record fits in the overflow block of this bucket.

However, the ratio of the number of records to buckets has exceeded 1.7, so we must create a new bucket, numbered 11. Coincidentally, this bucket is the one we wanted for the new record. We split the four records in bucket 01, with 0001 and 0101 remaining, and 0111 and 1111 going to the new bucket. Since bucket 01 now has only two records, we can delete the overflow block. The hash table is now as shown in Fig. 14.29.

Notice that the next time we insert a record into Fig. 14.29, we shall exceed

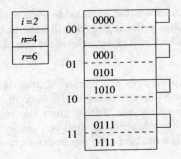

Figure 14.29: Adding a fourth bucket

the 1.7 ratio of records to buckets. Then, we shall raise n to 5 and i becomes 3. □

Lookup in a linear hash table follows the procedure we described for selecting the bucket in which an inserted record belongs. If the record we wish to look up is not in that bucket, it cannot be anywhere.

14.3.9 Exercises for Section 14.3

Exercise 14.3.1: We did not discuss how deletions can be carried out in a linear or extensible hash table. The mechanics of locating the record(s) to be deleted should be obvious. What method would you suggest for executing the deletion? In particular, what are the advantages and disadvantages of restructuring the table if its smaller size after deletion allows for compression of certain blocks?

! **Exercise 14.3.2:** The material of this section assumes that search keys are unique. However, only small modifications are needed to allow the techniques to work for search keys with duplicates. Describe the necessary changes to insertion, deletion, and lookup algorithms, and suggest the major problems that arise when there are duplicates in each of the following kinds of hash tables: (a) simple (b) linear (c) extensible.

Exercise 14.3.3: Show what happens to the buckets in Fig. 14.20 if the following insertions and deletions occur:

   i. Records g through j are inserted into buckets 0 through 3, respectively.

   ii. Records a and b are deleted.

   iii. Records k through n are inserted into buckets 0 through 3, respectively.

   iv. Records c and d are deleted.

Exercise 14.3.4: In an extensible hash table with n records per block, what is the probability that an overflowing block will have to be handled recursively; i.e., all members of the block will go into the same one of the two blocks created in the split?

Exercise 14.3.5: Suppose keys are hashed to four-bit sequences, as in our examples of extensible and linear hashing in this section. However, also suppose that blocks can hold three records, rather than the two-record blocks of our examples. If we start with a hash table with two empty blocks (corresponding to 0 and 1), show the organization after we insert records with hashed keys:

a) $1111, 1110, \ldots, 0000$, and the method of hashing is extensible hashing.

b) $1111, 1110, \ldots, 0000$, and the method of hashing is linear hashing with a capacity threshold of 75%.

c) $0000, 0001, \ldots, 1111$, and the method of hashing is extensible hashing.

d) $0000, 0001, \ldots, 1111$, and the method of hashing is linear hashing with a capacity threshold of 100%.

Exercise 14.3.6: Suppose we use a linear or extensible hashing scheme, but there are pointers to records from outside. These pointers prevent us from moving records between blocks, as is sometimes required by these hashing methods. Suggest several ways that we could modify the structure to allow pointers from outside.

! **Exercise 14.3.7:** Some hash functions do not work as well as theoretically possible. Suppose that we use the hash function on integer keys i defined by $h(i) = i^2 \bmod B$, where B is the number of buckets.

a) What is wrong with this hash function if $B = 10$?

b) How good is this hash function if $B = 16$?

c) Are there values of B for which this hash function is useful?

!! **Exercise 14.3.8:** A linear-hashing scheme with blocks that hold k records uses a threshold constant c, such that the current number of buckets n and the current number of records r are related by $r = ckn$. For instance, in Example 14.24 we used $k = 2$ and $c = 0.85$, so there were 1.7 records per bucket; i.e., $r = 1.7n$.

a) Suppose for convenience that each key occurs exactly its expected number of times.[7] As a function of c, k, and n, how many blocks, including overflow blocks, are needed for the structure?

---

[7]This assumption does not mean all buckets have the same number of records, because some buckets represent twice as many keys as others.

b) Keys will not generally distribute equally, but rather the number of records with a given key (or suffix of a key) will be *Poisson distributed*. That is, if λ is the expected number of records with a given key suffix, then the actual number of such records will be i with probability $e^{-\lambda}\lambda^i/i!$. Under this assumption, calculate the expected number of blocks used, as a function of c, k, and n.

! **Exercise 14.3.9:** Suppose we have a file of 1,000,000 records that we want to hash into a table with 2000 buckets. 100 records will fit in a block, and we wish to keep blocks as full as possible, but not allow two buckets to share a block. What are the minimum and maximum number of blocks that we could need to store this hash table?

14.4 Multidimensional Indexes

All the index structures discussed so far are *one dimensional*; that is, they assume a single search key, and they retrieve records that match a given search-key value. Although the search key may involve several attributes, the one-dimensional nature of indexes such as B-trees comes from the fact that values must be provided for all attributes of the search key, or the index is useless. So far in this chapter, we took advantage of a one-dimensional search-key space in several ways:

- Indexes on sequential files and B-trees both take advantage of having a single linear order for the keys.

- Hash tables require that the search key be completely known for any lookup. If a key consists of several fields, and even one is unknown, we cannot apply the hash function, but must instead search all the buckets.

In the balance of this chapter, we shall look at index structures that are suitable for multidimensional data. In these structures, any nonempty subset of the fields that form the dimensions can be given values, and some speedup will result.

14.4.1 Applications of Multidimensional Indexes

There are a number of applications that require us to view data as existing in a 2-dimensional space, or sometimes in higher dimensions. Some of these applications can be supported by conventional DBMS's, but there are also some specialized systems designed for multidimensional applications. One way in which these specialized systems distinguish themselves is by using data structures that support certain kinds of queries that are not common in SQL applications.

One important application of multidimensional indexes involves geographic data. A *geographic information system* stores objects in a (typically) two-dimensional space. The objects may be points or shapes. Often, these databases are maps, where the stored objects could represent houses, roads, bridges, pipelines, and many other physical objects. A suggestion of such a map is in Fig. 14.30.

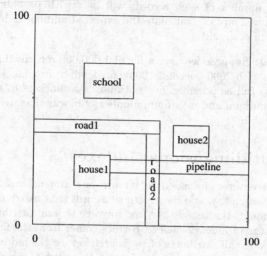

Figure 14.30: Some objects in 2-dimensional space

However, there are many other uses as well. For instance, an integrated-circuit design is a two-dimensional map of regions, often rectangles, composed of specific materials, called "layers." Likewise, we can think of the windows and icons on a screen as a collection of objects in two-dimensional space.

The queries asked of geographic information systems are not typical of SQL queries, although many can be expressed in SQL with some effort. Examples of these types of queries are:

1. *Partial match queries.* We specify values for one or more dimensions and look for all points matching those values in those dimensions.

2. *Range queries.* We give ranges for one or more of the dimensions, and we ask for the set of points within those ranges. If shapes are represented, then we may ask for the shapes that are partially or wholly within the range. These queries generalize the one-dimensional range queries that we considered in Section 14.2.4.

3. *Nearest-neighbor queries.* We ask for the closest point to a given point. For instance, if points represent cities, we might want to find the city of over 100,000 population closest to a given small city.

4. *Where-am-I queries.* We are given a point and we want to know in which shape, if any, the point is located. A familiar example is what happens

when you click your mouse, and the system determines which of the displayed elements you were clicking.

14.4.2 Executing Range Queries Using Conventional Indexes

Now, let us consider to what extent one-dimensional indexes help in answering range queries. Suppose for simplicity that there are two dimensions, x and y. We could put a secondary index on each of the dimensions, x and y. Using a B-tree for each would make it especially easy to get a range of values for each dimension.

Given ranges in both dimensions, we could begin by using the B-tree for x to get pointers to all of the records in the range for x. Next, we use the B-tree for y to get pointers to the records for all points whose y-coordinate is in the range for y. Then, we intersect these pointers, using the idea of Section 14.1.7. If the pointers fit in main memory, then the total number of disk I/O's is the number of leaf nodes of each B-tree that need to be examined, plus a few I/O's for finding our way down the B-trees (see Section 14.2.7). To this amount we must add the disk I/O's needed to retrieve all the matching records, however many they may be.

Example 14.26: Let us consider a hypothetical set of 1,000,000 points distributed randomly in a space in which both the x- and y-coordinates range from 0 to 1000. Suppose that 100 point records fit on a block, and an average B-tree leaf has about 200 key-pointer pairs (recall that not all slots of a B-tree block are necessarily occupied, at any given time). We shall assume there are B-tree indexes on both x and y.

Imagine we are given the range query asking for points in the square of side 100 surrounding the center of the space, that is, $450 \leq x \leq 550$ and $450 \leq y \leq 550$. Using the B-tree for x, we can find pointers to all the records with x in the range; there should be about 100,000 pointers, and this number of pointers should fit in main memory. Similarly, we use the B-tree for y to get the pointers to all the records with y in the desired range; again there are about 100,000 of them. Approximately 10,000 pointers will be in the intersection of these two sets, and it is the records reached by the 10,000 pointers in the intersection that form our answer.

Now, let us estimate the number of disk I/O's needed to answer the range query. First, as we pointed out in Section 14.2.7, it is generally feasible to keep the root of any B-tree in main memory. Section 14.2.4 showed how to access the 100,000 pointers in either dimension by examining one intermediate-level node and all the leaves that contain the desired pointers. Since we assumed leaves have about 200 key-pointer pairs each, we shall have to look at about 500 leaf blocks in each of the B-trees. When we add in one intermediate node per B-tree, we have a total of 1002 disk I/O's.

Finally, we have to retrieve the blocks containing the 10,000 desired records.

If they are stored randomly, we must expect that they will be on almost 10,000 different blocks. Since the entire file of a million records is assumed stored over 10,000 blocks, packed 100 to a block, we essentially have to look at every block of the data file anyway. Thus, in this example at least, conventional indexes have been little if any help in answering the range query. Of course, if the range were smaller, then constructing the intersection of the two pointer sets would allow us to limit the search to a fraction of the blocks in the data file. □

14.4.3 Executing Nearest-Neighbor Queries Using Conventional Indexes

Almost any data structure we use will allow us to answer a nearest-neighbor query by picking a range in each dimension, asking the range query, and selecting the point closest to the target within that range. Unfortunately, there are two things that could go wrong:

1. There is no point within the selected range.

2. The closest point within the range might not be the closest point overall, as suggested by Fig. 14.31.

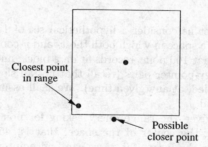

Figure 14.31: The point is in the range, but there could be a closer point outside the range

The general technique we shall use for answering nearest-neighbor queries is to begin by estimating a range in which the nearest point is likely to be found, and executing the corresponding range query. If no points are found within that range, we repeat with a larger range, until eventually we find at least one point. We then consider whether there is the possibility that a closer point exists, but that point is outside the range just used, as in Fig. 14.31. If so, we increase the range once more and retrieve all points in the larger range, to check.

14.4.4 Overview of Multidimensional Index Structures

Most data structures for supporting queries on multidimensional data fall into one of two categories:

1. Hash-table-like approaches.

2. Tree-like approaches.

For each of these structures, we give up something that we have in one-dimensional index structures. With the hash-based schemes — grid files and partitioned hash functions in Section 14.5 — we no longer have the advantage that the answer to our query is in exactly one bucket. However, each of these schemes limit our search to a subset of the buckets. With the tree-based schemes, we give up at least one of these important properties of B-trees:

1. The balance of the tree, where all leaves are at the same level.

2. The correspondence between tree nodes and disk blocks.

3. The speed with which modifications to the data may be performed.

As we shall see in Section 14.6, trees often will be deeper in some parts than in others; often the deep parts correspond to regions that have many points. We shall also see that it is common that the information corresponding to a tree node is considerably smaller than what fits in one block. It is thus necessary to group nodes into blocks in some useful way.

14.5 Hash Structures for Multidimensional Data

In this section we shall consider two data structures that generalize hash tables built using a single key. In each case, the bucket for a point is a function of all the attributes or dimensions. One scheme, called the "grid file," usually doesn't "hash" values along the dimensions, but rather partitions the dimensions by sorting the values along that dimension. The other, called "partitioned hashing," does "hash" the various dimensions, with each dimension contributing to the bucket number.

14.5.1 Grid Files

One of the simplest data structures that often outperforms single-dimension indexes for queries involving multidimensional data is the *grid file*. Think of the space of points partitioned in a grid. In each dimension, *grid lines* partition the space into *stripes*. Points that fall on a grid line will be considered to belong to the stripe for which that grid line is the lower boundary. The number of grid lines in different dimensions may vary, and there may be different spacings between adjacent grid lines, even between lines in the same dimension.

Example 14.27: Let us introduce a running example for multidimensional indexes: "who buys gold jewelry?" Imagine a database of customers who have bought gold jewelry. To make things simple, we assume that the only relevant attributes are the customer's age and salary. Our example database has twelve customers, which we can represent by the following age-salary pairs:

$$\begin{array}{llll}
(25, 60) & (45, 60) & (50, 75) & (50, 100) \\
(50, 120) & (70, 110) & (85, 140) & (30, 260) \\
(25, 400) & (45, 350) & (50, 275) & (60, 260)
\end{array}$$

In Fig. 14.32 we see these twelve points located in a 2-dimensional space. We have also selected some grid lines in each dimension. For this simple example, we have chosen two lines in each dimension, dividing the space into nine rectangular regions, but there is no reason why the same number of lines must be used in each dimension. In general, a rectangle includes points on its lower and left boundaries, but not on its upper and right boundaries. For instance, the central rectangle in Fig. 14.32 represents points with $40 \le age < 55$ and $90 \le salary < 225$. □

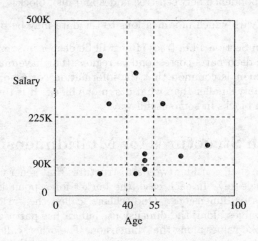

Figure 14.32: A grid file

14.5.2 Lookup in a Grid File

Each of the regions into which a space is partitioned can be thought of as a bucket of a hash table, and each of the points in that region has its record placed in a block belonging to that bucket. If needed, overflow blocks can be used to increase the size of a bucket.

Instead of a one-dimensional array of buckets, as is found in conventional hash tables, the grid file uses an array whose number of dimensions is the same as for the data file. To locate the proper bucket for a point, we need to know, for each dimension, the list of values at which the grid lines occur. Hashing a point is thus somewhat different from applying a hash function to the values of its components. Rather, we look at each component of the point and determine the position of the point in the grid for that dimension. The positions of the point in each of the dimensions together determine the bucket.

Example 14.28: Figure 14.33 shows the data of Fig. 14.32 placed in buckets. Since the grids in both dimensions divide the space into three regions, the bucket array is a 3×3 matrix. Two of the buckets:

1. Salary between $90K and $225K and age between 0 and 40, and

2. Salary below $90K and age above 55

are empty, and we do not show a block for that bucket. The other buckets are shown, with the artificially low maximum of two data points per block. In this simple example, no bucket has more than two members, so no overflow blocks are needed.   □

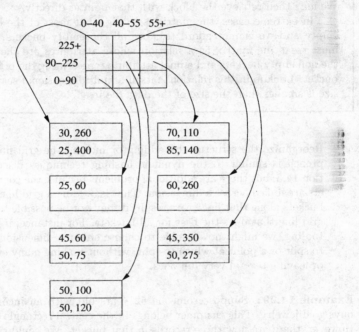

Figure 14.33: A grid file representing the points of Fig. 14.32

14.5.3   Insertion Into Grid Files

When we insert a record into a grid file, we follow the procedure for lookup of the record, and we place the new record in that bucket. If there is room in the block for the bucket then there is nothing more to do. The problem occurs when there is no room in the bucket. There are two general approaches:

1. Add overflow blocks to the buckets, as needed.

Accessing Buckets of a Grid File

While finding the proper coordinates for a point in a three-by-three grid like Fig. 14.33 is easy, we should remember that the grid file may have a very large number of stripes in each dimension. If so, then we must create an index for each dimension. The search key for an index is the set of partition values in that dimension.

Given a value v in some coordinate, we search for the greatest key value w less than or equal to v. Associated with w in that index will be the row or column of the matrix into which v falls. Given values in each dimension, we can find where in the matrix the pointer to the bucket falls. We may then retrieve the block with that pointer directly.

In extreme cases, the matrix is so big, that most of the buckets are empty and we cannot afford to store all the empty buckets. Then, we must treat the matrix as a relation whose attributes are the corners of the nonempty buckets and a final attribute representing the pointer to the bucket. Lookup in this relation is itself a multidimensional search, but its size is smaller than the size of the data file itself.

---

2. Reorganize the structure by adding or moving the grid lines. This approach is similar to the dynamic hashing techniques discussed in Section 14.3, but there are additional problems because the contents of buckets are linked across a dimension. That is, adding a grid line splits all the buckets along that line. As a result, it may not be possible to select a new grid line that does the best for all buckets. For instance, if one bucket is too big, we might not be able to choose either a dimension along which to split or a point at which to split, without making many empty buckets or leaving several very full ones.

Example 14.29: Suppose someone 52 years old with an income of $200K buys gold jewelry. This customer belongs in the central rectangle of Fig. 14.32. However, there are now three records in that bucket. We could simply add an overflow block. If we want to split the bucket, then we need to choose either the age or salary dimension, and we need to choose a new grid line to create the division. There are only three ways to introduce a grid line that will split the central bucket so two points are on one side and one on the other, which is the most even possible split in this case.

1. A vertical line, such as age $= 51$, that separates the two 50's from the 52. This line does nothing to split the buckets above or below, since both points of each of the other buckets for age 40–55 are to the left of the line age $= 51$.

2. A horizontal line that separates the point with salary = 200 from the other two points in the central bucket. We may as well choose a number like 130, which also splits the bucket to the right (that for age 55–100 and salary 90–225).

3. A horizontal line that separates the point with salary = 100 from the other two points. Again, we would be advised to pick a number like 115 that also splits the bucket to the right.

Choice (1) is probably not advised, since it doesn't split any other bucket; we are left with more empty buckets and have not reduced the size of any occupied buckets, except for the one we had to split. Choices (2) and (3) are equally good, although we might pick (2) because it puts the horizontal grid line at salary = 130, which is closer to midway between the upper and lower limits of 90 and 225 than we get with choice (3). The resulting partition into buckets is shown in Fig. 14.34. □

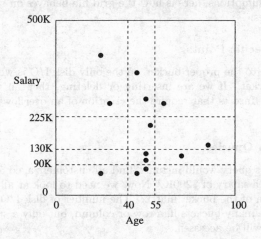

Figure 14.34: Insertion of the point $(52, 200)$ followed by splitting of buckets

14.5.4 Performance of Grid Files

Let us consider how many disk I/O's a grid file requires on various types of queries. We have been focusing on the two-dimensional version of grid files, although they can be used for any number of dimensions. One major problem in the high-dimensional case is that the number of buckets grows exponentially with the number of dimensions. If large portions of a space are empty, then there will be many empty buckets. We can envision the problem even in two dimensions. Suppose that there were a high correlation between age and salary, so all points in Fig. 14.32 lay along the diagonal. Then no matter where we placed the grid lines, the buckets off the diagonal would have to be empty.

However, if the data is well distributed, and the data file itself is not too large, then we can choose grid lines so that:

1. There are sufficiently few buckets that we can keep the bucket matrix in main memory, thus not incurring disk I/O to consult it, or to add rows or columns to the matrix when we introduce a new grid line.

2. We can also keep in memory indexes on the values of the grid lines in each dimension (as per the box "Accessing Buckets of a Grid File"), or we can avoid the indexes altogether and use main-memory binary search of the values defining the grid lines in each dimension.

3. The typical bucket does not have more than a few overflow blocks, so we do not incur too many disk I/O's when we search through a bucket.

Under those assumptions, here is how the grid file behaves on some important classes of queries.

Lookup of Specific Points

We are directed to the proper bucket, so the only disk I/O is what is necessary to read the bucket. If we are inserting or deleting, then an additional disk write is needed. Inserts that require the creation of an overflow block cause an additional write.

Partial-Match Queries

Examples of this query would include "find all customers aged 50," or "find all customers with a salary of $200K." Now, we need to look at all the buckets in a row or column of the bucket matrix. The number of disk I/O's can be quite high if there are many buckets in a row or column, but only a small fraction of all the buckets will be accessed.

Range Queries

A range query defines a rectangular region of the grid, and all points found in the buckets that cover that region will be answers to the query, with the exception of some of the points in buckets on the border of the search region. For example, if we want to find all customers aged 35–45 with a salary of 50–100, then we need to look in the four buckets in the lower left of Fig. 14.32. In this case, all buckets are on the border, so we may look at a good number of points that are not answers to the query. However, if the search region involves a large number of buckets, then most of them must be interior, and all their points are answers. For range queries, the number of disk I/O's may be large, as we may be required to examine many buckets. However, since range queries tend to produce large answer sets, we typically will examine not too many more blocks than the minimum number of blocks on which the answer could be placed by any organization whatsoever.

Nearest-Neighbor Queries

Given a point P, we start by searching the bucket in which that point belongs. If we find at least one point there, we have a candidate Q for the nearest neighbor. However, it is possible that there are points in adjacent buckets that are closer to P than Q is; the situation is like that suggested in Fig. 14.31. We have to consider whether the distance between P and a border of its bucket is less than the distance from P to Q. If there are such borders, then the adjacent buckets on the other side of each such border must be searched also. In fact, if buckets are severely rectangular — much longer in one dimension than the other — then it may be necessary to search even buckets that are not adjacent to the one containing point P.

Example 14.30: Suppose we are looking in Fig. 14.32 for the point nearest $P = (45, 200)$. We find that $(50, 120)$ is the closest point in the bucket, at a distance of 80.2. No point in the lower three buckets can be this close to $(45, 200)$, because their salary component is at most 90, so we can omit searching them. However, the other five buckets must be searched, and we find that there are actually two equally close points: $(30, 260)$ and $(60, 260)$, at a distance of 61.8 from P. Generally, the search for a nearest neighbor can be limited to a few buckets, and thus a few disk I/O's. However, since the buckets nearest the point P may be empty, we cannot easily put an upper bound on how costly the search is. □

14.5.5 Partitioned Hash Functions

Hash functions can take a list of values as arguments, although typically there is only one argument. For instance, if a is an integer-valued attribute and b is a character-string-valued attribute, then we could compute $h(a, b)$ by adding the value of a to the value of the ASCII code for each character of b, dividing by the number of buckets, and taking the remainder.

However, such a hash table could be used only in queries that specified values for both a and b. A preferable option is to design the hash function so it produces some number of bits, say k. These k bits are divided among n attributes, so that we produce k_i bits of the hash value from the ith attribute, and $\sum_{i=1}^{n} k_i = k$. More precisely, the hash function h is actually a list of hash functions $(h_1, h_2, \ldots, h_n)$, such that h_i applies to a value for the ith attribute and produces a sequence of k_i bits. The bucket in which to place a tuple with values $(v_1, v_2, \ldots, v_n)$ for the n attributes is computed by concatenating the bit sequences: $h_1(v_1)h_2(v_2) \cdots h_n(v_n)$.

Example 14.31: If we have a hash table with 10-bit bucket numbers (1024 buckets), we could devote four bits to attribute a and the remaining six bits to attribute b. Suppose we have a tuple with a-value A and b-value B, perhaps with other attributes that are not involved in the hash. If $h_a(A) = 0101$ and $h_b(B) = 111000$, then this tuple hashes to bucket 0101111000, the concatenation of the two bit sequences.

By partitioning the hash function this way, we get some advantage from knowing values for any one or more of the attributes that contribute to the hash function. For instance, if we are given a value A for attribute a, and we find that $h_a(A) = 0101$, then we know that the only tuples with a-value A are in the 64 buckets whose numbers are of the form $0101\cdots$, where the $\cdots$ represents any six bits. Similarly, if we are given the b-value B of a tuple, we can isolate the possible buckets of the tuple to the 16 buckets whose number ends in the six bits $h_b(B)$. ☐

Example 14.32: Suppose we have the "gold jewelry" data of Example 14.27, which we want to store in a partitioned hash table with eight buckets (i.e., three bits for bucket numbers). We assume as before that two records are all that can fit in one block. We shall devote one bit to the age attribute and the remaining two bits to the salary attribute.

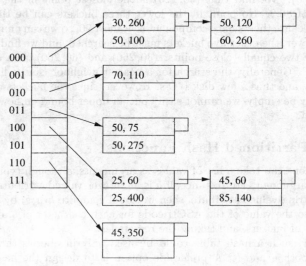

Figure 14.35: A partitioned hash table

For the hash function on age, we shall take the age modulo 2; that is, a record with an even age will hash into a bucket whose number is of the form $0xy$ for some bits x and y. A record with an odd age hashes to one of the buckets with a number of the form $1xy$. The hash function for salary will be the salary (in thousands) modulo 4. For example, a salary that leaves a remainder of 1 when divided by 4, such as 57K, will be in a bucket whose number is $z01$ for some bit z.

In Fig. 14.35 we see the data from Example 14.27 placed in this hash table. Notice that, because we have used mostly ages and salaries divisible by 10, the hash function does not distribute the points too well. Two of the eight buckets have four records each and need overflow blocks, while three other buckets are empty. □

14.5.6 Comparison of Grid Files and Partitioned Hashing

The performance of the two data structures discussed in this section are quite different. Here are the major points of comparison.

- Partitioned hash tables are actually quite useless for nearest-neighbor queries or range queries. The problem is that physical distance between points is not reflected by the closeness of bucket numbers. Of course we could design the hash function on some attribute a so the smallest values were assigned the first bit string (all 0's), the next values were assigned the next bit string $(00 \cdots 01)$, and so on. If we do so, then we have reinvented the grid file.

- A well chosen hash function will randomize the buckets into which points fall, and thus buckets will tend to be equally occupied. However, grid files, especially when the number of dimensions is large, will tend to leave many buckets empty or nearly so. The intuitive reason is that when there are many attributes, there is likely to be some correlation among at least some of them, so large regions of the space are left empty. For instance, we mentioned in Section 14.5.4 that a correlation between age and salary would cause most points of Fig. 14.32 to lie near the diagonal, with most of the rectangle empty. As a consequence, we can use fewer buckets, and/or have fewer overflow blocks in a partitioned hash table than in a grid file.

Thus, if we are required to support only partial match queries, where we specify some attributes' values and leave the other attributes completely unspecified, then the partitioned hash function is likely to outperform the grid file. Conversely, if we need to do nearest-neighbor queries or range queries frequently, then we would prefer to use a grid file.

14.5.7 Exercises for Section 14.5

Exercise 14.5.1: In Fig. 14.36 are specifications for twelve of the thirteen PC's introduced in Fig. 2.21. Suppose we wish to design an index on speed and hard-disk size only.

a) Choose five grid lines (total for the two dimensions), so that there are no more than two points in any bucket.

! b) Can you separate the points with at most two per bucket if you use only four grid lines? Either show how or argue that it is not possible.

model	speed	ram	hd
1001	2.66	1024	250
1002	2.10	512	250
1003	1.42	512	80
1004	2.80	1024	250
1005	3.20	512	250
1006	3.20	1024	320
1007	2.20	1024	200
1008	2.20	2048	250
1009	2.00	1024	250
1010	2.80	2048	300
1011	1.86	2048	160
1012	2.80	1024	160

Figure 14.36: Some PC's and their characteristics

! c) Suggest a partitioned hash function that will partition these points into four buckets with at most four points per bucket.

Exercise 14.5.2: Choose a partitioned hash function with one bit for each of the three attributes speed, ram, and hard-disk that divides the data of Fig. 14.36 well.

Exercise 14.5.3: Suppose we place the data of Fig. 14.36 in a grid file with dimensions for speed and ram only. The partitions are at speeds of 2.00, 2.20, and 2.80, and at ram of 1024 and 2048. Suppose also that only two points can fit in one bucket. Suggest good splits if we insert a point with speed 2.5 and ram 1536.

! **Exercise 14.5.4:** Suppose we wish to place the data of Fig. 14.36 in a three-dimensional grid file, based on the speed, ram, and hard-disk attributes. Suggest a partition in each dimension that will divide the data well.

Exercise 14.5.5: Suppose we store a relation $R(x,y)$ in a grid file. Both attributes have a range of values from 0 to 1000. The partitions of this grid file happen to be uniformly spaced; for x there are partitions every 20 units, at 20, 40, 60, and so on, while for y the partitions are every 50 units, at 50, 100, 150, and so on.

a) How many buckets do we have to examine to answer the range query

```
SELECT * FROM R
WHERE 330 < x AND x < 400 AND 620 < y AND y < 860;
```

! b) We wish to perform a nearest-neighbor query for the point $(110, 245)$. We begin by searching the bucket with lower-left corner at $(100, 200)$ and upper-right corner at $(120, 250)$, and we find that the closest point in this bucket is $(115, 230)$. What other buckets must be searched to verify that this point is the closest?

!! **Exercise 14.5.6:** Suppose we have a hash table whose buckets are numbered 0 to $2^n - 1$; i.e., bucket addresses are n bits long. We wish to store in the table a relation with two attributes x and y. A query will specify either a value for x or y, but never both. With probability p, it is x whose value is specified.

a) Suppose we partition the hash function so that m bits are devoted to x and the remaining $n - m$ bits to y. As a function of m, n, and p, what is the expected number of buckets that must be examined to answer a random query?

b) For what value of m (as a function of n and p) is the expected number of buckets minimized? Do not worry that this m is unlikely to be an integer.

14.6 Tree Structures for Multidimensional Data

We shall now consider four more structures that are useful for range queries or nearest-neighbor queries on multidimensional data. In order, we shall consider:

1. Multiple-key indexes.

2. *kd*-trees.

3. Quad trees.

4. R-trees.

The first three are intended for sets of points. The R-tree is commonly used to represent sets of regions; it is also useful for points.

14.6.1 Multiple-Key Indexes

Suppose we have several attributes representing dimensions of our data points, and we want to support range queries or nearest-neighbor queries on these points. A simple tree scheme for accessing these points is an index of indexes, or more generally a tree in which the nodes at each level are indexes for one attribute.

The idea is suggested in Fig. 14.37 for the case of two attributes. The "root of the tree" is an index for the first of the two attributes. This index could be any type of conventional index, such as a B-tree or a hash table. The index associates with each of its search-key values — i.e., values for the first attribute — a pointer to another index. If V is a value of the first attribute,

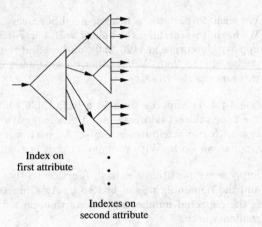

Index on
first attribute   •
                       •
                       •
              Indexes on
          second attribute

Figure 14.37: Using nested indexes on different keys

then the index we reach by following key V and its pointer is an index into the set of points that have V for their value in the first attribute and any value for the second attribute.

Example 14.33: Figure 14.38 shows a multiple-key index for our running "gold jewelry" example, where the first attribute is age, and the second attribute is salary. The root index, on age, is suggested at the left of Fig. 14.38. At the right of Fig. 14.38 are seven indexes that provide access to the points themselves. For example, if we follow the pointer associated with age 50 in the root index, we get to a smaller index where salary is the key, and the four key values in the index are the four salaries associated with points that have age 50: salaries 75, 100, 120, and 275.   □

In a multiple-key index, some of the second- or higher-level indexes may be very small. For example, Fig 14.38 has four second-level indexes with but a single pair. Thus, it may be appropriate to implement these indexes as simple tables that are packed several to a block.

14.6.2   Performance of Multiple-Key Indexes

Let us consider how a multiple key index performs on various kinds of multidimensional queries. We shall concentrate on the case of two attributes, although the generalization to more than two attributes is unsurprising.

Partial-Match Queries

If the first attribute is specified, then the access is quite efficient. We use the root index to find the one subindex that leads to the points we want. On the

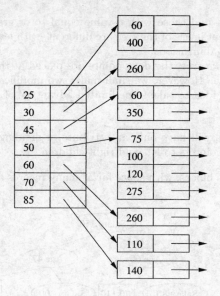

Figure 14.38: Multiple-key indexes for age/salary data

other hand, if the first attribute does not have a specified value, then we must search every subindex, a potentially time-consuming process.

Range Queries

The multiple-key index works quite well for a range query, provided the individual indexes themselves support range queries on their attribute — B-trees or indexed-sequential files, for instance. To answer a range query, we use the root index and the range of the first attribute to find all of the subindexes that might contain answer points. We then search each of these subindexes, using the range specified for the second attribute.

Nearest-Neighbor Queries

These queries can be answered by a series of range queries, as described in Section 14.4.3.

14.6.3 kd-Trees

A kd-tree (k-dimensional search tree) is a main-memory data structure generalizing the binary search tree to multidimensional data. We shall present the idea and then discuss how the idea has been adapted to the block model of storage. A kd-tree is a binary tree in which interior nodes have an associated attribute a and a value V that splits the data points into two parts: those with *a*-value less than V and those with *a*-value equal to or greater than V. The attributes at different levels of the tree are different, with levels rotating among the attributes of all dimensions.

In the classical *kd*-tree, the data points are placed at the nodes, just as in a binary search tree. However, we shall make two modifications in our initial presentation of the idea to take some limited advantage of the block model of storage.

1. Interior nodes will have only an attribute, a dividing value for that attribute, and pointers to left and right children.

2. Leaves will be blocks, with space for as many records as a block can hold.

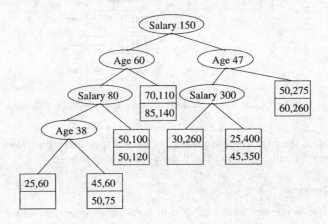

Figure 14.39: A *kd*-tree

Example 14.34: In Fig. 14.39 is a *kd*-tree for the twelve points of our running gold-jewelry example. We use blocks that hold only two records for simplicity; these blocks and their contents are shown as square leaves. The interior nodes are ovals with an attribute — either age or salary — and a value. For instance, the root splits by salary, with all records in the left subtree having a salary less than $150K, and all records in the right subtree having a salary at least $150K.

At the second level, the split is by age. The left child of the root splits at age 60, so everything in its left subtree will have age less than 60 and salary less than $150K. Its right subtree will have age at least 60 and salary less than $150K. Figure 14.40 suggests how the various interior nodes split the space of points into leaf blocks. For example, the horizontal line at salary = 150 represents the split at the root. The space below that line is split vertically at age 60, while the space above is split at age 47, corresponding to the decision at the right child of the root. □

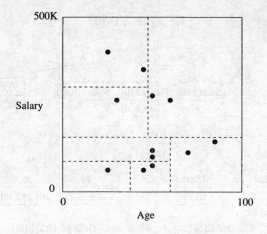

Figure 14.40: The partitions implied by the tree of Fig. 14.39

14.6.4 Operations on *kd*-Trees

A lookup of a tuple, given values for all dimensions, proceeds as in a binary search tree. We make a decision which way to go at each interior node and are directed to a single leaf, whose block we search.

To perform an insertion, we proceed as for a lookup. We are eventually directed to a leaf, and if its block has room we put the new data point there. If there is no room, we split the block into two, and we divide its contents according to whatever attribute is appropriate at the level of the leaf being split. We create a new interior node whose children are the two new blocks, and we install at that interior node a splitting value that is appropriate for the split we have just made.[8]

Example 14.35 : Suppose someone 35 years old with a salary of $500K buys gold jewelry. Starting at the root, since the salary is at least $150K we go to the right. There, we compare the age 35 with the age 47 at the node, which directs us to the left. At the third level, we compare salaries again, and our salary is greater than the splitting value, $300K. We are thus directed to a leaf containing the points $(25, 400)$ and $(45, 350)$, along with the new point $(35, 500)$.

There isn't room for three records in this block, so we must split it. The fourth level splits on age, so we have to pick some age that divides the records as evenly as possible. The median value, 35, is a good choice, so we replace the leaf by an interior node that splits on age = 35. To the left of this interior node is a leaf block with only the record $(25, 400)$, while to the right is a leaf block with the other two records, as shown in Fig. 14.41. □

---

[8]One problem that might arise is a situation where there are so many points with the same value in a given dimension that the bucket has only one value in that dimension and cannot be split. We can try splitting along another dimension, or we can use an overflow block.

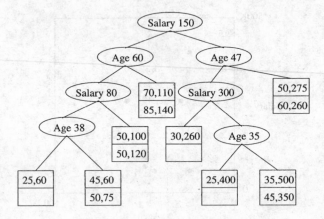

Figure 14.41: Tree after insertion of $(35, 500)$

The more complex queries discussed in this chapter are also supported by a *kd*-tree. Here are the key ideas and synopses of the algorithms:

Partial-Match Queries

If we are given values for some of the attributes, then we can go one way when we are at a level belonging to an attribute whose value we know. When we don't know the value of the attribute at a node, we must explore both of its children. For example, if we ask for all points with age = 50 in the tree of Fig. 14.39, we must look at both children of the root, since the root splits on salary. However, at the left child of the root, we need go only to the left, and at the right child of the root we need only explore its right subtree. For example, if the tree is perfectly balanced and the index has two dimensions, one of which is specified in the search, then we would have to explore both ways at every other level, ultimately reaching about the square root of the total number of leaves.

Range Queries

Sometimes, a range will allow us to move to only one child of a node, but if the range straddles the splitting value at the node then we must explore both children. For example, given the range of ages 35 to 55 and the range of salaries from $100K to $200K, we would explore the tree of Fig. 14.39 as follows. The salary range straddles the $150K at the root, so we must explore both children. At the left child, the range is entirely to the left, so we move to the node with salary $80K. Now, the range is entirely to the right, so we reach the leaf with records $(50, 100)$ and $(50, 120)$, both of which meet the range query. Returning to the right child of the root, the splitting value age = 47 tells us to look at both subtrees. At the node with salary $300K, we can go only to the left, finding the point (30, 260), which is actually outside the range. At the right child of the node for age = 47, we find two other points, both of which are outside the range.

14.6.5 Adapting kd-Trees to Secondary Storage

Suppose we store a file in a kd-tree with n leaves. Then the average length of a path from the root to a leaf will be about $\log_2 n$, as for any binary tree. If we store each node in a block, then as we traverse a path we must do one disk I/O per node. For example, if $n = 1000$, then we need about 10 disk I/O's, much more than the 2 or 3 disk I/O's that would be typical for a B-tree, even on a much larger file. In addition, since interior nodes of a kd-tree have relatively little information, most of the block would be wasted space. Two approaches to the twin problems of long paths and unused space are:

1. *Multiway Branches at Interior Nodes.* Interior nodes of a kd-tree could look more like B-tree nodes, with many key-pointer pairs. If we had n keys at a node, we could split values of an attribute a into $n+1$ ranges. If there were $n+1$ pointers, we could follow the appropriate one to a subtree that contained only points with attribute a in that range.

2. *Group Interior Nodes Into Blocks.* We could pack many interior nodes, each with two children, into a single block. To minimize the number of blocks that we must read from disk while traveling down one path, we are best off including in one block a node and all its descendants for some number of levels. That way, once we retrieve the block with this node, we are sure to use some additional nodes on the same block, saving disk I/O's.

14.6.6 Quad Trees

In a *quad tree*, each interior node corresponds to a square region in two dimensions, or to a k-dimensional cube in k dimensions. As with the other data structures in this chapter, we shall consider primarily the two-dimensional case. If the number of points in a square is no larger than what will fit in a block, then we can think of this square as a leaf of the tree, and it is represented by the block that holds its points. If there are too many points to fit in one block, then we treat the square as an interior node, with children corresponding to its four quadrants.

Example 14.36: Figure 14.42 shows the gold-jewelry data points organized into regions that correspond to nodes of a quad tree. For ease of calculation, we have restricted the usual space so salary ranges between 0 and $400K, rather than up to $500K as in other examples of this chapter. We continue to make the assumption that only two records can fit in a block.

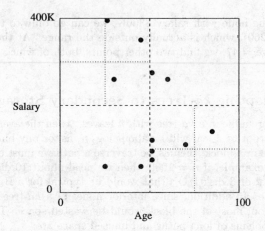

Figure 14.42: Data organized in a quad tree

Figure 14.43 shows the tree explicitly. We use the compass designations for the quadrants and for the children of a node (e.g., SW stands for the southwest quadrant — the points to the left and below the center). The order of children is always as indicated at the root. Each interior node indicates the coordinates of the center of its region.

Since the entire space has 12 points, and only two will fit in one block, we must split the space into quadrants, which we show by the dashed line in Fig. 14.42. Two of the resulting quadrants — the southwest and northeast — have only two points. They can be represented by leaves and need not be split further.

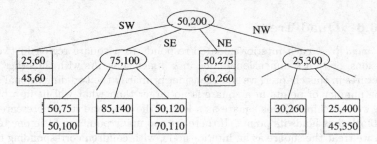

Figure 14.43: A quad tree

The remaining two quadrants each have more than two points. Both are split into subquadrants, as suggested by the dotted lines in Fig. 14.42. Each of the resulting quadrants has at most two points, so no more splitting is necessary.
□

Since interior nodes of a quad tree in k dimensions have 2^k children, there is a range of k where nodes fit conveniently into blocks. For instance, if 128, or 2^7, pointers can fit in a block, then $k = 7$ is a convenient number of dimensions. However, for the 2-dimensional case, the situation is not much better than for kd-trees; an interior node has four children. Moreover, while we can choose the splitting point for a kd-tree node, we are constrained to pick the center of a quad-tree region, which may or may not divide the points in that region evenly. Especially when the number of dimensions is large, we expect to find many null pointers (corresponding to empty quadrants) in interior nodes. Of course we can be somewhat clever about how high-dimension nodes are represented, and keep only the non-null pointers and a designation of which quadrant the pointer represents, thus saving considerable space.

We shall not go into detail regarding the standard operations that we discussed in Section 14.6.4 for kd-trees. The algorithms for quad trees resemble those for kd-trees.

14.6.7   R-Trees

An *R-tree* (region tree) is a data structure that captures some of the spirit of a B-tree for multidimensional data. Recall that a B-tree node has a set of keys that divide a line into segments. Points along that line belong to only one segment, as suggested by Fig. 14.44. The B-tree thus makes it easy for us to find points; if we think the point is somewhere along the line represented by a B-tree node, we can determine a unique child of that node where the point could be found.

Figure 14.44: A B-tree node divides keys along a line into disjoint segments

An R-tree, on the other hand, represents data that consists of 2-dimensional, or higher-dimensional regions, which we call *data regions*. An interior node of an R-tree corresponds to some *interior region*, or just "region," which is not normally a data region. In principle, the region can be of any shape, although in practice it is usually a rectangle or other simple shape. The R-tree node has, in place of keys, subregions that represent the contents of its children. The subregions are allowed to overlap, although it is desirable to keep the overlap small.

Figure 14.45 suggests a node of an R-tree that is associated with the large solid rectangle. The dotted rectangles represent the subregions associated with four of its children. Notice that the subregions do not cover the entire region, which is satisfactory as long as each data region that lies within the large region is wholly contained within one of the small regions.

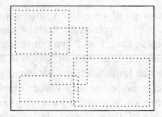

Figure 14.45: The region of an R-tree node and subregions of its children

14.6.8 Operations on R-Trees

A typical query for which an R-tree is useful is a "where-am-I" query, which specifies a point P and asks for the data region or regions in which the point lies. We start at the root, with which the entire region is associated. We examine the subregions at the root and determine which children of the root correspond to interior regions that contain point P. Note that there may be zero, one, or several such regions.

If there are zero regions, then we are done; P is not in any data region. If there is at least one interior region that contains P, then we must recursively search for P at the child corresponding to *each* such region. When we reach one or more leaves, we shall find the actual data regions, along with either the complete record for each data region or a pointer to that record.

When we insert a new region R into an R-tree, we start at the root and try to find a subregion into which R fits. If there is more than one such region, then we pick one, go to its corresponding child, and repeat the process there. If there is no subregion that contains R, then we have to expand one of the subregions. Which one to pick may be a difficult decision. Intuitively, we want to expand regions as little as possible, so we might ask which of the children's subregions would have their area increased as little as possible, change the boundary of that region to include R, and recursively insert R at the corresponding child.

Eventually, we reach a leaf, where we insert the region R. However, if there is no room for R at that leaf, then we must split the leaf. How we split the leaf is subject to some choice. We generally want the two subregions to be as small as possible, yet they must, between them, cover all the data regions of the original leaf. Having split the leaf, we replace the region and pointer for the original leaf at the node above by a pair of regions and pointers corresponding to the two new leaves. If there is room at the parent, we are done. Otherwise, as in a B-tree, we recursively split nodes going up the tree.

Example 14.37: Let us consider the addition of a new region to the map of Fig. 14.30. Suppose that leaves have room for six regions. Further suppose that the six regions of Fig. 14.30 are together on one leaf, whose region is represented by the outer (solid) rectangle in Fig. 14.46.

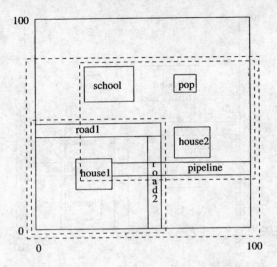

Figure 14.46: Splitting the set of objects

Now, suppose the local cellular phone company adds a POP (point of presence, or base station) at the position shown in Fig. 14.46. Since the seven data regions do not fit on one leaf, we shall split the leaf, with four in one leaf and three in the other. Our options are many; we have picked in Fig. 14.46 the division (indicated by the inner, dashed rectangles) that minimizes the overlap, while splitting the leaves as evenly as possible.

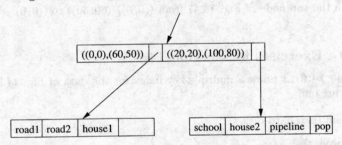

Figure 14.47: An R-tree

We show in Fig. 14.47 how the two new leaves fit into the R-tree. The parent of these nodes has pointers to both leaves, and associated with the pointers are the lower-left and upper-right corners of the rectangular regions covered by each leaf. □

Example 14.38 : Suppose we inserted another house below house2, with lower-left coordinates $(70, 5)$ and upper-right coordinates $(80, 15)$. Since this house is

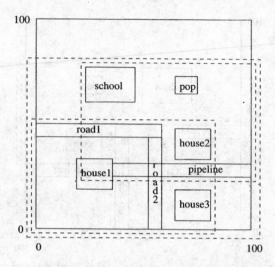

Figure 14.48: Extending a region to accommodate new data

not wholly contained within either of the leaves' regions, we must choose which region to expand. If we expand the lower subregion, corresponding to the first leaf in Fig. 14.47, then we add 1000 square units to the region, since we extend it 20 units to the right. If we extend the other subregion by lowering its bottom by 15 units, then we add 1200 square units. We prefer the first, and the new regions are changed in Fig. 14.48. We also must change the description of the region in the top node of Fig. 14.47 from $((0,0),\ (60,50))$ to $((0,0),\ (80,50))$. □

14.6.9 Exercises for Section 14.6

Exercise 14.6.1: Show a multiple-key index for the data of Fig. 14.36 if the indexes are on:

a) Ram then hard-disk.

b) Speed, then ram.

c) Speed, then hard-disk, then ram.

Exercise 14.6.2: Place the data of Fig. 14.36 in a *kd*-tree. Assume two records can fit in one block. At each level, pick a separating value that divides the data as evenly as possible. For an order of the splitting attributes choose:

a) Speed, then ram, alternating.

b) Speed, then ram, then hard-disk, alternating.

c) Whatever attribute produces the most even split at each node.

Exercise 14.6.3: Suppose we have a relation $R(x, y, z)$, where the pair of attributes x and y together form the key. Attribute x ranges from 1 to 100, and y ranges from 1 to 1000. For each x there are records with 50 different values of y, and for each y there are records with 5 different values of x. Note that there are thus 5000 records in R. We wish to use a multiple-key index that will help us to answer queries of the form

```
SELECT z
FROM R
WHERE x = C AND y = D;
```

where C and D are constants. Assume that blocks can hold ten key-pointer pairs, and we wish to create dense indexes at each level, perhaps with sparse higher-level indexes above them, so that each index starts from a single block. Also assume that initially all index and data blocks are on disk.

a) How many disk I/O's are necessary to answer a query of the above form if the first index is on y?

b) How many disk I/O's are necessary to answer a query of the above form if the first index is on x?

! c) Suppose you were allowed to buffer 6 blocks in memory at all times. Which blocks would you choose, and would you make x or y the first index, if you wanted to minimize the number of additional disk I/O's needed?

Exercise 14.6.4: For the structure of Exercise 14.6.3(a), how many disk I/O's are required to answer the range query in which $20 \leq x \leq 35$ and $200 \leq y \leq 350$. Assume data is distributed uniformly; i.e., the expected number of points will be found within any given range.

Exercise 14.6.5: In the tree of Fig. 14.39, what new points would be directed to:

a) The block with points $(45, 60)$ and $(50, 75)$?

b) The block with points $(25, 400)$ and $(45, 350)$?

Exercise 14.6.6: Show a possible evolution of the tree of Fig. 14.41 if we insert the points $(40, 200)$ and then $(20, 175)$.

! **Exercise 14.6.7:** We mentioned that if a kd-tree were perfectly balanced, and we execute a partial-match query in which one of two attributes has a value specified, then we wind up looking at about $\sqrt{n}$ out of the n leaves.

a) Explain why.

b) If the tree split alternately in d dimensions, and we specified values for m of those dimensions, what fraction of the leaves would we expect to have to search?

c) How does the performance of (b) compare with a partitioned hash table?

! **Exercise 14.6.8:** If we are allowed to put the central point in a quadrant of a quad tree wherever we want, can we always divide a quadrant into subquadrants with an equal number of points (or as equal as possible, if the number of points in the quadrant is not divisible by 4)? Justify your answer.

! **Exercise 14.6.9:** Suppose we have a database of 1,000,000 regions, which may overlap. Nodes (blocks) of an R-tree can hold 100 regions and pointers. The region represented by any node has 100 subregions, and the overlap among these regions is such that the total area of the 100 subregions is 150% of the area of the region. If we perform a "where-am-I" query for a given point, how many blocks do we expect to retrieve?

Exercise 14.6.10: Place the data of Fig. 14.36 in a quad tree with dimensions speed and ram. Assume the range for speed is 1.00 to 5.00, and for ram it is 500 to 3500. No leaf of the quad tree should have more than two points.

Exercise 14.6.11: Repeat Exercise 14.6.10 with the addition of a third dimension, hard-disk, that ranges from 0 to 500.

14.7   Bitmap Indexes

Let us now turn to a type of index that is rather different from those seen so far. We begin by imagining that records of a file have permanent numbers, $1, 2, \ldots, n$. Moreover, there is some data structure for the file that lets us find the ith record easily for any i. A *bitmap index* for a field F is a collection of bit-vectors of length n, one for each possible value that may appear in the field F. The vector for value v has 1 in position i if the ith record has v in field F, and it has 0 there if not.

Example 14.39: Suppose a file consists of records with two fields, F and G, of type integer and string, respectively. The current file has six records, numbered 1 through 6, with the following values in order: (30, foo), (30, bar), (40, baz), (50, foo), (40, bar), (30, baz).

A bitmap index for the first field, F, would have three bit-vectors, each of length 6. The first, for value 30, is 110001, because the first, second, and sixth records have $F = 30$. The other two, for 40 and 50, respectively, are 001010 and 000100.

A bitmap index for G would also have three bit-vectors, because there are three different strings appearing there. The three bit-vectors are:

Value	Vector
foo	100100
bar	010010
baz	001001

In each case, 1's indicate the records in which the corresponding string appears.
□

14.7.1 Motivation for Bitmap Indexes

It might at first appear that bitmap indexes require much too much space, especially when there are many different values for a field, since the total number of bits is the product of the number of records and the number of values. For example, if the field is a key, and there are n records, then n^2 bits are used among all the bit-vectors for that field. However, compression can be used to make the number of bits closer to n, independent of the number of different values, as we shall see in Section 14.7.2.

You might also suspect that there are problems managing the bitmap indexes. For example, they depend on the number of a record remaining the same throughout time. How do we find the ith record as the file adds and deletes records? Similarly, values for a field may appear or disappear. How do we find the bitmap for a value efficiently? These and related questions are discussed in Section 14.7.4.

The compensating advantage of bitmap indexes is that they allow us to answer partial-match queries very efficiently in many situations. In a sense they offer the advantages of buckets that we discussed in Example 14.7, where we found the Movie tuples with specified values in several attributes without first retrieving all the records that matched in each of the attributes. An example will illustrate the point.

Example 14.40: Recall Example 14.7, where we queried the Movie relation with the query

```
SELECT title FROM Movie
WHERE studioName = 'Disney' AND year = 2005;
```

Suppose there are bitmap indexes on both attributes studioName and year. Then we can intersect the vectors for year = 2005 and studioName = 'Disney'; that is, we take the bitwise AND of these vectors, which will give us a vector with a 1 in position i if and only if the ith Movie tuple is for a movie made by Disney in 2005.

If we can retrieve tuples of Movie given their numbers, then we need to read only those blocks containing one or more of these tuples, just as we did in Example 14.7. To intersect the bit vectors, we must read them into memory, which requires a disk I/O for each block occupied by one of the two vectors. As mentioned, we shall later address both matters: accessing records given their numbers in Section 14.7.4 and making sure the bit-vectors do not occupy too much space in Section 14.7.2. □

Bitmap indexes can also help answer range queries. We shall consider an example next that both illustrates their use for range queries and shows in detail with short bit-vectors how the bitwise AND and OR of bit-vectors can be used to discover the answer to a query without looking at any records but the ones we want.

Example 14.41: Consider the gold-jewelry data first introduced in Example 14.27. Suppose that the twelve points of that example are records numbered from 1 to 12 as follows:

1:	(25, 60)	2:	(45, 60)	3:	(50, 75)	4:	(50, 100)
5:	(50, 120)	6:	(70, 110)	7:	(85, 140)	8:	(30, 260)
9:	(25, 400)	10:	(45, 350)	11:	(50, 275)	12:	(60, 260)

For the first component, age, there are seven different values, so the bitmap index for age consists of the following seven vectors:

25:	100000001000	30:	000000010000	45:	010000000100
50:	001110000010	60:	000000000001	70:	000001000000
85:	000000100000				

For the salary component, there are ten different values, so the salary bitmap index has the following ten bit-vectors:

60:	110000000000	75:	001000000000	100:	000100000000
110:	000001000000	120:	000010000000	140:	000000100000
260:	000000010001	275:	000000000010	350:	000000000100
400:	000000001000				

Suppose we want to find the jewelry buyers with an age in the range 45–55 and a salary in the range 100–200. We first find the bit-vectors for the age values in this range; in this example there are only two: 010000000100 and 001110000010, for 45 and 50, respectively. If we take their bitwise OR, we have a new bit-vector with 1 in position i if and only if the ith record has an age in the desired range. This bit-vector is 011110000110.

Next, we find the bit-vectors for the salaries between 100 and 200 thousand. There are four, corresponding to salaries 100, 110, 120, and 140; their bitwise OR is 000111100000.

The last step is to take the bitwise AND of the two bit-vectors we calculated by OR. That is:

$$011110000110 \text{ AND } 000111100000 = 000110000000$$

We thus find that only the fourth and fifth records, which are (50, 100) and (50, 120), are in the desired range. □

Binary Numbers Won't Serve as a Run-Length Encoding

Suppose we represented a run of i 0's followed by a 1 with the integer i in binary. Then the bit-vector 000101 consists of two runs, of lengths 3 and 1, respectively. The binary representations of these integers are 11 and 1, so the run-length encoding of 000101 is 111. However, a similar calculation shows that the bit-vector 010001 is also encoded by 111; bit-vector 010101 is a third vector encoded by 111. Thus, 111 cannot be decoded uniquely into one bit-vector.

14.7.2 Compressed Bitmaps

Suppose we have a bitmap index on field F of a file with n records, and there are m different values for field F that appear in the file. Then the number of bits in all the bit-vectors for this index is mn. If, say, blocks are 4096 bytes long, then we can fit 32,768 bits in one block, so the number of blocks needed is $mn/32768$. That number can be small compared to the number of blocks needed to hold the file itself, but the larger m is, the more space the bitmap index takes.

But if m is large, then 1's in a bit-vector will be very rare; precisely, the probability that any bit is 1 is $1/m$. If 1's are rare, then we have an opportunity to encode bit-vectors so that they take much less than n bits on the average. A common approach is called *run-length encoding*, where we represent a *run*, that is, a sequence of i 0's followed by a 1, by some suitable binary encoding of the integer i. We concatenate the codes for each run together, and that sequence of bits is the encoding of the entire bit-vector.

We might imagine that we could just represent integer i by expressing i as a binary number. However, that simple a scheme will not do, because it is not possible to break a sequence of codes apart to determine uniquely the lengths of the runs involved (see the box on "Binary Numbers Won't Serve as a Run-Length Encoding"). Thus, the encoding of integers i that represent a run length must be more complex than a simple binary representation.

We shall study one of many possible schemes for encoding. There are some better, more complex schemes that can improve on the amount of compression achieved here, by almost a factor of 2, but only when typical runs are very long. In our scheme, we first determine how many bits the binary representation of i has. This number j, which is approximately $\log_2 i$, is represented in "unary," by $j - 1$ 1's and a single 0. Then, we can follow with i in binary.[9]

Example 14.42: If $i = 13$, then $j = 4$; that is, we need 4 bits in the binary

---

[9]Actually, except for the case that $j = 1$ (i.e., $i = 0$ or $i = 1$), we can be sure that the binary representation of i begins with 1. Thus, we can save about one bit per number if we omit this 1 and use only the remaining $j - 1$ bits.

representation of i. Thus, the encoding for i begins with 1110. We follow with i in binary, or 1101. Thus, the encoding for 13 is 11101101.

The encoding for $i = 1$ is 01, and the encoding for $i = 0$ is 00. In each case, $j = 1$, so we begin with a single 0 and follow that 0 with the one bit that represents i. □

If we concatenate a sequence of integer codes, we can always recover the sequence of run lengths and therefore recover the original bit-vector. Suppose we have scanned some of the encoded bits, and we are now at the beginning of a sequence of bits that encodes some integer i. We scan forward to the first 0, to determine the value of j. That is, j equals the number of bits we must scan until we get to the first 0 (including that 0 in the count of bits). Once we know j, we look at the next j bits; i is the integer represented there in binary. Moreover, once we have scanned the bits representing i, we know where the next code for an integer begins, so we can repeat the process.

Example 14.43 : Let us decode the sequence 11101101001011. Starting at the beginning, we find the first 0 at the 4th bit, so $j = 4$. The next 4 bits are 1101, so we determine that the first integer is 13. We are now left with 001011 to decode.

Since the first bit is 0, we know the next bit represents the next integer by itself; this integer is 0. Thus, we have decoded the sequence 13, 0, and we must decode the remaining sequence 1011.

We find the first 0 in the second position, whereupon we conclude that the final two bits represent the last integer, 3. Our entire sequence of run-lengths is thus 13, 0, 3. From these numbers, we can reconstruct the actual bit-vector, 0000000000000110001. □

Technically, every bit-vector so decoded will end in a 1, and any trailing 0's will not be recovered. Since we presumably know the number of records in the file, the additional 0's can be added. However, since 0 in a bit-vector indicates the corresponding record is not in the described set, we don't even have to know the total number of records, and can ignore the trailing 0's.

Example 14.44 : Let us convert some of the bit-vectors from Example 14.42 to our run-length code. The vectors for the first three ages, 25, 30, and 45, are 100000001000, 000000010000, and 010000000100, respectively. The first of these has the run-length sequence $(0, 7)$. The code for 0 is 00, and the code for 7 is 110111. Thus, the bit-vector for age 25 becomes 00110111.

Similarly, the bit-vector for age 30 has only one run, with seven 0's. Thus, its code is 110111. The bit-vector for age 45 has two runs, $(1, 7)$. Since 1 has the code 01, and we determined that 7 has the code 110111, the code for the third bit-vector is 01110111. □

The compression in Example 14.44 is not great. However, we cannot see the true benefits when n, the number of records, is small. To appreciate the value of the encoding, suppose that $m = n$, i.e., each value for the field on which the bitmap index is constructed, occurs once. Notice that the code for a run of length i has about $2\log_2 i$ bits. If each bit-vector has a single 1, then it has a single run, and the length of that run cannot be longer than n. Thus, $2\log_2 n$ bits is an upper bound on the length of a bit-vector's code in this case.

Since there are n bit-vectors in the index, the total number of bits to represent the index is at most $2n \log_2 n$. In comparison, the uncompressed bit-vectors for this data would require n^2 bits.

14.7.3 Operating on Run-Length-Encoded Bit-Vectors

When we need to perform bitwise AND or OR on encoded bit-vectors, we have little choice but to decode them and operate on the original bit-vectors. However, we do not have to do the decoding all at once. The compression scheme we have described lets us decode one run at a time, and we can thus determine where the next 1 is in each operand bit-vector. If we are taking the OR, we can produce a 1 at that position of the output, and if we are taking the AND we produce a 1 if and only if both operands have their next 1 at the same position. The algorithms involved are complex, but an example may make the idea adequately clear.

Example 14.45: Consider the encoded bit-vectors we obtained in Example 14.44 for ages 25 and 30: 00110111 and 110111, respectively. We can decode their first runs easily; we find they are 0 and 7, respectively. That is, the first 1 of the bit-vector for 25 occurs in position 1, while the first 1 in the bit-vector for 30 occurs at position 8. We therefore generate 1 in position 1.

Next, we must decode the next run for age 25, since that bit-vector may produce another 1 before age 30's bit-vector produces a 1 at position 8. However, the next run for age 25 is 7, which says that this bit-vector next produces a 1 at position 9. We therefore generate six 0's and the 1 at position 8 that comes from the bit-vector for age 30. The 1 at position 9 from age 25's bit-vector is produced. Neither bit-vector produces any more 1's for the output. We conclude that the OR of these bit-vectors is 100000011. Technically, we must append 000, since uncompressed bit-vectors are of length twelve in this example. □

14.7.4 Managing Bitmap Indexes

We have described operations on bitmap indexes without addressing three important issues:

1. When we want to find the bit-vector for a given value, or the bit-vectors corresponding to values in a given range, how do we find these efficiently?

2. When we have selected a set of records that answer our query, how do we retrieve those records efficiently?

3. When the data file changes by insertion or deletion of records, how do we adjust the bitmap index on a given field?

Finding Bit-Vectors

Think of each bit-vector as a record whose key is the value corresponding to this bit-vector (although the value itself does not appear in this "record"). Then any secondary index technique will take us efficiently from values to their bit-vectors.

We also need to store the bit-vectors somewhere. It is best to think of them as variable-length records, since they will generally grow as more records are added to the data file. The techniques of Section 13.7 are useful.

Finding Records

Now let us consider the second question: once we have determined that we need record k of the data file, how do we find it? Again, techniques we have seen already may be adapted. Think of the kth record as having search-key value k (although this key does not actually appear in the record). We may then create a secondary index on the data file, whose search key is the number of the record.

Handling Modifications to the Data File

There are two aspects to the problem of reflecting data-file modifications in a bitmap index.

1. Record numbers must remain fixed once assigned.

2. Changes to the data file require the bitmap index to change as well.

The consequence of point (1) is that when we delete record i, it is easiest to "retire" its number. Its space is replaced by a "tombstone" in the data file. The bitmap index must also be changed, since the bit-vector that had a 1 in position i must have that 1 changed to 0. Note that we can find the appropriate bit-vector, since we know what value record i had before deletion.

Next consider insertion of a new record. We keep track of the next available record number and assign it to the new record. Then, for each bitmap index, we must determine the value the new record has in the corresponding field and modify the bit-vector for that value by appending a 1 at the end. Technically, all the other bit-vectors in this index get a new 0 at the end, but if we are using a compression technique such as that of Section 14.7.2, then no change to the compressed values is needed.

As a special case, the new record may have a value for the indexed field that has not been seen before. In that case, we need a new bit-vector for this value, and this bit-vector and its corresponding value need to be inserted into the secondary-index structure that is used to find a bit-vector given its corresponding value.

Lastly, consider a modification to a record i of the data file that changes the value of a field that has a bitmap index, say from value v to value w. We must find the bit-vector for v and change the 1 in position i to 0. If there is a bit-vector for value w, then we change its 0 in position i to 1. If there is not yet a bit-vector for w, then we create it as discussed in the paragraph above for the case when an insertion introduces a new value.

14.7.5 Exercises for Section 14.7

Exercise 14.7.1: For the data of Fig. 14.36, show the bitmap indexes for the attributes: (a) speed (b) ram (c) hd, both in (i) uncompressed form, and (ii) compressed form using the scheme of Section 14.7.2.

Exercise 14.7.2: Using the bitmaps of Example 14.41, find the jewelry buyers with an age in the range 40–60 and a salary in the range 100–200.

Exercise 14.7.3: Consider a file of 100,000 records, with a field F that has m different values.

a) As a function of m, how many bytes does the bitmap index for F have?

! b) Suppose that the records numbered from 1 to 100,000 are given values for the field F in a round-robin fashion, so each value appears every m records. How many bytes would be consumed by a compressed index?

Exercise 14.7.4: Encode, using the scheme of Section 14.7.2, the following bitmaps:

a) 01100000010000000100.

b) 10000000100000100101010001.

c) 000100000000000001000010000.

!! **Exercise 14.7.5:** We suggested in Section 14.7.2 that it was possible to reduce the number of bits taken to encode number i from the $2\log_2 i$ that we used in that section until it is close to $\log_2 i$. Show how to approach that limit as closely as you like, as long as i is large. *Hint*: We used a unary encoding of the length of the binary encoding that we used for i. Can you encode the length of the code in binary?

14.8 Summary of Chapter 14

✦ *Sequential Files*: Several simple file organizations begin by sorting the data file according to some sort key and placing an index on this file.

✦ *Dense and Sparse Indexes*: Dense indexes have a key-pointer pair for every record in the data file, while sparse indexes have one key-pointer pair for each block of the data file.

✦ *Multilevel Indexes*: It is sometimes useful to put an index on the index file itself, an index file on that, and so on. Higher levels of index must be sparse.

✦ *Secondary Indexes*: An index on a search key K can be created even if the data file is not sorted by K. Such an index must be dense.

✦ *Inverted Indexes*: The relation between documents and the words they contain is often represented by an index structure with word-pointer pairs. The pointer goes to a place in a "bucket" file where is found a list of pointers to places where that word occurs.

✦ *B-trees*: These structures are essentially multilevel indexes, with graceful growth capabilities. Blocks with n keys and $n + 1$ pointers are organized in a tree, with the leaves pointing to records. All nonroot blocks are between half-full and completely full at all times.

✦ *Hash Tables*: We can create hash tables out of blocks in secondary memory, much as we can create main-memory hash tables. A hash function maps search-key values to buckets, effectively partitioning the records of a data file into many small groups (the buckets). Buckets are represented by a block and possible overflow blocks.

✦ *Extensible Hashing*: This method allows the number of buckets to double whenever any bucket has too many records. It uses an array of pointers to blocks that represent the buckets. To avoid having too many blocks, several buckets can be represented by the same block.

✦ *Linear Hashing*: This method grows the number of buckets by 1 each time the ratio of records to buckets exceeds a threshold. Since the population of a single bucket cannot cause the table to expand, overflow blocks for buckets are needed in some situations.

✦ *Queries Needing Multidimensional Indexes*: The sorts of queries that need to be supported on multidimensional data include partial-match (all points with specified values in a subset of the dimensions), range queries (all points within a range in each dimension), nearest-neighbor (closest point to a given point), and where-am-I (region or regions containing a given point).

✦ *Executing Nearest-Neighbor Queries*: Many data structures allow nearest-neighbor queries to be executed by performing a range query around the target point, and expanding the range if there is no point in that range. We must be careful, because finding a point within a rectangular range may not rule out the possibility of a closer point outside that rectangle.

✦ *Grid Files*: The grid file slices the space of points in each of the dimensions. The grid lines can be spaced differently, and there can be different numbers of lines for each dimension. Grid files support range queries, partial-match queries, and nearest-neighbor queries well, as long as data is fairly uniform in distribution.

✦ *Partitioned Hash Tables*: A partitioned hash function constructs some bits of the bucket number from each dimension. They support partial-match queries well, and are not dependent on the data being uniformly distributed.

✦ *Multiple-Key Indexes*: A simple multidimensional structure has a root that is an index on one attribute, leading to a collection of indexes on a second attribute, which can lead to indexes on a third attribute, and so on. They are useful for range and nearest-neighbor queries.

✦ kd-*Trees*: These trees are like binary search trees, but they branch on different attributes at different levels. They support partial-match, range, and nearest-neighbor queries well. Some careful packing of tree nodes into blocks must be done to make the structure suitable for secondary-storage operations.

✦ *Quad Trees*: The quad tree divides a multidimensional cube into quadrants, and recursively divides the quadrants the same way if they have too many points. They support partial-match, range, and nearest-neighbor queries.

✦ *R-Trees*: This form of tree normally represents a collection of regions by grouping them into a hierarchy of larger regions. It helps with where-am-I queries and, if the atomic regions are actually points, will support the other types of queries studied in this chapter, as well.

✦ *Bitmap Indexes*: Multidimensional queries are supported by a form of index that orders the points or records and represents the positions of the records with a given value in an attribute by a bit vector. These indexes support range, nearest-neighbor, and partial-match queries.

✦ *Compressed Bitmaps*: In order to save space, the bitmap indexes, which tend to consist of vectors with very few 1's, are compressed by using a run-length encoding.

14.9 References for Chapter 14

The B-tree was the original idea of Bayer and McCreight [2]. Unlike the B+ tree described here, this formulation had pointers to records at the interior nodes as well as at the leaves. [8] is a survey of B-tree varieties.

Hashing as a data structure goes back to Peterson [19]. Extensible hashing was developed by [9], while linear hashing is from [15]. The book by Knuth [14] contains much information on data structures, including techniques for selecting hash functions and designing hash tables, as well as a number of ideas concerning B-tree variants. The B+ tree formulation (without key values at interior nodes) appeared in the 1973 edition of [14].

Secondary indexes and other techniques for retrieval of documents are covered by [23]. Also, [10] and [1] are surveys of index methods for text documents.

The *kd*-tree is from [4]. Modifications suitable for secondary storage appeared in [5] and [21]. Partitioned hashing and its use in partial-match retieval is from [20] and [7]. However, the design idea from Exercise 14.5.6 is from [22].

Grid files first appeared in [16] and the quad tree in [11]. The R-tree is from [13], and two extensions [24] and [3] are well known.

The bitmap index has an interesting history. There was a company called Nucleus, founded by Ted Glaser, that patented the idea and developed a DBMS in which the bitmap index was both the index structure and the data representation. The company failed in the late 1980's, but the idea has recently been incorporated into several major commercial database systems. The first published work on the subject was [17]. [18] is a recent expansion of the idea.

There are a number of surveys of multidimensional storage structures. One of the earliest is [6]. More recent surveys are found in [25] and [12]. The former also includes surveys of several other important database topics.

1. R. Baeza-Yates, "Integrating contents and structure in text retrieval," *SIGMOD Record* **25**:1 (1996), pp. 67–79.

2. R. Bayer and E. M. McCreight, "Organization and maintenance of large ordered indexes," *Acta Informatica* **1**:3 (1972), pp. 173–189.

3. N. Beckmann, H.-P. Kriegel, R. Schneider, and B. Seeger, "The R*-tree: an efficient and robust access method for points and rectangles," *Proc. ACM SIGMOD Intl. Conf. on Management of Data* (1990), pp. 322–331.

4. J. L. Bentley, "Multidimensional binary search trees used for associative searching," *Comm. ACM* **18**:9 (1975), pp. 509–517.

5. J. L. Bentley, "Multidimensional binary search trees in database applications," *IEEE Trans. on Software Engineering* **SE-5**:4 (1979), pp. 333-340.

6. J. L. Bentley and J. H. Friedman, "Data structures for range searching," *Computing Surveys* **13**:3 (1979), pp. 397–409.

7. W. A. Burkhard, "Hashing and trie algorithms for partial match retrieval," *ACM Trans. on Database Systems* **1**:2 (1976), pp. 175–187.

8. D. Comer, "The ubiquitous B-tree," *Computing Surveys* **11**:2 (1979), pp. 121–137.

9. R. Fagin, J. Nievergelt, N. Pippenger, and H. R. Strong, "Extendible hashing — a fast access method for dynamic files," *ACM Trans. on Database Systems* **4**:3 (1979), pp. 315–344.

10. C. Faloutsos, "Access methods for text," *Computing Surveys* **17**:1 (1985), pp. 49–74.

11. R. A. Finkel and J. L. Bentley, "Quad trees, a data structure for retrieval on composite keys," *Acta Informatica* **4**:1 (1974), pp. 1–9.

12. V. Gaede and O. Gunther, "Multidimensional access methods," *Computing Surveys* **30**:2 (1998), pp. 170–231.

13. A. Guttman, "R-trees: a dynamic index structure for spatial searching," *Proc. ACM SIGMOD Intl. Conf. on Management of Data* (1984), pp. 47–57.

14. D. E. Knuth, *The Art of Computer Programming, Vol. III, Sorting and Searching, Second Edition*, Addison-Wesley, Reading MA, 1998.

15. W. Litwin, "Linear hashing: a new tool for file and table addressing," *Intl. Conf. on Very Large Databases*, pp. 212–223, 1980.

16. J. Nievergelt, H. Hinterberger, and K. Sevcik, "The grid file: an adaptable, symmetric, multikey file structure," *ACM Trans. on Database Systems* **9**:1 (1984), pp. 38–71.

17. P. O'Neil, "Model 204 architecture and performance," *Proc. Second Intl. Workshop on High Performance Transaction Systems*, Springer-Verlag, Berlin, 1987.

18. P. O'Neil and D. Quass, "Improved query performance with variant indexes," *Proc. ACM SIGMOD Intl. Conf. on Management of Data* (1997), pp. 38–49.

19. W. W. Peterson, "Addressing for random access storage," *IBM J. Research and Development* **1**:2 (1957), pp. 130–146.

20. R. L. Rivest, "Partial match retrieval algorithms," *SIAM J. Computing* **5**:1 (1976), pp. 19–50.

21. J. T. Robinson, "The K-D-B-tree: a search structure for large multidimensional dynamic indexes," *Proc. ACM SIGMOD Intl. Conf. on Mamagement of Data* (1981), pp. 10–18.

22. J. B. Rothnie Jr. and T. Lozano, "Attribute based file organization in a paged memory environment, *Comm. ACM* **17**:2 (1974), pp. 63–69.

23. G. Salton, *Introduction to Modern Information Retrieval*, McGraw-Hill, New York, 1983.

24. T. K. Sellis, N. Roussopoulos, and C. Faloutsos, "The R+-tree: a dynamic index for multidimensional objects," *Intl. Conf. on Very Large Databases*, pp. 507–518, 1987.

25. C. Zaniolo, S. Ceri, C. Faloutsos, R. T. Snodgrass, V. S. Subrahmanian, and R. Zicari, *Advanced Database Systems*, Morgan-Kaufmann, San Francisco, 1997.

Chapter 15

Query Execution

The broad topic of query processing will be covered in this chapter and Chapter 16. The *query processor* is the group of components of a DBMS that turns user queries and data-modification commands into a sequence of database operations and executes those operations. Since SQL lets us express queries at a very high level, the query processor must supply much detail regarding how the query is to be executed. Moreover, a naive execution strategy for a query may take far more time than necessary.

Figure 15.1 suggests the division of topics between Chapters 15 and 16. In this chapter, we concentrate on query execution, that is, the algorithms that manipulate the data of the database. We focus on the operations of the extended relational algebra, described in Section 5.2. Because SQL uses a bag model, we also assume that relations are bags, and thus use the bag versions of the operators from Section 5.1.

We shall cover the principal methods for execution of the operations of relational algebra. These methods differ in their basic strategy; scanning, hashing, sorting, and indexing are the major approaches. The methods also differ on their assumption as to the amount of available main memory. Some algorithms assume that enough main memory is available to hold at least one of the relations involved in an operation. Others assume that the arguments of the operation are too big to fit in memory, and these algorithms have significantly different costs and structures.

Preview of Query Compilation

To set the context for query execution, we offer a very brief outline of the content of the next chapter. Query compilation is divided into the three major steps shown in Fig. 15.2.

a) *Parsing*. A *parse tree* for the query is constructed.

b) *Query Rewrite*. The parse tree is converted to an initial query plan, which is usually an algebraic representation of the query. This initial plan is then

701

query

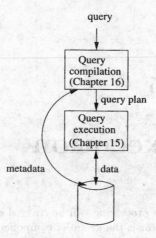

Figure 15.1: The major parts of the query processor

transformed into an equivalent plan that is expected to require less time to execute.

c) *Physical Plan Generation.* The abstract query plan from (b), often called a *logical query plan*, is turned into a *physical query plan* by selecting algorithms to implement each of the operators of the logical plan, and by selecting an order of execution for these operators. The physical plan, like the result of parsing and the logical plan, is represented by an expression tree. The physical plan also includes details such as how the queried relations are accessed, and when and if a relation should be sorted.

Parts (b) and (c) are often called the *query optimizer*, and these are the hard parts of query compilation. To select the best query plan we need to decide:

1. Which of the algebraically equivalent forms of a query leads to the most efficient algorithm for answering the query?

2. For each operation of the selected form, what algorithm should we use to implement that operation?

3. How should the operations pass data from one to the other, e.g., in a pipelined fashion, in main-memory buffers, or via the disk?

Each of these choices depends on the metadata about the database. Typical metadata that is available to the query optimizer includes: the size of each relation; statistics such as the approximate number and frequency of different values for an attribute; the existence of certain indexes; and the layout of data on disk.

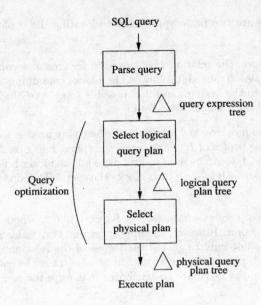

Figure 15.2: Outline of query compilation

15.1 Introduction to Physical-Query-Plan Operators

Physical query plans are built from operators, each of which implements one step of the plan. Often, the physical operators are particular implementations for one of the operations of relational algebra. However, we also need physical operators for other tasks that do not involve an operation of relational algebra. For example, we often need to "scan" a table, that is, bring into main memory each tuple of some relation. The relation is typically an operand of some other operation.

In this section, we shall introduce the basic building blocks of physical query plans. Later sections cover the more complex algorithms that implement operators of relational algebra efficiently; these algorithms also form an essential part of physical query plans. We also introduce here the "iterator" concept, which is an important method by which the operators comprising a physical query plan can pass requests for tuples and answers among themselves.

15.1.1 Scanning Tables

Perhaps the most basic thing we can do in a physical query plan is to read the entire contents of a relation R. A variation of this operator involves a simple predicate, where we read only those tuples of the relation R that satisfy the predicate. There are two basic approaches to locating the tuples of a relation R.

1. In many cases, the relation R is stored in an area of secondary memory, with its tuples arranged in blocks. The blocks containing the tuples of R are known to the system, and it is possible to get the blocks one by one. This operation is called *table-scan*.

2. If there is an index on any attribute of R, we may be able to use this index to get all the tuples of R. For example, a sparse index on R, as discussed in Section 14.1.3, can be used to lead us to all the blocks holding R, even if we don't know otherwise which blocks these are. This operation is called *index-scan*.

We shall take up index-scan again in Section 15.6.2, when we talk about implementing selection. However, the important observation for now is that we can use the index not only to get *all* the tuples of the relation it indexes, but to get only those tuples that have a particular value (or sometimes a particular range of values) in the attribute or attributes that form the search key for the index.

15.1.2 Sorting While Scanning Tables

There are a number of reasons why we might want to sort a relation as we read its tuples. For one, the query could include an ORDER BY clause, requiring that a relation be sorted. For another, some approaches to implementing relational-algebra operations require one or both arguments to be sorted relations. These algorithms appear in Section 15.4 and elsewhere.

The physical-query-plan operator *sort-scan* takes a relation R and a specification of the attributes on which the sort is to be made, and produces R in that sorted order. There are several ways that sort-scan can be implemented. If relation R must be sorted by attribute a, and there is a B-tree index on a, then a scan of the index allows us to produce R in the desired order. If R is small enough to fit in main memory, then we can retrieve its tuples using a table scan or index scan, and then use a main-memory sorting algorithm. If R is too large to fit in main memory, then we can use a multiway merge-sort, as will be discussed Section 15.4.1.

15.1.3 The Computation Model for Physical Operators

A query generally consists of several operations of relational algebra, and the corresponding physical query plan is composed of several physical operators. Since choosing physical-plan operators wisely is an essential of a good query processor, we must be able to estimate the "cost" of each operator we use. We shall use the number of disk I/O's as our measure of cost for an operation. This measure is consistent with our view (see Section 13.3.1) that it takes longer to get data from disk than to do anything useful with it once the data is in main memory.

When comparing algorithms for the same operations, we shall make an assumption that may be surprising at first:

- We assume that the arguments of any operator are found on disk, but the result of the operator is left in main memory.

If the operator produces the final answer to a query, and that result is indeed written to disk, then the cost of doing so depends only on the size of the answer, and not on how the answer was computed. We can simply add the final write-back cost to the total cost of the query. However, in many applications, the answer is not stored on disk at all, but printed or passed to some formatting program. Then, the disk I/O cost of the output either is zero or depends upon what some unknown application program does with the data. In either case, the cost of writing the answer does not influence our choice of algorithm for executing the operator.

Similarly, the result of an operator that forms part of a query (rather than the whole query) often is not written to disk. In Section 15.1.6 we shall discuss "iterators," where the result of one operator O_1 is constructed in main memory, perhaps a small piece at a time, and passed as an argument to another operator O_2. In this situation, we never have to write the result of O_1 to disk, and moreover, we save the cost of reading from disk an argument of O_2.

15.1.4 Parameters for Measuring Costs

Now, let us introduce the parameters (sometimes called statistics) that we use to express the cost of an operator. Estimates of cost are essential if the optimizer is to determine which of the many query plans is likely to execute fastest. Section 16.5 will show how to exploit these cost estimates.

We need a parameter to represent the portion of main memory that the operator uses, and we require other parameters to measure the size of its argument(s). Assume that main memory is divided into buffers, whose size is the same as the size of disk blocks. Then M will denote the number of main-memory buffers available to an execution of a particular operator.

Sometimes, we can think of M as the entire main memory, or most of the main memory. However, we shall also see situations where several operations share the main memory, so M could be much smaller than the total main memory. In fact, as we shall discuss in Section 15.7, the number of buffers available to an operation may not be a predictable constant, but may be decided during execution, based on what other processes are executing at the same time. If so, M is really an estimate of the number of buffers available to the operation.

Next, let us consider the parameters that measure the cost of accessing argument relations. These parameters, measuring size and distribution of data in a relation, are often computed periodically to help the query optimizer choose physical operators.

We shall make the simplifying assumption that data is accessed one block at a time from disk. In practice, one of the techniques discussed in Section 13.3 might be able to speed up the algorithm if we are able to read many blocks of the relation at once, and they can be read from consecutive blocks on a track. There are three parameter families, B, T, and V:

- When describing the size of a relation R, we most often are concerned with the number of blocks that are needed to hold all the tuples of R. This number of blocks will be denoted $B(R)$, or just B if we know that relation R is meant. Usually, we assume that R is *clustered*; that is, it is stored in B blocks or in approximately B blocks.

- Sometimes, we also need to know the number of tuples in R, and we denote this quantity by $T(R)$, or just T if R is understood. If we need the number of tuples of R that can fit in one block, we can use the ratio T/B.

- Finally, we shall sometimes want to refer to the number of distinct values that appear in a column of a relation. If R is a relation, and one of its attributes is a, then $V(R,a)$ is the number of distinct values of the column for a in R. More generally, if $[a_1, a_2, \ldots, a_n]$ is a list of attributes, then $V(R, [a_1, a_2, \ldots, a_n])$ is the number of distinct n-tuples in the columns of R for attributes $a_1, a_2, \ldots, a_n$. Put formally, it is the number of tuples in $\delta\big(\pi_{a_1, a_2, \ldots, a_n}(R)\big)$.

15.1.5   I/O Cost for Scan Operators

As a simple application of the parameters that were introduced, we can represent the number of disk I/O's needed for each of the table-scan operators discussed so far. If relation R is clustered, then the number of disk I/O's for the table-scan operator is approximately B. Likewise, if R fits in main-memory, then we can implement sort-scan by reading R into memory and performing an in-memory sort, again requiring only B disk I/O's.

However, if R is not clustered, then the number of required disk I/O's is generally much higher. If R is distributed among tuples of other relations, then a table-scan for R may require reading as many blocks as there are tuples of R; that is, the I/O cost is T. Similarly, if we want to sort R, but R fits in memory, then T disk I/O's are what we need to get all of R into memory.

Finally, let us consider the cost of an index-scan. Generally, an index on a relation R occupies many fewer than $B(R)$ blocks. Therefore, a scan of the entire R, which takes at least B disk I/O's, will require significantly more I/O's than does examining the entire index. Thus, even though index-scan requires examining both the relation and its index,

- We continue to use B or T, respectively, to estimate the cost of accessing a clustered or unclustered relation in its entirety, using an index.

However, if we only want part of R, we often are able to avoid looking at the entire index and the entire R. We shall defer analysis of these uses of indexes to Section 15.6.2.

15.1.6 Iterators for Implementation of Physical Operators

Many physical operators can be implemented as an *iterator*, which is a group of three methods that allows a consumer of the result of the physical operator to get the result one tuple at a time. The three methods forming the iterator for an operation are:

1. Open(). This method starts the process of getting tuples, but does not get a tuple. It initializes any data structures needed to perform the operation and calls Open() for any arguments of the operation.

2. GetNext(). This method returns the next tuple in the result and adjusts data structures as necessary to allow subsequent tuples to be obtained. In getting the next tuple of its result, it typically calls GetNext() one or more times on its argument(s). If there are no more tuples to return, GetNext() returns a special value NotFound, which we assume cannot be mistaken for a tuple.

3. Close(). This method ends the iteration after all tuples, or all tuples that the consumer wanted, have been obtained. Typically, it calls Close() on any arguments of the operator.

When describing iterators and their methods, we shall assume that there is a "class" for each type of iterator (i.e., for each type of physical operator implemented as an iterator), and the class defines Open(), GetNext(), and Close() methods on instances of the class.

Example 15.1: Perhaps the simplest iterator is the one that implements the table-scan operator. The iterator is implemented by a class TableScan, and a table-scan operator in a query plan is an instance of this class parameterized by the relation R we wish to scan. Let us assume that R is a relation clustered in some list of blocks, which we can access in a convenient way; that is, the notion of "get the next block of R" is implemented by the storage system and need not be described in detail. Further, we assume that within a block there is a directory of records (tuples), so it is easy to get the next tuple of a block or tell that the last tuple has been reached.

Figure 15.3 sketches the three methods for this iterator. We imagine a block pointer b and a tuple pointer t that points to a tuple within block b. We assume that both pointers can point "beyond" the last block or last tuple of a block, respectively, and that it is possible to identify when these conditions occur. Notice that Close() in this example does nothing. In practice, a Close() method for an iterator might clean up the internal structure of the DBMS in various ways. It might inform the buffer manager that certain buffers are no

```
Open() {
    b := the first block of R;
    t := the first tuple of block b;
}


GetNext() {
    IF (t is past the last tuple on block b) {
        increment b to the next block;
        IF (there is no next block)
            RETURN NotFound;
        ELSE /* b is a new block */
            t := first tuple on block b;
    } /* now we are ready to return t and increment */
    oldt := t;
    increment t to the next tuple of b;
    RETURN oldt;
}


Close() {
}
```

Figure 15.3: Iterator methods for the table-scan operator over relation R

longer needed, or inform the concurrency manager that the read of a relation has completed. □

Example 15.2: Now, let us consider an example where the iterator does most of the work in its Open() method. The operator is sort-scan, where we read the tuples of a relation R but return them in sorted order. We cannot return even the first tuple until we have examined each tuple of R. For simplicity, assume that R is small enough to fit in main memory.

Open() must read the entire R into main memory. It might also sort the tuples of R, in which case GetNext() needs only to return each tuple in turn, in the sorted order. Alternatively, Open() could leave R unsorted, and GetNext() could select the first of the remaining tuples, in effect performing one pass of a selection sort. □

Example 15.3: Finally, let us consider a simple example of how iterators can be combined by calling other iterators. The operation is the bag union $R \cup S$, in which we produce first all the tuples of R and then all the tuples of S, without regard for the existence of duplicates. Let $\mathcal{R}$ and $\mathcal{S}$ denote the iterators that produce relations R and S, and thus are the "children" of the union operator in a query plan for $R \cup S$. Iterators $\mathcal{R}$ and $\mathcal{S}$ could be table scans applied to stored relations R and S, or they could be iterators that call a network

---

Why Iterators?

We shall see in Section 16.7 how iterators support efficient execution when they are composed within query plans. They contrast with a *materialization* strategy, where the result of each operator is produced in its entirety — and either stored on disk or allowed to take up space in main memory. When iterators are used, many operations are active at once. Tuples pass between operators as needed, thus reducing the need for storage. Of course, as we shall see, not all physical operators support the iteration approach, or "pipelining," in a useful way. In some cases, almost all the work would need to be done by the Open() method, which is tantamount to materialization.

---

of other iterators to compute R and S. Regardless, all that is important is that we have available methods R.Open(), R.GetNext(), and R.Close(), and analogous methods for iterator S.

The iterator methods for the union are sketched in Fig. 15.4. One subtle point is that the methods use a shared variable CurRel that is either R or S, depending on which relation is being read from currently. □

15.2 One-Pass Algorithms

We shall now begin our study of a very important topic in query optimization: how should we execute each of the individual steps — for example, a join or selection — of a logical query plan? The choice of algorithm for each operator is an essential part of the process of transforming a logical query plan into a physical query plan. While many algorithms for operators have been proposed, they largely fall into three classes:

1. Sorting-based methods (Section 15.4).

2. Hash-based methods (Sections 15.5 and 20.1).

3. Index-based methods (Section 15.6).

In addition, we can divide algorithms for operators into three "degrees" of difficulty and cost:

a) Some methods involve reading the data only once from disk. These are the *one-pass* algorithms, and they are the topic of this section. Usually, they require at least one of the arguments to fit in main memory, although there are exceptions, especially for selection and projection as discussed in Section 15.2.1.

```
Open() {
    R.Open();
    CurRel := R;
}

GetNext() {
    IF (CurRel = R) {
        t := R.GetNext();
        IF (t <> NotFound) /* R is not exhausted */
            RETURN t;
        ELSE /* R is exhausted */ {
            S.Open();
            CurRel := S;
        }
    }
    /* here, we must read from S */
    RETURN S.GetNext();
    /* notice that if S is exhausted, S.GetNext()
       will return NotFound, which is the correct
       action for our GetNext as well */
}

Close() {
    R.Close();
    S.Close();
}
```

Figure 15.4: Building a union iterator from iterators $\mathcal{R}$ and $\mathcal{S}$

b) Some methods work for data that is too large to fit in available main
   memory but not for the largest imaginable data sets. These *two-pass*
   algorithms are characterized by reading data a first time from disk, processing it in some way, writing all, or almost all, of it to disk, and then
   reading it a second time for further processing during the second pass.
   We meet these algorithms in Sections 15.4 and 15.5.

c) Some methods work without a limit on the size of the data. These methods use three or more passes to do their jobs, and are natural, recursive generalizations of the two-pass algorithms. We shall study multipass
   methods in Section 15.8.

In this section, we shall concentrate on the one-pass methods. Here and
subsequently, we shall classify operators into three broad groups:

1. *Tuple-at-a-time, unary operations.* These operations — selection and projection — do not require an entire relation, or even a large part of it, in memory at once. Thus, we can read a block at a time, use one main-memory buffer, and produce our output.

2. *Full-relation, unary operations.* These one-argument operations require seeing all or most of the tuples in memory at once, so one-pass algorithms are limited to relations that are approximately of size M (the number of main-memory buffers available) or less. The operations of this class are γ (the grouping operator) and δ (the duplicate-elimination operator).

3. *Full-relation, binary operations.* All other operations are in this class: set and bag versions of union, intersection, difference, joins, and products. Except for bag union, each of these operations requires at least one argument to be limited to size M, if we are to use a one-pass algorithm.

15.2.1 One-Pass Algorithms for Tuple-at-a-Time Operations

The tuple-at-a-time operations $\sigma(R)$ and $\pi(R)$ have obvious algorithms, regardless of whether the relation fits in main memory. We read the blocks of R one at a time into an input buffer, perform the operation on each tuple, and move the selected tuples or the projected tuples to the output buffer, as suggested by Fig. 15.5. Since the output buffer may be an input buffer of some other operator, or may be sending data to a user or application, we do not count the output buffer as needed space. Thus, we require only that $M \geq 1$ for the input buffer, regardless of B.

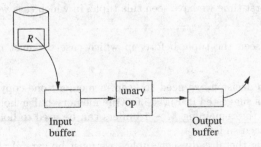

Figure 15.5: A selection or projection being performed on a relation R

The disk I/O requirement for this process depends only on how the argument relation R is provided. If R is initially on disk, then the cost is whatever it takes to perform a table-scan or index-scan of R. The cost was discussed in Section 15.1.5; typically, the cost is B if R is clustered and T if it is not clustered. However, remember the important exception where the operation being performed is a selection, and the condition compares a constant to an

---

Extra Buffers Can Speed Up Operations

Although tuple-at-a-time operations can get by with only one input buffer and one output buffer, as suggested by Fig. 15.5, we can often speed up processing if we allocate more input buffers. The idea appeared first in Section 13.3.2. If R is stored on consecutive blocks within cylinders, then we can read an entire cylinder into buffers, while paying for the seek time and rotational latency for only one block per cylinder. Similarly, if the output of the operation can be stored on full cylinders, we waste almost no time writing.

---

attribute that has an index. In that case, we can use the index to retrieve only a subset of the blocks holding R, thus improving performance, often markedly.

15.2.2   One-Pass Algorithms for Unary, Full-Relation Operations

Now, let us consider the unary operations that apply to relations as a whole, rather than to one tuple at a time: duplicate elimination (δ) and grouping (γ).

Duplicate Elimination

To eliminate duplicates, we can read each block of R one at a time, but for each tuple we need to make a decision as to whether:

1. It is the first time we have seen this tuple, in which case we copy it to the output, or

2. We have seen the tuple before, in which case we must not output this tuple.

To support this decision, we need to keep in memory one copy of every tuple we have seen, as suggested in Fig. 15.6. One memory buffer holds one block of R's tuples, and the remaining $M - 1$ buffers can be used to hold a single copy of every tuple seen so far.

When storing the already-seen tuples, we must be careful about the main-memory data structure we use. Naively, we might just list the tuples we have seen. When a new tuple from R is considered, we compare it with all tuples seen so far, and if it is not equal to any of these tuples we both copy it to the output and add it to the in-memory list of tuples we have seen.

However, if there are n tuples in main memory, each new tuple takes processor time proportional to n, so the complete operation takes processor time proportional to n^2. Since n could be very large, this amount of time calls into serious question our assumption that only the disk I/O time is significant. Thus,

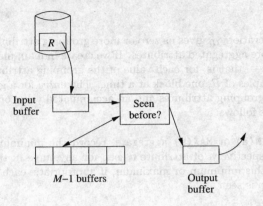

Figure 15.6: Managing memory for a one-pass duplicate-elimination

we need a main-memory structure that allows each us to add a new tuple and to tell whether a given tuple is already there, in time that grows slowly with n.

For example, we could use a hash table with a large number of buckets, or some form of balanced binary search tree.[1] Each of these structures has some space overhead in addition to the space needed to store the tuples; for instance, a main-memory hash table needs a bucket array and space for pointers to link the tuples in a bucket. However, the overhead tends to be small compared with the space needed to store the tuples, and we shall in this chpater neglect this overhead.

On this assumption, we may store in the $M - 1$ available buffers of main memory as many tuples as will fit in $M - 1$ blocks of R. If we want one copy of each distinct tuple of R to fit in main memory, then $B\big(\delta(R)\big)$ must be no larger than $M - 1$. Since we expect M to be much larger than 1, a simpler approximation to this rule, and the one we shall generally use, is:

- $B\big(\delta(R)\big) \leq M$

Note that we cannot in general compute the size of $\delta(R)$ without computing $\delta(R)$ itself. Should we underestimate that size, so $B\big(\delta(R)\big)$ is actually larger than M, we shall pay a significant penalty due to thrashing, as the blocks holding the distinct tuples of R must be brought into and out of main memory frequently.

---

[1]See Aho, A. V., J. E. Hopcroft, and J. D. Ullman, *Data Structures and Algorithms*, Addison-Wesley, 1983 for discussions of suitable main-memory structures. In particular, hashing takes on average $O(n)$ time to process n items, and balanced trees take $O(n \log n)$ time; either is sufficiently close to linear for our purposes.

Grouping

A grouping operation γ_L gives us zero or more grouping attributes and presumably one or more aggregated attributes. If we create in main memory one entry for each group — that is, for each value of the grouping attributes — then we can scan the tuples of R, one block at a time. The *entry* for a group consists of values for the grouping attributes and an accumulated value or values for each aggregation, as follows:

- For a MIN(a) or MAX(a) aggregate, record the minimum or maximum value, respectively, of attribute a seen for any tuple in the group so far. Change this minimum or maximum, if appropriate, each time a tuple of the group is seen.

- For any COUNT aggregation, add one for each tuple of the group that is seen.

- For SUM(a), add the value of attribute a to the accumulated sum for its group, provided a is not NULL.

- AVG(a) is the hard case. We must maintain two accumulations: the count of the number of tuples in the group and the sum of the a-values of these tuples. Each is computed as we would for a COUNT and SUM aggregation, respectively. After all tuples of R are seen, we take the quotient of the sum and count to obtain the average.

When all tuples of R have been read into the input buffer and contributed to the aggregation(s) for their group, we can produce the output by writing the tuple for each group. Note that until the last tuple is seen, we cannot begin to create output for a γ operation. Thus, this algorithm does not fit the iterator framework very well; the entire grouping has to be done by the Open method before the first tuple can be retrieved by GetNext.

In order that the in-memory processing of each tuple be efficient, we need to use a main-memory data structure that lets us find the entry for each group, given values for the grouping attributes. As discussed above for the δ operation, common main-memory data structures such as hash tables or balanced trees will serve well. We should remember, however, that the search key for this structure is the grouping attributes only.

The number of disk I/O's needed for this one-pass algorithm is B, as must be the case for any one-pass algorithm for a unary operator. The number of required memory buffers M is not related to B in any simple way, although typically M will be less than B. The problem is that the entries for the groups could be longer or shorter than tuples of R, and the number of groups could be anything equal to or less than the number of tuples of R. However, in most cases, group entries will be no longer than R's tuples, and there will be many fewer groups than tuples.

Operations on Nonclustered Data

All our calculations regarding the number of disk I/O's required for an operation are predicated on the assumption that the operand relations are clustered. In the (typically rare) event that an operand R is not clustered, then it may take us $T(R)$ disk I/O's, rather than $B(R)$ disk I/O's to read all the tuples of R. Note, however, that any relation that is the result of an operator may always be assumed clustered, since we have no reason to store a temporary relation in a nonclustered fashion.

15.2.3 One-Pass Algorithms for Binary Operations

Let us now take up the binary operations: union, intersection, difference, product, and join. Since in some cases we must distinguish the set- and bag-versions of these operators, we shall subscript them with B or S for "bag" and "set," respectively; e.g., $\cup_B$ for bag union or $-_S$ for set difference. To simplify the discussion of joins, we shall consider only the natural join. An equijoin can be implemented the same way, after attributes are renamed appropriately, and theta-joins can be thought of as a product or equijoin followed by a selection for those conditions that cannot be expressed in an equijoin.

Bag union can be computed by a very simple one-pass algorithm. To compute $R \cup_B S$, we copy each tuple of R to the output and then copy every tuple of S, as we did in Example 15.3. The number of disk I/O's is $B(R) + B(S)$, as it must be for a one-pass algorithm on operands R and S, while $M = 1$ suffices regardless of how large R and S are.

Other binary operations require reading the smaller of the operands R and S into main memory and building a suitable data structure so tuples can be both inserted quickly and found quickly, as discussed in Section 15.2.2. As before, a hash table or balanced tree suffices. Thus, the approximate requirement for a binary operation on relations R and S to be performed in one pass is:

- $\min\big(B(R), B(S)\big) \leq M$

More preceisely, one buffer is used to read the blocks of the larger relation, while approximately M buffers are needed to house the entire smaller relation and its main-memory data structure.

We shall now give the details of the various operations. In each case, we assume R is the larger of the relations, and we house S in main memory.

Set Union

We read S into $M - 1$ buffers of main memory and build a search structure whose search key is the entire tuple. All these tuples are also copied to the output. We then read each block of R into the Mth buffer, one at a time. For each tuple t of R, we see if t is in S, and if not, we copy t to the output. If t is also in S, we skip t.

Set Intersection

Read S into $M - 1$ buffers and build a search structure with full tuples as the search key. Read each block of R, and for each tuple t of R, see if t is also in S. If so, copy t to the output, and if not, ignore t.

Set Difference

Since difference is not commutative, we must distinguish between $R -_S S$ and $S -_S R$, continuing to assume that R is the larger relation. In each case, read S into $M - 1$ buffers and build a search structure with full tuples as the search key.

To compute $R -_S S$, we read each block of R and examine each tuple t on that block. If t is in S, then ignore t; if it is not in S then copy t to the output.

To compute $S -_S R$, we again read the blocks of R and examine each tuple t in turn. If t is in S, then we delete t from the copy of S in main memory, while if t is not in S we do nothing. After considering each tuple of R, we copy to the output those tuples of S that remain.

Bag Intersection

We read S into $M - 1$ buffers, but we associate with each distinct tuple a *count*, which initially measures the number of times this tuple occurs in S. Multiple copies of a tuple t are not stored individually. Rather we store one copy of t and associate with it a count equal to the number of times t occurs.

This structure could take slightly more space than $B(S)$ blocks if there were few duplicates, although frequently the result is that S is compacted. Thus, we shall continue to assume that $B(S) \leq M$ is sufficient for a one-pass algorithm to work, although the condition is only an approximation.

Next, we read each block of R, and for each tuple t of R we see whether t occurs in S. If not we ignore t; it cannot appear in the intersection. However, if t appears in S, and the count associated with t is still positive, then we output t and decrement the count by 1. If t appears in S, but its count has reached 0, then we do not output t; we have already produced as many copies of t in the output as there were copies in S.

Bag Difference

To compute $S -_B R$, we read the tuples of S into main memory, and count the number of occurrences of each distinct tuple, as we did for bag intersection. When we read R, for each tuple t we see whether t occurs in S, and if so, we decrement its associated count. At the end, we copy to the output each tuple in main memory whose count is positive, and the number of times we copy it equals that count.

To compute $R -_B S$, we also read the tuples of S into main memory and count the number of occurrences of distinct tuples. We may think of a tuple t with a count of c as c reasons not to copy t to the output as we read tuples of R. That is, when we read a tuple t of R, we see if t occurs in S. If not, then we copy t to the output. If t does occur in S, then we look at the current count c associated with t. If $c = 0$, then copy t to the output. If $c > 0$, do not copy t to the output, but decrement c by 1.

Product

Read S into $M - 1$ buffers of main memory; no special data structure is needed. Then read each block of R, and for each tuple t of R concatenate t with each tuple of S in main memory. Output each concatenated tuple as it is formed.

This algorithm may take a considerable amount of processor time per tuple of R, because each such tuple must be matched with $M - 1$ blocks full of tuples. However, the output size is also large, and the time per output tuple is small.

Natural Join

In this and other join algorithms, let us take the convention that $R(X, Y)$ is being joined with $S(Y, Z)$, where Y represents all the attributes that R and S have in common, X is all attributes of R that are not in the schema of S, and Z is all attributes of S that are not in the schema of R. We continue to assume that S is the smaller relation. To compute the natural join, do the following:

1. Read all the tuples of S and form them into a main-memory search structure with the attributes of Y as the search key. Use $M - 1$ blocks of memory for this purpose.

2. Read each block of R into the one remaining main-memory buffer. For each tuple t of R, find the tuples of S that agree with t on all attributes of Y, using the search structure. For each matching tuple of S, form a tuple by joining it with t, and move the resulting tuple to the output.

Like all the one-pass, binary algorithms, this one takes $B(R) + B(S)$ disk I/O's to read the operands. It works as long as $B(S) \leq M - 1$, or approximately, $B(S) \leq M$.

We shall not discuss joins other than the natural join. Remember that an equijoin is executed in essentially the same way as a natural join, but we must account for the fact that "equal" attributes from the two relations may have different names. A theta-join that is not an equijoin can be replaced by an equijoin or product followed by a selection.

15.2.4   Exercises for Section 15.2

Exercise 15.2.1: For each of the operations below, write an iterator that uses the algorithm described in this section: (a) distinct (δ) (b) grouping (γ_L) (c) set union (d) set intersection (e) set difference (f) bag intersection (g) bag difference (h) product (i) natural join. (j) projection

Exercise 15.2.2: For each of the operators in Exercise 15.2.1, tell whether the operator is *blocking*, by which we mean that the first output cannot be produced until all the input has been read. Put another way, a blocking operator is one whose only possible iterators have all the important work done by Open.

! **Exercise 15.2.3:** Give one-pass algorithms for each of the following join-like operators:

a) $R \overset{\circ}{\bowtie}_L S$, assuming R fits in memory (see Section 5.2.7 for definitions involving outerjoins).

b) $R \overset{\circ}{\bowtie}_L S$, assuming S fits in memory.

c) $R \overset{\circ}{\bowtie}_R S$, assuming R fits in memory.

d) $R \overset{\circ}{\bowtie}_R S$, assuming S fits in memory.

e) $R \overset{\circ}{\bowtie} S$, assuming R fits in memory.

f) $R \ltimes S$, assuming R fits in memory (see Exercise 2.4.8 for a definition of the semijoin).

g) $R \ltimes S$, assuming S fits in memory.

h) $R \overline{\ltimes} S$, assuming R fits in memory (see Exercise 2.4.9 for a definition of the antisemijoin).

i) $R \overline{\ltimes} S$, assuming S fits in memory.

Exercise 15.2.4: Figure 15.9 summarizes the memory and disk-I/O requirements of the algorithms of this section and the next. However, it assumes all arguments are clustered. How would the entries change if one or both arguments were not clustered?

15.3   Nested-Loop Joins

Before proceeding to the more complex algorithms in the next sections, we shall turn our attention to a family of algorithms for the join operator called "nested-loop" joins. These algorithms are, in a sense, "one-and-a-half" passes, since in each variation one of the two arguments has its tuples read only once, while the other argument will be read repeatedly. Nested-loop joins can be used for relations of any size; it is not necessary that one relation fit in main memory.

15.3.1   Tuple-Based Nested-Loop Join

The simplest variation of nested-loop join has loops that range over individual tuples of the relations involved. In this algorithm, which we call *tuple-based nested-loop join*, we compute the join $R(X, Y) \bowtie S(Y, Z)$ as follows:

```
FOR each tuple s in S DO
    FOR each tuple r in R DO
        IF r and s join to make a tuple t THEN
            output t;
```

If we are careless about how we buffer the blocks of relations R and S, then this algorithm could require as many as $T(R)T(S)$ disk I/O's. However, there are many situations where this algorithm can be modified to have much lower cost. One case is when we can use an index on the join attribute or attributes of R to find the tuples of R that match a given tuple of S, without having to read the entire relation R. We discuss index-based joins in Section 15.6.3. A second improvement looks much more carefully at the way tuples of R and S are divided among blocks, and uses as much of the memory as it can to reduce the number of disk I/O's as we go through the inner loop. We shall consider this block-based version of nested-loop join in Section 15.3.3.

15.3.2   An Iterator for Tuple-Based Nested-Loop Join

One advantage of a nested-loop join is that it fits well into an iterator framework, and thus, as we shall see in Section 16.7.3, allows us to avoid storing intermediate relations on disk in some situations. The iterator for $R \bowtie S$ is easy to build from the iterators for R and S, which support methods R.Open(), and so on, as in Section 15.1.6. The code for the three iterator methods for nested-loop join is in Fig. 15.7. It makes the assumption that neither relation R nor S is empty.

15.3.3   Block-Based Nested-Loop Join Algorithm

We can improve on the tuple-based nested-loop join of Section 15.3.1 if we compute $R \bowtie S$ by:

1. Organizing access to both argument relations by blocks, and

2. Using as much main memory as we can to store tuples belonging to the relation S, the relation of the outer loop.

Point (1) makes sure that when we run through the tuples of R in the inner loop, we use as few disk I/O's as possible to read R. Point (2) enables us to join each tuple of R that we read with not just one tuple of S, but with as many tuples of S as will fit in memory.

```
Open() {
    R.Open();
    S.Open();
    s := S.GetNext();
}

GetNext() {
    REPEAT {
        r := R.GetNext();
        IF (r = NotFound) { /* R is exhausted for
                the current s */
            R.Close();
            s := S.GetNext();
            IF (s = NotFound) RETURN NotFound;
                /* both R and S are exhausted */
            R.Open();
            r := R.GetNext();
        }
    }
    UNTIL (r and s join);
    RETURN the join of r and s;
}

Close() {
    R.Close();
    S.Close();
}
```

Figure 15.7: Iterator methods for tuple-based nested-loop join of R and S

As in Section 15.2.3, let us assume $B(S) \leq B(R)$, but now let us also assume that $B(S) > M$; i.e., neither relation fits entirely in main memory. We repeatedly read $M-1$ blocks of S into main-memory buffers. A search structure, with search key equal to the common attributes of R and S, is created for the tuples of S that are in main memory. Then we go through all the blocks of R, reading each one in turn into the last block of memory. Once there, we compare all the tuples of R's block with all the tuples in all the blocks of S that are currently in main memory. For those that join, we output the joined tuple. The nested-loop structure of this algorithm can be seen when we describe the algorithm more formally, in Fig. 15.8. The algorithm of Fig. 15.8 is sometimes called "nested-block join." We shall continue to call it simply *nested-loop join*, since it is the variant of the nested-loop idea most commonly implemented in practice.

```
FOR each chunk of M-1 blocks of S DO BEGIN
    read these blocks into main-memory buffers;
    organize their tuples into a search structure whose
        search key is the common attributes of R and S;
    FOR each block b of R DO BEGIN
        read b into main memory;
        FOR each tuple t of b DO BEGIN
            find the tuples of S in main memory that
                join with t;
            output the join of t with each of these tuples;
        END;
    END;
END;
```

Figure 15.8: The nested-loop join algorithm

The program of Fig. 15.8 appears to have three nested loops. However, there really are only two loops if we look at the code at the right level of abstraction. The first, or outer loop, runs through the tuples of S. The other two loops run through the tuples of R. However, we expressed the process as two loops to emphasize that the order in which we visit the tuples of R is not arbitrary. Rather, we need to look at these tuples a block at a time (the role of the second loop), and within one block, we look at all the tuples of that block before moving on to the next block (the role of the third loop).

Example 15.4: Let $B(R) = 1000$, $B(S) = 500$, and $M = 101$. We shall use 100 blocks of memory to buffer S in 100-block chunks, so the outer loop of Fig. 15.8 iterates five times. At each iteration, we do 100 disk I/O's to read the chunk of S, and we must read R entirely in the second loop, using 1000 disk I/O's. Thus, the total number of disk I/O's is 5500.

Notice that if we reversed the roles of R and S, the algorithm would use slightly more disk I/O's. We would iterate 10 times through the outer loop and do 600 disk I/O's at each iteration, for a total of 6000. In general, there is a slight advantage to using the smaller relation in the outer loop. □

15.3.4 Analysis of Nested-Loop Join

The analysis of Example 15.4 can be repeated for any $B(R)$, $B(S)$, and M. Assuming S is the smaller relation, the number of chunks, or iterations of the outer loop is $B(S)/(M-1)$. At each iteration, we read $M-1$ blocks of S and $B(R)$ blocks of R. The number of disk I/O's is thus $B(S)\big(M-1+B(R)\big)/(M-1)$, or $B(S)+\big(B(S)B(R)\big)/(M-1)$.

Assuming all of M, $B(S)$, and $B(R)$ are large, but M is the smallest of these, an approximation to the above formula is $B(S)B(R)/M$. That is, the cost is proportional to the product of the sizes of the two relations, divided by the amount of available main memory. We can do much better than a nested-loop join when both relations are large. But for reasonably small examples such as Example 15.4, the cost of the nested-loop join is not much greater than the cost of a one-pass join, which is 1500 disk I/O's for this example. In fact, if $B(S) \leq M - 1$, the nested-loop join becomes identical to the one-pass join algorithm of Section 15.2.3.

Although nested-loop join is generally not the most efficient join algorithm possible, we should note that in some early relational DBMS's, it was the only method available. Even today, it is needed as a subroutine in more efficient join algorithms in certain situations, such as when large numbers of tuples from each relation share a common value for the join attribute(s). For an example where nested-loop join is essential, see Section 15.4.6.

15.3.5   Summary of Algorithms so Far

The main-memory and disk I/O requirements for the algorithms we have discussed in Sections 15.2 and 15.3 are shown in Fig. 15.9. The memory requirements for γ and δ are actually more complex than shown, and $M = B$ is only a loose approximation. For γ, M depends on the number of groups, and for δ, M depends on the number of distinct tuples.

Operators	Approximate M required	Disk I/O	Section
σ, π	1	B	15.2.1
γ, δ	B	B	15.2.2
$\cup$, $\cap$, $-$, $\times$, $\bowtie$	$\min(B(R), B(S))$	$B(R) + B(S)$	15.2.3
$\bowtie$	any $M \geq 2$	$B(R)B(S)/M$	15.3.3

Figure 15.9: Main memory and disk I/O requirements for one-pass and nested-loop algorithms

15.3.6   Exercises for Section 15.3

Exercise 15.3.1: Suppose $B(R) = B(S) = 10,000$, and $M = 1000$. Calculate the disk I/O cost of a nested-loop join.

Exercise 15.3.2: For the relations of Exercise 15.3.1, what value of M would we need to compute $R \bowtie S$ using the nested-loop algorithm with no more than (a) 200,000   ! (b) 25,000   ! (c) 15,000 disk I/O's?

Exercise 15.3.3: Give the three iterator methods for the block-based version of nested-loop join.

! Exercise 15.3.4: The iterator of Fig. 15.7 will not work properly if either R or S is empty. Rewrite the methods so they will work, even if one or both relations are empty.

! Exercise 15.3.5: If R and S are both unclustered, it seems that nested-loop join would require about $T(R)T(S)/M$ disk I/O's.

a) How can you do significantly better than this cost?

b) If only one of R and S is unclustered, how would you perform a nested-loop join? Consider both the cases that the larger is unclustered and that the smaller is unclustered.

15.4   Two-Pass Algorithms Based on Sorting

We shall now begin the study of multipass algorithms for performing relational-algebra operations on relations that are larger than what the one-pass algorithms of Section 15.2 can handle. We concentrate on *two-pass algorithms*, where data from the operand relations is read into main memory, processed in some way, written out to disk again, and then reread from disk to complete the operation. We can naturally extend this idea to any number of passes, where the data is read many times into main memory. However, we concentrate on two-pass algorithms because:

a) Two passes are usually enough, even for very large relations.

b) Generalizing to more than two passes is not hard; we discuss these extensions in Section 15.4.1 and more generally in Section 15.8.

We begin with an implementation of the sorting operator τ that illustrates the general approach: divide a relation R for which $B(R) > M$ into chucks of size M, sort them, and then process the sorted sublists in some fashion that requires only one block of each sorted sublist in main memory at any one time.

15.4.1   Two-Phase, Multiway Merge-Sort

It is possible to sort very large relations in two passes using an algorithm called *Two-Phase, Multiway Merge-Sort* (TPMMS), Suppose we have M main-memory buffers to use for the sort. TPMMS sorts a relation R as follows:

- *Phase 1*: Repeatedly fill the M buffers with new tuples from R and sort them, using any main-memory sorting algorithm. Write out each *sorted sublist* to secondary storage.

- *Phase 2*: Merge the sorted sublists. For this phase to work, there can be at most $M - 1$ sorted sublists, which limits the size of R. We allocate one input block to each sorted sublist and one block to the output. The

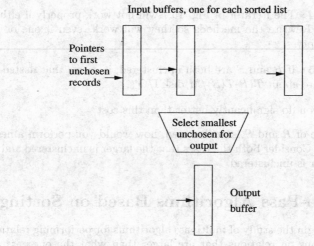

Figure 15.10: Main-memory organization for multiway merging

use of buffers is suggested by Fig. 15.10. A pointer to each input block indicates the first element in the sorted order that has not yet been moved to the output. We merge the sorted sublists into one sorted list with all the records as follows.

1. Find the smallest key among the first remaining elements of all the lists. Since this comparison is done in main memory, a linear search is sufficient, taking a number of machine instructions proportional to the number of sublists. However, if we wish, there is a method based on "priority queues"[2] that takes time proportional to the logarithm of the number of sublists to find the smallest element.

2. Move the smallest element to the first available position of the output block.

3. If the output block is full, write it to disk and reinitialize the same buffer in main memory to hold the next output block.

4. If the block from which the smallest element was just taken is now exhausted of records, read the next block from the same sorted sublist into the same buffer that was used for the block just exhausted. If no blocks remain, then leave its buffer empty and do not consider elements from that list in any further competition for smallest remaining elements.

In order for TPMMS to work, there must be no more than $M - 1$ sublists. Suppose R fits on B blocks. Since each sublist consists of M blocks, the number

---

[2] See Aho, A. V. and J. D. Ullman, *Foundations of Computer Science*, Computer Science Press, 1992.

of sublists is B/M. We thus require $B/M \leq M - 1$, or $B \leq M(M-1)$ (or about $B \leq M^2$).

The algorithm requires us to read B blocks in the first pass, and another B disk I/O's to write the sorted sublists. The sorted sublists are each read again in the second pass, resulting in a total of $3B$ disk I/O's. If, as is customary, we do not count the cost of writing the result to disk (since the result may be pipelined and never written to disk), then $3B$ is all that the sorting operator τ requires. However, if we need to store the result on disk, then the requirement is $4B$.

Example 15.5 : Suppose blocks are 64K bytes, and we have one gigabyte of main memory. Then we can afford M of 16K. Thus, a relation fitting in B blocks can be sorted as long as B is no more than $(16K)^2 = 2^{28}$. Since blocks are of size 64K $= 2^{14}$, a relation can be sorted as long as its size is no greater than 2^{42} bytes, or 4 terabytes. □

Example 15.5 shows that even on a modest machine, 2PMMS is sufficient to sort all but an incredibly large relation in two passes. However, if you have an even bigger relation, then the same idea can be applied recursively. Divide the relation into chunks of size $M(M-1)$, use 2PMMS to sort each one, and then treat the resulting sorted lists as sublists for a third pass. The idea extends similarly to any number of passes.

15.4.2 Duplicate Elimination Using Sorting

To perform the $\delta(R)$ operation in two passes, we sort the tuples of R in sublists as in 2PMMS. In the second pass, we use the available main memory to hold one block from each sorted sublist and one output block, as we did for 2PMMS. However, instead of sorting on the second pass, we reapeatedly select the first (in sorted order) unconsidered tuple t among all the sorted sublists. We write one copy of t to the output and eliminate from the input blocks all occurrences of t. Thus, the output will consist of exactly one copy of any tuple in R; they will in fact be produced in sorted order. When an output block is full or an input block empty, we manage the buffers exactly as in 2PMMS.

The number of disk I/O's performed by this algorithm, as always ignoring the handling of the output, is the same as for sorting: $3B(R)$. This figure can be compared with $B(R)$ for the single-pass algorithm of Section 15.2.2. On the other hand, we can handle much larger files using the two-pass algorithm than with the one-pass algorithm. As for 2PMMS, approximately $B \leq M^2$ is required for the two-pass algorithm to be feasible, compared with $B \leq M$ for the one-pass algorithm. Put another way, to eliminate duplicates with the two-pass algorithm requires only $\sqrt{B(R)}$ blocks of main memory, rather than the $B(R)$ blocks required for a one-pass algorithm.

15.4.3   Grouping and Aggregation Using Sorting

The two-pass algorithm for $\gamma_L(R)$ is quite similar to the algorithm for $\delta(R)$ or 2PMMS. We summarize it as follows:

1. Read the tuples of R into memory, M blocks at a time. Sort the tuples in each set of M blocks, using the grouping attributes of L as the sort key. Write each sorted sublist to disk.

2. Use one main-memory buffer for each sublist, and initially load the first block of each sublist into its buffer.

3. Repeatedly find the least value of the sort key (grouping attributes) present among the first available tuples in the buffers. This value, v, becomes the next group, for which we:

   (a) Prepare to compute all the aggregates on list L for this group. As in Section 15.2.2, use a count and sum in place of an average.

   (b) Examine each of the tuples with sort key v, and accumulate the needed aggregates.

   (c) If a buffer becomes empty, replace it with the next block from the same sublist.

   When there are no more tuples with sort key v available, output a tuple consisting of the grouping attributes of L and the associated values of the aggregations we have computed for the group.

As for the δ algorithm, this two-pass algorithm for γ takes $3B(R)$ disk I/O's, and will work as long as $B(R) \leq M^2$.

15.4.4   A Sort-Based Union Algorithm

When bag-union is wanted, the one-pass algorithm of Section 15.2.3, where we simply copy both relations, works regardless of the size of the arguments, so there is no need to consider a two-pass algorithm for $\cup_B$. However, the one-pass algorithm for $\cup_S$ only works when at least one relation is smaller than the available main memory, so we must consider a two-pass algorithm for set union. The methodology we present works for the set and bag versions of intersection and difference as well, as we shall see in Section 15.4.5. To compute $R \cup_S S$, we modify 2PMMS as follows:

1. In the first phase, create sorted sublists from both R and S.

2. Use one main-memory buffer for each sublist of R and S. Initialize each with the first block from the corresponding sublist.

3. Repeatedly find the first remaining tuple t among all the buffers. Copy t to the output, and remove from the buffers all copies of t (if R and S are sets there should be at most two copies). Manage empty input buffers and a full output buffer as for 2PMMS.

We observe that each tuple of R and S is read twice into main memory, once when the sublists are being created, and the second time as part of one of the sublists. The tuple is also written to disk once, as part of a newly formed sublist. Thus, the cost in disk I/O's is $3\big(B(R) + B(S)\big)$.

The algorithm works as long as the total number of sublists among the two relations does not exceed $M - 1$, because we need one buffer for each sublist and one for the output Thus, approximately, the sum of the sizes of the two relations must not exceed M^2; that is, $B(R) + B(S) \leq M^2$.

15.4.5 Sort-Based Intersection and Difference

Whether the set version or the bag version is wanted, the algorithms are essentially the same as that of Section 15.4.4, except that the way we handle the copies of a tuple t at the fronts of the sorted sublists differs. For each algorithm, we repeatedly consider the tuple t that is least in the sorted order among all tuples remaining in the input buffers. We produce output as follows, and then remove all copies of t from the input buffers.

- For set intersection, output t if it appears in both R and S.

- For bag intersection, output t the minimum of the number of times it appears in R and in S. Note that t is not output if either of these counts is 0; that is, if t is missing from one or both of the relations.

- For set difference, $R -_S S$, output t if and only if it appears in R but not in S.

- For bag difference, $R -_B S$, output t the number of times it appears in R minus the number of times it appears in S. Of course, if t appears in S at least as many times as it appears in R, then do not output t at all.

One subtlely must be remembered for the bag operations. When counting occurrences of t, it is possible that all remaining tuples in an input buffer are t. If so, there may be more t's on the next block for that sublist. Thus, when a buffer has only t's remaining, we must load the next block for that sublist, continuing the count of t's. This process may continue for several blocks and may need to be done for several sublists.

The analysis of this family of algorithms is the same as for the set-union algorithm described in Section 15.4.4:

- $3\big(B(R) + B(S)\big)$ disk I/O's.

- Approximately $B(R) + B(S) \leq M^2$ for the algorithm to work.

15.4.6 A Simple Sort-Based Join Algorithm

There are several ways that sorting can be used to join large relations. Before examining the join algorithms, let us observe one problem that can occur when we compute a join but was not an issue for the binary operations considered so far. When taking a join, the number of tuples from the two relations that share a common value of the join attribute(s), and therefore need to be in main memory simultaneously, can exceed what fits in memory. The extreme example is when there is only one value of the join attribute(s), and every tuple of one relation joins with every tuple of the other relation. In this situation, there is really no choice but to take a nested-loop join of the two sets of tuples with a common value in the join-attribute(s).

To avoid facing this situation, we can try to reduce main-memory use for other aspects of the algorithm, and thus make available a large number of buffers to hold the tuples with a given join-attribute value. In this section we shall discuss the algorithm that makes the greatest possible number of buffers available for joining tuples with a common value. In Section 15.4.8 we consider another sort-based algorithm that uses fewer disk I/O's, but can present problems when there are large numbers of tuples with a common join-attribute value.

Given relations $R(X, Y)$ and $S(Y, Z)$ to join, and given M blocks of main memory for buffers, we do the following:

1. Sort R, using 2PMMS, with Y as the sort key.

2. Sort S similarly.

3. Merge the sorted R and S. We use only two buffers: one for the current block of R and the other for the current block of S. The following steps are done repeatedly:

    (a) Find the least value y of the join attributes Y that is currently at the front of the blocks for R and S.

    (b) If y does not appear at the front of the other relation, then remove the tuple(s) with sort key y.

    (c) Otherwise, identify all the tuples from both relations having sort key y. If necessary, read blocks from the sorted R and/or S, until we are sure there are no more y's in either relation. As many as M buffers are available for this purpose.

    (d) Output all the tuples that can be formed by joining tuples from R and S that have a common Y-value y.

    (e) If either relation has no more unconsidered tuples in main memory, reload the buffer for that relation.

Example 15.6: Let us consider the relations R and S from Example 15.4. Recall these relations occupy 1000 and 500 blocks, respectively, and there are $M = 101$ main-memory buffers. When we use 2PMMS on a relation and store the result on disk, we do four disk I/O's per block, two in each of the two phases. Thus, we use $4(B(R) + B(S))$ disk I/O's to sort R and S, or 6000 disk I/O's.

When we merge the sorted R and S to find the joined tuples, we read each block of R and S a fifth time, using another 1500 disk I/O's. In this merge we generally need only two of the 101 blocks of memory. However, if necessary, we could use all 101 blocks to hold the tuples of R and S that share a common Y-value y. Thus, it is sufficient that for no y do the tuples of R and S that have Y-value y together occupy more than 101 blocks.

Notice that the total number of disk I/O's performed by this algorithm is 7500, compared with 5500 for nested-loop join in Example 15.4. However, nested-loop join is inherently a quadratic algorithm, taking time proportional to $B(R)B(S)$, while sort-join has linear I/O cost, taking time proportional to $B(R) + B(S)$. It is only the constant factors and the small size of the example (each relation is only 5 or 10 times larger than a relation that fits entirely in the allotted buffers) that make nested-loop join preferable. $\square$

15.4.7 Analysis of Simple Sort-Join

As we noted in Example 15.6, the algorithm of Section 15.4.6 performs five disk I/O's for every block of the argument relations. We also need to consider how big M needs to be in order for the simple sort-join to work. The primary constraint is that we need to be able to perform the two-phase, multiway merge sorts on R and S. As we observed in Section 15.4.1, we need $B(R) \leq M^2$ and $B(S) \leq M^2$ to perform these sorts. In addition, we require that all the tuples with a common Y-value must fit in M buffers. In summary:

- The simple sort-join uses $5(B(R) + B(S))$ disk I/O's.

- It requires $B(R) \leq M^2$ and $B(S) \leq M^2$ to work.

- It also requires that the tuples with a common value for the join attributes fit in M blocks.

15.4.8 A More Efficient Sort-Based Join

If we do not have to worry about very large numbers of tuples with a common value for the join attribute(s), then we can save two disk I/O's per block by combining the second phase of the sorts with the join itself. We call this algorithm *sort-join*; other names by which it is known include "merge-join" and "sort-merge-join." To compute $R(X, Y) \bowtie S(Y, Z)$ using M main-memory buffers:

1. Create sorted sublists of size M, using Y as the sort key, for both R and S.

2. Bring the first block of each sublist into a buffer; we assume there are no more than M sublists in all.

3. Repeatedly find the least Y-value y among the first available tuples of all the sublists. Identify all the tuples of both relations that have Y-value y, perhaps using some of the M available buffers to hold them, if there are fewer than M sublists. Output the join of all tuples from R with all tuples from S that share this common Y-value. If the buffer for one of the sublists is exhausted, then replenish it from disk.

Example 15.7: Let us again consider the problem of Example 15.4: joining relations R and S of sizes 1000 and 500 blocks, respectively, using 101 buffers. We divide R into 10 sublists and S into 5 sublists, each of length 100, and sort them.[3] We then use 15 buffers to hold the current blocks of each of the sublists. If we face a situation in which many tuples have a fixed Y-value, we can use the remaining 86 buffers to store these tuples.

We perform three disk I/O's per block of data. Two of those are to create the sorted sublists. Then, every block of every sorted sublist is read into main memory one more time in the multiway merging process. Thus, the total number of disk I/O's is 4500. □

This sort-join algorithm is more efficient than the algorithm of Section 15.4.6 when it can be used. As we observed in Example 15.7, the number of disk I/O's is $3(B(R) + B(S))$. We can perform the algorithm on data that is almost as large as that of the previous algorithm. The sizes of the sorted sublists are M blocks, and there can be at most M of them among the two lists. Thus, $B(R) + B(S) \leq M^2$ is sufficient.

15.4.9 Summary of Sort-Based Algorithms

In Fig. 15.11 is a table of the analysis of the algorithms we have discussed in Section 15.4. As discussed in Sections 15.4.6 and 15.4.8, the join algorithms have limitiations on how many tuples can share a common value of the join attribute(s). If this limit is violated, we may have to use a nest-loop join instead.

15.4.10 Exercises for Section 15.4

Exercise 15.4.1: For each of the following operations, write an iterator that uses the algorithm described in this section: (a) grouping (γ_L) (b) set intersection (c) bag difference (d) natural join. (e) distinct (δ)

---

[3]Technically, we could have arranged for the sublists to have length 101 blocks each, with the last sublist of R having 91 blocks and the last sublist of S having 96 blocks, but the costs would turn out exactly the same.

Operators	Approximate M required	Disk I/O	Section
τ, γ, δ	$\sqrt{B}$	$3B$	15.4.1, 15.4.2, 15.4.3
$\cup, \cap, -$	$\sqrt{B(R) + B(S)}$	$3\big(B(R) + B(S)\big)$	15.4.4, 15.4.5
$\bowtie$	$\sqrt{\max\big(B(R), B(S)\big)}$	$5\big(B(R) + B(S)\big)$	15.4.6
$\bowtie$	$\sqrt{B(R) + B(S)}$	$3\big(B(R) + B(S)\big)$	15.4.8

Figure 15.11: Main memory and disk I/O requirements for sort-based algorithms

Exercise 15.4.2: How much memory do we need to use a two-pass, sort-based algorithm for relations of 20,000 blocks each, if the operation is: (a) δ (b) γ (c) a binary operation such as join or union.

Exercise 15.4.3: Describe a two-pass, sort-based algorithm for each of the join-like operators of Exercise 15.2.3.

Exercise 15.4.4: If $B(R) = B(S) = 10,000$ and $M = 500$, what are the disk I/O requirements of: (a) simple sort-join (b) the more efficient sort-join of Section 15.4.8. (c) set union

! **Exercise 15.4.5:** Suppose that the second pass of an algorithm described in this section does not need all M buffers, because there are fewer than M sublists. How might we save disk I/O's by using the extra buffers?

! **Exercise 15.4.6:** In Example 15.6 we discussed the join of two relations R and S, with 1000 and 500 blocks, respectively, and $M = 101$. However, we need additional additional disk I/O's if there are so many tuples with a given value that neither relation's tuples could fit in main memory. Calculate the total number of disk I/O's needed if:

a) There are only two Y-values, each appearing in half the tuples of R and half the tuples of S (recall Y is the join attribute or attributes).

b) There are five Y-values, each equally likely in each relation.

c) There are 10 Y-values, each equally likely in each relation.

! **Exercise 15.4.7:** Repeat Exercise 15.4.6 for the more efficient sort-join of Section 15.4.8.

!! **Exercise 15.4.8**: Sometimes, it is possible to save some disk I/O's if we leave the last sublist in memory. It may even make sense to use sublists of fewer than M blocks to take advantage of this effect. How many disk I/O's can be saved this way?

! **Exercise 15.4.9**: Suppose records could be larger than blocks, i.e., we could have spanned records. How would the memory requirements of two-pass, sort-based algorithms change?

15.5   Two-Pass Algorithms Based on Hashing

There is a family of hash-based algorithms that attack the same problems as in Section 15.4. The essential idea behind all these algorithms is as follows. If the data is too big to store in main-memory buffers, hash all the tuples of the argument or arguments using an appropriate hash key. For all the common operations, there is a way to select the hash key so all the tuples that need to be considered together when we perform the operation fall into the same bucket.

We then perform the operation by working on one bucket at a time (or on a pair of buckets with the same hash value, in the case of a binary operation). In effect, we have reduced the size of the operand(s) by a factor equal to the number of buckets, which is roughly M. Notice that the sort-based algorithms of Section 15.4 also gain a factor of M by preprocessing, although the sorting and hashing approaches achieve their similar gains by rather different means.

15.5.1   Partitioning Relations by Hashing

To begin, let us review the way we would take a relation R and, using M buffers, partition R into $M - 1$ buckets of roughly equal size. We shall assume that h is the hash function, and that h takes complete tuples of R as its argument (i.e., all attributes of R are part of the hash key). We associate one buffer with each bucket. The last buffer holds blocks of R, one at a time. Each tuple t in the block is hashed to bucket $h(t)$ and copied to the appropriate buffer. If that buffer is full, we write it out to disk, and initialize another block for the same bucket. At the end, we write out the last block of each bucket if it is not empty. The algorithm is given in more detail in Fig. 15.12.

15.5.2   A Hash-Based Algorithm for Duplicate Elimination

We shall now consider the details of hash-based algorithms for the various operations of relational algebra that might need two-pass algorithms. First, consider duplicate elimination, that is, the operation $\delta(R)$. We hash R to $M - 1$ buckets, as in Fig. 15.12. Note that two copies of the same tuple t will hash to the same bucket. Thus, we can examine one bucket at a time, perform δ on that bucket in isolation, and take as the answer the union of $\delta(R_i)$, where

```
initialize M-1 buckets using M-1 empty buffers;
FOR each block b of relation R DO BEGIN
    read block b into the Mth buffer;
    FOR each tuple t in b DO BEGIN
        IF the buffer for bucket h(t) has no room for t THEN
            BEGIN
                copy the buffer to disk;
                initialize a new empty block in that buffer;
            END;
        copy t to the buffer for bucket h(t);
    END;
END;
FOR each bucket DO
    IF the buffer for this bucket is not empty THEN
        write the buffer to disk;
```

Figure 15.12: Partitioning a relation R into $M - 1$ buckets

R_i is the portion of R that hashes to the ith bucket. The one-pass algorithm of Section 15.2.2 can be used to eliminate duplicates from each R_i in turn and write out the resulting unique tuples.

This method will work as long as the individual R_i's are sufficiently small to fit in main memory and thus allow a one-pass algorithm. Since we may assume the hash function h partitions R into equal-sized buckets, each R_i will be approximately $B(R)/(M - 1)$ blocks in size. If that number of blocks is no larger than M, i.e., $B(R) \leq M(M-1)$, then the two-pass, hash-based algorithm will work. In fact, as we discussed in Section 15.2.2, it is only necessary that the number of distinct tuples in one bucket fit in M buffers. Thus, a conservative estimate (assuming M and $M - 1$ are essentially the same) is $B(R) \leq M^2$, exactly as for the sort-based, two-pass algorithm for δ.

The number of disk I/O's is also similar to that of the sort-based algorithm. We read each block of R once as we hash its tuples, and we write each block of each bucket to disk. We then read each block of each bucket again in the one-pass algorithm that focuses on that bucket. Thus, the total number of disk I/O's is $3B(R)$.

15.5.3 Hash-Based Grouping and Aggregation

To perform the $\gamma_L(R)$ operation, we again start by hashing all the tuples of R to $M - 1$ buckets. However, in order to make sure that all tuples of the same group wind up in the same bucket, we must choose a hash function that depends only on the grouping attributes of the list L.

Having partitioned R into buckets, we can then use the one-pass algorithm for γ from Section 15.2.2 to process each bucket in turn. As we discussed for δ in Section 15.5.2, we can process each bucket in main memory provided $B(R) \leq M^2$.

However, on the second pass, we need only one record per group as we process each bucket. Thus, even if the size of a bucket is larger than M, we can handle the bucket in one pass provided the records for all the groups in the bucket take no more than M buffers. As a consequence, if groups are large, then we may actually be able to handle much larger relations R than is indicated by the $B(R) \leq M^2$ rule. On the other hand, if M exceeds the number of groups, then we cannot fill all buckets. Thus, the actual limitation on the size of R as a function of M is complex, but $B(R) \leq M^2$ is a conservative estimate. Finally, we observe that the number of disk I/O's for γ, as for δ, is $3B(R)$.

15.5.4 Hash-Based Union, Intersection, and Difference

When the operation is binary, we must make sure that we use the same hash function to hash tuples of both arguments. For example, to compute $R \cup_S S$, we hash both R and S to $M - 1$ buckets each, say $R_1, R_2, \ldots, R_{M-1}$ and $S_1, S_2, \ldots, S_{M-1}$. We then take the set-union of R_i with S_i for all i, and output the result. Notice that if a tuple t appears in both R and S, then for some i we shall find t in both R_i and S_i. Thus, when we take the union of these two buckets, we shall output only one copy of t, and there is no possibility of introducing duplicates into the result. For $\cup_B$, the simple bag-union algorithm of Section 15.2.3 is preferable to any other approach for that operation.

To take the intersection or difference of R and S, we create the $2(M - 1)$ buckets exactly as for set-union and apply the appropriate one-pass algorithm to each pair of corresponding buckets. Notice that all these one-pass algorithms require $B(R) + B(S)$ disk I/O's. To this quantity we must add the two disk I/O's per block that are necessary to hash the tuples of the two relations and store the buckets on disk, for a total of $3(B(R) + B(S))$ disk I/O's.

In order for the algorithms to work, we must be able to take the one-pass union, intersection, or difference of R_i and S_i, whose sizes will be approximately $B(R)/(M - 1)$ and $B(S)/(M - 1)$, respectively. Recall that the one-pass algorithms for these operations require that the smaller operand occupies at most $M - 1$ blocks. Thus, the two-pass, hash-based algorithms require that $\min(B(R), B(S)) \leq M^2$, approximately.

15.5.5 The Hash-Join Algorithm

To compute $R(X, Y) \bowtie S(Y, Z)$ using a two-pass, hash-based algorithm, we act almost as for the other binary operations discussed in Section 15.5.4. The only difference is that we must use as the hash key just the join attributes, Y. Then we can be sure that if tuples of R and S join, they will wind up in corresponding buckets R_i and S_i for some i. A one-pass join of all pairs of corresponding buckets completes this algorithm, which we call *hash-join.*[4]

Example 15.8: Let us renew our discussion of the two relations R and S from Example 15.4, whose sizes were 1000 and 500 blocks, respectively, and for which 101 main-memory buffers are made available. We may hash each relation to 100 buckets, so the average size of a bucket is 10 blocks for R and 5 blocks for S. Since the smaller number, 5, is much less than the number of available buffers, we expect to have no trouble performing a one-pass join on each pair of buckets.

The number of disk I/O's is 1500 to read each of R and S while hashing into buckets, another 1500 to write all the buckets to disk, and a third 1500 to read each pair of buckets into main memory again while taking the one-pass join of corresponding buckets. Thus, the number of disk I/O's required is 4500, just as for the efficient sort-join of Section 15.4.8. □

We may generalize Example 15.8 to conclude that:

- Hash join requires $3\big(B(R) + B(S)\big)$ disk I/O's to perform its task.

- The two-pass hash-join algorithm will work as long as approximately $\min\big(B(R), B(S)\big) \leq M^2$.

The argument for the latter point is the same as for the other binary operations: one of each pair of buckets must fit in $M - 1$ buffers.

15.5.6 Saving Some Disk I/O's

If there is more memory available on the first pass than we need to hold one block per bucket, then we have some opportunities to save disk I/O's. One option is to use several blocks for each bucket, and write them out as a group, in consecutive blocks of disk. Strictly speaking, this technique doesn't save disk I/O's, but it makes the I/O's go faster, since we save seek time and rotational latency when we write.

However, there are several tricks that have been used to avoid writing some of the buckets to disk and then reading them again. The most effective of them, called *hybrid hash-join*, works as follows. In general, suppose we decide that to join $R \bowtie S$, with S the smaller relation, we need to create k buckets, where k is much less than M, the available memory. When we hash S, we can choose to keep m of the k buckets entirely in main memory, while keeping only one block for each of the other $k - m$ buckets. We can manage to do so provided the expected size of the buckets in memory, plus one block for each of the other buckets, does not exceed M; that is:

$$mB(S)/k + k - m \leq M \qquad (15.1)$$

---

[4]Sometimes, the term "hash-join" is reserved for the variant of the one-pass join algorithm of Section 15.2.3 in which a hash table is used as the main-memory search structure. Then, the two-pass hash-join algorithm described here is called "partition hash-join."

In explanation, the expected size of a bucket is $B(S)/k$, and there are m buckets in memory.

Now, when we read the tuples of the other relation, R, to hash that relation into buckets, we keep in memory:

1. The m buckets of S that were never written to disk, and

2. One block for each of the $k-m$ buckets of R whose corresponding buckets of S were written to disk.

If a tuple t of R hashes to one of the first m buckets, then we immediately join it with all the tuples of the corresponding S-bucket, as if this were a one-pass, hash-join. It is necessary to organize each of the in-memory buckets of S into an efficient search structure to facilitate this join, just as for the one-pass hash-join. If t hashes to one of the buckets whose corresponding S-bucket is on disk, then t is sent to the main-memory block for that bucket, and eventually migrates to disk, as for a two-pass, hash-based join.

On the second pass, we join the corresponding buckets of R and S as usual. However, there is no need to join the pairs of buckets for which the S-bucket was left in memory; these buckets have already been joined and their result output.

The savings in disk I/O's is equal to two for every block of the buckets of S that remain in memory, and their corresponding R-buckets. Since m/k of the buckets are in memory, the savings is $2(m/k)(B(R) + B(S))$. We must thus ask how to maximize m/k, subject to the constraint of Equation (15.1). The surprising answer is: pick $m = 1$, and then make k as small as possible.

The intuitive justification is that all but $k - m$ of the main-memory buffers can be used to hold tuples of S in main memory, and the more of these tuples, the fewer the disk I/O's. Thus, we want to minimize k, the total number of buckets. We do so by making each bucket about as big as can fit in main memory; that is, buckets are of size M, and therefore $k = B(S)/M$. If that is the case, then there is only room for one bucket in the extra main memory; i.e., $m = 1$.

In fact, we really need to make the buckets slightly smaller than $B(S)/M$, or else we shall not quite have room for one full bucket and one block for the other $k-1$ buckets in memory at the same time. Assuming, for simplicity, that k is about $B(S)/M$ and $m = 1$, the savings in disk I/O's is

$$2M(B(R) + B(S))/B(S)$$

and the total cost is $(3 - 2M/B(S))(B(R) + B(S))$.

Example 15.9: Consider the problem of Example 15.4, where we had to join relations R and S, of 1000 and 500 blocks, respectively, using $M = 101$. If we use a hybrid hash-join, then we want k, the number of buckets, to be about $500/101$. Suppose we pick $k = 5$. Then the average bucket will have 100 blocks of S's tuples. If we try to fit one of these buckets and four extra blocks for the other four buckets, we need 104 blocks of main memory, and we cannot take the chance that the in-memory bucket will overflow memory.

Thus, we are advised to choose $k = 6$. Now, when hashing S on the first pass, we have five buffers for five of the buckets, and we have up to 96 buffers for the in-memory bucket, whose expected size is 500/6 or 83. The number of disk I/O's we use for S on the first pass is thus 500 to read all of S, and $500 - 83 = 417$ to write five buckets to disk. When we process R on the first pass, we need to read all of R (1000 disk I/O's) and write 5 of its 6 buckets (833 disk I/O's).

On the second pass, we read all the buckets written to disk, or $417 + 833 = 1250$ additional disk I/O's. The total number of disk I/O's is thus 1500 to read R and S, 1250 to write 5/6 of these relations, and another 1250 to read those tuples again, or 4000 disk I/O's. This figure compares with the 4500 disk I/O's needed for the straightforward hash-join or sort-join. □

15.5.7 Summary of Hash-Based Algorithms

Figure 15.13 gives the memory requirements and disk I/O's needed by each of the algorithms discussed in this section. As with other types of algorithms, we should observe that the estimates for γ and δ may be conservative, since they really depend on the number of duplicates and groups, respectively, rather than on the number of tuples in the argument relation.

Operators	Approximate M required	Disk I/O	Section
γ, δ	$\sqrt{B}$	$3B$	15.5.2, 15.5.3
$\cup, \cap, -$	$\sqrt{B(S)}$	$3(B(R) + B(S))$	15.5.4
$\bowtie$	$\sqrt{B(S)}$	$3(B(R) + B(S))$	15.5.5
$\bowtie$	$\sqrt{B(S)}$	$(3 - 2M/B(S))(B(R) + B(S))$	15.5.6

Figure 15.13: Main memory and disk I/O requirements for hash-based algorithms; for binary operations, assume $B(S) \leq B(R)$

Notice that the requirements for sort-based and the corresponding hash-based algorithms are almost the same. The significant differences between the two approaches are:

1. Hash-based algorithms for binary operations have a size requirement that depends only on the smaller of two arguments rather than on the sum of the argument sizes, that sort-based algorithms require.

2. Sort-based algorithms sometimes allow us to produce a result in sorted order and take advantage of that sort later. The result might be used in another sort-based algorithm for a subsequent operator, or it could be the answer to a query that is required to be produced in sorted order.

3. Hash-based algorithms depend on the buckets being of equal size. Since there is generally at least a small variation in size, it is not possible to use buckets that, on average, occupy M blocks; we must limit them to a slightly smaller figure. This effect is especially prominent if the number of different hash keys is small, e.g., performing a group-by on a relation with few groups or a join with very few values for the join attributes.

4. In sort-based algorithms, the sorted sublists may be written to consecutive blocks of the disk if we organize the disk properly. Thus, one of the three disk I/O's per block may require little rotational latency or seek time and therefore may be much faster than the I/O's needed for hash-based algorithms.

5. Moreover, if M is much larger than the number of sorted sublists, then we may read in several consecutive blocks at a time from a sorted sublist, again saving some latency and seek time.

6. On the other hand, if we can choose the number of buckets to be less than M in a hash-based algorithm, then we can write out several blocks of a bucket at once. We thus obtain the same benefit on the write step for hashing that the sort-based algorithms have for the second read, as we observed in (5). Similarly, we may be able to organize the disk so that a bucket eventually winds up on consecutive blocks of tracks. If so, buckets can be read with little latency or seek time, just as sorted sublists were observed in (4) to be writable efficiently.

15.5.8   Exercises for Section 15.5

Exercise 15.5.1: If $B(S) = B(R) = 10,000$ and $M = 500$, what is the number of disk I/O's required for a hybrid hash join?

Exercise 15.5.2: Write iterators that implement the two-pass, hash-based algorithms for (a) $\cap_B$ (b) $-_S$ (c) $\bowtie$ (d) δ (e) γ.

Exercise 15.5.3: The hybrid-hash-join idea, storing one bucket in main memory, can also be applied to other operations. Show how to save the cost of storing and reading one bucket from each relation when implementing a two-pass, hash-based algorithm for: (a) $\cap_B$ (b) $-_S$. (c) δ (d) γ

! **Exercise 15.5.4:** Suppose we are performing a two-pass, hash-based grouping operation on a relation R of the appropriate size; i.e., $B(R) \leq M^2$. However, there are so few groups, that some groups are larger than M; i.e., they will not fit in main memory at once. What modifications, if any, need to be made to the algorithm given here?

! **Exercise 15.5.5:** Suppose that we are using a disk where the time to move the head to a block is 100 milliseconds, and it takes 1/2 millisecond to read one block. Therefore, it takes $k/2$ milliseconds to read k consecutive blocks, once the head is positioned. Suppose we want to compute a two-pass hash-join $R \bowtie S$, where $B(R) = 1000$, $B(S) = 500$, and $M = 101$. To speed up the join, we want to use as few buckets as possible (assuming tuples distribute evenly among buckets), and read and write as many blocks as we can to consecutive positions on disk. Counting 100.5 milliseconds for a random disk I/O and $100 + k/2$ milliseconds for reading or writing k consecutive blocks from or to disk:

  a) How much time does the disk I/O take?

  b) How much time does the disk I/O take if we use a hybrid hash-join as described in Example 15.9?

  c) How much time does a sort-based join take under the same conditions, assuming we write sorted sublists to consecutive blocks of disk?

15.6 Index-Based Algorithms

The existence of an index on one or more attributes of a relation makes available some algorithms that would not be feasible without the index. Index-based algorithms are especially useful for the selection operator, but algorithms for join and other binary operators also use indexes to very good advantage. In this section, we shall introduce these algorithms. We also continue with the discussion of the index-scan operator for accessing a stored table with an index that we began in Section 15.1.1. To appreciate many of the issues, we first need to digress and consider "clustering" indexes.

15.6.1 Clustering and Nonclustering Indexes

Recall from Section 15.1.3 that a relation is "clustered" if its tuples are packed into roughly as few blocks as can possibly hold those tuples. All the analyses we have done so far assume that relations are clustered.

We may also speak of *clustering indexes*, which are indexes on an attribute or attributes such that all the tuples with a fixed value for the search key of this index appear on roughly as few blocks as can hold them. Note that a relation that isn't clustered cannot have a clustering index,[5] but even a clustered relation

---

[5]Technically, if the index is on a key for the relation, so only one tuple with a given value in the index key exists, then the index is always "clustering," even if the relation is not clustered. However, if there is only one tuple per index-key value, then there is no advantage from clustering, and the performance measure for such an index is the same as if it were considered nonclustering.

can have nonclustering indexes.

Example 15.10: A relation $R(a, b)$ that is sorted on attribute a and stored in that order, packed into blocks, is surely clustered. An index on a is a clustering index, since for a given a-value a_1, all the tuples with that value for a are consecutive. They thus appear packed into blocks, except possibly for the first and last blocks that contain a-value a_1, as suggested in Fig. 15.14. However, an index on b is unlikely to be clustering, since the tuples with a fixed b-value will be spread all over the file unless the values of a and b are very closely correlated. □

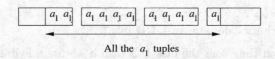

All the a_1 tuples

Figure 15.14: A clustering index has all tuples with a fixed value packed into (close to) the minimum possible number of blocks

15.6.2   Index-Based Selection

In Section 15.1.1 we discussed implementing a selection $\sigma_C(R)$ by reading all the tuples of relation R, seeing which meet the condition C, and outputting those that do. If there are no indexes on R, then that is the best we can do; the number of disk I/O's used by the operation is $B(R)$, or even $T(R)$, the number of tuples of R, should R not be a clustered relation.[6] However, suppose that the condition C is of the form $a = v$, where a is an attribute for which an index exists, and v is a value. Then one can search the index with value v and get pointers to exactly those tuples of R that have a-value v. These tuples constitute the result of $\sigma_{a=v}(R)$, so all we have to do is retrieve them.

If the index on $R.a$ is a clustering index, then the number of disk I/O's to retrieve the set $\sigma_{a=v}(R)$ will average $B(R)/V(R, a)$. The actual number may be somewhat higher for several reasons:

1. Often, the index is not kept entirely in main memory, and some disk I/O's are needed to support the index lookup.

2. Even though all the tuples with $a = v$ might fit in b blocks, they could be spread over $b + 1$ blocks because they don't start at the beginning of a block.

---

[6]Recall from Section 15.1.3 the notation we developed: $T(R)$ for the number of tuples in R, $B(R)$ for the number of blocks in which R fits, and $V(R, L)$ for the number of distinct tuples in $\pi_L(R)$.

3. Even though the tuples of R may be clustered, they may not be packed as tightly as possible into blocks. For example, there could be extra space for tuples to be inserted into R later, or R could be in a clustered file, as discussed in Section 14.1.6.

Moreover, we of course must round up if the ratio $B(R)/V(R,a)$ is not an integer. Most significant is that should a be a key for R, then $V(R,a) = T(R)$, which is presumably much bigger than $B(R)$, yet we surely require one disk I/O to retrieve the tuple with key value v, plus whatever disk I/O's are needed to access the index.

Now, let us consider what happens when the index on $R.a$ is nonclustering. To a first approximation, each tuple we retrieve will be on a different block, and we must access $T(R)/V(R,a)$ tuples. Thus, $T(R)/V(R,a)$ is an estimate of the number of disk I/O's we need. The number could be higher because we may also need to read some index blocks from disk; it could be lower because fortuitously some retrieved tuples appear on the same block, and that block remains buffered in memory.

Example 15.11: Suppose $B(R) = 1000$, and $T(R) = 20{,}000$. That is, R has 20,000 tuples, packed at most 20 to a block. Let a be one of the attributes of R, suppose there is an index on a, and consider the operation $\sigma_{a=0}(R)$. Here are some possible situations and the worst-case number of disk I/O's required. We shall ignore the cost of accessing the index blocks in all cases.

1. If R is clustered, but we do not use the index, then the cost is 1000 disk I/O's. That is, we must retrieve every block of R.

2. If R is not clustered and we do not use the index, then the cost is 20,000 disk I/O's.

3. If $V(R,a) = 100$ and the index is clustering, then the index-based algorithm uses $1000/100 = 10$ disk I/O's, plus whatever is needed to access the index.

4. If $V(R,a) = 10$ and the index is nonclustering, then the index-based algorithm uses $20{,}000/10 = 2000$ disk I/O's. Notice that this cost is higher than scanning the entire relation R, if R is clustered but the index is not.

5. If $V(R,a) = 20{,}000$, i.e., a is a key, then the index-based algorithm takes 1 disk I/O plus whatever is needed to access the index, regardless of whether the index is clustering or not.

□

Index-scan as an access method can help in several other kinds of selection operations.

a) An index such as a B-tree lets us access the search-key values in a given range efficiently. If such an index on attribute a of relation R exists, then we can use the index to retrieve just the tuples of R in the desired range for selections such as $\sigma_{a \geq 10}(R)$, or even $\sigma_{a \geq 10 \text{ AND } a \leq 20}(R)$.

b) A selection with a complex condition C can sometimes be implemented by an index-scan followed by another selection on only those tuples retrieved by the index-scan. If C is of the form $a = v$ AND C', where C' is any condition, then we can split the selection into a cascade of two selections, the first checking only for $a = v$, and the second checking condition C'. The first is a candidate for use of the index-scan operator. This splitting of a selection operation is one of many improvements that a query optimizer may make to a logical query plan; it is discussed particularly in Section 16.7.1.

15.6.3   Joining by Using an Index

All the binary operations we have considered, and the unary full-relation operations of γ and δ as well, can use certain indexes profitably. We shall leave most of these algorithms as exercises, while we focus on the matter of joins. In particular, let us examine the natural join $R(X, Y) \bowtie S(Y, Z)$; recall that X, Y, and Z can stand for sets of attributes, although it is sufficient to think of them as single attributes.

For our first index-based join algorithm, suppose that S has an index on the attribute(s) Y. Then one way to compute the join is to examine each block of R, and within each block consider each tuple t. Let t_Y be the component or components of t corresponding to the attribute(s) Y. Use the index to find all those tuples of S that have t_Y in their Y-component(s). These are exactly the tuples of S that join with tuple t of R, so we output the join of each of these tuples with t.

The number of disk I/O's depends on several factors. First, assuming R is clustered, we shall have to read $B(R)$ blocks to get all the tuples of R. If R is not clustered, then up to $T(R)$ disk I/O's may be required.

For each tuple t of R we must read an average of $T(S)/V(S, Y)$ tuples of S. If S has a nonclustered index on Y, then the number of disk I/O's required to read S is $T(R)T(S)/V(S, Y)$, but if the index is clustered, then only $T(R)B(S)/V(S, Y)$ disk I/O's suffice.[7] In either case, we may have to add a few disk I/O's per Y-value, to account for the reading of the index itself.

Regardless of whether or not R is clustered, the cost of accessing tuples of S dominates. Ignoring the cost of reading R, we shall take $T(R)T(S)/V(S, Y)$ or $T(R)\big(\max(1, B(S)/V(S, Y))\big)$ as the cost of this join method, for the cases of nonclustered and clustered indexes on S, respectively.

---

[7]But remember that $B(S)/V(S, Y)$ must be replaced by 1 if it is less, as discussed in Section 15.6.2.

Example 15.12: Let us consider our running example, relations $R(X, Y)$ and $S(Y, Z)$ covering 1000 and 500 blocks, respectively. Assume ten tuples of either relation fit on one block, so $T(R) = 10,000$ and $T(S) = 5000$. Also, assume $V(S, Y) = 100$; i.e., there are 100 different values of Y among the tuples of S.

Suppose that R is clustered, and there is a clustering index on Y for S. Then the approximate number of disk I/O's, excluding what is needed to access the index itself, is 1000 to read the blocks of R plus $10,000 \times 500 / 100 = 50,000$ disk I/O's. This number is considerably above the cost of other methods for the same data discussed previously. If either R or the index on S is not clustered, then the cost is even higher. □

While Example 15.12 makes it look as if an index-join is a very bad idea, there are other situations where the join $R \bowtie S$ by this method makes much more sense. Most common is the case where R is very small compared with S, and $V(S, Y)$ is large. We discuss in Exercise 15.6.5 a typical query in which selection before a join makes R tiny. In that case, most of S will never be examined by this algorithm, since most Y-values don't appear in R at all. However, both sort- and hash-based join methods will examine every tuple of S at least once.

15.6.4 Joins Using a Sorted Index

When the index is a B-tree, or any other structure from which we easily can extract the tuples of a relation in sorted order, we have a number of other opportunities to use the index. Perhaps the simplest is when we want to compute $R(X, Y) \bowtie S(Y, Z)$, and we have such an index on Y for either R or S. We can then perform an ordinary sort-join, but we do not have to perform the intermediate step of sorting one of the relations on Y.

As an extreme case, if we have sorting indexes on Y for both R and S, then we need to perform only the final step of the simple sort-based join of Section 15.4.6. This method is sometimes called *zig-zag join*, because we jump back and forth between the indexes finding Y-values that they share in common. Notice that tuples from R with a Y-value that does not appear in S need never be retrieved, and similarly, tuples of S whose Y-value does not appear in R need not be retrieved.

Example 15.13: Suppose that we have relations $R(X, Y)$ and $S(Y, Z)$ with indexes on Y for both relations. In a tiny example, let the search keys (Y-values) for the tuples of R be in order $1, 3, 4, 4, 4, 5, 6$, and let the search key values for S be $2, 2, 4, 4, 6, 7$. We start with the first keys of R and S, which are 1 and 2, respectively. Since $1 < 2$, we skip the first key of R and look at the second key, 3. Now, the current key of S is less than the current key of R, so we skip the two 2's of S to reach 4.

At this point, the key 3 of R is less than the key of S, so we skip the key of R. Now, both current keys are 4. We follow the pointers associated with all the keys 4 from both relations, retrieve the corresponding tuples, and join them. Notice that until we met the common key 4, no tuples of the relation were retrieved.

Having dispensed with the 4's, we go to key 5 of R and key 6 of S. Since $5 < 6$, we skip to the next key of R. Now the keys are both 6, so we retrieve the corresponding tuples and join them. Since R is now exhausted, we know there are no more pairs of tuples from the two relations that join.   □

If the indexes are B-trees, then we can scan the leaves of the two B-trees in order from the left, using the pointers from leaf to leaf that are built into the structure, as suggested in Fig. 15.15. If R and S are clustered, then retrieval of all the tuples with a given key will result in a number of disk I/O's proportional to the fractions of these two relations read. Note that in extreme cases, where there are so many tuples from R and S that neither fits in the available main memory, we shall have to use a fixup like that discussed in Section 15.4.6. However, in typical cases, the step of joining all tuples with a common Y-value can be carried out with only as many disk I/O's as it takes to read them.

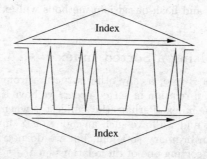

Figure 15.15: A zig-zag join using two indexes

Example 15.14 : Let us continue with Example 15.12, to see how joins using a combination of sorting and indexing would typically perform on this data. First, assume that there is an index on Y for S that allows us to retrieve the tuples of S sorted by Y. We shall, in this example, also assume both relations and the index are clustered. For the moment, we assume there is no index on R.

Assuming 101 available blocks of main memory, we may use them to create 10 sorted sublists for the 1000-block relation R. The number of disk I/O's is 2000 to read and write all of R. We next use 11 blocks of memory — 10 for the sublists of R and one for a block of S's tuples, retrieved via the index. We neglect disk I/O's and memory buffers needed to manipulate the index, but if the index is a B-tree, these numbers will be small anyway. In this second pass, we read all the tuples of R and S, using a total of 1500 disk I/O's, plus the small amount needed for reading the index blocks once each. We thus estimate the total number of disk I/O's at 3500, which is less than that for other methods considered so far.

Now, assume that both R and S have indexes on Y. Then there is no need to sort either relation. We use just 1500 disk I/O's to read the blocks of R and S through their indexes. In fact, if we determine from the indexes alone that a large fraction of R or S cannot match tuples of the other relation, then the total cost could be considerably less than 1500 disk I/O's. However, in any event we should add the small number of disk I/O's needed to read the indexes themselves. □

15.6.5 Exercises for Section 15.6

Exercise 15.6.1: Suppose $B(R) = 10,000$ and $T(R) = 500,000$. Let there be an index on $R.a$, and let $V(R, a) = k$ for some number k. Give the cost of $\sigma_{a=0}(R)$, as a function of k, under the following circumstances. You may neglect disk I/O's needed to access the index itself.

a) The index is not clustering.

b) The index is clustering.

c) R is clustered, and the index is not used.

Exercise 15.6.2: Repeat Exercise 15.6.1 if the operation is the range query $\sigma_{C \le a \text{ AND } a \le D}(R)$. You may assume that C and D are constants such that $k/10$ of the values are in the range.

Exercise 15.6.3: Suppose there is an index on attribute $R.a$. Describe how this index could be used to improve the execution of the following operations. Under what circumstances would the index-based algorithm be more efficient than sort- or hash-based algorithms?

a) $\delta(R)$.

b) $R \cup_S S$ (assume that R and S have no duplicates, although they may have tuples in common).

c) $R \cap_S S$ (again, with R and S sets).

! **Exercise 15.6.4:** If R is clustered, but the index on $R.a$ is *not* clustering, then depending on k we may prefer to implement a query by performing a table-scan of R or using the index. For what values of k would we prefer to use the index if the relation and query are as in (a) Exercise 15.6.1 (b) Exercise 15.6.2.

Exercise 15.6.5: Consider the SQL query:

```
SELECT birthdate FROM StarsIn, MovieStar
WHERE movieTitle = 'King Kong' AND starName = name;
```

This query uses the "movie" relations:

    StarsIn(movieTitle, movieYear, starName)
    MovieStar(name, address, gender, birthdate)

If we translate it to relational algebra, the heart is an equijoin between

$$\sigma_{movieTitle='\text{King Kong}'}(\text{StarsIn})$$

and MovieStar, which can be implemented much as a natural join $R \bowtie S$. Since there were only three movies named "King Kong," $T(R)$ is very small. Suppose that S, the relation MovieStar, has an index on name. Compare the cost of an index-join for this $R \bowtie S$ with the cost of a sort- or hash-based join.

! Exercise 15.6.6: In Example 15.14 we discussed the disk-I/O cost of a join $R \bowtie S$ in which one or both of R and S had sorting indexes on the join attribute(s). However, the methods described in that example can fail if there are too many tuples with the same value in the join attribute(s). What are the limits (in number of blocks occupied by tuples with the same value) under which the methods described will not need to do additional disk I/O's?

15.7 Buffer Management

We have assumed that operators on relations have available some number M of main-memory buffers that they can use to store needed data. In practice, these buffers are rarely allocated in advance to the operator, and the value of M may vary depending on system conditions. The central task of making main-memory buffers available to processes, such as queries, that act on the database is given to the *buffer manager*. It is the responsibility of the buffer manager to allow processes to get the memory they need, while minimizing the delay and unsatisfiable requests. The role of the buffer manager is illustrated in Fig. 15.16.

15.7.1 Buffer Management Architecture

There are two broad architectures for a buffer manager:

1. The buffer manager controls main memory directly, as in many relational DBMS's, or

2. The buffer manager allocates buffers in virtual memory, allowing the operating system to decide which buffers are actually in main memory at any time and which are in the "swap space" on disk that the operating system manages. Many "main-memory" DBMS's and "object-oriented" DBMS's operate this way.

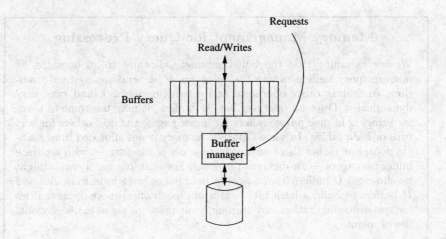

Figure 15.16: The buffer manager responds to requests for main-memory access to disk blocks

Whichever approach a DBMS uses, the same problem arises: the buffer manager should limit the number of buffers in use so they fit in the available main memory. When the buffer manager controls main memory directly, and requests exceed available space, it has to select a buffer to empty, by returning its contents to disk. If the buffered block has not been changed, then it may simply be erased from main memory, but if the block has changed it must be written back to its place on the disk. When the buffer manager allocates space in virtual memory, it has the option to allocate more buffers than can fit in main memory. However, if all these buffers are really in use, then there will be "thrashing," a common operating-system problem, where many blocks are moved in and out of the disk's swap space. In this situation, the system spends most of its time swapping blocks, while very little useful work gets done.

Normally, the number of buffers is a parameter set when the DBMS is initialized. We would expect that this number is set so that the buffers occupy the available main memory, regardless of whether the buffers are allocated in main or virtual memory. In what follows, we shall not concern ourselves with which mode of buffering is used, and simply assume that there is a fixed-size *buffer pool*, a set of buffers available to queries and other database actions.

15.7.2 Buffer Management Strategies

The critical choice that the buffer manager must make is what block to throw out of the buffer pool when a buffer is needed for a newly requested block. The *buffer-replacement strategies* in common use may be familiar to you from other applications of scheduling policies, such as in operating systems. These include:

Memory Management for Query Processing

We are assuming that the buffer manager allocates to an operator M main-memory buffers, where the value for M depends on system conditions (including other operators and queries underway), and may vary dynamically. Once an operator has M buffers, it may use some of them for bringing in disk pages, others for index pages, and still others for sort runs or hash tables. In some DBMS's, memory is not allocated from a single pool, but rather there are separate pools of memory — with separate buffer managers — for different purposes. For example, an operator might be allocated D buffers from a pool to hold pages brought in from disk and H buffers to build a hash table. This approach offers more opportunities for system configuration and "tuning," but may not make the best global use of memory.

Least-Recently Used (LRU)

The LRU rule is to throw out the block that has not been read or written for the longest time. This method requires that the buffer manager maintain a table indicating the last time the block in each buffer was accessed. It also requires that each database access make an entry in this table, so there is significant effort in maintaining this information. However, LRU is an effective strategy; intuitively, buffers that have not been used for a long time are less likely to be accessed sooner than those that have been accessed recently.

First-In-First-Out (FIFO)

When a buffer is needed, under the FIFO policy the buffer that has been occupied the longest by the same block is emptied and used for the new block. In this approach, the buffer manager needs to know only the time at which the block currently occupying a buffer was loaded into that buffer. An entry into a table can thus be made when the block is read from disk, and there is no need to modify the table when the block is accessed. FIFO requires less maintenance than LRU, but it can make more mistakes. A block that is used repeatedly, say the root block of a B-tree index, will eventually become the oldest block in a buffer. It will be written back to disk, only to be reread shortly thereafter into another buffer.

The "Clock" Algorithm ("Second Chance")

This algorithm is a commonly implemented, efficient approximation to LRU. Think of the buffers as arranged in a circle, as suggested by Fig. 15.17. A "hand" points to one of the buffers, and will rotate clockwise if it needs to find a buffer in which to place a disk block. Each buffer has an associated "flag," which is either 0 or 1. Buffers with a 0 flag are vulnerable to having their contents sent back to disk; buffers with a 1 are not. When a block is read into a buffer, its flag is set to 1. Likewise, when the contents of a buffer is accessed, its flag is set to 1.

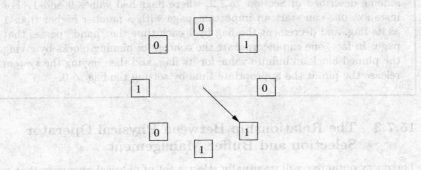

Figure 15.17: The clock algorithm visits buffers in a round-robin fashion and replaces $01 \cdots 1$ with $10 \cdots 0$

When the buffer manager needs a buffer for a new block, it looks for the first 0 it can find, rotating clockwise. If it passes 1's, it sets them to 0. Thus, a block is only thrown out of its buffer if it remains unaccessed for the time it takes the hand to make a complete rotation to set its flag to 0 and then make another complete rotation to find the buffer with its 0 unchanged. For instance, in Fig. 15.17, the hand will set to 0 the 1 in the buffer to its left, and then move clockwise to find the buffer with 0, whose block it will replace and whose flag it will set to 1.

System Control

The query processor or other components of a DBMS can give advice to the buffer manager in order to avoid some of the mistakes that would occur with a strict policy such as LRU, FIFO, or Clock. Recall from Section 13.6.5 that there are sometimes technical reasons why a block in main memory can *not* be moved to disk without first modifying certain other blocks that point to it. These blocks are called "pinned," and any buffer manager has to modify its buffer-replacement strategy to avoid expelling pinned blocks. This fact gives us the opportunity to force other blocks to remain in main memory by declaring them "pinned," even if there is no technical reason why they could not be written to disk. For example, a cure for the problem with FIFO mentioned above regarding the root of a B-tree is to "pin" the root, forcing it to remain in memory at all times. Similarly, for an algorithm like a one-pass hash-join, the query processor may "pin" the blocks of the smaller relation in order to assure that it will remain in main memory during the entire time.

More Tricks Using the Clock Algorithm

The "clock" algorithm for choosing buffers to free is not limited to the scheme described in Section 15.7.2, where flags had values 0 and 1. For instance, one can start an important page with a number higher than 1 as its flag, and decrement the flag by 1 each time the "hand" passes that page. In fact, one can incorporate the concept of pinning blocks by giving the pinned block an infinite value for its flag, and then having the system release the pin at the appropriate time by setting the flag to 0.

15.7.3   The Relationship Between Physical Operator Selection and Buffer Management

The query optimizer will eventually select a set of physical operators that will be used to execute a given query. This selection of operators may assume that a certain number of buffers M is available for execution of each of these operators. However, as we have seen, the buffer manager may not be willing or able to guarantee the availability of these M buffers when the query is executed. There are thus two related questions to ask about the physical operators:

1. Can the algorithm adapt to changes in the value of M, the number of main-memory buffers available?

2. When the expected M buffers are not available, and some blocks that are expected to be in memory have actually been moved to disk by the buffer manager, how does the buffer-replacement strategy used by the buffer manager impact the number of additional I/O's that must be performed?

Example 15.15: As an example of the issues, let us consider the block-based nested-loop join of Fig. 15.8. The basic algorithm does not really depend on the value of M, although its performance depends on M. Thus, it is sufficient to find out what M is just before execution begins.

It is even possible that M will change at different iterations of the outer loop. That is, each time we load main memory with a portion of the relation S (the relation of the outer loop), we can use all but one of the buffers available at that time; the remaining buffer is reserved for a block of R, the relation of the inner loop. Thus, the number of times we go around the outer loop depends on the average number of buffers available at each iteration. However, as long as M buffers are available *on average*, then the cost analysis of Section 15.3.4 will hold. In the extreme, we might have the good fortune to find that at the first iteration, enough buffers are available to hold all of S, in which case nested-loop join gracefully becomes the one-pass join of Section 15.2.3.

As another example of how nested-loop join interacts with buffering, suppose that we use an LRU buffer-replacement strategy, and there are k buffers available to hold blocks of R. As we read each block of R, in order, the blocks that remain in buffers at the end of this iteration of the outer loop will be the last k blocks of R. We next reload the $M - 1$ buffers for S with new blocks of S and start reading the blocks of R again, in the next iteration of the outer loop. However, if we start from the beginning of R again, then the k buffers for R will need to be replaced, and we do not save disk I/O's just because $k > 1$.

A better implementation of nested-loop join, when an LRU buffer-replacement strategy is used, visits the blocks of R in an order that alternates: first-to-last and then last-to-first (called *rocking*). In that way, if there are k buffers available to R, we save k disk I/O's on each iteration of the outer loop except the first. That is, the second and subsequent iterations require only $B(R) - k$ disk I/O's for R. Notice that even if $k = 1$ (i.e., no *extra* buffers are available to R), we save one disk I/O per iteration. $\Box$

Other algorithms also are impacted by the fact that M can vary and by the buffer-replacement strategy used by the buffer manager. Here are some useful observations.

- If we use a sort-based algorithm for some operator, then it is possible to adapt to changes in M. If M shrinks, we can change the size of a sublist, since the sort-based algorithms we discussed do not depend on the sublists being the same size. The major limitation is that as M shrinks, we could be forced to create so many sublists that we cannot then allocate a buffer for each sublist in the merging process.

- If the algorithm is hash-based, we can reduce the number of buckets if M shrinks, as long as the buckets do not then become so large that they do not fit in allotted main memory. However, unlike sort-based algorithms, we cannot respond to changes in M while the algorithm runs. Rather, once the number of buckets is chosen, it remains fixed throughout the first pass, and if buffers become unavailable, the blocks belonging to some of the buckets will have to be swapped out.

15.7.4 Exercises for Section 15.7

Exercise 15.7.1: Suppose that we wish to execute a join $R \bowtie S$, and the available memory will vary between M and $M/2$. In terms of M, $B(R)$, and $B(S)$, give the conditions under which we can guarantee that the following algorithms can be executed:

a) A two-pass, hash-based join.

b) A two-pass, sort-based join.

c) A one-pass join.

! **Exercise 15.7.2:** How would the number of disk I/O's taken by a nested-loop join improve if extra buffers became available and the buffer-replacement policy were:

a) The clock algorithm.

b) First-in-first-out.

!! **Exercise 15.7.3:** In Example 15.15, we suggested that it was possible to take advantage of extra buffers becoming available during the join by keeping more than one block of R buffered and visiting the blocks of R in reverse order on even-numbered iterations of the outer loop. However, we could also maintain only one buffer for R and increase the number of buffers used for S. Which strategy yields the fewest disk I/O's?

15.8   Algorithms Using More Than Two Passes

While two passes are enough for operations on all but the largest relations, we should observe that the principal techniques discussed in Sections 15.4 and 15.5 generalize to algorithms that, by using as many passes as necessary, can process relations of arbitrary size. In this section we shall consider the generalization of both sort- and hash-based approaches.

15.8.1   Multipass Sort-Based Algorithms

In Section 15.4.1 we alluded to how 2PMMS could be extended to a three-pass algorithm. In fact, there is a simple recursive approach to sorting that will allow us to sort a relation, however large, completely, or if we prefer, to create n sorted sublists for any desired n.

Suppose we have M main-memory buffers available to sort a relation R, which we shall assume is stored clustered. Then do the following:

BASIS: If R fits in M blocks (i.e., $B(R) \leq M$), then read R into main memory, sort it using any main-memory sorting algorithm, and write the sorted relation to disk.

INDUCTION: If R does not fit into main memory, partition the blocks holding R into M groups, which we shall call $R_1, R_2, \ldots, R_M$. Recursively sort R_i for each $i = 1, 2, \ldots, M$. Then, merge the M sorted sublists, as in Section 15.4.1.

If we are not merely sorting R, but performing a unary operation such as γ or δ on R, then we modify the above so that at the final merge we perform the operation on the tuples at the front of the sorted sublists. That is,

- For a δ, output one copy of each distinct tuple, and skip over copies of the tuple.

- For a γ, sort on the grouping attributes only, and combine the tuples with a given value of these grouping attributes in the appropriate manner, as discussed in Section 15.4.3.

When we want to perform a binary operation, such as intersection or join, we use essentially the same idea, except that the two relations are first divided into a total of M sublists. Then, each sublist is sorted by the recursive algorithm above. Finally, we read each of the M sublists, each into one buffer, and we perform the operation in the manner described by the appropriate subsection of Section 15.4.

We can divide the M buffers between relations R and S as we wish. However, to minimize the total number of passes, we would normally divide the buffers in proportion to the number of blocks taken by the relations. That is, R gets $M \times B(R)/(B(R) + B(S))$ of the buffers, and S gets the rest.

15.8.2 Performance of Multipass, Sort-Based Algorithms

Now, let us explore the relationship between the number of disk I/O's required, the size of the relation(s) operated upon, and the size of main memory. Let $s(M, k)$ be the maximum size of a relation that we can sort using M buffers and k passes. Then we can compute $s(M, k)$ as follows:

BASIS: If $k = 1$, i.e., one pass is allowed, then we must have $B(R) \leq M$. Put another way, $s(M, 1) = M$.

INDUCTION: Suppose $k > 1$. Then we partition R into M pieces, each of which must be sortable in $k - 1$ passes. If $B(R) = s(M, k)$, then $s(M, k)/M$, which is the size of each of the M pieces of R, cannot exceed $s(M, k-1)$. That is: $s(M, k) = M s(M, k - 1)$.

If we expand the above recursion, we find

$$s(M, k) = M s(M, k - 1) = M^2 s(M, k - 2) = \cdots = M^{k-1} s(M, 1)$$

Since $s(M, 1) = M$, we conclude that $s(M, k) = M^k$. That is, using k passes, we can sort a relation R if $B(R) \leq M^k$. Put another way, if we want to sort R in k passes, then the minimum number of buffers we can use is $M = (B(R))^{1/k}$.

Each pass of a sorting algorithm reads all the data from disk and writes it out again. Thus, a k-pass sorting algorithm requires $2kB(R)$ disk I/O's.

Now, let us consider the cost of a multipass join $R(X, Y) \bowtie S(Y, Z)$, as representative of a binary operation on relations. Let $j(M, k)$ be the largest number of blocks such that in k passes, using M buffers, we can join relations of $j(M, k)$ or fewer total blocks. That is, the join can be accomplished provided $B(R) + B(S) \leq j(M, k)$.

On the final pass, we merge M sorted sublists from the two relations. Each of the sublists is sorted using $k - 1$ passes, so they can be no longer than $s(M, k - 1) = M^{k-1}$ each, or a total of $M s(M, k - 1) = M^k$. That is,

$B(R) + B(S) \leq M^k$. Reversing the role of the parameters, we can also state that to compute the join in k passes requires $\left(B(R) + B(S)\right)^{1/k}$ buffers.

To calculate the number of disk I/O's needed in the multipass algorithms, we should remember that, unlike for sorting, we do not count the cost of writing the final result to disk for joins or other relational operations. Thus, we use $2(k-1)\left(B(R)+B(S)\right)$ disk I/O's to sort the sublists, and another $B(R) + B(S)$ disk I/O's to read the sorted sublists in the final pass. The result is a total of $(2k-1)\left(B(R) + B(S)\right)$ disk I/O's.

15.8.3 Multipass Hash-Based Algorithms

There is a corresponding recursive approach to using hashing for operations on large relations. We hash the relation or relations into $M - 1$ buckets, where M is the number of available memory buffers. We then apply the operation to each bucket individually, in the case of a unary operation. If the operation is binary, such as a join, we apply the operation to each pair of corresponding buckets, as if they were the entire relations. We can describe this approach recursively as:

BASIS: For a unary operation, if the relation fits in M buffers, read it into memory and perform the operation. For a binary operation, if either relation fits in $M - 1$ buffers, perform the operation by reading this relation into main memory and then read the second relation, one block at a time, into the Mth buffer.

INDUCTION: If no relation fits in main memory, then hash each relation into $M-1$ buckets, as discussed in Section 15.5.1. Recursively perform the operation on each bucket or corresponding pair of buckets, and accumulate the output from each bucket or pair.

15.8.4 Performance of Multipass Hash-Based Algorithms

In what follows, we shall make the assumption that when we hash a relation, the tuples divide as evenly as possible among the buckets. In practice, this assumption will be met approximately if we choose a truly random hash function, but there will always be some unevenness in the distribution of tuples among buckets.

First, consider a unary operation, like γ or δ on a relation R using M buffers. Let $u(M, k)$ be the number of blocks in the largest relation that a k-pass hashing algorithm can handle. We can define u recursively by:

BASIS: $u(M, 1) = M$, since the relation R must fit in M buffers; i.e., $B(R) \leq M$.

INDUCTION: We assume that the first step divides the relation R into $M - 1$ buckets of equal size. Thus, we can compute $u(M, k)$ as follows. The buckets for the next pass must be sufficiently small that they can be handled in $k - 1$

passes; that is, the buckets are of size $u(M, k-1)$. Since R is divided into $M-1$ buckets, we must have $u(M, k) = (M-1)u(M, k-1)$.

If we expand the recurrence above, we find that $u(M, k) = M(M-1)^{k-1}$, or approximately, assuming M is large, $u(M, k) = M^k$. Equivalently, we can perform one of the unary relational operations on relation R in k passes with M buffers, provided $M \geq (B(R))^{1/k}$.

We may perform a similar analysis for binary operations. As in Section 15.8.2, let us consider the join. Let $j(M, k)$ be an upper bound on the size of the smaller of the two relations R and S involved in $R(X, Y) \bowtie S(Y, Z)$. Here, as before, M is the number of available buffers and k is the number of passes we can use.

BASIS: $j(M, 1) = M - 1$; that is, if we use the one-pass algorithm to join, then either R or S must fit in $M - 1$ blocks, as we discussed in Section 15.2.3.

INDUCTION: $j(M, k) = (M-1)j(M, k-1)$; that is, on the first of k passes, we can divide each relation into $M - 1$ buckets, and we may expect each bucket to be $1/(M-1)$ of its entire relation, but we must then be able to join each pair of corresponding buckets in $M - 1$ passes.

By expanding the recurrence for $j(M, k)$, we conclude that $j(M, k) = (M-1)^k$. Again assuming M is large, we can say approximately $j(M, k) = M^k$. That is, we can join $R(X, Y) \bowtie S(Y, Z)$ using k passes and M buffers provided $\min(B(R), B(S)) \leq M^k$.

15.8.5 Exercises for Section 15.8

Exercise 15.8.1: Suppose $B(R) = 10,000$, $B(S) = 40,000$, and $M = 101$. Describe the behavior of the following algorithms to compute $R \bowtie S$:

a) A three-pass, hash-based algorithm.

b) A three-pass, sort-based algorithm.

! **Exercise 15.8.2:** There are several "tricks" we have discussed for improving the performance of two-pass algorithms. For the following, tell whether the trick could be used in a multipass algorithm, and if so, how?

a) Improving a sort-based algorithm by storing blocks consecutively on disk (Section 15.5.7).

b) Improving a hash-based algorithm by storing blocks consecutively on disk (Section 15.5.7).

c) The hybrid-hash-join trick of Section 15.5.6.

15.9   Summary of Chapter 15

✦ *Query Processing*: Queries are compiled, which involves extensive optimization, and then executed. The study of query execution involves knowing methods for executing operations of relational algebra with some extensions to match the capabilities of SQL.

✦ *Query Plans*: Queries are compiled first into logical query plans, which are often like expressions of relational algebra, and then converted to a physical query plan by selecting an implementation for each operator, ordering joins and making other decisions, as will be discussed in Chapter 16.

✦ *Table Scanning*: To access the tuples of a relation, there are several possible physical operators. The table-scan operator simply reads each block holding tuples of the relation. Index-scan uses an index to find tuples, and sort-scan produces the tuples in sorted order.

✦ *Cost Measures for Physical Operators*: Commonly, the number of disk I/O's taken to execute an operation is the dominant component of the time. In our model, we count only disk I/O time, and we charge for the time and space needed to read arguments, but not to write the result.

✦ *Iterators*: Several operations involved in the execution of a query can be meshed conveniently if we think of their execution as performed by an iterator. This mechanism consists of three methods, to open the construction of a relation, to produce the next tuple of the relation, and to close the construction.

✦ *One-Pass Algorithms*: As long as one of the arguments of a relational-algebra operator can fit in main memory, we can execute the operator by reading the smaller relation to memory, and reading the other argument one block at a time.

✦ *Nested-Loop Join*: This simple join algorithm works even when neither argument fits in main memory. It reads as much as it can of the smaller relation into memory, and compares that with the entire other argument; this process is repeated until all of the smaller relation has had its turn in memory.

✦ *Two-Pass Algorithms*: Except for nested-loop join, most algorithms for arguments that are too large to fit into memory are either sort-based, hash-based, or index-based.

✦ *Sort-Based Algorithms*: These partition their argument(s) into main-memory-sized, sorted sublists. The sorted sublists are then merged appropriately to produce the desired result. For instance, if we merge the tuples of all sublists in sorted order, then we have the important two-phase-multiway-merge sort.

✦ *Hash-Based Algorithms*: These use a hash function to partition the argument(s) into buckets. The operation is then applied to the buckets individually (for a unary operation) or in pairs (for a binary operation).

✦ *Hashing Versus Sorting*: Hash-based algorithms are often superior to sort-based algorithms, since they require only one of their arguments to be "small." Sort-based algorithms, on the other hand, work well when there is another reason to keep some of the data sorted.

✦ *Index-Based Algorithms*: The use of an index is an excellent way to speed up a selection whose condition equates the indexed attribute to a constant. Index-based joins are also excellent when one of the relations is small, and the other has an index on the join attribute(s).

✦ *The Buffer Manager*: The availability of blocks of memory is controlled by the buffer manager. When a new buffer is needed in memory, the buffer manager uses one of the familiar replacement policies, such as least-recently-used, to decide which buffer is returned to disk.

✦ *Coping With Variable Numbers of Buffers*: Often, the number of main-memory buffers available to an operation cannot be predicted in advance. If so, the algorithm used to implement an operation needs to degrade gracefully as the number of available buffers shrinks.

✦ *Multipass Algorithms*: The two-pass algorithms based on sorting or hashing have natural recursive analogs that take three or more passes and will work for larger amounts of data.

15.10 References for Chapter 15

Two surveys of query optimization are [6] and [2]. [8] is a survey of distributed query optimization.

An early study of join methods is in [5]. Buffer-pool management was analyzed, surveyed, and improved by [3].

The use of sort-based techniques was pioneered by [1]. The advantage of hash-based algorithms for join was expressed by [7] and [4]; the latter is the origin of the hybrid hash-join.

1. M. W. Blasgen and K. P. Eswaran, "Storage access in relational databases," *IBM Systems J.* **16**:4 (1977), pp. 363–378.

2. S. Chaudhuri, "An overview of query optimization in relational systems," *Proc. Seventeenth Annual ACM Symposium on Principles of Database Systems*, pp. 34–43, June, 1998.

3. H.-T. Chou and D. J. DeWitt, "An evaluation of buffer management strategies for relational database systems," *Intl. Conf. on Very Large Databases*, pp. 127–141, 1985.

4. D. J. DeWitt, R. H. Katz, F. Olken, L. D. Shapiro, M. Stonebraker, and D. Wood, "Implementation techniques for main-memory database systems," *Proc. ACM SIGMOD Intl. Conf. on Management of Data* (1984), pp. 1–8.

5. L. R. Gotlieb, "Computing joins of relations," *Proc. ACM SIGMOD Intl. Conf. on Management of Data* (1975), pp. 55–63.

6. G. Graefe, "Query evaluation techniques for large databases," *Computing Surveys* **25**:2 (June, 1993), pp. 73–170.

7. M. Kitsuregawa, H. Tanaka, and T. Moto-oka, "Application of hash to data base machine and its architecture," *New Generation Computing* **1**:1 (1983), pp. 66–74.

8. D. Kossman, "The state of the art in distributed query processing," *Computing Surveys* **32**:4 (Dec., 2000), pp. 422–469.

Chapter 16

The Query Compiler

We shall now take up the architecture of the query compiler and its optimizer. As we noted in Fig. 15.2, there are three broad steps that the query processor must take:

1. The query, written in a language like SQL, is *parsed*, that is, turned into a parse tree representing the structure of the query in a useful way.

2. The parse tree is transformed into an expression tree of relational algebra (or a similar notation), which we term a *logical query plan*.

3. The logical query plan must be turned into a *physical query plan*, which indicates not only the operations performed, but the order in which they are performed, the algorithm used to perform each step, and the ways in which stored data is obtained and data is passed from one operation to another.

The first step, parsing, is the subject of Section 16.1. The result of this step is a parse tree for the query. The other two steps involve a number of choices. In picking a logical query plan, we have opportunities to apply many different algebraic operations, with the goal of producing the best logical query plan. Section 16.2 discusses the algebraic laws for relational algebra in the abstract. Then, Section 16.3 discusses the conversion of parse trees to initial logical query plans and shows how the algebraic laws from Section 16.2 can be used in strategies to improve the initial logical plan.

When producing a physical query plan from a logical plan, we must evaluate the predicted cost of each possible option. Cost estimation is a science of its own, which we discuss in Section 16.4. We show how to use cost estimates to evaluate plans in Section 16.5, and the special problems that come up when we order the joins of several relations are the subject of Section 16.6. Finally, Section 16.7 covers additional issues and strategies for selecting the physical query plan: algorithm choice, and pipelining versus materialization.

16.1   Parsing and Preprocessing

The first stages of query compilation are illustrated in Fig. 16.1. The four boxes in that figure correspond to the first two stages of Fig. 15.2.

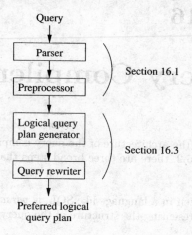

Figure 16.1: From a query to a logical query plan

In this section, we discuss parsing of SQL and give rudiments of a grammar that can be used for that language. We also discuss how to handle a query that involves a virtual view and other steps of preprocessing.

16.1.1   Syntax Analysis and Parse Trees

The job of the parser is to take text written in a language such as SQL and convert it to a *parse tree*, which is a tree whose nodes correspond to either:

1. *Atoms*, which are lexical elements such as keywords (e.g., SELECT), names of attributes or relations, constants, parentheses, operators such as + or <, and other schema elements, or

2. *Syntactic categories*, which are names for families of query subparts that all play a similar role in a query. We shall represent syntactic categories by triangular brackets around a descriptive name. For example, <Query> will be used to represent some queries in the common select-from-where form, and <Condition> will represent any expression that is a condition; i.e., it can follow WHERE in SQL.

If a node is an atom, then it has no children. However, if the node is a syntactic category, then its children are described by one of the *rules* of the grammar for the language. We shall present these ideas by example. The details of how one designs grammars for a language, and how one "parses," i.e., turns a program or query into the correct parse tree, is properly the subject of a course on compiling.[1]

16.1.2 A Grammar for a Simple Subset of SQL

We shall illustrate the parsing process by giving some rules that describe a small subset of SQL queries.

Queries

The syntactic category <Query> is intended to represent (some of the) queries of SQL. We give it only one rule:

```
<Query> ::= SELECT <SelList> FROM <FromList> WHERE <Condition>
```

Symbol ::= means "can be expressed as." The syntactic categories <SelList> and <FromList> represent lists that can follow SELECT and FROM, respectively. We shall describe limited forms of such lists shortly. The syntactic category <Condition> represents SQL conditions (expressions that are either true or false); we shall give some simplified rules for this category later.

Note this rule does not provide for the various optional clauses such as GROUP BY, HAVING, or ORDER BY, nor for options such as DISTINCT after SELECT, nor for query expressions using UNION, JOIN, or other binary operators.

Select-Lists

```
        <SelList> ::= <Attribute> , <SelList>
        <SelList> ::= <Attribute>
```

These two rules say that a select-list can be any comma-separated list of attributes: either a single attribute or an attribute, a comma, and any list of one or more attributes. Note that in a full SQL grammar we would also need provision for expressions and aggregation functions in the select-list and for aliasing of attributes and expressions.

From-Lists

```
        <FromList> ::= <Relation> , <FromList>
        <FromList> ::= <Relation>
```

Here, a from-list is defined to be any comma-separated list of relations. For simplification, we omit the possibility that elements of a from-list can be expressionsa, such as joins or subqueries. Likewise, a full SQL grammar would have to allow tuple variables for relations.

---

[1]Those unfamiliar with the subject may wish to examine A. V. Aho, M. Lam, R. Sethi, and J. D. Ullman, *Compilers: Principles, Techniques, and Tools*, Addison-Wesley, 2007, although the examples of Section 16.1.2 should be sufficient to place parsing in the context of the query processor.

Conditions

The rules we shall use are:

```
<Condition> ::= <Condition> AND <Condition>
<Condition> ::= <Attribute> IN ( <Query> )
<Condition> ::= <Attribute> = <Attribute>
<Condition> ::= <Attribute> LIKE <Pattern>
```

Although we have listed more rules for conditions than for other categories, these rules only scratch the surface of the forms of conditions. We have omitted rules introducing operators OR, NOT, and EXISTS, comparisons other than equality and LIKE, constant operands, and a number of other structures that are needed in a full SQL grammar.

Base Syntactic Categories

Syntactic categories <Attribute>, <Relation>, and <Pattern> are special, in that they are not defined by grammatical rules, but by rules about the atoms for which they can stand. For example, in a parse tree, the one child of <Attribute> can be any string of characters that identifies an attribute of the current database schema. Similarly, <Relation> can be replaced by any string of characters that makes sense as a relation in the current schema, and <Pattern> can be replaced by any quoted string that is a legal SQL pattern.

Example 16.1: Recall two relations from the running movies example:

```
StarsIn(movieTitle, movieYear, starName)
MovieStar(name, address, gender, birthdate)
```

Our study of parsing and query rewriting will center around two versions of the query "find the titles of movies that have at least one star born in 1960." We identify stars born in 1960 by asking if their birthdate (a SQL string) ends in '1960', using the LIKE operator.

One way to ask this query is to construct the set of names of those stars born in 1960 as a subquery, and ask about each StarsIn tuple whether the starName in that tuple is a member of the set returned by this subquery. The SQL for this variation of the query is shown in Fig. 16.2.

The parse tree for the query of Fig. 16.2, according to the grammar we have sketched, is shown in Fig. 16.3. At the root is the syntactic category <Query>, as must be the case for any parse tree of a query. Working down the tree, we see that this query is a select-from-where form; the select-list consists of only the attribute movieTitle, and the from-list is only the one relation StarsIn.

The condition in the outer WHERE-clause is more complex. It has the form of attribute-IN-parenthesized-query. The subquery has its own singleton select- and from-lists and a simple condition involving a LIKE operator. □

```
SELECT movieTitle
FROM StarsIn
WHERE starName IN (
    SELECT name
    FROM MovieStar
    WHERE birthdate LIKE '%1960'
);
```

Figure 16.2: Find the movies with stars born in 1960

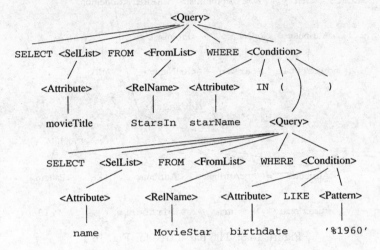

Figure 16.3: The parse tree for Fig. 16.2

Example 16.2 : Now, let us consider another version of the query of Fig. 16.2, this time without using a subquery. We may instead equijoin the relations StarsIn and MovieStar, using the condition starName = name, to require that the star mentioned in both relations be the same. Note that starName is an attribute of relation StarsIn, while name is an attribute of MovieStar. This form of the query of Fig. 16.2 is shown in Fig. 16.4.[2]

The parse tree for Fig. 16.4 is seen in Fig. 16.5. Many of the rules used in this parse tree are the same as in Fig. 16.3. However, notice a from-list with more than one relation and two conditions connected by AND. □

---

[2]There is a small difference between the two queries in that Fig. 16.4 can produce duplicates if a movie has more than one star born in 1960. Strictly speaking, we should add DISTINCT to Fig. 16.4, but our example grammar was simplified to the extent of omitting that option.

```
SELECT movieTitle
FROM StarsIn, MovieStar
WHERE starName = name AND
      birthdate LIKE '%1960';
```

Figure 16.4: Another way to ask for the movies with stars born in 1960

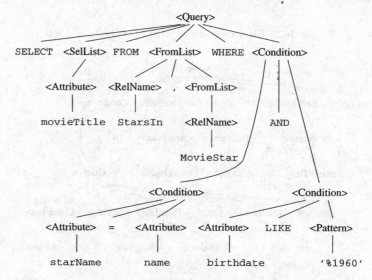

Figure 16.5: The parse tree for Fig. 16.4

16.1.3 The Preprocessor

The *preprocessor* has several important functions. If a relation used in the query is actually a virtual view, then each use of this relation in the from-list must be replaced by a parse tree that describes the view. This parse tree is obtained from the definition of the view, which is essentially a query. We discuss the preprocessing of view references in Section 16.1.4.

The preprocessor is also responsible for *semantic checking*. Even if the query is valid syntactically, it actually may violate one or more semantic rules on the use of names. For instance, the preprocessor must:

1. *Check relation uses.* Every relation mentioned in a FROM-clause must be a relation or view in the current schema.

2. *Check and resolve attribute uses.* Every attribute that is mentioned in the SELECT- or WHERE-clause must be an attribute of some relation in the current scope. For instance, attribute movieTitle in the first select-list of Fig. 16.3 is in the scope of only relation StarsIn. Fortunately,

movieTitle is an attribute of StarsIn, so the preprocessor validates this use of movieTitle. The typical query processor would at this point *resolve* each attribute by attaching to it the relation to which it refers, if that relation was not attached explicitly in the query (e.g., StarsIn.movieTitle). It would also check ambiguity, signaling an error if the attribute is in the scope of two or more relations with that attribute.

3. *Check types.* All attributes must be of a type appropriate to their uses. For instance, birthdate in Fig. 16.3 is used in a LIKE comparison, which requires that birthdate be a string or a type that can be coerced to a string. Since birthdate is a date, and dates in SQL normally can be treated as strings, this use of an attribute is validated. Likewise, operators are checked to see that they apply to values of appropriate and compatible types.

16.1.4   Preprocessing Queries Involving Views

When an operand in a query is a virtual view, the preprocessor needs to replace the operand by a piece of parse tree that represents how the view is constructed from base tables. The idea is illustrated in Fig. 16.6. A query Q is represented by its expression tree in relational algebra, and that tree may have some leaves that are views. We have suggested two such leaves, the views V and W. To interpret Q in terms of base tables, we find the definition of the views V and W. These definitions are also queries, so they can be expressed in relational algebra or as parse trees.

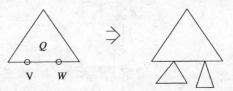

Figure 16.6: Substituting view definitions for view references

To form the query over base tables, we substitute, for each leaf in the tree for Q that is a view, the root of a copy of the tree that defines that view. Thus, in Fig. 16.6 we have shown the leaves labeled V and W replaced by the definitions of these views. The resulting tree is a query over base tables that is equivalent to the original query about views.

Example 16.3: Let us consider the view definition and query of Example 8.3. Recall the definition of view ParamountMovies is:

```
CREATE VIEW ParamountMovies AS
    SELECT title, year
```

```
FROM Movies
WHERE studioName = 'Paramount';
```

The tree in Fig. 16.7 is a relational-algebra expression for the query; we use relational algebra here because it is more succinct than the parse trees we have been using.

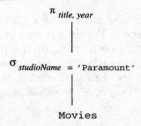

$\pi_{title, year}$

$\sigma_{studioName = 'Paramount'}$

Movies

Figure 16.7: Expression tree for view `ParamountMovies`

The query of Example 8.3 is

```
SELECT title
FROM ParamountMovies
WHERE year = 1979;
```

asking for the Paramount movies made in 1979. This query has the expression tree shown in Fig. 16.8. Note that the one leaf of this tree represents the view `ParamountMovies`.

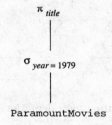

π_{title}

$\sigma_{year = 1979}$

ParamountMovies

Figure 16.8: Expression tree for the query

We substitute the tree of Fig. 16.7 for the leaf `ParamountMovies` in Fig. 16.8. The resulting tree is shown in Fig. 16.9.

This tree, while the formal result of the view preprocessing, is not a very good way to express the query. In Section 16.2 we shall discuss ways to improve expression trees such as Fig. 16.9. In particular, we can push selections and projections down the tree, and combine them in many cases. Figure 16.10 is an improved representation that we can obtain by standard query-processing techniques.   □

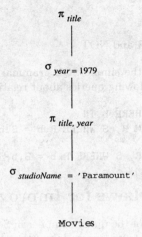

Figure 16.9: Expressing the query in terms of base tables

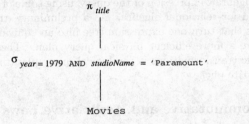

Figure 16.10: Simplifying the query over base tables

16.1.5 Exercises for Section 16.1

Exercise 16.1.1: Add to or modify the rules for <Query> to include simple versions of the following features of SQL select-from-where expressions:

  a) A query with no where-clause.

  b) The ability to produce a set with the DISTINCT keyword.

  c) A GROUP BY clause and a HAVING clause.

  d) Sorted output with the ORDER BY clause.

Exercise 16.1.2: Add to the rules for <Condition> to allow the following features of SQL conditionals:

  a) Comparisons other than =.

  b) Parenthesized conditions.

   c) EXISTS expressions.

   d) Logical operators OR and NOT.

Exercise 16.1.3: Using the simple SQL grammar exhibited in this section, give parse trees for the following queries about relations $R(a, b)$ and $S(b, c)$:

a)   SELECT a FROM R WHERE b IN
            (SELECT a FROM R, S WHERE R.b = S.b);

b)   SELECT a, c FROM R, S WHERE R.b = S.b;

16.2 Algebraic Laws for Improving Query Plans

We resume our discussion of the query compiler in Section 16.3, where we shall transform the parse tree into an expression of the extended relational algebra. Also in Section 16.3, we shall see how to apply heuristics that we hope will improve the algebraic expression of the query, using some of the many algebraic laws that hold for relational algebra. As a preliminary, this section catalogs algebraic laws that turn one expression tree into an equivalent expression tree that may have a more efficient physical query plan. The result of applying these algebraic transformations is the logical query plan that is the output of the query-rewrite phase.

16.2.1 Commutative and Associative Laws

A *commutative law* about an operator says that it does not matter in which order you present the arguments of the operator; the result will be the same. For instance, $+$ and $\times$ are commutative operators of arithmetic. More precisely, $x + y = y + x$ and $x \times y = y \times x$ for any numbers x and y. On the other hand, $-$ is not a commutative arithmetic operator: $x - y \neq y - x$.

An *associative law* about an operator says that we may group two uses of the operator either from the left or the right. For instance, $+$ and $\times$ are associative arithmetic operators, meaning that $(x + y) + z = x + (y + z)$ and $(x \times y) \times z = x \times (y \times z)$. On the other hand, $-$ is not associative: $(x - y) - z \neq x - (y - z)$. When an operator is both associative and commutative, then any number of operands connected by this operator can be grouped and ordered as we wish without changing the result. For example, $((w + x) + y) + z = (y + x) + (z + w)$.

Several of the operators of relational algebra are both associative and commutative. Particularly:

- $R \times S = S \times R$; $(R \times S) \times T = R \times (S \times T)$.

- $R \bowtie S = S \bowtie R$; $(R \bowtie S) \bowtie T = R \bowtie (S \bowtie T)$.

- $R \cup S = S \cup R$; $(R \cup S) \cup T = R \cup (S \cup T)$.

- $R \cap S = S \cap R$; $(R \cap S) \cap T = R \cap (S \cap T)$.

Note that these laws hold for both sets and bags. We shall not prove each of these laws, although we give one example of a proof, below.

Example 16.4: Let us verify the commutative law for $\bowtie$: $R \bowtie S = S \bowtie R$. First, suppose a tuple t is in the result of $R \bowtie S$, the expression on the left. Then there must be a tuple r in R and a tuple s in S that agree with t on every attribute that each shares with t. Thus, when we evaluate the expression on the right, $S \bowtie R$, the tuples s and r will again combine to form t.

We might imagine that the order of components of t will be different on the left and right, but formally, tuples in relational algebra have no fixed order of attributes. Rather, we are free to reorder components, as long as we carry the proper attributes along in the column headers, as was discussed in Section 2.2.5.

We are not done yet with the proof. Since our relational algebra is an algebra of bags, not sets, we must also verify that if t appears n times on the left, then it appears n times on the right, and vice-versa. Suppose t appears n times on the left. Then it must be that the tuple r from R that agrees with t appears some number of times n_R, and the tuple s from S that agrees with t appears some n_S times, where $n_R n_S = n$. Then when we evaluate the expression $S \bowtie R$ on the right, we find that s appears n_S times, and r appears n_R times, so we get $n_S n_R$ copies of t, or n copies.

We are still not done. We have finished the half of the proof that says everything on the left appears on the right, but we must show that everything on the right appears on the left. Because of the obvious symmetry, the argument is essentially the same, and we shall not go through the details here. $\square$

We did not include the theta-join among the associative-commutative operators. True, this operator is commutative:

- $R \bowtie_C S = S \bowtie_C R$.

Moreover, if the conditions involved make sense where they are positioned, then the theta-join is associative. However, there are examples, such as the following, where we cannot apply the associative law because the conditions do not apply to attributes of the relations being joined.

Example 16.5: Suppose we have three relations $R(a,b)$, $S(b,c)$, and $T(c,d)$. The expression

$$(R \bowtie_{R.b > S.b} S) \bowtie_{a < d} T$$

is transformed by a hypothetical associative law into:

$$R \bowtie_{R.b > S.b} (S \bowtie_{a < d} T)$$

However, we cannot join S and T using the condition $a < d$, because a is an attribute of neither S nor T. Thus, the associative law for theta-join cannot be applied arbitrarily. $\square$

Laws for Bags and Sets Can Differ

Be careful about applying familiar laws about sets to relations that are bags. For instance, you may have learned set-theoretic laws such as $A \cap_S (B \cup_S C) = (A \cap_S B) \cup_S (A \cap_S C)$, which is formally the "distributive law of intersection over union." This law holds for sets, but not for bags.

As an example, suppose bags A, B, and C were each $\{x\}$. Then $A \cap_B (B \cup_B C) = \{x\} \cap_B \{x, x\} = \{x\}$. But $(A \cap_B B) \cup_B (A \cap_B C) = \{x\} \cup_B \{x\} = \{x, x\}$, which differs from the left-hand-side, $\{x\}$.

16.2.2 Laws Involving Selection

Since selections tend to reduce the size of relations markedly, one of the most important rules of efficient query processing is to move the selections down the tree as far as they will go without changing what the expression does. Indeed early query optimizers used variants of this transformation as their primary strategy for selecting good logical query plans. As we shall see shortly, the transformation of "push selections down the tree" is not quite general enough, but the idea of "pushing selections" is still a major tool for the query optimizer.

To start, when the condition of a selection is complex (i.e., it involves conditions connected by AND or OR), it helps to break the condition into its constituent parts. The motivation is that one part, involving fewer attributes than the whole condition, may be moved to a convenient place where the entire condition cannot be evaluated. Thus, our first two laws for σ are the *splitting laws*:

- $\sigma_{C_1 \text{ AND } C_2}(R) = \sigma_{C_1}\big(\sigma_{C_2}(R)\big)$.

- $\sigma_{C_1 \text{ OR } C_2}(R) = \big(\sigma_{C_1}(R)\big) \cup_S \big(\sigma_{C_2}(R)\big)$.

However, the second law, for OR, works only if the relation R is a set. Notice that if R were a bag, the set-union would have the effect of eliminating duplicates incorrectly.

Notice that the order of C_1 and C_2 is flexible. For example, we could just as well have written the first law above with C_2 applied after C_1, as $\sigma_{C_2}\big(\sigma_{C_1}(R)\big)$. In fact, more generally, we can swap the order of any sequence of σ operators:

- $\sigma_{C_1}\big(\sigma_{C_2}(R)\big) = \sigma_{C_2}\big(\sigma_{C_1}(R)\big)$.

Example 16.6 : Let $R(a, b, c)$ be a relation. Then $\sigma_{(a=1 \text{ OR } a=3) \text{ AND } b<c}(R)$ can be split as $\sigma_{a=1 \text{ OR } a=3}\big(\sigma_{b<c}(R)\big)$. We can then split this expression at the OR into $\sigma_{a=1}\big(\sigma_{b<c}(R)\big) \cup \sigma_{a=3}\big(\sigma_{b<c}(R)\big)$. In this case, because it is impossible for a tuple to satisfy both $a = 1$ and $a = 3$, this transformation holds regardless

of whether or not R is a set, as long as $\cup_B$ is used for the union. However, in general the splitting of an OR requires that the argument be a set and that $\cup_S$ be used.

Alternatively, we could have started to split by making $\sigma_{b<c}$ the outer operation, as $\sigma_{b<c}\big(\sigma_{a=1 \text{ OR } a=3}(R)\big)$. When we then split the OR, we would get $\sigma_{b<c}\big(\sigma_{a=1}(R) \cup \sigma_{a=3}(R)\big)$, an expression that is equivalent to, but somewhat different from the first expression we derived. $\square$

The next family of laws involving σ allow us to push selections through the binary operators: product, union, intersection, difference, and join. There are three types of laws, depending on whether it is optional or required to push the selection to each of the arguments:

1. For a union, the selection *must* be pushed to both arguments.

2. For a difference, the selection must be pushed to the first argument and optionally may be pushed to the second.

3. For the other operators it is only required that the selection be pushed to one argument. For joins and products, it may not make sense to push the selection to both arguments, since an argument may or may not have the attributes that the selection requires. When it is possible to push to both, it may or may not improve the plan to do so; see Exercise 16.2.6.

Thus, the law for union is:

- $\sigma_C(R \cup S) = \sigma_C(R) \cup \sigma_C(S)$.

Here, it is mandatory to move the selection down both branches of the tree.
For difference, one version of the law is:

- $\sigma_C(R - S) = \sigma_C(R) - S$.

However, it is also permissible to push the selection to both arguments, as:

- $\sigma_C(R - S) = \sigma_C(R) - \sigma_C(S)$.

The next laws allow the selection to be pushed to one or both arguments. If the selection is σ_C, then we can only push this selection to a relation that has all the attributes mentioned in C, if there is one. We shall show the laws below assuming that the relation R has all the attributes mentioned in C.

- $\sigma_C(R \times S) = \sigma_C(R) \times S$.

- $\sigma_C(R \bowtie S) = \sigma_C(R) \bowtie S$.

- $\sigma_C(R \bowtie_D S) = \sigma_C(R) \bowtie_D S$.

- $\sigma_C(R \cap S) = \sigma_C(R) \cap S$.

If C has only attributes of S, then we can instead write:

- $\sigma_C(R \times S) = R \times \sigma_C(S)$.

and similarly for the other three operators $\bowtie$, $\bowtie_D$, and $\cap$. Should relations R and S both happen to have all attributes of C, then we can use laws such as:

- $\sigma_C(R \bowtie S) = \sigma_C(R) \bowtie \sigma_C(S)$.

Note that it is impossible for this variant to apply if the operator is $\times$ or $\bowtie_D$, since in those cases R and S have no shared attributes. On the other hand, for $\cap$ this form of law always applies, since the schemas of R and S must then be the same.

Example 16.7: Consider relations $R(a, b)$ and $S(b, c)$ and the expression

$$\sigma_{(a=1 \text{ OR } a=3) \text{ AND } b<c}(R \bowtie S)$$

The condition $b < c$ applies only to to S, and the condition $a = 1$ OR $a = 3$ applies only to R. We thus begin by splitting the AND of the two conditions as we did in the first alternative of Example 16.6:

$$\sigma_{a=1 \text{ OR } a=3}\big(\sigma_{b<c}(R \bowtie S)\big)$$

Next, we can push the selection $\sigma_{b<c}$ to S, giving us the expression:

$$\sigma_{a=1 \text{ OR } a=3}\big(R \bowtie \sigma_{b<c}(S)\big)$$

Finally, push the first condition to R, yielding: $\sigma_{a=1 \text{ OR } a=3}(R) \bowtie \sigma_{b<c}(S)$. □

16.2.3 Pushing Selections

As was illustrated in Example 16.3, pushing a selection down an expression tree — that is, replacing the left side of one of the rules in Section 16.2.2 by its right side — is one of the most powerful tools of the query optimizer. However, when queries involve virtual views, it is sometimes necessary first to move a selection as far *up* the tree as it can go, and then push the selections down all possible branches. An example will illustrate the proper selection-pushing approach.

Example 16.8: Suppose we have the relations

```
StarsIn(title, year, starName)
Movies(title, year, length, genre, studioName, producerC#)
```

Note that we have altered the first two attributes of StarsIn from the usual movieTitle and movieYear to make this example simpler to follow. Define view MoviesOf1996 by:

Some Trivial Laws

We are not going to state every true law for the relational algebra. The reader should be alert, in particular, for laws about extreme cases: a relation that is empty, a selection or theta-join whose condition is always true or always false, or a projection onto the list of all attributes, for example. A few of the many possible special-case laws:

- Any selection on an empty relation is empty.

- If C is an always-true condition (e.g., $x > 10$ OR $x \le 10$ on a relation that forbids $x = $ NULL), then $\sigma_C(R) = R$.

- If R is empty, then $R \cup S = S$.

```
CREATE VIEW MoviesOf1996 AS
    SELECT *
    FROM Movies
    WHERE year = 1996;
```

We can ask the query "which stars worked for which studios in 1996?" by the SQL query:

```
SELECT starName, studioName
FROM MoviesOf1996 NATURAL JOIN StarsIn;
```

The view MoviesOf1996 is defined by the relational-algebra expression

$$\sigma_{year=1996}(\text{Movies})$$

Thus, the query, which is the natural join of this expression with StarsIn, followed by a projection onto attributes starName and studioName, has the expression shown in Fig. 16.11.

Here, the selection is already as far down the tree as it will go, so there is no way to "push selections down the tree." However, the rule $\sigma_C(R \bowtie S) = \sigma_C(R) \bowtie S$ can be applied "backwards," to bring the selection $\sigma_{year=1996}$ above the join in Fig. 16.11. Then, since $year$ is an attribute of both Movies and StarsIn, we may push the selection down to *both* children of the join node. The resulting logical query plan is shown in Fig. 16.12. It is likely to be an improvement, since we reduce the size of the relation StarsIn before we join it with the movies of 1996. □

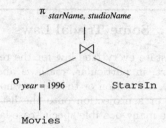

Figure 16.11: Logical query plan constructed from definition of a query and view

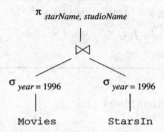

Figure 16.12: Improving the query plan by moving selections up and down the tree

16.2.4   Laws Involving Projection

Projections, like selections, can be "pushed down" through many other operators. Pushing projections differs from pushing selections in that when we push projections, it is quite usual for the projection also to remain where it is. Put another way, "pushing" projections really involves introducing a new projection somewhere below an existing projection.

Pushing projections is useful, but generally less so than pushing selections. The reason is that while selections often reduce the size of a relation by a large factor, projection keeps the number of tuples the same and only reduces the length of tuples. In fact, the extended projection operator of Section 5.2.5 can actually increase the length of tuples.

To describe the transformations of extended projection, we need to introduce some terminology. Consider a term $E \to x$ on the list for a projection, where E is an attribute or an expression involving attributes and constants. We say all attributes mentioned in E are *input* attributes of the projection, and x is an *output* attribute. If a term is a single attribute, then it is both an input and output attribute. If a projection list consists only of attributes, with no renaming or expressions other than a single attribute, then we say the projection is *simple*.

Example 16.9: Projection $\pi_{a,b,c}(R)$ is simple; a, b, and c are both its input attributes and its output attributes. On the other hand, $\pi_{a+b\to x,\ c}(R)$ is not simple. It has input attributes a, b, and c, and its output attributes are x and c. □

The principle behind laws for projection is that:

- We may introduce a projection anywhere in an expression tree, as long as it eliminates only attributes that are neither used by an operator above nor are in the result of the entire expression.

In the most basic form of these laws, the introduced projections are always simple, although the pre-existing projections, such as L below, need not be.

- $\pi_L(R \bowtie S) = \pi_L\big(\pi_M(R) \bowtie \pi_N(S)\big)$, where M and N are the join attributes and the input attributes if L that are found among the attributes of R and S, respectively.

- $\pi_L(R \bowtie_C S) = \pi_L\big(\pi_M(R) \bowtie_C \pi_N(S)\big)$, where M and N are the join attributes (i.e., those mentioned in condition C) and the input attributes of L that are found among the attributes of R and S respectively.

- $\pi_L(R \times S) = \pi_L\big(\pi_M(R) \times \pi_N(S)\big)$, where M and N are the lists of all attributes of R and S, respectively, that are input attributes of L.

Example 16.10: Let $R(a,b,c)$ and $S(c,d,e)$ be two relations. Consider the expression $\pi_{a+e\to x,\ b\to y}(R \bowtie S)$. The input attributes of the projection are a, b, and e, and c is the only join attribute. We may apply the law for pushing projections below joins to get the equivalent expression:

$$\pi_{a+e\to x,\ b\to y}\big(\pi_{a,b,c}(R) \bowtie \pi_{c,e}(S)\big)$$

Notice that the projection $\pi_{a,b,c}(R)$ is trivial; it projects onto all the attributes of R. We may thus eliminate this projection and get a third equivalent expression: $\pi_{a+e\to x,\ b\to y}(R \bowtie \pi_{c,e}(S))$. That is, the only change from the original is that we remove the attribute d from S before the join. □

We can perform a projection entirely before a bag union. That is:

- $\pi_L(R \cup_B S) = \pi_L(R) \cup_B \pi_L(S)$.

On the other hand, projections cannot be pushed below set unions or either the set or bag versions of intersection or difference at all.

Example 16.11: Let $R(a,b)$ consist of the one tuple $\{(1,2)\}$ and $S(a,b)$ consist of the one tuple $\{(1,3)\}$. Then $\pi_a(R \cap S) = \pi_a(\emptyset) = \emptyset$. However, $\pi_a(R) \cap \pi_a(S) = \{(1)\} \cap \{(1)\} = \{(1)\}$. □

If the projection involves some computations, and the input attributes of a term on the projection list belong entirely to one of the arguments of a join or product below the projection, then we have the option, although not the obligation, to perform the computation directly on that argument. An example should help illustrate the point.

Example 16.12: Again let $R(a, b, c)$ and $S(c, d, e)$ be relations, and consider the join and projection $\pi_{a+b\to x,\ d+e\to y}(R \bowtie S)$. We can move the sum $a + b$ and its renaming to x directly onto the relation R, and move the sum $d + e$ to S similarly. The resulting equivalent expression is

$$\pi_{x,y}\big(\pi_{a+b\to x,\ c}(R) \bowtie \pi_{d+e\to y,\ c}(S)\big)$$

One special case to handle is if x or y were c. Then, we could not rename a sum to c, because a relation cannot have two attributes named c. Thus, we would have to invent a temporary name and do another renaming in the projection above the join. For example, $\pi_{a+b\to c,\ d+e\to y}(R \bowtie S)$ could become $\pi_{z\to c,\ y}\big(\pi_{a+b\to z,\ c}(R) \bowtie \pi_{d+e\to y,\ c}(S)\big)$. $\square$

It is also possible to push a projection below a selection.

- $\pi_L\big(\sigma_C(R)\big) = \pi_L\Big(\sigma_C\big(\pi_M(R)\big)\Big)$, where M is the list of all attributes that are either input attributes of L or mentioned in condition C.

As in Example 16.12, we have the option of performing computations on the list L in the list M instead, provided the condition C does not need the input attributes of L that are involved in a computation.

16.2.5   Laws About Joins and Products

We saw in Section 16.2.1 many of the important laws involving joins and products: their commutative and associative laws. However, there are a few additional laws that follow directly from the definition of the join, as was mentioned in Section 2.4.12.

- $R \bowtie_C S = \sigma_C(R \times S)$.

- $R \bowtie S = \pi_L\big(\sigma_C(R \times S)\big)$, where C is the condition that equates each pair of attributes from R and S with the same name, and L is a list that includes one attribute from each equated pair and all the other attributes of R and S.

In practice, we usually want to apply these rules from right to left. That is, we identify a product followed by a selection as a join of some kind. The reason for doing so is that the algorithms for computing joins are generally much faster than algorithms that compute a product followed by a selection on the (very large) result of the product.

16.2.6 Laws Involving Duplicate Elimination

The operator δ, which eliminates duplicates from a bag, can be pushed through many, but not all operators. In general, moving a δ down the tree reduces the size of intermediate relations and may therefore be beneficial. Moreover, we can sometimes move the δ to a position where it can be eliminated altogether, because it is applied to a relation that is known not to possess duplicates:

- $\delta(R) = R$ if R has no duplicates. Important cases of such a relation R include

  a) A stored relation with a declared primary key, and

  b) The result of a γ operation, since grouping creates a relation with no duplicates.

  c) The result of a set union, intersection, or difference.

Several laws that "push" δ through other operators are:

- $\delta(R \times S) = \delta(R) \times \delta(S)$.

- $\delta(R \bowtie S) = \delta(R) \bowtie \delta(S)$.

- $\delta(R \bowtie_C S) = \delta(R) \bowtie_C \delta(S)$.

- $\delta\big(\sigma_C(R)\big) = \sigma_C\big(\delta(R)\big)$.

We can also move the δ to either or both of the arguments of an intersection:

- $\delta(R \cap_B S) = \delta(R) \cap_B S = R \cap_B \delta(S) = \delta(R) \cap_B \delta(S)$.

On the other hand, δ generally cannot be pushed through the operators $\cup_B$, $-_B$, or π.

Example 16.13 : Let R have two copies of the tuple t and S have one copy of t. Then $\delta(R \cup_B S)$ has one copy of t, while $\delta(R) \cup_B \delta(S)$ has two copies of t. Also, $\delta(R -_B S)$ has one copy of t, while $\delta(R) -_B \delta(S)$ has no copy of t.

Now, consider relation $T(a, b)$ with one copy each of the tuples $(1, 2)$ and $(1, 3)$, and no other tuples. Then $\delta\big(\pi_a(T)\big)$ has one copy of the tuple (1), while $\pi_a\big(\delta(T)\big)$ has two copies of (1). $\square$

16.2.7 Laws Involving Grouping and Aggregation

When we consider the operator γ, we find that the applicability of many transformations depends on the details of the aggregate operators used. Thus, we cannot state laws in the generality that we used for the other operators. One exception is the law, mentioned in Section 16.2.6, that a γ absorbs a δ. Precisely:

- $\delta\big(\gamma_L(R)\big) = \gamma_L(R)$.

Another general rule is that we may project useless attributes from the argument should we wish, prior to applying the γ operation. This law can be written:

- $\gamma_L(R) = \gamma_L\big(\pi_M(R)\big)$ if M is a list containing at least all those attributes of R that are mentioned in L.

The reason that other transformations depend on the aggregation(s) involved in a γ is that some aggregations — MIN and MAX in particular — are not affected by the presence or absence of duplicates. The other aggregations — SUM, COUNT, and AVG — generally produce different values if duplicates are eliminated prior to application of the aggregation.

Thus, let us call an operator γ_L *duplicate-impervious* if the only aggregations in L are MIN and/or MAX. Then:

- $\gamma_L(R) = \gamma_L\big(\delta(R)\big)$ provided γ_L is duplicate-impervious.

Example 16.14: Suppose we have the relations

```
MovieStar(name, addr, gender, birthdate)
StarsIn(movieTitle, movieYear, starName)
```

and we want to know for each year the birthdate of the youngest star to appear in a movie that year. We can express this query as

```
SELECT movieYear, MAX(birthdate)
FROM MovieStar, StarsIn
WHERE name = starName
GROUP BY movieYear;
```

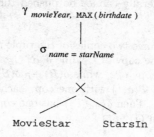

Figure 16.13: Initial logical query plan for the query of Example 16.14

An initial logical query plan constructed directly from the query is shown in Fig. 16.13. The FROM list is expressed by a product, and the WHERE clause by a selection above it. The grouping and aggregation are expressed by the γ operator above those. Some transformations that we could apply to Fig. 16.13 if we wished are:

1. Combine the selection and product into an equijoin.

2. Generate a δ below the γ, since the γ is duplicate-impervious.

3. Generate a π between the γ and the introduced δ to project onto movie-
Year and birthdate, the only attributes relevant to the γ.

The resulting plan is shown in Fig. 16.14.

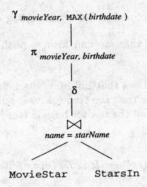

Figure 16.14: Another query plan for the query of Example 16.14

We can now push the δ below the $\bowtie$ and introduce π's below that if we wish.
This new query plan is shown in Fig. 16.15. If name is a key for MovieStar, the
δ can be eliminated along the branch leading to that relation.   □

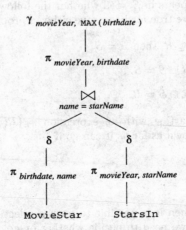

Figure 16.15: A third query plan for Example 16.14

16.2.8   Exercises for Section 16.2

Exercise 16.2.1: Give examples to show that:

a) Duplicate elimination (δ) cannot be pushed below projection.

b) Duplicate elimination cannot be pushed below bag union or difference.

c) Projection cannot be pushed below set union.

d) Projection cannot be pushed below set or bag difference.

! **Exercise 16.2.2:** Prove that we can always push a projection below both branches of a bag union.

! **Exercise 16.2.3:** Some laws that hold for sets hold for bags; others do not. For each of the laws below that are true for sets, tell whether or not it is true for bags. Either give a proof the law for bags is true, or give a counterexample.

a) $R - R = \emptyset$.

b) $R \cup (S \cap T) = (R \cup S) \cap (R \cup T)$ (distribution of union over intersection).

c) $R \cup R = R$ (the idempotent law for union).

d) $R \cap R = R$ (the idempotent law for intersection).

! **Exercise 16.2.4:** We can define $\subseteq$ for bags by: $R \subseteq S$ if and only if for every element x, the number of times x appears in R is less than or equal to the number of times it appears in S. Tell whether the following statements (which are all true for sets) are true for bags; give either a proof or a counterexample:

a) If $R \subseteq S$ and $S \subseteq R$, then $R = S$.

b) If $R \subseteq S$, then $R \cup S = S$.

c) If $R \subseteq S$, then $R \cap S = R$.

Exercise 16.2.5: Starting with an expression $\pi_L\big(R(a,b,c) \bowtie S(b,c,d,e)\big)$, push the projection down as far as it can go if L is:

a) $a,\ b,\ a + d \to z$.

b) $b + c \to x,\ c + d \to y$.

Exercise 16.2.6: When it is possible to push a selection to both arguments of a binary operator, we need to decide whether or not to do so. How would the existence of indexes on one of the arguments affect our choice? Consider, for instance, an expression $\sigma_C(R \cap S)$, where there is an index on S.

! Exercise 16.2.7: The following are possible equalities involving operations on a relation $R(a, b)$. Tell whether or not they are true; give either a proof or a counterexample.

   a) $\gamma_{MIN(a)\to y, \ x}\left(\gamma_{a, \ SUM(b)\to x}(R)\right) = \gamma_{y, SUM(b)\to x}\left(\gamma_{MIN(a)\to y, \ b}(R)\right)$.

   b) $\gamma_{MIN(a)\to y, \ x}\left(\gamma_{a, \ MAX(b)\to x}(R)\right) = \gamma_{y, MAX(b)\to x}\left(\gamma_{MIN(a)\to y, \ b}(R)\right)$.

!! Exercise 16.2.8: The join-like operators of Exercise 15.2.3 obey some of the familiar laws, and others do not. Tell whether each of the following is or is not true. Give either a proof that the law holds or a counterexample.

   a) $R \bowtie S = S \bowtie R$.

   b) $\sigma_C(R \bowtie S) = \sigma_C(R) \bowtie S$.

   c) $\sigma_C(R \overset{\circ}{\bowtie} S) = \sigma_C(R) \overset{\circ}{\bowtie} S$.

   d) $\sigma_C(R \overset{\circ}{\bowtie}_L S) = \sigma_C(R) \overset{\circ}{\bowtie}_L S$, where C involves only attributes of R.

   e) $\sigma_C(R \overset{\circ}{\bowtie}_L S) = R \overset{\circ}{\bowtie}_L \sigma_C(S)$, where C involves only attributes of S.

   f) $\pi_L(R \overline{\bowtie} S) = \pi_L(R) \overline{\bowtie} S$.

   g) $(R \overset{\circ}{\bowtie} S) \overset{\circ}{\bowtie} T = R \overset{\circ}{\bowtie} (S \overset{\circ}{\bowtie} T)$.

   h) $R \overset{\circ}{\bowtie} S = S \overset{\circ}{\bowtie} R$.

   i) $R \overset{\circ}{\bowtie}_L S = S \overset{\circ}{\bowtie}_L R$.

!! Exercise 16.2.9: While it is not precisely an algebraic law, because it involves an indeterminate number of operands, it is generally true that

$$\text{SUM}(a_1, a_2, \dots, a_n) = a_1 + a_2 + \dots + a_n$$

SQL has both a SUM operator and addition for integers and reals. Considering the possibility that one or more of the a_i's could be NULL, rather than an integer or real, does this "law" hold in SQL?

! Exercise 16.2.10: We mentioned in Example 16.14 that none of the plans we showed is necessarily the best plan. Can you think of a better plan?

16.3 From Parse Trees to Logical Query Plans

We now resume our discussion of the query compiler. Having constructed a parse tree for a query in Section 16.1, we next need to turn the parse tree into the preferred logical query plan. There are two steps, as was suggested in Fig. 16.1.

The first step is to replace the nodes and structures of the parse tree, in appropriate groups, by an operator or operators of relational algebra. We shall suggest some of these rules and leave some others for exercises. The second step is to take the relational-algebra expression produced by the first step and to turn it into an expression that we expect can be converted to the most efficient physical query plan.

16.3.1 Conversion to Relational Algebra

We shall now describe informally some rules for transforming SQL parse trees to algebraic logical query plans. The first rule, perhaps the most important, allows us to convert all "simple" select-from-where constructs to relational algebra directly. Its informal statement:

- If we have a <Query> with a <Condition> that has no subqueries, then we may replace the entire construct — the select-list, from-list, and condition — by a relational-algebra expression consisting, from bottom to top, of:

  1. The product of all the relations mentioned in the <FromList>, which is the argument of:

  2. A selection σ_C, where C is the <Condition> expression in the construct being replaced, which in turn is the argument of:

  3. A projection π_L, where L is the list of attributes in the <SelList>.

Example 16.15: Let us consider the parse tree of Fig. 16.5. The select-from-where transformation applies to the entire tree of Fig. 16.5. We take the product of the two relations StarsIn and MovieStar of the from-list, select for the condition in the subtree rooted at <Condition>, and project onto the select-list, movieTitle. The resulting relational-algebra expression is Fig. 16.16.

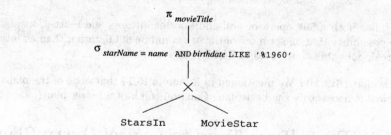

Figure 16.16: Translation of a parse tree to an algebraic expression tree

The same transformation does not apply to the outer query of Fig. 16.3. The reason is that the condition involves a subquery, a matter we defer to Section 16.3.2. However, we can apply the transformation to the subquery in

---

Limitations on Selection Conditions

One might wonder why we do not allow C, in a selection operator σ_C, to involve a subquery. It is conventional in relational algebra for the *arguments* of an operator — the elements that do not appear in subscripts — to be expressions that yield relations. On the other hand, *parameters* — the elements that appear in subscripts — have a type other than relations. For instance, parameter C in σ_C is a boolean-valued condition, and parameter L in π_L is a list of attributes or formulas.

If we follow this convention, then whatever calculation is implied by a parameter can be applied to each tuple of the relation argument(s). That limitation on the use of parameters simplifies query optimization. Suppose, in contrast, that we allowed an operator like $\sigma_C(R)$, where C involves a subquery. Then the application of C to each tuple of R involves computing the subquery. Do we compute it anew for every tuple of R? That would be unnecessarily expensive, unless the subquery were *correlated*, i.e., its value depends on something defined outside the query, as the subquery of Fig. 16.3 depends on the value of starName. Even correlated subqueries can be evaluated without recomputation for each tuple, in most cases, provided we organize the computation correctly.

Fig. 16.3. The expression of relational algebra that we get from the subquery is $\pi_{name}\left(\sigma_{birthdate\ \text{LIKE}\ \text{'%1960'}}(\text{MovieStar})\right)$. □

16.3.2 Removing Subqueries From Conditions

For parse trees with a <Condition> that has a subquery, we shall introduce an intermediate form of operator, between the syntactic categories of the parse tree and the relational-algebra operators that apply to relations. This operator is often called *two-argument selection*. We shall represent a two-argument selection in a transformed parse tree by a node labeled σ, with no parameter. Below this node is a left child that represents the relation R upon which the selection is being performed, and a right child that is an expression for the condition applied to each tuple of R. Both arguments may be represented as parse trees, as expression trees, or as a mixture of the two.

Example 16.16: In Fig. 16.17 is a rewriting of the parse tree of Fig. 16.3 that uses a two-argument selection. Several transformations have been made to construct Fig. 16.17 from Fig. 16.3:

1. The subquery in Fig. 16.3 has been replaced by an expression of relational algebra, as discussed at the end of Example 16.15.

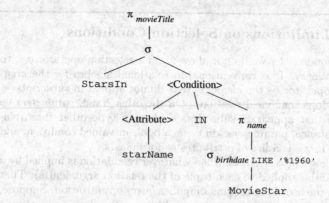

Figure 16.17: An expression using a two-argument σ, midway between a parse tree and relational algebra

2. The outer query has also been replaced, using the rule for select-from-where expressions from Section 16.3.1. However, we have expressed the necessary selection as a two-argument selection, rather than by the conventional σ operator of relational algebra. As a result, the upper node of the parse tree labeled <Condition> has not been replaced, but remains as an argument of the selection, with its parentheses and <Query> replaced by relational algebra, per point (1).

This tree needs further transformation, which we discuss next.   □

We need rules that allow us to replace a two-argument selection by a one-argument selection and other operators of relational algebra. Each form of condition may require its own rule. In common situations, it is possible to remove the two-argument selection and reach an expression that is pure relational algebra. However, in extreme cases, the two-argument selection can be left in place and considered part of the logical query plan.

We shall give, as an example, the rule that lets us deal with the condition in Fig. 16.17 involving the IN operator. Note that the subquery in this condition is uncorrelated; that is, the subquery's relation can be computed once and for all, independent of the tuple being tested. The rule for eliminating such a condition is stated informally as follows:

• Suppose we have a two-argument selection in which the first argument represents some relation R and the second argument is a <Condition> of the form t IN S, where expression S is an uncorrelated subquery, and t is a tuple composed of (some) attributes of R. We transform the tree as follows:

   a) Replace the <Condition> by the tree that is the expression for S. If S may have duplicates, then it is necessary to include a δ operation at the root of the expression for S, so the expression being formed does not produce more copies of tuples than the original query does.

  b) Replace the two-argument selection by a one-argument selection σ_C, where C is the condition that equates each component of the tuple t to the corresponding attribute of the relation S.

  c) Give σ_C an argument that is the product of R and S.

Figure 16.18 illustrates this transformation.

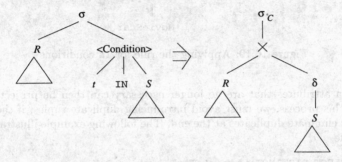

Figure 16.18: This rule handles a two-argument selection with a condition involving IN

Example 16.17: Consider the tree of Fig. 16.17, to which we shall apply the rule for IN conditions described above. In this figure, relation R is StarsIn, and relation S is the result of the relational-algebra expression consisting of the subtree rooted at π_{name}. The tuple t has one component, the attribute starName.

The two-argument selection is replaced by $\sigma_{starName=name}$; its condition C equates the one component of tuple t to the attribute of the result of query S. The child of the σ node is a × node, and the arguments of the × node are the node labeled StarsIn and the root of the expression for S. Notice that, because name is the key for MovieStar, there is no need to introduce a duplicate-eliminating δ in the expression for S. The new expression is shown in Fig. 16.19. It is completely in relational algebra, and is equivalent to the expression of Fig. 16.16, although its structure is quite different. □

The strategy for translating subqueries to relational algebra is more complex when the subquery is correlated. Since correlated subqueries involve unknown values defined outside themselves, they cannot be translated in isolation. Rather, we need to translate the subquery so that it produces a relation in which certain extra attributes appear — the attributes that must later be compared with the externally defined attributes. The conditions that relate attributes from the subquery to attributes outside are then applied to this relation, and

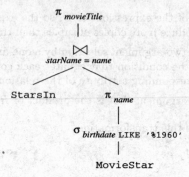

Figure 16.19: Applying the rule for IN conditions

the extra attributes that are no longer necessary can then be projected out.
During this process, we must avoid introducing duplicate tuples, if the query
does not eliminate duplicates at the end. The following example illustrates this
technique.

```
SELECT DISTINCT m1.movieTitle, m1.movieYear
FROM StarsIn m1
WHERE m1.movieYear - 40 <= (
    SELECT AVG(birthdate)
    FROM StarsIn m2, MovieStar s
    WHERE m2.starName = s.name AND
        m1.movieTitle = m2.movieTitle AND
        m1.movieYear = m2.movieYear
);
```

Figure 16.20: Finding movies with high average star age

Example 16.18: Figure 16.20 is a SQL rendition of the query: "find the
movies where the average age of the stars was at most 40 when the movie was
made." To simplify, we treat birthdate as a birth year, so we can take its
average and get a value that can be compared with the movieYear attribute of
StarsIn. We have also written the query so that each of the three references
to relations has its own tuple variable, in order to help remind us where the
various attributes come from.

Fig. 16.21 shows the result of parsing the query and performing a partial
translation to relational algebra. During this initial translation, we split the
WHERE-clause of the subquery in two, and used part of it to convert the product
of relations to an equijoin. We have retained the aliases m1, m2, and s in
the nodes of this tree, in order to make clearer the origin of each attribute.

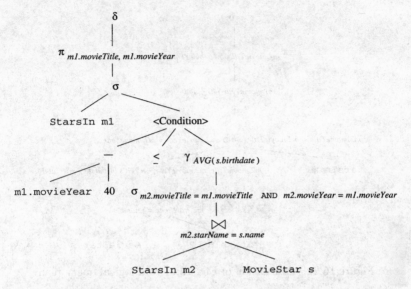

Figure 16.21: Partially transformed parse tree for Fig. 16.20

Alternatively, we could have used projections to rename attributes and thus avoid conflicting attribute names, but the result would be harder to follow.

In order to remove the <Condition> node and eliminate the two-argument σ, we need to create an expression that describes the relation in the right branch of the <Condition>. However, because the subquery is correlated, there is no way to obtain the attributes m1.movieTitle or m1.movieYear from the relations mentioned in the subquery, which are StarsIn (with alias m2) and MovieStar. Thus, we need to defer the selection

$$\sigma_{m2.movieTitle=m1.movieTitle \text{ AND } m2.movieYear=m1.movieYear}$$

until after the relation from the subquery is combined with the copy of StarsIn from the outer query (the copy aliased m1). To transform the logical query plan in this way, we need to modify the γ to group by the attributes m2.movieTitle and m2.movieYear, so these attributes will be available when needed by the selection. The net effect is that we compute for the subquery a relation consisting of movies, each represented by its title and year, and the average star birth year for that movie.

The modified group-by operator appears in Fig. 16.22; in addition to the two grouping attributes, we need to rename the average abd (average birthdate) so we can refer to it later. Figure 16.22 also shows the complete translation to relational algebra. Above the γ, the StarsIn from the outer query is joined with the result of the subquery. The selection from the subquery is then applied to the product of StarsIn and the result of the subquery; we show this selection as

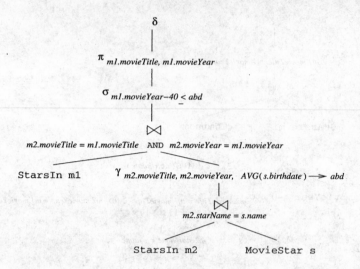

Figure 16.22: Translation of Fig. 16.21 to a logical query plan

a theta-join, which it would become after normal application of algebraic laws. Above the theta-join is another selection, this one corresponding to the selection of the outer query, in which we compare the movie's year to the average birth year of its stars. The algebraic expression finishes at the top like the expression of Fig. 16.21, with the projection onto the desired attributes and the elimination of duplicates.

As we shall see in Section 16.3.3, there is much more that a query optimizer can do to improve the query plan. This particular example satisfies three conditions that let us improve the plan considerably. The conditions are:

1. Duplicates are eliminated at the end,

2. Star names from StarsIn m1 are projected out, and

3. The join between StarsIn m1 and the rest of the expression equates the title and year attributes from StarsIn m1 and StarsIn m2.

Because these conditions hold, we can replace all uses of m1.movieTitle and m1.movieYear by m2.movieTitle and m2.movieYear, respectively. Thus, the upper join in Fig. 16.22 is unnecessary, as is the argument StarsIn m1. This logical query plan is shown in Fig. 16.23. □

16.3.3 Improving the Logical Query Plan

When we convert our query to relational algebra we obtain one possible logical query plan. The next step is to rewrite the plan using the algebraic laws outlined

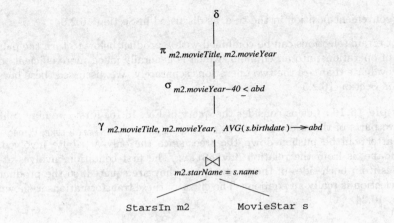

Figure 16.23: Simplification of Fig. 16.22

in Section 16.2. Alternatively, we could generate more than one logical plan, representing different orders or combinations of operators. But in this book we shall assume that the query rewriter chooses a single logical query plan that it believes is "best," meaning that it is likely to result ultimately in the cheapest physical plan.

We do, however, leave open the matter of what is known as "join ordering," so a logical query plan that involves joining relations can be thought of as a family of plans, corresponding to the different ways a join could be ordered and grouped. We discuss choosing a join order in Section 16.6. Similarly, a query plan involving three or more relations that are arguments to the other associative and commutative operators, such as union, should be assumed to allow reordering and regrouping as we convert the logical plan to a physical plan. We begin discussing the issues regarding ordering and physical plan selection in Section 16.4.

There are a number of algebraic laws from Section 16.2 that tend to improve logical query plans. The following are most commonly used in optimizers:

- Selections can be pushed down the expression tree as far as they can go. If a selection condition is the AND of several conditions, then we can split the condition and push each piece down the tree separately. This strategy is probably the most effective improvement technique, but we should recall the discussion in Section 16.2.3, where we saw that in some circumstances it was necessary to push the selection up the tree first.

- Similarly, projections can be pushed down the tree, or new projections can be added. As with selections, the pushing of projections should be done with care, as discussed in Section 16.2.4.

- Duplicate eliminations can sometimes be removed, or moved to a more convenient position in the tree, as discussed in Section 16.2.6.

- Certain selections can be combined with a product below to turn the pair of operations into an equijoin, which is generally much more efficient to evaluate than are the two operations separately. We discussed these laws in Section 16.2.5.

Example 16.19: Let us consider the query of Fig. 16.16. First, we may split the two parts of the selection into $\sigma_{starName=name}$ and $\sigma_{birthdate\ \text{LIKE}\ \text{'%1960'}}$. The latter can be pushed down the tree, since the only attribute involved, `birthdate`, is from the relation `MovieStar`. The first condition involves attributes from both sides of the product, but they are equated, so the product and selection is really an equijoin. The effect of these transformations is shown in Fig. 16.24. □

Figure 16.24: The effect of query rewriting

16.3.4 Grouping Associative/Commutative Operators

An operator that is associative and commutative operators may be thought of as having any number of operands. Thinking of an operator such as join as having any number of operands lets us reorder those operands so that when the multiway join is executed as a sequence of binary joins, they take less time than if we had executed the joins in the order implied by the parse tree. We discuss ordering multiway joins in Section 16.6.

Thus, we shall perform a last step before producing the final logical query plan: for each portion of the subtree that consists of nodes with the same associative and commutative operator, we group the nodes with these operators into a single node with many children. Recall that the usual associative/commutative operators are natural join, union, and intersection. Natural joins and theta-joins can also be combined with each other under certain circumstances:

1. We must replace the natural joins with theta-joins that equate the attributes of the same name.

2. We must add a projection to eliminate duplicate copies of attributes involved in a natural join that has become a theta-join.

3. The theta-join conditions must be associative. Recall there are cases, as discussed in Section 16.2.1, where theta-joins are not associative.

In addition, products can be considered as a special case of natural join and combined with joins if they are adjacent in the tree. Figure 16.25 illustrates this transformation in a situation where the logical query plan has a cluster of two union operators and a cluster of three natural join operators. Note that the letters R through W stand for any expressions, not necessarily for stored relations.

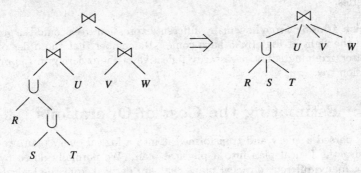

Figure 16.25: Final step in producing the logical query plan: group the associative and commutative operators

16.3.5 Exercises for Section 16.3

Exercise 16.3.1: Convert to relational algebra your parse trees from Exercise 16.1.3(a) and (b). For (a), show both the form with a two-argument selection and its eventual conversion to a one-argument (conventional σ_C) selection.

Exercise 16.3.2: Replace the natural joins in the following expressions by equivalent theta-joins and projections. Tell whether the resulting theta-joins form a commutative and associative group.

a) $\big(R(a,b) \bowtie S(b,c)\big) \bowtie \big(T(c,d) \bowtie U(d,e)\big)$.

b) $\big(R(a,b) \bowtie S(b,c)\big) \bowtie \big(T(c,d) \bowtie U(a,d)\big)$.

c) $\big(R(a,b) \bowtie S(b,c)\big) \bowtie_{R.a<T.c} T(c,d)$.

! **Exercise 16.3.3:** Give a rule for converting each of the following forms of <Condition> to relational algebra. All conditions may be assumed to be applied (by a two-argument selection) to a relation R. You may assume that the subquery is not correlated with R. Be careful that you do not introduce or eliminate duplicates in opposition to the formal definition of SQL.

a) A condition of the form $a =$ ANY $<$Query$>$, where a is an attribute of R.

b) A condition of the form $a =$ ALL $<$Query$>$, where a is an attribute of R.

c) A condition of the form EXISTS($<$Query$>$).

!! **Exercise 16.3.4:** Repeat Exercise 16.3.3, but allow the subquery to be corollated with R. For simplicity, you may assume that the subquery has the simple form of select-from-where expression described in this section, with *no* further subqueries.

!! **Exercise 16.3.5:** From how many different expression trees could the grouped tree on the right of Fig. 16.25 have come? Remember that the order of children after grouping is not necessarily reflective of the ordering in the original expression tree.

16.4   Estimating the Cost of Operations

Having parsed a query and transformed it into a logical query plan, we must next turn the logical plan into a physical plan. We normally do so by considering many different physical plans that are derived from the logical plan, and evaluating or estimating the cost of each. After this evaluation, often called *cost-based enumeration*, we pick the physical query plan with the least estimated cost; that plan is the one passed to the query-execution engine. When enumerating possible physical plans derivable from a given logical plan, we select for each physical plan:

1. An order and grouping for associative-and-commutative operations like joins, unions, and intersections.

2. An algorithm for each operator in the logical plan, for instance, deciding whether a nested-loop join or a hash-join should be used.

3. Additional operators — scanning, sorting, and so on — that are needed for the physical plan but that were not present explicitly in the logical plan.

4. The way in which arguments are passed from one operator to the next, for instance, by storing the intermediate result on disk or by using iterators and passing an argument one tuple or one main-memory buffer at a time.

To make each of these choices, we need to understand what the costs of the various physical plans are. We cannot know these costs exactly without executing the plan. But almost always, the cost of executing a query plan is

---

Review of Notation

Recall from Section 15.1.3 the following size parameters:

- $B(R)$ is the number of blocks needed to hold relation R.

- $T(R)$ is the number of tuples of relation R.

- $V(R, a)$ is the *value count* for attribute a of relation R, that is, the number of distinct values relation R has in attribute a. Also, $V(R, [a_1, a_2, \ldots, a_n])$ is the number of distinct values R has when all of attributes $a_1, a_2, \ldots, a_n$ are considered together, that is, the number of tuples in $\delta\big(\pi_{a_1, a_2, \ldots, a_n}(R)\big)$.

---

significantly greater than all the work done by the query compiler in selecting a plan. Thus, we do not want to execute more than one plan for one query, and we are forced to estimate the cost of any plan without executing it.

Therefore, our first problem is how to estimate costs of plans accurately. Such estimates are based on parameters of the data (see the box on "Review of Notation") that must be either computed exactly from the data or estimated by a process of "statistics gathering" that we discuss in Section 16.5.1. Given values for these parameters, we may make a number of reasonable estimates of relation sizes that can be used to predict the cost of a complete physical plan.

16.4.1 Estimating Sizes of Intermediate Relations

The physical plan is selected to minimize the estimated cost of evaluating the query. No matter what method is used for executing query plans, and no matter how costs of query plans are estimated, the sizes of intermediate relations of the plan have a profound influence on costs. Ideally, we want rules for estimating the number of tuples in an intermediate relation so that the rules:

1. Give accurate estimates.

2. Are easy to compute.

3. Are logically consistent; that is, the size estimate for an intermediate relation should not depend on how that relation is computed. For instance, the size estimate for a join of several relations should not depend on the order in which we join the relations.

There is no universally agreed-upon way to meet these three conditions. We shall give some simple rules that serve in most situations. Fortunately, the goal of size estimation is not to predict the exact size; it is to help select a physical query plan. Even an inaccurate size-estimation method will serve that purpose well if it errs consistently, that is, if the size estimator assigns the least cost to the best physical query plan, even if the actual cost of that plan turns out to be different from what was predicted.

16.4.2 Estimating the Size of a Projection

The extended projection of Section 5.2.5 is a bag projection and does not eliminate duplicates. We shall treat a clasical, duplicate-eliminating projection as a bag-projection followed by a δ. The extended projection of bags is different from the other operators, in that the size of the result is computable exactly. Normally, tuples shrink during a projection, as some components are eliminated. However, the extended projection allows the creation of new components that are combinations of attributes, and so there are situations where a π operator actually increases the size of the relation.

Example 16.20: Suppose $R(a, b, c)$ is a relation, where a and b are integers of four bytes each, and c is a string of 100 bytes. Let tuple headers require 12 bytes. Then each tuple of R requires 120 bytes. Let blocks be 1024 bytes long, with block headers of 24 bytes. We can thus fit 8 tuples in one block. Suppose $T(R) = 10,000$; i.e., there are 10,000 tuples in R. Then $B(R) = 1250$.

Consider $S = \pi_{a+b \to x, c}(R)$; that is, we replace a and b by their sum. Tuples of S require 116 bytes: 12 for header, 4 for the sum, and 100 for the string. Although tuples of S are slightly smaller than tuples of R, we can still fit only 8 tuples in a block. Thus, $T(S) = 10,000$ and $B(S) = 1250$.

Now consider $U = \pi_{a,b}(R)$, where we eliminate the string component. Tuples of U are only 20 bytes long. $T(U)$ is still 10,000. However, we can now pack 50 tuples of U into one block, so $B(U) = 200$. This projection thus shrinks the relation by a factor slightly more than 6. $\square$

16.4.3 Estimating the Size of a Selection

When we perform a selection, we generally reduce the number of tuples, although the sizes of tuples remain the same. In the simplest kind of selection, where an attribute is equated to a constant, there is an easy way to estimate the size of the result, provided we know, or can estimate, the number of different values the attribute has. Let $S = \sigma_{A=c}(R)$, where A is an attribute of R and c is a constant. Then we recommend as an estimate:

- $T(S) = T(R)/V(R, A)$

This rule surely holds if the value of A is chosen randomly from among all the possible values.

The size estimate is more problematic when the selection involves an inequality comparison, for instance, $S = \sigma_{a<10}(R)$. One might think that on the average, half the tuples would satisfy the comparison and half not, so $T(R)/2$

The Zipfian Distribution

In estimating the size of a selection $\sigma_{A=c}$ it is not necessary to assume that values of A appear equally often. In fact, many attributes have values whose occurrences follow a *Zipfian distribution*, where the frequencies of the ith most common values are in proportion to $1/\sqrt{i}$. For example, if the most common value appears 1000 times, then the second most common value would be expected to appear about $1000/\sqrt{2}$ times, or 707 times, and the third most common value would appear about $1000/\sqrt{3}$ times, or 577 times. Originally postulated as a way to describe the relative frequencies of words in English sentences, this distribution has been found to appear in many sorts of data. For example, in the US, state populations follow an approximate Zipfian distribution. The three most populous states, California, Texas, and New York, have populations in ratio approximately 1:0.62:0.56, compared with the Zipfian ideal of 1:0.71:0.58. Thus, if state were an attribute of a relation describing US people, say a list of magazine subscribers, we would expect the values of state to distribute in the Zipfian, rather than uniform manner.

As long as the constant in the selection condition is chosen randomly, it doesn't matter whether the values of the attribute involved have a uniform, Zipfian, or other distribution; the *average* size of the matching set will still be $T(R)/V(R,a)$. However, if the constants are also chosen with a Zipfian distribution, then we would expect the average size of the selected set to be somewhat larger than $T(R)/V(R,a)$.

---

would estimate the size of S. However, there is an intuition that queries involving an inequality tend to retrieve a small fraction of the possible tuples.[3] Thus, we propose a rule that acknowledges this tendency, and assumes the typical inequality will return about one third of the tuples, rather than half the tuples. If $S = \sigma_{a<c}(R)$, then our estimate for $T(S)$ is:

- $T(S) = T(R)/3$

The case of a "not equals" comparison is rare. However, should we encounter a selection like $S = \sigma_{a\neq 10}(R)$, we recommend assuming that essentially all tuples will satisfy the condition. That is, take $T(S) = T(R)$ as an estimate. Alternatively, we may use $T(S) = T(R)\big(V(R,a)-1\big)/V(R,a)$, which is slightly less, as an estimate, acknowledging that about fraction $1/V(R,a)$ tuples of R will fail to meet the condition because their a-value *does* equal the constant.

When the selection condition C is the AND of several equalities and inequalities, we can treat the selection $\sigma_C(R)$ as a cascade of simple selections, each of

---

[3]For instance, if you had data about faculty salaries, would you be more likely to query for those faculty who made *less* than $200,000 or *more* than $200,000?

which checks for one of the conditions. Note that the order in which we place these selections doesn't matter. The effect will be that the size estimate for the result is the size of the original relation multiplied by the *selectivity* factor for each condition. That factor is 1/3 for any inequality, 1 for $\neq$, and $1/V(R, A)$ for any attribute A that is compared to a constant in the condition C.

Example 16.21: Let $R(a, b, c)$ be a relation, and $S = \sigma_{a=10 \text{ AND } b<20}(R)$. Also, let $T(R) = 10,000$, and $V(R, a) = 50$. Then our best estimate of $T(S)$ is $T(R)/(50 \times 3)$, or 67. That is, 1/50th of the tuples of R will survive the $a = 10$ filter, and 1/3 of those will survive the $b < 20$ filter.

An interesting special case where our analysis breaks down is when the condition is contradictory. For instance, consider $S = \sigma_{a=10 \text{ AND } a>20}(R)$. According to our rule, $T(S) = T(R)/3V(R, a)$, or 67 tuples. However, it should be clear that no tuple can have both $a = 10$ and $a > 20$, so the correct answer is $T(S) = 0$. When rewriting the logical query plan, the query optimizer can look for instances of many special-case rules. In the above instance, the optimizer can apply a rule that finds the selection condition logically equivalent to FALSE and replaces the expression for S by the empty set. □

When a selection involves an OR of conditions, say $S = \sigma_{C_1 \text{ OR } C_2}(R)$, then we have less certainty about the size of the result. One simple assumption is that no tuple will satisfy both conditions, so the size of the result is the sum of the number of tuples that satisfy each. That measure is generally an overestimate, and in fact can sometimes lead us to the absurd conclusion that there are more tuples in S than in the original relation R.

A less simple, but possibly more accurate estimate of the size of

$$S = \sigma_{C_1 \text{ OR } C_2}(R)$$

is to assume that C_1 and C_2 are independent. Then, if R has n tuples, m_1 of which satisfy C_1 and m_2 of which satisfy C_2, we would estimate the number of tuples in S as $n\bigl(1 - (1 - m_1/n)(1 - m_2/n)\bigr)$. In explanation, $1 - m_1/n$ is the fraction of tuples that do not satisfy C_1, and $1 - m_2/n$ is the fraction that do not satisfy C_2. The product of these numbers is the fraction of R's tuples that are *not* in S, and 1 minus this product is the fraction that are in S.

Example 16.22: Suppose $R(a, b)$ has $T(R) = 10,000$ tuples, and

$$S = \sigma_{a=10 \text{ OR } b<20}(R)$$

Let $V(R, a) = 50$. Then the number of tuples that satisfy $a = 10$ we estimate at 200, i.e., $T(R)/V(R, a)$. The number of tuples that satisfy $b < 20$ we estimate at $T(R)/3$, or 3333.

The simplest estimate for the size of S is the sum of these numbers, or 3533. The more complex estimate based on independence of the conditions $a = 10$ and $b < 20$ gives $10000\bigl(1 - (1 - 200/10000)(1 - 3333/10000)\bigr)$, or 3466. In this case, there is little difference between the two estimates, and it is very unlikely that choosing one over the other would change our estimate of the best physical query plan. □

The final operator that could appear in a selection condition is NOT. The estimated number of tuples of R that satisfy condition NOT C is $T(R)$ minus the estimated number that satisfy C.

16.4.4 Estimating the Size of a Join

We shall consider here only the natural join. Other joins can be handled according to the following outline:

1. The number of tuples in the result of an equijoin can be computed exactly as for a natural join, after accounting for the change in variable names. Example 16.24 will illustrate this point.

2. Other theta-joins can be estimated as if they were a selection following a product. Note that the number of tuples in a product is the product of the number of tuples in the relations involved.

We shall begin our study with the assumption that the natural join of two relations involves only the equality of two attributes. That is, we study the join $R(X, Y) \bowtie S(Y, Z)$, but initially we assume that Y is a single attribute although X and Z can represent any set of attributes.

The problem is that we don't know how the Y-values in R and S relate. For instance:

1. The two relations could have disjoint sets of Y-values, in which case the join is empty and $T(R \bowtie S) = 0$.

2. Y might be the key of S and the corresponding foreign key of R, so each tuple of R joins with exactly one tuple of S, and $T(R \bowtie S) = T(R)$.

3. Almost all the tuples of R and S could have the same Y-value, in which case $T(R \bowtie S)$ is about $T(R)T(S)$.

To focus on the most common situations, we shall make two simplifying assumptions:

- *Containment of Value Sets.* If Y is an attribute appearing in several relations, then each relation chooses its values from the front of a fixed list of values $y_1, y_2, y_3, \ldots$ and has all the values in that prefix. As a consequence, if R and S are two relations with an attribute Y, and $V(R, Y) \leq V(S, Y)$, then every Y-value of R will be a Y-value of S.

- *Preservation of Value Sets.* If we join a relation R with another relation, then an attribute A that is not a join attribute (i.e., not present in both relations) does not lose values from its set of possible values. More precisely, if A is an attribute of R but not of S, then $V(R \bowtie S, A) = V(R, A)$.

Assumption (1), containment of value sets, clearly might be violated, but it *is* satisfied when Y is a key in S and the corresponding foreign key in R. It also is approximately true in many other cases, since we would intuitively expect that if S has many Y-values, then a given Y-value that appears in R has a good chance of appearing in S.

Assumption (2), preservation of value sets, also might be violated, but it is true when the join attribute(s) of $R \bowtie S$ are a key for S and the corresponding foreign key of R. In fact, (2) can only be violated when there are "dangling tuples" in R, that is, tuples of R that join with no tuple of S; and even if there *are* dangling tuples in R, the assumption might still hold.

Under these assumptions, we can estimate the size of $R(X, Y) \bowtie S(Y, Z)$ as follows. Suppose r is a tuple in R, and S is a tuple in S. What is the probability that r and s agree on attribute Y? Suppose that $V(R, Y) \geq V(S, Y)$. Then the Y-value of s is surely one of the Y values that appear in R, by the containment-of-value-sets assumption. Hence, the chance that r has the same Y-value as s is $1/V(R, Y)$. Similarly, if $V(R, Y) < V(S, Y)$, then the value of Y in r will appear in S, and the probability is $1/V(S, Y)$ that r and s will share the same Y-value. In general, we see that the probability of agreement on the Y value is $1/\max(V(R, Y), V(S, Y))$. Thus:

- $T(R \bowtie S) = T(R)T(S)/\max(V(R, Y), V(S, Y))$

That is, the estimated number of tuples in $T(R \bowtie S)$ is the number of pairs of tuples — one from R and one from S, times the probability that such a pair shares a common Y value.

Example 16.23: Let us consider the following three relations and their important statistics:

$R(a, b)$	$S(b, c)$	$U(c, d)$
$T(R) = 1000$	$T(S) = 2000$	$T(U) = 5000$
$V(R, b) = 20$	$V(S, b) = 50$	
	$V(S, c) = 100$	$V(U, c) = 500$

Suppose we want to compute the natural join $R \bowtie S \bowtie U$. One way is to group R and S first, as $(R \bowtie S) \bowtie U$. Our estimate for $T(R \bowtie S)$ is $T(R)T(S)/\max(V(R, b), V(S, b))$, which is $1000 \times 2000/50$, or 40,000.

We then need to join $R \bowtie S$ with U. Our estimate for the size of the result is $T(R \bowtie S)T(U)/\max(V(R \bowtie S, c), V(U, c))$. By our assumption that value sets are preserved, $V(R \bowtie S, c)$ is the same as $V(S, c)$, or 100; that is no values of attribute c disappeared when we performed the join. In that case, we get as our estimate for the number of tuples in $R \bowtie S \bowtie U$ the value $40{,}000 \times 5000/\max(100, 500)$, or 400,000.

We could also start by joining S and U. If we do, then we get the estimate $T(S \bowtie U) = T(S)T(U)/\max(V(S, c), V(U, c)) = 2000 \times 5000/500 = 20{,}000$.

By our assumption that value sets are preserved, $V(S \bowtie U, b) = V(S, b) = 50$, so the estimated size of the result is

$$T(R)T(S \bowtie U) / \max(V(R, b), V(S \bowtie U, b))$$

which is $1000 \times 20{,}000/50$, or $400{,}000$. □

16.4.5 Natural Joins With Multiple Join Attributes

When the set of attributes Y in the join $R(X, Y) \bowtie S(Y, Z)$ consists of more than one attribute, the same argument as we used for a single attribute Y applies to each attribute in Y. That is:

- The estimate of the size of $R \bowtie S$ is computed by multiplying $T(R)$ by $T(S)$ and dividing by the larger of $V(R, y)$ and $V(S, y)$ for each attribute y that is common to R and S.

Example 16.24: The following example uses the rule above. It also illustrates that the analysis we have been doing for natural joins applies to any equijoin. Consider the join

$$R(a, b, c) \bowtie_{R.b=S.d \text{ AND } R.c=S.e} S(d, e, f)$$

Suppose we have the following size parameters:

$R(a, b, c)$	$S(d, e, f)$
$T(R) = 1000$	$T(S) = 2000$
$V(R, b) = 20$	$V(S, d) = 50$
$V(R, c) = 100$	$V(S, e) = 50$

We can think of this join as a natural join if we regard $R.b$ and $S.d$ as the same attribute and also regard $R.c$ and $S.e$ as the same attribute. Then the rule given above tells us the estimate for the size of $R \bowtie S$ is the product 1000×2000 divided by the larger of 20 and 50 and also divided by the larger of 100 and 50. Thus, the size estimate for the join is $1000 \times 2000/(50 \times 100) = 400$ tuples. □

Example 16.25: Let us reconsider Example 16.23, but consider the third possible order for the joins, where we first take $R(a, b) \bowtie U(c, d)$. This join is actually a product, and the number of tuples in the result is $T(R)T(U) = 1000 \times 5000 = 5{,}000{,}000$. Note that the number of different b's in the product is $V(R, b) = 20$, and the number of different c's is $V(U, c) = 500$.

When we join this product with $S(b, c)$, we multiply the numbers of tuples and divide by both $\max(V(R, b), V(S, b))$ and $\max(V(U, c), V(S, c))$. This quantity is $2000 \times 5{,}000{,}000/(50 \times 500) = 400{,}000$. Note that this third way of joining gives the same estimate for the size of the result that we found in Example 16.23. □

16.4.6 Joins of Many Relations

Finally, let us consider the general case of a natural join:

$$S = R_1 \bowtie R_2 \bowtie \cdots \bowtie R_n$$

Suppose that attribute A appears in k of the R_i's, and the numbers of its sets of values in these k relations — that is, the various values of $V(R_i, A)$ for $i = 1, 2, \ldots, k$ — are $v_1 \leq v_2 \leq \cdots \leq v_k$, in order from smallest to largest. Suppose we pick a tuple from each relation. What is the probability that all tuples selected agree on attribute A?

In answer, consider the tuple t_1 chosen from the relation that has the smallest number of A-values, v_1. By the containment-of-value-sets assumption, each of these v_1 values is among the A-values found in the other relations that have attribute A. Consider the relation that has v_i values in attribute A. Its selected tuple t_i has probability $1/v_i$ of agreeing with t_1 on A. Since this claim is true for all $i = 2, 3, \ldots, k$, the probability that all k tuples agree on A is the product $1/v_2 v_3 \cdots v_k$. This analysis gives us the rule for estimating the size of any join.

- Start with the product of the number of tuples in each relation. Then, for each attribute A appearing at least twice, divide by all but the least of the $V(R, A)$'s.

Likewise, we can estimate the number of values that will remain for attribute A after the join. By the preservation-of-value-sets assumption, it is the least of these $V(R, A)$'s.

Example 16.26: Consider the join $R(a, b, c) \bowtie S(b, c, d) \bowtie U(b, e)$, and suppose the important statistics are as given in Fig. 16.26. To estimate the size of this join, we begin by multiplying the relation sizes; $1000 \times 2000 \times 5000$. Next, we look at the attributes that appear more than once; these are b, which appears three times, and c, which appears twice. We divide by the two largest of $V(R, b)$, $V(S, b)$, and $V(U, b)$; these are 50 and 200. Finally, we divide by the larger of $V(R, c)$ and $V(S, c)$, which is 200. The resulting estimate is

$$1000 \times 2000 \times 5000/(50 \times 200 \times 200) = 5000$$

We can also estimate the number of values for each of the attributes in the join. Each estimate is the least value count for the attribute among all the relations in which it appears. These numbers are, for a, b, c, d, e respectively: 100, 20, 100, 400, and 500. □

Based on the two assumptions we have made — containment and preservation of value sets — we have a surprising and convenient property of the estimating rule given above.

- No matter how we group and order the terms in a natural join of n relations, the estimation rules, applied to each join individually, yield the

$R(a, b, c)$	$S(b, c, d)$	$U(b, e)$
$T(R) = 1000$	$T(S) = 2000$	$T(U) = 5000$
$V(R, a) = 100$		
$V(R, b) = 20$	$V(S, b) = 50$	$V(U, b) = 200$
$V(R, c) = 200$	$V(S, c) = 100$	
	$V(S, d) = 400$	
		$V(U, e) = 500$

Figure 16.26: Parameters for Example 16.26

same estimate for the size of the result. Moreover, this estimate is the same that we get if we apply the rule for the join of all n relations as a whole.

Examples 16.23 and 16.25 form an illustration of this rule for the three groupings of a three-relation join, including the grouping where one of the "joins" is actually a product.

16.4.7 Estimating Sizes for Other Operations

We have seen two operations — selection and join — with reasonable estimating techniques. In addition, projections do not change the number of tuples in a relation, and products multiply the numbers of tuples in the argument relations. However, for the remaining operations, the size of the result is not easy to determine. We shall review the other relational-algebra operators and give some suggestions as to how this estimation could be done.

Union

If the bag union is taken, then the size is exactly the sum of the sizes of the arguments. A set union can be as large as the sum of the sizes or as small as the larger of the two arguments. We suggest that something in the middle be chosen, e.g., the larger plus half the smaller.

Intersection

The result can have as few as 0 tuples or as many as the smaller of the two arguments, regardless of whether set- or bag-intersection is taken. One approach is to take the average of the extremes, which is half the smaller.

Difference

When we compute $R - S$, the result can have between $T(R)$ and $T(R) - T(S)$ tuples. We suggest the average as an estimate: $T(R) - T(S)/2$.

Duplicate Elimination

If $R(a_1, a_2, \ldots, a_n)$ is a relation, then $V(R, [a_1, a_2, \ldots, a_n])$ is the size of $\delta(R)$. However, often we shall not have this statistic available, so it must be approximated. In the extremes, the size of $\delta(R)$ could be the same as the size of R (no duplicates) or as small as 1 (all tuples in R are the same).[4] Another upper limit on the number of tuples in $\delta(R)$ is the maximum number of distinct tuples that could exist: the product of $V(R, a_i)$ for $i = 1, 2, \ldots, n$. That number could be smaller than other estimates of $T(\delta(R))$. There are several rules that could be used to estimate $T(\delta(R))$. One reasonable one is to take the smaller of $T(R)/2$ and the product of all the $V(R, a_i)$'s.

Grouping and Aggregation

Suppose we have an expression $\gamma_L(R)$, the size of whose result we need to estimate. If the statistic $V(R, [g_1, g_2, \ldots, g_k])$, where the g_i's are the grouping attributes in L, is available, then that is our answer. However, that statistic may well not be obtainable, so we need another way to estimate the size of $\gamma_L(R)$. The number of tuples in $\gamma_L(R)$ is the same as the number of groups. There could be as few as one group in the result or as many groups as there are tuples in R. As with δ, we can also upper-bound the number of groups by a product of $V(R, A)$'s, but here attribute A ranges over only the grouping attributes of L. We again suggest an estimate that is the smaller of $T(R)/2$ and this product.

16.4.8 Exercises for Section 16.4

Exercise 16.4.1: Below are the vital statistics for four relations, W, X, Y, and Z:

$W(a,b)$	$X(b,c)$	$Y(c,d)$	$Z(d,e)$
$T(W) = 400$	$T(X) = 300$	$T(Y) = 200$	$T(Z) = 100$
$V(W,a) = 50$	$V(X,b) = 60$	$V(Y,c) = 50$	$V(Z,d) = 10$
$V(W,b) = 40$	$V(X,c) = 100$	$V(Y,d) = 20$	$V(Z,e) = 50$

Estimate the sizes of relations that are the results of the following expressions:

(a) $W \bowtie X \bowtie Y \bowtie Z$ (b) $\sigma_{a=10}(W)$ (c) $\sigma_{c=20}(Y)$

(d) $\sigma_{c=20}(Y) \bowtie Z$ (e) $W \times Y$ (f) $\sigma_{d>10}(Z)$

(g) $\sigma_{a=1 \text{ AND } b=2}(W)$ (h) $\sigma_{a=1 \text{ AND } b>2}(W)$ (i) $X \bowtie_{X.c < Y.c} Y$

Exercise 16.4.2: Here are the statistics for four relations E, F, G, and H:

---

[4]Strictly speaking, if R is empty there are no tuples in either R or $\delta(R)$, so the lower bound is 0. However, we are rarely interested in this special case.

$E(a,b,c)$	$F(a,b,d)$	$G(a,c,d)$	$H(b,c,d)$
$T(E) = 1000$	$T(F) = 2000$	$T(G) = 3000$	$T(H) = 4000$
$V(E,a) = 500$	$V(F,a) = 50$	$V(G,a) = 500$	$V(H,b) = 400$
$V(E,b) = 100$	$V(F,b) = 200$	$V(G,c) = 300$	$V(H,c) = 200$
$V(E,c) = 20$	$V(F,d) = 100$	$V(G,d) = 100$	$V(H,d) = 800$

How many tuples does the join of these tuples have, using the techniques for estimation from this section?

!! **Exercise 16.4.3:** Suppose we compute $R(a,b) \bowtie S(a,c)$, where R and S each have 1000 tuples. The a attribute of each relation has 100 different values, and they are the *same* 100 values. If the distribution of values was uniform; i.e., each a-value appeared in exactly 10 tuples of each relation, then there would be 10,000 tuples in the join. Suppose instead that the 100 a-values have the same Zipfian distribution in each relation. Precisely, let the values be $a_1, a_2, \ldots, a_{100}$. Then the number of tuples of both R and S that have a-value a_i is proportional to $1/\sqrt{i}$. Under these circumstances, how many tuples does the join have? You should ignore the fact that the number of tuples with a given a-value may not be an integer.

! **Exercise 16.4.4:** How would you estimate the size of a semijoin?

16.5 Introduction to Cost-Based Plan Selection

Whether selecting a logical query plan or constructing a physical query plan from a logical plan, the query optimizer needs to estimate the cost of evaluating certain expressions. We study the issues involved in cost-based plan selection here, and in Section 16.6 we consider in detail one of the most important and difficult problems in cost-based plan selection: the selection of a join order for several relations.

As before, we shall assume that the "cost" of evaluating an expression is approximated well by the number of disk I/O's performed. The number of disk I/O's, in turn, is influenced by:

1. The particular logical operators chosen to implement the query, a matter decided when we choose the logical query plan.

2. The sizes of intermediate results, whose estimation we discussed in Section 16.4.

3. The physical operators used to implement logical operators, e.g., the choice of a one-pass or two-pass join, or the choice to sort or not sort a given relation; this matter is discussed in Section 16.7.

4. The ordering of similar operations, especially joins as discussed in Section 16.6.

5. The method of passing arguments from one physical operator to the next, which is also discussed in Section 16.7.

Many issues need to be resolved in order to perform effective cost-based plan selection. In this section, we first consider how the size parameters, which were so essential for estimating relation sizes in Section 16.4, can be obtained from the database efficiently. We then revisit the algebraic laws we introduced to find the preferred logical query plan. Cost-based analysis justifies the use of many of the common heuristics for transforming logical query plans, such as pushing selections down the tree. Finally, we consider the various approaches to enumerating all the physical query plans that can be derived from the selected logical plan. Especially important are methods for reducing the number of plans that need to be evaluated, while making it likely that the least-cost plan is still considered.

16.5.1   Obtaining Estimates for Size Parameters

The formulas of Section 16.4 were predicated on knowing certain important parameters, especially $T(R)$, the number of tuples in a relation R, and $V(R, a)$, the number of different values in the column of relation R for attribute a. A modern DBMS generally allows the user or administrator explicitly to request the gathering of statistics, such as $T(R)$ and $V(R, a)$. These statistics are then used in query optimization, unchanged until the next command to gather statistics.

By scanning an entire relation R, it is straightforward to count the number of tuples $T(R)$ and also to discover the number of different values $V(R, a)$ for each attribute a. The number of blocks in which R can fit, $B(R)$, can be estimated either by counting the actual number of blocks used (if R is clustered), or by dividing $T(R)$ by the number of R's tuples that can fit in one block.

In addition, a DBMS may compute a *histogram* of the values for a given attribute. If $V(R, A)$ is not too large, then the histogram may consist of the number (or fraction) of the tuples having each of the values of attribute A. If there are many values of this attribute, then only the most frequent values may be recorded individually, while other values are counted in groups. The most common types of histograms are:

1. *Equal-width.* A width w is chosen, along with a constant v_0. Counts are provided of the number of tuples with values v in the ranges $v_0 \leq v < v_0 + w$, $v_0 + w \leq v < v_0 + 2w$, and so on. The value v_0 may be the lowest possible value or a lower bound on values seen so far. In the latter case, should a new, lower value be seen, we can lower the value of v_0 by w and add a new count to the histogram.

2. *Equal-height.* These are the common "percentiles." We pick some fraction p, and list the lowest value, the value that is fraction p from the lowest, the fraction $2p$ from the lowest, and so on, up to the highest value.

3. *Most-frequent-values.* We may list the most common values and their numbers of occurrences. This information may be provided along with a count of occurrences for all the other values as a group, or we may record frequent values in addition to an equal-width or equal-height histogram for the other values.

One advantage of keeping a histogram is that the sizes of joins can be estimated more accurately than by the simplified methods of Section 16.4. In particular, if a value of the join attribute appears explicitly in the histograms of both relations being joined, then we know exactly how many tuples of the result will have this value. For those values of the join attribute that do not appear explicitly in the histogram of one or both relations, we estimate their effect on the join as in Section 16.4. However, if we use an equal-width histogram, with the same bands for the join attributes of both relations, then we can estimate the size of the joins of corresponding bands, and sum those estimates. The result will be a good estimate, because only tuples in corresponding bands can join. The following examples will suggest how to carry out histogram-based estimation; we shall not use histograms in estimates subsequently.

Example 16.27: Consider histograms that mention the three most frequent values and their counts, and group the remaining values. Suppose we want to compute the join $R(a, b) \bowtie S(b, c)$. Let the histogram for $R.b$ be:

$$1: 200, \quad 0: 150, \quad 5: 100, \quad \text{others: } 550$$

That is, of the 1000 tuples in R, 200 of them have b-value 1, 150 have b-value 0, and 100 have b-value 5. In addition, 550 tuples have b-values other than 0, 1, or 5, and none of these other values appears more than 100 times.

Let the histogram for $S.b$ be:

$$0: 100, \quad 1: 80, \quad 2: 70, \quad \text{others: } 250$$

Suppose also that $V(R, b) = 14$ and $V(S, b) = 13$. That is, the 550 tuples of R with unknown b-values are divided among eleven values, for an average of 50 tuples each, and the 250 tuples of S with unknown b-values are divided among ten values, each with an average of 25 tuples each.

Values 0 and 1 appear explicitly in both histograms, so we can calculate that the 150 tuples of R with $b = 0$ join with the 100 tuples of S having the same b-value, to yield 15,000 tuples in the result. Likewise, the 200 tuples of R with $b = 1$ join with the 80 tuples of S having $b = 1$ to yield 16,000 more tuples in the result.

The estimate of the effect of the remaining tuples is more complex. We shall continue to make the assumption that every value appearing in the relation with the smaller set of values (S in this case) will also appear in the set of values of the other relation. Thus, among the eleven remaining b-values of S, we know one of those values is 2, and we shall assume another of the values is 5, since that is one of the most frequent values in R. We estimate that 2 appears 50 times in R, and 5 appears 25 times in S. These estimates are each obtained by assuming that the value is one of the "other" values for its relation's histogram. The number of additional tuples from b-value 2 is thus $70 \times 50 = 3500$, and the number of additional tuples from b-value 5 is $100 \times 25 = 2500$.

Finally, there are nine other b-values that appear in both relations, and we estimate that each of them appears in 50 tuples of R and 25 tuples of S. Each of the nine values thus contributes $50 \times 25 = 1250$ tuples to the result. The estimate of the output size is thus:

$$15000 + 16000 + 3500 + 2500 + 9 \times 1250$$

or 48,250 tuples. Note that the simpler estimate from Section 16.4 would be $1000 \times 500/14$, or 35,714, based on the assumptions of equal numbers of occurrences of each value in each relation. □

Example 16.28: In this example, we shall assume an equal-width histogram, and we shall demonstrate how knowing that values of two relations are almost disjoint can impact the estimate of a join size. Our relations are:

    Jan(day, temp)
    July(day, temp)

and the query is:

    SELECT Jan.day, July.day
    FROM Jan, July
    WHERE Jan.temp = July.temp;

That is, find pairs of days in January and July that had the same temperature. The query plan is to equijoin Jan and July on the temperature, and project onto the two day attributes.

Suppose the histogram of temperatures for the relations Jan and July are as given in the table of Fig. 16.27.[5] In general, if both join attributes have equal-width histograms with the same set of bands, then we can estimate the size of the join by considering each pair of corresponding bands and summing.

If two corresponding bands have T_1 and T_2 tuples, respectively, and the number of values in a band is V, then the estimate for the number of tuples in the join of those bands is $T_1 T_2 / V$, following the principles laid out in Section 16.4.4. For the histograms of Fig. 16.27, many of these products are 0, because one or the other of T_1 and T_2 is 0. The only bands for which neither is 0 are 40–49 and 50–59. Since $V = 10$ is the width of a band, the 40–49 band contributes $10 \times 5/10 = 5$ tuples, and the 50–59 band contributes $5 \times 20/10 = 10$ tuples.

---

[5] Our friends south of the equator should reverse the columns for January and July, and convert to centigrade as well.

Range	Jan	July
0–9	40	0
10–19	60	0
20–29	80	0
30–39	50	0
40–49	10	5
50–59	5	20
60–69	0	50
70–79	0	100
80–89	0	60
90–99	0	10

Figure 16.27: Histograms of temperature

Thus our estimate for the size of this join is $5 + 10 = 15$ tuples. If we had no histogram, and knew only that each relation had 245 tuples distributed among 100 values from 0 to 99, then our estimate of the join size would be $245 \times 245/100 = 600$ tuples. □

16.5.2 Computation of Statistics

Statistics normally are computed only periodically, for several reasons. First, statistics tend not to change radically in a short time. Second, even somewhat inaccurate statistics are useful as long as they are applied consistently to all the plans. Third, the alternative of keeping statistics up-to-date can make the statistics themselves into a "hot-spot" in the database; because statistics are read frequently, we prefer not to update them frequently too.

The recomputation of statistics might be triggered automatically after some period of time, or after some number of updates. However, a database administrator, noticing that poor-performing query plans are being selected by the query optimizer on a regular basis, might request the recomputation of statistics in an attempt to rectify the problem.

Computing statistics for an entire relation R can be very expensive, particularly if we compute $V(R, a)$ for each attribute a in the relation (or even worse, compute histograms for each a). One common approach is to compute approximate statistics by sampling only a fraction of the data. For example, let us suppose we want to sample a small fraction of the tuples to obtain an estimate for $V(R, a)$. A statistically reliable calculation can be complex, depending on a number of assumptions, such as whether values for a are distributed uniformly, according to a Zipfian distribution, or according to some other distribution. However, the intuition is as follows. If we look at a small sample of R, say 1% of its tuples, and we find that most of the a-values we see are different, then it is likely that $V(R, a)$ is close to $T(R)$. If we find that the sample has very few different values of a, then it is likely that we have seen most of the a-values that exist in the current relation.

16.5.3 Heuristics for Reducing the Cost of Logical Query Plans

One important use of cost estimates for queries or subqueries is in the application of heuristic transformations of the query. We already have observed in Section 16.3.3 how certain heuristics, such as pushing selections down the tree, can be expected almost certainly to improve the cost of a logical query plan, regardless of relation sizes. However, there are other points in the query optimization process where estimating the cost both before and after a transformation will allow us to apply a transformation where it appears to reduce cost and avoid the transformation otherwise. In particular, when the preferred logical query plan is being generated, we may consider a number of optional transformations and the costs before and after.

Because we are estimating the cost of a *logical* query plan, and so we have not yet made decisions about the physical operators that will be used to implement the operators of relational algebra, our cost estimate cannot be based on disk I/O's. Rather, we estimate the sizes of all intermediate results using the techniques of Section 16.4, and their sum is our heuristic estimate for the cost of the entire logical plan. One example will serve to illustrate the issues and process.

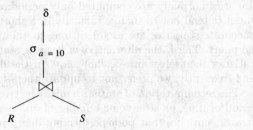

Figure 16.28: Logical query plan for Example 16.29

Example 16.29: Consider the initial logical query plan of Fig. 16.28, and let the statistics for the relations R and S be as follows:

$R(a,b)$	$S(b,c)$
$T(R) = 5000$	$T(S) = 2000$
$V(R,a) = 50$	
$V(R,b) = 100$	$V(S,b) = 200$
	$V(S,c) = 100$

To generate a final logical query plan from Fig. 16.28, we shall insist that the selection be pushed down as far as possible. However, we are not sure whether it makes sense to push the δ below the join or not. Thus, we generate from Fig. 16.28 the two query plans shown in Fig. 16.29; they differ in whether we have chosen to eliminate duplicates before or after the join. Notice that in plan (a) the δ is pushed down both branches of the tree. If R and/or S is known to have no duplicates, then the δ along its branch could be eliminated.

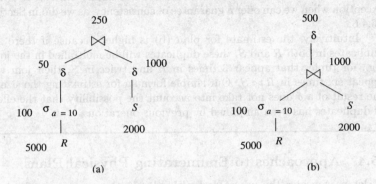

Figure 16.29: Two candidates for the best logical query plan

We know how to estimate the size of the result of the selections, from Section 16.4.3; we divide $T(R)$ by $V(R,a) = 50$. We also know how to estimate the size of the joins; we multiply the sizes of the arguments and divide by $\max(V(R,b), V(S,b))$, which is 200. What we don't know is how to estimate the size of the relations with duplicates eliminated.

First, consider the size estimate for $\delta(\sigma_{a=10}(R))$. Since $\sigma_{a=10}(R)$ has only one value for a and up to 100 values for b, and there are an estimated 100 tuples in this relation, the rule from Section 16.4.7 tells us that the product of the value counts for each of the attributes is not a limiting factor. Thus, we estimate the size of the result of δ as half the tuples in $\sigma_{a=10}(R)$, and Fig. 16.29(a) shows an estimate of 50 tuples for $\delta(\sigma_{a=10}(R))$.

Now, consider the estimate of the result of the δ in Fig. 16.29(b). The join has one value for a, an estimated $\min(V(R,b), V(S,b)) = 100$ values for b, and an estimated $V(S,c) = 100$ values for c. Thus again the product of the value counts does not limit how big the result of the δ can be. We estimate this result as 500 tuples, or half the number of tuples in the join.

To compare the two plans of Fig. 16.29, we add the estimated sizes for all the nodes except the root and the leaves. We exclude the root and leaves, because these sizes are not dependent on the plan chosen. For plan (a) this cost, the sum of the estimated sizes of the interior nodes, is $100 + 50 + 1000 = 1150$, while for plan (b) the sum is $100 + 1000 = 1100$. Thus, by a small margin we conclude that deferring the duplicate elimination to the end is a better plan. We would come to the opposite conclusion if, say, R or S had fewer b-values. Then the join size would be greater, making the cost of plan (b) greater. $\square$

Estimates for Result Sizes Need Not Be the Same

Notice that in Fig. 16.29 the estimates at the roots of the two trees are different: 250 in one case and 500 in the other. Because estimation is an inexact science, these sorts of anomalies will occur. In fact, it is the exception when we can offer a guarantee of consistency, as we did in Section 16.4.6.

Intuitively, the estimate for plan (b) is higher because if there are duplicates in both R and S, these duplicates will be multiplied in the join; e.g., for tuples that appear 3 times in R and twice in S, their join will appear six times in $R \bowtie S$. Our simple formula for estimating the size of the result of a δ does not take into account the possibility that the effect of duplicates has been amplified by previous operations.

16.5.4   Approaches to Enumerating Physical Plans

Now, let us consider the use of cost estimates in the conversion of a logical query plan to a physical query plan. The baseline approach, called *exhaustive*, is to consider all combinations of choices for each of the issues outlined at the beginning of Section 16.4 (order of joins, physical implementation of operators, and so on). Each possible physical plan is assigned an estimated cost, and the one with the smallest cost is selected.

However, there are a number of other approaches to selection of a physical plan. In this section, we shall outline various approaches that have been used, while Section 16.6 focuses on selecting a join order. Before proceeding, let us comment that there are two broad approaches to exploring the space of possible physical plans:

- *Top-down*: Here, we work down the tree of the logical query plan from the root. For each possible implementation of the operation at the root, we consider each possible way to evaluate its argument(s), and compute the cost of each combination, taking the best.[6]

- *Bottom-up*: For each subexpression of the logical-query-plan tree, we compute the costs of all possible ways to compute that subexpression. The possibilities and costs for a subexpression E are computed by considering the options for the subexpressions of E, and combining them in all possible ways with implementations for the root operator of E.

There is actually not much difference between the two approaches in their broadest interpretations, since either way, all possible combinations of ways to

---

[6]Remember from Section 16.3.4 that a single node of the logical-query-plan tree may represent many uses of a single commutative and associative operator, such as join. Thus, the consideration of all possible plans for a single node may itself involve enumeration of very many choices.

implement each operator in the query tree are considered. We shall concentrate on bottom-up methods in what follows.

You may, in fact, have noticed that there is an apparent simplification of the bottom-up method, where we consider only the *best* plan for each subexpression when we compute the plans for a larger subexpression. This approach, called *dynamic programming* in the list of methods below, is not guaranteed to yield the best overall plan, although often it does. The approach called *Selinger-style* (or *System-R-style*) optimization, also listed below, exploits additional properties that some of the plans for a subexpression may have, in order to produce optimal overall plans from plans that are not optimal for certain subexpressions.

Heuristic Selection

One option is to use the same approach to selecting a physical plan that is generally used for selecting a logical plan: make a sequence of choices based on heuristics. In Section 16.6.6, we shall discuss a "greedy" heuristic for join ordering, where we start by joining the pair of relations whose result has the smallest estimated size, then repeat the process for the result of that join and the other relations in the set to be joined. There are many other heuristics that may be applied; here are some of the most commonly used ones:

1. If the logical plan calls for a selection $\sigma_{A=c}(R)$, and stored relation R has an index on attribute A, then perform an index-scan (as in Section 15.1.1) to obtain only the tuples of R with A-value equal to c.

2. More generally, if the selection involves one condition like $A = c$ above, and other conditions as well, we can implement the selection by an index-scan followed by a further selection on the tuples, which we shall represent by the physical operator *filter*. This matter is discussed further in Section 16.7.1.

3. If an argument of a join has an index on the join attribute(s), then use an index-join with that relation in the inner loop.

4. If one argument of a join is sorted on the join attribute(s), then prefer a sort-join to a hash-join, although not necessarily to an index-join if one is possible.

5. When computing the union or intersection of three or more relations, group the smallest relations first.

Branch-and-Bound Plan Enumeration

This approach, often used in practice, begins by using heuristics to find a good physical plan for the entire logical query plan. Let the cost of this plan be C. Then as we consider other plans for subqueries, we can eliminate any plan for a subquery that has a cost greater than C, since that plan for the subquery could not possibly participate in a plan for the complete query that is better than what we already know. Likewise, if we construct a plan for the complete query that has cost less than C, we replace C by the cost of this better plan in subsequent exploration of the space of physical query plans.

An important advantage of this approach is that we can choose when to cut off the search and take the best plan found so far. For instance, if the cost C is small, then even if there are much better plans to be found, the time spent finding them may exceed C, so it does not make sense to continue the search. However, if C is large, then investing time in the hope of finding a faster plan is wise.

Hill Climbing

This approach, in which we really search for a "valley" in the space of physical plans and their costs, starts with a heuristically selected physical plan. We can then make small changes to the plan, e.g., replacing one method for executing an operator by another, or reordering joins by using the associative and/or commutative laws, to find "nearby" plans that have lower cost. When we find a plan such that no small modification yields a plan of lower cost, we make that plan our chosen physical query plan.

Dynamic Programming

In this variation of the general bottom-up strategy, we keep for each subexpression only the plan of least cost. As we work up the tree, we consider possible implementations of each node, assuming the best plan for each subexpression is also used. We examine this approach extensively in Section 16.6.

Selinger-Style Optimization

This approach improves upon the dynamic-programming approach by keeping for each subexpression not only the plan of least cost, but certain other plans that have higher cost, yet produce a result that is sorted in an order that may be useful higher up in the expression tree. Examples of such *interesting* orders are when the result of the subexpression is sorted on one of:

1. The attribute(s) specified in a sort (τ) operator at the root.

2. The grouping attribute(s) of a later group-by (γ) operator.

3. The join attribute(s) of a later join.

If we take the cost of a plan to be the sum of the sizes of the intermediate relations, then there appears to be no advantage to having an argument sorted. However, if we use the more accurate measure, disk I/O's, as the cost, then the advantage of having an argument sorted becomes clear if we can use one of the sort-based algorithms of Section 15.4, and save the work of the first pass for the argument that is sorted already.

16.5.5   Exercises for Section 16.5

Exercise 16.5.1: Estimate the size of the join $R(a, b) \bowtie S(b, c)$ using histograms for $R.b$ and $S.b$. Assume $V(R, b) = V(S, b) = 20$, and the histograms for both attributes give the frequency of the four most common values, as tabulated below:

	0	1	2	3	4	others
$R.b$	5	4	10	5		36
$S.b$	10	8	5		7	50

How does this estimate compare with the simpler estimate, assuming that all 20 values are equally likely to occur, with $T(R) = 60$ and $T(S) = 80$?

Exercise 16.5.2: Estimate the size of the join $R(a, b) \bowtie S(b, c)$ if we have the following histogram information:

	$b < 0$	$b = 0$	$b > 0$
R	400	100	200
S	400	300	800

! Exercise 16.5.3: In Example 16.29 we suggested that reducing the number of values that either attribute named b had could make plan (a) better than plan (b) of Fig. 16.29. For what values of:

a) $V(S, b)$

b) $V(R, b)$

will plan (a) have a lower estimated cost than plan (b)?

! Exercise 16.5.4: Consider four relations R, S, T, and V. Respectively, they have 100, 200, 300, and 400 tuples, chosen randomly and independently from the same pool of 1000 tuples (e.g., the probabilities of a given tuple being in R is 1/10, in S is 1/5, and in both is 1/50).

a) What is the expected size of $R \cap S \cap T \cap V$?

b) What order of intersections gives the least cost (estimated sum of the sizes of the intermediate relations)?

c) What is the expected size of $R \cup S \cup T \cup V$?

d) What order of unions gives the least cost (estimated sum of the sizes of the intermediate relations)?

! Exercise 16.5.5: Repeat Exercise 16.5.4 if all four relations have 250 of the 1000 tuples, at random.

!! **Exercise 16.5.6:** Suppose we wish to compute the expression

$$\tau_b\big(R(a,b) \bowtie S(b,c) \bowtie T(d,a)\big)$$

That is, we join the three relations and produce the result sorted on attribute b. Let us make the simplifying assumptions:

    i. We shall not "join" R and T first, because that is a product.

   ii. Any other join can be performed with a two-pass sort-join or hash-join, but in no other way.

  iii. Any relation, or the result of any expression, can be sorted by a two-phase, multiway merge-sort, but in no other way.

  iv. The result of the first join will be passed as an argument to the last join one block at a time and not stored temporarily on disk.

   v. Each relation occupies 1000 blocks, and the result of either join of two relations occupies 5000 blocks.

Answer the following based on these assumptions:

  a) What are all the subexpressions and orders that a Selinger-style optimization would consider?

  b) Which query plan uses the fewest disk I/O's?[7]

!! **Exercise 16.5.7:** Give an example of a logical query plan of the form $E \bowtie F$, for some expressions E and F (which you may choose), where using the best plans to evaluate E and F does not allow any choice of algorithm for the final join that minimizes the total cost of evaluating the entire expression. Make whatever assumptions you wish about the number of available main-memory buffers and the sizes of relations mentioned in E and F.

16.6   Choosing an Order for Joins

In this section we focus on a critical problem in cost-based optimization: selecting an order for the (natural) join of three or more relations. Similar ideas can be applied to other binary operations like union or intersection, but these operations are less important in practice, because they typically take less time to execute than joins, and they more rarely appear in clusters of three or more.

---

[7]Notice that, because we have made some very specific assumptions about the join methods to be used, we can estimate disk I/O's, instead of relying on the simpler, but less accurate, counts of tuples as our cost measure.

16.6.1 Significance of Left and Right Join Arguments

When ordering a join, we should remember that many of the join methods discussed in Chapter 15 are asymmetric. That is, the roles played by the two argument relations are different, and the cost of the join depends on which relation plays which role. Perhaps most important, the one-pass join of Section 15.2.3 reads one relation — preferably the smaller — into main memory, creating a structure such as a hash table to facilitate matching of tuples from the other relation. It then reads the other relation, one block at a time, to join its tuples with the tuples stored in memory.

For instance, suppose that when we select a physical plan we decide to use a one-pass join. Then we shall assume the left argument of the join is the smaller relation and store it in a main-memory data structure. This relation is called the *build relation*. The right argument of the join, called the *probe relation*, is read a block at a time and its tuples are matched in main memory with those of the build relation. Other join algorithms that distinguish between their arguments include:

1. Nested-loop join, where we assume the left argument is the relation of the outer loop.

2. Index-join, where we assume the right argument has the index.

16.6.2 Join Trees

When we have the join of two relations, we need to order the arguments. We shall conventionally select the one whose estimated size is the smaller as the left argument. It is quite common for there to be a significant and discernible difference in the sizes of arguments, because a query involving joins often also involves a selection on at least one attribute, and that selection reduces the estimated size of one of the relations greatly.

Example 16.30 : Recall the query

```
SELECT movieTitle
FROM StarsIn, MovieStar
WHERE starName = name AND
      birthdate LIKE '%1960';
```

from Fig. 16.4, which leads to the preferred logical query plan of Fig. 16.24, in which we take the join of relation StarsIn and the result of a selection on relation MovieStar. We have not given estimates for the sizes of relations StarsIn or MovieStar, but we can assume that selecting for stars born in a single year will produce about 1/50th of the tuples in MovieStar. Since there are generally several stars per movie, we expect StarsIn to be larger than MovieStar to begin with, so the second argument of the join, $\sigma_{birthdate \text{ LIKE } '\%1960'}(\text{MovieStar})$, is much smaller than the first argument StarsIn. We conclude that the order of arguments in Fig. 16.24 should be reversed, so that the selection on MovieStar is the left argument. ☐

There are only two choices for a join tree when there are two relations — take either of the two relations to be the left argument. When the join involves more than two relations, the number of possible join trees grows rapidly. For example, Fig. 16.30 shows three of the five shapes of trees in which four relations R, S, T, and U, are joined. However, each of these trees has the four relations in alphabetical order from the left. Since order of arguments matters, and there are $n!$ ways to order n things, each tree represents $4! = 24$ different trees when the possible labelings of the leaves are considered.

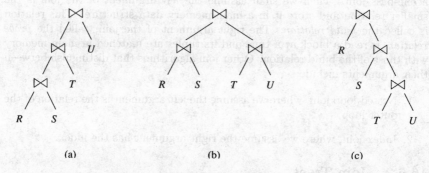

(a)   (b)   (c)

Figure 16.30: Ways to join four relations

16.6.3 Left-Deep Join Trees

Figure 16.30(a) is an example of what is called a *left-deep* tree. In general, a binary tree is left-deep if all right children are leaves. Similarly, a tree like Fig. 16.30(c), all of whose left children are leaves, is called a *right-deep* tree. A tree such as Fig. 16.30(b), that is neither left-deep nor right-deep, is called *bushy*. We shall argue below that there is a two-fold advantage to considering only left-deep trees as possible join orders.

1. The number of possible left-deep trees with a given number of leaves is large, but not nearly as large as the number of all trees. Thus, searches for query plans can be used for larger queries if we limit the search to left-deep trees.

2. Left-deep trees for joins interact well with common join algorithms — nested-loop joins and one-pass joins in particular. Query plans based on left-deep trees plus these join implementations will tend to be more efficient than the same algorithms used with non-left-deep trees.

The "leaves" in a left- or right-deep join tree can actually be interior nodes, with operators other than a join. Thus, for instance, Fig. 16.24 is technically a left-deep join tree with one join operator. The fact that a selection is applied to the right operand of the join does not take the tree out of the left-deep join class.

The number of left-deep trees does not grow nearly as fast as the number of all trees for the multiway join of a given number of relations. For n relations, there is only one left-deep tree shape, to which we may assign the relations in $n!$ ways. There are the same number of right-deep trees for n relations. However, the total number of tree shapes $T(n)$ for n relations is given by the recurrence:

$$T(1) = 1$$
$$T(n) = \sum_{i=1}^{n-1} T(i)T(n-i)$$

The explanation for the second equation is that we may pick any number i between 1 and $n-1$ to be the number of leaves in the left subtree of the root, and those leaves may be arranged in any of the $T(i)$ ways that trees with i leaves can be arranged. Similarly, the remaining $n-i$ leaves in the right subtree can be arranged in any of $T(n-i)$ ways.

The first few values of $T(n)$ are:

n	1	2	3	4	5	6
$T(n)$	1	1	2	5	14	42

To get the total number of trees once relations are assigned to the leaves, we multiply $T(n)$ by $n!$. Thus, for instance, the number of leaf-labeled trees of 6 leaves is $42 \times 6!$ or 30,240, of which 6!, or 720, are left-deep trees and another 720 are right-deep trees.

Now, let us consider the second advantage mentioned for left-deep join trees: their tendency to produce efficient plans. We shall give two examples:

1. If one-pass joins are used, and the build relation is on the left, then the amount of memory needed at any one time tends to be smaller than if we used a right-deep tree or a bushy tree for the same relations.

2. If we use nested-loop joins, with the relation of the outer loop on the left, then we avoid constructing any intermediate relation more than once.

Example 16.31: Consider the left-deep tree in Fig. 16.30(a), and suppose that we use a simple one-pass join for each of the three $\bowtie$ operators. As always, the left argument is the build relation; i.e., it will be held in main memory. To compute $R \bowtie S$, we need to keep R in main memory, and as we compute $R \bowtie S$ we need to keep the result in main memory as well. Thus, we need $B(R) + B(R \bowtie S)$ main-memory buffers. If we pick R to be the smallest of the relations, and a selection has made R be rather small, then there is likely to be no problem making this number of buffers available.

Having computed $R \bowtie S$, we must join this relation with T. However, the buffers used for R are no longer needed and can be reused to hold (some of) the result of $(R \bowtie S) \bowtie T$. Similarly, when we join this relation with U, the

---

Role of the Buffer Manager

The reader may notice a difference between our approach in the series of examples such as Example 15.4 and 15.6, where we assumed that there was a fixed limit on the number of main-memory buffers available for a join, and the more flexible assumption taken here, where we assume that as many buffers as necessary are available, but we try not to use "too many." Recall from Section 15.7 that the buffer manager has significant flexibility to allocate buffers to operations. However, if too many buffers are allocated at once, there will be thrashing, thus degrading the assumed performance of the algorithm being used.

---

relation $R \bowtie S$ is no longer needed, and its buffers can be reused for the result of the final join. In general, a left-deep join tree that is computed by one-pass joins requires main-memory space for at most two of the temporary relations any time.

Now, let us consider a similar implementation of the right-deep tree of Fig. 16.30(c). The first thing we need to do is load R into main-memory buffers, since left arguments are always the build relation. Then, we need to construct $S \bowtie (T \bowtie U)$ and use that as the probe relation for the join at the root. To compute $S \bowtie (T \bowtie U)$ we need to bring S into buffers and then compute $T \bowtie U$ as the probe relation for S. But $T \bowtie U$ requires that we first bring T into buffers. Now we have all three of R, S, and T in memory at the same time. In general, if we try to compute a right-deep join tree with n leaves, we shall have to bring $n - 1$ relations into memory simultaneously.

Of course it is possible that the total size $B(R) + B(S) + B(T)$ is less than the amount of space we need at either of the two intermediate stages of the computation of the left-deep tree, which are $B(R) + B(R \bowtie S)$ and $B(R \bowtie S) + B((R \bowtie S) \bowtie T)$, respectively. However, as we pointed out in Example 16.30, queries with several joins often will have a small relation with which we can start as the leftmost argument in a left-deep tree. If R is small, we might expect $R \bowtie S$ to be significantly smaller than S and $(R \bowtie S) \bowtie T$ to be smaller than T, further justifying the use of a left-deep tree. □

Example 16.32: Now, let us suppose we are going to implement the four-way join of Fig. 16.30 by nested-loop joins, and that we use an iterator (as in Section 15.1.6) for each of the three joins involved. Also, assume for simplicity that each of the relations R, S, T, and U are stored relations, rather than expressions. If we use the left-deep tree of Fig. 16.30(a), then the iterator at the root gets a main-memory-sized chunk of its left argument $(R \bowtie S) \bowtie T$. It then joins the chunk with all of U, but as long as U is a stored relation, it is only necessary to scan U, not to construct it. When the next chunk of the left argument is obtained and put in memory, U will be read again, but nested-loop join requires that repetition, which cannot be avoided if both arguments are large.

Similarly, to get a chunk of $(R \bowtie S) \bowtie T$, we get a chunk of $R \bowtie S$ into memory and scan T. Several scans of T may eventually be necessary, but cannot be avoided. Finally, to get a chunk of $R \bowtie S$ requires reading a chunk of R and comparing it with S, perhaps several times. However, in all this action, only stored relations are read multiple times, and this repeated reading is an artifact of the way nested-loop join works when the main memory is insufficient to hold an entire relation.

Now, compare the behavior of iterators on the left-deep tree with the behavior of iterators on the right-deep tree of Fig. 16.30(c). The iterator at the root starts by reading a chunk of R. It must then construct the entire relation $S \bowtie (T \bowtie U)$ and compare it with that chunk of R. When we read the next chunk of R into memory, $S \bowtie (T \bowtie U)$ must be constructed again. Each subsequent chunk of R likewise requires constructing this same relation.

Of course, we could construct $S \bowtie (T \bowtie U)$ once and store it, either in memory or on disk. If we store it on disk, we are using extra disk I/O's compared with the left-deep tree's plan, and if we store it in memory, then we run into the same problem with overuse of memory that we discussed in Example 16.31. □

16.6.4 Dynamic Programming to Select a Join Order and Grouping

To pick an order for the join of many relations we have three choices:

1. Consider them all.

2. Consider a subset.

3. Use a heuristic to pick one.

We shall here consider a sensible approach to enumeration called *dynamic programming*. It can be used either to consider all orders, or to consider certain subsets only, such as orders restricted to left-deep trees. In Section 16.6.6 we consider a heuristic for selecting a single ordering. Dynamic programming is a common algorithmic paradigm.[8] The idea behind dynamic programming is that we fill in a table of costs, remembering only the minimum information we need to proceed to a conclusion.

Suppose we want to join $R_1 \bowtie R_2 \bowtie \cdots \bowtie R_n$. In a dynamic programming algorithm, we construct a table with an entry for each subset of one or more of the n relations. In that table we put:

1. The estimated size of the join of these relations. For this quantity we may use the formula of Section 16.4.6.

---

[8]See Aho, Hopcroft and Ullman, *Data Structures and Algorithms*, Addison-Wesley, 1983, for a general treatment of dynamic programming.

2. The least cost of computing the join of these relations. We shall use in our examples the sum of the sizes of the intermediate relations (not including the R_i's themselves or the join of the full set of relations associated with this table entry).

3. The expression that yields the least cost. This expression joins the set of relations in question, with some grouping. We can optionally restrict ourselves to left-deep expressions, in which case the expression is just an ordering of the relations.

The construction of this table is an induction on the subset size. There are two variations, depending on whether we wish to consider all possible tree shapes or only left-deep trees. We explain the difference when we discuss the inductive step of table construction.

BASIS: The entry for a single relation R consists of the size of R, a cost of 0, and an expression that is just R itself. The entry for a pair of relations $\{R_i, R_j\}$ is also easy to compute. The cost is 0, since there are no intermediate relations involved, and the size estimate is given by the rule of Section 16.4.6; it is the product of the sizes of R_i and R_j divided by the larger value-set size for each attribute shared by R_i and R_j, if any. The expression is either $R_i \bowtie R_j$ or $R_j \bowtie R_i$. Following the idea introduced in Section 16.6.1, we pick the smaller of R_i and R_j as the left argument.

INDUCTION: Now, we can build the table, computing entries for all subsets of size 3, 4, and so on, until we get an entry for the one subset of size n. That entry tells us the best way to compute the join of all the relations; it also gives us the estimated cost of that method, which is needed as we compute later entries. We need to see how to compute the entry for a set of k relations $\mathcal{R}$.

If we wish to consider only left-deep trees, then for each of the k relations R in $\mathcal{R}$ we consider the possibility that we compute the join for $\mathcal{R}$ by first computing the join of $\mathcal{R} - \{R\}$ and then joining it with R. The cost of the join for $\mathcal{R}$ is the cost of $\mathcal{R} - \{R\}$ plus the size of the result for $\mathcal{R} - \{R\}$. We pick whichever R yields the least cost. The expression for $\mathcal{R}$ has the best join expression for $\mathcal{R} - \{R\}$ as the left argument of a final join, and R as the right argument. The size for $\mathcal{R}$ is whatever the formula from Section 16.4.6 gives.

If we wish to consider all trees, then computing the entry for a set of relations $\mathcal{R}$ is somewhat more complex. We need to consider all ways to partition $\mathcal{R}$ into disjoint sets $\mathcal{R}_1$ and $\mathcal{R}_2$. For each such subset, we consider the sum of:

1. The best costs of $\mathcal{R}_1$ and $\mathcal{R}_2$.

2. The sizes of the results for $\mathcal{R}_1$ and $\mathcal{R}_2$.

For whichever partition gives the best cost, we use this sum as the cost for $\mathcal{R}$, and the expression for $\mathcal{R}$ is the join of the best join orders for $\mathcal{R}_1$ and $\mathcal{R}_2$.

Example 16.33: Consider the join of four relations R, S, T, and U. For simplicity, we shall assume they each have 1000 tuples. Their attributes and the estimated sizes of values sets for the attributes in each relation are summarized in Fig. 16.31.

$R(a,b)$	$S(b,c)$	$T(c,d)$	$U(d,a)$
$V(R,a) = 100$			$V(U,a) = 50$
$V(R,b) = 200$	$V(S,b) = 100$		
	$V(S,c) = 500$	$V(T,c) = 20$	
		$V(T,d) = 50$	$V(U,d) = 1000$

Figure 16.31: Parameters for Example 16.33

For the singleton sets, the sizes, costs, and best plans are as in the table of Fig. 16.32. That is, for each single relation, the size is as given, 1000 for each, the cost is 0 since there are no intermediate relations needed, and the best (and only) expression is the relation itself.

	$\{R\}$	$\{S\}$	$\{T\}$	$\{U\}$
Size	1000	1000	1000	1000
Cost	0	0	0	0
Best plan	R	S	T	U

Figure 16.32: The table for singleton sets

Now, consider the pairs of relations. The cost for each is 0, since there are still no intermediate relations in a join of two. There are two possible plans, since either of the two relations can be the left argument, but since the sizes happen to be the same for each relation we have no basis on which to choose between the plans. We shall take the first, in alphabetical order, to be the left argument in each case. The sizes of the resulting relations are computed by the usual formula. The results are summarized in Fig. 16.33.

	$\{R,S\}$	$\{R,T\}$	$\{R,U\}$	$\{S,T\}$	$\{S,U\}$	$\{T,U\}$
Size	5000	1,000,000	10,000	2000	1,000,000	1000
Cost	0	0	0	0	0	0
Best plan	$R \bowtie S$	$R \bowtie T$	$R \bowtie U$	$S \bowtie T$	$S \bowtie U$	$T \bowtie U$

Figure 16.33: The table for pairs of relations

Now, consider the table for joins of three out of the four relations. The only way to compute a join of three relations is to pick two to join first. The size estimate for the result is computed by the standard formula, and we omit the details of this calculation; remember that we'll get the same size regardless of which way we compute the join.

The cost estimate for each triple of relations is the size of the one intermediate relation — the join of the first two chosen. Since we want this cost to be as small as possible, we consider each pair of two out of the three relations and take the pair with the smallest size.

For the expression, we group the two chosen relations first, but these could be either the left or right argument. Let us suppose that we are only interested in left-deep trees, so we always use the join of the first two relations as the left argument. Since in all cases the estimated size for the join of two of our relations is at least 1000 (the size of each individual relation), were we to allow non-left-deep trees we would always select the single relation as the left argument in this example. The summary table for the triples is shown in Fig. 16.34.

	$\{R,S,T\}$	$\{R,S,U\}$	$\{R,T,U\}$	$\{S,T,U\}$
Size	10,000	50,000	10,000	2,000
Cost	2,000	5,000	1,000	1,000
Best plan	$(S \bowtie T) \bowtie R$	$(R \bowtie S) \bowtie U$	$(T \bowtie U) \bowtie R$	$(T \bowtie U) \bowtie S$

Figure 16.34: The table for triples of relations

Let us consider $\{R,S,T\}$ as an example of the calculation. We must consider each of the three pairs in turn. If we start with $R \bowtie S$, then the cost is the size of this relation, which is 5000 (see Fig. 16.33). Starting with $R \bowtie T$ gives us a cost of 1,000,000 for the intermediate relation, and starting with $S \bowtie T$ has a cost of 2000. Since the latter is the smallest cost of the three options, we choose that plan. The choice is reflected not only in the cost entry of the $\{R,S,T\}$ column, but in the best-plan row, where the plan that groups S and T first appears.

Now, we must consider the situation for the join of all four relations. There are two general ways we can compute the join of all four:

1. Pick three to join in the best possible way, and then join in the fourth.

2. Divide the four relations into two pairs of two, join the pairs and then join the results.

Of course, if we consider only left-deep trees then the second type of plan is excluded, because it yields bushy trees. The table of Fig. 16.35 summarizes the seven possible ways to group the joins, based on the preferred groupings from Figs. 16.33 and 16.34.

For instance, consider the first expression in Fig. 16.35. It represents joining R, S, and T first, and then joining that result with U. From Fig. 16.34, we know that the best way to join R, S, and T is to join S and T first. We have used the left-deep form of this expression, and joined U on the right to continue

Grouping	Cost
$((S \bowtie T) \bowtie R) \bowtie U$	12,000
$((R \bowtie S) \bowtie U) \bowtie T$	55,000
$((T \bowtie U) \bowtie R) \bowtie S$	11,000
$((T \bowtie U) \bowtie S) \bowtie R$	3,000
$(T \bowtie U) \bowtie (R \bowtie S)$	6,000
$(R \bowtie T) \bowtie (S \bowtie U)$	2,000,000
$(S \bowtie T) \bowtie (R \bowtie U)$	12,000

Figure 16.35: Join groupings and their costs

the left-deep form. If we consider only left-deep trees, then this expression and relation order is the only option. If we allowed bushy trees, we would join U on the left, since it is smaller than the join of the other three. The cost of this join is 12,000, which is the sum of the cost and size of $(S \bowtie T) \bowtie R$, which are 2000 and 10,000, respectively.

The last three expressions in Fig. 16.35 represent additional options if we include bushy trees. These are formed by joining relations first in two pairs. For example, the last line represents the strategy of joining $R \bowtie U$ and $S \bowtie T$, and then joining the result. The cost of this expression is the sum of the sizes and costs of the two pairs. The costs are 0, as must be the case for any pair, and the sizes are 10,000 and 2000, respectively. Since we generally select the smaller relation to be the left argument, we show the expression as $(S \bowtie T) \bowtie (R \bowtie U)$.

In this example, we see that the least of all costs is associated with the fourth expression: $((T \bowtie U) \bowtie S) \bowtie R$. This expression is the one we select for computing the join; its cost is 3000. Since it is a left-deep tree, it is the selected logical query plan regardless of whether our dynamic-programming strategy considers all plans or just left-deep plans. □

16.6.5 Dynamic Programming With More Detailed Cost Functions

Using relation sizes as the cost estimate simplifies the calculations in a dynamic-programming algorithm. However, a disadvantage of this simplification is that it does not involve the actual costs of the joins in the calculation. As an extreme example, if one possible join $R(a, b) \bowtie S(b, c)$ involves a relation R with one tuple and another relation S that has an index on the join attribute b, then the join takes almost no time. On the other hand, if S has no index, then we must scan it, taking $B(S)$ disk I/O's, even when R is a singleton. A cost measure that only involved the sizes of R, S, and $R \bowtie S$ cannot distinguish these two cases, so the cost of using $R \bowtie S$ in the grouping will be either overestimated or underestimated.

However, modifying the dynamic programming algorithm to take join algorithms into account is not hard. First, the cost measure we use becomes disk

I/O's. When computing the cost of $\mathcal{R}_1 \bowtie \mathcal{R}_2$, we sum the cost of $\mathcal{R}_1$, the cost of $\mathcal{R}_2$, and the least cost of joining these two relations using the best available algorithm. Since the latter cost usually depends on the sizes of $\mathcal{R}_1$ and $\mathcal{R}_2$, we must also compute estimates for these sizes as we did in Example 16.33.

An even more powerful version of dynamic programming is based on the Selinger-style optimization mentioned in Section 16.5.4. Now, for each set of relations that might be joined, we keep not only one cost, but several costs. Recall that Selinger-style optimization considers not only the least cost of producing the result of the join, but also the least cost of producing that relation sorted in any of a number of "interesting" orders. These interesting sorts include any that might be used to advantage in a later sort-join or that could be used to produce the output of the entire query in the sorted order desired by the user. When sorted relations must be produced, the use of sort-join, either one-pass or multipass, must be considered as an option, while without considering the value of sorting a result, hash-joins are always at least as good as the corresponding sort-join.

16.6.6   A Greedy Algorithm for Selecting a Join Order

As Example 16.33 suggests, even the carefully limited search of dynamic programming leads to a number of calculations that is exponential in the number of relations joined. It is reasonable to use an exhaustive method like dynamic programming or branch-and-bound search to find optimal join orders of five or six relations. However, when the number of joins grows beyond that, or if we choose not to invest the time necessary for an exhaustive search, then we can use a join-order heuristic in our query optimizer.

The most common choice of heuristic is a *greedy* algorithm, where we make one decision at a time about the order of joins and never backtrack or reconsider decisions once made. We shall consider a greedy algorithm that only selects a left-deep tree. The "greediness" is based on the idea that we want to keep the intermediate relations as small as possible at each level of the tree.

BASIS: Start with the pair of relations whose estimated join size is smallest. The join of these relations becomes the *current tree*.

INDUCTION: Find, among all those relations not yet included in the current tree, the relation that, when joined with the current tree, yields the relation of smallest estimated size. The new current tree has the old current tree as its left argument and the selected relation as its right argument.

Example 16.34 : Let us apply the greedy algorithm to the relations of Example 16.33. The basis step is to find the pair of relations that have the smallest join. Consulting Fig. 16.33, we see that this honor goes to the join $T \bowtie U$, with a cost of 1000. Thus, $T \bowtie U$ is the "current tree."

We now consider whether to join R or S into the tree next. Thus we compare the sizes of $(T \bowtie U) \bowtie R$ and $(T \bowtie U) \bowtie S$. Figure 16.34 tells us that the

---

Join Selectivity

A useful way to view heuristics such as the greedy algorithm for selecting a left-deep join tree is that each relation R, when joined with the current tree, has a *selectivity*, which is the ratio of the size of the join result to size of the current tree's result. Since we usually do not have the exact sizes of either relation, we estimate these sizes as we have done previously. A greedy approach to join ordering is to pick that relation with the smallest selectivity.

For example, if a join attribute is a key for R, then the selectivity is at most 1, which is usually a favorable situation. Notice that, judging from the statistics of Fig. 16.31, attribute d is a key for U, and there are no keys for other relations, which suggests why joining T with U is the best way to start the join.

---

latter, with a size of 2000 is better than the former, with a size of 10,000. Thus, we pick as the new current tree $(T \bowtie U) \bowtie S$.

Now there is no choice; we must join R at the last step, leaving us with a total cost of 3000, the sum of the sizes of the two intermediate relations. Note that the tree resulting from the greedy algorithm is the same as that selected by the dynamic-programming algorithm in Example 16.33. However, there are examples where the greedy algorithm fails to find the best solution, while the dynamic-programming algorithm guarantees to find the best; see Exercise 16.6.4. □

16.6.7 Exercises for Section 16.6

Exercise 16.6.1: For the relations of Exercise 16.4.1, give the dynamic-programming table entries that evaluates all possible join orders allowing: a) Left-deep trees only. b) All trees What is the best choice in each case?

Exercise 16.6.2: Repeat Exercise 16.6.1 with the following modifications:

  i. The schema for Z is changed to $Z(d, a)$.

  ii. $V(Z, a) = 50$.

Exercise 16.6.3: Repeat Exercise 16.6.1 with the relations of Exercise 16.4.2.

Exercise 16.6.4: Consider the join of relations $R(a, b)$, $S(b, c)$, $T(c, d)$, and $U(a, d)$, where R and U each have 1000 tuples, while S and T each have 200 tuples. Further, there are 200 values of all attributes of all relations, except for attribute c, where $V(S, c) = V(T, c) = 20$.

a) What is the order selected by the greedy algorithm? What is its cost?

b) What is the optimum join ordering and its cost?

! **Exercise 16.6.5:** Suppose we wish to join the relations R, S, T, and U in one of the tree structures of Fig. 16.30, and we want to keep all intermediate relations in memory until they are no longer needed. Following our usual assumption, the result of the join of all four will be consumed by some other process as it is generated, so no memory is needed for that relation. In terms of the number of blocks required for the stored relations and the intermediate relations [e.g., $B(R)$ or $B(R \bowtie S)$], give a lower bound on M, the number of blocks of memory needed, for each of the trees in Fig. 16.30? What assumptions let us conclude that one tree is certain to use less memory than another?

! **Exercise 16.6.6:** If we use dynamic programming to select an order for the join of k relations, how many entries of the table do we have to fill?

Exercise 16.6.7: How many trees are there for the join of (a) eight (b) nine relations? How many of these are neither left-deep nor right-deep?

16.7 Completing the Physical-Query-Plan

We have parsed the query, converted it to an initial logical query plan, and improved that logical query plan with transformations described in Section 16.3. Part of the process of selecting the physical query plan is enumeration and cost-estimation for all of our options, which we discussed in Section 16.5. Section 16.6 focused on the question of enumeration, cost estimation, and ordering for joins of several relations. By extension, we can use similar techniques to order groups of unions, intersections, or any associative/commutative operation.

There are still several steps needed to turn the logical plan into a complete physical query plan. The principal issues that we must yet cover are:

1. Selection of algorithms to implement the operations of the query plan, when algorithm-selection was not done as part of some earlier step such as selection of a join order by dynamic programming.

2. Decisions regarding when intermediate results will be *materialized* (created whole and stored on disk), and when they will be *pipelined* (created only in main memory, and not necessarily kept in their entirety at any one time).

3. Notation for physical-query-plan operators, which must include details regarding access methods for stored relations and algorithms for implementation of relational-algebra operators.

We shall not discuss the subject of selection of algorithms for operators in its entirety. Rather, we sample the issues by discussing two of the most important operators: selection in Section 16.7.1 and joins in Section 16.7.2.

Then, we consider the choice between pipelining and materialization in Sections 16.7.3 through 16.7.5. A notation for physical query plans is presented in Section 16.7.6.

16.7.1 Choosing a Selection Method

One of the important steps in choosing a physical query plan is to pick algorithms for each selection operator. In Section 15.2.1 we mentioned the obvious implementation of a $\sigma_C(R)$ operator, where we access the entire relation R and see which tuples satisfy condition C. Then in Section 15.6.2 we considered the possibility that C was of the form "attribute equals constant," and we had an index on that attribute. If so, then we can find the tuples that satisfy condition C without looking at all of R. Now, let us consider the generalization of this problem, where we have a selection condition that is the AND of several conditions. Assume at least one condition is of the form $A\theta c$, where A is an attribute with an index, c is a constant, and θ is a comparison operator such as $=$ or $<$.

Each physical plan uses some number of attributes that each:

a) Have an index, and

b) Are compared to a constant in one of the terms of the selection.

We then use these indexes to identify the sets of tuples that satisfy each of the conditions. Sections 14.1.7 and 14.4.3 discussed how we could use pointers obtained from these indexes to find only the tuples that satisfied all the conditions before we read these tuples from disk.

For simplicity, we shall not consider the use of several indexes in this way. Rather, we limit our discussion to physical plans that:

1. Retrieve all tuples that satisfy a comparison for which an index exists, using the index-scan physical operator discussed in Section 15.1.1.

2. Consider each tuple selected in (1) to decide whether it satisfies the rest of the selection condition. The physical operator that performs this step is callled Filter.

In addition to physical plans of this form, we must also consider the plan that uses no index but reads the entire relation (using the table-scan physical operator) and passes each tuple to the Filter operator to check for satisfaction of the selection condition.

We decide among the possible physical plans for a selection by estimating the cost of reading data with each plan. To compare costs of alternative plans we cannot continue using the simplified cost estimate of intermediate-relation size. The reason is that we are now considering implementations of a single step of the logical query plan, and intermediate relations are independent of implementation.

Thus, we shall refocus our attention and resume counting disk I/O's, as we did when we discussed algorithms and their costs in Chapter 15. To simplify as before, we shall count only the cost of accessing the data blocks, not the index blocks. Recall that the number of index blocks needed is generally much smaller than the number of data blocks needed, so this approximation to disk I/O cost is usually accurate enough.

The following is an outline of how costs for the various plans are estimated. We assume that the operation is $\sigma_C(R)$, where condition C is the AND of one or more terms.

1. The cost of the table-scan algorithm coupled with a filter step is:

    (a) $B(R)$ if R is clustered, and

    (b) $T(R)$ if R is not clustered.

2. The cost of a plan that picks an equality term such as $a = 10$ for which an index on attribute a exists, uses index-scan to find the matching tuples, and then filters the retrieved tuples to see if they satisfy the full condition C is:

    (a) $B(R)/V(R, a)$ if the index is clustering, and

    (b) $T(R)/V(R, a)$ if the index is not clustering.

3. The cost of a plan that picks an inequality term such as $b < 20$ for which an index on attribute b exists, uses index-scan to retrieve the matching tuples, and then filters the retrieved tuples to see if they satisfy the full condition C is:

    (a) $B(R)/3$ if the index is clustering,[9] and

    (b) $T(R)/3$ if the index is not clustering.

Example 16.35: Consider selection $\sigma_{x=1 \text{ AND } y=2 \text{ AND } z<5}(R)$, where $R(x, y, z)$ has the following parameters: $T(R) = 5000$, $B(R) = 200$, $V(R, x) = 100$, and $V(R, y) = 500$. Further, suppose R is clustered, and there are indexes on all of x, y, and z, but only the index on z is clustering. The following are the options for implementing this selection:

1. Table-scan followed by filter. The cost is $B(R)$, or 200 disk I/O's, since R is clustered.

2. Use the index on x and the index-scan operator to find those tuples with $x = 1$, then use the filter operator to check that $y = 2$ and $z < 5$. Since there are about $T(R)/V(R, x) = 50$ tuples with $x = 1$, and the index is not clustering, we require about 50 disk I/O's.

---

[9]Recall that we assume the typical inequality retrieves only 1/3 the tuples, for reasons discussed in Section 16.4.3.

3. Use the index on y and index-scan to find those tuples with $y = 2$, then filter these tuples to see that $x = 1$ and $z < 5$. The cost for using this nonclustering index is about $T(R)/V(R,y)$, or 10 disk I/O's.

4. Use the clustering index on z and index-scan to find those tuples with $z < 5$, then filter these tuples to see that $x = 1$ and $y = 2$. The number of disk I/O's is about $B(R)/3 = 67$.

We see that the least cost plan is the third, with an estimated cost of 10 disk I/O's. Thus, the preferred physical plan for this selection retrieves all tuples with $y = 2$ and then filters for the other two conditions. □

16.7.2 Choosing a Join Method

We saw in Chapter 15 the costs associated with the various join algorithms. On the assumption that we know (or can estimate) how many buffers are available to perform the join, we can apply the formulas in Section 15.4.9 for sort-joins, Section 15.5.7 for hash-joins, and Sections 15.6.3 and 15.6.4 for indexed joins.

However, if we are not sure of, or cannot know, the number of buffers that will be available during the execution of this query (because we do not know what else the DBMS is doing at the same time), or if we do not have estimates of important size parameters such as the $V(R,a)$'s, then there are still some principles we can apply to choosing a join method. Similar ideas apply to other binary operations such as unions, and to the full-relation, unary operators, γ and δ.

- One approach is to call for the one-pass join, hoping that the buffer manager can devote enough buffers to the join, or that the buffer manager can come close, so thrashing is not a major cost. An alternative (for joins only, not for other binary operators) is to choose a nested-loop join, hoping that if the left argument cannot be granted enough buffers to fit in memory at once, then that argument will not have to be divided into too many pieces, and the resulting join will still be reasonably efficient.

- A sort-join is a good choice when either:

  1. One or both arguments are already sorted on their join attribute(s), or

  2. There are two or more joins on the same attribute, such as

  $$(R(a,b) \bowtie S(a,c)) \bowtie T(a,d)$$

  where sorting R and S on a will cause the result of $R \bowtie S$ to be sorted on a and used directly in a second sort-join.

- If there is an index opportunity such as a join $R(a,b) \bowtie S(b,c)$, where R is expected to be small (perhaps the result of a selection on a key that must yield only one tuple), and there is an index on the join attribute $S.b$, then we should choose an index-join.

- If there is no opportunity to use already-sorted relations or indexes, and a multipass join is needed, then hashing is probably the best choice, because the number of passes it requires depends on the size of the smaller argument rather than on both arguments.

16.7.3 Pipelining Versus Materialization

The last major issue we shall discuss in connection with choice of a physical query plan is pipelining of results. The naive way to execute a query plan is to order the operations appropriately (so an operation is not performed until the argument(s) below it have been performed), and store the result of each operation on disk until it is needed by another operation. This strategy is called *materialization*, since each intermediate relation is materialized on disk.

A more subtle, and generally more efficient, way to execute a query plan is to interleave the execution of several operations. The tuples produced by one operation are passed directly to the operation that uses it, without ever storing the intermediate tuples on disk. This approach is called *pipelining*, and it typically is implemented by a network of iterators (see Section 15.1.6), whose methods call each other at appropriate times. Since it saves disk I/O's, there is an obvious advantage to pipelining, but there is a corresponding disadvantage. Since several operations must share main memory at any time, there is a chance that algorithms with higher disk-I/O requirements must be chosen, or thrashing will occur, thus giving back all the disk-I/O savings that were gained by pipelining, and possibly more.

16.7.4 Pipelining Unary Operations

Unary operations — selection and projection — are excellent candidates for pipelining. Since these operations are tuple-at-a-time, we never need to have more than one block for input, and one block for the output. This mode of operation was suggested by Fig. 15.5.

We may implement a pipelined unary operation by iterators, as discussed in Section 15.1.6. The consumer of the pipelined result calls GetNext() each time another tuple is needed. In the case of a projection, it is only necessary to call GetNext() once on the source of tuples, project that tuple appropriately, and return the result to the consumer. For a selection σ_C (technically, the physical operator Filter(C)), it may be necessary to call GetNext() several times at the source, until one tuple that satisfies condition C is found. Figure 16.36 illustrates this process.

16.7.5 Pipelining Binary Operations

The results of binary operations can also be pipelined. We use one buffer to pass the result to its consumer, one block at a time. However, the number of other buffers needed to compute the result and to consume the result varies,

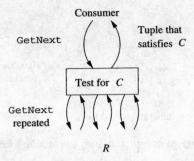

Figure 16.36: Execution of a pipelined selection using iterators

---

Materialization in Memory

One might imagine that there is an intermediate approach, between pipelining and materialization, where the entire result of one operation is stored in main-memory buffers (not on disk) before being passed to the consuming operation. We regard this possible mode of operation as pipelining, where the first thing that the consuming operation does is organize the entire relation, or a large portion of it, in memory. An example of this sort of behavior is a selection whose result becomes the left (build) argument to one of several join algorithms, including the simple one-pass join, multipass hash-join, or sort-join.

---

depending on the size of the result and the sizes of the arguments. We shall use an extended example to illustrate the tradeoffs and opportunities.

Example 16.36: Let us consider physical query plans for the expression

$$(R(w, x) \bowtie S(x, y)) \bowtie U(y, z)$$

We make the following assumptions:

1. R occupies 5000 blocks; S and U each occupy 10,000 blocks.

2. The intermediate result $R \bowtie S$ occupies k blocks for some k.

3. Both joins will be implemented as hash-joins, either one-pass or two-pass, depending on k.

4. There are 101 buffers available. This number, as usual, is set artificially low.

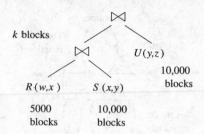

Figure 16.37: Logical query plan and parameters for Example 16.36

A sketch of the expression with key parameters is in Fig. 16.37.

First, consider the join $R \bowtie S$. Neither relation fits in main memory, so we need a two-pass hash-join. If the smaller relation R is partitioned into the maximum-possible 100 buckets on the first pass, then each bucket for R occupies 50 blocks.[10] If R's buckets have 50 blocks, then the second pass of the hash-join $R \bowtie S$ uses 51 buffers, leaving 50 buffers to use for the join of the result of $R \bowtie S$ with U.

Now, suppose that $k \leq 49$; that is, the result of $R \bowtie S$ occupies at most 49 blocks. Then we can pipeline the result of $R \bowtie S$ into 49 buffers, organize them for lookup as a hash table, and we have one buffer left to read each block of U in turn. We may thus execute the second join as a one-pass join. The total number of disk I/O's is:

a) 45,000 to perform the two-pass hash join of R and S.

b) 10,000 to read U in the one-pass hash-join of $(R \bowtie S) \bowtie U$.

The total is 55,000 disk I/O's.

Now, suppose $k > 49$, but $k \leq 5000$. We can still pipeline the result of $R \bowtie S$, but we need to use another strategy, in which this relation is joined with U in a 50-bucket, two-pass hash-join.

1. Before we start on $R \bowtie S$, we hash U into 50 buckets of 200 blocks each.

2. Next, we perform a two-pass hash join of R and S using 51 buckets as before, but as each tuple of $R \bowtie S$ is generated, we place it in one of the 50 remaining buffers that is used to help form the 50 buckets for the join of $R \bowtie S$ with U. These buffers are written to disk when they get full, as is normal for a two-pass hash-join.

3. Finally, we join $R \bowtie S$ with U bucket by bucket. Since $k \leq 5000$, the buckets of $R \bowtie S$ will be of size at most 100 blocks, so this join is feasible. The fact that buckets of U are of size 200 blocks is not a problem, since

---

[10]We shall assume for convenience that all buckets wind up with exactly their fair share of tuples.

we are using buckets of $R \bowtie S$ as the build relation and buckets of U as the probe relation in the one-pass joins of buckets.

The number of disk I/O's for this pipelined join is:

a) 20,000 to read U and write its tuples into buckets.

b) 45,000 to perform the two-pass hash-join $R \bowtie S$.

c) k to write out the buckets of $R \bowtie S$.

d) $k + 10,000$ to read the buckets of $R \bowtie S$ and U in the final join.

The total cost is thus $75,000 + 2k$. Note that there is an apparent discontinuity as k grows from 49 to 50, since we had to change the final join from one-pass to two-pass. In practice, the cost would not change so precipitously, since we could use the one-pass join even if there were not enough buffers and a small amount of thrashing occurred.

Last, let us consider what happens when $k > 5000$. Now, we cannot perform a two-pass join in the 50 buffers available if the result of $R \bowtie S$ is pipelined. We could use a three-pass join, but that would require an extra 2 disk I/O's per block of either argument, or $20,000 + 2k$ more disk I/O's. We can do better if we instead decline to pipeline $R \bowtie S$. Now, an outline of the computation of the joins is:

1. Compute $R \bowtie S$ using a two-pass hash join and store the result on disk.

2. Join $R \bowtie S$ with U, also using a two-pass hash-join. Note that since $B(U) = 10,000$, we can perform a two-pass hash-join using 100 buckets, regardless of how large k is. Technically, U should appear as the left argument of its join in Fig. 16.37 if we decide to make U the build relation for the hash join.

The number of disk I/O's for this plan is:

a) 45,000 for the two-pass join of R and S.

b) k to store $R \bowtie S$ on disk.

c) $30,000 + 3k$ for the two-pass hash-join of U with $R \bowtie S$.

The total cost is thus $75,000 + 4k$, which is less than the cost of going to a three-pass join at the final step. The three complete plans are summarized in the table of Fig. 16.38. □

Range of k	Pipeline or Materialize	Algorithm for final join	Total Disk I/O's
$k \leq 49$	Pipeline	one-pass	55,000
$50 \leq k \leq 5000$	Pipeline	50-bucket, two-pass	$75,000 + 2k$
$5000 < k$	Materialize	100-bucket, two-pass	$75,000 + 4k$

Figure 16.38: Costs of physical plans as a function of the size of $R \bowtie S$

16.7.6 Notation for Physical Query Plans

We have seen many examples of the operators that can be used to form a physical query plan. In general, each operator of the logical plan becomes one or more operators of the physical plan, and leaves (stored relations) of the logical plan become, in the physical plan, one of the scan operators applied to that relation. In addition, materialization would be indicated by a Store operator applied to the intermediate result that is to be materialized, followed by a suitable scan operator (usually TableScan, since there is no index on the intermediate relation unless one is constructed explicitly) when the materialized result is accessed by its consumer. However, for simplicity, in our physical-query-plan trees we shall indicate that a certain intermediate relation is materialized by a double line crossing the edge between that relation and its consumer. All other edges are assumed to represent pipelining between the supplier and consumer of tuples.

We shall now catalog the various operators that are typically found in physical query plans. Unlike the relational algebra, whose notation is fairly standard, each DBMS will use its own internal notation for physical query plans.

Operators for Leaves

Each relation R that is a leaf operand of the logical-query-plan tree will be replaced by a scan operator. The options are:

1. TableScan(R): All blocks holding tuples of R are read in arbitrary order.

2. SortScan(R,L): Tuples of R are read in order, sorted according to the attribute(s) on list L.

3. IndexScan(R,C): Here, C is a condition of the form $A\theta c$, where A is an attribute of R, θ is a comparison such as $=$ or $<$, and c is a constant. Tuples of R are accessed through an index on attribute A. If the comparison θ is not $=$, then the index must be one, such as a B-tree, that supports range queries.

4. IndexScan(R,A): Here A is an attribute of R. The entire relation R is retrieved via an index on $R.A$. This operator behaves like TableScan,

but may be more efficient if R is not clustered.

Physical Operators for Selection

A logical operator $\sigma_C(R)$ is often combined, or partially combined, with the access method for relation R, when R is a stored relation. Other selections, where the argument is not a stored relation or an appropriate index is not available, will be replaced by the corresponding physical operator we have called Filter. Recall the strategy for choosing a selection implementation, which we discussed in Section 16.7.1. The notation we shall use for the various selection implementations are:

1. We may simply replace $\sigma_C(R)$ by the operator Filter(C). This choice makes sense if there is no index on R, or no index on an attribute that condition C mentions. If R, the argument of the selection, is actually an intermediate relation being pipelined to the selection, then no other operator besides Filter is needed. If R is a stored or materialized relation, then we must use an operator, TableScan or SortScan(R,L), to access R. We prefer sort-scan if the result of $\sigma_C(R)$ will later be passed to an operator that requires its argument sorted.

2. If condition C can be expressed as $A\theta c$ AND D for some other condition D, and there is an index on $R.A$, then we may:

   (a) Use the operator IndexScan(R,Aθc) to access R, and

   (b) Use Filter(D) in place of the selection $\sigma_C(R)$.

Physical Sort Operators

Sorting of a relation can occur at any point in the physical query plan. We have already introduced the SortScan(R,L) operator, which reads a stored relation R and produces it sorted according to the list of attributes L. When we apply a sort-based algorithm for operations such as join or grouping, there is an initial phase in which we sort the argument according to some list of attributes. It is common to use an explicit physical operator Sort(L) to perform this sort on an operand relation that is not stored. This operator can also be used at the top of the physical-query-plan tree if the result needs to be sorted because of an ORDER BY clause in the original query, thus playing the same role as the τ operator of Section 5.2.6.

Other Relational-Algebra Operations

All other operations are replaced by a suitable physical operator. These operators can be given designations that indicate:

1. The operation being performed, e.g., join or grouping.

2. Necessary parameters, e.g., the condition in a theta-join or the list of elements in a grouping.

3. A general strategy for the algorithm: sort-based, hash-based, or index-based, e.g.

4. A decision about the number of passes to be used: one-pass, two-pass, or multipass (recursive, using as many passes as necessary for the data at hand). Alternatively, this choice may be left until run-time.

5. An anticipated number of buffers the operation will require.

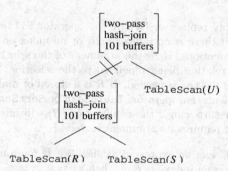

Figure 16.39: A physical plan from Example 16.36

Example 16.37 : Figure 16.39 shows the physical plan developed in Example 16.36 for the case $k > 5000$. In this plan, we access each of the three relations by a table-scan. We use a two-pass hash-join for the first join, materialize it, and use a two-pass hash-join for the second join. By implication of the double-line symbol for materialization, the left argument of the top join is also obtained by a table-scan, and the result of the first join is stored using the Store operator.

In contrast, if $k \leq 49$, then the physical plan developed in Example 16.36 is that shown in Fig. 16.40. Notice that the second join uses a different number of passes, a different number of buffers, and a left argument that is pipelined, not materialized. □

Example 16.38 : Consider the selection operation in Example 16.35, where we decided that the best of options was to use the index on y to find those tuples with $y = 2$, then check these tuples for the other conditions $x = 1$ and $z < 5$. Figure 16.41 shows the physical query plan. The leaf indicates that R will be accessed through its index on y, retrieving only those tuples with $y = 2$. The filter operator says that we complete the selection by further selecting those of the retrieved tuples that have both $x = 1$ and $z < 5$. □

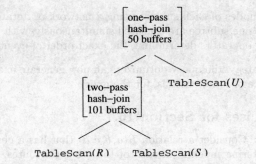

Figure 16.40: Another physical plan for the case where $R \bowtie S$ is expected to be very small

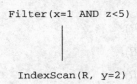

Figure 16.41: Annotating a selection to use the most appropriate index

16.7.7 Ordering of Physical Operations

Our final topic regarding physical query plans is the matter of order of operations. The physical query plan is generally represented as a tree, and trees imply something about order of operations, since data must flow up the tree. However, since bushy trees may have interior nodes that are neither ancestors nor descendants of one another, the order of evaluation of interior nodes may not always be clear. Moreover, since iterators can be used to implement operations in a pipelined manner, it is possible that the times of execution for various nodes overlap, and the notion of "ordering" nodes makes no sense.

If materialization is implemented in the obvious store-and-later-retrieve way, and pipelining is implemented by iterators, then we may establish a fixed sequence of events whereby each operation of a physical query plan is executed. The following rules summarize the ordering of events implicit in a physical-query-plan tree:

1. Break the tree into subtrees at each edge that represents materialization. The subtrees will be executed one-at-a-time.

2. Order the execution of the subtrees in a bottom-up, left-to-right manner. To be precise, perform a preorder traversal of the entire tree. Order the subtrees in the order in which the preorder traversal exits from the subtrees.

3. Execute all nodes of each subtree using a network of iterators. Thus, all the nodes in one subtree are executed simultaneously, with GetNext calls among their operators determining the exact order of events.

Following this strategy, the query optimizer can now generate executable code, perhaps a sequence of function calls, for the query.

16.7.8   Exercises for Section 16.7

Exercise 16.7.1: Consider a relation $R(a, b, c, d)$ that has a clustering index on a and nonclustering indexes on each of the other attributes. The relevant parameters are: $B(R) = 500$, $T(R) = 5000$, $V(R, a) = 50$, $V(R, b) = 1000$, $V(R, c) = 5000$, and $V(R, d) = 500$. Give the best query plan (index-scan or table-scan followed by a filter step) and the disk-I/O cost for each of the following selections:

a) $\sigma_{a=1 \text{ AND } b=2 \text{ AND } c \geq 3}(R)$.

b) $\sigma_{a=1 \text{ AND } b \leq 2 \text{ AND } c \geq 3}(R)$.

c) $\sigma_{a=1 \text{ AND } b=2 \text{ AND } d=3}(R)$.

Exercise 16.7.2: How would the conclusions about when to pipeline in Example 16.36 change if the size of relation R were not 5000 blocks, but: (a) 1000 blocks   ! (b) 100 blocks   ! (c) 10,000 blocks?

! **Exercise 16.7.3:** In terms of $B(R)$, $T(R)$, $V(R, x)$, and $V(R, y)$, express the following conditions about the cost of implementing a selection on R:

a) It is better to use index-scan with a nonclustering index on x and a term that equates x to a constant than a clustering index on y and a term that equates y to a constant.

b) It is better to use index-scan with a nonclustering index on x and a term that equates x to a constant than a clustering index on y and a term of the form $y > C$ for some constant C.

c) It is better to use index-scan with a nonclustering index on x and a term that equates x to a constant than a nonclustering index on y and a term that equates y to a constant.

! **Exercise 16.7.4:** Suppose we want to compute $(R(a, b) \bowtie S(a, c)) \bowtie T(a, d)$ in the order indicated. We have $M = 101$ main-memory buffers, and $B(R) = B(S) = 2000$. Because the join attribute a is the same for both joins, we decide to implement the first join $R \bowtie S$ by a two-pass sort-join, and we shall use the appropriate number of passes for the second join, first dividing T into some number of sublists sorted on a, and merging them with the sorted and pipelined stream of tuples from the join $R \bowtie S$. For what values of $B(T)$ should we choose for the join of T with $R \bowtie S$:

a) A one-pass join; i.e., we read T into memory, and compare its tuples with the tuples of $R \bowtie S$ as they are generated.

b) A two-pass join; i.e., we create sorted sublists for T and keep one buffer in memory for each sorted sublist, while we generate tuples of $R \bowtie S$.

16.8   Summary of Chapter 16

✦ *Compilation of Queries*: Compilation turns a query into a physical query plan, which is a sequence of operations that can be implemented by the query-execution engine. The principal steps of query compilation are parsing, semantic checking, selection of the preferred logical query plan (algebraic expression), and generation from that of the best physical plan.

✦ *The Parser*: The first step in processing a SQL query is to parse it, as one would for code in any programming language. The result of parsing is a parse tree with nodes corresponding to SQL constructs.

✦ *View Expansion*: Queries that refer to virtual views must have these references in the parse tree replaced by the tree for the expression that defines the view. This expansion often introduces several opportunities to optimize the complete query.

✦ *Semantic Checking*: A preprocessor examines the parse tree, checks that the attributes, relation names, and types make sense, and resolves attribute references.

✦ *Conversion to a Logical Query Plan*: The query processor must convert the semantically checked parse tree to an algebraic expression. Much of the conversion to relational algebra is straightforward, but subqueries present a problem. One approach is to introduce a two-argument selection that puts the subquery in the condition of the selection, and then apply appropriate transformations for the common special cases.

✦ *Algebraic Transformations*: There are many ways that a logical query plan can be transformed to a better plan by using algebraic transformations. Section 16.2 enumerates the principal ones.

✦ *Choosing a Logical Query Plan*: The query processor must select that query plan that is most likely to lead to an efficient physical plan. In addition to applying algebraic transformations, it is useful to group associative and commutative operators, especially joins, so the physical query plan can choose the best order and grouping for these operations.

✦ *Estimating Sizes of Relations*: When selecting the best logical plan, or when ordering joins or other associative-commutative operations, we use the estimated size of intermediate relations as a surrogate for the true running time. Knowing, or estimating, both the size (number of tuples) of relations and the number of distinct values for each attribute of each relation helps us get good estimates of the sizes of intermediate relations.

✦ *Histograms*: Some systems keep histograms of the values for a given attribute. This information can be used to obtain better estimates of intermediate-relation sizes than the simple methods stressed here.

✦ *Cost-Based Optimization*: When selecting the best physical plan, we need to estimate the cost of each possible plan. Various strategies are used to generate all or some of the possible physical plans that implement a given logical plan.

✦ *Plan-Enumeration Strategies*: The common approaches to searching the space of physical plans for the best include dynamic programming (tabularizing the best plan for each subexpression of the given logical plan), Selinger-style dynamic programming (which includes the sort-order of results as part of the table, giving best plans for each sort-order and for an unsorted result), greedy approaches (making a series of locally optimal decisions, given the choices for the physical plan that have been made so far), and branch-and-bound (enumerating only plans that are not immediately known to be worse than the best plan found so far).

✦ *Left-Deep Join Trees*: When picking a grouping and order for the join of several relations, it is common to restrict the search to left-deep trees, which are binary trees with a single spine down the left edge, with only leaves as right children. This form of join expression tends to yield efficient plans and also limits significantly the number of physical plans that need to be considered.

✦ *Physical Plans for Selection*: If possible, a selection should be broken into an index-scan of the relation to which the selection is applied (typically using a condition in which the indexed attribute is equated to a constant), followed by a filter operation. The filter examines the tuples retrieved by the index-scan and passes through only those that meet the portions of the selection condition other than that on which the index scan is based.

✦ *Pipelining Versus Materialization*: Ideally, the result of each physical operator is consumed by another operator, with the result being passed between the two in main memory ("pipelining"), perhaps using an iterator to control the flow of data from one to the other. However, sometimes there is an advantage to storing ("materializing") the result of one operator to save space in main memory for other operators. Thus, the physical-query-plan generator should consider both pipelining and materialization of intermediates.

16.9 References for Chapter 16

The surveys mentioned in the bibliographic notes to Chapter 15 also contain material relevant to query compilation. In addition, we recommend the survey [1], which contains material on the query optimizers of commercial systems.

Three of the earliest studies of query optimization are [4], [5], and [3]. Paper [6], another early study, incorporates the idea of pushing selections down the tree with the greedy algorithm for join-order choice. [2] is the source for "Selinger-style optimization" as well as describing the System R optimizer, which was one of the most ambitious attempts at query optimization of its day.

1. G. Graefe (ed.), *Data Engineering* **16**:4 (1993), special issue on query processing in commercial database management systems, IEEE.

2. P. Griffiths-Selinger, M. M. Astrahan, D. D. Chamberlin, R. A. Lorie, and T. G. Price, "Access path selection in a relational database system," *Proc. ACM SIGMOD Intl. Conf. on Management of Data* (1979), pp. 23–34.

3. P. A. V. Hall, "Optimization of a single relational expression in a relational database system," *IBM J. Research and Development* **20**:3 (1976), pp. 244–257.

4. F. P. Palermo, "A database search problem," in: J. T. Tou (ed.) *Information Systems COINS IV*, Plenum, New York, 1974.

5. J. M. Smith and P. Y. Chang, "Optimizing the performance of a relational algebra database interface," *Comm. ACM* **18**:10 (1975), pp. 568–579.

6. E. Wong and K. Youssefi, "Decomposition — a strategy for query processing," *ACM Trans. on Database Systems* **1**:3 (1976), pp. 223–241.

Chapter 17

Coping With System Failures

Starting with this chapter, we focus our attention on those parts of a DBMS that control access to data. There are two major issues to address:

1. Data must be protected in the face of a system failure. This chapter deals with techniques for supporting the goal of *resilience*, that is, integrity of the data when the system fails in some way.

2. Data must not be corrupted simply because several error-free queries or database modifications are being done at once. This matter is addressed in Chapters 18 and 19.

The principal technique for supporting resilience is a *log*, which records securely the history of database changes. We shall discuss three different styles of logging, called "undo," "redo," and "undo/redo." We also discuss *recovery*, the process whereby the log is used to reconstruct what has happened to the database when there has been a failure. An important aspect of logging and recovery is avoidance of the situation where the log must be examined into the distant past. Thus, we shall learn about "checkpointing," which limits the length of log that must be examined during recovery.

In a final section, we discuss "archiving," which allows the database to survive not only temporary system failures, but situations where the entire database is lost. Then, we must rely on a recent copy of the database (the archive) plus whatever log information survives, to reconstruct the database as it existed at some point in the recent past.

17.1 Issues and Models for Resilient Operation

We begin our discussion of coping with failures by reviewing the kinds of things that can go wrong, and what a DBMS can and should do about them. We

843

initially focus on "system failures" or "crashes," the kinds of errors that the logging and recovery methods are designed to fix. We also introduce in Section 17.1.4 the model for buffer management that underlies all discussions of recovery from system errors. The same model is needed in the next chapter as we discuss concurrent access to the database by several transactions.

17.1.1 Failure Modes

There are many things that can go wrong as a database is queried and modified. Problems range from the keyboard entry of incorrect data to an explosion in the room where the database is stored on disk. The following items are a catalog of the most important failure modes and what the DBMS can do about them.

Erroneous Data Entry

Some data errors are impossible to detect. For example, if a clerk mistypes one digit of your phone number, the data will still look like a phone number that *could* be yours. On the other hand, if the clerk omits a digit from your phone number, then the data is evidently in error, since it does not have the form of a phone number. The principal technique for addressing data-entry errors is to write constraints and triggers that detect data believed to be erroneous.

Media Failures

A local failure of a disk, one that changes only a bit or a few bits, can normally be detected by parity checks associated with the sectors of the disk, as we discussed in Section 13.4.2. Head crashes, where the entire disk becomes unreadable, are generally handled by one or both of the following approaches:

1. Use one of the RAID schemes discussed in Section 13.4, so the lost disk can be restored.

2. Maintain an *archive*, a copy of the database on a medium such as tape or optical disk. The archive is periodically created, either fully or incrementally, and stored at a safe distance from the database itself. We shall discuss archiving in Section 17.5.

3. Instead of an archive, one could keep redundant copies of the database on-line, distributed among several sites. These copies are kept consistent by mechanisms we shall discuss in Section 20.6.

Catastrophic Failure

In this category are a number of situations in which the media holding the database is completely destroyed. Examples include explosions, fires, or vandalism at the site of the database. RAID will not help, since all the data disks and their parity check disks become useless simultaneously. However, the other approaches that can be used to protect against media failure — archiving and redundant, distributed copies — will also protect against a catastrophic failure.

System Failures

The processes that query and modify the database are called *transactions*. A transaction, like any program, executes a number of steps in sequence; often, several of these steps will modify the database. Each transaction has a *state*, which represents what has happened so far in the transaction. The state includes the current place in the transaction's code being executed and the values of any local variables of the transaction that will be needed later on.

System failures are problems that cause the state of a transaction to be lost. Typical system failures are power loss and software errors. Since main memory is "volatile," as we discussed in Section 13.1.3, a power failure will cause the contents of main memory to disappear, along with the result of any transaction step that was kept only in main memory, rather than on (nonvolatile) disk. Similarly, a software error may overwrite part of main memory, possibly including values that were part of the state of the program.

When main memory is lost, the transaction state is lost; that is, we can no longer tell what parts of the transaction, including its database modifications, were made. Running the transaction again may not fix the problem. For example, if the transaction must add 1 to a value in the database, we do not know whether to repeat the addition of 1 or not. The principal remedy for the problems that arise due to a system error is logging of all database changes in a separate, nonvolatile log, coupled with recovery when necessary. However, the mechanisms whereby such logging can be done in a fail-safe manner are surprisingly intricate, as we shall see starting in Section 17.2.

17.1.2 More About Transactions

We introduced the idea of transactions from the point of view of the SQL programmer in Section 6.6. Before proceeding to our study of database resilience and recovery from failures, we need to discuss the fundamental notion of a transaction in more detail.

The transaction is the unit of execution of database operations. For example, if we are issuing ad-hoc commands to a SQL system, then each query or database modification statement (plus any resulting trigger actions) is a transaction. When using an embedded SQL interface, the programmer controls the extent of a transaction, which may include several queries or modifications, as well as operations performed in the host language. In the typical embedded SQL system, transactions begin as soon as operations on the database are executed and end with an explicit COMMIT or ROLLBACK ("abort") command.

As we shall discuss in Section 17.1.3, a transaction must execute atomically, that is, all-or-nothing and as if it were executed at an instant in time. Assuring that transactions are executed correctly is the job of a *transaction manager*, a subsystem that performs several functions, including:

1. Issuing signals to the log manager (described below) so that necessary information in the form of "log records" can be stored on the log.

2. Assuring that concurrently executing transactions do not interfere with each other in ways that introduce errors ("scheduling"; see Section 18.1).

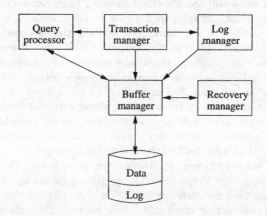

Figure 17.1: The log manager and transaction manager

The transaction manager and its interactions are suggested by Fig. 17.1. The transaction manager will send messages about actions of transactions to the log manager, to the buffer manager about when it is possible or necessary to copy the buffer back to disk, and to the query processor to execute the queries and other database operations that comprise the transaction.

The log manager maintains the log. It must deal with the buffer manager, since space for the log initially appears in main-memory buffers, and at certain times these buffers must be copied to disk. The log, as well as the data, occupies space on the disk, as we suggest in Fig. 17.1.

Finally, we show a recovery manager in Fig. 17.1. When there is a crash, the recovery manager is activated. It examines the log and uses it to repair the data, if necessary. As always, access to the disk is through the buffer manager.

17.1.3   Correct Execution of Transactions

Before we can deal with correcting system errors, we need to understand what it means for a transaction to be executed "correctly." To begin, we assume that the database is composed of "elements." We shall not specify precisely what an "element" is, except to say it has a value and can be accessed or modified by transactions. Different database systems use different notions of elements, but they are usually chosen from one or more of the following:

1. Relations.

2. Disk blocks or pages.

3. Individual tuples or objects.

In examples to follow, one can imagine that database elements are tuples, or in many examples, simply integers. However, there are several good reasons in practice to use choice (2) — disk blocks or pages — as the database element. In this way, buffer-contents become single elements, allowing us to avoid some serious problems with logging and transactions that we shall explore periodically as we learn various techniques. Avoiding database elements that are bigger than disk blocks also prevents a situation where part but not all of an element has been placed in nonvolatile storage when a crash occurs.

A database has a *state*, which is a value for each of its elements.[1] Intuitively, we regard certain states as *consistent*, and others as inconsistent. Consistent states satisfy all constraints of the database schema, such as key constraints and constraints on values. However, consistent states must also satisfy implicit constraints that are in the mind of the database designer. The implicit constraints may be maintained by triggers that are part of the database schema, but they might also be maintained only by policy statements concerning the database, or warnings associated with the user interface through which updates are made.

A fundamental assumption about transactions is:

- *The Correctness Principle*: If a transaction executes in the absence of any other transactions or system errors, and it starts with the database in a consistent state, then the database is also in a consistent state when the transaction ends.

There is a converse to the correctness principle that forms the motivation for both the logging techniques discussed in this chapter and the concurrency control mechanisms discussed in Chapter 18. This converse involves two points:

1. A transaction is *atomic*; that is, it must be executed as a whole or not at all. If only part of a transaction executes, then the resulting database state may not be consistent.

2. Transactions that execute simultaneously are likely to lead to an inconsistent state unless we take steps to control their interactions, as we shall in Chapter 18.

---

[1] We should not confuse the database state with the state of a transaction; the latter is values for the transaction's local variables, not database elements.

Is the Correctness Principle Believable?

Given that a database transaction could be an ad-hoc modification command issued at a terminal, perhaps by someone who doesn't understand the implicit constraints in the mind of the database designer, is it plausible to assume all transactions take the database from a consistent state to another consistent state? Explicit constraints are enforced by the database, so any transaction that violates them will be rejected by the system and not change the database at all. As for implicit constraints, one cannot characterize them exactly under any circumstances. Our position, justifying the correctness principle, is that if someone is given authority to modify the database, then they also have the authority to judge what the implicit constraints are.

17.1.4 The Primitive Operations of Transactions

Let us now consider in detail how transactions interact with the database. There are three address spaces that interact in important ways:

1. The space of disk blocks holding the database elements.

2. The virtual or main memory address space that is managed by the buffer manager.

3. The local address space of the transaction.

For a transaction to read a database element, that element must first be brought to a main-memory buffer or buffers, if it is not already there. Then, the contents of the buffer(s) can be read by the transaction into its own address space. Writing a new value for a database element by a transaction follows the reverse route. The new value is first created by the transaction in its own space. Then, this value is copied to the appropriate buffer(s).

The buffer may or may not be copied to disk immediately; that decision is the responsibility of the buffer manager in general. As we shall soon see, one of the principal tools for assuring resilience is forcing the buffer manager to write the block in a buffer back to disk at appropriate times. However, in order to reduce the number of disk I/O's, database systems can and will allow a change to exist only in volatile main-memory storage, at least for certain periods of time and under the proper set of conditions.

In order to study the details of logging algorithms and other transaction-management algorithms, we need a notation that describes all the operations that move data between address spaces. The primitives we shall use are:

1. INPUT(X): Copy the disk block containing database element X to a memory buffer.

Buffers in Query Processing and in Transactions

If you got used to the analysis of buffer utilization in the chapters on query processing, you may notice a change in viewpoint here. In Chapters 15 and 16 we were interested in buffers principally as they were used to compute temporary relations during the evaluation of a query. That is one important use of buffers, but there is never a need to preserve a temporary value, so these buffers do not generally have their values logged. On the other hand, those buffers that hold data retrieved from the database *do* need to have those values preserved, especially when the transaction updates them.

---

2. READ(X,t): Copy the database element X to the transaction's local variable t. More precisely, if the block containing database element X is not in a memory buffer then first execute INPUT(X). Next, assign the value of X to local variable t.

3. WRITE(X,t): Copy the value of local variable t to database element X in a memory buffer. More precisely, if the block containing database element X is not in a memory buffer then execute INPUT(X). Next, copy the value of t to X in the buffer.

4. OUTPUT(X): Copy the block containing X from its buffer to disk.

The above operations make sense as long as database elements reside within a single disk block, and therefore within a single buffer. If a database element occupies several blocks, we shall imagine that each block-sized portion of the element is an element by itself. The logging mechanism to be used will assure that the transaction cannot complete without the write of X being atomic; i.e., either all blocks of X are written to disk, or none are. Thus, we shall assume for the entire discussion of logging that

- A database element is no larger than a single block.

Different DBMS components issue the various commands we just introduced. READ and WRITE are issued by transactions. INPUT and OUTPUT are normally issued by the buffer manager. OUTPUT can also be initiated by the log manager under certain conditions, as we shall see.

Example 17.1: To see how the above primitive operations relate to what a transaction might do, let us consider a database that has two elements, A and B, with the constraint that they must be equal in all consistent states.[2]
Transaction T consists logically of the following two steps:

---

[2]One reasonably might ask why we should bother to have two different elements that are constrained to be equal, rather than maintaining only one element. However, this simple

```
A := A*2;
B := B*2;
```

If T starts in a consistent state (i.e., $A = B$) and completes its activities without interference from another transaction or system error, then the final state must also be consistent. That is, T doubles two equal elements to get new, equal elements.

Execution of T involves reading A and B from disk, performing arithmetic in the local address space of T, and writing the new values of A and B to their buffers. The relevant steps of T are thus:

```
READ(A,t); t := t*2; WRITE(A,t); READ(B,t); t := t*2; WRITE(B,t);
```

In addition, the buffer manager will eventually execute the OUTPUT steps to write these buffers back to disk. Figure 17.2 shows the primitive steps of T, followed by the two OUTPUT commands from the buffer manager. We assume that initially $A = B = 8$. The values of the memory and disk copies of A and B and the local variable t in the address space of transaction T are indicated for each step.

Action	t	Mem A	Mem B	Disk A	Disk B
READ(A,t)	8	8		8	8
t := t*2	16	8		8	8
WRITE(A,t)	16	16		8	8
READ(B,t)	8	16	8	8	8
t := t*2	16	16	8	8	8
WRITE(B,t)	16	16	16	8	8
OUTPUT(A)	16	16	16	16	8
OUTPUT(B)	16	16	16	16	16

Figure 17.2: Steps of a transaction and its effect on memory and disk

At the first step, T reads A, which generates an INPUT(A) command for the buffer manager if A's block is not already in a buffer. The value of A is also copied by the READ command into local variable t of T's address space. The second step doubles t; it has no affect on A, either in a buffer or on disk. The third step writes t into A of the buffer; it does not affect A on disk. The next three steps do the same for B, and the last two steps copy A and B to disk.

Observe that as long as all these steps execute, consistency of the database is preserved. If a system error occurs before OUTPUT(A) is executed, then there is no effect to the database stored on disk; it is as if T never ran, and consistency is preserved. However, if there is a system error after OUTPUT(A) but before

---

numerical constraint captures the spirit of many more realistic constraints, e.g., the number of seats sold on a flight must not exceed the number of seats on the plane by more than 10%, or the sum of the loan balances at a bank must equal the total debt of the bank.

OUTPUT(B), then the database is left in an inconsistent state. We cannot prevent this situation from ever occurring, but we can arrange that when it does occur, the problem can be repaired — either both A and B will be reset to 8, or both will be advanced to 16. □

17.1.5 Exercises for Section 17.1

Exercise 17.1.1: Suppose that the consistency constraint on the database is $0 \leq A \leq B$. Tell whether each of the following transactions preserves consistency.

  a) B := A+B; A := A+B;

  b) A := B+1; B := A+1;

  c) A := A+B; B := A+B;

Exercise 17.1.2: For each of the transactions of Exercise 17.1.1, add the read- and write-actions to the computation and show the effect of the steps on main memory and disk. Assume that initially $A = 50$ and $B = 25$. Also, tell whether it is possible, with the appropriate order of OUTPUT actions, to assure that consistency is preserved even if there is a crash while the transaction is executing.

17.2 Undo Logging

A *log* is a file of *log records*, each telling something about what some transaction has done. If log records appear in nonvolatile storage, we can use them to restore the database to a consistent state after a system crash. Our first style of logging — *undo logging* — makes repairs to the database state by undoing the effects of transactions that may not have completed before the crash.

Additionally, in this section we introduce the basic idea of log records, including the *commit* (successful completion of a transaction) action and its effect on the database state and log. We shall also consider how the log itself is created in main memory and copied to disk by a "flush-log" operation. Finally, we examine the undo log specifically, and learn how to use it in recovery from a crash. In order to avoid having to examine the entire log during recovery, we introduce the idea of "checkpointing," which allows old portions of the log to be thrown away.

17.2.1 Log Records

Imagine the log as a file opened for appending only. As transactions execute, the *log manager* has the job of recording in the log each important event. One block of the log at a time is filled with log records, each representing one of these events. Log blocks are initially created in main memory and are allocated

---

Why Might a Transaction Abort?

One might wonder why a transaction would abort rather than commit. There are actually several reasons. The simplest is when there is some error condition in the code of the transaction itself, e.g., an attempted division by zero. The DBMS may also abort a transaction for one of several reasons. For instance, a transaction may be involved in a deadlock, where it and one or more other transactions each hold some resource that the other needs. Then, one or more transactions must be forced by the system to abort (see Section 19.2).

---

by the buffer manager like any other blocks that the DBMS needs. The log blocks are written to nonvolatile storage on disk as soon as is feasible; we shall have more to say about this matter in Section 17.2.2.

There are several forms of log record that are used with each of the types of logging we discuss in this chapter. These are:

1. $<$START $T>$: This record indicates that transaction T has begun.

2. $<$COMMIT $T>$: Transaction T has completed successfully and will make no more changes to database elements. Any changes to the database made by T should appear on disk. However, because we cannot control when the buffer manager chooses to copy blocks from memory to disk, we cannot in general be sure that the changes are already on disk when we see the $<$COMMIT $T>$ log record. If we insist that the changes already be on disk, this requirement must be enforced by the log manager (as is the case for undo logging).

3. $<$ABORT $T>$: Transaction T could not complete successfully. If transaction T aborts, no changes it made can have been copied to disk, and it is the job of the transaction manager to make sure that such changes never appear on disk, or that their effect on disk is cancelled if they do. We shall discuss the matter of repairing the effect of aborted transactions in Section 19.1.1.

For an undo log, the only other kind of log record we need is an *update record*, which is a triple $<T, X, v>$. The meaning of this record is: transaction T has changed database element X, and its former value was v. The change reflected by an update record normally occurs in memory, not disk; i.e., the log record is a response to a WRITE action into memory, not an OUTPUT action to disk. Notice also that an undo log does not record the new value of a database element, only the old value. As we shall see, should recovery be necessary in a system using undo logging, the only thing the recovery manager will do is cancel the possible effect of a transaction on disk by restoring the old value.

Preview of Other Logging Methods

In "redo logging" (Section 17.3), on recovery we redo any transaction that has a COMMIT record, and we ignore all others. Rules for redo logging assure that we may ignore transactions whose COMMIT records never reached the log on disk. "Undo/redo logging" (Section 17.4) will, on recovery, undo any transaction that has not committed, and will redo those transactions that have committed. Again, log-management and buffering rules will assure that these steps successfully repair any damage to the database.

17.2.2   The Undo-Logging Rules

An undo log is sufficient to allow recovery from a system failure, provided transactions and the buffer manager obey two rules:

U_1: If transaction T modifies database element X, then the log record of the form $<T, X, v>$ must be written to disk *before* the new value of X is written to disk.

U_2: If a transaction commits, then its COMMIT log record must be written to disk only *after* all database elements changed by the transaction have been written to disk, but as soon thereafter as possible.

To summarize rules U_1 and U_2, material associated with one transaction must be written to disk in the following order:

a) The log records indicating changed database elements.

b) The changed database elements themselves.

c) The COMMIT log record.

However, the order of (a) and (b) applies to each database element individually, not to the group of update records for a transaction as a whole.

In order to force log records to disk, the log manager needs a *flush-log* command that tells the buffer manager to copy to disk any log blocks that have not previously been copied to disk or that have been changed since they were last copied. In sequences of actions, we shall show FLUSH LOG explicitly. The transaction manager also needs to have a way to tell the buffer manager to perform an OUTPUT action on a database element. We shall continue to show the OUTPUT action in sequences of transaction steps.

Example 17.2: Let us reconsider the transaction of Example 17.1 in the light of undo logging. Figure 17.3 expands on Fig. 17.2 to show the log entries and flush-log actions that have to take place along with the actions of the transaction

Step	Action	t	M-A	M-B	D-A	D-B	Log
1)							$<$START $T>$
2)	READ(A,t)	8	8		8	8	
3)	t := t*2	16	8		8	8	
4)	WRITE(A,t)	16	16		8	8	$<T, A, 8>$
5)	READ(B,t)	8	16	8	8	8	
6)	t := t*2	16	16	8	8	8	
7)	WRITE(B,t)	16	16	16	8	8	$<T, B, 8>$
8)	FLUSH LOG						
9)	OUTPUT(A)	16	16	16	16	8	
10)	OUTPUT(B)	16	16	16	16	16	
11)							$<$COMMIT $T>$
12)	FLUSH LOG						

Figure 17.3: Actions and their log entries

T. Note we have shortened the headers to M-A for "the copy of A in a memory buffer" or D-B for "the copy of B on disk," and so on.

In line (1) of Fig. 17.3, transaction T begins. The first thing that happens is that the $<$START $T>$ record is written to the log. Line (2) represents the read of A by T. Line (3) is the local change to t, which affects neither the database stored on disk nor any portion of the database in a memory buffer. Neither lines (2) nor (3) require any log entry, since they have no affect on the database.

Line (4) is the write of the new value of A to the buffer. This modification to A is reflected by the log entry $<T, A, 8>$ which says that A was changed by T and its former value was 8. Note that the new value, 16, is not mentioned in an undo log.

Lines (5) through (7) perform the same three steps with B instead of A. At this point, T has completed and must commit. The changed A and B must migrate to disk, but in order to follow the two rules for undo logging, there is a fixed sequence of events that must happen.

First, A and B cannot be copied to disk until the log records for the changes are on disk. Thus, at step (8) the log is flushed, assuring that these records appear on disk. Then, steps (9) and (10) copy A and B to disk. The transaction manager requests these steps from the buffer manager in order to commit T.

Now, it is possible to commit T, and the $<$COMMIT $T>$ record is written to the log, which is step (11). Finally, we must flush the log again at step (12) to make sure that the $<$COMMIT $T>$ record of the log appears on disk. Notice that without writing this record to disk, we could have a situation where a transaction has committed, but for a long time a review of the log does not tell us that it has committed. That situation could cause strange behavior if there were a crash, because, as we shall see in Section 17.2.3, a transaction that appeared to the user to have completed long ago would then be undone and effectively aborted. □

Background Activity Affects the Log and Buffers

As we look at a sequence of actions and log entries like Fig. 17.3, it is tempting to imagine that these actions occur in isolation. However, the DBMS may be processing many transactions simultaneously. Thus, the four log records for transaction T may be interleaved on the log with records for other transactions. Moreover, if one of these transactions flushes the log, then the log records from T may appear on disk earlier than is implied by the flush-log actions of Fig. 17.3. There is no harm if log records reflecting a database modification appear earlier than necessary. The essential policy for undo logging is that we don't write the <COMMIT T> record until the OUTPUT actions for T are completed.

A trickier situation occurs if two database elements A and B share a block. Then, writing one of them to disk writes the other as well. In the worst case, we can violate rule U_1 by writing one of these elements prematurely. It may be necessary to adopt additional constraints on transactions in order to make undo logging work. For instance, we might use a locking scheme where database elements are disk blocks, as described in Section 18.3, to prevent two transactions from accessing the same block at the same time. This and other problems that appear when database elements are fractions of a block motivate our suggestion that blocks *be* the database elements.

17.2.3 Recovery Using Undo Logging

Suppose now that a system failure occurs. It is possible that certain database changes made by a given transaction were written to disk, while other changes made by the same transaction never reached the disk. If so, the transaction was not executed atomically, and there may be an inconsistent database state. The *recovery manager* must use the log to restore the database to some consistent state.

In this section we consider only the simplest form of recovery manager, one that looks at the entire log, no matter how long, and makes database changes as a result of its examination. In Section 17.2.4 we consider a more sensible approach, where the log is periodically "checkpointed," to limit the distance back in history that the recovery manager must go.

The first task of the recovery manager is to divide the transactions into committed and uncommitted transactions. If there is a log record <COMMIT T>, then by undo rule U_2 all changes made by transaction T were previously written to disk. Thus, T by itself could not have left the database in an inconsistent state when the system failure occurred.

However, suppose that we find a <START T> record on the log but no <COMMIT T> record. Then there could have been some changes to the database made by T that were written to disk before the crash, while other changes by T either were not made, or were made in the main-memory buffers but not copied to disk. In this case, T is an *incomplete transaction* and must be *undone*. That is, whatever changes T made must be reset to their previous value. Fortunately, rule U_1 assures us that if T changed X on disk before the crash, then there will be a $<T, X, v>$ record on the log, and that record will have been copied to disk before the crash. Thus, during the recovery, we must write the value v for database element X. Note that this rule begs the question whether X had value v in the database anyway; we don't even bother to check.

Since there may be several uncommitted transactions in the log, and there may even be several uncommitted transactions that modified X, we have to be systematic about the order in which we restore values. Thus, the recovery manager must scan the log from the end (i.e., from the most recently written record to the earliest written). As it travels, it remembers all those transactions T for which it has seen a $<$COMMIT $T>$ record or an $<$ABORT $T>$ record. Also as it travels backward, if it sees a record $<T, X, v>$, then:

1. If T is a transaction whose COMMIT record has been seen, then do nothing. T is committed and must not be undone.

2. Otherwise, T is an incomplete transaction, or an aborted transaction. The recovery manager must change the value of X in the database to v, in case X had been altered just before the crash.

After making these changes, the recovery manager must write a log record $<$ABORT $T>$ for each incomplete transaction T that was not previously aborted, and then flush the log. Now, normal operation of the database may resume, and new transactions may begin executing.

Example 17.3 : Let us consider the sequence of actions from Fig. 17.3 and Example 17.2. There are several different times that the system crash could have occurred; let us consider each significantly different one.

1. The crash occurs after step (12). Then the $<$COMMIT $T>$ record reached disk before the crash. When we recover, we do not undo the results of T, and all log records concerning T are ignored by the recovery manager.

2. The crash occurs between steps (11) and (12). It is possible that the log record containing the COMMIT got flushed to disk; for instance, the buffer manager may have needed the buffer containing the end of the log for another transaction, or some other transaction may have asked for a log flush. If so, then the recovery is the same as in case (1) as far as T is concerned. However, if the COMMIT record never reached disk, then the recovery manager considers T incomplete. When it scans the log backward, it comes first to the record $<T, B, 8>$. It therefore stores 8 as the value of B on disk. It then comes to the record $<T, A, 8>$ and makes A have value 8 on disk. Finally, the record $<$ABORT $T>$ is written to the log, and the log is flushed.

Crashes During Recovery

Suppose the system again crashes while we are recovering from a previous crash. Because of the way undo-log records are designed, giving the old value rather than, say, the change in the value of a database element, the recovery steps are *idempotent*; that is, repeating them many times has exactly the same effect as performing them once. We already observed that if we find a record $<T, X, v>$, it does not matter whether the value of X is already v — we may write v for X regardless. Similarly, if we repeat the recovery process, it does not matter whether the first recovery attempt restored some old values; we simply restore them again. The same reasoning holds for the other logging methods we discuss in this chapter. Since the recovery operations are idempotent, we can recover a second time without worrying about changes made the first time.

---

3. The crash occurs between steps (10) and (11). Now, the COMMIT record surely was not written, so T is incomplete and is undone as in case (2).

4. The crash occurs between steps (8) and (10). Again, T is undone. In this case the change to A and/or B may not have reached disk. Nevertheless, the proper value, 8, is restored for each of these database elements.

5. The crash occurs prior to step (8). Now, it is not certain whether any of the log records concerning T have reached disk. However, we know by rule U_1 that if the change to A and/or B reached disk, then the corresponding log record reached disk. Therefore if there were changes to A and/or B made on disk by T, then the corresponding log record will cause the recovery manager to undo those changes.

□

17.2.4 Checkpointing

As we observed, recovery requires that the entire log be examined, in principle. When logging follows the undo style, once a transaction has its COMMIT log record written to disk, the log records of that transaction are no longer needed during recovery. We might imagine that we could delete the log prior to a COMMIT, but sometimes we cannot. The reason is that often many transactions execute at once. If we truncated the log after one transaction committed, log records pertaining to some other active transaction T might be lost and could not be used to undo T if recovery were necessary.

The simplest way to untangle potential problems is to *checkpoint* the log periodically. In a simple checkpoint, we:

1. Stop accepting new transactions.

2. Wait until all currently active transactions commit or abort and have written a COMMIT or ABORT record on the log.

3. Flush the log to disk.

4. Write a log record <CKPT>, and flush the log again.

5. Resume accepting transactions.

Any transaction that executed prior to the checkpoint will have finished, and by rule U_2 its changes will have reached the disk. Thus, there will be no need to undo any of these transactions during recovery. During a recovery, we scan the log backwards from the end, identifying incomplete transactions as in Section 17.2.3. However, when we find a <CKPT> record, we know that we have seen all the incomplete transactions. Since no transactions may begin until the checkpoint ends, we must have seen every log record pertaining to the incomplete transactions already. Thus, there is no need to scan prior to the <CKPT>, and in fact the log before that point can be deleted or overwritten safely.

Example 17.4: Suppose the log begins:

$$<\text{START } T_1>$$
$$<T_1, A, 5>$$
$$<\text{START } T_2>$$
$$<T_2, B, 10>$$

At this time, we decide to do a checkpoint. Since T_1 and T_2 are the active (incomplete) transactions, we shall have to wait until they complete before writing the <CKPT> record on the log.

A possible extension of the log is shown in Fig. 17.4. Suppose a crash occurs at this point. Scanning the log from the end, we identify T_3 as the only incomplete transaction, and restore E and F to their former values 25 and 30, respectively. When we reach the <CKPT> record, we know there is no need to examine prior log records and the restoration of the database state is complete. □

17.2.5 Nonquiescent Checkpointing

A problem with the checkpointing technique described in Section 17.2.4 is that effectively we must shut down the system while the checkpoint is being made. Since the active transactions may take a long time to commit or abort, the system may appear to users to be stalled. Thus, a more complex technique known as *nonquiescent checkpointing*, which allows new transactions to enter the system during the checkpoint, is usually preferred. The steps in a nonquiescent checkpoint are:

$$<\text{START } T_1>$$
$$<T_1, A, 5>$$
$$<\text{START } T_2>$$
$$<T_2, B, 10>$$
$$<T_2, C, 15>$$
$$<T_1, D, 20>$$
$$<\text{COMMIT } T_1>$$
$$<\text{COMMIT } T_2>$$
$$<\text{CKPT}>$$
$$<\text{START } T_3>$$
$$<T_3, E, 25>$$
$$<T_3, F, 30>$$

Figure 17.4: An undo log

1. Write a log record <START CKPT $(T_1, \ldots, T_k)$> and flush the log. Here, $T_1, \ldots, T_k$ are the names or identifiers for all the *active* transactions (i.e., transactions that have not yet committed and written their changes to disk).

2. Wait until all of $T_1, \ldots, T_k$ commit or abort, but do not prohibit other transactions from starting.

3. When all of $T_1, \ldots, T_k$ have completed, write a log record <END CKPT> and flush the log.

With a log of this type, we can recover from a system crash as follows. As usual, we scan the log from the end, finding all incomplete transactions as we go, and restoring old values for database elements changed by these transactions. There are two cases, depending on whether, scanning backwards, we first meet an <END CKPT> record or a <START CKPT $(T_1, \ldots, T_k)$> record.

- If we first meet an <END CKPT> record, then we know that all incomplete transactions began after the previous <START CKPT $(T_1, \ldots, T_k)$> record. We may thus scan backwards as far as the next START CKPT, and then stop; previous log is useless and may as well have been discarded.

- If we first meet a record <START CKPT $(T_1, \ldots, T_k)$>, then the crash occurred during the checkpoint. However, the only incomplete transactions are those we met scanning backwards before we reached the START CKPT and those of $T_1, \ldots, T_k$ that did not complete before the crash. Thus, we need scan no further back than the start of the earliest of these incomplete transactions. The previous START CKPT record is certainly prior to any of these transaction starts, but often we shall find the starts of the

Finding the Last Log Record

It is common to recycle blocks of the log file on disk, since checkpoints allow us to drop old portions of the log. However, if we overwrite old log records, then we need to keep a serial number, which may only increase, as suggested by:

1̸ 9	2̸ 10	3̸ 11	4	5	6	7	8

Then, we can find the record whose serial number is greater than that of the next record; the latter record will be the current end of the log, and the entire log is found by ordering the current records by their present serial numbers.

   In practice, a large log may be composed of many files, with a "top" file whose records indicate the files that comprise the log. Then, to recover, we find the last record of the top file, go to the file indicated, and find the last record there.

incomplete transactions long before we reach the previous checkpoint.[3] Moreover, if we use pointers to chain together the log records that belong to the same transaction, then we need not search the whole log for records belonging to active transactions; we just follow their chains back through the log.

As a general rule, once an <END CKPT> record has been written to disk, we can delete the log prior to the previous START CKPT record.

Example 17.5: Suppose that, as in Example 17.4, the log begins:

$$<\text{START } T_1>$$
$$<T_1, A, 5>$$
$$<\text{START } T_2>$$
$$<T_2, B, 10>$$

Now, we decide to do a nonquiescent checkpoint. Since T_1 and T_2 are the active (incomplete) transactions at this time, we write a log record

$$<\text{START CKPT } (T_1, T_2)>$$

Suppose that while waiting for T_1 and T_2 to complete, another transaction, T_3, initiates. A possible continuation of the log is shown in Fig. 17.5.

   Suppose that at this point there is a system crash. Examining the log from the end, we find that T_3 is an incomplete transaction and must be undone.

---

[3]Notice, however, that because the checkpoint is nonquiescent, one of the incomplete transactions could have begun between the start and end of the previous checkpoint.

$$<\text{START } T_1>$$
$$<T_1, A, 5>$$
$$<\text{START } T_2>$$
$$<T_2, B, 10>$$
$$<\text{START CKPT } (T_1, T_2)>$$
$$<T_2, C, 15>$$
$$<\text{START } T_3>$$
$$<T_1, D, 20>$$
$$<\text{COMMIT } T_1>$$
$$<T_3, E, 25>$$
$$<\text{COMMIT } T_2>$$
$$<\text{END CKPT}>$$
$$<T_3, F, 30>$$

Figure 17.5: An undo log using nonquiescent checkpointing

The final log record tells us to restore database element F to the value 30. When we find the $<\text{END CKPT}>$ record, we know that all incomplete transactions began after the previous START CKPT. Scanning further back, we find the record $<T_3, E, 25>$, which tells us to restore E to value 25. Between that record, and the START CKPT there are no other transactions that started but did not commit, so no further changes to the database are made.

$$<\text{START } T_1>$$
$$<T_1, A, 5>$$
$$<\text{START } T_2>$$
$$<T_2, B, 10>$$
$$<\text{START CKPT } (T_1, T_2)>$$
$$<T_2, C, 15>$$
$$<\text{START } T_3>$$
$$<T_1, D, 20>$$
$$<\text{COMMIT } T_1>$$
$$<T_3, E, 25>$$

Figure 17.6: Undo log with a system crash during checkpointing

Now suppose the crash occurs during the checkpoint, and the end of the log after the crash is as shown in Fig. 17.6. Scanning backwards, we identify T_3 and then T_2 as incomplete transactions and undo changes they have made. When we find the $<\text{START CKPT } (T_1, T_2)>$ record, we know that the only other possible incomplete transaction is T_1. However, we have already scanned the $<\text{COMMIT } T_1>$ record, so we know that T_1 is *not* incomplete. Also, we have already seen the $<\text{START } T_3>$ record. Thus, we need only to continue backwards until we meet the START record for T_2, restoring database element B to value

10 as we go.   □

17.2.6 Exercises for Section 17.2

Exercise 17.2.1: For each of the sequences of log records representing the actions of one transaction T, tell all the sequences of events that are legal according to the rules of undo logging, where the events of interest are the writing to disk of the blocks containing database elements, and the blocks of the log containing the update and commit records. You may assume that log records are written to disk in the order shown; i.e., it is not possible to write one log record to disk while a previous record is not written to disk.

a) <START T>; <$T, A, 10$>; <$T, B, 20$>; <COMMIT T>;

b) <START T>; <$T, A, 10$>; <$T, B, 20$>; <$T, C, 30$><COMMIT T>;

! **Exercise 17.2.2:** The pattern introduced in Exercise 17.2.1 can be extended to a transaction that writes new values for n database elements. How many legal sequences of events are there for such a transaction, if the undo-logging rules are obeyed?

Exercise 17.2.3: The following is a sequence of undo-log records written by two transactions T and U: <START U>; <$U, A, 10$>; <START T>; <$T, B, 20$>; <$U, C, 30$>; <$T, D, 40$>; <COMMIT T>; <$U, E, 50$>; <COMMIT U>. Describe the action of the recovery manager, including changes to both disk and the log, if there is a crash and the last log record to appear on disk is:

(a) <START T> (b) <COMMIT T> (c) <$U, E, 50$> (d) <COMMIT U>.

Exercise 17.2.4: For each of the situations described in Exercise 17.2.3, what values written by T and U *must* appear on disk? Which values *might* appear on disk?

! **Exercise 17.2.5:** Suppose that the transaction U in Exercise 17.2.3 is changed so that the record <$U, D, 40$> becomes <$U, A, 40$>. What is the effect on the disk value of A if there is a crash at some point during the sequence of events? What does this example say about the ability of logging by itself to preserve atomicity of transactions?

Exercise 17.2.6: Show the undo-log records for each of the transactions (call each T) of Exercise 17.1.1, assuming that initially $A = 50$ and $B = 25$.

Exercise 17.2.7: Consider the following sequence of log records: <START S>; <$S, A, 60$>; <COMMIT S>; <START T>; <$T, A, 10$>; <START U>; <$U, B, 20$>; <$T, C, 30$>; <START V>; <$U, D, 40$>; <$V, F, 70$>; <COMMIT U>; <$T, E, 50$>; <COMMIT T>; <$V, B, 80$>; <COMMIT V>. Suppose that we begin a nonquiescent checkpoint immediately after one of the following log records has been written (in memory):

(a) $<S, A, 60>$ (b) $<T, A, 10>$ (c) $<U, B, 20>$
(d) $<U, D, 40>$ (e) $<T, E, 50>$

For each, tell:

i. When the $<$END CKPT$>$ record is written, and

ii. For each possible point at which a crash could occur, how far back in the log we must look to find all possible incomplete transactions.

17.3   Redo Logging

Undo logging has a potential problem that we cannot commit a transaction without first writing all its changed data to disk. Sometimes, we can save disk I/O's if we let changes to the database reside only in main memory for a while. As long as there is a log to fix things up in the event of a crash, it is safe to do so.

The requirement for immediate backup of database elements to disk can be avoided if we use a logging mechanism called *redo logging*. The principal differences between redo and undo logging are:

1. While undo logging cancels the effect of incomplete transactions and ignores committed ones during recovery, redo logging ignores incomplete transactions and repeats the changes made by committed transactions.

2. While undo logging requires us to write changed database elements to disk before the COMMIT log record reaches disk, redo logging requires that the COMMIT record appear on disk before any changed values reach disk.

3. While the old values of changed database elements are exactly what we need to recover when the undo rules U_1 and U_2 are followed, to recover using redo logging, we need the new values instead.

17.3.1   The Redo-Logging Rule

In redo logging the meaning of a log record $<T, X, v>$ is "transaction T wrote new value v for database element X." There is no indication of the old value of X in this record. Every time a transaction T modifies a database element X, a record of the form $<T, X, v>$ must be written to the log.

For redo logging, the order in which data and log entries reach disk can be described by a single "redo rule," called the *write-ahead logging rule*.

R_1: Before modifying any database element X on disk, it is necessary that all log records pertaining to this modification of X, including both the update record $<T, X, v>$ and the $<$COMMIT $T>$ record, must appear on disk.

The COMMIT record for a transaction can only be written to the log when the transaction completes, so the commit record must follow all the update log records. Thus, when redo logging is in use, the order in which material associated with one transaction gets written to disk is:

1. The log records indicating changed database elements.

2. The COMMIT log record.

3. The changed database elements themselves.

Example 17.6: Let us consider the same transaction T as in Example 17.2. Figure 17.7 shows a possible sequence of events for this transaction.

Step	Action	t	M-A	M-B	D-A	D-B	Log
1)							<START T>
2)	READ(A,t)	8	8		8	8	
3)	t := t*2	16	8		8	8	
4)	WRITE(A,t)	16	16		8	8	<$T, A, 16$>
5)	READ(B,t)	8	16	8	8	8	
6)	t := t*2	16	16	8	8	8	
7)	WRITE(B,t)	16	16	16	8	8	<$T, B, 16$>
8)							<COMMIT T>
9)	FLUSH LOG						
10)	OUTPUT(A)	16	16	16	16	8	
11)	OUTPUT(B)	16	16	16	16	16	

Figure 17.7: Actions and their log entries using redo logging

The major differences between Figs. 17.7 and 17.3 are as follows. First, we note in lines (4) and (7) of Fig. 17.7 that the log records reflecting the changes have the new values of A and B, rather than the old values. Second, we see that the <COMMIT T> record comes earlier, at step (8). Then, the log is flushed, so all log records involving the changes of transaction T appear on disk. Only then can the new values of A and B be written to disk. We show these values written immediately, at steps (10) and (11), although in practice they might occur later. □

17.3.2 Recovery With Redo Logging

An important consequence of the redo rule R_1 is that unless the log has a <COMMIT T> record, we know that no changes to the database made by transaction T have been written to disk. Thus, incomplete transactions may be treated during recovery as if they had never occurred. However, the committed transactions present a problem, since we do not know which of their database changes have been written to disk. Fortunately, the redo log has exactly the

---

Order of Redo Matters

Since several committed transactions may have written new values for the same database element X, we have required that during a redo recovery, we scan the log from earliest to latest. Thus, the final value of X in the database will be the one written last, as it should be. Similarly, when describing undo recovery, we required that the log be scanned from latest to earliest. Thus, the final value of X will be the value that it had before any of the incomplete transactions changed it.

However, if the DBMS enforces atomicity, then we would not expect to find, in an undo log, two uncommitted transactions, each of which had written the same database element. In contrast, with redo logging we focus on the committed transactions, as these need to be redone. It is quite normal for there to be two *committed* transactions, each of which changed the same database element at different times. Thus, order of redo is always important, while order of undo might not be if the right kind of concurrency control were in effect.

---

information we need: the new values, which we may write to disk regardless of whether they were already there. To recover, using a redo log, after a system crash, we do the following.

1. Identify the committed transactions.

2. Scan the log forward from the beginning. For each log record $<T, X, v>$ encountered:

   (a) If T is not a committed transaction, do nothing.

   (b) If T is committed, write value v for database element X.

3. For each incomplete transaction T, write an $<$ABORT $T>$ record to the log and flush the log.

Example 17.7: Let us consider the log written in Fig. 17.7 and see how recovery would be performed if the crash occurred after different steps in that sequence of actions.

1. If the crash occurs any time after step (9), then the $<$COMMIT $T>$ record has been flushed to disk. The recovery system identifies T as a committed transaction. When scanning the log forward, the log records $<T, A, 16>$ and $<T, B, 16>$ cause the recovery manager to write values 16 for A and B. Notice that if the crash occurred between steps (10) and (11), then the write of A is redundant, but the write of B had not occurred and

changing B to 16 is essential to restore the database state to consistency. If the crash occurred after step (11), then both writes are redundant but harmless.

2. If the crash occurs between steps (8) and (9), then although the record <COMMIT T> was written to the log, it may not have gotten to disk (depending on whether the log was flushed for some other reason). If it did get to disk, then the recovery proceeds as in case (1), and if it did not get to disk, then recovery is as in case (3), below.

3. If the crash occurs prior to step (8), then <COMMIT T> surely has not reached disk. Thus, T is treated as an incomplete transaction. No changes to A or B on disk are made on behalf of T, and eventually an <ABORT T> record is written to the log.

□

17.3.3 Checkpointing a Redo Log

Redo logs present a checkpointing problem that we do not see with undo logs. Since the database changes made by a committed transaction can be copied to disk much later than the time at which the transaction commits, we cannot limit our concern to transactions that are active at the time we decide to create a checkpoint. Regardless of whether the checkpoint is quiescent or nonquiescent, between the start and end of the checkpoint we must write to disk all database elements that have been modified by committed transactions. To do so requires that the buffer manager keep track of which buffers are *dirty*, that is, they have been changed but not written to disk. It is also required to know which transactions modified which buffers.

On the other hand, we can complete the checkpoint without waiting for the active transactions to commit or abort, since they are not allowed to write their pages to disk at that time anyway. The steps to perform a nonquiescent checkpoint of a redo log are as follows:

1. Write a log record <START CKPT $(T_1, \ldots, T_k)$>, where $T_1, \ldots, T_k$ are all the active (uncommitted) transactions, and flush the log.

2. Write to disk all database elements that were written to buffers but not yet to disk by transactions that had already committed when the START CKPT record was written to the log.

3. Write an <END CKPT> record to the log and flush the log.

Example 17.8 : Figure 17.8 shows a possible redo log, in the middle of which a checkpoint occurs. When we start the checkpoint, only T_2 is active, but the value of A written by T_1 may have reached disk. If not, then we must copy A

$$
\begin{aligned}
&<\text{START } T_1> \\
&<T_1, A, 5> \\
&<\text{START } T_2> \\
&<\text{COMMIT } T_1> \\
&<T_2, B, 10> \\
&<\text{START CKPT } (T_2)> \\
&<T_2, C, 15> \\
&<\text{START } T_3> \\
&<T_3, D, 20> \\
&<\text{END CKPT}> \\
&<\text{COMMIT } T_2> \\
&<\text{COMMIT } T_3>
\end{aligned}
$$

Figure 17.8: A redo log

to disk before the checkpoint can end. We suggest the end of the checkpoint occurring after several other events have occurred: T_2 wrote a value for database element C, and a new transaction T_3 started and wrote a value of D. After the end of the checkpoint, the only things that happen are that T_2 and T_3 commit. □

17.3.4 Recovery With a Checkpointed Redo Log

As for an undo log, the insertion of records to mark the start and end of a checkpoint helps us limit our examination of the log when a recovery is necessary. Also as with undo logging, there are two cases, depending on whether the last checkpoint record is START or END.

Suppose first that the last checkpoint record on the log before a crash is <END CKPT>. Now, we know that every value written by a transaction that committed before the corresponding <START CKPT $(T_1, \ldots, T_k)$> has had its changes written to disk, so we need not concern ourselves with recovering the effects of these transactions. However, any transaction that is either among the T_i's or that started after the beginning of the checkpoint can still have changes it made not yet migrated to disk, even though the transaction has committed. Thus, we must perform recovery as described in Section 17.3.2, but may limit our attention to the transactions that are either one of the T_i's mentioned in the last <START CKPT $(T_1, \ldots, T_k)$> or that started after that log record appeared in the log. In searching the log, we do not have to look further back than the earliest of the <START T_i> records. Notice, however, that these START records could appear prior to any number of checkpoints. Linking backwards all the log records for a given transaction helps us to find the necessary records, as it did for undo logging.

Now, suppose the last checkpoint record on the log is

<START CKPT $(T_1, \ldots, T_k)$>

We cannot be sure that committed transactions prior to the start of this checkpoint had their changes written to disk. Thus, we must search back to the previous <END CKPT> record, find its matching <START CKPT $(S_1, \ldots, S_m)$> record,[4] and redo all those committed transactions that either started after that START CKPT or are among the S_i's.

Example 17.9: Consider again the log of Fig. 17.8. If a crash occurs at the end, we search backwards, finding the <END CKPT> record. We thus know that it is sufficient to consider as candidates to redo all those transactions that either started after the <START CKPT (T_2)> record was written or that are on its list (i.e., T_2). Thus, our candidate set is $\{T_2, T_3\}$. We find the records <COMMIT T_2> and <COMMIT T_3>, so we know that each must be redone. We search the log as far back as the <START T_2> record, and find the update records <$T_2, B, 10$>, <$T_2, C, 15$>, and <$T_3, D, 20$> for the committed transactions. Since we don't know whether these changes reached disk, we rewrite the values 10, 15, and 20 for B, C, and D, respectively.

Now, suppose the crash occurred between the records <COMMIT T_2> and <COMMIT T_3>. The recovery is similar to the above, except that T_3 is no longer a committed transaction. Thus, its change <$T_3, D, 20$> must *not* be redone, and no change is made to D during recovery, even though that log record is in the range of records that is examined. Also, we write an <ABORT T_3> record to the log after recovery.

Finally, suppose that the crash occurs just prior to the <END CKPT> record. In principal, we must search back to the next-to-last START CKPT record and get its list of active transactions. However, in this case there is no previous checkpoint, and we must go all the way to the beginning of the log. Thus, we identify T_1 as the only committed transaction, redo its action <$T_1, A, 5$>, and write records <ABORT T_2> and <ABORT T_3> to the log after recovery. □

Since transactions may be active during several checkpoints, it is convenient to include in the <START CKPT $(T_1, \ldots, T_k)$> records not only the names of the active transactions, but pointers to the place on the log where they started. By doing so, we know when it is safe to delete early portions of the log. When we write an <END CKPT>, we know that we shall never need to look back further than the earliest of the <START T_i> records for the active transactions T_i. Thus, anything prior to that START record may be deleted.

17.3.5 Exercises for Section 17.3

Exercise 17.3.1: Show the redo-log records for each of the transactions (call each T) of Exercise 17.1.1, assuming that initially $A = 50$ and $B = 25$.

---

[4]There is a small technicality that there could be a START CKPT record that, because of a previous crash, has no matching <END CKPT> record. Therefore, we must look not just for the previous START CKPT, but first for an <END CKPT> and then the previous START CKPT.

Exercise 17.3.2: Using the data of Exercise 17.2.7, answer for each of the positions (a) through (e) of that exercise:

   i. At what points could the <END CKPT> record be written, and

   ii. For each possible point at which a crash could occur, how far back in the log we must look to find all possible incomplete transactions. Consider both the case that the <END CKPT> record was or was not written prior to the crash.

Exercise 17.3.3: Repeat Exercise 17.2.1 for redo logging.

Exercise 17.3.4: Repeat Exercise 17.2.3 for redo logging.

Exercise 17.3.5: Repeat Exercise 17.2.4 for redo logging.

17.4 Undo/Redo Logging

We have seen two different approaches to logging, differentiated by whether the log holds old values or new values when a database element is updated. Each has certain drawbacks:

- Undo logging requires that data be written to disk immediately after a transaction finishes, perhaps increasing the number of disk I/O's that need to be performed.

- On the other hand, redo logging requires us to keep all modified blocks in buffers until the transaction commits and the log records have been flushed, perhaps increasing the average number of buffers required by transactions.

- Both undo and redo logs may put contradictory requirements on how buffers are handled during a checkpoint, unless the database elements are complete blocks or sets of blocks. For instance, if a buffer contains one database element A that was changed by a committed transaction and another database element B that was changed in the same buffer by a transaction that has not yet had its COMMIT record written to disk, then we are required to copy the buffer to disk because of A but also forbidden to do so, because rule R_1 applies to B.

We shall now see a kind of logging called *undo/redo logging*, that provides increased flexibility to order actions, at the expense of maintaining more information on the log.

17.4.1 The Undo/Redo Rules

An undo/redo log has the same sorts of log records as the other kinds of log, with one exception. The update log record that we write when a database element changes value has four components. Record $<T, X, v, w>$ means that transaction T changed the value of database element X; its former value was v, and its new value is w. The constraints that an undo/redo logging system must follow are summarized by the following rule:

UR_1 Before modifying any database element X on disk because of changes made by some transaction T, it is necessary that the update record $<T, X, v, w>$ appear on disk.

Rule UR_1 for undo/redo logging thus enforces only the constraints enforced by *both* undo logging and redo logging. In particular, the <COMMIT T> log record can precede or follow any of the changes to the database elements on disk.

Example 17.10: Figure 17.9 is a variation in the order of the actions associated with the transaction T that we last saw in Example 17.6. Notice that the log records for updates now have both the old and the new values of A and B. In this sequence, we have written the <COMMIT T> log record in the middle of the output of database elements A and B to disk. Step (10) could also have appeared before step (8) or step (9), or after step (11). □

Step	Action	t	M-A	M-B	D-A	D-B	Log
1)							<START T>
2)	READ(A,t)	8	8		8	8	
3)	t := t*2	16	8		8	8	
4)	WRITE(A,t)	16	16		8	8	$<T, A, 8, 16>$
5)	READ(B,t)	8	16	8	8	8	
6)	t := t*2	16	16	8	8	8	
7)	WRITE(B,t)	16	16	16	8	8	$<T, B, 8, 16>$
8)	FLUSH LOG						
9)	OUTPUT(A)	16	16	16	16	8	
10)							<COMMIT T>
11)	OUTPUT(B)	16	16	16	16	16	

Figure 17.9: A possible sequence of actions and their log entries using undo/redo logging

17.4.2 Recovery With Undo/Redo Logging

When we need to recover using an undo/redo log, we have the information in the update records either to undo a transaction T by restoring the old values of

---

A Problem With Delayed Commitment

Like undo logging, a system using undo/redo logging can exhibit a behavior where a transaction appears to the user to have been completed (e.g., they booked an airline seat over the Web and disconnected), and yet because the <COMMIT T> record was not flushed to disk, a subsequent crash causes the transaction to be undone rather than redone. If this possibility is a problem, we suggest the use of an additional rule for undo/redo logging:

UR_2 A <COMMIT T> record must be flushed to disk as soon as it appears in the log.

For instance, we would add FLUSH LOG after step (10) of Fig. 17.9.

---

the database elements that T changed, or to redo T by repeating the changes it has made. The undo/redo recovery policy is:

1. Redo all the committed transactions in the order earliest-first, and

2. Undo all the incomplete transactions in the order latest-first.

Notice that it is necessary for us to do both. Because of the flexibility allowed by undo/redo logging regarding the relative order in which COMMIT log records and the database changes themselves are copied to disk, we could have either a committed transaction with some or all of its changes not on disk, or an uncommitted transaction with some or all of its changes on disk.

Example 17.11: Consider the sequence of actions in Fig. 17.9. Here are the different ways that recovery would take place on the assumption that there is a crash at various points in the sequence.

1. Suppose the crash occurs after the <COMMIT T> record is flushed to disk. Then T is identified as a committed transaction. We write the value 16 for both A and B to the disk. Because of the actual order of events, A already has the value 16, but B may not, depending on whether the crash occurred before or after step (11).

2. If the crash occurs prior to the <COMMIT T> record reaching disk, then T is treated as an incomplete transaction. The previous values of A and B, 8 in each case, are written to disk. If the crash occurs between steps (9) and (10), then the value of A was 16 on disk, and the restoration to value 8 is necessary. In this example, the value of B does not need to be undone, and if the crash occurs before step (9) then neither does the value of A. However, in general we cannot be sure whether restoration is necessary, so we always perform the undo operation.

□

Strange Behavior of Transactions During Recovery

You may have noticed that we did not specify whether undo's or redo's are done first during recovery using an undo/redo log. In fact, whether we perform the redo's or undo's first, we are open to the following situation: a transaction T has committed and is redone. However, T read a value X written by some transaction U that has not committed and is undone. The problem is not whether we redo first, and leave X with its value prior to U, or we undo first and leave X with its value written by T. The situation makes no sense either way, because the final database state does not correspond to the effect of any sequence of atomic transactions.

In reality, the DBMS must do more than log changes. It must assure that such situations do not occur at all. In Chapter 18, there is a discussion about the means to isolate transactions like T and U, so the interaction between them through database element X cannot occur. In Section 19.1, we explicitly address means for preventing this situation where T reads a "dirty" value of X — one that has not been committed.

17.4.3   Checkpointing an Undo/Redo Log

A nonquiescent checkpoint is somewhat simpler for undo/redo logging than for the other logging methods. We have only to do the following:

1. Write a <START CKPT $(T_1, \ldots, T_k)$> record to the log, where $T_1, \ldots, T_k$ are all the active transactions, and flush the log.

2. Write to disk all the buffers that are *dirty*, i.e., they contain one or more changed database elements. Unlike redo logging, we flush all dirty buffers, not just those written by committed transactions.

3. Write an <END CKPT> record to the log, and flush the log.

Notice in connection with point (2) that, because of the flexibility undo/redo logging offers regarding when data reaches disk, we can tolerate the writing to disk of data written by incomplete transactions. Therefore we can tolerate database elements that are smaller than complete blocks and thus may share buffers. The only requirement we must make on transactions is:

- A transaction must not write any values (even to memory buffers) until it is certain not to abort.

As we shall see in Section 19.1, this constraint is almost certainly needed anyway, in order to avoid inconsistent interactions between transactions. Notice that under redo logging, the above condition is not sufficient, since even if the transaction that wrote B is certain to commit, rule R_1 requires that the transaction's COMMIT record be written to disk before B is written to disk.

Example 17.12: Figure 17.10 shows an undo/redo log analogous to the redo log of Fig. 17.8. We have changed only the update records, giving them an old value as well as a new value. For simplicity, we have assumed that in each case the old value is one less than the new value.

<START T_1>

<$T_1, A, 4, 5$>

<START T_2>

<COMMIT T_1>

<$T_2, B, 9, 10$>

<START CKPT (T_2)>

<$T_2, C, 14, 15$>

<START T_3>

<$T_3, D, 19, 20$>

<END CKPT>

<COMMIT T_2>

<COMMIT T_3>

Figure 17.10: An undo/redo log

As in Example 17.8, T_2 is identified as the only active transaction when the checkpoint begins. Since this log is an undo/redo log, it is possible that T_2's new B-value 10 has been written to disk, which was not possible under redo logging. However, it is irrelevant whether or not that disk write has occurred. During the checkpoint, we shall surely flush B to disk if it is not already there, since we flush all dirty buffers. Likewise, we shall flush A, written by the committed transaction T_1, if it is not already on disk.

If the crash occurs at the end of this sequence of events, then T_2 and T_3 are identified as committed transactions. Transaction T_1 is prior to the checkpoint. Since we find the <END CKPT> record on the log, T_1 is correctly assumed to have both completed and had its changes written to disk. We therefore redo both T_2 and T_3, as in Example 17.8, and ignore T_1. However, when we redo a transaction such as T_2, we do not need to look prior to the <START CKPT (T_2)> record, even though T_2 was active at that time, because we know that T_2's changes prior to the start of the checkpoint were flushed to disk during the checkpoint.

For another instance, suppose the crash occurs just before the <COMMIT T_3> record is written to disk. Then we identify T_2 as committed but T_3 as incomplete. We redo T_2 by setting C to 15 on disk; it is not necessary to set B to 10 since we know that change reached disk before the <END CKPT>. However, unlike the situation with a redo log, we also undo T_3; that is, we set D to 19 on disk. If T_3 had been active at the start of the checkpoint, we would have had to look prior to the START-CKPT record to find if there were more actions by T_3 that may have reached disk and need to be undone. □

17.4.4   Exercises for Section 17.4

Exercise 17.4.1: For each of the sequences of log records representing the actions of one transaction T, tell all the sequences of events that are legal according to the rules of undo/redo logging, where the events of interest are the writing to disk of the blocks containing database elements, and the blocks of the log containing the update and commit records. You may assume that log records are written to disk in the order shown; i.e., it is not possible to write one log record to disk while a previous record is not written to disk.

a) <START T>; <$T, A, 10, 11$>; <$T, B, 20, 21$>; <COMMIT T>;

b) <START T>; <$T, A, 10, 21$>; <$T, B, 20, 21$>; <$T, C, 30, 31$>; <COMMIT T>;

Exercise 17.4.2: The following is a sequence of undo/redo-log records written by two transactions T and U: <START U>; <$U, A, 10, 11$>; <START T>; <$T, B, 20, 21$>; <$U, C, 30, 31$>; <$T, D, 40, 41$>; <COMMIT T>; <$U, E, 50, 51$>; <COMMIT U>. Describe the action of the recovery manager, including changes to both disk and the log, if there is a crash and the last log record to appear on disk is:

(a) <START T>   (b) <COMMIT T>   (c) <$U, E, 50, 51$>   (d) <COMMIT U>.

Exercise 17.4.3: For each of the situations described in Exercise 17.4.2, what values written by T and U *must* appear on disk? Which values *might* appear on disk?

Exercise 17.4.4: Consider the following sequence of log records: <START S>; <$S, A, 60, 61$>; <COMMIT S>; <START T>; <$T, A, 61, 62$>; <START U>; <$U, B, 20, 21$>; <$T, C, 30, 31$>; <START V>; <$U, D, 40, 41$>; <$V, F, 70, 71$>; <COMMIT U>; <$T, E, 50, 51$>; <COMMIT T>; <$V, B, 21, 22$>; <COMMIT V>. Suppose that we begin a nonquiescent checkpoint immediately after one of the following log records has been written (in memory):

(a) <$S, A, 60, 61$>   (b) <$T, A, 61, 62$>   (c) <$U, B, 20, 21$>
(d) <$U, D, 40, 41$>   (e) <$T, E, 50, 51$>

For each, tell:

i. At what points could the <END CKPT> record be written, and

ii. For each possible point at which a crash could occur, how far back in the log we must look to find all possible incomplete transactions. Consider both the case that the <END CKPT> record was or was not written prior to the crash.

Exercise 17.4.5: Show the undo/redo-log records for each of the transactions (call each T) of Exercise 17.1.1, assuming that initially $A = 50$ and $B = 25$.

17.5 Protecting Against Media Failures

The log can protect us against system failures, where nothing is lost from disk, but temporary data in main memory is lost. However, as we discussed in Section 17.1.1, more serious failures involve the loss of one or more disks. An archiving system, which we cover next, is needed to enable a database to survive losses involving disk-resident data.

17.5.1 The Archive

To protect against media failures, we are thus led to a solution involving *archiving* — maintaining a copy of the database separate from the database itself. If it were possible to shut down the database for a while, we could make a backup copy on some storage medium such as tape or optical disk, and store the copy remote from the database, in some secure location. The backup would preserve the database state as it existed at the time of the backup, and if there were a media failure, the database could be restored to this state.

To advance to a more recent state, we could use the log, provided the log had been preserved since the archive copy was made, and the log itself survived the failure. In order to protect against losing the log, we could transmit a copy of the log, almost as soon as it is created, to the same remote site as the archive. Then, if the log as well as the data is lost, we can use the archive plus remotely stored log to recover, at least up to the point that the log was last transmitted to the remote site.

Since writing an archive is a lengthy process, we try to avoid copying the entire database at each archiving step. Thus, we distinguish between two levels of archiving:

1. A *full dump*, in which the entire database is copied.

2. An *incremental dump*, in which only those database elements changed since the previous full or incremental dump are copied.

It is also possible to have several levels of dump, with a full dump thought of as a "level 0" dump, and a "level i" dump copying everything changed since the last dump at a level less than or equal to i.

We can restore the database from a full dump and its subsequent incremental dumps, in a process much like the way a redo or undo/redo log can be used to repair damage due to a system failure. We copy the full dump back to the database, and then in an earliest-first order, make the changes recorded by the later incremental dumps.

17.5.2 Nonquiescent Archiving

The problem with the simple view of archiving in Section 17.5.1 is that most databases cannot be shut down for the period of time (possibly hours) needed

---

Why Not Just Back Up the Log?

We might question the need for an archive, since we have to back up the log in a secure place anyway if we are not to be stuck at the state the database was in when the previous archive was made. While it may not be obvious, the answer lies in the typical rate of change of a large database. While only a small fraction of the database may change in a day, the changes, each of which must be logged, will over the course of a year become much larger than the database itself. If we never archived, then the log could never be truncated, and the cost of storing the log would soon exceed the cost of storing a copy of the database.

---

to make a backup copy. We thus need to consider *nonquiescent archiving*, which is analogous to nonquiescent checkpointing. Recall that a nonquiescent checkpoint attempts to make a copy on the disk of the (approximate) database state that existed when the checkpoint started. We can rely on a small portion of the log around the time of the checkpoint to fix up any deviations from that database state, due to the fact that during the checkpoint, new transactions may have started and written to disk.

Similarly, a nonquiescent dump tries to make a copy of the database that existed when the dump began, but database activity may change many database elements on disk during the minutes or hours that the dump takes. If it is necessary to restore the database from the archive, the log entries made during the dump can be used to sort things out and get the database to a consistent state. The analogy is suggested by Fig. 17.11.

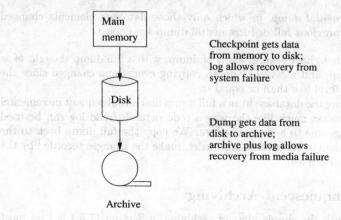

Figure 17.11: The analogy between checkpoints and dumps

A nonquiescent dump copies the database elements in some fixed order, possibly while those elements are being changed by executing transactions. As a result, the value of a database element that is copied to the archive may or may not be the value that existed when the dump began. As long as the log for the duration of the dump is preserved, the discrepancies can be corrected from the log.

Example 17.13: For a very simple example, suppose that our database consists of four elements, A, B, C, and D, which have the values 1 through 4, respectively, when the dump begins. During the dump, A is changed to 5, C is changed to 6, and B is changed to 7. However, the database elements are copied in order, and the sequence of events shown in Fig. 17.12 occurs. Then although the database at the beginning of the dump has values $(1, 2, 3, 4)$, and the database at the end of the dump has values $(5, 7, 6, 4)$, the copy of the database in the archive has values $(1, 2, 6, 4)$, a database state that existed at no time during the dump. ☐

Disk	Archive
	Copy A
$A := 5$	
	Copy B
$C := 6$	
	Copy C
$B := 7$	
	Copy D

Figure 17.12: Events during a nonquiescent dump

In more detail, the process of making an archive can be broken into the following steps. We assume that the logging method is either redo or undo/redo; an undo log is not suitable for use with archiving.

1. Write a log record <START DUMP>.

2. Perform a checkpoint appropriate for whichever logging method is being used.

3. Perform a full or incremental dump of the data disk(s), as desired, making sure that the copy of the data has reached the secure, remote site.

4. Make sure that enough of the log has been copied to the secure, remote site that at least the prefix of the log up to and including the checkpoint in item (2) will survive a media failure of the database.

5. Write a log record <END DUMP>.

At the completion of the dump, it is safe to throw away log prior to the beginning of the checkpoint *previous* to the one performed in item (2) above.

Example 17.14: Suppose that the changes to the simple database in Example 17.13 were caused by two transactions T_1 (which writes A and B) and T_2 (which writes C) that were active when the dump began. Figure 17.13 shows a possible undo/redo log of the events during the dump.

<START DUMP>
<START CKPT (T_1, T_2)>
<$T_1, A, 1, 5$>
<$T_2, C, 3, 6$>
<COMMIT T_2>
<$T_1, B, 2, 7$>
<END CKPT>
Dump completes
<END DUMP>

Figure 17.13: Log taken during a dump

Notice that we did not show T_1 committing. It would be unusual that a transaction remained active during the entire time a full dump was in progress, but that possibility doesn't affect the correctness of the recovery method that we discuss next. □

17.5.3 Recovery Using an Archive and Log

Suppose that a media failure occurs, and we must reconstruct the database from the most recent archive and whatever prefix of the log has reached the remote site and has not been lost in the crash. We perform the following steps:

1. Restore the database from the archive.

    (a) Find the most recent full dump and reconstruct the database from it (i.e., copy the archive into the database).

    (b) If there are later incremental dumps, modify the database according to each, earliest first.

2. Modify the database using the surviving log. Use the method of recovery appropriate to the log method being used.

Example 17.15: Suppose there is a media failure after the dump of Example 17.14 completes, and the log shown in Fig. 17.13 survives. Assume, to make the process interesting, that the surviving portion of the log does not include a <COMMIT T_1> record, although it does include the <COMMIT T_2> record shown in that figure. The database is first restored to the values in the archive, which is, for database elements A, B, C, and D, respectively, $(1, 2, 6, 4)$.

Now, we must look at the log. Since T_2 has completed, we redo the step that sets C to 6. In this example, C already had the value 6, but it might be that:

a) The archive for C was made before T_2 changed C, or

b) The archive actually captured a later value of C, which may or may not have been written by a transaction whose commit record survived. Later in the recovery, C will be restored to the value found in the archive *if* the transaction was committed.

Since T_1 does not have a COMMIT record, we must undo T_1. We use the log records for T_1 to determine that A must be restored to value 1 and B to 2. It happens that they had these values in the archive, but the actual archive value could have been different because the modified A and/or B had been included in the archive.   □

17.5.4   Exercises for Section 17.5

Exercise 17.5.1: If a redo log, rather than an undo/redo log, were used in Examples 17.14 and 17.15:

a) What would the log look like?

! b) If we had to recover using the archive and this log, what would be the consequence of T_1 not having committed?

c) What would be the state of the database after recovery?

17.6   Summary of Chapter 17

✦ *Transaction Management*: The two principal tasks of the transaction manager are assuring recoverability of database actions through logging, and assuring correct, concurrent behavior of transactions through the scheduler (discussed in the next chapter).

✦ *Database Elements*: The database is divided into elements, which are typically disk blocks, but could be tuples or relations, for instance. Database elements are the units for both logging and scheduling.

✦ *Logging*: A record of every important action of a transaction — beginning, changing a database element, committing, or aborting — is stored on a log. The log must be backed up on disk at a time that is related to when the corresponding database changes migrate to disk, but that time depends on the particular logging method used.

✦ *Recovery*: When a system crash occurs, the log is used to repair the database, restoring it to a consistent state.

✦ *Logging Methods*: The three principal methods for logging are undo, redo, and undo/redo, named for the way(s) that they are allowed to fix the database during recovery.

✦ *Undo Logging*: This method logs the old value, each time a database element is changed. With undo logging, a new value of a database element can be written to disk only after the log record for the change has reached disk, but before the commit record for the transaction performing the change reaches disk. Recovery is done by restoring the old value for every uncommitted transaction.

✦ *Redo Logging*: Here, only the new value of database elements is logged. With this form of logging, values of a database element can be written to disk only after both the log record of its change and the commit record for its transaction have reached disk. Recovery involves rewriting the new value for every committed transaction.

✦ *Undo/Redo Logging* In this method, both old and new values are logged. Undo/redo logging is more flexible than the other methods, since it requires only that the log record of a change appear on the disk before the change itself does. There is no requirement about when the commit record appears. Recovery is effected by redoing committed transactions and undoing the uncommitted transactions.

✦ *Checkpointing*: Since all recovery methods require, in principle, looking at the entire log, the DBMS must occasionally checkpoint the log, to assure that no log records prior to the checkpoint will be needed during a recovery. Thus, old log records can eventually be thrown away and their disk space reused.

✦ *Nonquiescent Checkpointing*: To avoid shutting down the system while a checkpoint is made, techniques associated with each logging method allow the checkpoint to be made while the system is in operation and database changes are occurring. The only cost is that some log records prior to the nonquiescent checkpoint may need to be examined during recovery.

✦ *Archiving*: While logging protects against system failures involving only the loss of main memory, archiving is necessary to protect against failures where the contents of disk are lost. Archives are copies of the database stored in a safe place.

✦ *Incremental Backups*: Instead of copying the entire database to an archive periodically, a single complete backup can be followed by several incremental backups, where only the changed data is copied to the archive.

♦ *Nonquiescent Archiving*: We can create a backup of the data while the database is in operation. The necessary techniques involve making log records of the beginning and end of the archiving, as well as performing a checkpoint for the log during the archiving.

♦ *Recovery From Media Failures*: When a disk is lost, it may be restored by starting with a full backup of the database, modifying it according to any later incremental backups, and finally recovering to a consistent database state by using an archived copy of the log.

17.7 References for Chapter 17

The major textbook on all aspects of transaction processing, including logging and recovery, is by Gray and Reuter [5]. This book was partially fed by some informal notes on transaction processing by Jim Gray [3] that were widely circulated; the latter, along with [4] and [8] are the primary sources for much of the logging and recovery technology.

[2] is an earlier, more concise description of transaction-processing technology. [7] is a recent treatment of recovery.

Two early surveys, [1] and [6] both represent much of the fundamental work in recovery and organized the subject in the undo-redo-undo/redo tricotomy that we followed here.

1. P. A. Bernstein, N. Goodman, and V. Hadzilacos, "Recovery algorithms for database systems," *Proc. 1983 IFIP Congress*, North Holland, Amsterdam, pp. 799–807.

2. P. A. Bernstein, V. Hadzilacos, and N. Goodman, *Concurrency Control and Recovery in Database Systems*, Addison-Wesley, Reading MA, 1987.

3. J. N. Gray, "Notes on database operating systems," in *Operating Systems: an Advanced Course*, pp. 393–481, Springer-Verlag, 1978.

4. J. N. Gray, P. R. McJones, and M. Blasgen, "The recovery manager of the System R database manager," *Computing Surveys* **13**:2 (1981), pp. 223–242.

5. J. N. Gray and A. Reuter, *Transaction Processing: Concepts and Techniques*, Morgan-Kaufmann, San Francisco, 1993.

6. T. Haerder and A. Reuter, "Principles of transaction-oriented database recovery — a taxonomy," *Computing Surveys* **15**:4 (1983), pp. 287–317.

7. V. Kumar and M. Hsu, *Recovery Mechanisms in Database Systems*, Prentice-Hall, Englewood Cliffs NJ, 1998.

8. C. Mohan, D. J. Haderle, B. G. Lindsay, H. Pirahesh, and P. Schwarz, "ARIES: a transaction recovery method supporting fine-granularity locking and partial rollbacks using write-ahead logging," *ACM Trans. on Database Systems* **17**:1 (1992), pp. 94–162.

Chapter 18

Concurrency Control

Interactions among concurrently executing transactions can cause the database state to become inconsistent, even when the transactions individually preserve correctness of the state, and there is no system failure. Thus, the timing of individual steps of different transactions needs to be regulated in some manner. This regulation is the job of the *scheduler* component of the DBMS, and the general process of assuring that transactions preserve consistency when executing simultaneously is called *concurrency control*. The role of the scheduler is suggested by Fig. 18.1.

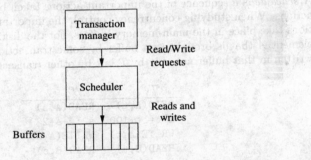

Figure 18.1: The scheduler takes read/write requests from transactions and either executes them in buffers or delays them

As transactions request reads and writes of database elements, these requests are passed to the scheduler. In most situations, the scheduler will execute the reads and writes directly, first calling on the buffer manager if the desired database element is not in a buffer. However, in some situations, it is not safe for the request to be executed immediately. The scheduler must delay the request; in some concurrency-control techniques, the scheduler may even abort the transaction that issued the request.

883

We begin by studying how to assure that concurrently executing transactions preserve correctness of the database state. The abstract requirement is called *serializability*, and there is an important, stronger condition called *conflict-serializability* that most schedulers actually enforce. We consider the most important techniques for implementing schedulers: locking, timestamping, and validation. Our study of lock-based schedulers includes the important concept of "two-phase locking," which is a requirement widely used to assure serializability of schedules.

18.1   Serial and Serializable Schedules

Recall the "correctness principle" from Section 17.1.3: every transaction, if executed in isolation (without any other transactions running concurrently), will transform any consistent state to another consistent state. In practice, transactions often run concurrently with other transactions, so the correctness principle doesn't apply directly. This section introduces the notion of "schedules," the sequence of actions performed by transactions and "serializable schedules," which produce the same result as if the transactions executed one-at-a-time.

18.1.1   Schedules

A *schedule* is a sequence of the important actions taken by one or more transactions. When studying concurrency control, the important read and write actions take place in the main-memory buffers, not the disk. That is, a database element A that is brought to a buffer by some transaction T may be read or written in that buffer not only by T but by other transactions that access A.

T_1	T_2
READ(A,t)	READ(A,s)
t := t+100	s := s*2
WRITE(A,t)	WRITE(A,s)
READ(B,t)	READ(B,s)
t := t+100	s := s*2
WRITE(B,t)	WRITE(B,s)

Figure 18.2: Two transactions

Example 18.1: Let us consider two transactions and the effect on the database when their actions are executed in certain orders. The important actions of the transactions T_1 and T_2 are shown in Fig. 18.2. The variables t and s are local variables of T_1 and T_2, respectively; they are *not* database elements.

We shall assume that the only consistency constraint on the database state is that $A = B$. Since T_1 adds 100 to both A and B, and T_2 multiplies both

A and B by 2, we know that each transaction, run in isolation, will preserve consistency. □

18.1.2 Serial Schedules

A schedule is *serial* if its actions consist of all the actions of one transaction, then all the actions of another transaction, and so on. No mixing of the actions is allowed.

T_1	T_2	A	B
		25	25
READ(A,t)			
t := t+100			
WRITE(A,t)		125	
READ(B,t)			
t := t+100			
WRITE(B,t)			125
	READ(A,s)		
	s := s*2		
	WRITE(A,s)	250	
	READ(B,s)		
	s := s*2		
	WRITE(B,s)		250

Figure 18.3: Serial schedule in which T_1 precedes T_2

Example 18.2: For the transactions of Fig. 18.2, there are two serial schedules, one in which T_1 precedes T_2 and the other in which T_2 precedes T_1. Figure 18.3 shows the sequence of events when T_1 precedes T_2, and the initial state is $A = B = 25$. We shall take the convention that when displayed vertically, time proceeds down the page. Also, the values of A and B shown refer to their values in main-memory buffers, not necessarily to their values on disk.

Figure 18.4 shows another serial schedule in which T_2 precedes T_1; the initial state is again assumed to be $A = B = 25$. Notice that the final values of A and B are different for the two schedules; they both have value 250 when T_1 goes first and 150 when T_2 goes first. In general, we would not expect the final state of a database to be independent of the order of transactions. □

We can represent a serial schedule as in Fig. 18.3 or Fig. 18.4, listing each of the actions in the order they occur. However, since the order of actions in a serial schedule depends only on the order of the transactions themselves, we shall sometimes represent a serial schedule by the list of transactions. Thus, the schedule of Fig. 18.3 is represented (T_1, T_2), and that of Fig. 18.4 is (T_2, T_1).

T_1	T_2	A	B
		25	25
	READ(A,s)		
	s := s*2		
	WRITE(A,s)	50	
	READ(B,s)		
	s := s*2		
	WRITE(B,s)		50
READ(A,t)			
t := t+100			
WRITE(A,t)		150	
READ(B,t)			
t := t+100			
WRITE(B,t)			150

Figure 18.4: Serial schedule in which T_2 precedes T_1

18.1.3   Serializable Schedules

The correctness principle for transactions tells us that every serial schedule will preserve consistency of the database state. But are there any other schedules that also are guaranteed to preserve consistency? There are, as the following example shows. In general, we say a schedule S is *serializable* if there is a serial schedule S' such that for every initial database state, the effects of S and S' are the same.

T_1	T_2	A	B
		25	25
READ(A,t)			
t := t+100			
WRITE(A,t)		125	
	READ(A,s)		
	s := s*2		
	WRITE(A,s)	250	
READ(B,t)			
t := t+100			
WRITE(B,t)			125
	READ(B,s)		
	s := s*2		
	WRITE(B,s)		250

Figure 18.5: A serializable, but not serial, schedule

Example 18.3: Figure 18.5 shows a schedule of the transactions from Example 18.1 that is serializable but not serial. In this schedule, T_2 acts on A after T_1 does, but before T_1 acts on B. However, we see that the effect of the two transactions scheduled in this manner is the same as for the serial schedule (T_1, T_2) from Fig. 18.3. To convince ourselves of the truth of this statement, we must consider not only the effect from the database state $A = B = 25$, which we show in Fig. 18.5, but from any consistent database state. Since all consistent database states have $A = B = c$ for some constant c, it is not hard to deduce that in the schedule of Fig. 18.5, both A and B will be left with the value $2(c + 100)$, and thus consistency is preserved from any consistent state.

T_1	T_2	A	B
		25	25
READ(A,t)			
t := t+100			
WRITE(A,t)		125	
	READ(A,s)		
	s := s*2		
	WRITE(A,s)	250	
	READ(B,s)		
	s := s*2		
	WRITE(B,s)		50
READ(B,t)			
t := t+100			
WRITE(B,t)			150

Figure 18.6: A nonserializable schedule

On the other hand, consider the schedule of Fig. 18.6, which is not serializable. The reason we can be sure it is not serializable is that it takes the consistent state $A = B = 25$ and leaves the database in an inconsistent state, where $A = 250$ and $B = 150$. Notice that in this order of actions, where T_1 operates on A first, but T_2 operates on B first, we have in effect applied different computations to A and B, that is $A := 2(A + 100)$ versus $B := 2B + 100$. The schedule of Fig. 18.6 is the sort of behavior that concurrency control mechanisms must avoid. □

18.1.4 The Effect of Transaction Semantics

In our study of serializability so far, we have considered in detail the operations performed by the transactions, to determine whether or not a schedule is serializable. The details of the transactions do matter, as we can see from the following example.

T_1	T_2	A	B
		25	25
READ(A,t)			
t := t+100			
WRITE(A,t)		125	
	READ(A,s)		
	s := s+200		
	WRITE(A,s)	325	
	READ(B,s)		
	s := s+200		
	WRITE(B,s)		225
READ(B,t)			
t := t+100			
WRITE(B,t)			325

Figure 18.7: A schedule that is serializable only because of the detailed behavior of the transactions

Example 18.4 : Consider the schedule of Fig. 18.7, which differs from Fig. 18.6 only in the computation that T_2 performs. That is, instead of multiplying A and B by 2, T_2 adds 200 to each. One can easily check that regardless of the consistent initial state, the final state is the one that results from the serial schedule (T_1, T_2). Coincidentally, it also results from the other serial schedule, (T_2, T_1). □

Unfortunately, it is not realistic for the scheduler to concern itself with the details of computation undertaken by transactions. Since transactions often involve code written in a general-purpose programming language as well as SQL or other high-level-language statements, it is impossible to say for certain what a transaction is doing. However, the scheduler does get to see the read and write requests from the transactions, so it can know what database elements each transaction reads, and what elements it *might* change. To simplify the job of the scheduler, it is conventional to assume that:

- Any database element A that a transaction T writes is given a value that depends on the database state in such a way that no arithmetic coincidences occur.

An example of a "coincidence" is that in Example 18.4, where $A + 100 + 200 = B + 200 + 100$ whenever $A = B$, even though the two operations are carried out in different orders on the two variables. Put another way, if there is something that T could do to a database element to make the database state inconsistent, then T will do that.

18.1.5 A Notation for Transactions and Schedules

If we assume "no coincidences," then only the reads and writes performed by the transaction matter, not the actual values involved. Thus, we shall represent transactions and schedules by a shorthand notation, in which the actions are $r_T(X)$ and $w_T(X)$, meaning that transaction T reads, or respectively writes, database element X. Moreover, since we shall usually name our transactions $T_1, T_2, \ldots$, we adopt the convention that $r_i(X)$ and $w_i(X)$ are synonyms for $r_{T_i}(X)$ and $w_{T_i}(X)$, respectively.

Example 18.5: The transactions of Fig. 18.2 can be written:

$$T_1: r_1(A); w_1(A); r_1(B); w_1(B);$$
$$T_2: r_2(A); w_2(A); r_2(B); w_2(B);$$

As another example,

$$r_1(A); w_1(A); r_2(A); w_2(A); r_1(B); w_1(B); r_2(B); w_2(B);$$

is the serializable schedule from Fig. 18.5. □

To make the notation precise:

1. An *action* is an expression of the form $r_i(X)$ or $w_i(X)$, meaning that transaction T_i reads or writes, respectively, the database element X.

2. A *transaction* T_i is a sequence of actions with subscript i.

3. A *schedule* S of a set of transactions $\mathcal{T}$ is a sequence of actions, in which for each transaction T_i in $\mathcal{T}$, the actions of T_i appear in S in the same order that they appear in the definition of T_i itself. We say that S is an *interleaving* of the actions of the transactions of which it is composed.

For instance, the schedule of Example 18.5 has all the actions with subscript 1 appearing in the same order that they have in the definition of T_1, and the actions with subscript 2 appear in the same order that they appear in the definition of T_2.

18.1.6 Exercises for Section 18.1

Exercise 18.1.1: A transaction T_1, executed by an airline-reservation system, performs the following steps:

   i. The customer is queried for a desired flight time and cities. Information about the desired flights is located in database elements (perhaps disk blocks) A and B, which the system retrieves from disk.

   ii. The customer is told about the options, and selects a flight whose data, including the number of reservations for that flight is in B. A reservation on that flight is made for the customer.

   iii. The customer selects a seat for the flight; seat data for the flight is in database element C.

   iv. The system gets the customer's credit-card number and appends the bill for the flight to a list of bills in database element D.

   v. The customer's phone and flight data is added to another list on database element E for a fax to be sent confirming the flight.

Express transaction T_1 as a sequence of r and w actions.

! Exercise 18.1.2: If two transactions each consist of 5 actions, how many interleavings of these transactions are there?

18.2   Conflict-Serializability

Schedulers in commercial systems generally enforce a condition, called "conflict-serializability," that is stronger than the general notion of serializability introduced in Section 18.1.3. It is based on the idea of a *conflict*: a pair of consecutive actions in a schedule such that, if their order is interchanged, then the behavior of at least one of the transactions involved can change.

18.2.1   Conflicts

To begin, let us observe that most pairs of actions do *not* conflict. In what follows, we assume that T_i and T_j are different transactions; i.e., $i \neq j$.

1. $r_i(X); r_j(Y)$ is never a conflict, even if $X = Y$. The reason is that neither of these steps change the value of any database element.

2. $r_i(X); w_j(Y)$ is not a conflict provided $X \neq Y$. The reason is that should T_j write Y before T_i reads X, the value of X is not changed. Also, the read of X by T_i has no effect on T_j, so it does not affect the value T_j writes for Y.

3. $w_i(X); r_j(Y)$ is not a conflict if $X \neq Y$, for the same reason as (2).

4. Similarly, $w_i(X); w_j(Y)$ is not a conflict as long as $X \neq Y$.

On the other hand, there are three situations where we may not swap the order of actions:

   a) Two actions of the same transaction, e.g., $r_i(X); w_i(Y)$, always conflict. The reason is that the order of actions of a single transaction are fixed and may not be reordered.

b) Two writes of the same database element by different transactions conflict. That is, $w_i(X)$; $w_j(X)$ is a conflict. The reason is that as written, the value of X remains afterward as whatever T_j computed it to be. If we swap the order, as $w_j(X)$; $w_i(X)$, then we leave X with the value computed by T_i. Our assumption of "no coincidences" tells us that the values written by T_i and T_j will be different, at least for some initial states of the database.

c) A read and a write of the same database element by different transactions also conflict. That is, $r_i(X)$; $w_j(X)$ is a conflict, and so is $w_i(X)$; $r_j(X)$. If we move $w_j(X)$ ahead of $r_i(X)$, then the value of X read by T_i will be that written by T_j, which we assume is not necessarily the same as the previous value of X. Thus, swapping the order of $r_i(X)$ and $w_j(X)$ affects the value T_i reads for X and could therefore affect what T_i does.

The conclusion we draw is that any two actions of different transactions may be swapped unless:

1. They involve the same database element, and

2. At least one is a write.

Extending this idea, we may take any schedule and make as many nonconflicting swaps as we wish, with the goal of turning the schedule into a serial schedule. If we can do so, then the original schedule is serializable, because its effect on the database state remains the same as we perform each of the nonconflicting swaps.

We say that two schedules are *conflict-equivalent* if they can be turned one into the other by a sequence of nonconflicting swaps of adjacent actions. We shall call a schedule *conflict-serializable* if it is conflict-equivalent to a serial schedule. Note that conflict-serializability is a sufficient condition for serializability; i.e., a conflict-serializable schedule is a serializable schedule. Conflict-serializability is not required for a schedule to be serializable, but it is the condition that the schedulers in commercial systems generally use when they need to guarantee serializability.

Example 18.6 : Consider the schedule

$$r_1(A); w_1(A); r_2(A); w_2(A); r_1(B); w_1(B); r_2(B); w_2(B);$$

from Example 18.5. We claim this schedule is conflict-serializable. Figure 18.8 shows the sequence of swaps in which this schedule is converted to the serial schedule (T_1, T_2), where all of T_1's actions precede all those of T_2. We have underlined the pair of adjacent actions about to be swapped at each step. □

$$r_1(A);\ w_1(A);\ r_2(A);\ \underline{w_2(A)};\ \underline{r_1(B)};\ w_1(B);\ r_2(B);\ w_2(B);$$
$$r_1(A);\ w_1(A);\ \underline{r_2(A)};\ \underline{r_1(B)};\ w_2(A);\ w_1(B);\ r_2(B);\ w_2(B);$$
$$r_1(A);\ w_1(A);\ r_1(B);\ \underline{r_2(A)};\ \underline{w_2(A)};\ w_1(B);\ r_2(B);\ w_2(B);$$
$$r_1(A);\ w_1(A);\ r_1(B);\ \underline{r_2(A)};\ \underline{w_1(B)};\ w_2(A);\ r_2(B);\ w_2(B);$$
$$r_1(A);\ w_1(A);\ r_1(B);\ \underline{w_1(B)};\ \underline{r_2(A)};\ w_2(A);\ r_2(B);\ w_2(B);$$

Figure 18.8: Converting a conflict-serializable schedule to a serial schedule by swaps of adjacent actions

18.2.2 Precedence Graphs and a Test for Conflict-Serializability

It is relatively simple to examine a schedule S and decide whether or not it is conflict-serializable. When a pair of conflicting actions appears anywhere in S, the transactions performing those actions must appear in the same order in any conflict-equivalent serial schedule as the actions appear in S. Thus, conflicting pairs of actions put constraints on the order of transactions in the hypothetical, conflict-equivalent serial schedule. If these constraints are not contradictory, we can find a conflict-equivalent serial schedule. If they are contradictory, we know that no such serial schedule exists.

Given a schedule S, involving transactions T_1 and T_2, perhaps among other transactions, we say that T_1 *takes precedence over* T_2, written $T_1 <_S T_2$, if there are actions A_1 of T_1 and A_2 of T_2, such that:

1. A_1 is ahead of A_2 in S,

2. Both A_1 and A_2 involve the same database element, and

3. At least one of A_1 and A_2 is a write action.

Notice that these are exactly the conditions under which we cannot swap the order of A_1 and A_2. Thus, A_1 will appear before A_2 in any schedule that is conflict-equivalent to S. As a result, a conflict-equivalent serial schedule must have T_1 before T_2.

We can summarize these precedences in a *precedence graph*. The nodes of the precedence graph are the transactions of a schedule S. When the transactions are T_i for various i, we shall label the node for T_i by only the integer i. There is an arc from node i to node j if $T_i <_S T_j$.

Example 18.7: The following schedule S involves three transactions, T_1, T_2, and T_3.

$$S:\ r_2(A);\ r_1(B);\ w_2(A);\ r_3(A);\ w_1(B);\ w_3(A);\ r_2(B);\ w_2(B);$$

If we look at the actions involving A, we find several reasons why $T_2 <_S T_3$. For example, $r_2(A)$ comes ahead of $w_3(A)$ in S, and $w_2(A)$ comes ahead of both

---

Why Conflict-Serializability is not Necessary for Serializability

Consider three transactions T_1, T_2, and T_3 that each write a value for X. T_1 and T_2 also write values for Y before they write values for X. One possible schedule, which happens to be serial, is

$$S_1: w_1(Y); w_1(X); w_2(Y); w_2(X); w_3(X);$$

S_1 leaves X with the value written by T_3 and Y with the value written by T_2. However, so does the schedule

$$S_2: w_1(Y); w_2(Y); w_2(X); w_1(X); w_3(X);$$

Intuitively, the values of X written by T_1 and T_2 have no effect, since T_3 overwrites their values. Thus, X has the same value after either S_1 or S_2, and likewise Y has the same value after either S_1 or S_2. Since S_1 is serial, and S_2 has the same effect as S_1 on any database state, we know that S_2 is serializable. However, since we cannot swap $w_1(Y)$ with $w_2(Y)$, and we cannot swap $w_1(X)$ with $w_2(X)$, therefore we cannot convert S_2 to any serial schedule by swaps. That is, S_2 is serializable, but not conflict-serializable.

Figure 18.9: The precedence graph for the schedule S of Example 18.7

$r_3(A)$ and $w_3(A)$. Any one of these three observations is sufficient to justify the arc in the precedence graph of Fig. 18.9 from 2 to 3.

Similarly, if we look at the actions involving B, we find that there are several reasons why $T_1 <_S T_2$. For instance, the action $r_1(B)$ comes before $w_2(B)$. Thus, the precedence graph for S also has an arc from 1 to 2. However, these are the only arcs we can justify from the order of actions in schedule S. □

To tell whether a schedule S is conflict-serializable, construct the precedence graph for S and ask if there are any cycles. If so, then S is not conflict-serializable. But if the graph is acyclic, then S is conflict-serializable, and moreover, any topological order of the nodes[1] is a conflict-equivalent serial order.

---

[1]A *topological order* of an acyclic graph is any order of the nodes such that for every arc $a \rightarrow b$, node a precedes node b in the topological order. We can find a topological order for any acyclic graph by repeatedly removing nodes that have no predecessors among the remaining nodes.

Example 18.8: Figure 18.9 is acyclic, so the schedule S of Example 18.7 is conflict-serializable. There is only one order of the nodes or transactions consistent with the arcs of that graph: (T_1, T_2, T_3). Notice that it is indeed possible to convert S into the schedule in which all actions of each of the three transactions occur in this order; this serial schedule is:

$$S': r_1(B); \ w_1(B); \ r_2(A); \ w_2(A); \ r_2(B); \ w_2(B); \ r_3(A); \ w_3(A);$$

To see that we can get from S to S' by swaps of adjacent elements, first notice we can move $r_1(B)$ ahead of $r_2(A)$ without conflict. Then, by three swaps we can move $w_1(B)$ just after $r_1(B)$, because each of the intervening actions involves A and not B. We can then move $r_2(B)$ and $w_2(B)$ to a position just after $w_2(A)$, moving through only actions involving A; the result is S'. □

Example 18.9: Consider the schedule

$$S_1: r_2(A); \ r_1(B); \ w_2(A); \ r_2(B); \ r_3(A); \ w_1(B); \ w_3(A); \ w_2(B);$$

which differs from S only in that action $r_2(B)$ has been moved forward three positions. Examination of the actions involving A still give us only the precedence $T_2 <_{S_1} T_3$. However, when we examine B we get not only $T_1 <_{S_1} T_2$ [because $r_1(B)$ and $w_1(B)$ appear before $w_2(B)$], but also $T_2 <_{S_1} T_1$ [because $r_2(B)$ appears before $w_1(B)$]. Thus, we have the precedence graph of Fig. 18.10 for schedule S_1.

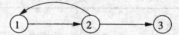

Figure 18.10: A cyclic precedence graph; its schedule is not conflict-serializable

This graph evidently has a cycle. We conclude that S_1 is not conflict-serializable. Intuitively, any conflict-equivalent serial schedule would have to have T_1 both ahead of and behind T_2, so therefore no such schedule exists. □

18.2.3   Why the Precedence-Graph Test Works

If there is a cycle involving n transactions $T_1 \rightarrow T_2 \rightarrow \ldots \rightarrow T_n \rightarrow T_1$, then in the hypothetical serial order, the actions of T_1 must precede those of T_2, which precede those of T_3, and so on, up to T_n. But the actions of T_n, which therefore come after those of T_1, are also required to precede those of T_1 because of the arc $T_n \rightarrow T_1$. Thus, if there is a cycle in the precedence graph, then the schedule is not conflict-serializable.

The converse is a bit harder. We must show that if the precedence graph has no cycles, then we can reorder the schedule's actions using legal swaps of adjacent actions, until the schedule becomes a serial schedule. If we can do so, then we have our proof that every schedule with an acyclic precedence graph is conflict-serializable. The proof is an induction on the number of transactions involved in the schedule.

BASIS: If $n = 1$, i.e., there is only one transaction in the schedule, then the schedule is already serial, and therefore surely conflict-serializable.

INDUCTION: Let the schedule S consist of the actions of n transactions

$$T_1, T_2, \ldots, T_n$$

We suppose that S has an acyclic precedence graph. If a finite graph is acyclic, then there is at least one node that has no arcs in; let the node i corresponding to transaction T_i be such a node. Since there are no arcs into node i, there can be no action A in S that:

1. Involves any transaction T_j other than T_i,

2. Precedes some action of T_i, and

3. Conflicts with that action.

For if there were, we should have put an arc from node j to node i in the precedence graph.

It is thus possible to swap all the actions of T_i, keeping them in order, but moving them to the front of S. The schedule has now taken the form

(Actions of T_i)(Actions of the other $n - 1$ transactions)

Let us now consider the tail of S — the actions of all transactions other than T_i. Since these actions maintain the same relative order that they did in S, the precedence graph for the tail is the same as the precedence graph for S, except that the node for T_i and any arcs out of that node are missing.

Since the original precedence graph was acyclic, and deleting nodes and arcs cannot make it cyclic, we conclude that the tail's precedence graph is acyclic. Moreover, since the tail involves $n - 1$ transactions, the inductive hypothesis applies to it. Thus, we know we can reorder the actions of the tail using legal swaps of adjacent actions to turn it into a serial schedule. Now, S itself has been turned into a serial schedule, with the actions of T_i first and the actions of the other transactions following in some serial order. The induction is complete, and we conclude that every schedule with an acyclic precedence graph is conflict-serializable.

18.2.4 Exercises for Section 18.2

Exercise 18.2.1: Below are two transactions, described in terms of their effect on two database elements A and B, which we may assume are integers.

T_1: READ(A,t); t:=t+2; WRITE(A,t); READ(B,t); t:=t*3; WRITE(B,t);
T_2: READ(B,s); s:=s*2; WRITE(B,s); READ(A,s); s:=s+3; WRITE(A,s);

We assume that, whatever consistency constraints there are on the database, these transactions preserve them in isolation. Note that $A = B$ is *not* the consistency constraint.

a) Give examples of a serializable schedule and a nonserializable schedule of the 12 actions above.

b) How many serial schedules of the 12 actions are there?

!! c) How many serializable schedules of the 12 actions are there?

d) It turns out that both serial orders have the same effect on the database; that is, (T_1, T_2) and (T_2, T_1) are equivalent. Demonstrate this fact by showing the effect of the two transactions on an arbitrary initial database state.

Exercise 18.2.2: The two transactions of Exercise 18.2.1 can be written in our notation that shows read- and write-actions only, as:

$$T_1: r_1(A); w_1(A); r_1(B); w_1(B);$$
$$T_2: r_2(B); w_2(B); r_2(A); w_2(A);$$

Answer the following:

a) Among the possible schedules of the eight actions above, how many are equivalent to the serial order (T_1, T_2)?

! b) How many schedules of the eight actions are conflict-equivalent to the serial order (T_2, T_1)?

!! c) How many schedules of the eight actions are equivalent (not necessarily conflict-equivalent) to the serial schedule (T_1, T_2), assuming the transactions have the effect on the database described in Exercise 18.2.1?

! d) Why are the answers to (c) above and Exercise 18.2.1(c) different?

! **Exercise 18.2.3:** Suppose the transactions of Exercise 18.2.2 are changed to be:

$$T_1: r_1(A); w_1(A); r_1(B); w_1(B);$$
$$T_2: r_2(A); w_2(A); r_2(B); w_2(B);$$

That is, the transactions retain their semantics from Exercise 18.2.1, but T_2 has been changed so A is processed before B. Give:

a) The number of serializable schedules, assuming the transactions have the same effect on the database state as in Exercise 18.2.1.

b) The number of conflict-serializable schedules.

! **Exercise 18.2.4:** Explain how, for any $n > 1$, one can find a schedule whose precedence graph has a cycle of length n, but no smaller cycle.

Exercise 18.2.5: For each of the following schedules:

a) $w_3(A); r_1(A); w_1(B); r_2(B): w_2(C); r_3(C);$

b) $r_1(A); r_2(A); w_1(B); w_2(B); r_1(B); r_2(B); w_2(C); w_1(D);$

c) $r_1(A); r_2(A); r_1(B); r_2(B); r_3(A); r_4(B); w_1(A); w_2(B);$

d) $r_1(A); r_2(A); r_3(B); w_1(A); r_2(C); r_2(B); w_2(B); w_1(C);$

e) $r_1(A); w_1(B); r_2(B): w_2(C); r_3(C); w_3(A);$

Answer the following questions:

i. What is the precedence graph for the schedule?

ii. Is the schedule conflict-serializable? If so, what are all the equivalent serial schedules?

! *iii.* Are there any serial schedules that must be equivalent (regardless of what the transactions do to the data), but are not conflict-equivalent?

!! **Exercise 18.2.6:** Say that a transaction T *precedes* a transaction U in a schedule S if every action of T precedes every action of U in S. Note that if T and U are the only transactions in S, then saying T precedes U is the same as saying that S is the serial schedule (T, U). However, if S involves transactions other than T and U, then S might not be serializable, and in fact, because of the effect of other transactions, S might not even be conflict-serializable. Give an example of a schedule S such that:

i. In S, T_1 precedes T_2, and

ii. S is conflict-serializable, but

iii. In every serial schedule conflict-equivalent to S, T_2 precedes T_1.

18.3 Enforcing Serializability by Locks

In this section we consider the most common architecture for a scheduler, one in which "locks" are maintained on database elements to prevent unserializable behavior. Intuitively, a transaction obtains locks on the database elements it accesses to prevent other transactions from accessing these elements at roughly the same time and thereby incurring the risk of unserializability.

In this section, we introduce the concept of locking with an (overly) simple locking scheme. In this scheme, there is only one kind of lock, which transactions must obtain on a database element if they want to perform any operation whatsoever on that element. In Section 18.4, we shall learn more realistic locking schemes, with several kinds of lock, including the common shared/exclusive locks that correspond to the privileges of reading and writing, respectively.

18.3.1 Locks

In Fig. 18.11 we see a scheduler that uses a lock table to help perform its job. Recall from the chapter introduction that the responsibility of the scheduler is to take requests from transactions and either allow them to operate on the database or block the transaction until such time as it is safe to allow it to continue. A lock table will be used to guide this decision in a manner that we shall discuss at length.

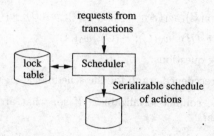

Figure 18.11: A scheduler that uses a lock table to guide decisions

Ideally, a scheduler would forward a request if and only if its execution cannot possibly lead to an inconsistent database state after all active transactions commit or abort. A locking scheduler, like most types of scheduler, instead enforces conflict-serializability, which as we learned is a more stringent condition than correctness, or even than serializability.

When a scheduler uses locks, transactions must request and release locks, in addition to reading and writing database elements. The use of locks must be proper in two senses, one applying to the structure of transactions, and the other to the structure of schedules.

- *Consistency of Transactions*: Actions and locks must relate in the expected ways:

    1. A transaction can only read or write an element if it previously was granted a lock on that element and hasn't yet released the lock.

    2. If a transaction locks an element, it must later unlock that element.

- *Legality of Schedules*: Locks must have their intended meaning: no two transactions may have locked the same element without one having first released the lock.

We shall extend our notation for actions to include locking and unlocking actions:

$l_i(X)$: Transaction T_i requests a lock on database element X.

$u_i(X)$: Transaction T_i releases ("unlocks") its lock on database element X.

Thus, the consistency condition for transactions can be stated as: "Whenever a transaction T_i has an action $r_i(X)$ or $w_i(X)$, then there is a previous action $l_i(X)$ with no intervening action $u_i(X)$, and there is a subsequent $u_i(X)$." The legality of schedules is stated: "If there are actions $l_i(X)$ followed by $l_j(X)$ in a schedule, then somewhere between these actions there must be an action $u_i(X)$."

Example 18.10: Let us consider the two transactions T_1 and T_2 that we introduced in Example 18.1. Recall that T_1 adds 100 to database elements A and B, while T_2 doubles them. Here are specifications for these transactions, in which we have included lock actions as well as arithmetic actions to help us remember what the transactions are doing.[2]

T_1: $l_1(A)$; $r_1(A)$; A := A+100; $w_1(A)$; $u_1(A)$; $l_1(B)$; $r_1(B)$; B := B+100; $w_1(B)$; $u_1(B)$;

T_2: $l_2(A)$; $r_2(A)$; A := A*2; $w_2(A)$; $u_2(A)$; $l_2(B)$; $r_2(B)$; B := B*2; $w_2(B)$; $u_2(B)$;

Each of these transactions is consistent. They each release the locks on A and B that they take. Moreover, they each operate on A and B only at steps where they have previously requested a lock on that element and have not yet released the lock.

T_1	T_2	A	B
		25	25
$l_1(A)$; $r_1(A)$;			
A := A+100;			
$w_1(A)$; $u_1(A)$;		125	
	$l_2(A)$; $r_2(A)$;		
	A := A*2;		
	$w_2(A)$; $u_2(A)$;	250	
	$l_2(B)$; $r_2(B)$;		
	B := B*2;		
	$w_2(B)$; $u_2(B)$;		50
$l_1(B)$; $r_1(B)$;			
B := B+100;			
$w_1(B)$; $u_1(B)$;			150

Figure 18.12: A legal schedule of consistent transactions; unfortunately it is not serializable

Figure 18.12 shows one legal schedule of these two transactions. To save space we have put several actions on one line. The schedule is legal because

---

[2]Remember that the actual computations of the transaction usually are not represented in our current notation, since they are not considered by the scheduler when deciding whether to grant or deny transaction requests.

the two transactions never hold a lock on A at the same time, and likewise for B. Specifically, T_2 does not execute $l_2(A)$ until after T_1 executes $u_1(A)$, and T_1 does not execute $l_1(B)$ until after T_2 executes $u_2(B)$. As we see from the trace of the values computed, the schedule, although legal, is not serializable. We shall see in Section 18.3.3 the additional condition, "two-phase locking," that we need to assure that legal schedules are conflict-serializable. □

18.3.2 The Locking Scheduler

It is the job of a scheduler based on locking to grant requests if and only if the request will result in a legal schedule. If a request is not granted, the requesting transaction is delayed; it waits until the scheduler grants its request at a later time. To aid its decisions, the scheduler has a *lock table* that tells, for every database element, the transaction (if any) that currently holds a lock on that element. We shall discuss the structure of a lock table in more detail in Section 18.5.2. However, when there is only one kind of lock, as we have assumed so far, the table may be thought of as a relation Locks(element, transaction), consisting of pairs (X, T) such that transaction T currently has a lock on database element X. The scheduler has only to query and modify this relation.

Example 18.11: The schedule of Fig. 18.12 is legal, as we mentioned, so the locking scheduler would grant every request in the order of arrival shown. However, sometimes it is not possible to grant requests. Here are T_1 and T_2 from Example 18.10, with simple but important changes, in which T_1 and T_2 each lock B before releasing the lock on A.

T_1: $l_1(A)$; $r_1(A)$; A := A+100; $w_1(A)$; $l_1(B)$; $u_1(A)$; $r_1(B)$; B := B+100; $w_1(B)$; $u_1(B)$;

T_2: $l_2(A)$; $r_2(A)$; A := A*2; $w_2(A)$; $l_2(B)$; $u_2(A)$; $r_2(B)$; B := B*2; $w_2(B)$; $u_2(B)$;

In Fig. 18.13, when T_2 requests a lock on B, the scheduler must deny the lock, because T_1 still holds a lock on B. Thus, T_2 is delayed, and the next actions are from T_1. Eventually, T_1 executes $u_1(B)$, which unlocks B. Now, T_2 can get its lock on B, which is executed at the next step. Notice that because T_2 was forced to wait, it wound up multiplying B by 2 after T_1 added 100, resulting in a consistent database state. □

18.3.3 Two-Phase Locking

There is a surprising condition, called *two-phase locking* (or *2PL*) under which we can guarantee that a legal schedule of consistent transactions is conflict-serializable:

- In every transaction, all lock actions precede all unlock actions.

T_1	T_2	A	B
		25	25
$l_1(A); r_1(A);$			
A := A+100;			
$w_1(A); l_1(B); u_1(A);$		125	
	$l_2(A); r_2(A);$		
	A := A*2;		
	$w_2(A);$	250	
	$l_2(B)$ **Denied**		
$r_1(B);$ B := B+100;			
$w_1(B); u_1(B);$			125
	$l_2(B); u_2(A); r_2(B);$		
	B := B*2;		
	$w_2(B); u_2(B);$		250

Figure 18.13: The locking scheduler delays requests that would result in an illegal schedule

The "two phases" referred to by 2PL are thus the first phase, where locks are obtained, and the second phase, where locks are relinquished. Two-phase locking is a condition, like consistency, on the order of actions in a transaction. A transaction that obeys the 2PL condition is said to be a *two-phase-locked transaction*, or 2PL transaction.

Example 18.12: In Example 18.10, the transactions do not obey the two-phase locking rule. For instance, T_1 unlocks A before it locks B. However, the versions of the transactions found in Example 18.11 *do* obey the 2PL condition. Notice that T_1 locks both A and B within the first five actions and unlocks them within the next five actions; T_2 behaves similarly. If we compare Figs. 18.12 and 18.13, we see how the 2PL transactions interact properly with the scheduler to assure consistency, while the non-2PL transactions allow non-conflict-serializable behavior. □

18.3.4 Why Two-Phase Locking Works

Intuitively, each two-phase-locked transaction may be thought to execute in its entirety at the instant it issues its first unlock request, as suggested by Fig. 18.14. Thus, there is always at least one conflict-equivalent serial schedule for a schedule S of 2PL transactions: the one in which the transactions appear in the same order as their first unlocks.

We shall show how to convert any legal schedule S of consistent, two-phase-locked transactions to a conflict-equivalent serial schedule. The conversion is best described as an induction on n, the number of transactions in S. In what follows, it is important to remember that the issue of conflict-equivalence refers

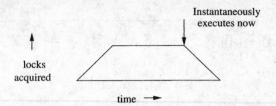

Figure 18.14: Every two-phase-locked transaction has a point at which it may be thought to execute instantaneously

to the read and write actions only. As we swap the order of reads and writes, we ignore the lock and unlock actions. Once we have the read and write actions ordered serially, we can place the lock and unlock actions around them as the various transactions require. Since each transaction releases all locks before its end, we know that the serial schedule is legal.

BASIS: If $n = 1$, there is nothing to do; S is already a serial schedule.

INDUCTION: Suppose S involves n transactions $T_1, T_2, \ldots, T_n$, and let T_i be the transaction with the first unlock action in the entire schedule S, say $u_i(X)$. We claim it is possible to move all the read and write actions of T_i forward to the beginning of the schedule without passing any conflicting reads or writes.

Consider some action of T_i, say $w_i(Y)$. Could it be preceded in S by some conflicting action, say $w_j(Y)$? If so, then in schedule S, actions $u_j(Y)$ and $l_i(Y)$ must intervene, in a sequence of actions

$$\cdots w_j(Y); \cdots; \ u_j(Y); \cdots; \ l_i(Y); \cdots; \ w_i(Y); \cdots$$

Since T_i is the first to unlock, $u_i(X)$ precedes $u_j(Y)$ in S; that is, S might look like:

$$\cdots; \ w_j(Y); \cdots; \ u_i(X); \cdots; \ u_j(Y); \cdots; \ l_i(Y); \cdots; \ w_i(Y); \cdots$$

or $u_i(X)$ could even appear before $w_j(Y)$. In any case, $u_i(X)$ appears before $l_i(Y)$, which means that T_i is *not* two-phase-locked, as we assumed. While we have only argued the nonexistence of conflicting pairs of writes, the same argument applies to any pair of potentially conflicting actions, one from T_i and the other from another T_j.

We conclude that it is indeed possible to move all the actions of T_i forward to the beginning of S, using swaps of nonconflicting read and write actions, followed by restoration of the lock and unlock actions of T_i. That is, S can be written in the form

(Actions of T_i)(Actions of the other $n - 1$ transactions)

The tail of $n - 1$ transactions is still a legal schedule of consistent, 2PL transactions, so the inductive hypothesis applies to it. We convert the tail to a

A Risk of Deadlock

One problem that is not solved by two-phase locking is the potential for deadlocks, where several transactions are forced by the scheduler to wait forever for a lock held by another transaction. For instance, consider the 2PL transactions from Example 18.11, but with T_2 changed to work on B first:

T_1: $l_1(A)$; $r_1(A)$; A := A+100; $w_1(A)$; $l_1(B)$; $u_1(A)$; $r_1(B)$; B := B+100; $w_1(B)$; $u_1(B)$;

T_2: $l_2(B)$; $r_2(B)$; B := B*2; $w_2(B)$; $l_2(A)$; $u_2(B)$; $r_2(A)$; A := A*2; $w_2(A)$; $u_2(A)$;

A possible interleaving of the actions of these transactions is:

T_1	T_2	A	B
		25	25
$l_1(A)$; $r_1(A)$;			
	$l_2(B)$; $r_2(B)$;		
A := A+100;			
	B := B*2;		
$w_1(A)$;		125	
	$w_2(B)$;		50
$l_1(B)$ **Denied**	$l_2(A)$ **Denied**		

Now, neither transaction can proceed, and they wait forever. In Section 19.2, we shall discuss methods to remedy this situation. However, observe that it is not possible to allow both transactions to proceed, since if we do so the final database state cannot possibly have $A = B$.

conflict-equivalent serial schedule, and now all of S has been shown conflict-serializable.

18.3.5 Exercises for Section 18.3

Exercise 18.3.1: Below are two transactions, with lock requests and the semantics of the transactions indicated. Recall from Exercise 18.2.1 that these transactions have the unusual property that they can be scheduled in ways that are not conflict-serializable, but, because of the semantics, are serializable.

T_1: $l_1(A)$; $r_1(A)$; A := A+2; $w_1(A)$; $u_1(A)$; $l_1(B)$; $r_1(B)$; B := B*3; $w_1(B)$; $u_1(B)$;

T_2: $l_2(B)$; $r_2(B)$; B := B*2; $w_2(B)$; $u_2(B)$; $l_2(A)$; $r_2(A)$; A := A+3; $w_2(A)$; $u_2(A)$;

In the questions below, consider only schedules of the read and write actions, not the lock, unlock, or assignment steps.

a) Give an example of a schedule that is prohibited by the locks.

! b) Of the $\binom{8}{4} = 70$ orders of the eight read and write actions, how many are legal schedules (i.e., they are permitted by the locks)?

! c) Of those schedules that are legal and serializable, how many are conflict-serializable?

! d) Of the legal schedules, how many are serializable (according to the semantics of the transactions given)?

!! e) Since T_1 and T_2 are not two-phase-locked, we would expect that some nonserializable behaviors would occur. Are there any legal schedules that are unserializable? If so, give an example, and if not, explain why.

Exercise 18.3.2: For each of the schedules of Exercise 18.2.5, assume that each transaction takes a lock on each database element immediately before it reads or writes the element, and that each transaction releases its locks immediately after the last time it accesses an element. Tell what the locking scheduler would do with each of these schedules; i.e., what requests would get delayed, and when would they be allowed to resume?

! **Exercise 18.3.3:** Here are the transactions of Exercise 18.3.1, with all unlocks moved to the end so they are two-phase-locked.

T_1: $l_1(A)$; $r_1(A)$; A := A+2; $w_1(A)$; $l_1(B)$; $r_1(B)$; B := B*3; $w_1(B)$; $u_1(A)$; $u_1(B)$;

T_2: $l_2(B)$; $r_2(B)$; B := B*2; $w_2(B)$; $l_2(A)$; $r_2(A)$; A := A+3; $w_2(A)$; $u_2(B)$; $u_2(A)$;

How many legal schedules of all the read and write actions of these transactions are there?

! **Exercise 18.3.4:** For each of the transactions described below, suppose that we insert one lock and one unlock action for each database element that is accessed.

a) $r_2(A)$; $w_2(A)$; $w_2(B)$;

b) $r_1(A)$; $w_1(B)$;

Tell how many orders of the lock, unlock, read, and write actions are:

   i. Consistent and two-phase locked.

   ii. Consistent, but not two-phase locked.

   iii. Inconsistent, but two-phase locked.

   iv. Neither consistent nor two-phase locked.

18.4 Locking Systems With Several Lock Modes

The locking scheme of Section 18.3 illustrates the important ideas behind locking, but it is too simple to be a practical scheme. The main problem is that a transaction T must take a lock on a database element X even if it only wants to read X and not write it. We cannot avoid taking the lock, because if we didn't, then another transaction might write a new value for X while T was active and cause unserializable behavior. On the other hand, there is no reason why several transactions could not read X at the same time, as long as none is allowed to write X.

We are thus motivated to introduce the most common locking scheme, where there are two different kinds of locks, one for reading (called a "shared lock" or "read lock"), and one for writing (called an "exclusive lock" or "write lock"). We then examine an improved scheme where transactions are allowed to take a shared lock and "upgrade" it to an exclusive lock later. We also consider "increment locks," which treat specially write actions that increment a database element; the important distinction is that increment operations commute, while general writes do not. These examples lead us to the general notion of a lock scheme described by a "compatibility matrix" that indicates what locks on a database element may be granted when other locks are held.

18.4.1 Shared and Exclusive Locks

The lock we need for writing is "stronger" than the lock we need to read, since it must prevent both reads and writes. Let us therefore consider a locking scheduler that uses two different kinds of locks: *shared locks* and *exclusive locks*. For any database element X there can be either one exclusive lock on X, or no exclusive locks but any number of shared locks. If we want to write X, we need to have an exclusive lock on X, but if we wish only to read X we may have either a shared or exclusive lock on X. If we want to read X but not write it, it is better to take only a shared lock.

We shall use $sl_i(X)$ to mean "transaction T_i requests a shared lock on database element X" and $xl_i(X)$ for "T_i requests an exclusive lock on X." We continue to use $u_i(X)$ to mean that T_i unlocks X; i.e., it relinquishes whatever lock(s) it has on X.

The three kinds of requirements — consistency and 2PL for transactions, and legality for schedules — each have their counterpart for a shared/exclusive lock system. We summarize these requirements here:

1. *Consistency of transactions*: A transaction may not write without holding an exclusive lock, and you may not read without holding some lock. More precisely, in any transaction T_i,

    (a) A read action $r_i(X)$ must be preceded by $sl_i(X)$ or $xl_i(X)$, with no intervening $u_i(X)$.

    (b) A write action $w_i(X)$ must be preceded by $xl_i(X)$, with no intervening $u_i(X)$.

    All locks must be followed by an unlock of the same element.

2. *Two-phase locking of transactions*: Locking must precede unlocking. To be more precise, in any two-phase locked transaction T_i, no action $sl_i(X)$ or $xl_i(X)$ can be preceded by an action $u_i(Y)$, for any Y.

3. *Legality of schedules*: An element may either be locked exclusively by one transaction or by several in shared mode, but not both. More precisely:

    (a) If $xl_i(X)$ appears in a schedule, then there cannot be a following $xl_j(X)$ or $sl_j(X)$, for some j other than i, without an intervening $u_i(X)$.

    (b) If $sl_i(X)$ appears in a schedule, then there cannot be a following $xl_j(X)$, for $j \neq i$, without an intervening $u_i(X)$.

Note that we *do* allow one transaction to request and hold both shared and exclusive locks on the same element, provided its doing so does not conflict with the lock(s) of other transactions. If transactions know in advance their needs for locks, then only the exclusive lock would have to be requested, but if lock needs are unpredictable, then it is possible that one transaction would request both shared and exclusive locks at different times.

Example 18.13: Let us examine a possible schedule of the following two transactions, using shared and exclusive locks:

$$T_1: sl_1(A); \ r_1(A); \ xl_1(B); \ r_1(B); \ w_1(B); \ u_1(A); \ u_1(B);$$
$$T_2: sl_2(A); \ r_2(A); \ sl_2(B); \ r_2(B); \ u_2(A); \ u_2(B);$$

Both T_1 and T_2 read A and B, but only T_1 writes B. Neither writes A.

In Fig. 18.15 is an interleaving of the actions of T_1 and T_2 in which T_1 begins by getting a shared lock on A. Then, T_2 follows by getting shared locks on both A and B. Now, T_1 needs an exclusive lock on B, since it will both read and write B. However, it cannot get the exclusive lock because T_2 already has a shared lock on B. Thus, the scheduler forces T_1 to wait. Eventually, T_2 releases the lock on B. At that time, T_1 may complete. □

T_1	T_2
$sl_1(A); r_1(A);$	
	$sl_2(A); r_2(A);$
	$sl_2(B); r_2(B);$
$xl_1(B)$ **Denied**	
	$u_2(A); u_2(B)$
$xl_1(B); r_1(B); w_1(B);$	
$u_1(A); u_1(B);$	

Figure 18.15: A schedule using shared and exclusive locks

Notice that the resulting schedule in Fig 18.15 is conflict-serializable. The conflict-equivalent serial order is (T_2, T_1), even though T_1 started first. The argument we gave in Section 18.3.4 to show that legal schedules of consistent, 2PL transactions are conflict-serializable applies to systems with shared and exclusive locks as well. In Fig. 18.15, T_2 unlocks before T_1, so we would expect T_2 to precede T_1 in the serial order.

18.4.2 Compatibility Matrices

If we use several lock modes, then the scheduler needs a policy about when it can grant a lock request, given the other locks that may already be held on the same database element. A *compatibility matrix* is a convenient way to describe lock-management policies. It has a row and column for each lock mode. The rows correspond to a lock that is already held on an element X by another transaction, and the columns correspond to the mode of a lock on X that is requested. The rule for using a compatibility matrix for lock-granting decisions is:

- We can grant the lock on X in mode C if and only if for every row R such that there is already a lock on X in mode R by some other transaction, there is a "Yes" in column C.

		Lock requested	
		S	X
Lock held	S	Yes	No
in mode	X	No	No

Figure 18.16: The compatibility matrix for shared and exclusive locks

Example 18.14: Figure 18.16 is the compatibility matrix for shared (S) and exclusive (X) locks. The column for S says that we can grant a shared lock on an element if the only locks held on that element currently are shared locks. The column for X says that we can grant an exclusive lock only if there are no other locks held currently.   □

18.4.3 Upgrading Locks

A transaction T that takes a shared lock on X is being "friendly" toward other transactions, since they are allowed to read X at the same time T is. Thus, we might wonder whether it would be friendlier still if a transaction T that wants to read and write a new value of X were first to take a shared lock on X, and only later, when T was ready to write the new value, *upgrade* the lock to exclusive (i.e., request an exclusive lock on X in addition to its already held shared lock on X). There is nothing that prevents a transaction from issuing requests for locks on the same database element in different modes. We adopt the convention that $u_i(X)$ releases all locks on X held by transaction T_i, although we could introduce mode-specific unlock actions if there were a use for them.

Example 18.15: In the following example, transaction T_1 is able to perform its computation concurrently with T_2, which would not be possible had T_1 taken an exclusive lock on B initially. The two transactions are:

T_1: $sl_1(A); r_1(A); sl_1(B); r_1(B); xl_1(B); w_1(B); u_1(A); u_1(B);$
T_2: $sl_2(A); r_2(A); sl_2(B); r_2(B); u_2(A); u_2(B);$

Here, T_1 reads A and B and performs some (possibly lengthy) calculation with them, eventually using the result to write a new value of B. Notice that T_1 takes a shared lock on B first, and later, after its calculation involving A and B is finished, requests an exclusive lock on B. Transaction T_2 only reads A and B, and does not write.

T_1	T_2
$sl_1(A); r_1(A);$	
	$sl_2(A); r_2(A);$
	$sl_2(B); r_2(B);$
$sl_1(B); r_1(B);$	
$xl_1(B)$ **Denied**	
	$u_2(A); u_2(B)$
$xl_1(B); w_1(B);$	
$u_1(A); u_2(B);$	

Figure 18.17: Upgrading locks allows more concurrent operation

Figure 18.17 shows a possible schedule of actions. T_2 gets a shared lock on B before T_1 does, but on the fourth line, T_1 is also able to lock B in shared mode. Thus, T_1 has both A and B and can perform its computation using their values. It is not until T_1 tries to upgrade its lock on B to exclusive that the scheduler must deny the request and force T_1 to wait until T_2 releases its lock on B. At that time, T_1 gets its exclusive lock on B, writes B, and finishes.

Notice that had T_1 asked for an exclusive lock on B initially, before reading B, then the request would have been denied, because T_2 already had a shared lock on B. T_1 could not perform its computation without reading B, and so T_1 would have more to do after T_2 releases its locks. As a result, T_1 finishes later using only an exclusive lock on B than it would if it used the upgrading strategy. □

Example 18.16: Unfortunately, indiscriminate use of upgrading introduces a new and potentially serious source of deadlocks. Suppose, that T_1 and T_2 each read database element A and write a new value for A. If both transactions use an upgrading approach, first getting a shared lock on A and then upgrading it to exclusive, the sequence of events suggested in Fig. 18.18 will happen whenever T_1 and T_2 initiate at approximately the same time.

T_1	T_2
$sl_1(A)$	
	$sl_2(A)$
$xl_1(A)$ **Denied**	
	$xl_2(A)$ **Denied**

Figure 18.18: Upgrading by two transactions can cause a deadlock

T_1 and T_2 are both able to get shared locks on A. Then, they each try to upgrade to exclusive, but the scheduler forces each to wait because the other has a shared lock on A. Thus, neither can make progress, and they will each wait forever, or until the system discovers that there is a deadlock, aborts one of the two transactions, and gives the other the exclusive lock on A. □

18.4.4 Update Locks

We can avoid the deadlock problem of Example 18.16 with a third lock mode, called *update locks*. An update lock $ul_i(X)$ gives transaction T_i only the privilege to read X, not to write X. However, only the update lock can be upgraded to a write lock later; a read lock cannot be upgraded. We can grant an update lock on X when there are already shared locks on X, but once there is an update lock on X we prevent additional locks of any kind — shared, update, or exclusive — from being taken on X. The reason is that if we don't deny such locks, then the updater might never get a chance to upgrade to exclusive, since there would always be other locks on X.

This rule leads to an asymmetric compatibility matrix, because the update (U) lock looks like a shared lock when we are requesting it and looks like an exclusive lock when we already have it. Thus, the columns for U and S locks are the same, and the rows for U and X locks are the same. The matrix is shown in Fig. 18.19.[3]

	S	X	U
S	Yes	No	Yes
X	No	No	No
U	No	No	No

Figure 18.19: Compatibility matrix for shared, exclusive, and update locks

Example 18.17: The use of update locks would have no effect on Example 18.15. As its third action, T_1 would take an update lock on B, rather than a shared lock. But the update lock would be granted, since only shared locks are held on B, and the same sequence of actions shown in Fig. 18.17 would occur.

However, update locks fix the problem shown in Example 18.16. Now, both T_1 and T_2 first request update locks on A and only later take exclusive locks. Possible descriptions of T_1 and T_2 are:

$$T_1: ul_1(A); r_1(A); xl_1(A); w_1(A); u_1(A);$$
$$T_2: ul_2(A); r_2(A); xl_2(A); w_2(A); u_2(A);$$

The sequence of events corresponding to Fig. 18.18 is shown in Fig. 18.20. Now, T_2, the second to request an update lock on A, is denied. T_1 is allowed to finish, and then T_2 may proceed. The lock system has effectively prevented concurrent execution of T_1 and T_2, but in this example, any significant amount of concurrent execution will result in either a deadlock or an inconsistent database state. □

T_1	T_2
$ul_1(A); r_1(A);$	
	$ul_2(A)$ **Denied**
$xl_1(A); w_1(A); u_1(A);$	
	$ul_2(A); r_2(A);$
	$xl_2(A); w_2(A); u_2(A);$

Figure 18.20: Correct execution using update locks

---

[3]Remember, however, that there is an additional condition regarding legality of schedules that is not reflected by this matrix: a transaction holding a shared lock but not an update lock on an element X cannot be given an exclusive lock on X, even though we do not in general prohibit a transaction from holding multiple locks on an element.

18.4.5 Increment Locks

Another interesting kind of lock that is useful in some situations is an "increment lock." Many transactions operate on the database only by incrementing or decrementing stored values. For example, consider a transaction that transfers money from one bank account to another.

The useful property of increment actions is that they commute with each other, since if two transactions add constants to the same database element, it does not matter which goes first, as the diagram of database state transitions in Fig. 18.21 suggests. On the other hand, incrementation commutes with neither reading nor writing; If you read A before or after it is incremented, you leave different values, and if you increment A before or after some other transaction writes a new value for A, you get different values of A in the database.

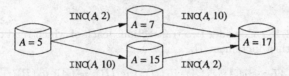

Figure 18.21: Two increment actions commute, since the final database state does not depend on which went first

Let us introduce as a possible action in transactions the *increment* action, written INC(A,c). Informally, this action adds constant c to database element A, which we assume is a single number. Note that c could be negative, in which case we are really decrementing A. In practice, we might apply INC to a component of a tuple, while the tuple itself, rather than one of its components, is the lockable element. More formally, we use INC(A,c) to stand for the atomic execution of the following steps: READ(A,t); $t := t+c$; WRITE(A,t);.

Corresponding to the increment action, we need an *increment lock*. We shall denote the action of T_i requesting an increment lock on X by $il_i(X)$. We also use shorthand $inc_i(X)$ for the action in which transaction T_i increments database element X by some constant; the exact constant doesn't matter.

The existence of increment actions and locks requires us to make several modifications to our definitions of consistent transactions, conflicts, and legal schedules. These changes are:

a) A consistent transaction can only have an increment action on X if it holds an increment lock on X at the time. An increment lock does not enable either read or write actions, however.

b) In a legal schedule, any number of transactions can hold an increment lock on X at any time. However, if an increment lock on X is held by some transaction, then no other transaction can hold either a shared or exclusive lock on X at the same time. These requirements are expressed by the compatibility matrix of Fig. 18.22, where I represents a lock in increment mode.

c) The action $inc_i(X)$ conflicts with both $r_j(X)$ and $w_j(X)$, for $j \neq i$, but does not conflict with $inc_j(X)$.

	S	X	I
S	Yes	No	No
X	No	No	No
I	No	No	Yes

Figure 18.22: Compatibility matrix for shared, exclusive, and increment locks

Example 18.18: Consider two transactions, each of which read database element A and then increment B.

$$T_1: \; sl_1(A); \; r_1(A); \; il_1(B); \; inc_1(B); \; u_1(A); \; u_1(B);$$
$$T_2: \; sl_2(A); \; r_2(A); \; il_2(B); \; inc_2(B); \; u_2(A); \; u_2(B);$$

Notice that the transactions are consistent, since they only perform an incrementation while they have an increment lock, and they only read while they have a shared lock. Figure 18.23 shows a possible interleaving of T_1 and T_2. T_1 reads A first, but then T_2 both reads A and increments B. However, T_1 is then allowed to get its increment lock on B and proceed.

T_1	T_2
$sl_1(A); \; r_1(A);$	
	$sl_2(A); \; r_2(A);$
	$il_2(B); \; inc_2(B);$
$il_1(B); \; inc_1(B);$	
	$u_2(A); \; u_2(B);$
$u_1(A); \; u_1(B);$	

Figure 18.23: A schedule of transactions with increment actions and locks

Notice that the scheduler did not have to delay any requests in Fig. 18.23. Suppose, for instance, that T_1 increments B by A, and T_2 increments B by $2A$. They can execute in either order, since the value of A does not change, and the incrementations may also be performed in either order.

Put another way, we may look at the sequence of non-lock actions in the schedule of Fig. 18.23; they are:

$$S: \; r_1(A); \; r_2(A); \; inc_2(B); \; inc_1(B);$$

We may move the last action, $inc_1(B)$, to the second position, since it does not conflict with another increment of the same element, and surely does not conflict with a read of a different element. This sequence of swaps shows that S is conflict-equivalent to the serial schedule $r_1(A)$; $inc_1(B)$; $r_2(A)$; $inc_2(B)$;. Similarly, we can move the first action, $r_1(A)$ to the third position by swaps, giving a serial schedule in which T_2 precedes T_1. □

18.4.6 Exercises for Section 18.4

Exercise 18.4.1: For each of the schedules of transactions T_1, T_2, and T_3 below:

a) $r_1(A)$; $r_2(B)$; $r_3(C)$; $w_1(B)$; $w_2(C)$; $w_3(A)$;

b) $r_1(A)$; $r_2(B)$; $r_3(C)$; $r_1(B)$; $r_2(C)$; $r_3(D)$; $w_1(C)$; $w_2(D)$; $w_3(E)$;

c) $r_1(A)$; $r_2(B)$; $r_3(C)$; $r_1(B)$; $r_2(C)$; $r_3(A)$; $w_1(A)$; $w_2(B)$; $w_3(C)$;

d) $r_1(A)$; $r_2(B)$; $r_3(C)$; $w_1(B)$; $w_2(C)$; $w_3(D)$;

e) $r_1(A)$; $r_2(B)$; $r_3(C)$; $r_1(B)$; $r_2(C)$; $r_3(D)$; $w_1(A)$; $w_2(B)$; $w_3(C)$;

do each of the following:

   i. Insert shared and exclusive locks, and insert unlock actions. Place a shared lock immediately in front of each read action that is not followed by a write action of the same element by the same transaction. Place an exclusive lock in front of every other read or write action. Place the necessary unlocks at the end of every transaction.

  ii. Tell what happens when each schedule is run by a scheduler that supports shared and exclusive locks.

 iii. Insert shared and exclusive locks in a way that allows upgrading. Place a shared lock in front of every read, an exclusive lock in front of every write, and place the necessary unlocks at the ends of the transactions.

 iv. Tell what happens when each schedule from (*iii*) is run by a scheduler that supports shared locks, exclusive locks, and upgrading.

  v. Insert shared, exclusive, and update locks, along with unlock actions. Place a shared lock in front of every read action that is not going to be upgraded, place an update lock in front of every read action that will be upgraded, and place an exclusive lock in front of every write action. Place unlocks at the ends of transactions, as usual.

 vi. Tell what happens when each schedule from (*v*) is run by a scheduler that supports shared, exclusive, and update locks.

Exercise 18.4.2: For each of the following schedules, insert appropriate locks (read, write, or increment) before each action, and unlocks at the ends of transactions. Then tell what happens when the schedule is run by a scheduler that supports these three types of locks.

a) $r_1(A); r_2(B); inc_1(B); inc_2(A); w_1(C); w_2(D);$

b) $inc_1(A); inc_2(B); inc_1(B); inc_2(C); w_1(C); w_2(D);$

c) $r_1(A); r_2(B); inc_1(B); inc_2(C); w_1(C); w_2(D);$

Exercise 18.4.3: In Exercise 18.1.1, we discussed a hypothetical transaction involving an airline reservation. If the transaction manager had available to it shared, exclusive, update, and increment locks, what lock would you recommend for each of the steps of the transaction?

Exercise 18.4.4: The action of multiplication by a constant factor can be modeled by an action of its own. Suppose MC(X,c) stands for an atomic execution of the steps READ(X,t); t := c*t; WRITE(X,t);. We can also introduce a lock mode that allows only multiplication by a constant factor.

a) Show the compatibility matrix for read, write, and multiplication-by-a-constant locks.

! b) Show the compatibility matrix for read, write, incrementation, and multiplication-by-a-constant locks.

! **Exercise 18.4.5:** Consider the two transactions:

$$T_1: r_1(A); r_1(B); inc_1(A); inc_1(B);$$
$$T_2: r_2(A); r_2(B); inc_2(A); inc_2(B);$$

Answer the following:

a) How many interleavings of these transactions are serializable?

b) If the order of incrementation in T_2 were reversed [i.e., $inc_2(B)$ followed by $inc_2(A)$], how many serializable interleavings would there be?

! **Exercise 18.4.6:** Suppose for sake of argument that database elements are two-dimensional vectors. There are four operations we can perform on vectors, and each will have its own type of lock.

i. Change the value along the x-axis (an X-lock).

ii. Change the value along the y-axis (a Y-lock).

iii. Change the angle of the vector (an A-lock).

iv. Change the magnitude of the vector (an M-lock).

Answer the following questions.

  a) Which pairs of operations commute? For example, if we rotate the vector so its angle is 120° and then change the x-coordinate to be 10, is that the same as first changing the x-coordinate to 10 and then changing the angle to 120°?

  b) Based on your answer to (a), what is the compatibility matrix for the four types of locks?

!! c) Suppose we changed the four operations so that instead of giving new values for a measure, the operations incremented the measure (e.g., "add 10 to the x-coordinate," or "rotate the vector 30° clockwise"). What would the compatibility matrix then be?

! **Exercise 18.4.7:** Here is a schedule with one action missing:

$$r_1(A);\ r_2(B);\ ???;\ w_1(C);\ w_2(A);$$

Your problem is to figure out what actions of certain types could replace the ??? and make the schedule not be serializable. Tell all possible nonserializable replacements for each of the following types of action: (a) Read (b) Increment (c) Update (d) Write.

18.5 An Architecture for a Locking Scheduler

Having seen a number of different locking schemes, we next consider how a scheduler that uses one of these schemes operates. We shall consider here only a simple scheduler architecture based on several principles:

  1. The transactions themselves do not request locks, or cannot be relied upon to do so. It is the job of the scheduler to insert lock actions into the stream of reads, writes, and other actions that access data.

  2. Transactions do not release locks. Rather, the scheduler releases the locks when the transaction manager tells it that the transaction will commit or abort.

18.5.1 A Scheduler That Inserts Lock Actions

Figure 18.24 shows a two-part scheduler that accepts requests such as read, write, commit, and abort, from transactions. The scheduler maintains a lock table, which, although it is shown as secondary-storage data, may be partially or completely in main memory. Normally, the main memory used by the lock table is not part of the buffer pool that is used for query execution and logging. Rather, the lock table is just another component of the DBMS, and will be

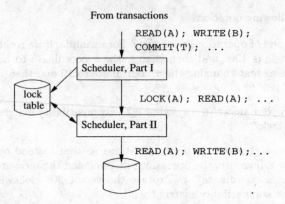

Figure 18.24: A scheduler that inserts lock requests into the transactions' request stream

allocated space by the operating system like other code and internal data of the DBMS.

Actions requested by a transaction are generally transmitted through the scheduler and executed on the database. However, under some circumstances a transaction is *delayed*, waiting for a lock, and its requests are not (yet) transmitted to the database. The two parts of the scheduler perform the following actions:

1. Part I takes the stream of requests generated by the transactions and inserts appropriate lock actions ahead of all database-access operations, such as read, write, increment, or update. The database access actions are then transmitted to Part II. Part I of the scheduler must select an appropriate lock mode from whatever set of lock modes the scheduler is using.

2. Part II takes the sequence of lock and database-access actions passed to it by Part I, and executes each appropriately. If a lock or database-access request is received by Part II, it determines whether the issuing transaction T is already delayed, because a lock has not been granted. If so, then the action is itself delayed and added to a list of actions that must eventually be performed for transaction T. If T is *not* delayed (i.e., all locks it previously requested have been granted already), then

   (a) If the action is a database access, it is transmitted to the database and executed.

   (b) If a lock action is received by Part II, it examines the lock table to see if the lock can be granted.

       i. If so, the lock table is modified to include the lock just granted.

      ii. If not, then an entry must be made in the lock table to indicate that the lock has been requested. Part II of the scheduler then delays transaction T until such time as the lock is granted.

3. When a transaction T commits or aborts, Part I is notified by the transaction manager, and releases all locks held by T. If any transactions are waiting for any of these locks, Part I notifies Part II.

4. When Part II is notified that a lock on some database element X is available, it determines the next transaction or transactions that can now be given a lock on X. The transaction(s) that receive a lock are allowed to execute as many of their delayed actions as can execute, until they either complete or reach another lock request that cannot be granted.

Example 18.19: If there is only one kind of lock, as in Section 18.3, then the task of Part I of the scheduler is simple. If it sees any action on database element X, and it has not already inserted a lock request on X for that transaction, then it inserts the request. When a transaction commits or aborts, Part I can forget about that transaction after releasing its locks, so the memory required for Part I does not grow indefinitely.

    When there are several kinds of locks, the scheduler may require advance notice of what future actions on the same database element will occur. Let us reconsider the case of shared-exclusive-update locks, using the transactions of Example 18.15, which we now write without any locks at all:

$$T_1: \ r_1(A); \ r_1(B); \ w_1(B);$$
$$T_2: \ r_2(A); \ r_2(B);$$

The messages sent to Part I of the scheduler must include not only the read or write request, but an indication of future actions on the same element. In particular, when $r_1(B)$ is sent, the scheduler needs to know that there will be a later $w_1(B)$ action (or might be such an action). There are several ways the information might be made available. For example, if the transaction is a query, we know it will not write anything. If the transaction is a SQL database modification command, then the query processor can determine in advance the database elements that might be both read and written. If the transaction is a program with embedded SQL, then the compiler has access to all the SQL statements (which are the only ones that can access the database) and can determine the potential database elements written.

    In our example, suppose that events occur in the order suggested by Fig. 18.17. Then T_1 first issues $r_1(A)$. Since there will be no future upgrading of this lock, the scheduler inserts $sl_1(A)$ ahead of $r_1(A)$. Next, the requests from T_2 — $r_2(A)$ and $r_2(B)$ — arrive at the scheduler. Again there is no future upgrade, so the sequence of actions $sl_2(A); \ r_2(A); \ sl_2(B); \ r_2(B)$ are issued by Part I.

    Then, the action $r_1(B)$ arrives at the scheduler, along with a warning that this lock may be upgraded. The scheduler Part I thus emits $ul_1(B); \ r_1(B)$ to

Part II. The latter consults the lock table and finds that it can grant the update lock on B to T_1, because there are only shared locks on B.

When the action $w_1(B)$ arrives at the scheduler, Part I emits $xl_1(B); w_1(B)$. However, Part II cannot grant the $xl_1(B)$ request, because there is a shared lock on B for T_2. This and any subsequent actions from T_1 are delayed, stored by Part II for future execution. Eventually, T_2 commits, and Part I releases the locks on A and B that T_2 held. At that time, it is found that T_1 is waiting for a lock on B. Part II of the scheduler is notified, and it finds the lock $xl_1(B)$ is now available. It enters this lock into the lock table and proceeds to execute stored actions from T_1 to the extent possible. In this case, T_1 completes. □

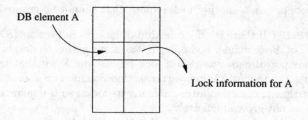

Figure 18.25: A lock table is a mapping from database elements to their lock information

18.5.2 The Lock Table

Abstractly, the lock table is a relation that associates database elements with locking information about that element, as suggested by Fig. 18.25. The table might, for instance, be implemented with a hash table, using (addresses of) database elements as the hash key. Any element that is not locked does not appear in the table, so the size is proportional to the number of locked elements only, not to the size of the entire database.

In Fig. 18.26 is an example of the sort of information we would find in a lock-table entry. This example structure assumes that the shared-exclusive-update lock scheme of Section 18.4.4 is used by the scheduler. The entry shown for a typical database element A is a tuple with the following components:

1. The *group mode* is a summary of the most stringent conditions that a transaction requesting a new lock on A faces. Rather than comparing the lock request with every lock held by another transaction on the same element, we can simplify the grant/deny decision by comparing the request with only the group mode.[4] For the shared-exclusive-update (SXU) lock scheme, the rule is simple: the group mode:

---

[4]The lock manager must, however, deal with the possibility that the requesting transaction already has a lock in another mode on the same element. For instance, in the SXU lock system discussed, the lock manager may be able to grant an X-lock request if the requesting

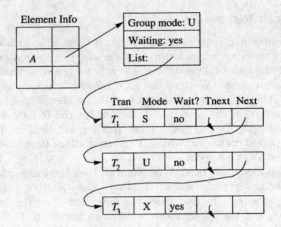

Figure 18.26: Structure of lock-table entries

(a) S means that only shared locks are held.

(b) U means that there is one update lock and perhaps one or more shared locks.

(c) X means there is one exclusive lock and no other locks.

For other lock schemes, there is usually an appropriate system of summaries by a group mode; we leave examples as exercises.

2. The *waiting* bit tells that there is at least one transaction waiting for a lock on A.

3. A list describing all those transactions that either currently hold locks on A or are waiting for a lock on A. Useful information that each list entry has might include:

   (a) The name of the transaction holding or waiting for a lock.

   (b) The mode of this lock.

   (c) Whether the transaction is holding or waiting for the lock.

We also show in Fig. 18.26 two links for each entry. One links the entries themselves, and the other links all entries for a particular transaction (Tnext in the figure). The latter link would be used when a transaction commits or aborts, so that we can easily find all the locks that must be released.

---

transaction is the one that holds a U lock on the same element. For systems that do not support multiple locks held by one transaction on one element, the group mode always tells what the lock manager needs to know.

Handling Lock Requests

Suppose transaction T requests a lock on A. If there is no lock-table entry for A, then surely there are no locks on A, so the entry is created and the request is granted. If the lock-table entry for A exists, we use it to guide the decision about the lock request. We find the group mode, which in Fig. 18.26 is U, or "update." Once there is an update lock on an element, no other lock can be granted (except in the case that T itself holds the U lock and other locks are compatible with T's request). Thus, this request by T is denied, and an entry will be placed on the list saying T requests a lock (in whatever mode was requested), and Wait? = 'yes'.

If the group mode had been X (exclusive), then the same thing would happen, but if the group mode were S (shared), then another shared or update lock could be granted. In that case, the entry for T on the list would have Wait? = 'no', and the group mode would be changed to U if the new lock were an update lock; otherwise, the group mode would remain S. Whether or not the lock is granted, the new list entry is linked properly, through its Tnext and Next fields. Notice that whether or not the lock is granted, the entry in the lock table tells the scheduler what it needs to know without having to examine the list of locks.

Handling Unlocks

Now suppose transaction T unlocks A. T's entry on the list for A is deleted. If the lock held by T is not the same as the group mode (e.g., T held an S lock, while the group mode was U), then there is no reason to change the group mode. On the other hand, if T's lock is in the group mode, we may have to examine the entire list to find the new group mode. In the example of Fig. 18.26, we know there can be only one U lock on an element, so if that lock is released, the new group mode could be only S (if there are shared locks remaining) or nothing (if no other locks are currently held).[5] If the group mode is X, we know there are no other locks, and if the group mode is S, we need to determine whether there are other shared locks.

If the value of Waiting is 'yes', then we need to grant one or more locks from the list of requested locks. There are several different approaches, each with its advantages:

1. *First-come-first-served*: Grant the lock request that has been waiting the longest. This strategy guarantees no *starvation*, the situation where a transaction can wait forever for a lock.

2. *Priority to shared locks*: First grant all the shared locks waiting. Then, grant one update lock, if there are any waiting. Only grant an exclusive lock if no others are waiting. This strategy can allow starvation, if a transaction is waiting for a U or X lock.

---

[5]We would never actually see a group mode of "nothing," since if there are no locks and no lock requests on an element, then there is no lock-table entry for that element.

3. *Priority to upgrading*: If there is a transaction with a U lock waiting to upgrade it to an X lock, grant that first. Otherwise, follow one of the other strategies mentioned.

18.5.3 Exercises for Section 18.5

Exercise 18.5.1: For each of the schedules of Exercise 18.2.5, tell the steps that the locking scheduler described in this section would execute.

Exercise 18.5.2: What are suitable group modes for a lock table if the lock modes used are:

a) Shared and exclusive locks.

! b) Shared, exclusive, and increment locks.

!! c) The lock modes of Exercise 18.4.6.

18.6 Hierarchies of Database Elements

Let us now return to the exploration of different locking schemes that we began in Section 18.4. In particular, we shall focus on two problems that come up when there is a tree structure to our data.

1. The first kind of tree structure we encounter is a hierarchy of lockable elements. We shall discuss in this section how to allow locks on both large elements, e.g., relations, and smaller elements contained within these, such as blocks holding several tuples of the relation, or individual tuples.

2. The second kind of hierarchy that is important in concurrency-control systems is data that is itself organized in a tree. A major example is B-tree indexes. We may view nodes of the B-tree as database elements, but if we do, then as we shall see in Section 18.7, the locking schemes studied so far perform poorly, and we need to use a new approach.

18.6.1 Locks With Multiple Granularity

Recall that the term "database element" was purposely left undefined, because different systems use different sizes of database elements to lock, such as tuples, pages or blocks, and relations. Some applications benefit from small database elements, such as tuples, while others are best off with large elements.

Example 18.20: Consider a database for a bank. If we treated relations as database elements, and therefore had only one lock for an entire relation such as the one giving account balances, then the system would allow very little concurrency. Since most transactions will change an account balance either positively or negatively, most transactions would need an exclusive lock on the accounts relation. Thus, only one deposit or withdrawal could take place at any time, no matter how many processors we had available to execute these transactions. A better approach is to lock individual pages or data blocks. Thus, two accounts whose tuples are on different blocks can be updated at the same time, offering almost all the concurrency that is possible in the system. The extreme would be to provide a lock for every tuple, so any set of accounts whatsoever could be updated at once, but this fine a grain of locks is probably not worth the extra effort.

In contrast, consider a database of documents. These documents may be edited from time to time, but most transactions will retrieve whole documents. The sensible choice of database element is a complete document. Since most transactions are *read-only* (i.e., they do not perform any write actions), locking is only necessary to avoid the reading of a document that is in the middle of being edited. Were we to use smaller-granularity locks, such as paragraphs, sentences, or words, there would be essentially no benefit but added expense. The only activity a smaller-granularity lock would support is the ability for two people to edit different parts of a document simultaneously. □

Some applications could use both large- and small-grained locks. For instance, the bank database discussed in Example 18.20 clearly needs block- or tuple-level locking, but might also at some time need a lock on the entire accounts relation in order to audit accounts (e.g., check that the sum of the accounts is correct). However, permitting a shared lock on the accounts relation, in order to compute some aggregation on the relation, while at the same time there are exclusive locks on individual account tuples, can lead easily to unserializable behavior. The reason is that the relation is actually changing while a supposedly frozen copy of it is being read by the aggregation query.

18.6.2 Warning Locks

The solution to the problem of managing locks at different granularities involves a new kind of lock called a "warning." These locks are useful when the database elements form a nested or hierarchical structure, as suggested in Fig. 18.27. There, we see three levels of database elements:

1. Relations are the largest lockable elements.

2. Each relation is composed of one or more block or pages, on which its tuples are stored.

3. Each block contains one or more tuples.

The rules for managing locks on a hierarchy of database elements constitute the *warning protocol*, which involves both "ordinary" locks and "warning" locks. We shall describe the lock scheme where the ordinary locks are S and X (shared and exclusive). The warning locks will be denoted by prefixing I (for "intention

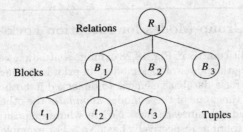

Figure 18.27: Database elements organized in a hierarchy

to") to the ordinary locks; for example IS represents the intention to obtain a shared lock on a subelement. The rules of the warning protocol are:

1. To place an ordinary S or X lock on any element, we must begin at the root of the hierarchy.

2. If we are at the element that we want to lock, we need look no further. We request an S or X lock on that element.

3. If the element we wish to lock is further down the hierarchy, then we place a warning at this node; that is, if we want to get a shared lock on a subelement we request an IS lock at this node, and if we want an exclusive lock on a subelement, we request an IX lock on this node. When the lock on the current node is granted, we proceed to the appropriate child (the one whose subtree contains the node we wish to lock). We then repeat step (2) or step (3), as appropriate, until we reach the desired node.

	IS	IX	S	X
IS	Yes	Yes	Yes	No
IX	Yes	Yes	No	No
S	Yes	No	Yes	No
X	No	No	No	No

Figure 18.28: Compatibility matrix for shared, exclusive, and intention locks

In order to decide whether or not one of these locks can be granted, we use the compatibility matrix of Fig. 18.28. To see why this matrix makes sense, consider first the IS column. When we request an IS lock on a node N, we intend to read a descendant of N. The only time this intent could create a problem is if some other transaction has already claimed the right to write a new copy of the entire database element represented by N; thus we see "No" in the row for X. Notice that if some other transaction plans to write only a subelement, indicated by an IX lock at N, then we can afford to grant the IS

Group Modes for Intention Locks

The compatibility matrix of Fig. 18.28 exhibits a situation we have not seen before regarding the power of lock modes. In prior lock schemes, whenever it was possible for a database element to be locked in both modes M and N at the same time, one of these modes *dominates* the other, in the sense that its row and column each has "No" in whatever positions the other mode's row or column, respectively, has "No." For example, in Fig. 18.19 we see that U dominates S, and X dominates both S and U. An advantage of knowing that there is always one dominant lock on an element is that we can summarize the effect of many locks with a "group mode," as discussed in Section 18.5.2.

As we see from Fig. 18.28, neither of modes S and IX dominate the other. Moreover, it is possible for an element to be locked in both modes S and IX at the same time, provided the locks are requested by the same transaction (recall that the "No" entries in a compatibility matrix only apply to locks held by some *other* transaction). A transaction might request both locks if it wanted to read an entire element and then write a few of its subelements. If a transaction has both S and IX locks on an element, then it restricts other transactions to the extent that either lock does. That is, we can imagine another lock mode SIX, whose row and column have "No" everywhere except in the entry for IS. The lock mode SIX serves as the group mode if there is a transaction with locks in S and IX modes, but not X mode.

Incidentally, we might imagine that the same situation occurs in the matrix of Fig 18.22 for increment locks. That is, one transaction could hold locks in both S and I modes. However, this situation is equivalent to holding a lock in X mode, so we could use X as the group mode in that situation.

lock at N, and allow the conflict to be resolved at a lower level, if indeed the intent to write and the intent to read happen to involve a common element.

Now consider the column for IX. If we intend to write a subelement of node N, then we must prevent either reading or writing of the entire element represented by N. Thus, we see "No" in the entries for lock modes S and X. However, per our discussion of the IS column, another transaction that reads or writes a subelement can have potential conflicts dealt with at that level, so IX does not conflict with another IX at N or with an IS at N.

Next, consider the column for S. Reading the element corresponding to node N cannot conflict with either another read lock on N or a read lock on some subelement of N, represented by IS at N. Thus, we see "Yes" in the rows for both S and IS. However, either an X or an IX means that some other transaction will write at least a part of the element represented by N. Thus, we cannot grant the right to read all of N, which explains the "No" entries in the column for S.

Finally, the column for X has only "No" entries. We cannot allow writing of all of node N if any other transaction already has the right to read or write N, or to acquire that right on a subelement.

Example 18.21: Consider the relation

```
Movie(title, year, length, studioName)
```

Let us postulate a lock on the entire relation and locks on individual tuples. Then transaction T_1, which consists of the query

```
SELECT *
FROM Movie
WHERE title = 'King Kong';
```

starts by getting an IS lock on the entire relation. It then moves to the individual tuples (there are three movies with the title *King Kong*), and gets S locks on each of them.

Now, suppose that while we are executing the first query, transaction T_2, which changes the year component of a tuple, begins:

```
UPDATE Movie
SET year = 1939
WHERE title = 'Gone With the Wind';
```

T_2 needs an IX lock on the relation, since it plans to write a new value for one of the tuples. T_1's IS lock on the relation is compatible, so the lock is granted. When T_2 goes to the tuple for *Gone With the Wind*, it finds no lock there, and so gets its X lock and rewrites the tuple. Had T_2 tried to write a new value in the tuple for one of the *King Kong* movies, it would have had to wait until T_1 released its S lock, since S and X are not compatible. The collection of locks is suggested by Fig. 18.29. □

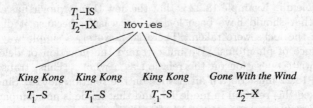

Figure 18.29: Locks granted to two transactions accessing `Movie` tuples

18.6.3   Phantoms and Handling Insertions Correctly

When transactions create new subelements of a lockable element, there are some opportunities to go wrong. The problem is that we can only lock existing items; there is no easy way to lock database elements that do not exist but might later be inserted. The following example illustrates the point.

Example 18.22 : Suppose we have the same `Movie` relation as in Example 18.21, and the first transaction to execute is T_3, which is the query

```
SELECT SUM(length)
FROM Movie
WHERE studioName = 'Disney';
```

T_3 needs to read the tuples of all the Disney movies, so it might start by getting an IS lock on the `Movie` relation and S locks on each of the tuples for Disney movies.[6]

Now, a transaction T_4 comes along and inserts a new Disney movie. It seems that T_4 needs no locks, but it has made the result of T_3 incorrect. That fact by itself is not a concurrency problem, since the serial order (T_3, T_4) is equivalent to what actually happened. However, there could also be some other element X that both T_3 and T_4 write, with T_4 writing first, so there *could* be an unserializable behavior of more complex transactions.

To be more precise, suppose that D_1 and D_2 are pre-existing Disney movies, and D_3 is the new Disney movie inserted by T_4. Let L be the sum of the lengths of the Disney movies computed by T_3, and assume the consistency constraint on the database is that L should be equal to the sum of all the lengths of the Disney movies that existed the last time L was computed. Then the following is a sequence of events that is legal under the warning protocol:

$$r_3(D_1);\ r_3(D_2);\ w_4(D_3);\ w_4(X);\ w_3(L);\ w_3(X);$$

Here, we have used $w_4(D_3)$ to represent the creation of D_3 by transaction T_4. The schedule above is not serializable. In particular, the value of L is not the sum of the lengths of D_1, D_2, and D_3, which are the current Disney movies. Moreover, the fact that X has the value written by T_3 and not T_4 rules out the possibility that T_3 was ahead of T_4 in a supposed equivalent serial order.   □

The problem in Example 18.22 is that the new Disney movie has a *phantom* tuple, one that should have been locked but wasn't, because it didn't exist at the time the locks were taken. There is, however, a simple way to avoid the occurrence of phantoms. We must regard the insertion or deletion of a tuple as a write operation on the relation as a whole. Thus, transaction T_4 in Example 18.22 must obtain an X lock on the relation `Movie`. Since T_3 has already locked this relation in mode IS, and that mode is not compatible with mode X, T_4 would have to wait until after T_3 completes.

---

[6]However, if there were many Disney movies, it might be more efficient just to get an S lock on the entire relation.

18.6.4 Exercises for Section 18.6

Exercise 18.6.1: Change the sequence of actions in Example 18.22 so that the $w_4(D_3)$ action becomes a write by T_4 of the entire relation Movie. Then, show the action of a warning-protocol-based scheduler on this sequence of requests.

Exercise 18.6.2: Consider, for variety, an object-oriented database. The objects of class C are stored on two blocks, B_1 and B_2. Block B_1 contains objects O_1, O_2, and O_3, while block B_2 contains objects O_4 and O_5. The entire set of objects of class C, the blocks, and the individual objects form a hierarchy of lockable database elements. Tell the sequence of lock requests and the response of a warning-protocol-based scheduler to the following sequences of requests. You may assume all requests occur just before they are needed, and all unlocks occur at the end of the transaction.

a) $r_1(O_5); w_2(O_5); r_2(O_3); w_1(O_4);$

b) $r_1(O_1); r_1(O_3); r_2(O_1); w_2(O_4); w_2(O_5);$

c) $r_1(O_1); w_2(O_2); r_2(O_3); w_1(O_4);$

d) $r_1(O_1); r_2(O_2); r_3(O_1); w_1(O_3); w_2(O_4); w_3(O_5); w_1(O_2);$

!! **Exercise 18.6.3:** Show how to add increment locks to a warning-protocol-based scheduler.

18.7 The Tree Protocol

Like Section 18.6, this section deals with data in the form of a tree. However, here, the nodes of the tree do not form a hierarchy based on containment. Rather, database elements are disjoint pieces of data, but the only way to get to a node is through its parent; B-trees are an important example of this sort of data. Knowing that we must traverse a particular path to an element gives us some important freedom to manage locks differently from the two-phase locking approaches we have seen so far.

18.7.1 Motivation for Tree-Based Locking

Let us consider a B-tree index in a system that treats individual nodes (i.e., blocks) as lockable database elements. The node is the right level of lock granularity, because treating smaller pieces as elements offers no benefit, and treating the entire B-tree as one database element prevents the sort of concurrent use of the index that can be achieved via the mechanisms that form the subject of this section.

If we use a standard set of lock modes, like shared, exclusive, and update locks, and we use two-phase locking, then concurrent use of the B-tree is almost impossible. The reason is that every transaction using the index must begin by locking the root node of the B-tree. If the transaction is 2PL, then it cannot unlock the root until it has acquired all the locks it needs, both on B-tree nodes and other database elements.[7] Moreover, since in principle any transaction that inserts or deletes could wind up rewriting the root of the B-tree, the transaction needs at least an update lock on the root node, or an exclusive lock if update mode is not available. Thus, only one transaction that is not read-only can access the B-tree at any time.

However, in most situations, we can deduce almost immediately that a B-tree node will not be rewritten, even if the transaction inserts or deletes a tuple. For example, if the transaction inserts a tuple, but the child of the root that we visit is not completely full, then we know the insertion cannot propagate up to the root. Similarly, if the transaction deletes a single tuple, and the child of the root we visit has more than the minimum number of keys and pointers, then we can be sure the root will not change.

Thus, as soon as a transaction moves to a child of the root and observes the (quite usual) situation that rules out a rewrite of the root, we would like to release the lock on the root. The same observation applies to the lock on any interior node of the B-tree. Unfortunately, releasing the lock on the root early will violate 2PL, so we cannot be sure that the schedule of several transactions accessing the B-tree will be serializable. The solution is a specialized protocol for transactions that access tree-structured data such as B-trees. The protocol violates 2PL, but uses the fact that accesses to elements must proceed down the tree to assure serializability.

18.7.2 Rules for Access to Tree-Structured Data

The following restrictions on locks form the *tree protocol*. We assume that there is only one kind of lock, represented by lock requests of the form $l_i(X)$, but the idea generalizes to any set of lock modes. We assume that transactions are consistent, and schedules must be legal (i.e., the scheduler will enforce the expected restrictions by granting locks on a node only when they do not conflict with locks already on that node), but there is no two-phase locking requirement on transactions.

1. A transaction's first lock may be at any node of the tree.[8]

2. Subsequent locks may only be acquired if the transaction currently has a lock on the parent node.

3. Nodes may be unlocked at any time.

4. A transaction may not relock a node on which it has released a lock, even if it still holds a lock on the node's parent.

---

[7]Additionally, there are good reasons why a transaction will hold all its locks until it is ready to commit; see Section 19.1.

[8]In the B-tree example of Section 18.7.1, the first lock would always be at the root.

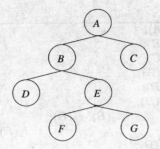

Figure 18.30: A tree of lockable elements

Example 18.23: Figure 18.30 shows a hierarchy of nodes, and Fig. 18.31 indicates the action of three transactions on this data. T_1 starts at the root A, and proceeds downward to B, C, and D. T_2 starts at B and tries to move to E, but its move is initially denied because of the lock by T_3 on E. Transaction T_3 starts at E and moves to F and G. Notice that T_1 is not a 2PL transaction, because the lock on A is relinquished before the lock on D is acquired. Similarly, T_3 is not a 2PL transaction, although T_2 happens to be 2PL. □

18.7.3 Why the Tree Protocol Works

The tree protocol implies a serial order on the transactions involved in a schedule. We can define an order of precedence as follows. Say that $T_i <_S T_j$ if in schedule S, the transactions T_i and T_j lock a node in common, and T_i locks the node first.

Example 18.24: In the schedule S of Fig 18.31, we find T_1 and T_2 lock B in common, and T_1 locks it first. Thus, $T_1 <_S T_2$. We also find that T_2 and T_3 lock E in common, and T_3 locks it first; thus $T_3 <_S T_2$. However, there is no precedence between T_1 and T_3, because they lock no node in common. Thus, the precedence graph derived from these precedence relations is as shown in Fig. 18.32. □

If the precedence graph drawn from the precedence relations that we defined above has no cycles, then we claim that any topological order of the transactions is an equivalent serial schedule. For example, either (T_1, T_3, T_2) or (T_3, T_1, T_2) is an equivalent serial schedule for Fig. 18.31. The reason is that in such a serial schedule, all nodes are touched in the same order as they are in the original schedule.

To understand why the precedence graph described above must always be acyclic if the tree protocol is obeyed, observe the following:

- If two transactions lock several elements in common, then they are all locked in the same order.

T_1	T_2	T_3
$l_1(A); r_1(A);$		
$l_1(B); r_1(B);$		
$l_1(C); r_1(C);$		
$w_1(A); u_1(A);$		
$l_1(D); r_1(D);$		
$w_1(B); u_1(B);$		
	$l_2(B); r_2(B);$	
		$l_3(E); r_3(E);$
$w_1(D); u_1(D);$		
$w_1(C); u_1(C);$		
	$l_2(E)$ **Denied**	
		$l_3(F); r_3(F);$
		$w_3(F); u_3(F);$
		$l_3(G); r_3(G)$
		$w_3(E); u_3(E);$
	$l_2(E); r_2(E);$	
		$w_3(G); u_3(G)$
	$w_2(B); u_2(B);$	
	$w_2(E); u_2(E);$	

Figure 18.31: Three transactions following the tree protocol

To see why, consider some transactions T and U, which lock two or more items in common. First, notice that each transaction locks a set of elements that form a tree, and the intersection of two trees is itself a tree. Thus, there is some one highest element X that both T and U lock. Suppose that T locks X first, but that there is some other element Y that U locks before T. Then there is a path in the tree of elements from X to Y, and both T and U must lock each element along the path, because neither can lock a node without having a lock on its parent.

Consider the first element along this path, say Z, that U locks first, as suggested by Fig. 18.33. Then T locks the parent P of Z before U does. But then T is still holding the lock on P when it locks Z, so U has not yet locked

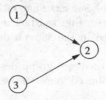

Figure 18.32: Precedence graph derived from the schedule of Fig. 18.31

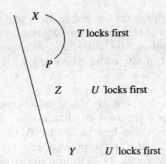

Figure 18.33: A path of elements locked by two transactions

P when it locks Z. It cannot be that Z is the first element U locks in common with T, since they both lock ancestor X (which could also be P, but not Z). Thus, U cannot lock Z until after it has acquired a lock on P, which is after T locks Z. We conclude that T precedes U at every node they lock in common.

Now, consider an arbitrary set of transactions $T_1, T_2, \ldots, T_n$ that obey the tree protocol and lock some of the nodes of a tree according to schedule S. First, among those that lock the root, they do so in some order, and by the rule just observed:

- If T_i locks the root before T_j, then T_i locks every node in common with T_j before T_j does. That is, $T_i <_S T_j$, but not $T_j <_S T_i$.

We can show by induction on the number of nodes of the tree that there is some serial order equivalent to S for the complete set of transactions.

BASIS: If there is only one node, the root, then as we just observed, the order in which the transactions lock the root serves.

INDUCTION: If there is more than one node in the tree, consider for each subtree of the root the set of transactions that lock one or more nodes in that subtree. Note that transactions locking the root may belong to more than one subtree, but a transaction that does not lock the root will belong to only one subtree. For instance, among the transactions of Fig. 18.31, only T_1 locks the root, and it belongs to both subtrees — the tree rooted at B and the tree rooted at C. However, T_2 and T_3 belong only to the tree rooted at B.

By the inductive hypothesis, there is a serial order for all the transactions that lock nodes in any one subtree. We have only to blend the serial orders for the various subtrees. Since the only transactions these lists of transactions have in common are the transactions that lock the root, and we established that these transactions lock every node in common in the same order that they lock the root, it is not possible that two transactions locking the root appear in different orders in two of the sublists. Specifically, if T_i and T_j appear on the list for some child C of the root, then they lock C in the same order as they lock the root and therefore appear on the list in that order. Thus, we can build a serial order for the full set of transactions by starting with the transactions that lock the root, in their appropriate order, and interspersing those transactions that do not lock the root in any order consistent with the serial order of their subtrees.

Example 18.25 : Suppose there are 10 transactions $T_1, T_2, \ldots, T_{10}$, and of these, T_1, T_2, and T_3 lock the root in that order. Suppose also that there are two children of the root, the first locked by T_1 through T_7 and the second locked by T_2, T_3, T_8, T_9, and T_{10}. Hypothetically, let the serial order for the first subtree be $(T_4, T_1, T_5, T_2, T_6, T_3, T_7)$; note that this order must include T_1, T_2, and T_3 in that order. Also, let the serial order for the second subtree be $(T_8, T_2, T_9, T_{10}, T_3)$. As must be the case, the transactions T_2 and T_3, which locked the root, appear in this sequence in the order in which they locked the root.

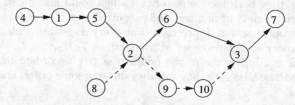

Figure 18.34: Combining serial orders for the subtrees into a serial order for all transactions

The constraints imposed on the serial order of these transactions are as shown in Fig. 18.34. Solid lines represent constraints due to the order at the first child of the root, while dashed lines represent the order at the second child. $(T_4, T_8, T_1, T_5, T_2, T_9, T_6, T_{10}, T_3, T_7)$ is one of the many topological sorts of this graph. □

18.7.4   Exercises for Section 18.7

Exercise 18.7.1 : Suppose we perform the following actions on the B-tree of Fig. 14.13. If we use the tree protocol, when can we release a write-lock on each of the nodes searched?

(a) Insert 4 (b) Insert 30 (c) Delete 37 (d) Delete 7.

! **Exercise 18.7.2 :** Consider the following transactions that operate on the tree of Fig. 18.30.

$$T_1: r_1(A); r_1(B); r_1(E);$$
$$T_2: r_2(A); r_2(C); r_2(B);$$
$$T_3: r_3(B); r_3(E); r_3(F);$$

If schedules follow the tree protocol, in how many ways can we interleave: (a) T_1 and T_3 (b) T_2 and T_3 !! (c) all three?

!! **Exercise 18.7.3:** Suppose we use the tree protocol with shared and exclusive locks for reading and writing, respectively. Rule (2), which requires a lock on the parent to get a lock on a node, must be changed to prevent unserializable behavior. What is the proper rule (2) for shared and exclusive locks? *Hint:* Does the lock on the parent have to be of the same type as the lock on the child?

! **Exercise 18.7.4:** Suppose there are eight transactions $T_1, T_2, \ldots, T_8$, of which the odd-numbered transactions, T_1, T_3, T_5, and T_7, lock the root of a tree, in that order. There are three children of the root, the first locked by T_1, T_2, T_3, and T_4 in that order. The second child is locked by T_3, T_6, and T_5, in that order, and the third child is locked by T_8 and T_7, in that order. How many serial orders of the transactions are consistent with these statements?

18.8 Concurrency Control by Timestamps

Next, we shall consider two methods other than locking that are used in some systems to assure serializability of transactions:

1. *Timestamping.* Assign a "timestamp" to each transaction. Record the timestamps of the transactions that last read and write each database element, and compare these values with the transactions timestamps, to assure that the serial schedule according to the transactions' timestamps is equivalent to the actual schedule of the transactions. This approach is the subject of the present section.

2. *Validation.* Examine timestamps of the transaction and the database elements when a transaction is about to commit; this process is called "validation" of the transaction. The serial schedule that orders transactions according to their validation time must be equivalent to the actual schedule. The validation approach is discussed in Section 18.9.

Both these approaches are *optimistic*, in the sense that they assume that no unserializable behavior will occur and only fix things up when a violation is apparent. In contrast, all locking methods assume that things will go wrong unless transactions are prevented in advance from engaging in nonserializable behavior. The optimistic approaches differ from locking in that the only remedy when something does go wrong is to abort and restart a transaction that tries to engage in unserializable behavior. In contrast, locking schedulers delay transactions, but do not abort them.[9] Generally, optimistic schedulers are

---

[9]That is not to say that a system using a locking scheduler will never abort a transaction; for instance, Section 19.2 discusses aborting transactions to fix deadlocks. However, a locking scheduler never uses a transaction abort simply as a response to a lock request that it cannot grant.

better than locking when many of the transactions are read-only, since those transactions can never, by themselves, cause unserializable behavior.

18.8.1 Timestamps

To use timestamping as a concurrency-control method, the scheduler needs to assign to each transaction T a unique number, its *timestamp* $\text{TS}(T)$. Timestamps must be issued in ascending order, at the time that a transaction first notifies the scheduler that it is beginning. Two approaches to generating timestamps are:

a) We can use the system clock as the timestamp, provided the scheduler does not operate so fast that it could assign timestamps to two transactions on one tick of the clock.

b) The scheduler can maintain a counter. Each time a transaction starts, the counter is incremented by 1, and the new value becomes the timestamp of the transaction. In this approach, timestamps have nothing to do with "time," but they have the important property that we need for any timestamp-generating system: a transaction that starts later has a higher timestamp than a transaction that starts earlier.

Whatever method of generating timestamps is used, the scheduler must maintain a table of currently active transactions and their timestamps.

To use timestamps as a concurrency-control method, we need to associate with each database element X two timestamps and an additional bit:

1. $\text{RT}(X)$, the *read time* of X, which is the highest timestamp of a transaction that has read X.

2. $\text{WT}(X)$, the *write time* of X, which is the highest timestamp of a transaction that has written X.

3. $\text{C}(X)$, the *commit bit* for X, which is true if and only if the most recent transaction to write X has already committed. The purpose of this bit is to avoid a situation where one transaction T reads data written by another transaction U, and U then aborts. This problem, where T makes a "dirty read" of uncommitted data, certainly can cause the database state to become inconsistent, and any scheduler needs a mechanism to prevent dirty reads.[10]

18.8.2 Physically Unrealizable Behaviors

In order to understand the architecture and rules of a timestamp scheduler, we need to remember that the scheduler assumes the timestamp order of transactions is also the serial order in which they must appear to execute. Thus,

---

[10] Although commercial systems generally give the user an option to allow dirty reads, as suggested by the SQL isolation level READ UNCOMMITTED in Section 6.6.5.

the job of the scheduler, in addition to assigning timestamps and updating RT, WT, and C for the database elements, is to check that whenever a read or write occurs, what happens in real time *could* have happened if each transaction had executed instantaneously at the moment of its timestamp. If not, we say the behavior is *physically unrealizable*. There are two kinds of problems that can occur:

1. *Read too late*: Transaction T tries to read database element X, but the write time of X indicates that the current value of X was written after T theoretically executed; that is, $\text{TS}(T) < \text{WT}(X)$. Figure 18.35 illustrates the problem. The horizontal axis represents the real time at which events occur. Dotted lines link the actual events to the times at which they theoretically occur — the timestamp of the transaction that performs the event. Thus, we see a transaction U that started after transaction T, but wrote a value for X before T reads X. T should not be able to read the value written by U, because theoretically, U executed after T did. However, T has no choice, because U's value of X is the one that T now sees. The solution is to abort T when the problem is encountered.

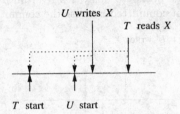

Figure 18.35: Transaction T tries to read too late

2. *Write too late*: Transaction T tries to write database element X. However, the read time of X indicates that some other transaction should have read the value written by T, but read some other value instead. That is, $\text{WT}(X) < \text{TS}(T) < \text{RT}(X)$. The problem is shown in Fig. 18.36. There we see a transaction U that started after T, but read X before T got a chance to write X. When T tries to write X, we find $\text{RT}(X) > \text{TS}(T)$, meaning that X has already been read by a transaction U that theoretically executed later than T. We also find $\text{WT}(X) < \text{TS}(T)$, which means that no other transaction wrote into X a value that would have overwritten T's value, thus, negating T's responsibility to get its value into X so transaction U could read it.

18.8.3 Problems With Dirty Data

There is a class of problems that the commit bit is designed to solve. One of these problems, a "dirty read," is suggested in Fig. 18.37. There, transaction

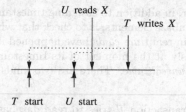

Figure 18.36: Transaction T tries to write too late

T reads X, and X was last written by U. The timestamp of U is less than that of T, and the read by T occurs after the write by U in real time, so the event seems to be physically realizable. However, it is possible that after T reads the value of X written by U, transaction U will abort; perhaps U encounters an error condition in its own data, such as a division by 0, or as we shall see in Section 18.8.4, the scheduler forces U to abort because it tries to do something physically unrealizable. Thus, although there is nothing physically unrealizable about T reading X, it is better to delay T's read until U commits or aborts. We can tell that U is not committed because the commit bit $C(X)$ will be false.

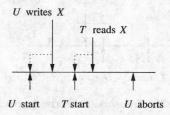

Figure 18.37: T could perform a dirty read if it reads X when shown

A second potential problem is suggested by Fig. 18.38. Here, U, a transaction with a later timestamp than T, has written X first. When T tries to write, the appropriate action is to do nothing. Evidently no other transaction V that should have read T's value of X got U's value instead, because if V tried to read X it would have aborted because of a too-late read. Future reads of X will want U's value or a later value of X, not T's value. This idea, that writes can be skipped when a write with a later write-time is already in place, is called the *Thomas write rule*.

There is a potential problem with the Thomas write rule, however. If U later aborts, as is suggested in Fig. 18.38, then its value of X should be removed and the previous value and write-time restored. Since T is committed, it would seem that the value of X should be the one written by T for future reading. However, we already skipped the write by T and it is too late to repair the damage.

While there are many ways to deal with the problems just described, we

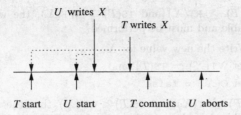

U writes X

T writes X

T start U start T commits U aborts

Figure 18.38: A write is cancelled because of a write with a later timestamp, but the writer then aborts

shall adopt a relatively simple policy based on the following assumed capability of the timestamp-based scheduler.

- When a transaction T writes a database element X, the write is "tentative" and may be undone if T aborts. The commit bit $C(X)$ is set to false, and the scheduler makes a copy of the old value of X and its previous $\text{WT}(X)$.

18.8.4 The Rules for Timestamp-Based Scheduling

We can now summarize the rules that a scheduler using timestamps must follow to make sure that nothing physically unrealizable may occur. The scheduler, in response to a read or write request from a transaction T has the choice of:

a) Granting the request,

b) Aborting T (if T would violate physical reality) and restarting T with a new timestamp (abort followed by restart is often called *rollback*), or

c) Delaying T and later deciding whether to abort T or to grant the request (if the request is a read, and the read might be dirty, as in Section 18.8.3).

The rules are as follows:

1. Suppose the scheduler receives a request $r_T(X)$.

   (a) If $\text{TS}(T) \geq \text{WT}(X)$, the read is physically realizable.

      i. If $C(X)$ is true, grant the request. If $\text{TS}(T) > \text{RT}(X)$, set $\text{RT}(X) := \text{TS}(T)$; otherwise do not change $\text{RT}(X)$.

      ii. If $C(X)$ is false, delay T until $C(X)$ becomes true, or the transaction that wrote X aborts.

   (b) If $\text{TS}(T) < \text{WT}(X)$, the read is physically unrealizable. Rollback T; that is, abort T and restart it with a new, larger timestamp.

2. Suppose the scheduler receives a request $w_T(X)$.

(a) If $TS(T) \geq RT(X)$ and $TS(T) \geq WT(X)$, the write is physically realizable and must be performed.

   i. Write the new value for X,

   ii. Set $WT(X) := TS(T)$, and

   iii. Set $C(X) := \texttt{false}$.

(b) If $TS(T) \geq RT(X)$, but $TS(T) < WT(X)$, then the write is physically realizable, but there is already a later value in X. If $C(X)$ is true, then the previous writer of X is committed, and we simply ignore the write by T; we allow T to proceed and make no change to the database. However, if $C(X)$ is false, then we must delay T as in point 1(a)ii.

(c) If $TS(T) < RT(X)$, then the write is physically unrealizable, and T must be rolled back.

3. Suppose the scheduler receives a request to commit T. It must find (using a list the scheduler maintains) all the database elements X written by T, and set $C(X) := \texttt{true}$. If any transactions are waiting for X to be committed (found from another scheduler-maintained list), these transactions are allowed to proceed.

4. Suppose the scheduler receives a request to abort T or decides to rollback T as in 1b or 2c. Then any transaction that was waiting on an element X that T wrote must repeat its attempt to read or write, and see whether the action is now legal after T's writes are cancelled.

Example 18.26: Figure 18.39 shows a schedule of three transactions, T_1, T_2, and T_3 that access three database elements, A, B, and C. The real time at which events occur increases down the page, as usual. We have also indicated the timestamps of the transactions and the read and write times of the elements. At the beginning, each of the database elements has both a read and write time of 0. The timestamps of the transactions are acquired when they notify the scheduler that they are beginning. Notice that even though T_1 executes the first data access, it does not have the least timestamp. Presumably T_2 was the first to notify the scheduler of its start, and T_3 did so next, with T_1 last to start.

In the first action, T_1 reads B. Since the write time of B is less than the timestamp of T_1, this read is physically realizable and allowed to happen. The read time of B is set to 200, the timestamp of T_1. The second and third read actions similarly are legal and result in the read time of each database element being set to the timestamp of the transaction that read it.

At the fourth step, T_1 writes B. Since the read time of B is not bigger than the timestamp of T_1, the write is physically realizable. Since the write time of B is no larger than the timestamp of T_1, we must actually perform the write. When we do, the write time of B is raised to 200, the timestamp of the writing transaction T_1.

T_1	T_2	T_3	A	B	C
200	150	175	RT=0	RT=0	RT=0
			WT=0	WT=0	WT=0
$r_1(B)$;				RT=200	
	$r_2(A)$;		RT=150		
		$r_3(C)$;			RT=175
$w_1(B)$;				WT=200	
$w_1(A)$;			WT=200		
	$w_2(C)$;				
	Abort;				
		$w_3(A)$;			

Figure 18.39: Three transactions executing under a timestamp-based scheduler

Next, T_2 tries to write C. However, C was already read by transaction T_3, which theoretically executed at time 175, while T_2 would have written its value at time 150. Thus, T_2 is trying to do something that s physically unrealizable, and T_2 must be rolled back.

The last step is the write of A by T_3. Since the read time of A, 150, is less than the timestamp of T_3, 175, the write is legal. However, there is already a later value of A stored in that database element, namely the value written by T_1, theoretically at time 200. Thus, T_3 is not rolled back, but neither does it write its value. □

18.8.5 Multiversion Timestamps

An important variation of timestamping maintains old versions of database elements in addition to the current version that is stored in the database itself. The purpose is to allow reads $r_T(X)$ that otherwise would cause transaction T to abort (because the current version of X was written in T's future) to proceed by reading the version of X that is appropriate for a transaction with T's timestamp. The method is especially useful if database elements are disk blocks or pages, since then all that must be done is for the buffer manager to keep in memory certain blocks that might be useful for some currently active transaction.

Example 18.27: Consider the set of transactions accessing database element A shown in Fig. 18.40. These transactions are operating under an ordinary timestamp-based scheduler, and when T_3 tries to read A, it finds WT(A) to be greater than its own timestamp, and must abort. However, there is an old value of A written by T_1 and overwritten by T_2 that would have been suitable for T_3 to read; this version of A had a write time of 150, which is less than T_3's timestamp of 175. If this old value of A were available, T_3 could be allowed to read it, even though it is not the "current" value of A. □

T_1	T_2	T_3	T_4	A
150	200	175	225	RT=0
				WT=0
$r_1(A)$				RT=150
$w_1(A)$				WT=150
	$r_2(A)$			RT=200
	$w_2(A)$			WT=200
		$r_3(A)$		
		Abort		
			$r_4(A)$	RT=225

Figure 18.40: T_3 must abort because it cannot access an old value of A

A multiversion-timestamp scheduler differs from the scheduler described in Section 18.8.4 in the following ways:

1. When a new write $w_T(X)$ occurs, if it is legal, then a new version of database element X is created. Its write time is $\text{TS}(T)$, and we shall refer to it as X_t, where $t = \text{TS}(T)$.

2. When a read $r_T(X)$ occurs, the scheduler finds the version X_t of X such that $t \leq \text{TS}(T)$, but there is no other version $X_{t'}$ with $t < t' \leq \text{TS}(T)$. That is, the version of X written immediately before T theoretically executed is the version that T reads.

3. Write times are associated with *versions* of an element, and they never change.

4. Read times are also associated with versions. They are used to reject certain writes, namely one whose time is less than the read time of the previous version. Figure 18.41 suggests the problem, where X has versions X_{50} and X_{100}, the former was read by a transaction with timestamp 80, and a new write by a transaction T whose timestamp is 60 occurs. This write must cause T to abort, because its value of X should have been read by the transaction with timestamp 80, had T been allowed to execute.

5. When a version X_t has a write time t such that no active transaction has a timestamp less than t, then we may delete any version of X *previous* to X_t.

Example 18.28 : Let us reconsider the actions of Fig. 18.40 if multiversion timestamping is used. First, there are three versions of A: A_0, which exists before these transactions start, A_{150}, written by T_1, and A_{200}, written by T_2. Figure 18.42 shows the sequence of events, when the versions are created, and when they are read. Notice in particular that T_3 does not have to abort, because it can read an earlier version of A. $\square$

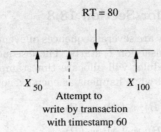

Figure 18.41: A transaction tries to write a version of X that would make events physically unrealizable

T_1	T_2	T_3	T_4	A_0	A_{150}	A_{200}
150	200	175	225			
$r_1(A)$				Read		
$w_1(A)$					Create	
	$r_2(A)$			Read		
	$w_2(A)$					Create
		$r_3(A)$		Read		
			$r_4(A)$			Read

Figure 18.42: Execution of transactions using multiversion concurrency control

18.8.6 Timestamps Versus Locking

Generally, timestamping is superior in situations where either most transactions are read-only, or it is rare that concurrent transactions will try to read and write the same element. In high-conflict situations, locking performs better. The argument for this rule-of-thumb is:

- Locking will frequently delay transactions as they wait for locks.

- But if concurrent transactions frequently read and write elements in common, then rollbacks will be frequent in a timestamp scheduler, introducing even more delay than a locking system.

There is an interesting compromise used in several commercial systems. The scheduler divides the transactions into read-only transactions and read/write transactions. Read/write transactions are executed using two-phase locking, to keep all transactions from accessing the elements they lock.

Read-only transactions are executed using multiversion timestamping. As the read/write transactions create new versions of a database element, those versions are managed as in Section 18.8.5. A read-only transaction is allowed to read whatever version of a database element is appropriate for its timestamp. A read-only transaction thus never has to abort, and will only rarely be delayed.

18.8.7   Exercises for Section 18.8

Exercise 18.8.1: Below are several sequences of events, including *start* events, where st_i means that transaction T_i starts. These sequences represent real time, and the timestamp scheduler will allocate timestamps to transactions in the order of their starts. Tell what happens as each executes.

   a) st_1; $r_1(A)$; st_2; $w_2(B)$; $r_2(A)$; $w_1(B)$;

   b) st_1; st_2; $r_1(A)$; $r_2(B)$; $w_2(A)$; $w_1(B)$;

   c) st_1; st_3; st_2; $r_1(A)$; $r_3(B)$; $w_1(C)$; $r_2(B)$; $r_2(C)$; $w_3(B)$; $w_2(A)$;

   d) st_1; st_2; st_3; $r_1(A)$; $r_3(B)$; $w_1(C)$; $r_2(B)$; $r_2(C)$; $w_3(B)$; $w_2(A)$;

!! **Exercise 18.8.2:** We observed in our study of lock-based schedulers that there are several reasons why transactions that obtain locks could deadlock. Can a timestamp scheduler using the commit bit $C(X)$ have a deadlock?

Exercise 18.8.3: Tell what happens during the following sequences of events if a multiversion, timestamp scheduler is used. What happens instead, if the scheduler does not maintain multiple versions?

   a) st_1; st_2; st_3; st_4; $w_1(A)$; $w_3(A)$; $r_4(A)$; $r_2(A)$;

   b) st_1; st_2; st_3; st_4; $w_1(A)$; $w_4(A)$; $r_3(A)$; $w_2(A)$;

   c) st_1; st_2; st_3; st_4; $w_1(A)$; $w_2(A)$; $w_3(A)$; $r_2(A)$; $r_4(A)$;

18.9   Concurrency Control by Validation

Validation is another type of optimistic concurrency control, where we allow transactions to access data without locks, and at the appropriate time we check that the transaction has behaved in a serializable manner. Validation differs from timestamping principally in that the scheduler maintains a record of what active transactions are doing, rather than keeping read and write times for all database elements. Just before a transaction starts to write values of database elements, it goes through a "validation phase," where the sets of elements it has read and will write are compared with the write sets of other active transactions. Should there be a risk of physically unrealizable behavior, the transaction is rolled back.

18.9.1   Architecture of a Validation-Based Scheduler

When validation is used as the concurrency-control mechanism, the scheduler must be told for each transaction T the sets of database elements T reads and writes, the *read set*, RS(T), and the *write set*, WS(T), respectively. Transactions are executed in three phases:

1. *Read.* In the first phase, the transaction reads from the database all the elements in its read set. The transaction also computes in its local address space all the results it is going to write.

2. *Validate.* In the second phase, the scheduler validates the transaction by comparing its read and write sets with those of other transactions. We shall describe the validation process in Section 18.9.2. If validation fails, then the transaction is rolled back; otherwise it proceeds to the third phase.

3. *Write.* In the third phase, the transaction writes to the database its values for the elements in its write set.

Intuitively, we may think of each transaction that successfully validates as executing at the moment that it validates. Thus, the validation-based scheduler has an assumed serial order of the transactions to work with, and it bases its decision to validate or not on whether the transactions' behaviors are consistent with this serial order.

To support the decision whether to validate a transaction, the scheduler maintains three sets:

1. *START*, the set of transactions that have started, but not yet completed validation. For each transaction T in this set, the scheduler maintains START(T), the time at which T started.

2. *VAL*, the set of transactions that have been validated but not yet finished the writing of phase 3. For each transaction T in this set, the scheduler maintains both START(T) and VAL(T), the time at which T validated. Note that VAL(T) is also the time at which T is imagined to execute in the hypothetical serial order of execution.

3. *FIN*, the set of transactions that have completed phase 3. For these transactions T, the scheduler records START(T), VAL(T), and FIN(T), the time at which T finished. In principle this set grows, but as we shall see, we do not have to remember transaction T if FIN(T) < START(U) for any active transaction U (i.e., for any U in *START* or *VAL*). The scheduler may thus periodically purge the *FIN* set to keep its size from growing beyond bounds.

18.9.2 The Validation Rules

The information of Section 18.9.1 is enough for the scheduler to detect any potential violation of the assumed serial order of the transactions — the order in which the transactions validate. To understand the rules, let us first consider what can be wrong when we try to validate a transaction T.

1. Suppose there is a transaction U such that:

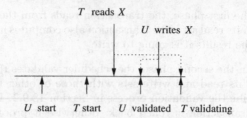

Figure 18.43: T cannot validate if an earlier transaction is now writing something that T should have read

 (a) U is in *VAL* or *FIN*; that is, U has validated.

 (b) $\text{FIN}(U) > \text{START}(T)$; that is, U did not finish before T started.[11]

 (c) $\text{RS}(T) \cap \text{WS}(U)$ is not empty; in particular, let it contain database element X.

Then it is possible that U wrote X after T read X. In fact, U may not even have written X yet. A situation where U wrote X, but not in time is shown in Fig. 18.43. To interpret the figure, note that the dotted lines connect the events in real time with the time at which they would have occurred had transactions been executed at the moment they validated. Since we don't know whether or not T got to read U's value, we must rollback T to avoid a risk that the actions of T and U will not be consistent with the assumed serial order.

 2. Suppose there is a transaction U such that:

 (a) U is in *VAL*; i.e., U has successfully validated.

 (b) $\text{FIN}(U) > \text{VAL}(T)$; that is, U did not finish before T entered its validation phase.

 (c) $\text{WS}(T) \cap \text{WS}(U) \neq \emptyset$; in particular, let X be in both write sets.

Then the potential problem is as shown in Fig. 18.44. T and U must both write values of X, and if we let T validate, it is possible that it will write X before U does. Since we cannot be sure, we rollback T to make sure it does not violate the assumed serial order in which it follows U.

The two problems described above are the only situations in which a write by T could be physically unrealizable. In Fig. 18.43, if U finished before T started, then surely T would read the value of X that either U or some later transaction wrote. In Fig. 18.44, if U finished before T validated, then surely

---

[11]Note that if U is in *VAL*, then U has not yet finished when T validates. In that case, $\text{FIN}(U)$ is technically undefined. However, we know it must be larger than $\text{START}(T)$ in this case.

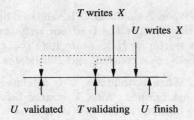

Figure 18.44: T cannot validate if it could then write something ahead of an earlier transaction

U wrote X before T did. We may thus summarize these observations with the following rule for validating a transaction T:

- Check that $\text{RS}(T) \cap \text{WS}(U) = \emptyset$ for any previously validated U that did not finish before T started, i.e., if $\text{FIN}(U) > \text{START}(T)$.

- Check that $\text{WS}(T) \cap \text{WS}(U) = \emptyset$ for any previously validated U that did not finish before T validated, i.e., if $\text{FIN}(U) > \text{VAL}(T)$.

Example 18.29: Figure 18.45 shows a time line during which four transactions T, U, V, and W attempt to execute and validate. The read and write sets for each transaction are indicated on the diagram. T starts first, although U is the first to validate.

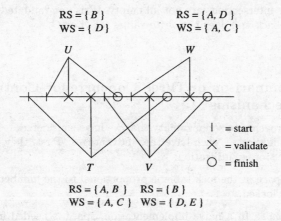

Figure 18.45: Four transactions and their validation

1. Validation of U: When U validates there are no other validated transactions, so there is nothing to check. U validates successfully and writes a value for database element D.

2. Validation of T: When T validates, U is validated but not finished. Thus, we must check that neither the read nor write set of T has anything in common with $\text{WS}(U) = \{D\}$. Since $\text{RS}(T) = \{A, B\}$, and $\text{WS}(T) = \{A, C\}$, both checks are successful, and T validates.

3. Validation of V: When V validates, U is validated and finished, and T is validated but not finished. Also, V started before U finished. Thus, we must compare both $\text{RS}(V)$ and $\text{WS}(V)$ against $\text{WS}(T)$, but only $\text{RS}(V)$ needs to be compared against $\text{WS}(U)$. we find:

   - $\text{RS}(V) \cap \text{WS}(T) = \{B\} \cap \{A, C\} = \emptyset$.
   - $\text{WS}(V) \cap \text{WS}(T) = \{D, E\} \cap \{A, C\} = \emptyset$.
   - $\text{RS}(V) \cap \text{WS}(U) = \{B\} \cap \{D\} = \emptyset$.

   Thus, V also validates successfully.

4. Validation of W: When W validates, we find that U finished before W started, so no comparison between W and U is performed. T is finished before W validates but did not finish before W started, so we compare only $\text{RS}(W)$ with $\text{WS}(T)$. V is validated but not finished, so we need to compare both $\text{RS}(W)$ and $\text{WS}(W)$ with $\text{WS}(V)$. These tests are:

   - $\text{RS}(W) \cap \text{WS}(T) = \{A, D\} \cap \{A, C\} = \{A\}$.
   - $\text{RS}(W) \cap \text{WS}(V) = \{A, D\} \cap \{D, E\} = \{D\}$.
   - $\text{WS}(W) \cap \text{WS}(V) = \{A, C\} \cap \{D, E\} = \emptyset$.

   Since the intersections are not all empty, W is not validated. Rather, W is rolled back and does not write values for A or C.

□

18.9.3 Comparison of Three Concurrency-Control Mechanisms

The three approaches to serializability that we have considered — locks, timestamps, and validation — each have their advantages. First, they can be compared for their storage utilization:

- *Locks*: Space in the lock table is proportional to the number of database elements locked.

- *Timestamps*: In a naive implementation, space is needed for read- and write-times with every database element, whether or not it is currently accessed. However, a more careful implementation will treat all timestamps that are prior to the earliest active transaction as "minus infinity" and not record them. In that case, we can store read- and write-times in a table analogous to a lock table, in which only those database elements that have been accessed recently are mentioned at all.

Just a Moment

You may have been concerned with a tacit notion that validation takes place in a moment, or indivisible instant of time. For example, we imagine that we can decide whether a transaction U has already validated before we start to validate transaction T. Could U perhaps finish validating while we are validating T?

If we are running on a uniprocessor system, and there is only one scheduler process, we can indeed think of validation and other actions of the scheduler as taking place in an instant of time. The reason is that if the scheduler is validating T, then it cannot also be validating U, so all during the validation of T, the validation status of U cannot change.

If we are running on a multiprocessor, and there are several scheduler processes, then it might be that one is validating T while the other is validating U. If so, then we need to rely on whatever synchronization mechanism the multiprocessor system provides to make validation an atomic action.

- *Validation*: Space is used for timestamps and read/write sets for each currently active transaction, plus a few more transactions that finished after some currently active transaction began.

Thus, the amounts of space used by each approach is approximately proportional to the sum over all active transactions of the number of database elements the transaction accesses. Timestamping and validation may use slightly more space because they keep track of certain accesses by recently committed transactions that a lock table would not record. A potential problem with validation is that the write set for a transaction must be known before the writes occur (but after the transaction's local computation has been completed).

We can also compare the methods for their effect on the ability of transactions to complete without delay. The performance of the three methods depends on whether *interaction* among transactions (the likelihood that a transaction will access an element that is also being accessed by a concurrent transaction) is high or low.

- Locking delays transactions but avoids rollbacks, even when interaction is high. Timestamps and validation do not delay transactions, but can cause them to rollback, which is a more serious form of delay and also wastes resources.

- If interference is low, then neither timestamps nor validation will cause many rollbacks, and may be preferable to locking because they generally have lower overhead than a locking scheduler.

- When a rollback is necessary, timestamps catch some problems earlier than validation, which always lets a transaction do all its internal work before considering whether the transaction must rollback.

18.9.4 Exercises for Section 18.9

Exercise 18.9.1: In the following sequences of events, we use $R_i(X)$ to mean "transaction T_i starts, and its read set is the list of database elements X." Also, V_i means "T_i attempts to validate," and $W_i(X)$ means that "T_i finishes, and its write set was X." Tell what happens when each sequence is processed by a validation-based scheduler.

a) $R_1(A,B)$; $R_2(B,C)$; $R_3(C)$; V_1; V_2; V_3; $W_1(A)$; $W_2(B)$; $W_3(C)$;

b) $R_1(A,B)$; $R_2(B,C)$; $R_3(C)$; V_1; V_2; V_3; $W_1(C)$; $W_2(B)$; $W_3(A)$;

c) $R_1(A,B)$; $R_2(B,C)$; $R_3(C)$; V_1; V_2; V_3; $W_1(A)$; $W_2(C)$; $W_3(B)$;

d) $R_1(A,B)$; $R_2(B,C)$; V_1; $R_3(C,D)$; V_3; $W_1(A)$; V_2; $W_2(A)$; $W_3(B)$;

e) $R_1(A,B)$; $R_2(B,C)$; V_1; $R_3(C,D)$; V_3; $W_1(A)$; V_2; $W_2(A)$; $W_3(D)$;

f) $R_1(A,B)$; $R_2(B,C)$; V_1; $R_3(C,D)$; V_3; $W_1(C)$; V_2; $W_2(A)$; $W_3(D)$;

18.10 Summary of Chapter 18

✦ *Consistent Database States*: Database states that obey whatever implied or declared constraints the designers intended are called consistent. It is essential that operations on the database preserve consistency, that is, they turn one consistent database state into another.

✦ *Consistency of Concurrent Transactions*: It is normal for several transactions to have access to a database at the same time. Transactions, run in isolation, are assumed to preserve consistency of the database. It is the job of the scheduler to assure that concurrently operating transactions also preserve the consistency of the database.

✦ *Schedules*: Transactions are broken into actions, mainly reading and writing from the database. A sequence of these actions from one or more transactions is called a schedule.

✦ *Serial Schedules*: If transactions execute one at a time, the schedule is said to be serial.

✦ *Serializable Schedules*: A schedule that is equivalent in its effect on the database to some serial schedule is said to be serializable. Interleaving of actions from several transactions is possible in a serializable schedule that is not itself serial, but we must be very careful what sequences of actions we allow, or an interleaving will leave the database in an inconsistent state.

✦ *Conflict-Serializability*: A simple-to-test, sufficient condition for serializability is that the schedule can be made serial by a sequence of swaps of adjacent actions without conflicts. Such a schedule is called conflict-serializable. A conflict occurs if we try to swap two actions of the same transaction, or to swap two actions that access the same database element, at least one of which actions is a write.

✦ *Precedence Graphs*: An easy test for conflict-serializability is to construct a precedence graph for the schedule. Nodes correspond to transactions, and there is an arc $T \to U$ if some action of T in the schedule conflicts with a later action of U. A schedule is conflict-serializable if and only if the precedence graph is acyclic.

✦ *Locking*: The most common approach to assuring serializable schedules is to lock database elements before accessing them, and to release the lock after finishing access to the element. Locks on an element prevent other transactions from accessing the element.

✦ *Two-Phase Locking*: Locking by itself does not assure serializability. However, two-phase locking, in which all transactions first enter a phase where they only acquire locks, and then enter a phase where they only release locks, will guarantee serializability.

✦ *Lock Modes*: To avoid locking out transactions unnecessarily, systems usually use several lock modes, with different rules for each mode about when a lock can be granted. Most common is the system with shared locks for read-only access and exclusive locks for accesses that include writing.

✦ *Compatibility Matrices*: A compatibility matrix is a useful summary of when it is legal to grant a lock in a certain lock mode, given that there may be other locks, in the same or other modes, on the same element.

✦ *Update Locks*: A scheduler can allow a transaction that plans to read and then write an element first to take an update lock, and later to upgrade the lock to exclusive. Update locks can be granted when there are already shared locks on the element, but once there, an update lock prevents other locks from being granted on that element.

✦ *Increment Locks*: For the common case where a transaction wants only to add or subtract a constant from an element, an increment lock is suitable. Increment locks on the same element do not conflict with each other, although they conflict with shared and exclusive locks.

✦ *Locking Elements With a Granularity Hierarchy*: When both large and small elements — relations, disk blocks, and tuples, perhaps — may need to be locked, a warning system of locks enforces serializability. Transactions place intention locks on large elements to warn other transactions that they plan to access one or more of its subelements.

✦ *Locking Elements Arranged in a Tree*: If database elements are only accessed by moving down a tree, as in a B-tree index, then a non-two-phase locking strategy can enforce serializability. The rules require a lock to be held on the parent while obtaining a lock on the child, although the lock on the parent can then be released and additional locks taken later.

✦ *Optimistic Concurrency Control*: Instead of locking, a scheduler can assume transactions will be serializable, and abort a transaction if some potentially nonserializable behavior is seen. This approach, called optimistic, is divided into timestamp-based, and validation-based scheduling.

✦ *Timestamp-Based Schedulers*: This type of scheduler assigns timestamps to transactions as they begin. Database elements have associated read- and write-times, which are the timestamps of the transactions that most recently performed those actions. If an impossible situation, such as a read by one transaction of a value that was written in that transaction's future is detected, the violating transaction is rolled back, i.e., aborted and restarted.

✦ *Multiversion Timestamps*: A common technique in practice is for read-only transactions to be scheduled by timestamps, but with multiple versions, where a write of an element does not overwrite earlier values of that element until all transactions that could possibly need the earlier value have finished. Writing transactions are scheduled by conventional locks.

✦ *Validation-Based Schedulers*: These schedulers validate transactions after they have read everything they need, but before they write. Transactions that have read, or will write, an element that some other transaction is in the process of writing, will have an ambiguous result, so the transaction is not validated. A transaction that fails to validate is rolled back.

18.11 References for Chapter 18

The book [6] is an important source for material on scheduling, as well as locking. [3] is another important source. Two recent surveys of concurrency control are [12] and [11].

Probably the most significant paper in the field of transaction processing is [4] on two-phase locking. The warning protocol for hierarchies of granularity is from [5]. Non-two-phase locking for trees is from [10]. The compatibility matrix was introduced to study behavior of lock modes in [7].

Timestamps as a concurrency control method appeared in [2] and [1]. Scheduling by validation is from [8]. The use of multiple versions was studied by [9].

1. P. A. Bernstein and N. Goodman, "Timestamp-based algorithms for concurrency control in distributed database systems," *Intl. Conf. on Very Large Databases*, pp. 285–300, 1980.

2. P. A. Bernstein, N. Goodman, J. B. Rothnie, Jr., and C. H. Papadimitriou, "Analysis of serializability in SDD-1: a system of distributed databases (the fully redundant case)," *IEEE Trans. on Software Engineering* **SE-4**:3 (1978), pp. 154–168.

3. P. A. Bernstein, V. Hadzilacos, and N. Goodman, *Concurrency Control and Recovery in Database Systems*, Addison-Wesley, Reading MA, 1987.

4. K. P. Eswaran, J. N. Gray, R. A. Lorie, and I. L. Traiger, "The notions of consistency and predicate locks in a database system," *Comm. ACM* **19**:11 (1976), pp. 624–633.

5. J. N. Gray, F. Putzolo, and I. L. Traiger, "Granularity of locks and degrees of consistency in a shared data base," in G. M. Nijssen (ed.), *Modeling in Data Base Management Systems*, North Holland, Amsterdam, 1976.

6. J. N. Gray and A. Reuter, *Transaction Processing: Concepts and Techniques*, Morgan-Kaufmann, San Francisco, 1993.

7. H. F. Korth, "Locking primitives in a database system," *J. ACM* **30**:1 (1983), pp. 55–79.

8. H.-T. Kung and J. T. Robinson, "Optimistic concurrency control," *ACM Trans. on Database Systems* **6**:2 (1981), pp. 312–326.

9. C. H. Papadimitriou and P. C. Kanellakis, "On concurrency control by multiple versions," *ACM Trans. on Database Systems* **9**:1 (1984), pp. 89–99.

10. A. Silberschatz and Z. Kedem, "Consistency in hierarchical database systems," *J. ACM* **27**:1 (1980), pp. 72–80.

11. A. Thomasian, "Concurrency control: methods, performance, and analysis," *Computing Surveys* **30**:1 (1998), pp. 70–119.

12. B. Thuraisingham and H.-P. Ko, "Concurrency control in trusted database management systems: a survey," *SIGMOD Record* **22**:4 (1993), pp. 52–60.

Chapter 19

More About Transaction Management

In this chapter we cover several issues about transaction management that were not addressed in Chapters 17 or 18. We begin by reconciling the points of view of these two chapters: how do the needs to recover from errors, to allow transactions to abort, and to maintain serializability interact? Then, we discuss the management of deadlocks among transactions, which typically result from several transactions each having to wait for a resource, such as a lock, that is held by another transaction.

Finally, we consider the problems that arise due to "long transactions." There are applications, such as CAD systems or "workflow" systems, in which human and computer processes interact, perhaps over a period of days. These systems, like short-transaction systems such as banking or airline reservations, need to preserve consistency of the database state. However, the concurrency-control methods discussed in Chapter 18 do not work reasonably when locks are held for days, or human decisions are part of a "transaction."

19.1 Serializability and Recoverability

In Chapter 17 we discussed the creation of a log and its use to recover the database state when a system crash occurs. We introduced the view of database computation in which values move between nonvolatile disk, volatile main-memory, and the local address space of transactions. The guarantee the various logging methods give is that, should a crash occur, it will be able to reconstruct the actions of the committed transactions on the disk copy of the database. A logging system makes no attempt to support serializability; it will blindly reconstruct a database state, even if it is the result of a nonserializable schedule of actions. In fact, commercial database systems do not always insist on serializability, and in some systems, serializability is enforced only on explicit request of the user.

On the other hand, Chapter 18 talked about serializability only. Schedulers designed according to the principles of that chapter may do things that the log manager cannot tolerate. For instance, there is nothing in the serializability definition that forbids a transaction with a lock on an element A from writing a new value of A into the database before committing, and thus violating a rule of the logging policy. Worse, a transaction might write into the database and then abort without undoing the write, which could easily result in an inconsistent database state, even though there is no system crash and the scheduler theoretically maintains serializability.

19.1.1   The Dirty-Data Problem

Recall from Section 6.6.5 that data is "dirty" if it has been written by a transaction that is not yet committed. The dirty data could appear either in the buffers, or on disk, or both; either can cause trouble.

T_1	T_2	A	B
		25	25
$l_1(A); r_1(A);$			
A := A+100;			
$w_1(A); l_1(B); u_1(A);$		125	
	$l_2(A); r_2(A);$		
	A := A*2;		
	$w_2(A);$	250	
	$l_2(B)$ **Denied**		
$r_1(B);$			
Abort; $u_1(B);$			
	$l_2(B); u_2(A); r_2(B);$		
	B := B*2;		
	$w_2(B); u_2(B);$		50

Figure 19.1: T_1 writes dirty data and then aborts

Example 19.1 : Let us reconsider the serializable schedule from Fig. 18.13, but suppose that after reading B, T_1 has to abort for some reason. Then the sequence of events is as in Fig. 19.1. After T_1 aborts, the scheduler releases the lock on B that T_1 obtained; that step is essential, or else the lock on B would be unavailable to any other transaction, forever.

However, T_2 has now read data that does not represent a consistent state of the database. That is, T_2 read the value of A that T_1 changed, but read the value of B that existed prior to T_1's actions. It doesn't matter in this case whether or not the value 125 for A that T_1 created was written to disk or not; T_2

gets that value from a buffer, regardless. Because it read an inconsistent state, T_2 leaves the database (on disk) with an inconsistent state, where $A \neq B$.

The problem in Fig. 19.1 is that A written by T_1 is dirty data, whether it is in a buffer or on disk. The fact that T_2 read A and used it in its own calculation makes T_2's actions questionable. As we shall see in Section 19.1.2, it is necessary, if such a situation is allowed to occur, to abort and roll back T_2 as well as T_1. □

T_1	T_2	T_3	A	B	C
200	150	175	RT=0	RT=0	RT=0
			WT=0	WT=0	WT=0
	$w_2(B)$;			WT=150	
$r_1(B)$;					
	$r_2(A)$;		RT=150		
		$r_3(C)$;			RT=175
	$w_2(C)$;				
	Abort;			WT=0	
		$w_3(A)$;	WT=175		

Figure 19.2: T_1 has read dirty data from T_2 and must abort when T_2 does

Example 19.2: Now, consider Fig. 19.2, which shows a sequence of actions under a timestamp-based scheduler as in Section 18.8. However, we imagine that this scheduler does not use the commit bit that was introduced in Section 18.8.1. Recall that the purpose of this bit is to prevent a value that was written by an uncommitted transaction to be read by another transaction. Thus, when T_1 reads B at the second step, there is no commit-bit check to tell T_1 to delay. T_1 can proceed and could even write to disk and commit; we have not shown further details of what T_1 does.

Eventually, T_2 tries to write C in a physically unrealizable way, and T_2 aborts. The effect of T_2's prior write of B is cancelled; the value and write-time of B is reset to what it was before T_2 wrote. Yet T_1 has been allowed to use this cancelled value of B and can do anything with it, such as using it to compute new values of A, B, and/or C and writing them to disk. Thus, T_1, having read a dirty value of B, can cause an inconsistent database state. Note that, had the commit bit been recorded and used, the read $r_1(B)$ at step (2) would have been delayed, and not allowed to occur until after T_2 aborted and the value of B had been restored to its previous (presumably committed) value. □

19.1.2 Cascading Rollback

As we see from the examples above, if dirty data is available to transactions, then we sometimes have to perform a *cascading rollback*. That is, when a transaction T aborts, we must determine which transactions have read data written by T, abort them, and recursively abort any transactions that have read data written by an aborted transaction. To cancel the effect of an aborted transaction, we can use the log, if it is one of the types (undo or undo/redo) that provides former values. We may also be able to restore the data from the disk copy of the database, if the effect of the dirty data has not migrated to disk.

As we have noted, a timestamp-based scheduler with a commit bit prevents a transaction that may have read dirty data from proceeding, so there is no possibility of cascading rollback with such a scheduler. A validation-based scheduler avoids cascading rollback, because writing to the database (even in buffers) occurs only after it is determined that the transaction will commit.

19.1.3 Recoverable Schedules

For any of the logging methods we have discussed in Chapter 17 to allow recovery, the set of transactions that are regarded as committed *after* recovery must be consistent. That is, if a transaction T_1 is, after recovery, regarded as committed, and T_1 used a value written by T_2, then T_2 must also remain committed, after recovery. Thus, we define:

- A schedule is *recoverable* if each transaction commits only after each transaction from which it has read has committed.

Example 19.3: In this and several subsequent examples of schedules with read- and write-actions, we shall use c_i for the action "transaction T_i commits." Here is an example of a recoverable schedule:

$$S_1: w_1(A); w_1(B); w_2(A); r_2(B); c_1; c_2;$$

Note that T_2 reads a value (B) written by T_1, so T_2 must commit after T_1 for the schedule to be recoverable.

Schedule S_1 above is evidently serial (and therefore serializable) as well as recoverable, but the two concepts are orthogonal. For instance, the following variation on S_1 is still recoverable, but not serializable.

$$S_2: w_2(A); w_1(B); w_1(A); r_2(B); c_1; c_2;$$

In schedule S_2, T_2 must precede T_1 in a serial order because of the writing of A, but T_1 must precede T_2 because of the writing and reading of B.

Finally, observe the following variation on S_1, which is serializable but not recoverable:

$$S_3: w_1(A); w_1(B); w_2(A); r_2(B); c_2; c_1;$$

In schedule S_3, T_1 precedes T_2, but their commitments occur in the wrong order. If before a crash, the commit record for T_2 reached disk, but the commit record for T_1 did not, then regardless of whether undo, redo, or undo/redo logging were used, T_2 would be committed after recovery, but T_1 would not. □

In order for recoverable schedules to be truly recoverable under any of the three logging methods, there is one additional assumption we must make regarding schedules:

- The log's commit records reach disk in the order in which they are written.

As we observed in Example 19.3 concerning schedule S_3, should it be possible for commit records to reach disk in the wrong order, then consistent recovery might be impossible. We shall return to and exploit this principle in Section 19.1.6.

19.1.4 Schedules That Avoid Cascading Rollback

Recoverable schedules sometimes require cascading rollback. For instance, if after the first four steps of schedule S_1 in Example 19.3 T_1 had to roll back, it would be necessary to roll back T_2 as well. To guarantee the absence of cascading rollback, we need a stronger condition than recoverability. We say that:

- A schedule *avoids cascading rollback* (or "is an *ACR schedule*") if transactions may read only values written by committed transactions.

Put another way, an ACR schedule forbids the reading of dirty data. As for recoverable schedules, we assume that "committed" means that the log's commit record has reached disk.

Example 19.4: The schedules of Example 19.3 are not ACR. In each case, T_2 reads B from the uncommitted transaction T_1. However, consider:

$$S_4: w_1(A); w_1(B); w_2(A); c_1; r_2(B); c_2;$$

Now, T_2 reads B only after T_1, the transaction that last wrote B, has committed, and its log record written to disk. Thus, schedule S_4 is ACR, as well as recoverable. ☐

Notice that should a transaction such as T_2 read a value written by T_1 after T_1 commits, then surely T_2 either commits or aborts after T_1 commits. Thus:

- Every ACR schedule is recoverable.

19.1.5 Managing Rollbacks Using Locking

Our prior discussion applies to schedules that are generated by any kind of scheduler. In the common case that the scheduler is lock-based, there is a simple and commonly used way to guarantee that there are no cascading rollbacks:

- *Strict Locking*: A transaction must not release any exclusive locks (or other locks, such as increment locks that allow values to be changed) until the transaction has either committed or aborted, and the commit or abort log record has been flushed to disk.

A schedule of transactions that follow the strict-locking rule is called a *strict schedule*. Two important properties of these schedules are:

1. *Every strict schedule is ACR*. The reason is that a transaction T_2 cannot read a value of element X written by T_1 until T_1 releases any exclusive lock (or similar lock that allows X to be changed). Under strict locking, the release does not occur until after commit.

2. *Every strict schedule is serializable.* To see why, observe that a strict schedule is equivalent to the serial schedule in which each transaction runs instantaneously at the time it commits.

With these observations, we can now picture the relationships among the different kinds of schedules we have seen so far. The containments are suggested in Fig. 19.3.

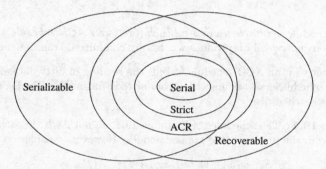

Figure 19.3: Containments and noncontainments among classes of schedules

Clearly, in a strict schedule, it is not possible for a transaction to read dirty data, since data written to a buffer by an uncommitted transaction remains locked until the transaction commits. However, we still have the problem of fixing the data in buffers when a transaction aborts, since these changes must have their effects cancelled. How difficult it is to fix buffered data depends on whether database elements are blocks or something smaller. We shall consider each.

Rollback for Blocks

If the lockable database elements are blocks, then there is a simple rollback method that never requires us to use the log. Suppose that a transaction T has obtained an exclusive lock on block A, written a new value for A in a buffer, and then had to abort. Since A has been locked since T wrote its value, no other transaction has read A. It is easy to restore the old value of A provided the following rule is followed:

- Blocks written by uncommitted transactions are pinned in main memory; that is, their buffers are not allowed to be written to disk.

In this case, we "roll back" T when it aborts by telling the buffer manager to ignore the value of A. That is, the buffer occupied by A is not written anywhere, and its buffer is added to the pool of available buffers. We can be sure that the value of A on disk is the most recent value written by a committed transaction, which is exactly the value we want A to have.

There is also a simple rollback method if we are using a multiversion system as in Sections 18.8.5 and 18.8.6. We must again assume that blocks written by uncommitted transactions are pinned in memory. Then, we simply remove the value of A that was written by T from the list of available values of A. Note that because T was a writing transaction, its value of A was locked from the time the value was written to the time it aborted (assuming the timestamp/lock scheme of Section 18.8.6 is used).

Rollback for Small Database Elements

When lockable database elements are fractions of a block (e.g., tuples or objects), then the simple approach to restoring buffers that have been modified by aborted transactions will not work. The problem is that a buffer may contain data changed by two or more transactions; if one of them aborts, we still must preserve the changes made by the other. We have several choices when we must restore the old value of a small database element A that was written by the transaction that has aborted:

1. We can read the original value of A from the database stored on disk and modify the buffer contents appropriately.

2. If the log is an undo or undo/redo log, then we can obtain the former value from the log itself. The same code used to recover from crashes may be used for "voluntary" rollbacks as well.

3. We can keep a separate main-memory log of the changes made by each transaction, preserved for only the time that transaction is active. The old value can be found from this "log."

None of these approaches is ideal. The first surely involves a disk access. The second (examining the log) might not involve a disk access, if the relevant portion of the log is still in a buffer. However, it could also involve extensive examination of portions of the log on disk, searching for the update record that tells the correct former value. The last approach does not require disk accesses, but may consume a large fraction of memory for the main-memory "logs."

19.1.6 Group Commit

Under some circumstances, we can avoid reading dirty data even if we do not flush every commit record on the log to disk immediately. As long as we flush log records in the order that they are written, we can release locks as soon as the commit record is written to the log in a buffer.

Example 19.5 : Suppose transaction T_1 writes X, finishes, writes its COMMIT record on the log, but the log record remains in a buffer. Even though T_1 has not committed in the sense that its commit record can survive a crash, we shall release T_1's locks. Then T_2 reads X and "commits," but its commit record, which follows that of T_1, also remains in a buffer. Since we are flushing log records in the order written, T_2 cannot be perceived as committed by a recovery manager (because its commit record reached disk) unless T_1 is also perceived as committed. Thus, the recovery manager will find either one of two things:

1. T_1 is committed on disk. Then regardless of whether or not T_2 is committed on disk, we know T_2 did not read X from an uncommitted transaction.

2. T_1 is not committed on disk. Then neither is T_2, and both are aborted by the recovery manager. In this case, the fact that T_2 read X from an uncommitted transaction has no effect on the database.

On the other hand, suppose that the buffer containing T_2's commit record got flushed to disk (say because the buffer manager decided to use the buffer for something else), but the buffer containing T_1's commit record did not. If there is a crash at that point, it will look to the recovery manager that T_1 did not commit, but T_2 did. The effect of T_2 will be permanently reflected in the database, but this effect was based on the dirty read of X by T_2. □

Our conclusion from Example 19.5 is that we can release locks earlier than the time that the transaction's commit record is flushed to disk. This policy, often called *group commit*, is:

• Do not release locks until the transaction finishes, and the commit log record at least appears in a buffer.

• Flush log blocks in the order that they were created.

Group commit, like the policy of requiring "recoverable schedules" as discussed in Section 19.1.3, guarantees that there is never a read of dirty data.

19.1.7   Logical Logging

We saw in Section 19.1.5 that dirty reads are easier to fix up when the unit of locking is the block or page. However, there are at least two problems presented when database elements are blocks.

1. All logging methods require either the old or new value of a database element, or both, to be recorded in the log. When the change to a block

---

When is a Transaction Really Committed?

The subtlety of group commit reminds us that a completed transaction can be in several different states between when it finishes its work and when it is truly "committed," in the sense that under no circumstances, including the occurrence of a system failure, will the effect of that transaction be lost. As we noted in Chapter 17, it is possible for a transaction to finish its work and even write its COMMIT record to the log in a main-memory buffer, yet have the effect of that transaction lost if there is a system crash and the COMMIT record has not yet reached disk. Moreover, we saw in Section 17.5 that even if the COMMIT record is on disk but not yet backed up in the archive, a media failure can cause the transaction to be undone and its effect to be lost.

In the absence of failure, all these states are equivalent, in the sense that each transaction will surely advance from being finished to having its effects survive even a media failure. However, when we need to take failures and recovery into account, it is important to recognize the differences among these states, which otherwise could all be referred to informally as "committed."

---

is small, e.g., a rewritten attribute of one tuple, or an inserted or deleted tuple, then there is a great deal of redundant information written on the log.

2. The requirement that the schedule be recoverable, releasing its locks only after commit, can inhibit concurrency severely. For example, recall our discussion in Section 18.7.1 of the advantage of early lock release as we access data through a B-tree index. If we require that locks be held until commit, then this advantage cannot be obtained, and we effectively allow only one writing transaction to access a B-tree at any time.

Both these concerns motivate the use of *logical logging*, where only the changes to the blocks are described. There are several degrees of complexity, depending on the nature of the change.

1. A small number of bytes of the database element are changed, e.g., the update of a fixed-length field. This situation can be handled in a straight-forward way, where we record only the changed bytes and their positions. Example 19.6 will show this situation and an appropriate form of update record.

2. The change to the database element is simply described, and easily restored, but it has the effect of changing most or all of the bytes in the database element. One common situation, discussed in Example 19.7, is

when a variable-length field is changed and much of its record, and even other records, must slide within the block. The new and old values of the block look very different unless we realize and indicate the simple cause of the change.

3. The change affects many bytes of a database element, and further changes can prevent this change from ever being undone. This situation is true "logical" logging, since we cannot even see the undo/redo process as occurring on the database elements themselves, but rather on some higher-level "logical" structure that the database elements represent. We shall, in Example 19.8, take up the matter of B-trees, a logical structure represented by database elements that are disk blocks, to illustrate this complex form of logical logging.

Example 19.6: Suppose database elements are blocks that each contain a set of tuples from some relation. We can express the update of an attribute by a log record that says something like "tuple t had its attribute a changed from value v_1 to v_2." An insertion of a new tuple into empty space on the block can be expressed as "a tuple t with value $(a_1, a_2, \ldots, a_k)$ was inserted beginning at offset position p." Unless the attribute changed or the tuple inserted are comparable in size to a block, the amount of space taken by these records will be much smaller than the entire block. Moreover, they serve for both undo and redo operations.

Notice that both these operations are idempotent; if you perform them several times on a block, the result is the same as performing them once. Likewise, their implied inverses, where the value of $t[a]$ is restored from v_2 back to v_1, or the tuple t is removed, are also idempotent. Thus, records of these types can be used for recovery in exactly the same way that update log records were used throughout Chapter 17. □

Example 19.7: Again assume database elements are blocks holding tuples, but the tuples have some variable-length fields. If a change to a field such as was described in Example 19.6 occurs, we may have to slide large portions of the block to make room for a longer field, or to preserve space if a field becomes smaller. In extreme cases, we could have to create an overflow block (recall Section 13.8) to hold part of the contents of the original block, or we could remove an overflow block if a shorter field allows us to combine the contents of two blocks into one.

As long as the block and its overflow block(s) are considered part of one database element, then it is straightforward to use the old and/or new value of the changed field to undo or redo the change. However, the block-plus-overflow-block(s) must be thought of as holding certain tuples at a "logical" level. We may not even be able to restore the bytes of these blocks to their original state after an undo or redo, because there may have been reorganization of the blocks due to other changes that varied the length of other fields. Yet if we think of a database element as being a collection of blocks that together represent certain tuples, then a redo or undo can indeed restore the logical "state" of the element. ☐

However, it may not be possible, as we suggested in Example 19.7, to treat blocks as expandable through the mechanism of overflow blocks. We may thus be able to undo or redo actions only at a level higher than blocks. The next example discusses the important case of B-tree indexes, where the management of blocks does not permit overflow blocks, and we must think of undo and redo as occurring at the "logical" level of the B-tree itself, rather than the blocks.

Example 19.8: Let us consider the problem of logical logging for B-tree nodes. Instead of writing the old and/or new value of an entire node (block) on the log, we write a short record that describes the change. These changes include:

1. Insertion or deletion of a key/pointer pair for a child.

2. Change of the key associated with a pointer.

3. Splitting or merging of nodes.

Each of these changes can be indicated with a short log record. Even the splitting operation requires only telling where the split occurs, and where the new nodes are. Likewise, merging requires only a reference to the nodes involved, since the manner of merging is determined by the B-tree management algorithms used.

Using logical update records of these types allows us to release locks earlier than would otherwise be required for a recoverable schedule. The reason is that dirty reads of B-tree blocks are never a problem for the transaction that reads them, provided its only purpose is to use the B-tree to locate the data the transaction needs to access.

For instance, suppose that transaction T reads a leaf node N, but the transaction U that last wrote N later aborts, and some change made to N (e.g., the insertion of a new key/pointer pair into N due to an insertion of a tuple by U) needs to be undone. If T has also inserted a key/pointer pair into N, then it is not possible to restore N to the way it was before U modified it. However, the effect of U on N can be undone; in this example we would delete the key/pointer pair that U had inserted. The resulting N is not the same as that which existed before U operated; it has the insertion made by T. However, there is no database inconsistency, since the B-tree as a whole continues to reflect only the changes made by committed transactions. That is, we have restored the B-tree at a logical level, but not at the physical level. ☐

19.1.8 Recovery From Logical Logs

If the logical actions are idempotent — i.e., they can be repeated any number of times without harm — then we can recover easily using a logical log. For instance, we discussed in Example 19.6 how a tuple insertion could be represented in the logical log by the tuple and the place within a block where the tuple was placed. If we write that tuple in the same place two or more times, then it is as if we had written it once. Thus, when recovering, should we need to redo a transaction that inserted a tuple, we can repeat the insertion into the proper block at the proper place, without worrying whether we had already inserted that tuple.

In contrast, consider a situation where tuples can move around within blocks or between blocks, as in Examples 19.7 and 19.8. Now, we cannot associate a particular place into which a tuple is to be inserted; the best we can do is place in the log an action such as "the tuple t was inserted somewhere on block B." If we need to redo the insertion of t during recovery, we may wind up with two copies of t in block B. Worse, we may not know whether the block B with the first copy of t made it to disk. Another transaction writing to another database element on block B may have caused a copy of B to be written to disk, for example.

To disambiguate situations such as this when we recover using a logical log, a technique called *log sequence numbers* has been developed.

- Each log record is given a number one greater than that of the previous log record.[1] Thus, a typical logical log record has the form $<L, T, A, B>$, where:

    - L is the log sequence number, an integer.
    - T is the transaction involved.
    - A is the action performed by T, e.g., "insert of tuple t."
    - B is the block on which the action was performed.

- For each action, there is a *compensating action* that logically undoes the action. As discussed in Example 19.8, the compensating action may not restore the database to exactly the same state S it would have been in had the action never occurred, but it restores the database to a state that is logically equivalent to S. For instance, the compensating action for "insert tuple t" is "delete tuple t."

- If a transaction T aborts, then for each action performed on the database by T, the compensating action is performed, and the fact that this action was performed is also recorded in the log.

- Each block maintains, in its header, the log sequence number of the last action that affected that block.

Suppose now that we need to use the logical log to recover after a crash. Here is an outline of the steps to take.

---

[1] Eventually the log sequence numbers must restart at 0, but the time between restarts of the sequence is so large that no ambiguity can occur.

1. Our first step is to reconstruct the state of the database at the time of the crash, including blocks whose current values were in buffers and therefore got lost. To do so:

    (a) Find the most recent checkpoint on the log, and determine from it the set of transactions that were active at that time.

    (b) For each log entry $<L, T, A, B>$, compare the log sequence number N on block B with the log sequence number L for this log record. If $N < L$, then redo action A; that action was never performed on block B. However, if $N \geq L$, then do nothing; the effect of A was already felt by B.

    (c) For each log entry that informs us that a transaction T started, committed, or aborted, adjust the set of active transactions accordingly.

2. The set of transactions that remain active when we reach the end of the log must be aborted. To do so:

    (a) Scan the log again, this time from the end back to the previous checkpoint. Each time we encounter a record $<L, T, A, B>$ for a transaction T that must be aborted, perform the compensating action for A on block B and record in the log the fact that that compensating action was performed.

    (b) If we must abort a transaction that began prior to the most recent checkpoint (i.e., that transaction was on the active list for the checkpoint), then continue back in the log until the start-records for all such transactions have been found.

    (c) Write abort-records in the log for each of the transactions we had to abort.

19.1.9 Exercises for Section 19.1

Exercise 19.1.1: What are all the ways to insert locks (of a single type only, as in Section 18.3) into the sequence of actions

$$r_1(A);\ r_1(B);\ w_1(A);\ w_1(B);$$

so that the transaction T_1 is:

a) Two-phase locked, but not strict.

b) Two-phase locked, and strict.

Exercise 19.1.2: Suppose that each of the sequences of actions below is followed by an abort action for transaction T_1. Tell which transactions need to be rolled back.

a) $r_1(A);\ w_1(B);\ r_3(B);\ w_3(C);\ r_2(C);\ w_2(D);$

b) $r_3(A); r_2(A); r_1(A); w_1(B); r_3(B); r_2(B); w_3(C); r_2(C);$

c) $r_3(A); r_2(A); r_1(A); w_1(B); r_2(B); w_3(C); r_2(C);$

d) $r_1(A); r_3(B); w_1(B); w_3(C); r_2(B); r_2(C); w_2(D);$

Exercise 19.1.3: Give an example of an ACR schedule with shared and exclusive locks that is not strict.

Exercise 19.1.4: Consider each of the sequences of actions in Exercise 19.1.2, but now suppose that all three transactions commit and write their commit record on the log immediately after their last action. However, a crash occurs, and a tail of the log was not written to disk before the crash and is therefore lost. Tell, depending on where the lost tail of the log begins:

    i. What transactions could be considered uncommitted?

    ii. Are any dirty reads created during the recovery process? If so, what transactions need to be rolled back?

    iii. What additional dirty reads could have been created if the portion of the log lost was not a tail, but rather some portions in the middle?

! Exercise 19.1.5: Consider the following two transactions:

$$T_1: w_1(A); w_1(B); r_1(C); c_1;$$
$$T_2: w_2(A); r_2(B); w_2(C); c_2;$$

a) How many schedules of T_1 and T_2 are recoverable?

b) Of these, how many are ACR schedules?

c) How many are both ACR and serializable?

d) How many are both recoverable and serializable?

19.2 Deadlocks

Several times we have observed that concurrently executing transactions can compete for resources and thereby reach a state where there is a *deadlock*: each of several transactions is waiting for a resource held by one of the others, and none can make progress.

- In Section 18.3.4 we saw how ordinary operation of two-phase-locked transactions can still lead to a deadlock, because each has locked something that another transaction also needs to lock.

- In Section 18.4.3 we saw how the ability to upgrade locks from shared to exclusive can cause a deadlock because each transaction holds a shared lock on the same element and wants to upgrade the lock.

There are two broad approaches to dealing with deadlock. We can detect deadlocks and fix them, or we can manage transactions in such a way that deadlocks are never able to form.

19.2.1 Deadlock Detection by Timeout

When a deadlock exists, it is generally impossible to repair the situation so that all transactions involved can proceed. Thus, at least one of the transactions will have to be aborted and restarted.

The simplest way to detect and resolve deadlocks is with a *timeout*. Put a limit on how long a transaction may be active, and if a transaction exceeds this time, roll it back. For example, in a simple transaction system, where typical transactions execute in milliseconds, a timeout of one minute would affect only transactions that are caught in a deadlock.

Notice that when one deadlocked transaction times out and rolls back, it releases its locks or other resources. Thus, there is a chance that the other transactions involved in the deadlock will complete before reaching their timeout limits. However, since transactions involved in a deadlock are likely to have started at approximately the same time (or else, one would have completed before another started), it is also possible that spurious timeouts of transactions that are no longer involved in a deadlock will occur.

19.2.2 The Waits-For Graph

Deadlocks that are caused by transactions waiting for locks held by another can be detected by a *waits-for graph*, indicating which transactions are waiting for locks held by another transaction. This graph can be used either to detect deadlocks after they have formed or to prevent deadlocks from ever forming. We shall assume the latter, which requires us to maintain the waits-for graph at all times, refusing to allow an action that creates a cycle in the graph.

Recall from Section 18.5.2 that a lock table maintains for each database element X a list of the transactions that are waiting for locks on X, as well as transactions that currently hold locks on X. The waits-for graph has a node for each transaction that currently holds any lock or is waiting for one. There is an arc from node (transaction) T to node U if there is some database element A such that:

1. U holds a lock on A,

2. T is waiting for a lock on A, and

3. T cannot get a lock on A in its desired mode unless U first releases its lock on A.[2]

---

[2]In common situations, such as shared and exclusive locks, every waiting transaction will have to wait until *all* current lock holders release their locks, but there are examples of systems of lock modes where a transaction can get its lock after only some of the current locks are released; see Exercise 19.2.5.

If there are no cycles in the waits-for graph, then each transaction can complete eventually. There will be at least one transaction waiting for no other transaction, and this transaction surely can complete. At that time, there will be at least one other transaction that is not waiting, which can complete, and so on.

However, if there is a cycle, then no transaction in the cycle can ever make progress, so there is a deadlock. Thus, a strategy for deadlock avoidance is to roll back any transaction that makes a request that would cause a cycle in the waits-for graph.

Example 19.9: Suppose we have the following four transactions, each of which reads one element and writes another:

T_1: $l_1(A)$; $r_1(A)$; $l_1(B)$; $w_1(B)$; $u_1(A)$; $u_1(B)$;

T_2: $l_2(C)$; $r_2(C)$; $l_2(A)$; $w_2(A)$; $u_2(C)$; $u_2(A)$;

T_3: $l_3(B)$; $r_3(B)$; $l_3(C)$; $w_3(C)$; $u_3(B)$; $u_3(C)$;

T_4: $l_4(D)$; $r_4(D)$; $l_4(A)$; $w_4(A)$; $u_4(D)$; $u_4(A)$;

	T_1	T_2	T_3	T_4
1)	$l_1(A)$; $r_1(A)$;			
2)		$l_2(C)$; $r_2(C)$;		
3)			$l_3(B)$; $r_3(B)$;	
4)				$l_4(D)$; $r_4(D)$;
5)		$l_2(A)$; **Denied**		
6)			$l_3(C)$; **Denied**	
7)				$l_4(A)$; **Denied**
8)	$l_1(B)$; **Denied**			

Figure 19.4: Beginning of a schedule with a deadlock

We use a simple locking system with only one lock mode, although the same effect would be noted if we were to use a shared/exclusive system. In Fig. 19.4 is the beginning of a schedule of these four transactions. In the first four steps, each transaction obtains a lock on the element it wants to read. At step (5), T_2 tries to lock A, but the request is denied because T_1 already has a lock on A. Thus, T_2 waits for T_1, and we draw an arc from the node for T_2 to the node for T_1.

Similarly, at step (6) T_3 is denied a lock on C because of T_2, and at step (7), T_4 is denied a lock on A because of T_1. The waits-for graph at this point is as shown in Fig. 19.5. There is no cycle in this graph.

At step (8), T_1 must wait for the lock on B held by T_3. If we allow T_1 to wait, there is a cycle in the waits-for graph involving T_1, T_2, and T_3, as seen

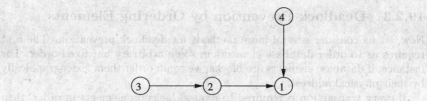

Figure 19.5: Waits-for graph after step (7) of Fig. 19.4

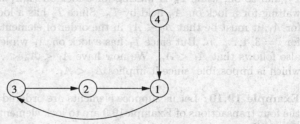

Figure 19.6: Waits-for graph with a cycle caused by step (8) of Fig. 19.4

in Fig. 19.6. Since each of these transactions is waiting for another to finish, none can make progress, and therefore there is a deadlock involving these three transactions. Incidentally, T_4 can not finish either, although it is not in the cycle, because T_4's progress depends on T_1 making progress.

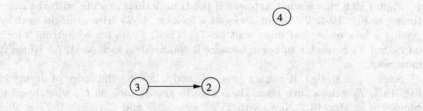

Figure 19.7: Waits-for graph after T_1 is rolled back

Since we roll back any transaction that causes a cycle, T_1 must be rolled back, yielding the waits-for graph of Fig. 19.7. T_1 relinquishes its lock on A, which may be given to either T_2 or T_4. Suppose it is given to T_2. Then T_2 can complete, whereupon it relinquishes its locks on A and C. Now T_3, which needs a lock on C, and T_4, which needs a lock on A, can both complete. At some time, T_1 is restarted, but it cannot get locks on A and B until T_2, T_3, and T_4 have completed. □

19.2.3   Deadlock Prevention by Ordering Elements

Now, let us consider several more methods for deadlock prevention. The first requires us to order database elements in some arbitrary but fixed order. For instance, if database elements are blocks, we could order them lexicographically by their physical address.

If every transaction is required to request locks on elements in order, then there can be no deadlock due to transactions waiting for locks. For suppose T_2 is waiting for a lock on A_1 held by T_1; T_3 is waiting for a lock on A_2 held by T_2, and so on, while T_n is waiting for a lock on A_{n-1} held by T_{n-1}, and T_1 is waiting for a lock on A_n held by T_n. Since T_2 has a lock on A_2 but is waiting for A_1, it must be that $A_2 < A_1$ in the order of elements. Similarly, $A_i < A_{i-1}$ for $i = 3, 4, \ldots, n$. But since T_1 has a lock on A_1 while it is waiting for A_n, it also follows that $A_1 < A_n$. We now have $A_1 < A_n < A_{n-1} < \cdots < A_2 < A_1$, which is impossible, since it implies $A_1 < A_1$.

Example 19.10: Let us suppose elements are ordered alphabetically. Then if the four transactions of Example19.9 are to lock elements in alphabetical order, T_2 and T_4 must be rewritten to lock elements in the opposite order. Thus, the four transactions are now:

T_1: $l_1(A)$; $r_1(A)$; $l_1(B)$; $w_1(B)$; $u_1(A)$; $u_1(B)$;

T_2: $l_2(A)$; $l_2(C)$; $r_2(C)$; $w_2(A)$; $u_2(C)$; $u_2(A)$;

T_3: $l_3(B)$; $r_3(B)$; $l_3(C)$; $w_3(C)$; $u_3(B)$; $u_3(C)$;

T_4: $l_4(A)$; $l_4(D)$; $r_4(D)$; $w_4(A)$; $u_4(D)$; $u_4(A)$;

Figure 19.8 shows what happens if the transactions execute with the same timing as Fig. 19.4. T_1 begins and gets a lock on A. T_2 tries to begin next by getting a lock on A, but must wait for T_1. Then, T_3 begins by getting a lock on B, but T_4 is unable to begin because it too needs a lock on A, for which it must wait.

Since T_2 is stalled, it cannot proceed, and following the order of events in Fig. 19.4, T_3 gets a turn next. It is able to get its lock on C, whereupon it completes at step (6). Now, with T_3's locks on B and C released, T_1 is able to complete, which it does at step (8). At this point, the lock on A becomes available, and we suppose that it is given on a first-come-first-served basis to T_2. Then, T_2 can get both locks that it needs and completes at step (11). Finally, T_4 can get its locks and completes.   □

19.2.4   Detecting Deadlocks by Timestamps

We can detect deadlocks by maintaining the waits-for graph, as we discussed in Section 19.2.2. However, this graph can be large, and analyzing it for cycles each time a transaction has to wait for a lock can be time-consuming. An

	T_1	T_2	T_3	T_4
1)	$l_1(A); r_1(A);$			
2)		$l_2(A);$ **Denied**		
3)			$l_3(B); r_3(B);$	
4)				$l_4(A);$ **Denied**
5)			$l_3(C); w_3(C);$	
6)			$u_3(B); u_3(C);$	
7)	$l_1(B); w_1(B);$			
8)	$u_1(A); u_1(B);$			
9)		$l_2(A); l_2(C);$		
10)		$r_2(C); w_2(A);$		
11)		$u_2(A); u_2(C);$		
12)				$l_4(A); l_4(D);$
13)				$r_4(D); w_4(A);$
14)				$u_4(A); u_4(D);$

Figure 19.8: Locking elements in alphabetical order prevents deadlock

alternative to maintaining the waits-for graph is to associate with each transaction a timestamp. This timestamp is for deadlock detection only; it is not the same as the timestamp used for concurrency control in Section 18.8, even if timestamp-based concurrency control is in use. In particular, if a transaction is rolled back, it restarts with a new, later concurrency timestamp, but its timestamp for deadlock detection never changes.

The timestamp is used when a transaction T has to wait for a lock that is held by another transaction U. Two different things happen, depending on whether T or U is *older* (has the earlier timestamp). There are two different policies that can be used to manage transactions and detect deadlocks.

1. The *Wait-Die Scheme*:

    (a) If T is older than U (i.e., the timestamp of T is smaller than U's timestamp), then T is allowed to wait for the lock(s) held by U.

    (b) If U is older than T, then T "dies"; it is rolled back.

2. The *Wound-Wait Scheme*:

    (a) If T is older than U, it "wounds" U. Usually, the "wound" is fatal: U must roll back and relinquish to T the lock(s) that T needs from U. There is an exception if, by the time the "wound" takes effect, U has already finished and released its locks. In that case, U survives and need not be rolled back.

    (b) If U is older than T, then T waits for the lock(s) held by U.

Example 19.11: Let us consider the wait-die scheme, using the transactions of Example 19.10. We shall assume that T_1, T_2, T_3, T_4 is the order of times; i.e., T_1 is the oldest transaction. We also assume that when a transaction rolls back, it does not restart soon enough to become active before the other transactions finish.

Figure 19.9 shows a possible sequence of events under the wait-die scheme. T_1 gets the lock on A first. When T_2 asks for a lock on A, it dies, because T_1 is older than T_2. In step (3), T_3 gets a lock on B, but in step (4), T_4 asks for a lock on A and dies because T_1, the holder of the lock on A, is older than T_4. Next, T_3 gets its lock on C and completes. When T_1 continues, it finds the lock on B available and also completes at step (8).

Now, the two transactions that rolled back — T_2 and T_4 — start again. Their timestamps, as far as deadlock is concerned, do not change; T_2 is still older than T_4. However, we assume that T_4 restarts first, at step (9), and when the older transaction T_2 requests a lock on A at step (10), it is forced to wait, but does not abort. T_4 completes at step (12), and then T_2 is allowed to run to completion, as shown in the last three steps.   □

Example 19.12: Next, let us consider the same transactions running under the wound-wait policy, as shown in Fig. 19.10. As in Fig. 19.9, T_1 begins by locking A. When T_2 requests a lock on A at step (2), it waits, since T_1 is older than T_2. After T_3 gets its lock on B at step (3), T_4 is also made to wait for the lock on A.

Then, suppose that T_1 continues at step (5) with its request for the lock on B. That lock is already held by T_3, but T_1 is older than T_3. Thus, T_1 "wounds" T_3. Since T_3 is not yet finished, the wound is fatal: T_3 relinquishes its lock and rolls back. Thus, T_1 is able to complete.

When T_1 makes the lock on A available, suppose it is given to T_2, which is then able to proceed. After T_2, the lock is given to T_4, which proceeds to completion. Finally, T_3 restarts and completes without interference.   □

19.2.5 Comparison of Deadlock-Management Methods

In both the wait-die and wound-wait schemes, older transactions kill off newer transactions. Since transactions restart with their old timestamp, eventually each transaction becomes the oldest in the system and is sure to complete. This guarantee, that every transaction eventually completes, is called *no starvation*. Notice that other schemes described in this section do not necessarily prevent starvation; if extra measures are not taken, a transaction could repeatedly start, get involved in a deadlock, and be rolled back. (see Exercise 19.2.6).

There is, however, a subtle difference in the way wait-die and wound-wait behave. In wound-wait, a newer transaction is killed whenever an old transaction asks for a lock held by the newer transaction. If we assume that transactions take their locks near the time that they begin, it will be rare that an old transaction was beaten to a lock by a new transaction. Thus, we expect rollback to be rare in wound-wait.

	T_1	T_2	T_3	T_4
1)	$l_1(A); r_1(A);$			
2)		$l_2(A);$ **Dies**		
3)			$l_3(B); r_3(B);$	
4)				$l_4(A);$ **Dies**
5)			$l_3(C); w_3(C);$	
6)			$u_3(B); u_3(C);$	
7)	$l_1(B); w_1(B);$			
8)	$u_1(A); u_1(B);$			
9)				$l_4(A); l_4(D);$
10)		$l_2(A);$ **Waits**		
11)				$r_4(D); w_4(A);$
12)				$u_4(A); u_4(D);$
13)		$l_2(A); l_2(C);$		
14)		$r_2(C); w_2(A);$		
15)		$u_2(A); u_2(C);$		

Figure 19.9: Actions of transactions detecting deadlock under the wait-die scheme

	T_1	T_2	T_3	T_4
1)	$l_1(A); r_1(A);$			
2)		$l_2(A);$ **Waits**		
3)			$l_3(B); r_3(B);$	
4)				$l_4(A);$ **Waits**
5)	$l_1(B); w_1(B);$		**Wounded**	
6)	$u_1(A); u_1(B);$			
7)		$l_2(A); l_2(C);$		
8)		$r_2(C); w_2(A);$		
9)		$u_2(A); u_2(C);$		
10)				$l_4(A); l_4(D);$
11)				$r_4(D); w_4(A);$
12)				$u_4(A); u_4(D);$
13)			$l_3(B); r_3(B);$	
14)			$l_3(C); w_3(C);$	
15)			$u_3(B); u_3(C);$	

Figure 19.10: Actions of transactions detecting deadlock under the wound-wait scheme

---

Why Timestamp-Based Deadlock Detection Works

We claim that in either the wait-die or wound-wait scheme, there can be no cycle in the waits-for graph, and hence no deadlock. Suppose there is a cycle such as $T_1 \rightarrow T_2 \rightarrow T_3 \rightarrow T_1$. One of the transactions is the oldest, say T_2.

In the wait-die scheme, you can only wait for younger transactions. Thus, it is not possible that T_1 is waiting for T_2, since T_2 is surely older than T_1. In the wound-wait scheme, you can only wait for older transactions. Thus, there is no way T_2 could be waiting for the younger T_3. We conclude that the cycle cannot exist, and therefore there is no deadlock.

On the other hand, when a rollback does occur, wait-die rolls back a transaction that is still in the stage of gathering locks, presumably the earliest phase of the transaction. Thus, although wait-die may roll back more transactions than wound-wait, these transactions tend to have done little work. In contrast, when wound-wait does roll back a transaction, it is likely to have acquired its locks and for substantial processor time to have been invested in its activity. Thus, either scheme may turn out to cause more wasted work, depending on the population of transactions processed.

We should also consider the advantages and disadvantages of both wound-wait and wait-die when compared with a straightforward construction and use of the waits-for graph. The important points are:

- Both wound-wait and wait-die are easier to implement than a system that maintains or periodically constructs the waits-for graph.

- Using the waits-for graph minimizes the number of times we must abort a transaction because of deadlock. If we abort a transaction, there really is a deadlock. On the other hand, either wound-wait or wait-die will sometimes roll back a transaction when there really is no deadlock.

19.2.6 Exercises for Section 19.2

Exercise 19.2.1: For each of the sequences of actions below, assume that shared locks are requested immediately before each read action, and exclusive locks are requested immediately before every write action. Also, unlocks occur immediately after the final action that a transaction executes. Tell what actions are denied, and whether deadlock occurs. Also tell how the waits-for graph evolves during the execution of the actions. If there are deadlocks, pick a transaction to abort, and show how the sequence of actions continues.

a) $r_1(A)$; $r_3(B)$; $r_2(C)$; $w_1(B)$; $w_3(C)$; $w_2(D)$;

b) $r_1(A); r_3(B); r_2(C); w_1(B); w_3(C); w_2(A);$

c) $r_1(A); r_3(B); w_1(C); w_3(D); r_2(C); w_1(B); w_4(D); w_3(A);$

d) $r_1(A); r_3(B); w_1(C); r_2(D); r_4(E); w_2(B); w_3(C); w_4(A); w_1(D);$

Exercise 19.2.2: For each of the action sequences in Exercise 19.2.1, tell what happens under the wait-die deadlock avoidance system. Assume the order of deadlock-timestamps is the same as the order of subscripts for the transactions, that is, T_1, T_2, T_3, T_4. Also assume that transactions that need to restart do so in the order that they were rolled back.

Exercise 19.2.3: For each of the action sequences in Exercise 19.2.1, tell what happens under the wound-wait deadlock avoidance system. Make the same assumptions as in Exercise 19.2.2.

!! **Exercise 19.2.4:** One approach to avoiding deadlocks is to require each transaction to announce all the locks it wants at the beginning, and to either grant all those locks or deny them all and make the transaction wait. Does this approach avoid deadlocks due to locking? Either explain why, or give an example of a deadlock that can arise.

! **Exercise 19.2.5:** Consider the intention-locking system of Section 18.6. Describe how to construct the waits-for graph for this system of lock modes. Especially, consider the possibility that a database element A is locked by different transactions in modes IS and also either S or IX. If a request for a lock on A has to wait, what arcs do we draw?

! **Exercise 19.2.6:** In Section 19.2.5 we pointed out that deadlock-detection methods other than wound-wait and wait-die do not necessarily prevent starvation, where a transaction is repeatedly rolled back and never gets to finish. Give an example of how using the policy of rolling back any transaction that would cause a cycle can lead to starvation. Does requiring that transactions request locks on elements in a fixed order necessarily prevent starvation? What about timeouts as a deadlock-resolution mechanism?

! **Exercise 19.2.7:** Can one have a waits-for graph with a cycle of length n, but no smaller cycle, for any integer $n > 1$? What about $n = 1$, i.e., a loop on a node?

19.3 Long-Duration Transactions

There is a family of applications for which a database system is suitable for maintaining data, but the model of many short transactions on which database concurrency-control mechanisms are predicated, is inappropriate. In this section we shall examine some examples of these applications and the problems that arise. We then discuss a solution based on "compensating transactions" that negate the effects of transactions that were committed, but shouldn't have been.

19.3.1   Problems of Long Transactions

Roughly, a *long transaction* is one that takes too long to be allowed to hold locks that another transaction needs. Depending on the environment, "too long" could mean seconds, minutes, or hours. Three broad classes of applications that involve long transactions are:

1. *Conventional DBMS Applications.* While common database applications run mostly short transactions, many applications require occasional long transactions. For example, one transaction might examine all of a bank's accounts to verify that the total balance is correct. Another application may require that an index be reconstructed occasionally to keep performance at its peak.

2. *Design Systems.* Whether the thing being designed is mechanical like an automobile, electronic like a microprocessor, or a software system, the common element of design systems is that the design is broken into a set of components (e.g., files of a software project), and different designers work on different components simultaneously. We do not want two designers taking a copy of a file, editing it to make design changes, and then writing the new file versions back, because then one set of changes would overwrite the other. Thus, a *check-out-check-in* system allows a designer to "check out" a file and check it in when the changes are finished, perhaps hours or days later. Even if the first designer is changing the file, another designer might want to look at the file to learn something about its contents. If the check-out operation were tantamount to an exclusive lock, then some reasonable and sensible actions would be delayed, possibly for days.

3. *Workflow Systems.* These systems involve collections of processes, some executed by software alone, some involving human interaction, and perhaps some involving human action alone. We shall give shortly an example of office paperwork involving the payment of a bill. Such applications may take days to perform, and during that entire time, some database elements may be subject to change. Were the system to grant an exclusive lock on data involved in a transaction, other transactions could be locked out for days.

Example 19.13: Consider the problem of an employee vouchering travel expenses. The intent of the traveler is to be reimbursed from account A123, and the process whereby the payment is made is shown in Fig. 19.11. The process begins with action A_1, where the traveler's secretary fills out an on-line form describing the travel, the account to be charged, and the amount. We assume in this example that the account is A123, and the amount is $1000.

The traveler's receipts are sent physically to the departmental authorization office, while the form is sent on-line to an automated action A_2. This process checks that there is enough money in the charged account (A123) and reserves the money for expenditure; i.e., it tentatively deducts $1000 from the account

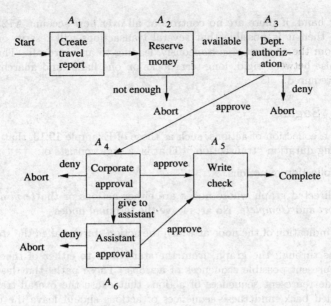

Figure 19.11: Workflow for a traveler requesting expense reimbursement

but does not issue a check for that amount. If there is not enough money in the account, the transaction aborts, and presumably it will restart when either enough money is in the account or after changing the account to be charged.

Action A_3 is performed by the departmental administrator, who examines the receipts and the on-line form. This action might take place the next day. If everything is in order, the form is approved and sent to the corporate administrator, along with the physical receipts. If not, the transaction is aborted. Presumably the traveler will be required to modify the request in some way and resubmit the form.

In action A_4, which may take place several days later, the corporate administrator either approves or denies the request, or passes the form to an assistant, who will then make the decision in action A_5. If the form is denied, the transaction again aborts and the form must be resubmitted. If the form is approved, then at action A_6 the check is written, and the deduction of $1000 from account A123 is finalized.

However, suppose that the only way we could implement this workflow is by conventional locking. In particular, since the balance of account A123 may be changed by the complete transaction, it has to be locked exclusively at action A_2 and not unlocked until either the transaction aborts or action A_6 completes. This lock may have to be held for days, while the people charged with authorizing the payment get a chance to look at the matter. If so, then there can be no other charges made to account A123, even tentatively. On the other hand, if there are no controls at all over how account A123 can be accessed, then it is possible that several transactions will reserve or deduct money from the account simultaneously, leading to an overdraft. Thus, some compromise between rigid, long-term locks on one hand, and anarchy on the other, is required. □

19.3.2 Sagas

A *saga* is a collection of actions, such as those of Example 19.13, that together form a long-duration "transaction." That is, a saga consists of:

1. A collection of actions.

2. A directed graph whose nodes are either actions or the *terminal* nodes *Abort* and *Complete*. No arcs leave the terminal nodes.

3. An indication of the node at which the action starts, called the *start node*.

The paths through the graph, from the start node to either of the terminal nodes, represent possible sequences of actions. Those paths that lead to the *Abort* node represent sequences of actions that cause the overall transaction to be rolled back, and these sequences of actions should leave the database unchanged. Paths to the *Complete* node represent successful sequences of actions, and all the changes to the database system that these actions perform will remain in the database.

Example 19.14: The paths in the graph of Fig. 19.11 that lead to the *Abort* node are: A_1A_2, $A_1A_2A_3$, $A_1A_2A_3A_4$, and $A_1A_2A_3A_4A_5$. The paths that lead to the *Complete* node are $A_1A_2A_3A_4A_6$, and $A_1A_2A_3A_4A_5A_6$. Notice that in this case the graph has no cycles, so there are a finite number of paths leading to a terminal node. However, in general, a graph can have cycles and an infinite number of paths. □

Concurrency control for sagas is managed by two facilities:

1. Each action may be considered itself a (short) transaction, that when executed uses a conventional concurrency-control mechanism, such as locking. For instance, A_2 may be implemented to (briefly) obtain a lock on account A123, decrement the amount indicated on the travel voucher, and release the lock. This locking prevents two transactions from trying to write new values of the account balance at the same time, thereby losing the effect of the first to write and making money "appear by magic."

2. The overall transaction, which can be any of the paths to a terminal node, is managed through the mechanism of "compensating transactions," which are inverses to the transactions at the nodes of the saga. Their job is to roll back the effect of a committed action in a way that does not depend on what has happened to the database between the time the action was executed and the time the compensating transaction is executed.

When are Database States "The Same"?

When discussing compensating transactions, we should be careful about what it means to return the database to "the same" state that it had before. We had a taste of the problem when we discussed logical logging for B-trees in Example 19.8. There we saw that if we "undid" an operation, the state of the B-tree might not be identical to the state before the operation, but would be equivalent to it as far as access operations on the B-tree were concerned. More generally, executing an action and its compensating transaction might not restore the database to a state literally identical to what existed before, but the differences must not be detectable by whatever application programs the database supports.

19.3.3 Compensating Transactions

In a saga, each action A has a *compensating transaction*, which we denote A^{-1}. Intuitively, if we execute A, and later execute A^{-1}, then the resulting database state is the same as if neither A nor A^{-1} had executed. More formally:

- If D is any database state, and $B_1 B_2 \cdots B_n$ is any sequence of actions and compensating transactions (whether from the saga in question or any other saga or transaction that may legally execute on the database) then the same database states result from running the sequences $B_1 B_2 \cdots B_n$ and $A B_1 B_2 \cdots B_n A^{-1}$ starting in database state D.

If a saga execution leads to the *Abort* node, then we roll back the saga by executing the compensating transactions for each executed action, in the reverse order of those actions. By the property of compensating transactions stated above, the effect of the saga is negated, and the database state is the same as if it had never happened. An explanation of why the effect is guaranteed to be negated is given in Section 19.3.4

Example 19.15 : Let us consider the actions in Fig. 19.11 and see what the compensating transactions for A_1 through A_6 might be. First, A_1 creates an on-line document. If the document is stored in the database, then A_1^{-1} must remove it from the database. Notice that this compensation obeys the fundamental property for compensating transactions: If we create the document, do any sequence of actions α (including deletion of the document if we wish), then the effect of $A_1 \alpha A_1^{-1}$ is the same as the effect of α.

A_2 must be implemented carefully. We "reserve" the money by deducting it from the account. The money will stay removed unless restored by the compensating transaction A_2^{-1}. We claim that this A_2^{-1} is a correct compensating transaction if the usual rules for how accounts may be managed are followed. To appreciate the point, it is useful to consider a similar transaction where the obvious compensation will not work; we consider such a case in Example 19.16, next.

The actions A_3, A_4, and A_6 each involve adding an approval to a form. Thus, their compensating transactions can remove that approval.[3]

Finally, A_5, which writes the check, does not have an obvious compensating transaction. In practice none is needed, because once A_5 is executed, this saga cannot be rolled back. However, technically A_5 does not affect the database anyway, since the money for the check was deducted by A_2. Should we need to consider the "database" as the larger world, where effects such as cashing a check affected the database, then we would have to design A_5^{-1} to first try to cancel the check, next write a letter to the payee demanding the money back, and if all remedies failed, restoring the money to the account by declaring a loss due to a bad debt.   □

Next, let us take up the example, alluded to in Example 19.15, where a change to an account cannot be compensated by an inverse change. The problem is that accounts normally are not allowed to go negative.

Example 19.16: Suppose B is a transaction that adds $1000 to an account that has $2000 in it initially, and B^{-1} is the compensating transaction that removes the same amount of money. Also, it is reasonable to assume that transactions may fail if they try to delete money from an account and the balance would thereby become negative. Let C be a transaction that deletes $2500 from the same account. Then $BCB^{-1} \not\equiv C$. The reason is that C by itself fails, and leaves the account with $2000, while if we execute B then C, the account is left with $500, whereupon B^{-1} fails.

Our conclusion that a saga with arbitrary transfers among accounts and a rule about accounts never being allowed to go negative cannot be supported simply by compensating transactions. Some modification to the system must be done, e.g., allowing negative balances in accounts.   □

19.3.4 Why Compensating Transactions Work

Let us say that two sequences of actions are *equivalent* ($\equiv$) if they take any database state D to the same state. The fundamental assumption about compensating transactions can be stated:

- If A is any action and α is any sequence of legal actions and compensating transactions, then $A\alpha A^{-1} \equiv \alpha$.

Now, we need to show that if a saga execution $A_1 A_2 \cdots A_n$ is followed by its compensating transactions in reverse order, $A_n^{-1} \cdots A_2^{-1} A_1^{-1}$, with any intervening actions whatsoever, then the effect is as if neither the actions nor the compensating transactions executed. The proof is an induction on n.

---

[3]In the saga of Fig. 19.11, the only time these actions are compensated is when we are going to delete the form anyway, but the definition of compensating transactions require that they work in isolation, regardless of whether some other compensating transaction was going to make their changes irrelevant.

BASIS: If $n = 1$, then the sequence of all actions between A_1 and its compensating transaction A_1^{-1} looks like $A_1 \alpha A_1^{-1}$. By the fundamental assumption about compensating transactions, $A_1 \alpha A_1^{-1} \equiv \alpha$.

INDUCTION: Assume the statement for paths of up to $n - 1$ actions, and consider a path of n actions, followed by its compensating transactions in reverse order, with any other transactions intervening. The sequence looks like

$$A_1 \alpha_1 A_2 \alpha_2 \cdots \alpha_{n-1} A_n \beta A_n^{-1} \gamma_{n-1} \cdots \gamma_2 A_2^{-1} \gamma_1 A_1^{-1} \qquad (19.1)$$

where all Greek letters represent sequences of zero or more actions. By the definition of compensating transaction, $A_n \beta A_n^{-1} \equiv \beta$. Thus, (19.1) is equivalent to

$$A_1 \alpha_1 A_2 \alpha_2 \cdots A_{n-1} \alpha_{n-1} \beta \gamma_{n-1} A_{n-1}^{-1} \gamma_{n-2} \cdots \gamma_2 A_2^{-1} \gamma_1 A_1^{-1} \qquad (19.2)$$

By the inductive hypothesis, expression (19.2) is equivalent to

$$\alpha_1 \alpha_2 \cdots \alpha_{n-1} \beta \gamma_{n-1} \cdots \gamma_2 \gamma_1$$

since there are only $n - 1$ actions in (19.2). That is, the saga and its compensation leave the database state the same as if the saga had never occurred.

19.3.5 Exercises for Section 19.3

! Exercise 19.3.1: The process of "uninstalling" software can be thought of as a compensating transaction for the action of installing the same software. In a simple model of installing and uninstalling, suppose that an action consists of *loading* one or more files from the source (e.g., a CD-ROM) onto the hard disk of the machine. To load a file f, we copy f from CD-ROM. If there was a file f' with the same path name, we back up f' before replacement. To distinguish files with the same path name, we may assume each file has a timestamp.

  a) What is the compensating transaction for the action that loads file f? Consider both the case where no file with that path name existed, and where there was a file f' with the same path name.

  b) Explain why your answer to (a) is guaranteed to compensate. *Hint*: Consider carefully the case where after replacing f' by f, a later action replaces f by another file with the same path name.

! Exercise 19.3.2: Describe the process of booking an airline seat as a saga. Consider the possibility that the customer will query about a seat but not book it. The customer may book the seat, but cancel it, or not pay for the seat within the required time limit. The customer may or may not show up for the flight. For each action, describe the corresponding compensating transaction.

19.4   Summary of Chapter 19

✦ *Dirty Data*: Data that has been written, either into main-memory buffers or on disk, by a transaction that has not yet committed is called "dirty."

✦ *Cascading Rollback*: A combination of logging and concurrency control that allows a transaction to read dirty data may have to roll back transactions that read such data from a transaction that later aborts.

✦ *Strict Locking*: The strict locking policy requires transactions to hold their locks (except for shared-locks) until not only have they committed, but the commit record on the log has been flushed to disk. Strict locking guarantees that no transaction can read dirty data, even retrospectively after a crash and recovery.

✦ *Group Commit*: We can relax the strict-locking condition that requires commit records to reach disk if we assure that log records are written to disk in the order that they are written. There is still then a guarantee of no dirty reads, even if a crash and recovery occurs.

✦ *Restoring Database State After an Abort*: If a transaction aborts but has written values to buffers, then we can restore old values either from the log or from the disk copy of the database. If the new values have reached disk, then the log may still be used to restore the old value.

✦ *Logical Logging*: For large database elements such as disk blocks, it saves much space if we record old and new values on the log incrementally, that is, by indicating only the changes. In some cases, recording changes logically, that is, in terms of an abstraction of what blocks contain, allows us to restore state logically after a transaction abort, even if it is impossible to restore the state literally.

✦ *Deadlocks*: These occur when each of a set of transactions is waiting for a resource, such as a lock, currently held by another transaction in the set.

✦ *Waits-For Graphs*: Create a node for each waiting transaction, with an arc to the transaction it is waiting for. The existence of a deadlock is the same as the existence of one or more cycles in the waits-for graph. We can avoid deadlocks if we maintain the waits-for graph and abort any transaction whose waiting would cause a cycle.

✦ *Deadlock Avoidance by Ordering Resources*: Requiring transactions to acquire resources according to some lexicographic order of the resources will prevent a deadlock from arising.

✦ *Timestamp-Based Deadlock Avoidance*: Other schemes maintain a timestamp and base their abort/wait decision on whether the requesting transaction is newer or older than the one with the resource it wants. In the wait-die scheme, an older requesting transaction waits, and a newer one is rolled back with the same timestamp. In the wound-wait scheme, a newer transaction waits and an older one forces the transaction with the resource to roll back and give up the resource.

✦ *Sagas*: When transactions involve long-duration steps that may take hours or days, conventional locking mechanisms may limit concurrency too much. A saga consists of a network of actions, each of which may lead to one or more other actions, to the completion of the entire saga, or to a requirement that the saga abort.

✦ *Compensating Transactions*: For a saga to make sense, each action must have a compensating action that will undo the effects of the first action on the database state, while leaving intact any other actions that have been made by other sagas that have completed or are currently in operation. If a saga aborts, the appropriate sequence of compensating actions is executed.

19.5 References for Chapter 19

Some useful general sources for topics covered here are [2], [1], and [7]. The material on logical logging follows [6].

Deadlock prevention was surveyed in [5]; the waits-for graph is from there. The wait-die and wound-wait schemes are from [8].

Long transactions were introduced by [4]. Sagas were described in [3].

1. N. S. Barghouti and G. E. Kaiser, "Concurrency control in advanced database applications," *Computing Surveys* **23**:3 (Sept., 1991), pp. 269–318.

2. S. Ceri and G. Pelagatti, *Distributed Databases: Principles and Systems*, McGraw-Hill, New York, 1984.

3. H. Garcia-Molina and K. Salem, "Sagas," *Proc. ACM SIGMOD Intl. Conf. on Management of Data* (1987), pp. 249–259.

4. J. N. Gray, "The transaction concept: virtues and limitations," *Intl. Conf. on Very Large Databases* (1981), pp. 144–154.

5. R. C. Holt, "Some deadlock properties of computer systems," *Computing Surveys* **4**:3 (1972), pp. 179–196.

6. C. Mohan, D. J. Haderle, B. G. Lindsay, H. Pirahesh, and P. Schwarz, "ARIES: a transaction recovery method supporting fine-granularity locking and partial rollbacks using write-ahead logging," *ACM Trans. on Database Systems* **17**:1 (1992), pp. 94–162.

7. M. T. Ozsu and P. Valduriez, *Principles of Distributed Database Systems*, Prentice-Hall, Englewood Cliffs NJ, 1999.

8. D. J. Rosenkrantz, R. E. Stearns, and P. M. Lewis II, "System-level concurrency control for distributed database systems," *ACM Trans. on Database Systems* **3**:2 (1978), pp. 178–198.

Chapter 20

Parallel and Distributed Databases

While many databases sit at a single machine, a database can also be distributed over many machines. There are other databases that reside at a single highly parallel machine. When computation is either parallel or distributed, there are many database-implementation issues that need to be reconsidered.

In this chapter, we first look at the different kinds of parallel architectures that have been used. On a parallel machine it is important that the most expensive operations take advantage of parallelism, and for databases, these operations are the full-relation operations such as join. We then discuss the map-reduce paradigm for expressing large-scale computations. This formulation of algorithms is especially amenable to execution on large-scale parallel machines, and it is simple to express important database processes in this manner.

We then turn to distributed architectures. These include grids and networks of workstations, as well as corporate databases that are distributed around the world. Now, we must worry not only about exploiting the many available processors for query execution, but some database operations become much harder to perform correctly in a distributed environment. Notable among these are distributed commitment of transactions and distributed locking.

The extreme case of a distributed architecture is a collection of independent machines, often called "peer-to-peer" networks, In these networks, even data lookup becomes problematic. We shall therefore discuss distributed hash tables and distributed search in peer-to-peer networks.

20.1 Parallel Algorithms on Relations

Database operations, frequently being time-consuming and involving a lot of data, can generally profit from parallel processing. In this section, we shall review the principal architectures for parallel machines. We then concentrate on the "shared-nothing" architecture, which appears to be the most cost effective for database operations, although it may not be superior for other parallel applications. There are simple modifications of the standard algorithms for most relational operations that will exploit parallelism almost perfectly. That is, the time to complete an operation on a p-processor machine is about $1/p$ of the time it takes to complete the operation on a uniprocessor.

20.1.1 Models of Parallelism

At the heart of all parallel machines is a collection of processors. Often the number of processors p is large, in the hundreds or thousands. We shall assume that each processor has its own local cache, which we do not show explicitly in our diagrams. In most organizations, each processor also has local memory, which we do show. Of great importance to database processing is the fact that along with these processors are many disks, perhaps one or more per processor, or in some architectures a large collection of disks accessible to all processors directly.

Additionally, parallel computers all have some communications facility for passing information among processors. In our diagrams, we show the communication as if there were a shared bus for all the elements of the machine. However, in practice a bus cannot interconnect as many processors or other elements as are found in the largest machines, so the interconnection system in many architectures is a powerful switch, perhaps augmented by busses that connect subsets of the processors in local clusters. For example, the processors in a single rack are typically connected.

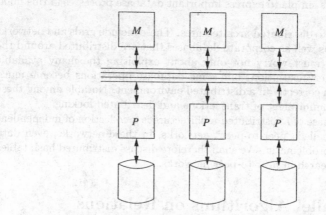

Figure 20.1: A shared-memory machine

We can classify parallel architectures into three broad groups. The most tightly coupled architectures share their main memory. A less tightly coupled architecture shares disk but not memory. Architectures that are often used for databases do not even share disk; these are called "shared nothing" architectures, although the processors are in fact interconnected and share data through message passing.

Shared-Memory Machines

In this architecture, illustrated in Fig. 20.1, each processor has access to all the memory of all the processors. That is, there is a single physical address space for the entire machine, rather than one address space for each processor. The diagram of Fig. 20.1 is actually too extreme, suggesting that processors have no private memory at all. Rather, each processor has some local main memory, which it typically uses whenever it can. However, it has direct access to the memory of other processors when it needs to. Large machines of this class are of the *NUMA* (nonuniform memory access) type, meaning that it takes somewhat more time for a processor to access data in a memory that "belongs" to some other processor than it does to access its "own" memory, or the memory of processors in its local cluster. However, the difference in memory-access times are not great in current architectures. Rather, all memory accesses, no matter where the data is, take much more time than a cache access, so the critical issue is whether or not the data a processor needs is in its own cache.

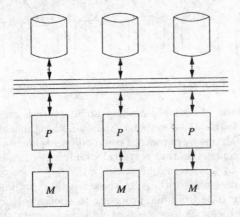

Figure 20.2: A shared-disk machine

Shared-Disk Machines

In this architecture, suggested by Fig. 20.2, every processor has its own memory, which is not accessible directly from other processors. However, the disks are accessible from any of the processors through the communication network. Disk controllers manage the potentially competing requests from different processors.

The number of disks and processors need not be identical, as it might appear from Fig. 20.2.

This architecture today appears in two forms, depending on the units of transfer between the disks and processors. Disk farms called *network attached storage* (NAS) store and transfer files. The alternative, *storage area networks* (SAN) transfer disk blocks to and from the processors.

Shared-Nothing Machines

Here, all processors have their own memory and their own disk or disks, as in Fig. 20.3. All communication is via the network, from processor to processor. For example, if one processor P wants to read tuples from the disk of another processor Q, then processor P sends a message to Q asking for the data. Q obtains the tuples from its disk and ships them over the network in another message, which is received by P.

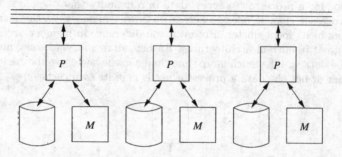

Figure 20.3: A shared-nothing machine

As we mentioned, the shared-nothing architecture is the most commonly used architecture for database systems. Shared-nothing machines are relatively inexpensive to build; one buys racks of commodity machines and connects them with the network connection that is typically built into the rack. Multiple racks can be connected by an external network.

But when we design algorithms for these machines we must be aware that it is costly to send data from one processor to another. Normally, data must be sent between processors in a message, which has considerable overhead associated with it. Both processors must execute a program that supports the message transfer, and there may be contention or delays associated with the communication network as well. Typically, the cost of a message can be broken into a large fixed overhead plus a small amount of time per byte transmitted. Thus, there is a significant advantage to designing a parallel algorithm so that communications between processors involve large amounts of data sent at once. For instance, we might buffer several blocks of data at processor P, all bound for processor Q. If Q does not need the data immediately, it may be much more efficient to wait until we have a long message at P and then send it to

Q. Fortunately, the best known parallel algorithms for database operations can use long messages effectively.

20.1.2 Tuple-at-a-Time Operations in Parallel

Let us begin our discussion of parallel algorithms for a shared-nothing machine by considering the selection operator. First, we must consider how data is best stored. As first suggested by Section 13.3.3, it is useful to distribute our data across as many disks as possible. For convenience, we shall assume there is one disk per processor. Then if there are p processors, divide any relation R's tuples evenly among the p processor's disks.

To compute $\sigma_C(R)$, we may use each processor to examine the tuples of R on its own disk. For each, it finds those tuples satisfying condition C and copies those to the output. To avoid communication among processors, we store those tuples t in $\sigma_C(R)$ at the same processor that has t on its disk. Thus, the result relation $\sigma_C(R)$ is divided among the processors, just like R is.

Since $\sigma_C(R)$ may be the input relation to another operation, and since we want to minimize the elapsed time and keep all the processors busy all the time, we would like $\sigma_C(R)$ to be divided evenly among the processors. If we were doing a projection, rather than a selection, then the number of tuples in $\pi_L(R)$ at each processor would be the same as the number of tuples of R at that processor. Thus, if R is distributed evenly, so would be its projection. However, a selection could radically change the distribution of tuples in the result, compared to the distribution of R.

Example 20.1 : Suppose the selection is $\sigma_{a=10}(R)$, that is, find all the tuples of R whose value in the attribute a is 10. Suppose also that we have divided R according to the value of the attribute a. Then all the tuples of R with $a = 10$ are at one processor, and the entire relation $\sigma_{a=10}(R)$ is at one processor. $\square$

To avoid the problem suggested by Example 20.1, we need to think carefully about the policy for partitioning our stored relations among the processors. Probably the best we can do is to use a hash function h that involves all the components of a tuple in such a way that changing one component of a tuple t can change $h(t)$ to be any possible bucket number. For example, if we want B buckets, we might convert each component somehow to an integer between 0 and $B - 1$, add the integers for each component, divide the result by B, and take the remainder as the bucket number. If B is also the number of processors, then we can associate each processor with a bucket and give that processor the contents of its bucket.

20.1.3 Parallel Algorithms for Full-Relation Operations

First, let us consider the operation $\delta(R)$. If we use a hash function to distribute the tuples of R as in Section 20.1.2, then we shall place duplicate tuples of R at the same processor. We can produce $\delta(R)$ in parallel by applying a standard, uniprocessor algorithm (as in Section 15.4.2 or 15.5.2, e.g.) to the portion of R at each processor. Likewise, if we use the same hash function to distribute the tuples of both R and S, then we can take the union, intersection, or difference of R and S by working in parallel on the portions of R and S at each processor.

However, suppose that R and S are not distributed using the same hash function, and we wish to take their union.[1] In this case, we first must make copies of all the tuples of R and S and distribute them according to a single hash function h.[2]

In parallel, we hash the tuples of R and S at each processor, using hash function h. The hashing proceeds as described in Section 15.5.1, but when the buffer corresponding to a bucket i at one processor j is filled, instead of moving it to the disk at j, we ship the contents of the buffer to processor i. If we have room for several blocks per bucket in main memory, then we may wait to fill several buffers with tuples of bucket i before shipping them to processor i.

Thus, processor i receives all the tuples of R and S that belong in bucket i. In the second stage, each processor performs the union of the tuples from R and S belonging to its bucket. As a result, the relation $R \cup S$ will be distributed over all the processors. If hash function h truly randomizes the placement of tuples in buckets, then we expect approximately the same number of tuples of $R \cup S$ to be at each processor.

The operations of intersection and difference may be performed just like a union; it does not matter whether these are set or bag versions of these operations. Moreover:

- To take a join $R(X,Y) \bowtie S(Y,Z)$, we hash the tuples of R and S to a number of buckets equal to the number of processors. However, the hash function h we use must depend only on the attributes of Y, not all the attributes, so that joining tuples are always sent to the same bucket. As with union, we ship tuples of bucket i to processor i. We may then perform the join at each processor using any uniprocessor join algorithm.

- To perform grouping and aggregation $\gamma_L(R)$, we distribute the tuples of R using a hash function h that depends only on the grouping attributes in list L. If each processor has all the tuples corresponding to one of the buckets of h, then we can perform the γ_L operation on these tuples locally, using any uniprocessor γ algorithm.

20.1.4 Performance of Parallel Algorithms

Now, let us consider how the running time of a parallel algorithm on a p-processor machine compares with the time to execute an algorithm for the

---

[1]In principle, this union could be either a set- or bag-union. But the simple bag-union technique from Section 15.2.3 of copying all the tuples from both arguments works in parallel, so we probably would not want to use the algorithm described here for a bag-union.

[2]If the hash function used to distribute tuples of R or S is known, we can use that hash function for the other and not distribute both relations.

same operation on the same data, using a uniprocessor. The total work — disk I/O's and processor cycles — cannot be smaller for a parallel machine than for a uniprocessor. However, because there are p processors working with p disks, we can expect the elapsed, or wall-clock, time to be much smaller for the multiprocessor than for the uniprocessor.

A unary operation such as $\sigma_C(R)$ can be completed in $1/p$th of the time it would take to perform the operation at a single processor, provided relation R is distributed evenly, as was supposed in Section 20.1.2. The number of disk I/O's is essentially the same as for a uniprocessor selection. The only difference is that there will, on average, be p half-full blocks of R, one at each processor, rather than a single half-full block of R had we stored all of R on one processor's disk.

Now, consider a binary operation, such as join. We use a hash function on the join attributes that sends each tuple to one of p buckets, where p is the number of processors. To distribute the tuples belonging to one processor, we must read each tuple from disk to memory, compute the hash function, and ship all tuples except the one out of p tuples that happens to belong to the bucket at its own processor.

If we are computing $R(X,Y) \bowtie S(Y,Z)$, then we need to do $B(R) + B(S)$ disk I/O's to read all the tuples of R and S and determine their buckets. We then must ship $((p-1)/p)(B(R) + B(S))$ blocks of data across the machine's internal interconnection network to their proper processors; only the $(1/p)$th of the tuples already at the right processor need not be shipped. The cost of shipment can be greater or less than the cost of the same number of disk I/O's, depending on the architecture of the machine. However, we shall assume that shipment across the internal network is significantly cheaper than movement of data between disk and memory, because no physical motion is involved in shipment among processors, while it is for disk I/O.

In principle, we might suppose that the receiving processor has to store the data on its own disk, then execute a local join on the tuples received. For example, if we used a two-pass sort-join at each processor, a naive parallel algorithm would use $3(B(R) + B(S))/p$ disk I/O's at each processor, since the sizes of the relations in each bucket would be approximately $B(R)/p$ and $B(S)/p$, and this type of join takes three disk I/O's per block occupied by each of the argument relations. To this cost we would add another $2(B(R) + B(S))/p$ disk I/O's per processor, to account for the first read of each tuple and the storing away of each tuple by the processor receiving the tuple during the hash and distribution of tuples. We should also add the cost of shipping the data, but we have elected to consider that cost negligible compared with the cost of disk I/O for the same data.

The above comparison demonstrates the value of the multiprocessor. While we do more disk I/O in total — five disk I/O's per block of data, rather than three — the elapsed time, as measured by the number of disk I/O's performed at each processor has gone down from $3(B(R) + B(S))$ to $5(B(R) + B(S))/p$, a significant win for large p.

Biiig Mistake

When using hash-based algorithms to distribute relations among processors and to execute operations, as in Example 20.2, we must be careful not to overuse one hash function. For instance, suppose we used a hash function h to hash the tuples of relations R and S among processors, in order to take their join. We might be tempted to use h to hash the tuples of S locally into buckets as we perform a one-pass hash-join at each processor. But if we do so, all those tuples will go to the same bucket, and the main-memory join suggested in Example 20.2 will be extremely inefficient.

Moreover, there are ways to improve the speed of the parallel algorithm so that the total number of disk I/O's is not greater than what is required for a uniprocessor algorithm. In fact, since we operate on smaller relations at each processor, we may be able to use a local join algorithm that uses fewer disk I/O's per block of data. For instance, even if R and S were so large that we need a two-pass algorithm on a uniprocessor, we may be able to use a one-pass algorithm on $(1/p)$th of the data.

We can avoid two disk I/O's per block if, when we ship a block to the processor of its bucket, that processor can use the block immediately as part of its join algorithm. Many algorithms known for join and the other relational operators allow this use, in which case the parallel algorithm looks just like a multipass algorithm in which the first pass uses the hashing technique of Section 15.8.3.

Example 20.2 : Consider our running example from Chapter 15 of the join $R(X, Y) \bowtie S(Y, Z)$, where R and S occupy 1000 and 500 blocks, respectively. Now, let there be 101 buffers at each processor of a 10-processor machine. Also, assume that R and S are distributed uniformly among these 10 processors.

We begin by hashing each tuple of R and S to one of 10 "buckets," using a hash function h that depends only on the join attributes Y. These 10 "buckets" represent the 10 processors, and tuples are shipped to the processor corresponding to their "bucket." The total number of disk I/O's needed to read the tuples of R and S is 1500, or 150 per processor. Each processor will have about 15 blocks worth of data for each other processor, so it ships 135 blocks to the other nine processors. The total communication is thus 1350 blocks.

We shall arrange that the processors ship the tuples of S before the tuples of R. Since each processor receives about 50 blocks of tuples from S, it can store those tuples in a main-memory data structure, using 50 of its 101 buffers. Then, when processors start sending R-tuples, each one is compared with the local S-tuples, and any resulting joined tuples are output.

In this way, the only cost of the join is 1500 disk I/O's. Moreover, the elapsed time is primarily the 150 disk I/O's performed at each processor, plus the time to ship tuples between processors and perform the main-memory computations. Note that 150 disk I/O's is less than 1/10th of the time to perform the same algorithm on a uniprocessor; we have not only gained because we had 10 processors working for us, but the fact that there are a total of 1010 buffers among those 10 processors gives us additional efficiency. ☐

20.1.5 Exercises for Section 20.1

Exercise 20.1.1: Suppose that a disk I/O takes 100 milliseconds. Let $B(R) = 200$, so the disk I/O's for computing $\sigma_C(R)$ on a uniprocessor machine will take about 20 seconds. What is the speedup if this selection is executed on a parallel machine with p processors, where: (a) $p = 1000$ (b) $p = 12$ (c) $p = 100$.

! Exercise 20.1.2: In Example 20.2 we described an algorithm that computed the join $R \bowtie S$ in parallel by first hash-distributing the tuples among the processors and then performing a one-pass join at the processors. In terms of $B(R)$ and $B(S)$, the sizes of the relations involved, p (the number of processors), and M (the number of blocks of main memory at each processor), give the condition under which this algorithm can be executed successfully.

20.2 The Map-Reduce Parallelism Framework

Map-reduce is a high-level programming system that allows many important database processes to be written simply. The user writes code for two functions, map and reduce. A master controller divides the input data into chunks, and assigns different processors to execute the map function on each chunk. Other processors, perhaps the same ones, are then assigned to perform the reduce function on pieces of the output from the map function.

20.2.1 The Storage Model

For the map-reduce framework to make sense, we should assume a massively parallel machine, most likely shared-nothing. Typically, the processors are commodity computers, mounted in racks with a simple communication network among the processors on a rank. If there is more than one rack, the racks are also connected by a simple network.

Data is assumed stored in files. Typically, the files are very large compared with the files found in conventional systems. For example, one file might be all the tuples of a very large relation. Or, the file might be a terabyte of "market-baskets," as discussed in Section 22.1.4. For another example of a single file, we shall talk in Section 23.2.2 of the "transition matrix of the Web," which is a representation of the graph with all Web pages as nodes and hyperlinks as edges.

Files are divided into *chunks*, which might be complete cylinders of a disk, and are typically many megabytes. For resiliency, each chunk is replicated several times, so it will not be lost if the disk holding it crashes.

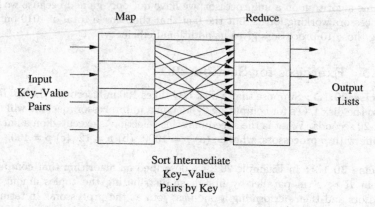

Figure 20.4: Execution of map and reduce functions

20.2.2   The Map Function

The outline of what user-defined map and reduce functions do is suggested in Fig. 20.4. The input is generally thought of as a set of key-value records, although in fact the input could be objects of any type.[3] The function *map* is executed by one or more processes, located at any number of processors. Each map process is given a chunk of the entire input data on which to work.

The map function is designed to take one key-value pair as input and to produce a list of key-value pairs as output. However:

- The types of keys and values for the output of the map function need not be the same as the types of input keys and values.

- The "keys" that are output from the map function are not true keys in the database sense. That is, there can be many pairs with the same key value. However, the key field of output pairs plays a special role in the reduce process to be explained next.

The result of executing all the *map* processes is a collection of key-value pairs called the *intermediate result*. These key-value pairs are the outputs of the map function applied to every input pair. Each pair appears at the processor that generated it. Remember that there may be many *map* processes executing the same algorithm on a different part of the input file at different processors.

---

[3]As we shall see, the output of a map-reduce algorithm is always a set of key-value pairs. Since it is useful in some applications to compose two or more map-reduce operations, it is conventional to assume that both input and output are sets of key-value pairs.

Example 20.3 : We shall consider as an example, constructing an inverted index for words in documents, as was discussed in Section 14.1.8. That is, our input is a collection of documents, and we desire to construct as the final output (not as the output of *map*) a list for each word of the documents that contain that word at least once. The input is a set of pairs each of whose keys are document ID's and whose values are the corresponding documents.

The map function takes a pair consisting of a document ID i and a document d. This function scans d character by character, and for each word w it finds, it emits the pair (w, i). Notice that in the output, the word is the key and the document ID is the associated value. The output of *map* for a single ID-document pair is a list of word-ID pairs. It is not necessary to catch duplicate words in the document; the elimination of duplicates can be done later, at the reduce phase. The intermediate result is the collection of all word-ID pairs created from all the documents in the input database. ☐

20.2.3 The Reduce Function

The second user-defined function, *reduce*, is also executed by one or more processes, located at any number of processors. The input to *reduce* is a single key value from the intermediate result, together with the list of all values that appear with this key in the intermediate result. Duplicate values are not eliminated.

In Fig. 20.4, we suggest that the output of *map* at each of four processors is distributed to four processors, each of which will execute *reduce* for a subset of the intermediate keys. However, there are a number of ways in which this distribution could be managed. For example, Each *map* process could leave its output on its local disk, and a *reduce* process could retrieve the portion of the intermediate result that it needed, over whatever network or bus interconnects the processors.

The reduce function itself combines the list of values associated with a given key k. The result is k paired with a value of some type. In many simple cases, the reduce function is associative and commutative, and the entire list of values is reduced to a single value of the same type as the list elements. For instance, if *reduce* is addition, the result is the some of a list of numbers.

When *reduce* is associative and commutative, it is possible to speed up the execution of *reduce* by starting to apply its operation to the pairs produced by the *map* processes, even before they finish. Moreover, if a given *map* process produces more than one intermediate pair with the same key, then the reduce operation can be applied on the spot to combine the pairs, without waiting for them to be passed to the *reduce* process for that key.

Example 20.4 : Let us consider the reduce function that lets us complete Example 20.3 to produce inverted indexes. The intermediate result consists of pairs of the form $(w, [i_1, i_2, \ldots, i_n])$, where the i's are a list of document ID's, one for each occurrence of word w. The reduce function we need takes a list of ID's, eliminates duplicates, and sorts the list of unique ID's.

Notice how this organization of the computation makes excellent use of whatever parallelism is available. The map function works on a single document, so we could have as many processes and processors as there are documents in the database. The reduce function works on a single word, so we could have as many processes and processors as there are words in the database. Of course, it is unlikely that we would use so many processors in practice. □

Example 20.5: Suppose rather than constructing an inverted index, we want to construct a word count. That is, for each word w that appears at least once in our database of documents, we want our output to have the pair (w, c), where c is the number of times w appears among all the documents. The map function takes an input document, goes through the document character by character, and each time it encounters another word w, it emits the pair $(w, 1)$. The intermediate result is a list of pairs $(w_1, 1), (w_2, 1), \ldots$.

In this example, the reduce function is addition of integers. That is, the input to *reduce* is a pair $(w, [1, 1, \ldots, 1])$, with a 1 for each occurrence of the word w. The reduce function sums the 1's, producing the count. □

Example 20.6: It is a little trickier to express the join of relations in the map-reduce framework. In this simple special case, we shall take the natural join of relations $R(A, B)$ and $S(B, C)$. First, the input to the map function is key-value pairs (x, t), where x is either R or S, and t is a tuple of the relation named by x. The output is a single pair consisting of the join value B taken from the tuple t and a pair consisting of x (to let us remember which relation this tuple came from) and the other component of t, either A (if $x = R$) or C (if $x = S$). All these records of the form $(b, (R, a))$ or $(b, (S, c))$ form the intermediate result.

The reduce function takes a B-value b, the key, together with a list that consists of pairs of the form (R, a) or (S, c). The result of the join will have as many tuples with B-value b as we can form by pairing an a from an (R, a) element on the list with a c from an (S, c) element on the list. Thus, *reduce* must extract from the list all the A-values associated with R and the list of all C-values associated with S. These are paired in all possible ways, with the b in the middle to form a tuple of the result. □

20.2.4 Exercises for Section 20.2

Exercise 20.2.1: Express, in the map-reduce framework, the following operations on relations: (a) π_L (b) σ_C (c) $R \cup S$ (d) $R \cap S$. (e) $R \bowtie_C S$

Exercise 20.2.2: Modify Example 20.5 to count the number of documents in which each word w appears.

20.3 Distributed Databases

We shall now consider the elements of distributed database systems. In a distributed system, there are many, relatively autonomous processors that may participate in database operations. The difference between a distributed system and a shared-nothing parallel system is in the assumption about the cost of communication. Shared-nothing parallel systems usually have a message-passing cost that is small compared with disk accesses and other costs. In a distributed system, the processors are typically physically distant, rather than in the same room. The network connecting processors may have much less capacity than the network in a shared-nothing system.

Distributed databases offer significant advantages. Like parallel systems, a distributed system can use many processors and thereby accelerate the response to queries. Further, since the processors are widely separated, we can increase resilience in the face of failures by replicating data at several sites.

On the other hand, distributed processing increases the complexity of every aspect of a database system, so we need to rethink how even the most basic components of a DBMS are designed. Since the cost of communicating may dominate the cost of processing in main memory, a critical issue is how many messages are sent between sites. In this section we shall introduce the principal issues, while the next sections concentrate on solutions to two important problems that come up in distributed databases: distributed commit and distributed locking.

20.3.1 Distribution of Data

One important reason to distribute data is that the organization is itself distributed among many sites, and the sites each have data that is germane primarily to that site. Some examples are:

1. A bank may have many branches. Each branch (or the group of branches in a given city) will keep a database of accounts maintained at that branch (or city). Customers can choose to bank at any branch, but will normally bank at "their" branch, where their account data is stored. The bank may also have data that is kept in the central office, such as employee records and policies such as current interest rates. Of course, a backup of the records at each branch is also stored, probably in a site that is neither a branch office nor the central office.

2. A chain of department stores may have many individual stores. Each store (or a group of stores in one city) has a database of sales at that store and inventory at that store. There may also be a central office with data about employees, a chain-wide inventory, data about credit-card customers, and information about suppliers such as unfilled orders, and what each is owed. In addition, there may be a copy of all the stores'

sales data in a data warehouse that is used to analyze and predict sales through ad-hoc queries issued by analysts.

3. A digital library may consist of a consortium of universities that each hold on-line books and other documents. Search at any site will examine the catalog of documents available at all sites and deliver an electronic copy of the document to the user if any site holds it.

In some cases, what we might think of logically as a single relation has been partitioned among many sites. For example, the chain of stores might be imagined to have a single sales relation, such as

    Sales(item, date, price, purchaser)

However, this relation does not exist physically. Rather, it is the union of a number of relations with the same schema, one at each of the stores in the chain. These local relations are called *fragments*, and the partitioning of a logical relation into physical fragments is called *horizontal decomposition* of the relation Sales. We regard the partition as "horizontal" because we may visualize a single Sales relation with its tuples separated, by horizontal lines, into the sets of tuples at each store.

In other situations, a distributed database appears to have partitioned a relation "vertically," by decomposing what might be one logical relation into two or more, each with a subset of the attributes, and with each relation at a different site. For instance, if we want to find out which sales at the Boston store were made to customers who are more than 90 days in arrears on their credit-card payments, it would be useful to have a relation (or view) that included the item, date, and purchaser information from Sales, along with the date of the last credit-card payment by that purchaser. However, in the scenario we are describing, this relation is decomposed vertically, and we would have to join the credit-card-customer relation at the central headquarters with the fragment of Sales at the Boston store.

20.3.2 Distributed Transactions

A consequence of the distribution of data is that a transaction may involve processes at several sites. Thus, our model of what a transaction is must change. No longer is a transaction a piece of code executed by a single processor communicating with a single scheduler and a single log manager at a single site. Rather, a transaction consists of communicating *transaction components*, each at a different site and communicating with the local scheduler and logger. Two important issues that must thus be looked at anew are:

1. How do we manage the commit/abort decision when a transaction is distributed? What happens if one component of the transaction wants to abort the whole transaction, while others encountered no problem and

want to commit? We discuss a technique called "two-phase commit" in Section 20.5; it allows the decision to be made properly and also frequently allows sites that are up to operate even if some other site(s) have failed.

2. How do we assure serializability of transactions that involve components at several sites? We look at locking in particular, in Section 20.6 and see how local lock tables can be used to support global locks on database elements and thus support serializability of transactions in a distributed environment.

20.3.3 Data Replication

One important advantage of a distributed system is the ability to *replicate* data, that is, to make copies of the data at different sites. One motivation is that if a site fails, there may be other sites that can provide the same data that was at the failed site. A second use is in improving the speed of query answering by making a copy of needed data available at the sites where queries are initiated. For example:

1. A bank may make copies of current interest-rate policy available at each branch, so a query about rates does not have to be sent to the central office.

2. A chain store may keep copies of information about suppliers at each store, so local requests for information about suppliers (e.g., the manager needs the phone number of a supplier to check on a shipment) can be handled without sending messages to the central office.

3. A digital library may temporarily cache a copy of a popular document at a school where students have been assigned to read the document.

However, there are several problems that must be faced when data is replicated.

a) How do we keep copies identical? In essence, an update to a replicated data element becomes a distributed transaction that updates all copies.

b) How do we decide where and how many copies to keep? The more copies, the more effort is required to update, but the easier queries become. For example, a relation that is rarely updated might have copies everywhere for maximum efficiency, while a frequently updated relation might have only one copy and a backup.

c) What happens when there is a communication failure in the network, and different copies of the same data have the opportunity to evolve separately and must then be reconciled when the network reconnects?

20.3.4   Exercises for Section 20.3

!! **Exercise 20.3.1:** The following exercise will allow you to address some of the problems that come up when deciding on a replication strategy for data. Suppose there is a relation R that is accessed from n sites. The ith site issues q_i queries about R and u_i updates to R per second, for $i = 1, 2, \ldots, n$. The cost of executing a query if there is a copy of R at the site issuing the query is c, while if there is no copy there, and the query must be sent to some remote site, then the cost is $8c$. The cost of executing an update is d for the copy of R at the issuing site and $12d$ for every copy of R that is not at the issuing site. As a function of these parameters, how would you choose, for large n, a set of sites at which to replicate R.

20.4   Distributed Query Processing

We now turn to optimizing queries on a network of distributed machines. When communication among processors is a significant cost, there are some query plans that can be more efficient than the ones we developed in Section 20.1 for processors that could communicate locally. Our principal objective is a new way of computing joins, using the semijoin operator that was introduced in Exercise 2.4.8.

20.4.1   The Distributed Join Problem

Suppose we want to compute $R(A, B) \bowtie S(B, C)$. However, R and S reside at different nodes of a network, as suggested in Fig. 20.5. There are two obvious ways to compute the join.

Figure 20.5: Joining relations at different nodes of a network

1. Send a copy of R to the site of S, and compute the join there.

2. Send a copy of S to the site of R and compute the join there.

In many situations, either of these methods is fine. However, problems can arise, such as:

a) What happens if the channel between the sites has low-capacity, e.g., a phone line or wireless link? Then, the cost of the join is primarily the time it takes to copy one of the relations, so we need to design our query plan to minimize communication.

b) Even if communication is fast, there may be a better query plan if the shared attribute B has values that are much smaller than the values of A and C. For example, B could be an identifier for documents or videos, while A and C are the documents or videos themselves.

20.4.2 Semijoin Reductions

Both these problems can be dealt with using the same type of query plan, in which only the relevant part of each relation is shipped to the site of the other. Recall that the semijoin of relations $R(X, Y)$ and $S(Y, Z)$, where X, Y, and Z are sets of attributes, is $R \ltimes S = R \bowtie (\pi_Y(S))$. That is, we project S onto the common attributes, and then take the natural join of that projection with R. $\pi_Y(S)$ is a set-projection, so duplicates are eliminated. It is unusual to take a natural join where the attributes of one argument are a subset of the attributes of the other, but the definition of the join covers this case. The effect is that $R \ltimes S$ contains all those tuples of R that join with at least one tuple of S. Put another way, the semijoin $R \ltimes S$ eliminates the dangling tuples of R.

Having sent $\pi_Y(S)$ to the site of R, we can compute $R \ltimes S$ there. We know those tuples of R that are not in $R \ltimes S$ cannot participate in $R \bowtie S$. Therefore it is sufficient to send $R \ltimes S$, rather than all of R, to the site of S and to compute the join there. This plan is suggested by Fig. 20.6 for the relations $R(A, B)$ and $S(B, C)$. Of course there is a symmetric plan where the roles of R and S are interchanged.

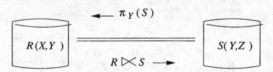

Figure 20.6: Exploiting the semijoin to minimize communication

Whether this semijoin plan, or the plan with R and S interchanged is more efficient than one of the obvious plans depends on several factors. First, if the projection of S onto Y results in a relation much smaller than S, then it is cheaper to send $\pi_Y(S)$ to the site of R, rather than S itself. $\pi_Y(S)$ will be small compared with S if either or both of the following hold:

1. There are many duplicates to be eliminated; i.e., many tuples of S share Y-values.

2. The components for the attributes of Z are large compared with the components of Y; e.g., Z includes attributes whose values are audios, videos, or documents.

In order for the semijoin plan to be superior, we also need to know that the size of $R \ltimes S$ is smaller than R. That is, R must contain many dangling tuples in its join with S.

20.4.3 Joins of Many Relations

When we want to take the natural join of two relations, only one semijoin is useful. The same holds for an equijoin, since we can act as if the equated pairs of attributes had the same name and treat the equijoin as if it were a natural join. However, when we take the natural join or equijoin of three or more relations at different sites, several surprising things happen.

- We may need several semijoins to eliminate all the dangling tuples from the relations before shipping them to other sites for joining.

- There are sets of relation schemas such that no finite sequence of semijoins eliminates all dangling tuples.

- It is possible to identify those sets of relation schemas such that there is a finite way to eliminate dangling tuples by semijoins.

Example 20.7: To see what can go wrong when we take the natural join of more than two relations, consider $R(A, B)$, $S(B, C)$, and $T(C, A)$. Suppose R and S have exactly the same n tuples: $\{(1, 1), (2, 2), \ldots, (n, n)\}$. T has $n - 1$ tuples: $\{(1, 2), (2, 3), \ldots, (n - 1, n)\}$. The relations are shown in Fig. 20.7.

A	B		B	C		C	A
1	1		1	1		1	2
2	2		2	2		2	3
.	.		.	.		.	.
.	.		.	.		.	.
.	.		.	.		.	.
n	n		n	n		$n-1$	n
R			S			T	

Figure 20.7: Three relations for which elimination of dangling tuples by semijoins is very slow

Notice that while R and S join to produce the n tuples

$$\{(1, 1, 1), (2, 2, 2), \ldots, (n, n, n)\}$$

none of these tuples can join with any tuple of T. The reason is that all tuples of $R \bowtie S$ agree in their A and C components, while the tuples of T disagree in their A and C components. That is, $R \bowtie S \bowtie T$ is empty, and *all* tuples of each relation are dangling.

However, no one semijoin can eliminate more than one tuple from any relation. For example, $S \ltimes T$ eliminates only (n, n) from S, because $\pi_C(T) = \{1, 2, \ldots, n - 1\}$. Similarly, $R \ltimes T$ eliminates only $(1, 1)$ from R, because $\pi_A(T) = \{2, 3, \ldots, n\}$. We can then continue, say, with $R \ltimes S$, which eliminates (n, n) from R, and $T \ltimes R$, which eliminates $(n - 1, n)$ from T. Now we can compute $S \ltimes T$ again and eliminate $(n-1, n-1)$ from S, and so on. While we shall not prove it, we in fact need $3n - 1$ semijoins to make all three relations empty. □

Since n in Example 20.7 is arbitrary, we see that for the particular relations discussed there, no fixed, finite sequence of semijoins is guaranteed to eliminate all dangling tuples, regardless of the data currently held in the relations. On the other hand, as we shall see, many typical joins of three or more relations do have fixed, finite sequences of semijoins that are guaranteed to eliminate all the dangling tuples. We call such a sequence of semijoins a *full reducer* for the relations in question.

20.4.4 Acyclic Hypergraphs

Let us assume that we are taking a natural join of several relations, although as mentioned, we can also handle equijoins by pretending the names of equated attributes from different relations are the same, and renaming attributes to make that pretense a reality. If we do, then we can draw a useful picture of every natural join as a *hypergraph*, that is a set of nodes with *hyperedges* that are sets of nodes. A traditional graph is then a hypergraph all of whose hyperedges are sets of size two.

The hypergraph for a natural join is formed by creating one node for each attribute name. Each relation is represented by a hyperedge containing all of its attributes.

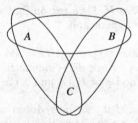

Figure 20.8: The hypergraph for Example 20.7

Example 20.8: Figure 20.8 is the hypergraph for the three relations from Example 20.7. The relation $R(A, B)$ is represented by the hyperedge $\{A, B\}$; S is represented by the hyperedge $\{B, C\}$, and T is the hyperedge $\{A, C\}$. Notice that this hypergraph is actually a graph, since the hyperedges are each pairs of nodes. Also observe that the three hyperedges form a cycle in the graph. As we shall see, it is this cyclicity that causes there to be no full reducer.

However, the question of when a hypergraph is cyclic has a somewhat unintuitive answer. In Fig. 20.9 is another hypergraph, which could be used, for instance, to represent the join of the relations $R(A, E, F)$, $S(A, B, C)$, $T(C, D, E)$, and $U(A, C, E)$. This hypergraph is a true hypergraph, since it has hyperedges with more than two nodes. It also happens to be an "acyclic" hypergraph, even though it appears to have cycles. □

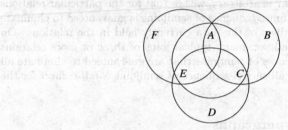

Figure 20.9: An acyclic hypergraph

To define acyclic hypergraphs correctly, and thus get the condition under which a full reducer exists, we first need the notion of an "ear" in a hypergraph. A hyperedge H is an *ear* if there is some other hyperedge G in the same hypergraph such that every node of H is either:

1. Found only in H, or

2. Also found in G.

We shall say that G *consumes* H, for a reason that will become apparent when we discuss reduction of the hypergraph.

Example 20.9 : In Fig. 20.9, hyperedge $H = \{A, E, F\}$ is an ear. The role of G is played by $\{A, C, E\}$. Node F is unique to H; it appears in no other hyperedge. The other two nodes of H (A and E) are also members of G. □

A hypergraph is *acyclic* if it can be reduced to a single hyperedge by a sequence of *ear reductions*. An ear reduction is simply the elimination of one ear from the hypergraph, along with any nodes that appear only in that ear. Note that an ear, if not eliminated at one step, remains an ear after another ear is eliminated. However, it is possible that a hyperedge that was not an ear, becomes an ear after another hyperedge is eliminated.

Example 20.10 : Figure 20.8 is not acyclic. No hyperedge is an ear, so we cannot get started with any ear reduction. For example, $\{A, B\}$ is not an ear because neither A nor B is unique to this hyperedge, and no other hyperedge contains both A and B.

On the other hand, Fig. 20.9 is acyclic. As we mentioned in Example 20.9, $\{A, E, F\}$ is an ear; so are $\{A, B, C\}$ and $\{C, D, E\}$. We can therefore eliminate hyperedge $\{A, E, F\}$ from the hypergraph. When we eliminate this ear, node F

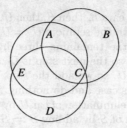

Figure 20.10: After one ear reduction

disappears, but the other five nodes and three hyperedges remain, as suggested in Fig. 20.10.

Since $\{A, B, C\}$ is an ear in Fig. 20.10, we may eliminate it and node B in a second ear reduction. Now, we are left with only hyperedges $\{A, C, E\}$ and $\{C, D, E\}$. Each is now an ear; notice that $\{A, C, E\}$ was not an ear until now. We can eliminate either, leaving a single hyperedge and proving that Fig. 20.9 is an acyclic hypergraph.   □

20.4.5   Full Reducers for Acyclic Hypergraphs

We can construct a full reducer for any acyclic hypergraph by following the sequence of ear reductions. We construct the sequence of semijoins as follows, by induction on the number of hyperedges in an acyclic hypergraph.

BASIS: If there is only one hyperedge, do nothing. The "join" of one relation is the relation itself, and there are surely no dangling tuples.

INDUCTION: If the acyclic hypergraph has more than one hyperedge, then it must have at least one ear. Pick one, say H, and suppose it is consumed by hyperedge G.

1. Execute the semijoin $G := G \ltimes H$; that is, eliminate from G any of its tuples that do not join with H.[4]

2. Recursively, find a semijoin sequence for the hypergraph with ear H eliminated.

3. Execute the semijoin $H := H \ltimes G$.

Example 20.11: Let us construct the full reducer for the relations $R(A, E, F)$, $S(A, B, C)$, $T(C, D, E)$, and $U(A, C, E)$, whose hypergraph we saw in Fig. 20.9.

---

[4]We are identifying hyperedges with the relations that they represent for convenience in notation. Moreover, if the sets of tuples corresponding to a hyperedge are stored tables, rather than temporary relations, we do not actually replace a relation by a semijoin, as would be suggested by a step like $G := G \ltimes H$, but instead we store the result in a new temporary, G'.

We shall use the sequence of ears R, then S, then U, as in Example 20.10. Since U consumes R, we begin with the semijoin $U := U \ltimes R$.

Recursively, we reduce the remaining three hyperedges. That reduction starts with U consuming S, so the next step is $U := U \ltimes S$. Another level of recursion has T consuming U, so we add the step $T := T \ltimes U$. With only T remaining, we have the basis case and do nothing.

Finally, we complete the elimination of ear U by adding $U := U \ltimes T$. Then, we complete the elimination of S by adding $S := S \ltimes U$, and we complete the elimination of R with $R := R \ltimes U$. The entire sequence of semijoins that forms a full reducer for Fig. 20.9 is shown in Fig. 20.11. □

$$U := U \ltimes R$$
$$U := U \ltimes S$$
$$T := T \ltimes U$$
$$U := U \ltimes T$$
$$S := S \ltimes U$$
$$R := R \ltimes U$$

Figure 20.11: A full reducer for Fig. 20.9

Once we have executed all the semijoins in the full reducer, we can copy all the reduced relations to the site of one of them, knowing that the relations to be shipped contain no dangling tuples and therefore are as small as can be. In fact, if we know at which site the join will be performed, then we do not have to eliminate all dangling tuples for relations at that site. We can stop applying semijoins to a relation as soon as that relation will no longer be used to reduce other relations.

Example 20.12: If the full reducer of Fig. 20.11 will be followed by a join at the site of S, then we do not have to do the step $S := S \ltimes U$. However, if the join is to be conducted at the site of T, then we still have to do the reduction $T := T \ltimes U$, because T is used to reduce other relations at later steps. □

20.4.6 Why the Full-Reducer Algorithm Works

We can show that the algorithm produces a full reducer for any acyclic hypergraph by induction on the number of hyperedges.

BASIS: One hyperedge. There are no dangling tuples, so nothing needs to be done.

INDUCTION: When we eliminate the ear H, we eliminate, from the hyperedge G that consumes H, all tuples that will not join with at least one tuple of H. Thus, whatever further reductions are done, the join of the relations for all the hyperedges besides H cannot contain a tuple that will not join with H.

Note that this statement is true because G is the only link between H and the remaining relations.

By induction, all tuples that are dangling in the join of the remaining relations are eliminated. When we do the final semijoin $H := H \ltimes G$ to eliminate dangling tuples from H, we know that no relation has dangling tuples.

20.4.7 Exercises for Section 20.4

Exercise 20.4.1: Determine which of the following hypergraphs are acyclic. Each hypergraph is represented by a list of its hyperedges.

a) $\{A, B\}$, $\{B, C, D\}$, $\{B, E, F\}$, $\{F, G, H\}$, $\{G, I\}$, $\{B, H\}$.

b) $\{A, B, C, D\}$, $\{A, B, E\}$, $\{B, D, F\}$, $\{C, D, G\}$, $\{A, C, H\}$.

c) $\{A, B\}$, $\{B, C, D\}$, $\{B, E, F\}$, $\{F, G, H\}$, $\{G, I\}$, $\{H, J\}$.

Exercise 20.4.2: For those hypergraphs of Exercise 20.4.1 that are acyclic, construct a full reducer.

! **Exercise 20.4.3:** Besides the full reducer of Example 20.11, how many other full reducers of six steps can be constructed for the hypergraph of Fig. 20.9 by choosing other orders for the elimination of ears?

! **Exercise 20.4.4:** A well known property of acyclic graphs is that if you delete an edge from an acyclic graph it remains acyclic. Is the analogous statement true for hypergraphs? That is, if you eliminate a hyperedge from an acyclic hypergraph, is the remaining hypergraph always acyclic? *Hint*: consider the acyclic hypergraph of Fig. 20.9.

! **Exercise 20.4.5:** Suppose we want to take the natural join of $R(A, B)$ and $S(B, C)$, where R and S are at different sites, and the size of the data communicated is the dominant cost of the join. Suppose the sizes of R and S are s_R and s_S, respectively. Suppose that the size of $\pi_B(R)$ is fraction p_R of the size of R and $\pi_B(S)$ is fraction p_S of the size of S. Finally, suppose that fractions d_R and d_S of relations R and S, respectively, are dangling. Write expressions, in terms of these six parameters, for the costs of the four strategies for evaluating $R \bowtie S$, and determine the conditions under which each is the best strategy. The four strategies are:

i) Ship R to the site of S.

ii) Ship S to the site of R.

iii) Ship $\pi_B(S)$ to the site of R, and then $R \ltimes S$ to the site of S.

iv) Ship $\pi_B(R)$ to the site of S, and then $S \ltimes R$ to the site of R.

!! **Exercise 20.4.6:** Not all binary operations on relations located at different nodes of a network can have their execution time reduced by preliminary operations like the semijoin. Is it possible to improve on the obvious algorithm (ship one of the relations to the other site) when the operation is (a) intersection (b) difference (c) union?

20.5 Distributed Commit

In this section, we shall address the problem of how a distributed transaction that has components at several sites can execute atomically. The next section discusses another important property of distributed transactions: executing them serializably.

20.5.1 Supporting Distributed Atomicity

We shall begin with an example that illustrates the problems that might arise.

Example 20.13: Consider our example of a chain of stores mentioned in Section 20.3. Suppose a manager of the chain wants to query all the stores, find the inventory of toothbrushes at each, and issue instructions to move toothbrushes from store to store in order to balance the inventory. The operation is done by a single global transaction T that has component T_i at the ith store and a component T_0 at the office where the manager is located. The sequence of activities performed by T are summarized below:

1. Component T_0 is created at the site of the manager.

2. T_0 sends messages to all the stores instructing them to create components T_i.

3. Each T_i executes a query at store i to discover the number of toothbrushes in inventory and reports this number to T_0.

4. T_0 takes these numbers and determines, by some algorithm we do not need to discuss, what shipments of toothbrushes are desired. T_0 then sends messages such as "store 10 should ship 500 toothbrushes to store 7" to the appropriate stores (stores 7 and 10 in this instance).

5. Stores receiving instructions update their inventory and perform the shipments.

□

There are a number of things that could go wrong in Example 20.13, and many of these result in violations of the atomicity of T. That is, some of the actions comprising T get executed, but others do not. Mechanisms such as logging and recovery, which we assume are present at each site, will assure that each T_i is executed atomically, but do not assure that T itself is atomic.

Example 20.14: Suppose a bug in the algorithm to redistribute toothbrushes might cause store 10 to be instructed to ship more toothbrushes than it has. T_{10} will therefore abort, and no toothbrushes will be shipped from store 10; neither will the inventory at store 10 be changed. However, T_7 detects no problems and commits at store 7, updating its inventory to reflect the supposedly shipped toothbrushes. Now, not only has T failed to execute atomically (since T_{10} never completes), but it has left the distributed database in an inconsistent state. □

Another source of problems is the possibility that a site will fail or be disconnected from the network while the distributed transaction is running.

Example 20.15: Suppose T_{10} replies to T_0's first message by telling its inventory of toothbrushes. However, the machine at store 10 then crashes, and the instructions from T_0 are never received by T_{10}. Can distributed transaction T ever commit? What should T_{10} do when its site recovers? □

20.5.2 Two-Phase Commit

In order to avoid the problems suggested in Section 20.5.1, distributed DBMS's use a complex protocol for deciding whether or not to commit a distributed transaction. In this section, we shall describe the basic idea behind these protocols, called *two-phase commit*.[5] By making a global decision about committing, each component of the transaction will commit, or none will. As usual, we assume that the atomicity mechanisms at each site assure that either the local component commits or it has no effect on the database state at that site; i.e., components of the transaction are atomic. Thus, by enforcing the rule that either all components of a distributed transaction commit or none does, we make the distributed transaction itself atomic.

Several salient points about the two-phase commit protocol follow:

- In a two-phase commit, we assume that each site logs actions at that site, but there is no global log.

- We also assume that one site, called the *coordinator*, plays a special role in deciding whether or not the distributed transaction can commit. For example, the coordinator might be the site at which the transaction originates, such as the site of T_0 in the examples of Section 20.5.1.

- The two-phase commit protocol involves sending certain messages between the coordinator and the other sites. As each message is sent, it is logged at the sending site, to aid in recovery should it be necessary.

With these points in mind, we can describe the two phases in terms of the messages sent between sites.

---

[5]Do not confuse two-phase commit with two-phase locking. They are independent ideas, designed to solve different problems.

Phase I

In phase 1 of the two-phase commit, the coordinator for a distributed transaction T decides when to attempt to commit T. Presumably the attempt to commit occurs after the component of T at the coordinator site is ready to commit, but in principle the steps must be carried out even if the coordinator's component wants to abort (but with obvious simplifications as we shall see). The coordinator polls the sites of all components of the transaction T to determine their wishes regarding the commit/abort decision, as follows:

1. The coordinator places a log record <Prepare T> on the log at its site.

2. The coordinator sends to each component's site (in principle including itself) the message prepare T.

3. Each site receiving the message prepare T decides whether to commit or abort its component of T. The site can delay if the component has not yet completed its activity, but must eventually send a response.

4. If a site wants to commit its component, it must enter a state called *precommitted*. Once in the precommitted state, the site cannot abort its component of T without a directive to do so from the coordinator. The following steps are done to become precommitted:

   (a) Perform whatever steps are necessary to be sure the local component of T will not have to abort, even if there is a system failure followed by recovery at the site. Thus, not only must all actions associated with the local T be performed, but the appropriate actions regarding the log must be taken so that T will be redone rather than undone in a recovery. The actions depend on the logging method, but surely the log records associated with actions of the local T must be flushed to disk.

   (b) Place the record <Ready T> on the local log and flush the log to disk.

   (c) Send to the coordinator the message ready T.

   However, the site does not commit its component of T at this time; it must wait for phase 2.

5. If, instead, the site wants to abort its component of T, then it logs the record <Don't commit T> and sends the message don't commit T to the coordinator. It is safe to abort the component at this time, since T will surely abort if even one component wants to abort.

The messages of phase 1 are summarized in Fig. 20.12.

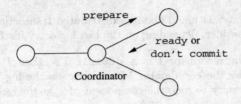

Figure 20.12: Messages in phase 1 of two-phase commit

Phase II

The second phase begins when responses `ready` or `don't commit` are received from each site by the coordinator. However, it is possible that some site fails to respond; it may be down, or it has been disconnected by the network. In that case, after a suitable timeout period, the coordinator will treat the site as if it had sent `don't commit`.

1. If the coordinator has received `ready` T from all components of T, then it decides to commit T. The coordinator logs <Commit T> at its site and then sends message `commit` T to all sites involved in T.

2. However, if the coordinator has received `don't commit` T from one or more sites, it logs <Abort T> at its site and then sends `abort` T messages to all sites involved in T.

3. If a site receives a `commit` T message, it commits the component of T at that site, logging <Commit T> as it does.

4. If a site receives the message `abort` T, it aborts T and writes the log record <Abort T>.

The messages of phase 2 are summarized in Fig. 20.13.

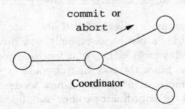

Figure 20.13: Messages in phase 2 of two-phase commit

20.5.3 Recovery of Distributed Transactions

At any time during the two-phase commit process, a site may fail. We need to make sure that what happens when the site recovers is consistent with the global decision that was made about a distributed transaction T. There are several cases to consider, depending on the last log entry for T.

1. If the last log record for T was <Commit T>, then T must have been committed by the coordinator. Depending on the log method used, it may be necessary to redo the component of T at the recovering site.

2. If the last log record is <Abort T>, then similarly we know that the global decision was to abort T. If the log method requires it, we undo the component of T at the recovering site.

3. If the last log record is <Don't commit T>, then the site knows that the global decision must have been to abort T. If necessary, effects of T on the local database are undone.

4. The hard case is when the last log record for T is <Ready T>. Now, the recovering site does not know whether the global decision was to commit or abort T. This site must communicate with at least one other site to find out the global decision for T. If the coordinator is up, the site can ask the coordinator. If the coordinator is not up at this time, some other site may be asked to consult its log to find out what happened to T. In the worst case, no other site can be contacted, and the local component of T must be kept active until the commit/abort decision is determined.

5. It may also be the case that the local log has no records about T that come from the actions of the two-phase commit protocol. If so, then the recovering site may unilaterally decide to abort its component of T, which is consistent with all logging methods. It is possible that the coordinator already detected a timeout from the failed site and decided to abort T. If the failure was brief, T may still be active at other sites, but it will never be inconsistent if the recovering site decides to abort its component of T and responds with don't commit T if later polled in phase 1.

The above analysis assumes that the failed site is not the coordinator. When the coordinator fails during a two-phase commit, new problems arise. First, the surviving participant sites must either wait for the coordinator to recover or elect a new coordinator. Since the coordinator could be down for an indefinite period, there is good motivation to elect a new leader, at least after a brief waiting period to see if the coordinator comes back up.

The matter of *leader election* is in its own right a complex problem of distributed systems, beyond the scope of this book. However, a simple method will work in most situations. For instance, we may assume that all participant sites have unique identifying numbers, e.g., IP addresses. Each participant sends messages announcing its availability as leader to all the other sites, giving its identifying number. After a suitable length of time, each participant acknowledges as the new coordinator the lowest-numbered site from which it has heard, and sends messages to that effect to all the other sites. If all sites receive consistent messages, then there is a unique choice for new coordinator, and everyone knows about it. If there is inconsistency, or a surviving site has failed to respond, that too will be universally known, and the election starts over.

Now, the new leader polls the sites for information about each distributed transaction T. Each site reports the last record on its log concerning T, if there is one. The possible cases are:

1. Some site has <Commit T> on its log. Then the original coordinator must have wanted to send commit T messages everywhere, and it is safe to commit T.

2. Similarly, if some site has <Abort T> on its log, then the original coordinator must have decided to abort T, and it is safe for the new coordinator to order that action.

3. Suppose now that no site has <Commit T> or <Abort T> on its log, but at least one site does *not* have <Ready T> on its log. Then since actions are logged before the corresponding messages are sent, we know that the old coordinator never received ready T from this site and therefore could not have decided to commit. It is safe for the new coordinator to decide to abort T.

4. The most problematic situation is when there is no <Commit T> or <Abort T> to be found, but every surviving site has <Ready T>. Now, we cannot be sure whether the old coordinator found some reason to abort T or not; it could have decided to do so because of actions at its own site, or because of a don't commit T message from another failed site, for example. Or the old coordinator may have decided to commit T and already committed its local component of T. Thus, the new coordinator is not able to decide whether to commit or abort T and must wait until the original coordinator recovers. In real systems, the database administrator has the ability to intervene and manually force the waiting transaction components to finish. The result is a possible loss of atomicity, but the person executing the blocked transaction will be notified to take some appropriate compensating action.

20.5.4 Exercises for Section 20.5

! **Exercise 20.5.1:** Consider a transaction T initiated at a home computer that asks bank B to transfer \$10,000 from an account at B to an account at another bank C.

a) What are the components of distributed transaction T? What should the components at B and C do?

b) What can go wrong if there is not \$10,000 in the account at B?

c) What can go wrong if one or both banks' computers crash, or if the network is disconnected?

d) If one of the problems suggested in (c) occurs, how could the transaction resume correctly when the computers and network resume operation?

Exercise 20.5.2: In this exercise, we need a notation for describing sequences of messages that can take place during a two-phase commit. Let (i, j, M) mean that site i sends the message M to site j, where the value of M and its meaning can be P (prepare), R (ready), D (don't commit), C (commit), or A (abort). We shall discuss a simple situation in which site 0 is the coordinator, but not otherwise part of the transaction, and sites 1 and 2 are the components. For instance, the following is one possible sequence of messages that could take place during a successful commit of the transaction:

$$(0,1,P), \ (0,2,P), \ (2,0,R), \ (1,0,R), \ (0,2,C), \ (0,1,C)$$

a) Give an example of a sequence of messages that could occur if site 1 wants to commit and site 2 wants to abort.

! b) How many possible sequences of messages such as the above are there, if the transaction successfully commits?

! c) If site 1 wants to commit, but site 2 does not, how many sequences of messages are there, assuming no failures occur?

! d) If site 1 wants to commit, but site 2 is down and does not respond to messages, how many sequences are there?

!! **Exercise 20.5.3:** Using the notation of Exercise 20.5.2, suppose the sites are a coordinator and n other sites that are the transaction components. As a function of n, how many sequences of messages are there if the transaction successfully commits?

20.6   Distributed Locking

In this section we shall see how to extend a locking scheduler to an environment where transactions are distributed and consist of components at several sites. We assume that lock tables are managed by individual sites, and that the component of a transaction at a site can request locks on the data elements only at that site.

When data is replicated, we must arrange that the copies of a single element X are changed in the same way by each transaction. This requirement introduces a distinction between locking the *logical* database element X and locking one or more of the copies of X. In this section, we shall offer a cost model for distributed locking algorithms that applies to both replicated and nonreplicated data. However, before introducing the model, let us consider an obvious (and sometimes adequate) solution to the problem of maintaining locks in a distributed database — centralized locking.

20.6.1 Centralized Lock Systems

Perhaps the simplest approach is to designate one site, the *lock site*, to maintain a lock table for logical elements, whether or not they have copies at that site. When a transaction wants a lock on logical element X, it sends a request to the lock site, which grants or denies the lock, as appropriate. Since obtaining a global lock on X is the same as obtaining a local lock on X at the lock site, we can be sure that global locks behave correctly as long as the lock site administers locks conventionally. The usual cost is three messages per lock (request, grant, and release), unless the transaction happens to be running at the lock site.

The use of a single lock site can be adequate in some situations, but if there are many sites and many simultaneous transactions, the lock site could become a bottleneck. Further, if the lock site crashes, no transaction at any site can obtain locks. Because of these problems with centralized locking, there are a number of other approaches to maintaining distributed locks, which we shall introduce after discussing how to estimate the cost of locking.

20.6.2 A Cost Model for Distributed Locking Algorithms

Suppose that each data element exists at exactly one site (i.e., there is no data replication) and that the lock manager at each site stores locks and lock requests for the elements at its site. Transactions may be distributed, and each transaction consists of components at one or more sites.

While there are several costs associated with managing locks, many of them are fixed, independent of the way transactions request locks over a network. The one cost factor over which we have control is the number of messages sent between sites when a transaction obtains and releases its locks. We shall thus count the number of messages required for various locking schemes on the assumption that all locks are granted when requested. Of course, a lock request may be denied, resulting in an additional message to deny the request and a later message when the lock is granted. However, since we cannot predict the rate of lock denials, and this rate is not something we can control anyway, we shall ignore this additional requirement for messages in our comparisons.

Example 20.16: As we mentioned in Section 20.6.1, in the central locking method, the typical lock request uses three messages, one to request the lock, one from the central site to grant the lock, and a third to release the lock. The exceptions are:

1. The messages are unnecessary when the requesting site is the central lock site, and

2. Additional messages must be sent when the initial request cannot be granted.

However, we assume that both these situations are relatively rare; i.e., most lock requests are from sites other than the central lock site, and most lock requests can be granted. Thus, three messages per lock is a good estimate of the cost of the centralized lock method.   □

Now, consider a situation more flexible than central locking, where there is no replication, but each database element X can maintain its locks at its own site. It might seem that, since a transaction wanting to lock X will have a component at the site of X, there are no messages between sites needed. The local component simply negotiates with the lock manager at that site for the lock on X. However, if the distributed transaction needs locks on several elements, say X, Y, and Z, then the transaction cannot complete its computation until it has locks on all three elements. If X, Y, and Z are at different sites, then the components of the transactions at those sites must at least exchange synchronization messages to prevent the transaction from proceeding before it has all the locks it needs.

Rather than deal with all the possible variations, we shall take a simple model of how transactions gather locks. We assume that one component of each transaction, the *lock coordinator* for that transaction, has the responsibility to gather all the locks that all components of the transaction require. The lock coordinator locks elements at its own site without messages, but locking an element X at any other site requires three messages:

1. A message to the site of X requesting the lock.

2. A reply message granting the lock (recall we assume all locks are granted immediately; if not, a denial message followed by a granting message later will be sent).

3. A message to the site of X releasing the lock.

If we pick as the lock coordinator the site where the most locks are needed by the transaction, then we minimize the requirement for messages. The number of messages required is three times the number of database elements at the other sites.

20.6.3 Locking Replicated Elements

When an element X has replicas at several sites, we must be careful how we interpret the locking of X.

Example 20.17 : Suppose there are two copies, X_1 and X_2, of a database element X. Suppose also that a transaction T gets a shared lock on the copy X_1 at the site of that copy, while transaction U gets an exclusive lock on the copy X_2 at its site. Now, U can change X_2 but cannot change X_1, resulting in the two copies of the element X becoming different. Moreover, since T and U may lock other elements as well, and the order in which they read and write X is not forced by the locks they hold on the copies of X, there is also an opportunity for T and U to engage in unserializable behavior.   □

The problem illustrated by Example 20.17 is that when data is replicated, we must distinguish between getting a shared or exclusive lock on the logical element X and getting a local lock on a copy of X. That is, in order to assure serializability, we need for transactions to take global locks on the logical elements. But the logical elements don't exist physically — only their copies do — and there is no global lock table. Thus, the only way that a transaction can obtain a global lock on X is to obtain local locks on one or more copies of X at the site(s) of those copies. We shall now consider methods for turning local locks into global locks that have the required property:

- A logical element X can have either one exclusive lock and no shared lock, or any number of shared locks and no exclusive locks.

20.6.4 Primary-Copy Locking

An improvement on the centralized locking approach, one which also allows replicated data, is to distribute the function of the lock site, but still maintain the principle that each logical element has a single site responsible for its global lock. This distributed-lock method, called *primary copy*, avoids the possibility that the central lock site will become a bottleneck, while still maintaining the simplicity of the centralized method.

In the primary copy lock method, each logical element X has one of its copies designated the "primary copy." In order to get a lock on logical element X, a transaction sends a request to the site of the primary copy of X. The site of the primary copy maintains an entry for X in its lock table and grants or denies the request as appropriate. Again, global (logical) locks will be administered correctly as long as each site administers the locks for the primary copies correctly.

Also as with a centralized lock site, most lock requests require three messages, except for those where the transaction and the primary copy are at the same site. However, if we choose primary copies wisely, then we expect that these sites will frequently be the same.

Example 20.18 : In the chain-of-stores example, we should make each store's sales data have its primary copy at the store. Other copies of this data, such as at the central office or at a data warehouse used by sales analysts, are not primary copies. Probably, the typical transaction is executed at a store and updates only sales data for that store. No messages are needed when this type of transaction takes its locks. Only if the transaction examined or modified data at another store would lock-related messages be sent. □

20.6.5 Global Locks From Local Locks

Another approach is to synthesize global locks from collections of local locks. In these schemes, no copy of a database element X is "primary"; rather they are symmetric, and local shared or exclusive locks can be requested on any of these

Distributed Deadlocks

There are many opportunities for transactions to get deadlocked as they try to acquire global locks on replicated data. There are also many ways to construct a global waits-for graph and thus detect deadlocks. However, in a distributed environment, it is often simplest and also most effective to use a timeout. Any transaction that has not completed after an appropriate amount of time is assumed to have gotten deadlocked and is rolled back.

copies. The key to a successful global locking scheme is to require transactions to obtain a certain number of local locks on copies of X before the transaction can assume it has a global lock on X.

Suppose database element A has n copies. We pick two numbers:

1. s is the number of copies of A that must be locked in shared mode in order for a transaction to have a global shared lock on A.

2. x is the number of copies of A that must be locked in exclusive mode in order for a transaction to have an exclusive lock on A.

As long as $2x > n$ and $s + x > n$, we have the desired properties: there can be only one global exclusive lock on A, and there cannot be both a global shared and global exclusive lock on A. The explanation is as follows. Since $2x > n$, if two transactions had global exclusive locks on A, there would be at least one copy that had granted local exclusive locks to both (because there are more local exclusive locks granted than there are copies of A). However, then the local locking method would be incorrect. Similarly, since $s + x > n$, if one transaction had a global shared lock on A and another had a global exclusive lock on A, then some copy granted both local shared and exclusive locks at the same time.

In general, the number of messages needed to obtain a global shared lock is $3s$, and the number to obtain a global exclusive lock is $3x$. That number seems excessive, compared with centralized methods that require 3 or fewer messages per lock on the average. However, there are compensating arguments, as the following two examples of specific (s, x) choices shows.

Read-Locks-One; Write-Locks-All

Here, $s = 1$ and $x = n$. Obtaining a global exclusive lock is very expensive, but a global shared lock requires three messages at the most. Moreover, this scheme has an advantage over the primary-copy method: while the latter allows us to avoid messages when we read the primary copy, the read-locks-one scheme allows us to avoid messages whenever the transaction is at the site of *any copy* of the database element we desire to read. Thus, this scheme can be superior when most transactions are read-only, but transactions to read an element X initiate at different sites. An example would be a distributed digital library that caches copies of documents where they are most frequently read.

Majority Locking

Here, $s = x = \lceil (n+1)/2 \rceil$. It seems that this system requires many messages no matter where the transaction is. However, there are several other factors that may make this scheme acceptable. First, many network systems support *broadcast*, where it is possible for a transaction to send out one general request for local locks on an element X, which will be received by all sites. Similarly, the release of locks may be achieved by a single message.

Moreover, this selection of s and x provides an advantage others do not: it allows partial operation even when the network is disconnected. As long as there is one component of the network that contains a majority of the sites with copies of X, then it is possible for a transaction to obtain a lock on X. Even if other sites are active while disconnected, we know that they cannot even get a shared lock on X, and thus there is no risk that transactions running in different components of the network will engage in behavior that is not serializable.

20.6.6 Exercises for Section 20.6

! **Exercise 20.6.1:** We showed how to create global shared and exclusive locks from local locks of that type. How would you create:

a) Global shared, exclusive, and update locks

b) Global shared, exclusive, and increment locks

!! c) Global shared, exclusive, and intention locks for each type

from local locks of the same types?

Exercise 20.6.2: Suppose there are five sites, each with a copy of a database element X. One of these sites P is the dominant site for X and will be used as X's primary site in a primary-copy distributed-lock system. The statistics regarding accesses to X are:

i. 50% of all accesses are read-only accesses originating at P.

ii. Each of the other four sites originates 10% of the accesses, and these are read-only.

iii. The remaining 10% of accesses require exclusive access and may originate at any of the five sites with equal probability (i.e., 2% originate at each).

For each of the lock methods below, give the average number of messages needed to obtain a lock. Assume that all requests are granted, so no denial messages are needed.

Grid Computing

Grid computing is a term that means almost the same as peer-to-peer computing. However, the applications of grids usually involve sharing of computing resources rather than data, and there is often a master node that controls what the others do. Popular examples include SETI, which attempts to distribute the analysis of signals for signs of extraterrestrial intelligence among participating nodes, and Folding-at-Home, which attempts to do the same for protein-folding.

---

a) Primary-copy locking, with the primary copy at P.

b) Read-locks-one; write-locks-all.

c) Majority locking.

20.7   Peer-to-Peer Distributed Search

In this section, we examine peer-to-peer distributed systems. When these systems are used to store and deliver data, the problem of search becomes surprisingly hard. That is, each node in the peer-to-peer network has a subset of the data elements, but there is no centralized index that says where something is located. The method called "distributed hashing" allows peer-to-peer networks to grow and shrink, yet allows us to find available data much more efficiently than sending messages to every node.

20.7.1   Peer-to-Peer Networks

A *peer-to-peer* network is a collection of *nodes* or *peers* (participating machines) that:

1. Are *autonomous*: participants do not respect any central control and can join or leave the network at will.

2. Are *loosely coupled*; they communicate over a general-purpose network such as the Internet, rather than being hard-wired together like the processors in a parallel machine.

3. Are equal in functionality; there is no leader or controlling node.

4. Share resources with one another.

Peer-to-peer networks initially received a bad name, because their first popular use was in sharing copyrighted files such as music. However, they have

---

Copyright Issues in Digital Libraries

In order for a distributed world-wide digital library to become a reality, there will have to be some resolution of the severe copyright issues that arise. Current, small-scale versions of this network have partial solutions. For example, on-line university libraries often pass accesses to the ACM digital library only from IP addresses in the university's domain. Other arrangements are based on the idea that only one user at a time can access a particular copyrighted document. The digital library can "loan" the right to another library, but then users of the first library cannot access the document. The world awaits a solution that is easily implementable and fair to all interests.

---

many legitimate uses. For example, as libraries replace books by digital images, it becomes feasible for all the world's libraries to share what they have. It should not be necessary for each library to store a copy of every book or document in the world. But then, when you request a book from your local library, that library's node needs to find a peer library that does have a copy of what you want.

As another example, we might imagine a peer-to-peer network for the sharing of personal collections of photographs or videos, that is, a peer-to-peer version of Flickr or YouTube. The images are housed on participants' personal computers, so they will be turned on and off periodically. There can be millions of participants, and each has only a small fraction of the resources of the entire network.

20.7.2 The Distributed-Hashing Problem

Early peer-to-peer networks such as Napster used a centralized table that told where data elements could be found. Later systems distributed the function of locating elements, either by replication or division of the task among the peers. When the database is truly large, such as a shared worldwide library or photo-sharing network, there is no choice but to share the task in some way.

We shall abstract the problem to one of lookup of records in a (very large) set of key-value pairs. Associated with each key K is a value V. For example, K might be the identifier of a document. V could be the document itself, or it could be the set of nodes at which the document can be found.

If the size of the key-value data is small, there are several simple solutions. We could use a central node that holds the entire key-value table. All nodes would query the central node when they wanted the value V associated with a given key K. In that case, a pair of query-response messages would answer any lookup question for any node. Alternatively, we could replicate the entire table at each node, so there would be no messages needed at all.

The problem becomes more interesting when the key-value table is too large to be handled by a single node. We shall consider this problem, using the following constraints:

1. At any time, only one node among the peers knows the value associated with any given key K.

2. The key-value pairs are distributed roughly equally among the peers.

3. Any node can ask the peers for the value V associated with a chosen key K. The value of V should be obtained in a way such that the number of messages sent among the peers grows much more slowly than the number of peers.

4. The amount of routing information needed at each node to help locate keys must also grow much more slowly than the number of nodes.

20.7.3 Centralized Solutions for Distributed Hashing

If the set of participants in the network is fixed once and for all, or the set of participants changes slowly, then there are straightforward ways to manage lookup of keys. For example, we could use a hash function h that hashes keys into node numbers. We place the key-value pair (K, V) at the node $h(K)$.

In fact, Google and similar search engines effectively maintain a centralized index of the entire Web and manage huge numbers of requests. They do so by behaving logically as if there were a centralized index, when in fact the index is replicated at a very large number of nodes. Each node consists of many machines that together share the index of the Web.

However, machines at Google are not really "peers." They cannot decide to leave the network, and they each have a specific function to perform. While machines can fail, their load is simply assumed by a node of similar machines until the failed machine is replaced. In the balance of this section, we shall consider the more complex solution that is needed when the data is maintained by a true collection of peer nodes.

20.7.4 Chord Circles

We shall now describe one of several possible algorithms for distributed hashing, an algorithm with the desirable property that it uses a number of messages that is logarithmic in the number of peers. In addition, the amount of information other than key-value peers needed at each node grows logarithmically in the number of nodes.

In this algorithm, we arrange the peers in a "chord circle." Each node knows its predecessor and successor around the circle, and nodes also have links to nodes located at an exponentially growing set of distances around the circle (these links are the "chords"). Figure 20.14 suggests what the chord circle looks like.

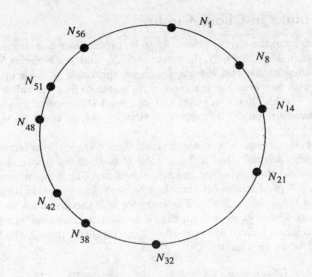

Figure 20.14: A chord circle

To place a node in the circle, we hash its ID i, and place it at position $h(i)$. We shall henceforth refer to this node as $N_{h(i)}$. Thus, for example, in Fig. 20.14, N_{21} is a node whose ID i has $h(i) = 21$. The successor of each node is the next higher one clockwise around the circle. For example, the successor of N_{21} is N_{32}, and N_1 is the successor of N_{56}. Likewise, N_{21} is the predecessor of N_{32}, and N_{56} is the predecessor of N_1.

The nodes are located around the circle using a hash function h that is capable of mapping both keys and node ID's (e.g., IP-addresses) to m-bit numbers, for some m. In Fig. 20.14, we suppose that $m = 6$, so there are 64 different possible locations for nodes around the circle. In a real application, m would be much larger.

Key-value pairs are also distributed around the circle using the hash function h. If (K, V) is a key-value pair, then we compute $h(K)$ and place (K, V) at the lowest numbered node N_j such that $h(K) \leq j$. As a special case, if $h(K)$ is above the highest-numbered node, then it is assigned to the lowest-numbered node. That is, key K goes to the first node at or clockwise of the position $h(K)$ in the circle.

Example 20.19: In Fig. 20.14, any (K, V) pair such that $42 < h(K) \leq 48$ would be stored at N_{48}. If $h(K)$ is any of $57, 58, \ldots, 63, 0, 1$, then (K, V) would be placed at N_1. $\square$

20.7.5   Links in Chord Circles

Each node around the circle stores links to its predecessor and successor. Thus, for example, in Fig. 20.14, N_1 has successor N_8 and predecessor N_{56}. These links are sufficient to send messages around the circle to look up the value associated with any key. For instance, if N_8 wants to find the value associated with a key K such that $h(K) = 54$, it can send the request forward around the circle until a node N_j is found such that $j \geq 54$; it would be node N_{56} in Fig. 20.14.

However, linear search is much too inefficient if the circle is large. To speed up the search, each node has a *finger table* that gives the first nodes found at distances around the circle that are a power of two. That is, suppose that the hash function h produces m-bit numbers. Node N_i has entries in its finger table for distances $1, 2, 4, 8, \ldots, 2^{m-1}$. The entry for 2^j is the first node we meet after going distance 2^j clockwise around the circle. Notice that some entries may be the same node, and there are only $m - 1$ entries, even though the number of nodes could be as high as 2^m.

Distance	1	2	4	8	16	32
Node	N_{14}	N_{14}	N_{14}	N_{21}	N_{32}	N_{42}

Figure 20.15: Finger table for N_8

Example 20.20: Referring to Fig. 20.14, let us construct the finger table for N_8; this table is shown in Fig. 20.15. For distance 1, we ask what is the lowest numbered node whose number is at least $8 + 1 = 9$. That node is N_{14}, since there are no nodes numbered $9, 10, \ldots, 13$. For distance 2, we ask for the lowest node that is at least $8 + 2 = 10$; the answer is N_{14} again. Likewise, for distance 4, N_{14} is is lowest-numbered node that is at least $8 + 4 = 12$.

For distance 8, we look for the lowest-numbered node that is at least $8 + 8 = 16$. Now, N_{14} is too low. The lowest-numbered node that is at least 16 is N_{21}, so that is the entry in the finger table for 8. For 16, we need a node numbered at least 24, so the entry for 16 is N_{32}. For 32, we need a node numbered at least 40, and the proper entry is N_{42}. Figure 20.16 shows the four links that are in the finger table for N_8. □

20.7.6   Search Using Finger Tables

Suppose we are at node N_i and we want to find the key-value pair (K, V) where $h(K) = j$. We know that (K, V), if it exists, will be at the lowest-numbered node that is at least j.[6] We can use the finger table and knowledge of successors

---

[6] As always, "lowest" must be taken in the circular sense, as the first node you meet traveling clockwise around the circle, after reaching the point j.

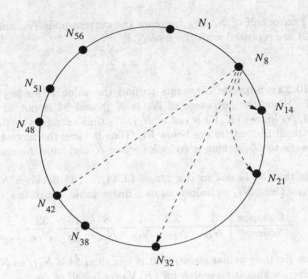

Figure 20.16: Links in the finger table for N_8

to find (K, V), if it exists, using at most $m+1$ messages, where m is the number of bits in the hash values produced by hash function h. Note that messages do not have to follow the entries of the finger table, which is needed only to help each node find out what other nodes exist.

Algorithm 20.21: Lookup in a Chord Circle.

INPUT: An initial request by a node N_i for the value associated with key value K, where $h(K) = j$.

OUTPUT: A sequence of messages sent by various nodes, resulting in a message to N_i with either the value of V in the key-value pair (K, V), or a statement that such a pair does not exist.

METHOD: The steps of the algorithm are actually executed by different nodes. At any time, activity is at some "current" node N_c, and initially N_c is N_i. Steps (1) and (2) below are done repeatedly. Note that N_i is a part of each request message, so the current node always knows that N_i is the node to which the answer must be sent.

1. End the search if $c < j \le s$, where N_s is the successor of N_c, around the circle. Then, N_c sends a message to N_s asking for (K, V) and informing N_s that the originator of the request is N_i. N_s will send a message to N_i with either the value V or a statement that (K, V) does not exist.

2. Otherwise, N_c consults its finger table to find the highest-numbered node N_h that is less than j. N_c sends N_h a message asking it to search for

(K, V) on behalf of N_i. N_h becomes the current node N_c, and steps (1) and (2) are repeated with the new N_c.

□

Example 20.22: Suppose N_8 wants to find the value V for key K, where $h(K) = 54$. Since the successor of N_8 is N_{14}, and 54 is not in the range $9, 10, \ldots, 14$, N_8 knows (K, V) is not at N_{14}. N_8 thus examines its finger table, and finds that all the entries are below 54. Thus it takes the largest, N_{42}, and sends a message to N_{42} asking it to look for key K and have the result sent to N_8.

N_{42} finds that 54 is not in the range $43, 44, \ldots, 48$ between N_{42} and its successor N_{48}. Thus, N_{42} examines its own finger table, which is:

Distance	1	2	4	8	16	32
Node	N_{48}	N_{48}	N_{48}	N_{51}	N_1	N_{14}

The last node (in the circular sense) that is less than 54 is N_{51}, so N_{42} sends a message to N_{51}, asking it to search for (K, V) on behalf of N_8.

N_{51} finds that 54 is no greater than its successor, N_{56}. Thus, if (K, V) exists, it is at N_{56}. N_{51} sends a request to N_{56}, which replies to N_8. The sequence of messages is shown in Fig. 20.17. □

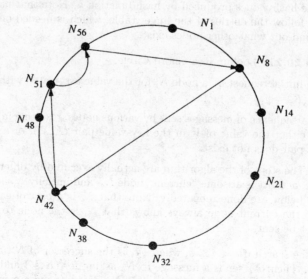

Figure 20.17: Message sequence in the search for (K, V)

In general, this recursive algorithm sends no more than m request messages. The reason is that whenever a node N_c has to consult its finger table, it messages

---

Dealing with Hash Collisions

Occasionally, when we insert a node, the hash value of its ID will be the same as that of some node already in the circle. The actual position of a particular node doesn't matter, as long as it knows its position and acts as if that position was the hash value of its ID. Thus, we can adjust the position of the new node up or down, until we find a position around the circle that is unoccupied.

---

a node that is no more than half the distance (measured clockwise around the circle) from the node holding (K, V) as N_c is. One response message is sent in all cases.

20.7.7 Adding New Nodes

Suppose a new node N_i (i.e., a node whose ID hashes to i) wants to join the network of peers. If N_i does not know how to communicate with any peer, it is not possible for N_i to join. However, if N_i knows even one peer, N_i can ask that peer what node would be N_i's successor around the circle. To answer, the known peer performs Algorithm 20.21 as if it were looking for a key that hashed to i. The node at which this hypothetical key would reside is the successor of N_i. Suppose that the successor of N_i is N_j.

We need to do two things:

1. Change predecessor and successor links, so N_i is properly linked into the circle.

2. Rearrange data so N_i gets all the data at N_j that belongs to N_i, that is, key-value pairs whose key hashes to something i or less.

We could link N into the circle at once, although it is difficult to do so correctly, because of concurrency problems. That is, several nodes whose successor would be N_j may be adding themselves at once. To avoid concurrency problems, we proceed in two steps. The first step is to set the successor of N to N_j and its predecessor to nil. N has no data at this time, and it has an empty finger table.

Example 20.23: Suppose we add to the circle of Fig. 20.14 a node N_{26}, i.e., a node whose ID hashes to 26. Whatever peer N_{26} contacted will be told that N_{26}'s successor is N_{32}. N_{26} sets its successor to N_{32} and its predecessor to nil. The predecessor of N_{32} remains N_{21} for the moment. The situation is suggested by Fig. 20.18. There, solid lines are successor links and dashed lines are predecessor links. □

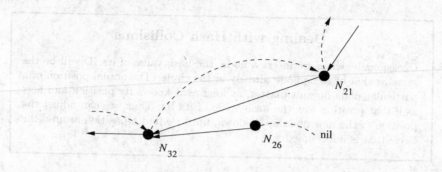

Figure 20.18: Adding node N_{26} to the network of peers

The second step is done automatically by all nodes, and is not a direct response to the insertion of N_i. All nodes must periodically perform a *stabilization* check, during which time predecessors and successors are updated, and if necessary, data is shared between a new node and its successor. Surely, N_{26} in Fig. 20.18 will have to perform a stabilization to get N_{32} to accept N_{26} as its predecessor, but N_{21} also needs to perform a stabilization in order to realize that N_{26} is its new successor. Note that N_{21} has not been informed of the existence of N_{26}, and will not be informed until N_{21} discovers this fact for itself during its own stabilization. The stabilization process at any node N is as follows.

1. Let S be the successor of N. N sends a message to S asking for P, the predecessor of S, and S replies. In normal cases, $P = N$, and if so, skip to step (4).

2. If P lies strictly between N and S, then N records that P is its successor.

3. Let S' be the current successor of N; S' could be either S or P, depending on what step (2) decided. If the predecessor of S' is nil or N lies strictly between S' and its predecessor, then N sends a message to S' telling S' that N is the predecessor of S'. S' sets its predecessor to N.

4. S' shares its data with N. That is, all (K, V) pairs at S' such that $h(K) \leq N$ are moved to N.

Example 20.24 : Following the events of Example 20.23, with the predecessor and successor links in the state of Fig. 20.18, node N_{26} will perform a stabilization. For this stabilization, $N = N_{26}$, $S = N_{32}$, and $P = N_{21}$. Since P does not lie between N and S, step (2) makes no change, so $S' = S = N_{32}$ at step (3). Since $N = N_{26}$ lies strictly between $S' = N_{32}$ and its predecessor N_{21}, we make N_{26} the predecessor of N_{32}. The state of the links is shown in Fig. 20.19. At step (4), all key-value pairs whose keys hash to 22 through 26 are moved from N_{32} to N_{26}.

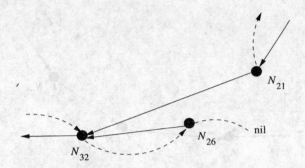

Figure 20.19: After making N_{26} the predecessor of N_{32}

The circle has still not stabilized, since N_{21} and many other nodes do not know about N_{26}. Searches for keys in the 22–26 range will still wind up at N_{32}. However, N_{32} knows that it no longer has keys in this range. N_{32}, which is N_c in Algorithm 20.21, simply continues the search according to this algorithm, which in effect causes the search to go around the circle again, possibly several times.

Eventually, N_{21} runs the stabilization operation, which it, like all nodes, does periodically. Now, $N = N_{21}$, $S = N_{32}$, and $P = N_{26}$. The test of step (2) is satisfied, so N_{26} becomes the successor of N_{21}. At step (3), $S' = N_{26}$. Since the predecessor of N_{26} is nil, we make N_{21} the predecessor of N_{26}. No data is shared at step (4), since all data at N_{26} belongs there. The final state of the predecessor and successor links is shown in Fig. 20.20.

At this time, the search for a key in the range 22–26 will reach N_{26} and be answered properly. It is possible, under rare circumstances, that insertion of many new nodes will keep the network from becoming completely stable for a long time. In that case, the search for a key in the range 22–26 could continue running until the network finally does stabilize. However, as soon as the network does stablize, the search comes to an end. □

There is still more to do, however. In terms of the running example, the finger table for N_{26} needs to be constructed, and other finger tables may now be wrong because they will link to N_{32} in some cases when they should link to N_{26}. Thus, it is necessary that every node N periodically checks its finger table. For each $i = 1, 2, 4, 8, \ldots$, node N must execute Algorithm 20.21 with $j = N + i \mod 2^m$. When it gets back the node at which the network thinks such a key would be located, N sets its finger-table entry for distance i to that value.

Notice that a new node, such as N_{26} in our running example, can construct its initial finger table this way, since the construction of any entry requires only entries that have already been constructed. That is, the entry for distance 1 is always the successor. For distance $2i$, either the successor is the correct entry, or we can find the correct entry by calling upon whatever node is the finger-table

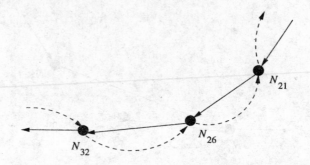

Figure 20.20: After N_{21} runs the stabilization algorithm

entry for distance i.

20.7.8 When a Peer Leaves the Network

A central tenet of peer-to-peer systems is that a node cannot be compelled to participate. Thus, a node can leave the circle at any time. The simple case is when a node leaves "gracefully," that is, cooperating with other nodes to keep the data available. To leave gracefully, a node:

1. Notifies its predecessor and successor that it is leaving, so they can become each other's predecessor and successor.

2. Transfers its data to its successor.

The network is still in a state that has errors; in particular the node that left may still appear in the finger tables of some nodes. These nodes will discover the error, either when they periodically update their finger tables, as discussed in Section 20.7.7, or when they try to communicate with the node that has disappeared. In the latter case, they can recompute the erroneous finger-table entry exactly as they would during periodic update.

20.7.9 When a Peer Fails

A harder problem occurs when a node fails, is turned off, or decides to leave without doing the "graceful" steps of Section 20.7.8. If the data is not replicated, then data at the failed node is now unavailable to the network. To avoid total unavailability of data, we can replicate it at several nodes. For example, we can place each (K, V) pair at three nodes: the correct node, its predecessor in the circle, and its successor.

To reestablish the circle when a node leaves, we can have each node record not only its predecessor and successor, but the predecessor of its predecessor and the successor of its successor. An alternative approach is to cluster nodes into groups of (say) three or more. Nodes in a cluster replicate their data and can substitute for one another, if one leaves or fails. When clusters get too large, they can be split into two clusters that are adjacent on the circle, using an algorithm similar to that described in Section 20.7.7 for node insertion. Similarly, clusters that get too small can be combined with a neighbor, a process similar to graceful leaving as in Section 20.7.8. Insertion of a new node is executed by having the node join its nearest cluster.

20.7.10 Exercises for Section 20.7

Exercise 20.7.1 : Given the circle of nodes of Fig. 20.14, where do key-value pairs reside if the key hashes to: (a) 35 (b) 20 (c) 60?

Exercise 20.7.2 : Given the circle of nodes of Fig. 20.14, construct the finger tables for: (a) N_{14} (b) N_{51}

Exercise 20.7.3 : Given the circle of nodes of Fig. 20.14, what is the sequence of messages sent if:

a) N_{14} searches for a key that hashes to 27.

b) N_8 searches for a key that hashes to 5.

c) N_{56} searches for a key that hashes to 54.

Exercise 20.7.4 : Show the sequence of steps that adjust successor and predecessor pointers and share data, for the circle of Fig. 20.14 when nodes are added that hash to: (a) 16 (b) 45.

! **Exercise 20.7.5 :** Suppose we want to guard against node failures by having each node maintain the predecessor information, successor information, and data of its predecessor and successor, as well as its own, as discussed in Section 20.7.9. How would you modify the node-insertion algorithm described in Section 20.7.7?

20.8 Summary of Chapter 20

✦ *Parallel Machines*: Parallel machines can be characterized as shared-memory, shared-disk, or shared-nothing. For database applications, the shared-nothing architecture is generally the most cost-effective.

✦ *Parallel Algorithms*: The operations of relational algebra can generally be sped up on a parallel machine by a factor close to the number of processors. The preferred algorithms start by hashing the data to buckets that correspond to the processors, and shipping data to the appropriate processor. Each processor then performs the operation on its local data.

✦ *The Map-Reduce Framework*: Often, highly parallel algorithms on massive files can be expressed by a map function and a reduce function. Many *map* processes execute on parts of the file in parallel, to produce key-value pairs. These pairs are then distributed so each key's pairs can be handled by one *reduce* process.

✦ *Distributed Data*: In a distributed database, data may be partitioned horizontally (one relation has its tuples spread over several sites) or vertically (a relation's schema is decomposed into several schemas whose relations are at different sites). It is also possible to replicate data, so presumably identical copies of a relation exist at several sites.

✦ *Distributed Joins*: In an environment with expensive communication, semijoins can speed up the join of two relations that are located at different sites. We project one relation onto the join attributes, send it to the other site, and return only the tuples of the second relation that are not dangling tuples.

✦ *Full Reducers*: When joining more than two relations at different sites, it may or may not be possible to eliminate all dangling tuples by performing semijoins. A finite sequence of semijoins that is guaranteed to eliminate all dangling tuples, no matter how large the relations are, is called a full reducer.

✦ *Hypergraphs*: A natural join of several relations can be represented by a hypergraph, which has a node for each attribute name and a hyperedge for each relation, which contains the nodes for all the attributes of that relation.

✦ *Acyclic Hypergraphs*: These are the hypergraphs that can be reduced to a single hyperedge by a series of ear-reductions — elimination of hyperedges all of whose nodes are either in no other hyperedge, or in one particular other hyperedge. Full reducers exist for all and only the hypergraphs that are acyclic.

✦ *Distributed Transactions*: In a distributed database, one logical transaction may consist of components, each executing at a different site. To preserve consistency, these components must all agree on whether to commit or abort the logical transaction.

✦ *Two-Phase Commit*: This algorithm enables transaction components to decide whether to commit or abort, often allowing a resolution even in the face of a system crash. In the first phase, a coordinator component polls the components whether they want to commit or abort. In the second phase, the coordinator tells the components to commit if and only if all have expressed a willingness to commit.

✦ *Distributed Locks*: If transactions must lock database elements found at several sites, a method must be found to coordinate these locks. In the centralized-site method, one site maintains locks on all elements. In the primary-copy method, the home site for an element maintains its locks.

✦ *Locking Replicated Data*: When database elements are replicated at several sites, global locks on an element must be obtained through locks on one or more replicas. The majority locking method requires a read- or write-lock on a majority of the replicas to obtain a global lock. Alternatively, we may allow a global read lock by obtaining a read lock on any copy, while allowing a global write lock only through write locks on every copy.

✦ *Peer-to-Peer Networks*: These networks consist of independent, autonomous nodes that all play the same role in the network. Such networks are generally used to share data among the peer nodes.

✦ *Distributed Hashing*: Distributed hashing is a central database problem in peer-to-peer networks. We are given a set of key-value pairs to distribute among the peers, and we must find the value associated with a given key without sending messages to all, or a large fraction of the peers, and without relying on any one peer that has all the key-value pairs.

✦ *Chord Circles*: A solution to the distributed hashing problem begins by using a hash function that hashes both node ID's and keys into the same m-bit values, which we perceive as forming a circle with 2^m positions. Keys are placed at the node at the position immediately clockwise of the position to which the key hashes. By use of a finger-table, which gives the nodes at distances $1, 2, 4, 8, \ldots$ around the circle from a given node, key lookup can be accomplished in time that is logarithmic in the number of nodes.

20.9 References for Chapter 20

The use of hashing in parallel join and other operations has been proposed several times. The earliest source we know of is [8]. The map-reduce framework for parallelism was expressed in [2]. There is an open-souce implementation available [6].

The relationship between full reducers and acyclic hypergraphs is from [1]. The test for whether a hypergraph is acyclic was discovered by [5] and [13].

The two-phase commit protocol was proposed in [7]. A more powerful scheme (not covered here) called three-phase commit is from [9]. The leader-election aspect of recovery was examined in [4].

Distributed locking methods have been proposed by [3] (the centralized locking method) [11] (primary-copy) and [12] (global locks from locks on copies). The chord algorithm for distributed hashing is from [10].

1. P. A. Bernstein and N. Goodman, "The power of natural semijoins," *SIAM J. Computing* **10**:4 (1981), pp. 751–771.

2. J. Dean and S. Ghemawat, "MapReduce: simplified processing on large clusters," *Sixth Symp. on Operating System Design and Implementation*, 2004.

3. H. Garcia-Molina, "Performance comparison of update algorithms for distributed databases," TR Nos. 143 and 146, Computer Systems Laboratory, Stanford Univ., 1979.

4. H. Garcia-Molina, "Elections in a distributed computer system," *IEEE Trans. on Computers* **C-31**:1 (1982), pp. 48–59.

5. M. H. Graham, "On the universal relation," Technical report, Dept. of CS, Univ. of Toronto, 1979.

6. Hadoop home page `lucene.apache.org/hadoop`.

7. B. Lampson and H. Sturgis, "Crash recovery in a distributed data storage system," Technical report, Xerox Palo Alto Research Center, 1976.

8. D. E. Shaw, "Knowledge-based retrieval on a relational database machine," Ph. D. thesis, Dept. of CS, Stanford Univ. (1980).

9. D. Skeen, "Nonblocking commit protocols," *Proc. ACM SIGMOD Intl. Conf. on Management of Data* (1981), pp. 133–142.

10. I. Stoica, R. Morris, D. Karger, M. Kaashoek, and H. Balakrishnan, "Chord: A scalabale peer-to-peer lookup service for Internet applications," *Proc. ACM SIGCOMM* (2001) pp. 149–160.

11. M. Stonebraker, "Retrospection on a database system," *ACM Trans. on Database Systems* **5**:2 (1980), pp. 225–240.

12. R. H. Thomas, "A majority consensus approach to concurrency control," *ACM Trans. on Database Systems* **4**:2 (1979), pp. 180–219.

13. C. T. Yu and M. Z. Ozsoyoglu, "An algorithm for tree-query membership of a distributed query," *Proc. IEEE COMPSAC* (1979), pp. 306–312.

Part V

Other Issues in Management of Massive Data

Chapter 21

Information Integration

Information integration is the process of taking several databases or other information sources and making the data in these sources work together as if they were a single database. The integrated database may be physical (a "warehouse") or virtual (a "mediator" or "middleware" that may be queried even though its does not exist physically). The sources may be conventional databases or other types of information, such as collections of Web pages.

We begin by exploring the ways in which seemingly similar databases can actually embody conflicts that are hard to resolve correctly. The solution lies in the design of "wrappers" — translators between the schema and data values at a source and the schema and data values at the integrated database.

Information-integration systems require special kinds of query-optimization techniques for their efficient operation. Mediator systems can be divided into two classes: "global-as-view" (the data at the integrated database is defined by how it is constructed from the sources) and "local-as-view" (the content of the sources is defined in terms of the schema that the integrated database supports). We examine capability-based optimization for global-as-view mediators. We also consider local-as-view mediation, which requires effort even to figure out how to compose the answer to a query from defined views, but which offers advantages in flexibility of operation.

In the last section, we examine another important issue in information integration, called "entity resolution." Different information sources may talk about the same entities (e.g., people) but contain discrepancies such as misspelled names or out-of-date addresses. We need to make a best estimate of which data elements at the different sources actually refer to the same entity.

21.1 Introduction to Information Integration

In this section, we discuss the ways in which information-integration is essential for many database applications. We then sample some of the problems that make information integration difficult.

21.1.1   Why Information Integration?

If we could start anew with an architecture and schema for all the data in the world, and we could put that data in a single database, there would be no need for information integration. However, in the real world, matters are rather different.

- Databases are created independently, even if they later need to work together.

- The use of databases evolves, so we cannot design a database to support every possible future use.

To see the need for information integration, we shall consider two typical scenarios: building applications for a university and integrating employee databases. In both scenarios, a key problem is that the overall data-management system must make use of *legacy* data sources — databases that were created independently of any other data source. Each legacy source is used by applications that expect the structure of "their" database not to change, so modification of the schema or data of legacy sources is not an option.

University Databases

As databases came into common use, each university started using them for several functions that were once done by hand. Here is a typical scenario. The Registrar builds a database of courses, and uses it to record the courses each student took and their grades. Applications are built using this database, such as a transcript generator.

The Bursar builds another database for recording tuition payments by students. The Human Resources Department builds a database for recording employees, including those students with teaching-assistant or research-assistant jobs. Applications include generation of payroll checks, calculation of taxes and social-security payments to the government, and many others. The Grants Office builds a database to keep track of expenditures on grants, which includes salaries to certain faculty, students, and staff. It may also include information about biohazards, use of human subjects, and many other matters related to research projects.

Pretty soon, the university realizes that all these databases are not helping nearly as much as they could, and are sometimes getting in the way. For example, suppose we want to make sure that the Registrar does not record grades for students that the Bursar says did not pay tuition. Someone has to get a list of students who paid tuition from the Bursar's database and compare that with a list of students from the Registrar's database. As another example, when Sally is appointed on grant 123 as a research assistant, someone needs to tell the Grants Office that her salary should be charged to grant 123. Someone also needs to tell Human Resources that they should pay her salary. And the salaries in the two databases had better be exactly the same.

So at some point, the university decides that it needs one database for all functions. The first thought might be: start over. Build one database that contains all the information of all the legacy databases and rewrite all the applications to use the new database. This approach has been tried, with great pain resulting. In addition to paying for a very expensive software-architecture task, the university has to run both the old and new systems in parallel for a long time to see that the new system actually works. And when they cut over to the new system, the users find that the applications do not work in the accustomed way, and turmoil results.

A better way is to build a layer of abstraction, called *middleware*, on top of all the legacy databases and allow the legacy databases to continue serving their current applications. The layer of abstraction could be relational views — either virtual or materialized. Then, SQL can be used to "query" the middleware layer. Often, this layer is defined by a collection of classes and queried in an object-oriented language. Or the middleware layer could use XML documents, which are queried using XQuery. We mentioned in Section 9.1 that this middleware may be an important component of the application tier in a 3-tier architecture, although we did not show it explicitly.

Once the middleware layer is built, new applications can be written to access this layer for data, while the legacy applications continue to run using the legacy databases. For example, we can write a new application that enters grades for students only if they have paid their tuition. Another new application could appoint a research assistant by getting their name, grant, and salary from the user. This application would then enter the name and salary into the Human-Resources database and the name, salary, and grant into the Grants-Office database.

Integrating Employee Databases

Compaq bought DEC and Tandem, and then Hewlett-Packard bought Compaq. Each company had a database of employees. Because the companies were previously independent, the schemas and architecture of their databases naturally differed. Moreover, each company actually had many databases about employees, and these databases probably differed on matters as basic as who is an employee. For example, the Payroll Department would not include retirees, but might include contractors. The Benefits Department would include retirees but not contractors. The Safety Office would include not only regular employees and contractors, but the employees of the company that runs the cafeteria.

For reasons we discussed in connection with the university database, it may not be practical to shut down these legacy databases and with them all the applications that run on them. However, it is possible to create a middleware layer that holds — virtually or physically — all information available for each employee.

21.1.2   The Heterogeneity Problem

When we try to connect information sources that were developed independently, we invariably find that the sources differ in many ways, even if they are intended to store the same kinds of data. Such sources are called *heterogeneous*, and the problem of integrating them is referred to as the *heterogeneity problem*. We shall introduce a running example of an automobile database and then discuss examples of the different levels at which heterogeneity can make integration difficult.

Example 21.1 : The Aardvark Automobile Co. has 1000 dealers, each of which maintains a database of their cars in stock. Aardvark wants to create an integrated database containing the information of all 1000 sources.[1] The integrated database will help dealers locate a particular model at another dealer, if they don't have one in stock. It also can be used by corporate analysts to predict the market and adjust production to provide the models most likely to sell.

However, the dealers' databases may differ in a great number of ways. We shall enumerate below the most important ways and give some examples in terms of the Aardvark database.   □

Communication Heterogeneity

Today, it is common to allow access to your information using the HTTP protocol that drives the Web. However, some dealers may not make their databases available on the Web, but instead accept remote accesses via remote procedure calls or anonymous FTP, for instance.

Query-Language Heterogeneity

The manner in which we query or modify a dealer's database may vary. It would be nice if the database accepted SQL queries and modifications, but not all do. Of those that do, each accepts a dialect of SQL — the version supported by the vendor of the dealer's DBMS. Another dealer may not have a relational database at all. They could use an Excel Spreadsheet, or an object-oriented database, or an XML database using XQuery as the language.

Schema Heterogeneity

Even assuming that all the dealers use a relational DBMS supporting SQL as the query language, we can find many sources of heterogeneity. At the highest level, the schemas can differ. For example, one dealer might store cars in a single relation that looks like:

---

[1] Most real automobile companies have similar facilities in place, and the history of their development may be different from our example; e.g., the centralized database may have come first, with dealers later able to download relevant portions to their own database. However, this scenario serves as an example of what companies in many industries are attempting today.

```
Cars(serialNo, model, color, autoTrans, navi,...)
```

with one boolean-valued attribute for every possible option. Another dealer might use a schema in which options are separated out into a second relation, such as:

```
Autos(serial, model, color)
Options(serial, option)
```

Notice that not only is the schema different, but apparently equivalent relation or attribute names have changed: `Cars` becomes `Autos`, and `serialNo` becomes `serial`.

Moreover, one dealer's schema might not record information that most of the other dealers provide. For instance, one dealer might not record colors at all. To deal with missing values, sometimes we can use NULL's or default values. However, because missing schema elements are a common problem, there is a trend toward using semistructured data such as XML as the data model for integrating middleware.

Data type differences

Serial numbers might be represented by character strings of varying length at one source and fixed length at another. The fixed lengths could differ, and some sources might use integers rather than character strings.

Value Heterogeneity

The same concept might be represented by different constants at different sources. The color black might be represented by an integer code at one source, the string BLACK at another, and the code BL at a third. The code BL might stand for "blue" at yet another source.

Semantic Heterogeneity

Terms may be given different interpretations at different sources. One dealer might include trucks in the `Cars` relation, while another puts only automobile data in the `Cars` relation. One dealer might distinguish station wagons from minivans, while another doesn't.

21.2 Modes of Information Integration

There are several ways that databases or other distributed information sources can be made to work together. In this section, we consider the three most common approaches:

1. *Federated databases.* The sources are independent, but one source can call on others to supply information.

2. *Warehousing.* Copies of data from several sources are stored in a single database, called a (*data*) *warehouse.* Possibly, the data stored at the warehouse is first processed in some way before storage; e.g., data may be filtered, and relations may be joined or aggregated. The warehouse is updated periodically, perhaps overnight. As the data is copied from the sources, it may need to be transformed in certain ways to make all data conform to the schema at the warehouse.

3. *Mediation.* A mediator is a software component that supports a *virtual database*, which the user may query as if it were *materialized* (physically constructed, like a warehouse). The mediator stores no data of its own. Rather, it translates the user's query into one or more queries to its sources. The mediator then synthesizes the answer to the user's query from the responses of those sources, and returns the answer to the user.

We shall introduce each of these approaches in turn. One of the key issues for all approaches is the way that data is transformed when it is extracted from an information source. We discuss the architecture of such transformers — called *wrappers*, *adapters*, or *extractors* — in Section 21.3.

21.2.1 Federated Database Systems

Perhaps the simplest architecture for integrating several databases is to implement one-to-one connections between all pairs of databases that need to talk to one another. These connections allow one database system D_1 to query another D_2 in terms that D_2 can understand. The problem with this architecture is that if n databases each need to talk to the $n - 1$ other databases, then we must write $n(n - 1)$ pieces of code to support queries between systems. The situation is suggested in Fig. 21.1. There, we see four databases in a federation. Each of the four needs three components, one to access each of the other three databases.

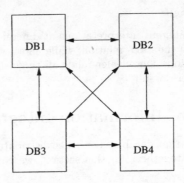

Figure 21.1: A federated collection of four databases needs 12 components to translate queries from one to another

Nevertheless, a federated system may be the easiest to build in some circumstances, especially when the communications between databases are limited in nature. An example will show how the translation components might work.

Example 21.2: Suppose the Aardvark Automobile dealers want to share inventory, but each dealer only needs to query the database of a few local dealers to see if they have a needed car. To be specific, consider Dealer 1, who has a relation

```
NeededCars(model, color, autoTrans)
```

whose tuples represent cars that customers have requested, by model, color, and whether or not they want an automatic transmission ('yes' or 'no' are the possible values). Dealer 2 stores inventory in the two-relation schema discussed in Example 21.1:

```
Autos(serial, model, color)
Options(serial, option)
```

Dealer 1 writes an application program that queries Dealer 2 remotely for cars that match each of the cars described in NeededCars. Figure 21.2 is a sketch of a program with embedded SQL that would find the desired cars. The intent is that the embedded SQL represents remote queries to the Dealer 2 database, with results returned to Dealer 1. We use the convention from standard SQL of prefixing a colon to variables that represent constants retrieved from a database.

These queries address the schema of Dealer 2. If Dealer 1 also wants to ask the same question of Dealer 3, who uses the first schema discussed in Example 21.1, with a single relation

```
Cars(serialNo, model, color, autoTrans,...)
```

the query would look quite different. But each query works properly for the database to which it is addressed. □

21.2.2 Data Warehouses

In the *data warehouse* integration architecture, data from several sources is extracted and combined into a *global* schema. The data is then stored at the warehouse, which looks to the user like an ordinary database. The arrangement is suggested by Fig. 21.3, although there may be many more than the two sources shown.

Once the data is in the warehouse, queries may be issued by the user exactly as they would be issued to any database. There are at least three approaches to constructing the data in the warehouse:

1. The warehouse is periodically closed to queries and reconstructed from the current data in the sources. This approach is the most common, with reconstruction occurring once a night or at even longer intervals.

```
for(each tuple (:m, :c, :a) in NeededCars) {
    if(:a = TRUE) { /* automatic transmission wanted */
        SELECT serial FROM Autos, Options
        WHERE Autos.serial = Options.serial AND
            Options.option = 'autoTrans' AND
            Autos.model = :m AND Autos.color = :c;
    }
    else { /* automatic transmission not wanted */
        SELECT serial
        FROM Autos
        WHERE Autos.model = :m AND Autos.color = :c AND
            NOT EXISTS (
                SELECT * FROM Options
                WHERE serial = Autos.serial AND
                    option = 'autoTrans'
            );
    }
}
```

Figure 21.2: Dealer 1 queries Dealer 2 for needed cars

2. The warehouse is updated periodically (e.g., each night), based on the changes that have been made to the sources since the last time the warehouse was modified. This approach can involve smaller amounts of data, which is very important if the warehouse needs to be modified in a short period of time, and the warehouse is large (multiterabyte warehouses are in common use). The disadvantage is that calculating changes to the warehouse, a process called *incremental update*, is complex, compared with algorithms that simply construct the warehouse from scratch.

Note that either of these approaches allow the warehouse to get out of date. However, it is generally too expensive to reflect immediately, at the warehouse, every change to the underlying databases.

Example 21.3: Suppose for simplicity that there are only two dealers in the Aardvark system, and they respectively use the schemas

```
Cars(serialNo, model, color, autoTrans, navi,...)
```

and

```
Autos(serial, model, color)
Options(serial, option)
```

We wish to create a warehouse with the schema

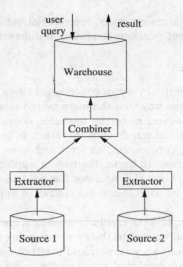

Figure 21.3: A data warehouse stores integrated information in a separate database

```
AutosWhse(serialNo, model, color, autoTrans, dealer)
```

That is, the global schema is like that of the first dealer, but we record only the option of having an automatic transmission, and we include an attribute that tells which dealer has the car.

The software that extracts data from the two dealers' databases and populates the global schema can be written as SQL queries. The query for the first dealer is simple:

```
INSERT INTO AutosWhse(serialNo, model, color,
        autoTrans, dealer)
    SELECT serialNo, model, color, autoTrans, 'dealer1'
    FROM Cars;
```

The extractor for the second dealer is more complex, since we have to decide whether or not a given car has an automatic transmission. We leave this SQL code as an exercise.

In this simple example, the combiner, shown in Fig. 21.3, for the data extracted from the sources is not needed. Since the warehouse is the union of the relations extracted from each source, the data may be loaded directly into the warehouse. However, many warehouses perform operations on the relations that they extract from each source. For instance relations extracted from two sources might be joined, and the result put at the warehouse. Or we might take the union of relations extracted from several sources and then aggregate the data of this union. More generally, several relations may be extracted from each source, and different relations combined in different ways. □

21.2.3 Mediators

A mediator supports a virtual view, or collection of views, that integrates several sources in much the same way that the materialized relation(s) in a warehouse integrate sources. However, since the mediator doesn't store any data, the mechanics of mediators and warehouses are rather different. Figure 21.4 shows a mediator integrating two sources; as for warehouses, there would typically be more than two sources. To begin, the user or application program issues a query to the mediator. Since the mediator has no data of its own, it must get the relevant data from its sources and use that data to form the answer to the user's query.

Thus, we see in Fig. 21.4 the mediator sending a query to each of its wrappers, which in turn send queries to their corresponding sources. The mediator may send several queries to a wrapper, and may not query all wrappers. The results come back and are combined at the mediator; we do not show an explicit combiner component as we did in the warehouse diagram, Fig. 21.3, because in the case of the mediator, the combining of results from the sources is one of the tasks performed by the mediator.

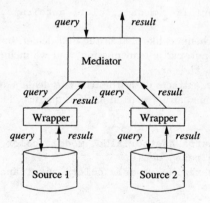

Figure 21.4: A mediator and wrappers translate queries into the terms of the sources and combine the answers

Example 21.4 : Let us consider a scenario similar to that of Example 21.3, but use a mediator. That is, the mediator integrates the same two automobile sources into a view that is a single relation with schema:

    AutosMed(serialNo, model, color, autoTrans, dealer)

Suppose the user asks the mediator about red cars, with the query:

```
SELECT serialNo, model
FROM AutosMed
WHERE color = 'red';
```

The mediator, in response to this user query, can forward the same query to each of the two wrappers. The way that wrappers can be designed and implemented to handle queries like this one is the subject of Section 21.3. In more complex scenarios, the mediator would first have to break the query into pieces, each of which is sent to a subset of the wrappers. However, in this case, the translation work can be done by the wrappers alone.

The wrapper for Dealer 1 translates the query into the terms of that dealer's schema, which we recall is

```
Cars(serialNo, model, color, autoTrans, navi,...)
```

A suitable translation is:

```
SELECT serialNo, model
FROM Cars
WHERE color = 'red';
```

An answer, which is a set of `serialNo-model` pairs, will be returned to the mediator by the first wrapper.

At the same time, the wrapper for Dealer 2 translates the same query into the schema of that dealer, which is:

```
Autos(serial, model, color)
Options(serial, option)
```

A suitable translated query for Dealer 2 is almost the same:

```
SELECT serial, model
FROM Autos
WHERE color = 'red';
```

It differs from the query at Dealer 1 only in the name of the relation queried, and in one attribute. The second wrapper returns to the mediator a set of `serial-model` pairs, which the mediator interprets as `serialNo-model` pairs. The mediator takes the union of these sets and returns the result to the user.
□

There are several options, not illustrated by Example 21.4, that a mediator may use to answer queries. For instance, the mediator may issue one query to one source, look at the result, and based on what is returned, decide on the next query or queries to issue. This method would be appropriate, for instance, if the user query asked whether there were any Aardvark "Gobi" model sport-utility vehicles available in blue. The first query could ask Dealer 1, and only if the result was an empty set of tuples would a query be sent to Dealer 2.

21.2.4 Exercises for Section 21.2

! **Exercise 21.2.1:** Computer company A keeps data about the PC models it sells in the schema:

```
Computers(number, proc, speed, memory, hd)
Monitors(number, screen, maxResX, maxResY)
```

For instance, the tuple $(123, \text{Athlon64}, 3.1, 512, 120)$ in `Computers` means that model 123 has an Athlon 64 processor running at 3.1 gigahertz, with 512M of memory and a 120G hard disk. The tuple $(456, 19, 1600, 1050)$ in `Monitors` means that model 456 has a 19-inch screen with a maximum resolution of 1600×1050.

Computer company B only sells complete systems, consisting of a computer and monitor. Its schema is

```
Systems(id, processor, mem, disk, screenSize)
```

The attribute `processor` is the speed in gigahertz; the type of processor (e.g., Athlon 64) is not recorded. Neither is the maximum resolution of the monitor recorded. Attributes `id`, `mem`, and `disk` are analogous to `number`, `memory`, and `hd` from company A, but the disk size is measured in megabytes instead of gigabytes.

a) If company A wants to insert into its relations information about the corresponding items from B, what SQL insert statements should it use?

b) If Company B wants to insert into `Systems` as much information about the systems that can be built from computers and monitors made by A, what SQL statements best allow this information to be obtained?

! **Exercise 21.2.2:** Suggest a global schema that would allow us to maintain as much information as we could about the products sold by companies A and B of Exercise 21.2.1.

Exercise 21.2.3: Suppose your global schema from Exercise 21.2.2 is used at a mediator. How would the mediator process the query that asks for the maximum amount of hard-disk available with any computer with a 3 gigahertz processor speed?

! **Exercise 21.2.4:** Suggest two other schemas that computer companies might use to hold data like that of Exercise 21.2.1. How would you integrate your schemas into your global schema from Exercise 21.2.2?

Exercise 21.2.5: Write SQL queries to gather the information from the data at companies A and B and put it in a warehouse with your global schema of Exercise 21.2.2.

Exercise 21.2.6: Go to the Web pages of several on-line booksellers, and see what information about this book you can find. How would you combine this information into a global schema suitable for a warehouse or mediator?

Exercise 21.2.7: In Example 21.3 we talked about a relation Cars at Dealer 1 that conveniently had an attribute autoTrans with only the values 'yes' and 'no'. Since these were the same values used for that attribute in the global schema, the construction of relation AutosWhse was especially easy. Suppose instead that the attribute Cars.autoTrans has values that are integers, with 0 meaning no automatic transmission, and $i > 0$ meaning that the car has an i-speed automatic transmission. Show how the translation from Cars to AutosWhse could be done by a SQL query.

Exercise 21.2.8: Write the insert-statements for the second dealer in Example 21.3. You may assume the values of autoTrans are 'y' and 'n'.

Exercise 21.2.9: How would the mediator of Example 21.4 translate the following queries?

a) Find the serial numbers of cars without automatic transmission.

b) Find the serial numbers of cars with automatic transmission.

! c) Find the serial numbers of the red cars from Dealer 2.

21.3 Wrappers in Mediator-Based Systems

In a data warehouse system like Fig. 21.3, the source extractors consist of:

1. One or more predefined queries that are executed at the source to produce data for the warehouse.

2. Suitable communication mechanisms, so the wrapper (extractor) can:

   (a) Pass ad-hoc queries to the source,

   (b) Receive responses from the source, and

   (c) Pass information to the warehouse.

The predefined queries to the source could be SQL queries if the source is a SQL database as in our examples of Section 21.2. Queries could also be operations in whatever language was appropriate for a source that was not a database system; e.g., the wrapper could fill out an on-line form at a Web page, issue a query to an on-line bibliography service in that system's own, specialized language, or use myriad other notations to pose the queries.

However, mediator systems require more complex wrappers than do most warehouse systems. The wrapper must be able to accept a variety of queries from the mediator and translate any of them to the terms of the source. Of course, the wrapper must then communicate the result to the mediator, just as a wrapper in a warehouse system communicates with the warehouse. In the balance of this section, we study the construction of flexible wrappers that are suitable for use with a mediator.

21.3.1 Templates for Query Patterns

A systematic way to design a wrapper that connects a mediator to a source is to classify the possible queries that the mediator can ask into *templates*, which are queries with parameters that represent constants. The mediator can provide the constants, and the wrapper executes the query with the given constants. An example should illustrate the idea; it uses the notation $T => S$ to express the idea that the template T is turned by the wrapper into the source query S.

Example 21.5 : Suppose we want to build a wrapper for the source of Dealer 1, which has the schema

```
Cars(serialNo, model, color, autoTrans, navi,...)
```

for use by a mediator with schema

```
AutosMed(serialNo, model, color, autoTrans, dealer)
```

Consider how the mediator could ask the wrapper for cars of a given color. If we denote the code representing that color by the parameter $c, then we can use the template shown in Fig. 21.5.

```
SELECT *
FROM AutosMed
WHERE color = '$c';
    =>
SELECT serialNo, model, color, autoTrans, 'dealer1'
FROM Cars
WHERE color = '$c';
```

Figure 21.5: A wrapper template describing queries for cars of a given color

Similarly, the wrapper could have another template that specified only the parameter $m representing a model, yet another template in which it was only specified whether an automatic transmission was wanted, and so on. In this case, there are eight choices, if queries are allowed to specify any of three attributes: model, color, and autoTrans. In general, there would be 2^n templates if we have the option of specifying n attributes.[2] Other templates would

---

[2]If the source is a database that can be queried in SQL, as in our example, you would rightly expect that one template could handle any number of attributes equated to constants,

be needed to deal with queries that asked for the total number of cars of certain types, or whether there exists a car of a certain type. The number of templates could grow unreasonably large, but some simplifications are possible by adding more sophistication to the wrapper, as we shall discuss starting in Section 21.3.3. □

21.3.2 Wrapper Generators

The templates defining a wrapper must be turned into code for the wrapper itself. The software that creates the wrapper is called a *wrapper generator*; it is similar in spirit to the parser generators (e.g., YACC) that produce components of a compiler from high-level specifications. The process, suggested in Fig. 21.6, begins when a specification, that is, a collection of templates, is given to the wrapper generator.

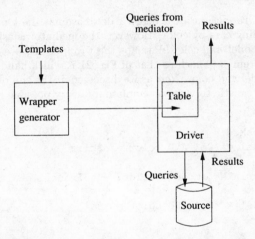

Figure 21.6: A wrapper generator produces tables for a driver; the driver and tables constitute the wrapper

The wrapper generator creates a table that holds the various query patterns contained in the templates, and the source queries that are associated with each. A *driver* is used in each wrapper; in general the driver can be the same for each generated wrapper. The task of the driver is to:

1. Accept a query from the mediator. The communication mechanism may be mediator-specific and is given to the driver as a "plug-in," so the same

---

simply by making the WHERE clause a parameter. While that approach will work for SQL sources and queries that only bind attributes to constants, we could not necessarily use the same idea with an arbitrary source, such as a Web site that allowed only certain forms as an interface. In the general case, we cannot assume that the way we translate one query resembles at all the way similar queries are translated.

driver can be used in systems that communicate differently.

2. Search the table for a template that matches the query. If one is found, then the parameter values from the query are used to instantiate a source query. If there is no matching template, the wrapper responds negatively to the mediator.

3. The source query is sent to the source, again using a "plug-in" communication mechanism. The response is collected by the wrapper.

4. The response is processed by the wrapper, if necessary, and then returned to the mediator. The next sections discuss how wrappers can support a larger class of queries by processing results.

21.3.3   Filters

Suppose that a wrapper on a car dealer's database has the template shown in Fig. 21.5 for finding cars by color. However, the mediator is asked to find cars of a particular model *and* color. Perhaps the wrapper has been designed with a more complex template such as that of Fig. 21.7, which handles queries that specify both model and color. Yet, as we discussed at the end of Example 21.5, it is not always realistic to write a template for every possible form of query.

```
SELECT *
FROM AutosMed
WHERE model = '$m' AND color = '$c';
    =>
SELECT serialNo, model, color, autoTrans, 'dealer1'
FROM Cars
WHERE model = '$m' AND color = '$c';
```

Figure 21.7: A wrapper template that gets cars of a given model and color

Another approach to supporting more queries is to have the wrapper *filter* the results of queries that it poses to the source. As long as the wrapper has a template that (after proper substitution for the parameters) returns a superset of what the query wants, then it is possible to filter the returned tuples at the wrapper and pass only the desired tuples to the mediator.

Example 21.6: Suppose the only template we have is the one in Fig. 21.5 that finds cars given a color. However, the wrapper is asked by the mediator to find blue Gobi model cars. A possible way to answer the query is to use the template of Fig. 21.5 with $c = $ 'blue' to find all the blue cars and store them in a temporary relation

```
TempAutos(serialNo, model, color, autoTrans, dealer)
```

Position of the Filter Component

We have, in our examples, supposed that the filtering operations take place at the wrapper. It is also possible that the wrapper passes raw data to the mediator, and the mediator filters the data. However, if most of the data returned by the template does not match the mediator's query, then it is best to filter at the wrapper and avoid the cost of shipping unneeded tuples.

The wrapper may then return to the mediator the desired set of automobiles by executing the local query:

```
SELECT *
FROM TempAutos
WHERE model = 'Gobi';
```

In practice, the tuples of TempAutos could be produced one-at-a-time and filtered one-at-a-time, in a pipelined fashion, rather than having the entire relation TempAutos materialized at the wrapper and then filtered. □

21.3.4 Other Operations at the Wrapper

It is possible to transform data in other ways at the wrapper, as long as we are sure that the source-query part of the template returns to the wrapper all the data needed in the transformation. For instance, columns may be projected out of the tuples before transmission to the mediator. It is even possible to take aggregations or joins at the wrapper and transmit the result to the mediator.

Example 21.7: Suppose the mediator wants to know about blue Gobis at the various dealers, but only asks for the serial number, dealer, and whether or not there is an automatic transmission, since the value of the model and color attributes are obvious from the query. The wrapper could proceed as in Example 21.6, but at the last step, when the result is to be returned to the mediator, the wrapper performs a projection in the SELECT clause as well as the filtering for the Gobi model in the WHERE clause. The query

```
SELECT serialNo, autoTrans, dealer
FROM TempAutos
WHERE model = 'Gobi';
```

does this additional filtering, although as in Example 21.6 relation TempAutos would probably be pipelined into the projection operator, rather than materialized at the wrapper. □

Example 21.8: For a more complex example, suppose the mediator is asked to find dealers and models such that the dealer has two red cars, of the same model, one with and one without an automatic transmission. Suppose also that the only useful template for Dealer 1 is the one about colors from Fig. 21.5. That is, the mediator asks the wrapper for the answer to the query of Fig. 21.8. Note that we do not have to specify a dealer for either A1 or A2, because this wrapper can only access data belonging to Dealer 1. The wrappers for all the other dealers will be asked the same query by the mediator.

```
SELECT A1.model A1.dealer
FROM AutosMed A1, AutosMed A2
WHERE A1.model = A2.model AND
      A1.color = 'red' AND
      A2.color = 'red' AND
      A1.autoTrans = 'no' AND
      A2.autoTrans = 'yes';
```

Figure 21.8: Query from mediator to wrapper

A cleverly designed wrapper could discover that it is possible to answer the mediator's query by first obtaining from the Dealer-1 source a relation with all the red cars at that dealer:

```
RedAutos(serialNo, model, color, autoTrans, dealer)
```

To get this relation, the wrapper uses its template from Fig. 21.5, which handles queries that specify a color only. In effect, the wrapper acts as if it were given the query:

```
SELECT *
FROM AutosMed
WHERE color = 'red';
```

The wrapper can then create the relation RedAutos from Dealer 1's database by using the template of Fig. 21.5 with $c = $ 'red'. Next, the wrapper joins RedAutos with itself, and performs the necessary selection, to get the relation asked for by the query of Fig. 21.8. The work performed by the wrapper for this step is shown in Fig. 21.9. □

21.3.5 Exercises for Section 21.3

Exercise 21.3.1: In Fig. 21.5 we saw a simple wrapper template that translated queries from the mediator for cars of a given color into queries at the dealer with relation Cars. Suppose that the color codes used by the mediator in its schema were different from the color codes used at this dealer, and there was

```
SELECT DISTINCT A1.model, A1.dealer
FROM RedAutos A1, RedAutos A2
WHERE A1.model = A2.model AND
      A1.autoTrans = 'no' AND
      A2.autoTrans = 'yes';
```

Figure 21.9: Query performed at the wrapper (or mediator) to complete the answer to the query of Fig. 21.8

a relation GtoL(globalColor, localColor) that translated between the two sets of codes. Rewrite the template so the correct query would be generated.

Exercise 21.3.2: In Exercise 21.2.1 we spoke of two computer companies, A and B, that used different schemas for information about their products. Suppose we have a mediator with schema

```
PCMed(manf, speed, mem, disk, screen)
```

with the intuitive meaning that a tuple gives the manufacturer (A or B), processor speed, main-memory size, hard-disk size, and screen size for one of the systems you could buy from that company. Write wrapper templates for the following types of queries. Note that you need to write two templates for each query, one for each of the manufacturers.

a) Given memory and disk sizes, find the matching tuples.

b) Given a speed, find the tuples with that speed.

c) Given a screen size, find the tuples with that size.

Exercise 21.3.3: Suppose you had the wrapper templates described in Exercise 21.3.2 available in the wrappers at each of the two sources (computer manufacturers). How could the mediator use these capabilities of the wrappers to answer the following queries?

a) Find all the systems with 1024M memory and a screen size (in inches) that ecceeds the disk size (in gigabytes).

b) Find the manufacturer, memory size, and screen size of all systems with a 2.8 gigahertz speed and a 120 gigabyte disk.

c) Find the maximum amount of hard disk available on a system with a 3.1 gigahertz processor.

21.4 Capability-Based Optimization

In Section 16.5 we introduced the idea of cost-based query optimization. A typical DBMS estimates the cost of each query plan and picks what it believes to be the best. When a mediator is given a query to answer, it often has little knowledge of how long its sources will take to answer the queries it sends them. Furthermore, many sources are not SQL databases, and often they will answer only a small subset of the kinds of queries that the mediator might like to pose. As a result, optimization of mediator queries cannot rely on cost measures alone to select a query plan.

Optimization by a mediator usually follows the simpler strategy known as *capability-based optimization*. The central issue is not what a query plan costs, but whether the plan can be executed at all. Only among plans found to be executable ("feasible") do we try to estimate costs.

21.4.1 The Problem of Limited Source Capabilities

Today, many useful sources have only Web-based interfaces, even if they are, behind the scenes, an ordinary database. Web sources usually permit querying only through a query form, which does not accept arbitrary SQL queries. Rather, we are invited to enter values for certain attributes and can receive a response that gives values for other attributes.

Example 21.9: The Amazon.com interface allows us to query about books in many different ways. We can specify an author and get all their books, or we can specify a book title and receive information about that book. We can specify keywords and get books that match the keywords. However, there is also information we can receive in answers but cannot specify. For instance, Amazon ranks books by sales, but we cannot ask "give me the top 10 sellers." Moreover, we cannot ask questions that are too general. For instance, the query:

```
SELECT * FROM Books;
```

"tell me everything you know about books," cannot be asked or answered through the Amazon Web interface, although it could be answered behind the scenes if we were able to access the Amazon database directly. □

There are a number of other reasons why a source may limit the ways in which queries can be asked. Among them are:

1. Many of the earliest data sources did not use a DBMS, surely not a relational DBMS that supports SQL queries. These systems were designed to be queried in certain very specific ways only.

2. For reasons of security, a source may limit the kinds of queries that it will accept. Amazon's unwillingness to answer the query "tell me about

all your books" is a rudimentary example; it protects against a rival exploiting the Amazon database. As another instance, a medical database may answer queries about averages, but won't disclose the details of a particular patient's medical history.

3. Indexes on large databases may make certain kinds of queries feasible, while others are too expensive to execute. For instance, if a books database were relational, and one of the attributes were author, then without an index on that attribute, it would be infeasible to answer queries that specified only an author.[3]

21.4.2 A Notation for Describing Source Capabilities

If data is relational, or may be thought of as relational, then we can describe the legal forms of queries by *adornments*. These are sequences of codes that represent the requirements for the attributes of the relation, in their standard order. The codes we shall use for adornments reflect the most common capabilities of sources. They are:

1. f (free) means that the attribute can be specified or not, as we choose.

2. b (bound) means that we must specify a value for the attribute, but any value is allowed.

3. u (unspecified) means that we are not permitted to specify a value for the attribute.

4. $c[S]$ (choice from set S) means that a value must be specified, and that value must be one of the values in the finite set S. This option corresponds, for instance, to values that are specified from a pulldown menu in a Web interface.

5. $o[S]$ (optional, from set S) means that we either do not specify a value, or we specify one of the values in the finite set S.

In addition, we place a prime (e.g., f') on a code to indicate that the attribute is not part of the output of the query.

A *capabilities specification* for a source is a set of adornments. The intent is that in order to query the source successfully, the query must match one of the adornments in its capabilities specification. Note that, if an adornment has free or optional components, then queries with different sets of attributes specified may match that adornment.

---

[3] We should be aware, however, that information like Amazon's about products is not accessed as if it were a relational database. Rather, the information about books is stored as text, with an inverted index, as we discussed in Section 14.1.8. Thus, queries about any aspect of books — authors, titles, words in titles, and perhaps words in descriptions of the book — are supported by this index.

Example 21.10 : Suppose we have two sources like those of the two dealers in Example 21.4. Dealer 1 is a source of data in the form:

    Cars(serialNo, model, color, autoTrans, navi)

Note that in the original, we suggested relation Cars could have additional attributes representing options, but for simplicity in this example, let us limit our thinking to automatic transmissions and navigation systems only. Here are two possible ways that Dealer 1 might allow this data to be queried:

1. The user specifies a serial number. All the information about the car with that serial number (i.e., the other four attributes) is produced as output. The adornment for this query form is $b'uuuu$. That is, the first attribute, serialNo must be specified and is not part of the output. The other attributes must *not* be specified and *are* part of the output.

2. The user specifies a model and color, and perhaps whether or not automatic transmission and navigation system are wanted. All five attributes are printed for all matching cars. An appropriate adornment is

$$ubbo[\text{yes, no}]o[\text{yes, no}]$$

This adornment says we must not specify the serial number; we must specify a model and color, but are allowed to give any possible value in these fields. Also, we may, if we wish, specify whether we want automatic transmission and/or a navigation system, but must do so by using only the values "yes" and "no" in those fields.

□

21.4.3 Capability-Based Query-Plan Selection

Given a query at the mediator, a capability-based query optimizer first considers what queries it can ask at the sources to help answer the query. If we imagine those queries asked and answered, then we have bindings for some more attributes, and these bindings may make some more queries at the sources possible. We repeat this process until either:

1. We have asked enough queries at the sources to resolve all the conditions of the mediator query, and therefore we may answer that query. Such a plan is called *feasible*.

2. We can construct no more valid forms of source queries, yet we still cannot answer the mediator query, in which case the mediator must give up; it has been given an impossible query.

What Do Adornments Guarantee?

It would be wonderful if a source that supported queries matching a given adornment would return all possible answers to the query. However, sources normally have only a subset of the possible answers to a query. For instance, Amazon does not stock every book that has ever been written, and the two dealers of our running automobiles example each have distinct sets of cars in their database. Thus, a more proper interpretation of an adornment is: "I will answer a query in the form described by this adornment, and every answer I give will be a true answer, but I do not guarantee to provide all true answers." An important consequence of this state of affairs is that if we want all available tuples for a relation R, then we must query every source that might contribute such tuples.

The simplest form of mediator query for which we need to apply the above strategy is a join of relations, each of which is available, with certain adornments, at one or more sources. If so, then the search strategy is to try to get tuples for each relation in the join, by providing enough argument bindings that some source allows a query about that relation to be asked and answered. A simple example will illustrate the point.

Example 21.11: Let us suppose we have sources like the relations of Dealer 2 in Example 21.4:

```
Autos(serial, model, color)
Options(serial, option)
```

Suppose that *ubf* is the sole adornment for Autos, while Options has two adornments, *bu* and *uc*[autoTrans, navi], representing two different kinds of queries that we can ask at that source. Let the query be "find the serial numbers and colors of Gobi models with a navigation system."

Here are three different query plans that the mediator must consider:

1. Specifying that the model is Gobi, query Autos and get the serial numbers and colors of all Gobis. Then, using the *bu* adornment for Options, for each such serial number, find the options for that car and filter to make sure it has a navigation system.

2. Specifying the navigation-system option, query Options using the

$$uc[\text{autoTrans, navi}]$$

adornment and get all the serial numbers for cars with a navigation system. Then query Autos as in (1), to get all the serial numbers and colors of Gobis, and intersect the two sets of serial numbers.

3. Query `Options` as in (2) to get the serial numbers for cars with a navigation system. Then use these serial numbers to query `Autos` and see which of these cars are Gobis.

Either of the first two plans are acceptable. However, the third plan is one of several plans that will not work; the system does not have the capability to execute this plan because the second part — the query to `Autos` — does not have a matching adornment. □

21.4.4 Adding Cost-Based Optimization

The mediator's query optimizer is not done when the capabilities of the sources are examined. Having found the feasible plans, it must choose among them. Making an intelligent, cost-based optimization requires that the mediator know a great deal about the costs of the queries involved. Since the sources are usually independent of the mediator, it is difficult to estimate the cost. For instance, a source may take less time during periods when it is lightly loaded, but when are those periods? Long-term observation by the mediator is necessary for the mediator even to guess what the response time might be.

In Example 21.11, we might simply count the number of queries to sources that must be issued. Plan (2) uses only two source queries, while plan (1) uses one plus the number of Gobis found in the `Autos` relation. Thus, it appears that plan (2) has lower cost. On the other hand, if the queries of `Options`, one with each serial number, could be combined into one query, then plan (1) might turn out to be the superior choice.

21.4.5 Exercises for Section 21.4

Exercise 21.4.1: Suppose each relation from Exercise 21.2.1:

```
Computers(number, proc, speed, memory, hd)
Monitors(number, screen, maxResX, maxResY)
```

is an information source. Using the notation from Section 21.4.2, write one or more adornments that express the following capabilities:

a) We can query for monitors if we specify either the number of the monitor, the screen size, or the maximum resolution in both dimensions.

b) We can query for computers having a given processor, which must be one of "P-IV," "G5," or "Athlon," a given speed, and (optionally) a given amount of memory.

c) We can query for computers having any specified hard-disk size and/or any given memory size.

d) We can query for monitors if we specify the screen size, which must be either 22, 24, 26, or 30 inches. All attributes except the screen size are returned.

! e) We can query for computers if we specify any two of the processor type, processor speed, memory size, or disk size.

Exercise 21.4.2: Suppose we have the two sources of Exercise 21.4.1, but understand the attribute **number** of both relations to refer to the number of a complete system, some of whose attributes are found in one source and some in the other. Suppose also that the adornments describing access to the Computers relation are *buuuu*, *ubbff*, and *uuubb*, while the adornments for Monitors are *bfff* and *ubbb*. Tell what plans are feasible for the following queries (exclude any plans that are obviously more expensive than other plans on your list):

a) Find the systems with a Pentium-IV processor running at 3.0 gigahertz with a 22-inch monitor and a maximum resolution of 1600-by-1050.

b) Find the systems with 1024 megabytes of memory, a 120-gigabyte hard disk, and a 24-inch monitor.

! c) Find all systems with a G5 processor running at 1.8 gigahertz, with 2 gigabytes of memory, a 200 gigabyte disk, and a 19-inch monitor.

21.5 Optimizing Mediator Queries

In this section, we shall give a greedy algorithm for answering queries at a mediator. This algorithm, called *chain*, always finds a way to answer the query by sending a sequence of requests to its sources, provided at least one solution exists. The class of queries that can be handled is those that involve joins of relations that come from the sources, followed by an optional selection and optional projection onto output attributes. This class of queries is exactly what can be expressed as Datalog rules (Section 5.3).

21.5.1 Simplified Adornment Notation

The Chain Algorithm concerns itself with Datalog rules and with whether prior source requests have provided bindings for any of the variables in the body of the rule. Since we care only about whether we have found all possible constants for a variable, we can limit ourselves, in the query at the mediator (although not at the sources), to the b (bound) and f (free) adornments. That is, a $c[S]$ adornment for an attribute of a source relation can be used as soon as we know all possible values of interest for that attribute (i.e., the corresponding position in the mediator query has a b adornment). Note that the source will not provide matches for the values outside S, so there is no point in asking questions about these values. The optional adornment $o[S]$ can be treated as free, since there is no need to have a binding for the corresponding attribute in the query at the mediator (although we could). Likewise, adornment u can be treated as free, since although we cannot then specify a value for the attribute at the source, we can have, or not have, a binding for the corresponding variable at the mediator.

Example 21.12: Let us use the same query and source relations as in Example 21.11, but with different capabilities at the sources. In what follows we shall use superscripts on the predicate or relation names to show the adornment or permitted set of adornments. In this example, the permitted adornments for the two source relations are:

$$\text{Autos}^{buu}(\text{serial, model, color})$$
$$\text{Options}^{uc[\text{autoTrans, navi}]}(\text{serial, option})$$

That is, we can only access Options by providing a binding "autoTrans" or "navi" for the option attribute, and we can only access Autos by providing a binding for the serial attribute.

The query "find the serial numbers and colors of Gobi models with a navigation system" is expressed in Datalog by:

$$\text{Answer(s,c)} \leftarrow \text{Autos}^{fbf}(\text{s,"Gobi",c}) \text{ AND Options}^{fb}(\text{s,"navi"})$$

Here, notice the adornments on the subgoals of the body. These, at the moment, are commentaries on what arguments of each subgoal are bound to a set of constants. Initially, only the middle argument of the Autos subgoal is bound (to the set containing only the constant "Gobi") and the second argument of the Options subgoal is bound to the set containing only "navi." We shall see shortly that as we use the sources to find tuples that match one or another subgoal, we get bindings for some of the variables in the Datalog rule, and thus change some of the f's to b's in the adornments. □

21.5.2 Obtaining Answers for Subgoals

We now need to formalize the comments made at the beginning of Section 21.5.1 about when a subgoal with some of its arguments bound can be answered by a source query. Suppose we have a subgoal $R^{x_1 x_2 \cdots x_n}(a_1, a_2, \ldots, a_n)$, where each x_i is either b or f. R is a relation that can be queried at some source, and which has some set of adornments.

Suppose $y_1 y_2 \cdots y_n$ is one of the adornments for R at its source. Each y_i can be any of b, f, u, $c[S]$ or $o[S]$ for any set S. Then it is possible to obtain a relation for the subgoal provided, for each $i = 1, 2, \ldots, n$, provided:

- If y_i is b or of the form $c[S]$, then $x_i = b$.

- If $x_i = f$, then y_i is not output restricted (i.e., not primed).

Note that if y_i is any of f, u, or $o[S]$, then x_i can be either b or f. We say that the adornment on the subgoal *matches* the adornment at the source.

Example 21.13 : Suppose the subgoal in question is $R^{bbff}(p,q,r,s)$, and the adornments for R at its source are $\alpha_1 = fc[S_1]uo[S_2]$ and $\alpha_2 = c[S_3]bfc[S_4]$. Then *bbff* matches adornment α_1, so we may use α_1 to get the relation for subgoal $R(p,q,r,s)$. That is, α_1 has no b's and only one c, in the second position. Since the adornment of the subgoal has b in the second position, we know that there is a set of constants to which the variable q (the variable in the second argument of the subgoal) has been bound. For each of those constants that are a member of the set S_1 we can issue a query to the source for R, using that constant as the binding for the second argument. We do not provide bindings for any other argument, even though α_1 allows us to provide a binding for the first and/or fourth argument as well.

However, *bbff* does not match α_2. The reason is that α_2 has $c[S_4]$ in the fourth position, while *bbff* has f in that position. If we were to try to obtain R using α_2, we would have to provide a binding for the fourth argument, which means that variable s in $R(p,q,r,s)$ would have to be bound to a set of constants. But we know that is not the case, or else the adornment on the subgoal would have had b in the fourth position. □

21.5.3 The Chain Algorithm

The *Chain Algorithm* is a greedy approach to selecting an order in which we obtain relations for each of the subgoals of a Datalog rule. It is not guaranteed to provide the most efficient solution, but it will provide a solution whenever one exists, and in practice, it is very likely to obtain the most efficient solution. The algorithm maintains two kinds of information:

- An adornment is maintained for each subgoal. Initially, the adornment for a subgoal has b if and only if the mediator query provides a constant binding for the corresponding argument of that subgoal, as for instance, the query in Example 21.12 provided bindings for the second arguments of both the Autos and Options subgoals. In all other places, the adornment has f's.

- A relation X that is (a projection of) the join of the relations for all the subgoals that have been *resolved*. We resolve a subgoal when the adornment for the subgoal matches one of the adornments at the source for this subgoal, and we have extracted from the source all possible tuples for that subgoal. Initially, since no subgoals have been resolved, X is a relation over no attributes, containing just the empty tuple (i.e., the tuple with zero components). Note that for empty X and any relation R, $X \bowtie R = R$; i.e., X is initially the identity relation for the natural-join operation. As the algorithm progresses, X will have attributes that are variables of the rule — those variables that correspond to b's in the adornments of the subgoals in which they appear.

The core of the Chain Algorithm is as follows. After initializing relation X and the adornments of the subgoals as above, we repeatedly select a subgoal that can be resolved. Let $R^\alpha(a_1, a_2, \ldots, a_n)$ be the subgoal to be resolved. We do so by:

1. Wherever α has a b, we shall find that either the corresponding argument of R is a constant rather than a variable, or it is one of the variables in the schema of the relation X. Project X onto those of its variables that appear in subgoal R. Each tuple in the projection, together with constants in the subgoal R, if any, provide sufficient bindings to use one of the adornments for the source relation R — whichever adornment α matches.

2. Issue a query to the source for each tuple t in the projection of X. We construct the query as follows, depending on the source adornment β that α matches.

   (a) If a component of β is b, then the corresponding component of α is too, and we can use the corresponding component of t (or a constant in the subgoal) to provide the necessary binding for the source query.

   (b) If a component of β is $c[S]$, then again the corresponding component of α will be b, and we can obtain a constant from the subgoal or the tuple t. However, if that constant is not in S, then there is no chance the source can produce any tuples that match t, so we do not generate any source query for t.

   (c) If a component of β is f, then produce a constant value for this component in the source query if we can; otherwise do not provide a value for this component in the source query. Note that we can provide a constant exactly when the corresponding component of α is b.

   (d) If a component of β is u, provide no binding for this component, even if the corresponding component of α is b.

   (e) If a component of β is $o[S]$, treat this component as if it were f in the case that the corresponding component of α is f, and as $c[S]$ if the corresponding component of α is b.

   For each tuple returned, extend the tuple so it has one component for each argument of the subgoal (i.e., n components). Note that the source will return every component of R that is not output restricted, so the only components that are not present have b in the adornment α. Thus, the returned tuples can be padded by using either the constant from the subgoal, or the constant from the tuple in the projection of X. The union of all the responses is the relation R for the subgoal $R(a_1, a_2, \ldots, a_n)$.

3. Every variable among $a_1, a_2, \ldots, a_n$ is now bound. For each subgoal that has not yet been resolved, change its adornment so any position holding one of these variables is now bound (b).

4. Replace X by $X \bowtie \pi_S(R)$, where S is all the variables among

$$a_1, a_2, \ldots, a_n$$

5. Project out of X all components that correspond to variables that do not appear in the head or in any unresolved subgoal. These components can never be useful in what follows.

The complete Chain Algorithm, then, consists of the initialization described above, followed by as many subgoal-resolution steps as we can manage. If we succeed in resolving every subgoal, then relation X will be the answer to the query. If at some point, there are unresolved subgoals, yet none can be resolved, then the algorithm fails. In that case, there can be no other sequence of resolution steps that answers the query.

Example 21.14: Consider the mediator query

$$Q: \quad \texttt{Answer(c)} \leftarrow \texttt{R}^{bf}\texttt{(1,a)} \text{ AND } \texttt{S}^{ff}\texttt{(a,b)} \text{ AND } \texttt{T}^{ff}\texttt{(b,c)}$$

There are three sources that provide answers to queries about R, S, and T, respectively. The contents of these relations at the sources and the only adornments supported by these sources are shown in Fig. 21.10.

Relation	R		S		T	
	w	x	x	y	y	z
Data	1	2	2	4	4	6
	1	3	3	5	5	7
	1	4			5	8
Adornment	bf		$c'[2,3,5]f$		bu	

Figure 21.10: Data for Example 21.14

Initially, the adornments on the subgoals are as shown in the query Q, and the relation X that we construct initially contains only the empty tuple. Since subgoals S and T have ff adornments, but the adornments at the corresponding sources each have a component with b or c, neither of these subgoals can be resolved. Fortunately, the first subgoal, $R(1, a)$, can be resolved, since the bf adornment at the corresponding source is matched by the adornment of the subgoal. Thus, we send the source for $R(w, x)$ a query with $w = 1$, and the response is the set of three tuples shown in the first column of Fig. 21.10.

We next project the subgoal's relation onto its second component, since only the second component of $R(1, a)$ is a variable. That gives us the relation

$$\frac{a}{\begin{array}{c} 2 \\ 3 \\ 4 \end{array}}$$

This relation is joined with X, which currently has no attributes and only the empty tuple. The result is that X becomes the relation above. Since a is now bound, we change the adornment on the S subgoal from ff to bf.

At this point, the second subgoal, $S^{bf}(a,b)$, can be resolved. We obtain bindings for the first component by projecting X onto a; the result is X itself. That is, we can go to the source for $S(x,y)$ with bindings 2, 3, and 4 for x. We do not need bindings for y, since the second component of the adornment for the source is f. The $c'[2,3,5]$ code for x says that we can give the source the value 2, 3, or 5 for the first argument. Since there is a prime on the c, we know that only the corresponding y value(s) will be returned, not the value of x that we supplied in the request. We care about values 2, 3, and 4, but 4 is not a possible value at the source for S, so we never ask about it.

When we ask about $x = 2$, we get one response: $y = 4$. We pad this response with the value 2 we supplied to conclude that $(2,4)$ is a tuple in the relation for the S subgoal. Similarly, when we ask about $x = 3$, we get $y = 5$ as the only response and we add $(3,5)$ to the set of tuples constructed for the S subgoal. There are no more requests to ask at the source for S, so we conclude that the relation for the S subgoal is

a	b
2	4
3	5

When we join this relation with the previous value of X, the result is just the relation above. However, variable a now appears neither in the head nor in any unresolved subgoal. Thus, we project it out, so X becomes

$$\frac{b}{\begin{array}{c} 4 \\ 5 \end{array}}$$

Since b is now bound, we change the adornment on the T subgoal, so it becomes $T^{bf}(b,c)$. Now this last subgoal can be resolved, which we do by sending requests to the source for $T(y,z)$ with $y = 4$ and $y = 5$. The responses we get back give us the following relation for the T subgoal:

b	c
4	6
5	7
5	8

We join it with the relation for X above, and then project onto the c attribute to get the relation for the head. That is, the answer to the query at the mediator is $\{(6),(7),(8)\}$. □

21.5.4 Incorporating Union Views at the Mediator

In our description of the Chain Algorithm, we assumed that each predicate in the Datalog query at the mediator was a "view" of data at one particular source. However, it is common for there to be several sources that can contribute tuples to the relation for the predicate. How we construct the relation for such a predicate depends on how we expect the sources for the predicate to interact.

The easy case is where we expect the sources for a predicate to contain replicated information. In that case, we can turn to any one of the sources to get the relation for a predicate. This case thus looks exactly like the case where there is a single source for a predicate, but there may be several adornments that allows us to query that source.

The more complex case is when the sources each contribute some tuples to the predicate that the other sources may not contribute. In that case, we should consult all the sources for the predicate. However, there is still a policy choice to be made. Either we can refuse to answer the query unless we can consult all the sources, or we can make best efforts to return all the answers to the query that we can obtain by combinations of sources.

Consult All Sources

If we must consult all sources to consider a subgoal resolved, then we can only resolve a subgoal when each source for its relation has an adornment matched by the current adornment of the subgoal. This rule is a small modification of the Chain Algorithm. However, not only does it make queries harder to answer, it makes queries impossible to answer when any source is "down," even if the Chain Algorithm provides a feasible ordering in which to resolve the subgoals. Thus, as the number of sources grows, this policy becomes progressively less practical.

Best Efforts

Under this assumption, we only need one source with a matching adornment to resolve a subgoal. However, we need to modify the chain algorithm to revisit each subgoal when that subgoal has new bound arguments. We may find that some source that could not be matched is now matched by the subgoal with its new adornment.

Example 21.15: Consider the mediator query

$$\text{answer(a,c)} \leftarrow \text{R}^{ff}\text{(a,b) AND S}^{ff}\text{(b,c)}$$

Suppose also that R has two sources, one described by adornment ff and the other by fb. Likewise, S has two sources, described by ff and bf. We could start by using either source with adornment ff; suppose we start with R's source. We query this source and get some tuples for R.

Now, we have some bindings, but perhaps not all, for the variable b. We can now use both sources for S to obtain tuples and the relation for S can be set to their union. At this point, we can project the relation for S onto variable b and get some b-values. These can be used to query the second source for R, the one with adornment fb. In this manner, we can get some additional R-tuples. It is only at this point that we can join the relations for R and S, and project onto a and c to get the best-effort answer to the query. □

21.5.5 Exercises for Section 21.5

Exercise 21.5.1: Describe all the source adornments that are matched by a subgoal with adornment R^{fb}.

Exercise 21.5.2: Apply the Chain Algorithm to the mediator query

$$\text{Answer(a,e)} \leftarrow \text{R(a,b,c) AND S(c,d) AND T(b,d,e)}$$

with the following adornments at the sources for R, S, and T. If there is more than one adornment for a predicate, either may be used.

a) R^{fbf}, S^{fb}, S^{bf}, T^{fff}.

b) R^{fff}, S^{bf}, T^{bff}, T^{fbf}.

c) R^{ffb}, S^{fb}, T^{fbf}, T^{bff}.

In each case:

   i. Indicate all possible orders in which the subgoals can be resolved.

   ii. Does the Chain Algorithm produce an answer to the query?

   iii. Give the sequence of relational-algebra operations needed to compute the intermediate relation X at each step and the result of the query.

! **Exercise 21.5.3:** Suppose that for the mediator query of Exercise 21.5.2, each predicate is a view defined by the union of two sources. For each predicate, one of the sources has an all-f adornment. The other sources have the following adornments: R^{fbb}, S^{bf}, and T^{bff}. Find a best-effort sequence of source requests that will produce all the answers to the mediator query that can be obtained from these sources.

!! **Exercise 21.5.4:** Prove that if there is any sequence of subgoal resolutions that will resolve all subgoals, then the Chain Algorithm will find one. *Hint*: Notice that if a subgoal can be resolved at a certain step, then if it is not selected for resolution, it can still be resolved at the next step.

21.6 Local-as-View Mediators

The mediators discussed so far are called *global-as-view* (GAV) mediators. The global data (i.e., the data available for querying at the mediator) is like a view; it doesn't exist physically, but pieces of it are constructed by the mediator, as needed, by asking queries of the sources.

In this section, we introduce another approach to connecting sources with a mediator. In a *local-as-view* (LAV) mediator, we define global predicates at the mediator, but we do not define these predicates as views of the source data. Rather, we define, for each source, one or more expressions involving the global predicates that describe the tuples that the source is able to produce. Queries are answered at the mediator by discovering all possible ways to construct the query using the views provided by the sources.

21.6.1 Motivation for LAV Mediators

In many applications, GAV mediators are easy to construct. You decide on the global predicates or relations that the mediator will support, and for each source, you consider which predicates it can support, and how it can be queried. That is, you determine the set of adornments for each predicate at each source. For instance, in our Aardvark Automobiles example, if we decide we want Autos and Options predicates at the mediator, we find a way to query each dealer's source for those concepts and let the Autos and Options predicates at the mediator represent the union of what the sources provide. Whenever we need one or both of those predicates to answer a mediator query, we make requests of each of the sources to obtain their data.

However, there are situations where the relationship between what we want to provide to users of the mediator and what the sources provide is more subtle. We shall look at an example where the mediator is intended to provide a single predicate $Par(c,p)$, meaning that p is a parent of c. As with all mediators, this predicate represents an abstract concept — in this case, the set of all child-parent facts that could ever exist — and the sources will provide information about whatever child-parent facts they know. Even put together, the sources probably do not know about everyone in the world, let along everyone who ever lived.

Life would be simple if each source held some child-parent information and nothing else that was relevant to the mediator. Then, all we would have to do is determine how to query each one for whatever facts they could provide. However, suppose we have a database maintained by the Association of Grandparents that doesn't provide any child-parent facts at all, but provides child-grandparent facts. We can never use this source to help answer a query about someone's parents or children, but we can use it to help answer a mediator query that uses the Par predicate several times to ask for the grandparents of an individual, or their great-grandparents, or another complex relationship among people.

GAV mediators do not allow us to use a grandparents source at all, if our goal is to produce a Par relation. Producing both a parent and a grandparent predicate at the mediator is possible, but it might be confusing to the user and would require us to figure out how to extract grandparents from all sources, including those that only allow queries for child-parent facts. However, LAV mediators allow us to say that a certain source provides grandparent facts. Moreover, the technology associated with LAV mediators lets us discover how and when to use that source in a given query.

21.6.2 Terminology for LAV Mediation

LAV mediators are always defined using a form of logic that serves as the language for defining views. In our presentation, we shall use Datalog. Both the queries at the mediator and the queries (view definitions) that describe the sources will be single Datalog rules. A query that is a single Datalog rule is often called a *conjunctive query*, and we shall use the term here.

A LAV mediator has a set of *global predicates*, which are used as the subgoals of mediator queries. There are other conjunctive queries that define *views*; i.e., their heads each have a unique view predicate that is the name of a view. Each view definition has a body consisting of global predicates and is associated with a particular source, from which that view can be constructed. We assume that each view can be constructed with an all-free adornment. If capabilities are limited, we can use the chain algorithm to decide whether solutions using the views are feasible.

Suppose we are given a conjunctive query Q whose subgoals are predicates defined at the mediator. We need to find all *solutions* — conjunctive queries whose bodies are composed of view predicates, but that can be "expanded" to produce a conjunctive query involving the global predicates. Moreover, this conjunctive query must produce only tuples that are also produced by Q. We say such expansions are *contained* in Q. An example may help with these tricky concepts, after which we shall define "expansion" formally.

Example 21.16 : Suppose there is one global predicate $Par(c,p)$ meaning that p is a parent of c. There is one source that produces some of the possible parent facts; its view is defined by the conjunctive query

$$V_1(c,p) \leftarrow Par(c,p)$$

There is another source that produces some grandparent facts; its view is defined by the conjunctive query

$$V_2(c,g) \leftarrow Par(c,p) \text{ AND } Par(p,g)$$

Our query at the mediator will ask for great-grandparent facts that can be obtained from the sources. That is, the mediator query is

$$Q(w,z) \leftarrow Par(w,x) \text{ AND } Par(x,y) \text{ AND } Par(y,z)$$

How might we answer this query? The source view V_1 contributes to the parent predicate directly, so we can use it three times in the obvious solution

$$Q(\text{w},\text{z}) \leftarrow V_1(\text{w},\text{x}) \text{ AND } V_1(\text{x},\text{y}) \text{ AND } V_1(\text{y},\text{z})$$

There are, however, other solutions that may produce additional answers, and thus must be part of the logical query plan for answering the query. In particular, we can use the view V_2 to get grandparent facts, some of which may not be inferrable by using two parent facts from V_1. We can use V_1 to make a step of one generation, and then use V_2 to make a step of two generations, as in the solution

$$Q(\text{w},\text{z}) \leftarrow V_1(\text{w},\text{x}) \text{ AND } V_2(\text{x},\text{z})$$

Or, we can use V_2 first, followed by V_1, as

$$Q(\text{w},\text{z}) \leftarrow V_2(\text{w},\text{y}) \text{ AND } V_1(\text{y},\text{z})$$

It turns out these are the only solutions we need; their union is all the great-grandparent facts that we can produce from the sources V_1 and V_2. There is still a great deal to explain. Why are these solutions guaranteed to produce only answers to the query? How do we tell whether a solution is part of the answer to a query? How do we find all the useful solutions to a query? We shall answer each of these questions in the next sections. □

21.6.3 Expanding Solutions

Given a query Q, a solution S has a body whose subgoals are views, and each view V is defined by a conjunctive query with that view as the head. We can substitute the body of V's conjunctive query for a subgoal in S that uses predicate V, as long as we are careful not to confuse variable names from one body with those of another. Once we substitute rule bodies for the views that are in S, we have a body that consists of global predicates only. The expanded solution can be compared with Q, to see if the results produced by the solution S are guaranteed to be answers to the query Q, in a manner we shall discuss later.

However, first we must be clear about the expansion algorithm. Suppose that there is a solution S that has a subgoal $V(a_1, a_2, \ldots, a_n)$. Here the a_i's can be any variables or constants, and it is possible that two or more of the a_i's are actually the same variable. Let the definition of view V be of the form

$$V(b_1, b_2, \ldots, b_n) \leftarrow B$$

where B represents the entire body. We may assume that the b_i's are distinct variables, since there is no need to have two identical components in a view, nor is there a need for components that are constant. We can replace $V(a_1, a_2, \ldots, a_n)$ in solution S by a version of body B that has all the subgoals of B, but with variables possibly altered. The rules for altering the variables of B are:

1. First, identify the *local variables* of B — those variables that appear in the body, but not in the head. Note that, within a conjunctive query, a local variable can be replaced by any other variable, as long as the replacing variable does not appear elsewhere in the conjunctive query. The idea is the same as substituting different names for local variables in a program.

2. If there are any local variables of B that appear in B or in S, replace each one by a distinct new variable that appears nowhere in the rule for V or in S.

3. In the body B, replace each b_i by a_i, for $i = 1, 2, \ldots, n$.

Example 21.17: Suppose we have the view definition

$$V(a,b,c,d) \leftarrow E(a,b,x,y) \text{ AND } F(x,y,c,d)$$

Suppose further that some solution S has in its body a subgoal $V(x, y, 1, x)$.

The local variables in the definition of V are x and y, since these do not appear in the head. We need to change them both, because they appear in the subgoal for which we are substituting. Suppose e and f are variable names that appear nowhere in S. We can rewrite the body of the rule for V as

$$V(a,b,c,d) \leftarrow E(a,b,e,f) \text{ AND } F(e,f,c,d)$$

Next, we must substitute the arguments of the V subgoal for a, b, c, and d. The correspondence is that a and d become x, b becomes y, and c becomes the constant 1. We therefore substitute for $V(x, y, 1, x)$ the two subgoals $E(x, y, e, f)$ and $F(e, f, 1, x)$. □

The expansion process is essentially the substitution described above for each subgoal of the solution S. There is one extra caution of which we must be aware, however. Since we may be substituting for the local variables of several view definitions, and may in fact need to create several versions of one view definition (if S has several subgoals with the same view predicate), we must make sure that in the substitution for each subgoal of S, we use unique local variables — ones that do not appear in any other substitution or in S itself. Only then can we be sure that when we do the expansion we do not use the same name for two variables that should be distinct.

Example 21.18: Let us resume the discussion we began in Example 21.16, where we had view definitions

$$V_1(c,p) \leftarrow Par(c,p)$$
$$V_2(c,g) \leftarrow Par(c,p) \text{ AND } Par(p,g)$$

One of the proposed solutions S is

$$Q(w,z) \leftarrow V_1(w,x) \text{ AND } V_2(x,z)$$

Let us expand this solution. The first subgoal, with predicate V_1 is easy to expand, because the rule for V_1 has no local variables. We substitute w and x for c and p respectively, so the body of the rule for V_1 becomes $Par(w, x)$. This subgoal will be substituted in S for $V_1(w, x)$.

We must also substitute for the V_2 subgoal. Its rule has local variable p. However, since p does not appear in S, nor has it been used as a local variable in another substitution, we are free to leave p as it is. We therefore have only to substitute x and z for the variables c and g, respectively. The two subgoals in the rule for V_2 become $Par(x, p)$ and $Par(p, z)$. When we substitute these two subgoals for $V_2(x, z)$ in S, we have constructed the complete expansion of S:

```
Q(w,z) ← Par(w,x) AND Par(x,p) AND Par(p,z)
```

Notice that this expansion is practically identical to the query in Example 21.16. The only difference is that the query uses local variable y where the expansion uses p. Since the names of local variables do not affect the result, it appears that the solution S is the answer to the query. However, that is not quite right. The query is looking for all great-grandparent facts, and all the expansion says is that the solution S provides only facts that answer the query. S might not produce all possible answers. For example, the source of V_2 might even be empty, in which case nothing is produced by solution S, even though another solution might produce some answers. $\Box$

21.6.4 Containment of Conjunctive Queries

In order for a conjunctive query S to be a solution to the given mediator query Q, the expansion of S, say E, must produce only answers that Q produces, regardless of what relations are represented by the predicates in the bodies of E and Q. If so, we say that $E \subseteq Q$.

There is an algorithm to tell whether $E \subseteq Q$; we shall see this test after introducing the following important concept. A *containment mapping* from Q to E is a function τ from the variables of Q to the variables and constants of E, such that:

1. If x is the ith argument of the head of Q, then $\tau(x)$ is the ith argument of the head of E.

2. Add to τ the rule that $\tau(c) = c$ for any constant c. If $P(x_1, x_2, \ldots, x_n)$ is a subgoal of Q, then $P(\tau(x_1), \tau(x_2), \ldots, \tau(x_n))$ is a subgoal of E.

Example 21.19: Consider the following two conjunctive queries:

$$Q_1: \quad H(x,y) \leftarrow A(x,z) \text{ AND } B(z,y)$$
$$Q_2: \quad H(a,b) \leftarrow A(a,c) \text{ AND } B(d,b) \text{ AND } A(a,d)$$

We claim that $Q_2 \subseteq Q_1$. In proof, we offer the following containment mapping: $\tau(x) = a$, $\tau(y) = b$, and $\tau(z) = d$. Notice that when we apply this substitution, the head of Q_1 becomes $H(a, b)$, which is the head of Q_2. The first subgoal of Q_1 becomes $A(a, d)$, which is the third subgoal of Q_2. Likewise, the second subgoal of Q_1 becomes the second subgoal of Q_2. That proves there is a containment mapping from Q_1 to Q_2, and therefore $Q_2 \subseteq Q_1$. Notice that no subgoal of Q_1 maps to the first subgoal of Q_2, but the containment-mapping definition does not require that there be one.

Surprisingly, there is also a containment mapping from Q_2 to Q_1, so the two conjunctive queries are in fact equivalent. That is, not only is one contained in the other, but on any relations A and B, they produce exactly the same set of tuples for the relation H. The containment mapping from Q_2 to Q_1 is $\rho(a) = x$, $\rho(b) = y$, and $\rho(c) = \rho(d) = z$. Under this mapping, the head of Q_2 becomes the head of Q_1, the first and third subgoals of Q_2 become the first subgoal of Q_1, and the second subgoal of Q_2 becomes the second subgoal of Q_1.

While it may appear strange that two such different looking conjunctive queries are equivalent, the following is the intuition. Think of A and B as two different colored edges on a graph. Then Q_1 asks for the pairs of nodes x and y such that there is an A-edge from x to some z and a B-edge from z to y. Q_2 asks for the same thing, using its second and third subgoals respectively, although it calls x, y, and z by the names a, b, and d respectively. In addition, Q_2 seems to have the added condition expressed by the first subgoal that there is an edge from node a to somewhere (node c). But we already know that there is an edge from a to somewhere, namely d. That is, we are always free to use the same node for c as we did for d, because there are no other constraints on c. □

Example 21.20: Here are two queries similar, but not identical, to those of Example 21.19:

$$P_1: \quad \text{H(x,y)} \leftarrow \text{A(x,z) AND A(z,y)}$$
$$P_2: \quad \text{H(a,b)} \leftarrow \text{A(a,c) AND A(c,d) AND A(d,b)}$$

Intuitively, if we think of A as representing edges in a graph, then P_1 asks for paths of length 2 and P_2 asks for paths of length 3. We do not expect either to be contained in the other, and indeed the containment-mapping test confirms that fact.

Consider a possible containment mapping τ from P_1 to P_2. Because of the conditions on heads, we know $\tau(x) = a$ and $\tau(y) = b$. To what does z map? Since we already know $\tau(x) = a$, the first subgoal $A(x, z)$ can only map to $A(a, c)$ of P_2. That means $\tau(z)$ must be c. However, since $\tau(y) = b$, the subgoal $A(z, y)$ of P_1 can only become $A(d, b)$ in P_2. That means $\tau(z)$ must be d. But z can only map to one value; it cannot map to both c and d. We conclude that no containment mapping from P_1 to P_2 exists.

A similar argument shows that there is no containment mapping from P_2 to P_1. We leave it as an exercise. □

Complexity of the Containment-Mapping Test

It is NP-complete to decide whether there is a containment mapping from one conjunctive query to another. However, in practice, it is usually quite easy to decide whether a containment mapping exists. Conjunctive queries in practice have few subgoals and few variables. Moreover, for the class of conjunctive queries that have no more than two subgoals with the same predicate — a very common condition — there is a linear-time test for the existence of a containment mapping.

The importance of containment mappings is expressed by the following theorem:

- If Q_1 and Q_2 are conjunctive queries, then $Q_2 \subseteq Q_1$ if and only if there is a containment mapping from Q_1 to Q_2.

Notice that the containment mapping goes in the opposite direction from the containment; that is, the containment mapping is from the conjunctive query that produces the larger set of answers to the one that produces the smaller, contained set.

21.6.5 Why the Containment-Mapping Test Works

We need to argue two points. First, if there is a containment mapping, why must there be a containment of conjunctive queries? Second, if there is containment, why must there be a containment mapping? We shall not give formal proofs, but will sketch the arguments.

First, suppose there is a containment mapping τ from Q_1 to Q_2. Recall from Section 5.3.4 that when we apply Q_2 to a database, we look for substitutions σ for all the variables of Q_2 that make all its relational subgoals be tuples of the corresponding relation of the database. The substitution for the head becomes a tuple t that is returned by Q_2. If we compose τ and then σ, we have a mapping from the variables of Q_1 to tuples of the database that produces the same tuple t for the head of Q_1. Thus, on any given database, everything that Q_2 produces is also produced by Q_1.

Conversely, suppose that $Q_2 \subseteq Q_1$. That is, on any database D, everything that Q_2 produces is also produced by Q_1. Construct a particular database D that has only the subgoals of Q_2. That is, pretend the variables of Q_2 are distinct constants, and for each subgoal $P(a_1, a_2, \ldots, a_n)$, put the tuple $(a_1, a_2, \ldots, a_n)$ in the relation for P. There are no other tuples in the relations of D.

When Q_2 is applied to database D, surely the tuple whose components are the arguments of the head of Q_2 is produced. Since $Q_2 \subseteq Q_1$, it must be that

Q_1 applied to D also produces the head of Q_2. Again, we use the definition in Section 5.3.4 of how a conjunctive query is applied to a database. That definition tells us that there is a substitution of constants of D for the variables of Q_1 that turns each subgoal of Q_1 into a tuple in D and turns the head of Q_1 into the tuple that is the head of Q_2. But remember that the constants of D are the variables of Q_2. Thus, this substitution is actually a containment mapping.

21.6.6 Finding Solutions to a Mediator Query

We have one more issue to resolve. We are given a mediator query Q, and we need to find all solutions S such that the expansion E of S is contained in Q. But there could be an infinite number of S built from the views using any number of subgoals and variables. The following theorem limits our search.

- If a query Q has n subgoals, then any answer produced by any solution is also produced by a solution that has at most n subgoals.

This theorem, often called the LMSS Theorem,[4] gives us a finite, although exponential task to find a sufficient set of solutions. There has been considerable work on making the test much more efficient in typical situations.

Example 21.21: Recall the query

$$Q_1: \quad \text{Q(w,z)} \leftarrow \text{Par(w,x) AND Par(x,y) AND Par(y,z)}$$

from Example 21.16. This query has three subgoals, so we don't have to look at solutions with more than three subgoals. One of the solutions we proposed was

$$S_1: \quad \text{Q(w,z)} \leftarrow \text{V}_1\text{(w,x) AND V}_2\text{(x,z)}$$

This solution has only two subgoals, and its expansion is contained in the query. Thus, it needs to be included among the set of solutions that we evaluate to answer the query.

However, consider the following solution:

$$S_2: \quad \text{Q(w,z)} \leftarrow \text{V}_1\text{(w,x) AND V}_2\text{(x,z) AND V}_1\text{(t,u) AND V}_2\text{(u,v)}$$

It has four subgoals, so we know by the LMSS Theorem that it does not need to be considered. However, it is truly a solution, since its expansion

$$E_2: \quad \text{Q(w,z)} \leftarrow \text{Par(w,x) AND Par(x,p) AND Par(p,z) AND Par(t,u)}$$
$$\text{AND Par(u,q) AND Par(q,v)}$$

---

[4]For the authors, A. Y. Levy, A. O. Mendelzon, Y. Sagiv, and D. Srivastava.

is contained in the query Q_1. To see why, use the containment mapping that maps w, x, and z to themselves and y to p.

However, E_2 is also contained in the expansion E_1 of the smaller solution S_1. Recall from Example 21.18 that the expansion of S_1 is

$$E_1: \quad \text{Q(w,z)} \leftarrow \text{Par(w,x) AND Par(x,p) AND Par(p,z)}$$

We can see immediately that $E_2 \subseteq E_1$, using the containment mapping that sends each variable of E_1 to the same variable in E_2. Thus, every answer to Q_1 produced by S_2 is also produced by S_1. Notice, incidentally, that S_2 is really S_1 with the two subgoals of S_1 repeated with different variables. □

In principle, to apply the LMSS Theorem, we must consider a number of possible solutions that is exponential in the query size. We must consider not only the choices of predicates for the subgoals, but which arguments of which subgoals hold the same variable. Note that within a conjunctive query, the names of the variables do not matter, but it matters which sets of arguments have the same variable. Most query processing is worst-case exponential in the query size anyway, as we learned in Chapter 16. Moreover, there are some powerful techniques known for limiting the search for solutions by looking at the structure of the conjunctive queries that define the views. We shall not go into depth here, but one easy but powerful idea is the following.

- If the conjunctive query that defines a view V has in its body a predicate P that does not appear in the body of the mediator query, then we need not consider any solution that uses V.

21.6.7 Why the LMSS Theorem Holds

Suppose we have a query Q with n subgoals, and there is a solution S with more than n subgoals. The expansion E of S must be contained in query Q, which means that there is a containment mapping from Q to the expansion E, as suggested in Fig. 21.11. If there are n subgoals ($n = 2$ in Fig. 21.11) in Q, then the containment mapping turns Q's subgoals into at most n of the subgoals of the expansion E. Moreover, these subgoals of E come from at most n of the subgoals of the solution S.

Suppose we removed from S all subgoals whose expansion was not the target of one of Q's subgoals under the containment mapping. We would have a new conjunctive query S' with at most n subgoals. Now S' must also be a solution to Q, because the same containment mapping that showed $E \subseteq Q$ in Fig. 21.11 also shows that $E' \subseteq Q$, where E' is the expansion of S'.

We must show one more thing: that any answer provided by S is also provided by S'. That is, $S \subseteq S'$. But there is an obvious containment mapping from S' to S: the identity mapping. Thus, there is no need for solution S among the solutions to query Q.

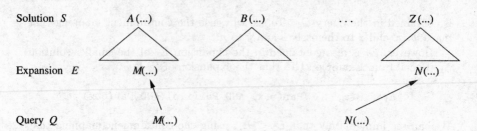

Figure 21.11: Why a query with n subgoals cannot need a solution with more than n subgoals

21.6.8 Exercises for Section 21.6

! **Exercise 21.6.1:** For the mediator and views of Example 21.16, find all the needed solutions to the great-great-grandparent query:

$$Q(x,y) \leftarrow Par(x,a) \text{ AND } Par(a,b) \text{ AND } Par(b,c) \text{ AND } Par(c,y)$$

! **Exercise 21.6.2:** Show that there is no containment mapping from P_2 to P_1 in Example 21.20.

! **Exercise 21.6.3:** Show that if conjunctive query Q_2 is constructed from conjunctive query Q_1 by removing one or more subgoals of Q_1, then $Q_1 \subseteq Q_2$.

Exercise 21.6.4: Find all the containments among the following four conjunctive queries:

Q_1:   P(x,y) ← Q(x,a) AND Q(a,b) AND Q(b,y)
Q_2:   P(x,y) ← Q(x,a) AND Q(a,1) AND Q(1,b) AND Q(b,y)
Q_3:   P(x,y) ← Q(x,a) AND Q(b,c) AND Q(d,y) AND Q(x,b) AND
                      Q(a,c) AND Q(c,y)
Q_4:   P(x,y) ← Q(x,a) AND Q(a,b) AND Q(b,c) AND Q(c,y)

21.7 Entity Resolution

We shall now take up a problem that must be solved in many information-integration scenarios. We have tacitly assumed that sources agree on the representation of entities or values, or at least that it is possible to perform a translation of data as we go through a wrapper. Thus, we are not afraid of two sources that report temperatures, one in Fahrenheit and one in Centigrade. Neither are we afraid of sources that support a concept like "employee" but have somewhat different sets of employees.

What happens, however, if two sources not only have different sets of employees, but it is unclear whether records at the two sources represent the same individual or not? Discrepancies can occur for many reasons, such as misspellings. In this section, we shall begin by discussing some of the reasons why *entity resolution* — determining whether two records or tuples do or do not represent the same person, organization, place, or other entity — is a hard problem. We then look at the process of comparing records and merging those that we believe represent the same entity. Under some fairly reasonable conditions, there is an algorithm for finding a unique way to group all sets of records that represent a common entity and to perform this grouping efficiently.

21.7.1 Deciding Whether Records Represent a Common Entity

Imagine we have a collection of records that represent members of an entity set. These records may be tuples derived from several different sources, or even from one source. We only need to know that the records each have the same fields (although some records may have null in some fields). We hope to compare the values in corresponding fields to decide whether or not two records represent the same entity.

To be concrete, suppose that the entities are people, and the records have three fields: name, address, and phone. Intuitively, we want to say that two records represent the same individual if the two records have similar values for each of the three fields. It is not sufficient to insist that the values of corresponding fields be identical for a number of reasons. Among them:

1. *Misspellings.* Often, data is entered by a clerk who hears something over the phone, or who copies a written form carelessly. Thus, "Smythe" may appear as "Smith," or "Jones" may appear as "Jomes" ("m" and "n" are adjacent on the keyboard). Two phone numbers or street addresses may differ in a digit, yet really represent the same phone or house.

2. *Variant Names.* A person may supply their middle initial or not. They may use their complete first name or just their initial, or a nickname. Thus, "Susan Williams" may appear as "Susan B. Williams," "S. Williams," or "Sue Williams" in different records.

3. *Misunderstanding of Names.* There are many different systems of names used throughout the world. In the US, it is sometimes not understood that Asian names generally begin with the family name. Thus, "Chen Li" and "Li Chen" may or may not turn out to be the same person. The first author of this book has been referred to as "Hector Garcia-Molina," "Hector Garcia," and even "Hector G. Molina."

4. *Evolution of Values.* Sometimes, two different records that represent the same entity were created at different times. A person may have moved in the interrim, so the address fields in the two records are completely different. Or they may have started using a cell phone, so the phone

fields are completely different. Area codes are sometimes changed. For example, every (650) number used to be a (415) number, so an old record may have (415) 555-1212 and a newer record (650) 555-1212, and yet these numbers refer to the same phone.

5. *Abbreviations.* Sometimes words in an address are spelled out; other times an abbreviation may be used. Thus, "Sesame St." and "Sesame Street" may be the same street.

Thus, when deciding whether two records represent the same entity, we need to look carefully at the kinds of discrepancies that occur and devise a scoring system or other test that measures the similarity of records. Ultimately, we must turn the score into a yes/no decision: do the records represent the same entity or not? We shall mention below two useful approaches to measuring the similarity of records.

Edit Distance

Values that are strings can be compared by counting the number of insertions and/or deletions of characters it takes to turn one string into another. Thus, Smythe and Smith are at distance 3 (delete the "y" and "e," then insert the "i").

An alternative edit distance counts 1 for a *mutation*, that is, a replacement of one letter by another. In this measure, Smythe and Smith are at distance 2 (mutate "y" to "i" and delete "e"). This edit distance makes mistyped characters "cost" less, and therefore may be appropriate if typing errors are common in the data.

Finally, we may devise a specialized distance that takes into account the way the data was constructed. For instance, if we decide that changes of area codes are a major source of errors, we might charge only 1 for changing the entire area code from one to another. We might decide that the problem of misinterpreted family names was severe and allow two components of a name to be swapped at low cost, so Chen Li and Li Chen are at distance 1.

Once we have decided on the appropriate edit distance for each field, we can define a similarity measure for records. For example, we could sum the edit distances of each of the pairs of corresponding fields in the two records, or we could compute the sum of the squares of those distances. Whatever formula we use, we have then to say that records represent the same entity if their similarity measure is below a given threshold.

Normalization

Before applying an edit distance, we might wish to "normalize" records by replacing certain substrings by others. The goal is that substrings representing the same "thing" will become identical. For instance, it may make sense to use a table of abbreviations and replace abbreviations by what they normally stand for. Thus, St. would be replaced by Street in street addresses and by Saint in town names. Also, we could use a table of nicknames and variant spellings, so Sue would become Susan and Jeffery would become Geoffrey.

One could even use the *Soundex* encoding of names, so names that sound the same are represented by the same string. This system, used by telephone information services, for example, would represent Smith and Smythe identically. Once we have normalized values in the records, we could base our similarity test on identical values only (e.g., a majority of fields have identical values in the two records), or we could further use an edit distance to measure the difference between normalized values in the fields.

21.7.2 Merging Similar Records

In many applications, when we find two records that are similar enough to merge, we would like to replace them by a single record that, in some sense, contains the information of both. For instance, if we want to compile a "dossier" on the entity represented, we might take the union of all the values in each field. Or we might somehow combine the values in corresponding fields to make a single value. If we try to combine values, there are many rules that we might follow, with no obvious best approach. For example, we might assume that a full name should replace a nickname or initials, and a middle initial should be used in place of no middle initial. Thus, "Susan Williams" and "S. B. Williams" would be combined into "Susan B. Williams."

It is less clear how to deal with misspellings. For instance, how would we combine the addresses "123 Oak St." and "123 Yak St."? Perhaps we could look at the town or zip-code and determine that there was an Oak St. there and no Yak St. But if both existed and had 123 in their range of addresses, there is no right answer.

Another problem that arises if we use certain combinations of a similarity test and a merging rule is that our decision to merge one pair of records may preclude our merging another pair. An example may help illustrate the risk.

	name	*address*	*phone*
(1)	Susan Williams	123 Oak St.	818-555-1234
(2)	Susan Williams	456 Maple St.	818-555-1234
(3)	Susan Williams	456 Maple St.	213-555-5678

Figure 21.12: Three records to be merged

Example 21.22: Suppose that we have the three name-address-phone records in Fig. 21.12. and our similarity rule is: "must agree exactly in at least two out of the three fields." Suppose also that our merge rule is: "set the field in which the records disagree to the empty string."

Then records (1) and (2) are similar; so are records (2) and (3). Note that records (1) and (3) are not similar to each other, which serves to remind us that "similarity" is not normally a transitive relationship. If we decide to replace (1) and (2) by their merger, we are left with the two tuples:

	name	address	phone
(1-2)	Susan Williams		818-555-1234
(3)	Susan Williams	456 Maple St.	213-555-5678

These records disagree in two fields, so they cannot be merged. Had we merged (1) and (3) first, we would again have a situation where the remaining record cannot be merged with the result.

Another choice for similarity and merge rules is:

1. Merge by taking the union of the values in each field, and

2. Declare two records similar if at least two of the three fields have a nonempty intersection.

Consider the three records in Fig. 21.12. Again, (1) is similar to (2) and (2) is similar to (3), but (1) is not similar to (3). If we choose to merge (1) and (2) first, we get:

	name	address	phone
(1-2)	Susan Williams	{123 Oak St.	818-555-1234
		456 Maple St.}	
(3)	Susan Williams	456 Maple St.	213-555-5678

Now, the remaining two tuples are similar, because 456 Maple St. is a member of both address sets and Susan Williams is a member of both name sets. The result is a single tuple:

	name	address	phone
(1-2-3)	Susan Williams	{123 Oak St.,	{818-555-1234,
		456 Maple St.}	213-555-5678}

□

21.7.3 Useful Properties of Similarity and Merge Functions

Any choice of similarity and merge functions allows us to test pairs of records for similarity and merge them if so. As we saw in the first part of Example 21.22, the result we get when no more records can be merged may depend on which pairs of mergeable records we consider first. Whether or not different ending configurations can result depends on properties of similarity and merger.

There are several properties that we would expect any merge function to satisfy. If ∧ is the operation that produces the merge of two records, it is reasonable to expect:

1. $r \wedge r = r$ (*Idempotence*). That is, the merge of a record with itself should surely be that record.

2. $r \wedge s = s \wedge r$ (*Commutativity*). If we merge two records, the order in which we list them should not matter.

3. $(r \wedge s) \wedge t = r \wedge (s \wedge t)$ (*Associativity*). The order in which we group records for a merger should not matter.

These three properties say that the merge operation is a semilattice. Note that both merger functions in Example 21.22 have these properties. The only tricky point is that we must remember that $r \wedge s$ need not defined for all records r and s. We do, however, assume that:

- If r and s are similar, then $r \wedge s$ is defined.

There are also some properties that we expect the similarity relationship to have, and ways that we expect similarity and merging to interact. We shall use $r \approx s$ to say that records r and s are similar.

a) $r \approx r$ (*Idempotence* for similarity). A record is always similar to itself.

b) $r \approx s$ if and only if $s \approx r$ (*Commutativity* of similarity). That is, in deciding whether two records are similar, it does not matter in which order we list them.

c) If $r \approx s$, then $r \approx (s \wedge t)$ (*Representability*). This rule requires that if r is similar to some other record s (and thus could be merged with s), but s is instead merged with some other record t, then r remains similar to the merger of s and t and can be merged with that record.

Note that representability is the property most likely to fail. In particular, it fails for the first merger rule in Example 21.22, where we merge by setting disagreeing fields to the empty string. In particular, representability fails when r is record (3) of Fig. 21.12, s is (2), and t is (1). On the other hand, the second merger rule of Example 21.22 satisfies the representability rule. If r and s have nonempty intersections in at least two fields, those shared values will still be present if we replace s by $s \wedge t$.

The collection of properties above are called the *ICAR properties*. The letters stand for Idempotence, Commutativity, Associativity, and Representability, respectively.

21.7.4 The R-Swoosh Algorithm for ICAR Records

When the similarity and merge functions satisfy the ICAR properties, there is a simple algorithm that merges all possible records. The representability property guarantees that if two records are similar, then as they are merged with other records, the resulting records are also similar and will eventually be merged. Thus, if we repeatedly replace any pair of similar records by their merger, until no more pairs of similar records remain, then we reach a unique set of records that is independent of the order in which we merge.

A useful way to think of the merger process is to imagine a graph whose nodes are the records. There is an edge between nodes r and s if $r \approx s$. Since similarity need not be transitive, it is possible that there are edges between r and s and between s and t, yet there is no edge between r and t. For instance, the records of Fig. 21.12 have the graph of Fig. 21.13.

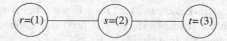

Figure 21.13: Similarity graph from Fig. 21.12

However, representability tells us that if we merge s and t, then because r is similar to s, it will be similar to $s \wedge t$. Thus, we can merge all three of r, s, and t. Likewise, if we merge r and s first, representability says that because $s \approx t$, we also have $(r \wedge s) \approx t$, so we can merge t with $r \wedge s$. Associativity tells us that the resulting record will be the same, regardless of the order in which we do the merge.

The idea described above extends to any set of ICAR nodes (records) that are connected in any way. That is, regardless of the order in which we do the merges, the result is that every connected component of the graph becomes a single record. This record is the merger of all the records in that component. Commutativity and associativity are enough to tell us that the order in which we perform the mergers does not matter.

Although computing connected components of a graph is simple in principle, when we have millions of records or more, it is not feasible to construct the graph. To do so would require us to test similarity of every pair of records. The "R-Swoosh" algorithm is an implementation of this idea that organizes the comparisons so we avoid, in many cases, comparing all pairs of records. Unfortunately, if no records at all are similar, then there is no algorithm that can avoid comparing all pairs of records to determine this fact.

Algorithm 21.23: R-Swoosh.

INPUT: A set of records I, a similarity function $\approx$, and a merge function $\wedge$. We assume that $\approx$ and $\wedge$ satisfy the ICAR properties. If they do not, then the algorithm will still merge some records, but the result may not be the maximum or best possible merging.

OUTPUT: A set of merged records O.

METHOD: Execute the steps of Fig. 21.14. The value of O at the end is the output.   □

```
O := emptyset;
WHILE I is not empty DO BEGIN
    let r be any record in I;
    find, if possible, some record s in O that is similar to r;
    IF no record s exists THEN
        move r from I to O
    ELSE BEGIN
        delete r from I;
        delete s from O;
        add the merger of r and s to I;
    END;
END;
```

Figure 21.14: The R-Swoosh Algorithm

Example 21.24: Suppose that I is the three records of Fig. 21.12, and that we use the ICAR similarity and merge functions from Example 21.22, where we take the union of possible values for a field to produce the corresponding field in the merged record. Initially, O is empty. We pick one of the records from I, say record (1) to be the record r in Fig. 21.14. Since O is empty, there is no possible record s, so we move record (1) from I to O.

We next pick a new record r. Suppose we pick record (3). Since record (3) is not similar to record (1), which is the only record in O, we again have no value of s, so we move record (3) from I to O. The third choice of r must be record (2). That record is similar to both of the records in O, so we must pick one to be s; say we pick record (1). Then we merge records (1) and (2) to get the record

	name	address	phone
(1-2)	Susan Williams	{123 Oak St., 456 Maple St.}	818-555-1234

We remove record (2) from I, remove record (1) from O, and insert the above record into I. At this point, I consists of only the record (1-2) and O consists of only the record (3).

The execution of the R-Swoosh Algorithm ends after we pick record (1-2) as r — the only choice — and pick record (3) as s — again the only choice. These records are merged, to produce

	name	address	phone
(1-2-3)	Susan Williams	{123 Oak St., 456 Maple St.}	{818-555-1234, 213-555-5678}

and deleted from I and O, respectively. The record (1-2-3) is put in I, at which point it is the only record in I, and O is empty. At the last step, this record is moved from I to O, and we are done. □

21.7.5 Why R-Swoosh Works

Recall that for ICAR similarity and merge functions, the goal is to merge records that form connected components. There is a loop invariant that holds for the while-loop of Fig. 21.14:

- If a connected component C is not completely merged into one record, then there is at least one record in I that is either in C or was formed by the merger of some records from C.

To see why this invariant must hold, suppose that the selected record r in some iteration of the loop is the last record in I from its connected component C. If r is the only record that is the merger of one or more records from C, then it may be moved to O without violating the loop invariant.

However, if there are other records that are the merger of one or more records from C, they are in O. Let r be the merger of the set of records $R \subseteq C$. Note that R could be only one record, or could be many records. However, since R is not all of C, there must be an original record r_1 in R that is similar to another original record r_2 that is in $C - R$. Suppose r_2 is currently merged into a record r' in O. By representability, perhaps applied several times, we can start with the known $r_1 \approx r_2$ and deduce that $r \approx r'$. Thus, r' can be s in Fig. 21.14. As a result, r will surely be merged with some record from O. The resulting merged record will be placed in I and is the merger of some or all records from C. Thus, the loop invariant continues to hold.

21.7.6 Other Approaches to Entity Resolution

There are many other algorithms known to discover and (optionally) merge similar records. We shall outline some of them briefly here.

Non-ICAR Datasets

First, suppose the ICAR properties do not hold, but we want to find all possible mergers of records, including cases where one record r_1 is merged with a record r_2, but later, r_1 (not the merger $r_1 \wedge r_2$) is also merged with r_3. If so, we need to systematically compare all records, including those we constructed by merger, with all other records, again including those constructed by merger.

To help control the proliferation of records, we can define a *dominance* relation $r \leq s$ that means record s contains all the information contained in record r. If so, we can eliminate record r from further consideration. If the merge function is a semilattice, then the only reasonable choice for $\leq$ is $a \leq b$ if and only if $a \wedge b = b$. This dominance function is always a partial order, regardless of what semilattice is used. If the merge operation is not even a semilattice, then the dominance function must be constructed in an ad-hoc manner.

Clustering

In some entity-resolution applications, we do not want to merge at all, but will instead group records into *clusters* such that members of a cluster are in some sense similar to each other and members of different clusters are not similar. For example, if we are looking for similar products sold on eBay, we might want the result to be not a single record for each kind of product, but rather a list of the records that represent a common product for sale. Clustering of large-scale data involves a complex set of options. We shall discuss the matter further in Section 22.5.

Partitioning

Since any algorithm for doing a complete merger of similar records may be forced to examine each pair of records, it may be infeasible to get an exact answer to a large entity-resolution problem. One solution is to group the records, perhaps several times, into groups that are likely to contain similar records, and look only within each group for pairs of similar records.

Example 21.25: Suppose we have millions of name-address-phone records, and our measure of similarity is that the total edit distance of the values in the three fields must be at most 5. We could partition the records into groups such that each group has the same name field. We could also partition the records according to the value in their address field, and a third time according to their phone numbers. Thus, each record appears in three groups and is compared only with the members of those groups. This method will not notice a pair of similar records that have edit distance 2 in their phone fields, 2 in their name fields, and 1 in their address fields. However, in practice, it will catch almost all similar pairs. □

The idea in Example 21.25 is actually a special case of an important idea: "locality-sensitive hashing." We discuss this topic in Section 22.4.

21.7.7 Exercises for Section 21.7

Exercise 21.7.1: A string s is a *subsequence* of a string t if s is formed from t by deleting 0 or more positions of t. For example, if $t = $ "acbac", then substrings of t include "aca" (delete positions 3 and 5), "cb" (delete positions 1, 4, and 5), and the empty string (delete all positions).

a) What are all the other subsequences of "acbac"?

b) What are the subsequences of "aacc"?

! c) If a string consists of n distinct characters, how many subsequences does it have?

Exercise 21.7.2: A *longest common subsequence* of two strings s and t is any string r that is a subsequence of both s and t and is as long as any other string that is a substring of both. For example, the longest common subsequences of "aba" and "bab" are "ab" and "ba". Give a the longest common subsequence for each pair of the following strings: "she", "hers", "they", and "theirs"?

Exercise 21.7.3: A *shortest common supersequence* of two strings s and t is any string r of which both s and t are subsequences, such that no string shorter than r has both s and t as subsequences. For example, the some of the shortest common supersequences of "acb" and "bc" are "acbc" and "abcb".

a) What are the shortest common supersequences of each pair of strings in Exercise 21.7.2?

! b) What are all the other shortest common supersequences of "acb" and "bc"?

!! c) If two strings have no characters in common, and are of lengths m and n, respectively, how many shortest common supersequences do the two strings have?

! **Exercise 21.7.4:** In Section 21.7.6 we suggested that if $\wedge$ is a semilattice, then the dominance relationship defined by $a \leq b$ if and only if $a \wedge b = b$ is a partial order. That is, $a \leq b$ and $b \leq c$ imply $a \leq c$ (transitivity) and $a \leq b$ and $b \leq a$ if and only if $a = b$ (antisymmetry). Prove that $\leq$ is a partial order, using the reflexivity, commutativity, and associativity properties of a semilattice.

!! **Exercise 21.7.5:** Suppose we merge records (whose fields are strings) by taking, for each field, the lexicographically first longest common subsequence of the strings in the corresponding fields.

a) Does this definition of merge satisfy the idempotent, commutative, and associative laws?

b) Repeat (a) if instead corresponding fields are merged by taking the lexicographically first shortest common supersequence.

! **Exercise 21.7.6:** Suppose we define the similarity and merge functions by:

i. Records are similar if in all fields, or in all but one field, either both records have the same value or one has NULL.

ii. Merge records by letting each field have the common value if both records agree in that field or have value NULL if the records disagree in that field. Note that NULL disagrees with any nonnull value.

Show that these similarity and merge functions have the ICAR properties.

21.8 Summary of Chapter 21

✦ *Integration of Information*: When many databases or other information sources contain related information, we have the opportunity to combine these sources into one. However, heterogeneities in the schemas often exist; these incompatibilities include differing types, codes or conventions for values, interpretations of concepts, and different sets of concepts represented in different schemas.

✦ *Approaches to Information Integration*: Early approaches involved "federation," where each database would query the others in the terms understood by the second. A more recent approach is warehousing, where data is translated to a global schema and copied to the warehouse. An alternative is mediation, where a virtual warehouse is created to allow queries to a global schema; the queries are then translated to the terms of the data sources.

✦ *Extractors and Wrappers*: Warehousing and mediation require components at each source, called extractors and wrappers, respectively. A major function of either is to translate queries and results between the global schema and the local schema at the source.

✦ *Wrapper Generators*: One approach to designing wrappers is to use templates, which describe how a query of a specific form is translated from the global schema to the local schema. These templates are tabulated and interpreted by a driver that tries to match queries to templates. The driver may also have the ability to combine templates in various ways, and/or perform additional work such as filtering, to answer more complex queries.

✦ *Capability-Based Optimization*: The sources for a mediator often are able or willing to answer only limited forms of queries. Thus, the mediator must select a query plan based on the capabilities of its sources, before it can even think about optimizing the cost of query plans as conventional DBMS's do.

✦ *Adornments*: These provide a convenient notation in which to describe the capabilities of sources. Each adornment tells, for each attribute of a relation, whether, in queries matching that adornment, this attribute requires or permits a contant value, and whether constants must be chosen from a menu.

✦ *Conjunctive Queries*: A single Datalog rule, used as a query, is a convenient representation for queries involving joins, possibly followed by selection and/or projection.

✦ *The Chain Algorithm*: This algorithm is a greedy approach to answering mediator queries that are in the form of a conjunctive query. Repeatedly look for a subgoal that matches one of the adornments at a source, and obtain the relation for that subgoal from the source. Doing so may provide a set of constant bindings for some variables of the query, so repeat the process, looking for additional subgoals that can be resolved.

✦ *Local-as-View Mediators*: These mediators have a set of global, virtual predicates or relations at the mediator, and each source is described by views, which are conjunctive queries whose subgoals use the global predicates. A query at the mediator is also a conjunctive query using the global predicates.

✦ *Answering Queries Using Views*: A local-as-view mediator searches for solutions to a query, which are conjunctive queries whose subgoals use the views as predicates. Each such subgoal of a proposed solution is expanded using the conjunctive query that defines the view, and it is checked that the expansion is contained in the query. If so, the proposed solution does indeed provide (some of the) answers to the query.

✦ *Containment of Conjunctive Queries*: We test for containment of conjunctive queries by looking for a containment mapping from the containing query to the contained query. A containment mapping is a substitution for variables that turns the head of the first into the head of the second and turns each subgoal of the first into some subgoal of the second.

✦ *Limiting the Search for Solutions*: The LMSS Theorem says that when seaching for solutions to a query at a local-as-view mediator, it is sufficient to consider solutions that have no more subgoals than the query does.

✦ *Entity Resolution*: The problem is to take records with a common schema, find pairs or groups of records that are likely to represent the same entity (e.g., a person) and merge these records into a single record that represents the information of the entire group.

✦ *ICAR Similarity and Merge Functions*: Certain choices of similarity and merge functions satisfy the properties of idempotence, commutativity, associativity, and representability. The latter is the key to efficient algorithms for merging, since it guarantees that if two records are similar, their successors will also be similar even as they are merged into records that represent progressively larger sets of original records.

✦ *The R-Swoosh Algorithm*: If similarity and merge functions have the ICAR properties, then the complete merger of similar records will group all records that are in a connected component of the graph formed from the similarity relation on the original records. The R-Swoosh algorithm is an efficient way to make all necessary mergers without determining similarity for every pair of records.

21.9 References for Chapter 21

Federated systems are surveyed in [11]. The concept of the mediator comes from [12]. Implementation of mediators and wrappers, especially the wrapper-generator approach, is covered in [4]. Capability-based optimization for mediators was explored in [10, 13]; the latter describes the Chain Algorithm.

Local-as-view mediators come from [7]. The LMSS Theorem is from [6], and the idea of containment mappings to decide containment of conjunctive queries is from [2]. [8] extends the idea to sources with limited capabilities. [5] is a survey of logical information-integration techniques.

Entity resolution was first studied informally by [9] and formally by [3]. The theory presented here, the R-Swoosh Algorithm, and related algorithms are from [1].

1. O. Benjelloun, H. Garcia-Molina, J. Jonas, Q. Su, S. E. Whang, and J. Widom, "Swoosh: a generic approach to entity resolution." Available as http://dbpubs.stanford.edu:8090/pub/2005-5.

2. A. K. Chandra and P. M. Merlin, "Optimal implementation of conjunctive queries in relational databases," *Proc. Ninth Annual Symposium on Theory of Computing*, pp. 77–90, 1977.

3. I. P. Fellegi and A. B. Sunter, "A theory for record linkage," *J. American Statistical Assn.* **64**, pp. 1183–1210, 1969.

4. H. Garcia-Molina, Y. Papakonstantinou, D. Quass, A. Rajaraman, Y. Sagiv, V. Vassalos, J. D. Ullman, and J. Widom, "The TSIMMIS approach to mediation: data models and languages," *J. Intelligent Information Systems* 8:2 (1997), pp. 117–132.

5. A. Y. Levy, "Logic-based techniques in data integration," *Logic-Based Artificial Intelligence* (J. Minker, ed.), pp. 575–595, Kluwer, Norwell, MA, 2000.

6. A. Y. Levy, A. O. Mendelzon, Y. Sagiv, and D. Srivastava, "Answering queries using views," *Proc. 25th Annual Symposium on Principles of Database Systems*, pp. 95–104, 1995.

7. A. Y. Levy, A. Rajaraman, and J. J. Ordille, "Querying heterogeneous information sources using source descriptions," *Intl. Conf. on Very Large Databases*, pp. 251–262, 1996.

8. A. Y. Levy, A. Rajaraman, and J. D. Ullman, "Answering queries using limited external query processors," *Proc. Fifteenth Annual Symposium on Principles of Database Systems*, pp. 227–237, 1996.

9. H. B. Newcombe, J. M. Kennedy, S. J. Axford, and A. P. James, "Automatic linkage of vital records," *Science* **130**, pp. 954–959, 1959.

10. Y. Papakonstantinou, A. Gupta, and L. Haas, "Capabilities-base query rewriting in mediator systems," *Conference on Parallel and Distributed Information Systems* (1996). Available as
    http://dbpubs.stanford.edu/pub/1995-2.

11. A. P. Sheth and J. A. Larson, "Federated databases for managing distributed, heterogeneous, and autonomous databases," *Computing Surveys* **22**:3 (1990), pp. 183–236.

12. G. Wiederhold, "Mediators in the architecture of future information systems," *IEEE Computer* **C-25**:1 (1992), pp. 38–49.

13. R. Yerneni, C. Li, H. Garcia-Molina, and J. D. Ullman, "Optimizing large joins in mediation systems," *Proc. Seventh Intl. Conf. on Database Theory*, pp. 348–364, 1999.

Chapter 22

Data Mining

"Data mining" is the process of examining data and finding simple rules or models that summarize the data. The rules can range from very general, such as "50% of the people who buy hot dogs also buy mustard," to the very specific: "these three individual's pattern of credit-card expenditures indicate that they are running a terrorist cell." Our discussion of data mining will concentrate on mining information from very large databases.

We begin by looking at "market-basket" data, records of the things people buy together, such as at a supermarket. This study leads to a number of efficient algorithms for finding "frequent itemsets" in large databases, including the "A-Priori" Algorithm and its extensions.

We next turn to finding "similar" items in a large collection. Example applications include finding documents on the Web that share a significant amount of common text or finding books that have been bought by many of the same Amazon customers. Two key techniques for this problem are "minhashing" and "locality-sensitive hashing."

We conclude the chapter with a discussion of the problem of large-scale clustering in high dimensions. An example application is clustering Web pages by the words they use. In that case, each word might be a dimension, and a document is placed in this space by counting the number of occurrences of each word.

22.1 Frequent-Itemset Mining

There is a family of problems that arise from attempts by marketers to use large databases of customer purchases to extract information about buying patterns. The fundamental problem is called "frequent itemsets" — what sets of items are often bought together? This information is sometimes further refined into "association rules" — implications that people who buy one set of items are likely to buy another particular item. The same technology has many other uses, from discovering combinations of genes related to certain diseases to finding plagiarism among documents on the Web.

22.1.1 The Market-Basket Model

In several important applications, the data involves a set of *items*, perhaps all the items that a supermarket sells, and a set of *baskets*; each basket is a subset of the set of items, typically a small subset. The baskets each represent a set of items that someone has bought together. Here are two typical examples of where market-basket data appears.

Supermarket Checkout

A supermarket chain may sell 10,000 different items. Daily, millions of customers wheel their shopping carts ("market baskets") to the checkout, and the cash register records the set of items they purchased. Each such set is one basket, in the sense used by the market-basket model. Some customers may have identified themselves, using a discount card that many supermarket chains provide, or by their credit card. However, the identity of the customer often is not necessary to get useful information from the data.

Stores analyze the data to learn what typical customers buy together. For example, if a large number of baskets contain both hot dogs and mustard, the supermarket manager can use this information in several ways.

1. Apparently, many people walk from where the hot dogs are to where the mustard is. We can put them close together, and put between them other foods that might also be bought with hot dogs and mustard, e.g., ketchup or potato chips. Doing so can generate additional "impulse" sales.

2. The store can run a sale on hot dogs and at the same time raise the price of mustard (without advertising that fact, of course). People will come to the store for the cheap hot dogs, and many will need mustard too. It is not worth the trouble to go to another store for cheaper mustard, so they buy that too. The store makes back on mustard what it loses on hot dogs, and also gets more customers into the store.

While the relationship between hot dogs and mustard may be obvious to those who think about the matter, even if they have no data to analyze, there are many pairs of items that are connected but may be less obvious. The most famous example is diapers and beer.[1]

There are some conditions on when a fact about co-occurrence of sets of items can be useful. Any useful pair (or larger set) of items must be bought by many customers. It is not even necessary that there be any connection between purchases of the items, as long as we know lots of customers buy them

---

[1] One theory: if you buy diapers, you probably have a baby at home. If so, you are not going out to a bar tonight, so you are more likely to buy beer at a supermarket.

all. Conversely, strongly linked, but rarely purchased items (e.g., caviar and champagne) are not very interesting to the supermarket, because it doesn't pay to advertise things that few customers are interested in buying anyway.

On-Line Purchases

Amazon.com offers several million different items for sale, and has several tens of millions of customers. While brick-and-mortar stores such as the supermarket discussed above can only make money on combinations of items that large numbers of people buy, Amazon and other on-line sellers have the opportunity to tailor their offers to every customer. Thus, an interesting question is to find pairs of items that many customers have bought together. Then, if one customer has bought one of these items but not the other, it might be good for Amazon to advertise the second item when this customer next logs in. We can treat the purchase data as a market-basket problem, where each "basket" is the set of items that one particular customer ever has bought.

But there is another way Amazon can use the same data. This approach, often called "collaborative filtering," has us look for customers that are similar in their purchase habits. For example, we could look for pairs, or even larger sets, of customers that have bought many of the same items. Then, if a customer logs in, Amazon might pitch an item that a similar customer bought, but this customer has not.

Finding similar customers also can be couched as a market-basket problem. Here, however, the "items" are the customers and the "baskets" are the items for sale by Amazon. That is, for each item I sold by Amazon there is a "basket" consisting of all the customers who bought I.

It is worth noting that the meaning of "many baskets" differs in the on-line and brick-and-mortar situations. In the brick-and-mortar case, we may need thousands of baskets containing a set of items before we can exploit that information profitably. For on-line stores, we need many fewer baskets containing a set of items, before we can use the information in the limited context we intend (pitching one item to one customer).

On the other hand, the brick-and-mortar store doesn't need too many examples of good sets of items to use; they can't run sales on millions of items. In contrast, the on-line store needs millions of good pairs to work with — at least one for each customer. As a result, the most effective techniques for analyzing on-line purchases may not be those of this section, which exploit the assumption that many occurrences of a pair of items are needed. Rather, we shall resume our discussion of finding correlated, but infrequent, pairs in Section 22.3.

22.1.2 Basic Definitions

Suppose we are given a set of items I and a set of baskets B. Each basket b in B is a subset of I. To talk about frequent sets of items, we need a *support threshold s*, which an integer. We say a set of items $J \subseteq I$ is *frequent* if there are at least s baskets that contain all the items in J (perhaps along with other items). Optionally, we can express the support s as a percentage of $|B|$, the number of baskets in B.

Example 22.1: Suppose our set of items I consists of the six movies

$$\{BI, BS, BU, HP1, HP2, HP3\}$$

standing for the *Bourne Identity, Bourne Supremacy, Bourne Ultimatum,* and *Harry Potter I, II,* and *III.* The table of Fig. 22.1 shows eight viewers (baskets of items) and the movies they have seen. An x indicates they saw the movie.

	BI	BS	BU	HP1	HP2	HP3
V_1	x	x	x			
V_2				x	x	x
V_3	x			x		
V_4	x	x		x	x	
V_5	x	x	x	x		
V_6	x		x			
V_7		x		x	x	
V_8	x	x		x	x	x

Figure 22.1: Market-basket data about viewers and movies

Suppose that $s = 3$. That is, in order for a set of items to be considered a frequent itemset, it must be a subset of at least three baskets. Technically, the empty set is a subset of all baskets, so it is frequent but uninteresting. In this example, all singleton sets except $\{HP3\}$ appear in at least three baskets. For example, $\{BI\}$ is contained in V_1, V_3, V_4, V_5, V_6, and V_8.

Now, consider which doubleton sets (pairs of items) are frequent. Since $HP3$ is not frequent by itself, it cannot be part of a frequent pair. However, each of the 10 pairs involving the other five movies might be frequent. For example, $\{BI, BS\}$ is frequent because it appears in at least three baskets; in fact it appears in four: V_1, V_4, V_5, and V_8.

Also:

- $\{BI, HP1\}$ is frequent appearing in V_3, V_4, V_5, and V_8.

- $\{BS, HP1\}$ is frequent, appearing in V_4, V_5, V_7, and V_8.

- $\{HP1, HP2\}$ is frequent, appearing in V_2, V_4, V_7, and V_8.

No other pair is frequent.

There is one frequent triple: $\{BI, BS, HP1\}$. This set is a subset of the baskets V_4, V_5, and V_8. There are no frequent itemsets of size greater than three. □

22.1.3 Association Rules

A natural query about market-basket data asks for implications among purchases that people make. That is, we want to find pairs of items such that people buying the first are likely to buy the second as well. More generally, people buying a particular set of items are also likely to buy yet another particular item. This idea is formalized by "association rules."

An *association rule* is a statement of the form $\{i_1, i_2, \ldots, i_n\} \Rightarrow j$, where the i's and j are items. In isolation, such a statement asserts nothing. However, three properties that we might want in useful rules of this form are:

1. High *Support*: the support of this association rule is the support of the itemset $\{i_1, i_2, \ldots, i_n, j\}$.

2. High *Confidence*: the probability of finding item j in a basket that has all of $\{i_1, i_2, \ldots, i_n\}$ is above a certain threshold, e.g., 50%, e.g., "at least 50% of the people who buy diapers buy beer."

3. *Interest*: the probability of finding item j in a basket that has all of $\{i_1, i_2, \ldots, i_n\}$ is significantly higher or lower than the probability of finding j in a random basket. In statistical terms, j correlates with

$$\{i_1, i_2, \ldots, i_n\}$$

either positively or negatively. The alleged relationship between diapers and beer is really a claim that the association rule $\{$diapers$\} \Rightarrow$ beer has high interest in the positive direction.

Note that even if an association rule has high confidence or interest, it will tend not to be useful unless it also has high support. The reason is that if the support is low, then the number of instances of the rule is not large, which limits the benefit of a strategy that exploits the rule. Also, it is important not to confuse an association rule, even with high values for support, confidence, and interest, with a causal rule. For instance, the "beer and diapers" example mentioned in Section 22.1.1 suggests that the association rule $\{$beer$\} \Rightarrow$ diapers has high confidence, but that does not mean beer "causes" diapers. Rather, the theory suggested there is that both are caused by a "hidden variable" — the baby at home.

Example 22.2: Using the data from Fig. 22.1, consider the association rule

$$\{BI, BS\} \Rightarrow BU$$

Its support is 2, since there are two baskets, V_1 and V_5 that contain all three "Bourne" movies. The confidence of the rule is $1/2$, since there are four baskets that contain both BI and BS, and two of these also contain BU. The rule is slightly interesting in the positive direction. That is, BU appears in $3/8$ of all baskets, but appears in $1/2$ of those baskets that contain the left side of the association rule. □

As long as high support is a significant requirement for a useful association rule, the search for high-confidence or high-interest association rules is really the search for high-support itemsets. Once we have these itemsets, we can consider each member of an itemset as the item on the right of the association rule. We may, as part of the process of finding frequent itemsets, already have computed the counts of baskets for the subsets of this frequent itemset, since they also must be frequent. If so, we can compute easily the confidence and interest of each potential association rule. We shall thus, in what follows, leave aside the problem of finding association rules and concentrate on efficient methods for finding frequent itemsets.

22.1.4   The Computation Model for Frequent Itemsets

Since we are studying database systems, our first thought might be that the market-basket data is stored in a relation such as:

```
Baskets(basket, item)
```

consisting of pairs that are a basket ID and the ID of one of the items in that basket. In principle, we could find frequent itemsets by a SQL query. For instance, the query in Fig. 22.2 finds all frequent pairs. It joins Baskets with itself, grouping the resulting tuples by the two items found in that tuple, and throwing away groups where the number of baskets is below the support threshold s. Note that the condition I.item < J.item in the WHERE-clause is there to prevent the same pair from being considered in both orders, or for a "pair" consisting of the same item twice from being considered at all.

```
SELECT I.item, J.item, COUNT(I.basket)
FROM Baskets I, Baskets J
WHERE I.basket = J.basket AND
      I.item < J.item
GROUP BY I.item, J.item
HAVING COUNT(I.basket) >= s;
```

Figure 22.2: Naive way to find all high-support pairs of items

However, if the size of the Baskets relation is very large, the join of the relation with itself will be too large to construct, or at least too time-consuming to construct. No matter how efficiently we compute the join, the result relation contains one tuple for each pair of items in a basket. For instance, if there are 1,000,000 baskets, and each basket contains 20 items, then there will be 190,000,000 tuples in the join [since $\binom{20}{2} = 190$]. We shall see in Section 22.2 that it is often possible to do much better by preprocessing the Baskets relation.

But in fact, it is not common to store market-basket data as a relation. It is far more efficient to put the data in a file or files consisting of the baskets, in some order. A basket is represented by a list of its items, and there is some punctuation between baskets.

Example 22.3: The data of Fig. 22.1 could be represented by a file that begins:

    {BI,BS,BU}{HP1,HP2,HP3}{BI,HP1}{BI,BS,HP1,HP2}{...

Here, we are using brackets to surround baskets and commas to separate items within a basket. □

When market-basket data is represented this way, the cost of an algorithm is relatively simple to estimate. Since we are interested only in cases where the data is too large to fit in main memory, we can count disk-I/O's as our measure of complexity.

However, the matter is even simpler than disk-I/O's. All the successful algorithms for finding frequent itemsets read the data file several times, in the order given. They thus make several passes over the data, and the information preserved from one pass to the next is small enough to fit in main memory. Thus, we do not even have to count disk-I/O's; it is sufficient to count the number of passes through the data.

22.1.5 Exercises for Section 22.1

Exercise 22.1.1: Suppose we are given the eight "market baskets" of Fig. 22.3.

$$B_1 = \{milk, coke, beer\}$$
$$B_2 = \{milk, pepsi, juice\}$$
$$B_3 = \{milk, beer\}$$
$$B_4 = \{coke, juice\}$$
$$B_5 = \{milk, pepsi, beer\}$$
$$B_6 = \{milk, beer, juice, pepsi\}$$
$$B_7 = \{coke, beer, juice\}$$
$$B_8 = \{beer, pepsi\}$$

Figure 22.3: Example market-basket data

a) As a percentage of the baskets, what is the support of the set {beer, milk}?

b) What is the support of the itemset {coke, pepsi}?

c) What is the confidence of beer given milk (i.e., of the association rule {milk} ⇒ beer)?

d) What is the confidence of milk given juice?

   e) What is the confidence of pepsi, given beer and milk?

   f) If the support threshold is 25% (i.e., 2 out of the eight baskets are needed), which pairs of items are frequent?

   g) If the support threshold is 37.5%, which pairs of items are frequent?

! h) What is the most interesting association rule with a singleton set on the left?

22.2 Algorithms for Finding Frequent Itemsets

We now look at how many passes are needed to find frequent itemsets of a certain size. We first argue why, in practice, finding frequent pairs is often the bottleneck. Then, we present the A-Priori Algorithm, a key step in minimizing the amount of main memory needed for a multipass algorithm. Several improvements on A-Priori make better use of main memory on the first pass, in order to make it more feasible to complete the algorithm without exceeding the capacity of main memory on later passes.

22.2.1 The Distribution of Frequent Itemsets

If we pick a support threshold $s = 1$, then all itemsets that appear in any basket are "frequent," so just producing the answer could be infeasible. However, in applications such as managing sales at a store, a small support threshold is not useful. Recall that we need many customers buying a set of items before we can exploit that itemset. Moreover, any data mining of market-basket data must produce a small number of answers, say tens or hundreds. If we get no answers, we cannot act, but if we get millions of answers, we cannot read them all, let alone act on them all.

The consequence of this reasoning is that the support threshold must be set high enough to make few itemsets frequent. Typically, a threshold around 1% of the baskets is used. Since the probability of an itemset being frequent goes down rapidly with size, most frequent itemsets will be small. However, an itemset of size one is generally not useful; we need at least two items in a frequent itemset in order to apply the marketing techniques mentioned in Section 22.1.1, for example.

Our conclusion is that in practical uses of algorithms to find frequent itemsets, we need to use a support threshold so that there will be a small number of frequent pairs, and very few frequent itemsets that are larger. Thus, our algorithms will focus on how to find frequent pairs in a few passes through the data. If larger frequent itemsets are wanted, the computing resources used to find the frequent pairs are usually sufficient to find the small number of frequent triples, quadruples, and so on.

What if Items Aren't Numbered Conveniently

We assume that items have integer ID's starting at 0. However, in practice, items could be represented by long ID's or by their full names. If so, we need to keep in main memory a hash table that maps each true item-ID to a unique integer in the range 0 to $k - 1$. This table consumes main memory proportional to the number of items k. No algorithm for finding frequent pairs or larger itemsets works if the number of items is not small compared with the available main memory. Thus, we neglect the possible need for a main-memory table whose size is proportional to the number of items.

22.2.2 The Naive Algorithm for Finding Frequent Itemsets

Let us suppose that there is some fixed number of bytes of main memory M, perhaps a gigabyte, or 16 gigabytes, or whatever our machine has. Let there be k different items in our market-basket dataset, and assume they are numbered $0, 1, \ldots, k - 1$. Finally, as suggested in Section 22.2.1, we shall focus on the counting of pairs, assuming that is the bottleneck for memory use.

If there is enough room in main memory to count all the pairs of items as we make a single pass over the baskets, then we can solve the frequent-pairs problem in a single pass. In that pass, we read one block of the data file at a time. We shall neglect the amount of main memory needed to hold this block (or even several blocks if baskets span two or more blocks), since we may assume that the space needed to represent a basket is tiny compared with M. For each basket found on this block, we execute a double loop through its items and for each pair of items in the basket, we add one to the count for that pair.

The essential problem we face, then, is how do we store the counts of the pairs of items in M bytes of memory. There are two reasonable ways to do so, and which is better depends on whether it is common or unlikely that a given pair of items occurs in at least one basket. In what follows, we shall make the simplifying assumption that all integers, whether used for a count or to represent an item, require four bytes. Here are the two contending approaches to maintaining counts.

Triangular Matrix

If most of the possible pairs of items are expected to appear at least once in the dataset, then the most efficient use of main memory is a triangular array. That is, let a be a one-dimensional integer array occupying all available main memory. We count the pair (i, j), where $0 \le i < j < k$ in $a[n]$, where:

$$n = (i+j)^2/4 + i - 1/4 \quad \text{if } i+j \text{ is odd}$$
$$n = (i+j)^2/4 + i \quad\quad\;\; \text{if } i+j \text{ is even}$$

As long as $M \geq 2k^2$, there is enough room to store array a, with four bytes per count. Notice that this method takes only half the space that would be used by a square array, of which we used only the upper or lower triangle to count the pairs (i, j) where $i < j$.

Table of Counts

If the probability of a pair of items ever occurring is small, then we can do with space less than $O(k^2)$. We instead construct a hash table of triples (i, j, c), where $i < j$ and $\{i, j\}$ is one of the itemsets that actually occurs in one or more of the baskets. Here, c is the count for that pair. We hash the pair (i, j) to find the bucket in which the count for that itemset is kept.

A triple (i, j, c) requires 12 bytes, so we can maintain counts for $M/12$ pairs.[2] Put another way, if p pairs ever occur in the data, we need main memory at least $M \geq 12p$.

Notice that there are approximately $k^2/2$ possible pairs if there are k different items. If the number of pairs $p = k^2/2$, then the table of counts requires three times as much main memory as the triangular matrix. However, if only 1/3 of all possible pairs occur, then the two methods have the same memory requirements, and if the probability that a given pair occurs is less than 1/3, then the table of counts is preferable.

Additional Comments About the Naive Algorithm

In summary, we can use the naive, one-pass algorithm to find all frequent pairs if the number of bytes of main memory M exceeds either $2k^2$ or $12p$, where k is the number of different items and p is the number of pairs of items that occur in at least one basket of the dataset.

The same approach can be used to count triples, provided that there is enough memory to count either all possible triples or all triples that actually occur in the data. Likewise, we can count quadruples or itemsets of any size, although the likelihood that we have enough memory goes down as the size goes up. We leave the formulas for how much memory is needed as an exercise.

22.2.3   The A-Priori Algorithm

The A-Priori Algorithm is a method for finding frequent itemsets of size n, for any n, in n passes. It normally uses much less main memory than the naive algorithm, and it is certain to use less memory if the support threshold is sufficiently high that some singleton sets are not frequent. The important

---

[2]Whatever kind of hash table we use, there will be some additional overhead, which we shall neglect. For example, if we use open addressing, then it is generally necessary to leave a small fraction of the buckets unfilled, to limit the average search for a triple.

insight that makes the algorithm work is *monotonicity* of the property of being frequent. That is:

- If an itemset S is frequent, so is each of its subsets.

The truth of the above statement is easy to see. If S is a subset of at least s baskets, where s is the support threshold, and $T \subseteq S$, then T is also a subset of the same baskets that contain S, and perhaps T is a subset of other baskets as well. The use of monotonicity is actually in its contrapositive form:

- If S is not a frequent itemset, then no superset of S is frequent.

On the first pass, the a-priori algorithm counts only the singleton sets of items. If some of those sets are not frequent by themselves, then their items cannot be part of any frequent pair. Thus, the nonfrequent items can be ignored on a second pass through the data, and only the pairs consisting of two frequent items need be counted. For example, if only half the items are frequent, then we need to count only $1/4$ of the number of pairs, so we can use $1/4$ as much main memory. Or put another way, with a fixed amount of main memory, we can deal with a dataset that has twice as many items.

We can continue to construct the frequent triples on another pass, the frequent quadruples on the fourth pass, and so on, as high as we like and that frequent itemsets exist. The generalization is that for the nth pass we begin with a *candidate set* of itemsets C_n, and we produce a subset F_n of C_n consisting of the frequent itemsets of size n. That is, C_1 is the set of all singletons, and F_1 is those singletons that are frequent. C_2 is the set of pairs of items, both of which are in F_1, and F_2 is those pairs that are frequent. The candidate set for the third pass, C_3, is those triples $\{i, j, k\}$ such that each doubleton subset, $\{i, j\}$, $\{i, k\}$, and $\{j, k\}$, is in F_2. The following gives the algorithm formally.

Algorithm 22.4: A-Priori Algorithm.

INPUT: A file D consisting of baskets of items, a support threshold s, and a size limit q for the size of frequent itemsets.

OUTPUT: The sets of itemsets $F_1, F_2, \ldots, F_q$, where F_i is the set of all itemsets of size i that appear in at least s baskets of D.

METHOD: Execute the algorithm of Fig. 22.4 and output each set F_n of frequent items, for $n = 1, 2, \ldots, q$. □

Example 22.5: Let us execute the A-Priori Algorithm on the data of Fig. 22.1 with support $s = 4$. Initially, C_1 is the set of all six movies. In the first pass, we count the singleton sets, and we find that BI, BS, $HP1$, and $HP2$ occur at least four times; the other two movies do not. Thus, $F_1 = \{BI, BS, HP1, HP2\}$, and C_2 is the set of six pairs that can be formed by choosing two of these four movies.

```
1)  LET C₁ = all items that appear in file F;
2)  FOR n := 1 TO q DO BEGIN
3)      Fₙ := those sets in Cₙ that occur at least
            s times in D;
4)      IF n = q BREAK;
5)      LET Cₙ₊₁ = all itemsets S of size n + 1 such that
            every subset of S of size n is in Fₙ;
    END
```

Figure 22.4: The A-Priori Algorithm

On the second pass, we count only these six pairs, and we find that $F_2 = \{\{BI, BS\}, \{HP1, HP2\}, \{BI, HP1\}, \{BS, HP1\}\}$; the other two pairs are not frequent. Assuming $q > 2$, we try to find frequent triples. C_3 consists of only the triple $\{BI, BS, HP1\}$, because that is the only set of three movies, all pairs of which are in F_2. However, these three movies appear together only in three rows: V_4, V_5, and V_8. Thus, F_3 is empty, and there are no more frequent itemsets, no matter how large q is. The algorithm returns $F_1 \cup F_2$. □

22.2.4 Implementation of the A-Priori Algorithm

Figure 22.4 is just an outline of the algorithm. We must consider carefully how the steps are implemented. The heart of the algorithm is line (3), which we shall implement, each time through, by a single pass through the input data. The let-statements of lines (1) and (5) are just definitions of what C_n is, rather than assignments to be executed. That is, as we run through the baskets in line (3), the definition of C_n tells us which sets of size n need to be counted in main memory, and which need not be counted.

The algorithm should be used only if there is enough main memory to satisfy the requirements to count all the candidate sets on each pass. If there is not enough memory, then either a more space-efficient algorithm must be used, or several passes must be used for a single value of n. Otherwise, the system will "thrash," with pages being moved in and out of main memory during a pass, thus greatly increasing the running time.

We can use either method discussed in Section 22.2.2 to organize the main-memory counts during a pass. It may not be obvious that the triangular-matrix method can be used with a-priori on the second pass, since the frequent items are not likely to have numbers $0, 1, \ldots$ up to as many frequent items as there are. However, after finding the frequent items on pass 1, we can construct a small main-memory table, no larger than the set of items itself, that translates the original items numbers into consecutive numbers for just the frequent items.

22.2.5   Making Better Use of Main Memory

We expect that the memory bottleneck comes on the second pass of Algorithm 22.4, that is, at the execution of line (3) of Fig. 22.4 with $n = 2$. That is, we assume counting candidate pairs takes more space than counting candidate triples, quadruples, and so on. Thus, let us concentrate on how we could reduce the number of candidate pairs for the second pass. To begin, the typical use of main memory on the first two passes of the A-Priori Algorithm is suggested by Fig. 22.5.

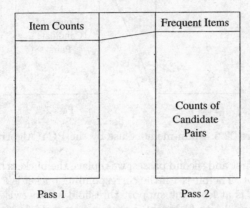

Figure 22.5: Main-memory use by the A-Priori Algorithm

On the first pass ($n = 1$), all we need is space to count all the items, which is typically very small compared with the amount of memory needed to count pairs. On the second pass ($n = 2$), the counts are replaced by a list of the frequent items, which is expected to take even less space than the counts took on the first pass. All the available memory is devoted, as needed, to counts of the candidate pairs.

Could we do anything with the unused memory on the first pass, in order to reduce the number of candidate pairs on the second pass? If so, data sets with larger numbers of frequent pairs could be handled on a machine with a fixed amount of main memory. The *PCY Algorithm*[3] exploits the unused memory by filling it entirely with an unusual sort of hash table. The "buckets" of this table do not hold pairs or other elements. Rather, each bucket is a single integer count, and thus occupies only four bytes. We could even use two-byte buckets if the support threshold were less than 2^{16}, since once a count gets above the threshold, we do not need to see how large it gets.

During the first pass, as we examine each basket, we not only add one to the count for each item in the basket, but we also hash each pair of items to its bucket in the hash table and add one to the count in that bucket. What we

---

[3]For the authors, J. S. Park, M.-S. Chen, and P. S. Yu.

hope for is that some buckets will wind up with a count less than s, the support threshold. If so, we know that no pair $\{i, j\}$ that hashes to that bucket can be frequent, even if both i and j are frequent as singletons.

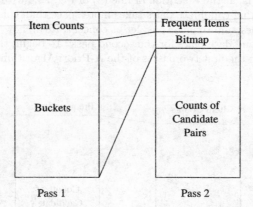

Figure 22.6: Main-memory use by the PCY Algorithm

Between the first and second passes, we replace the buckets by a *bitmap* with one bit per bucket. The bit is 1 if the corresponding bucket is a *frequent bucket*; that is, its count is at least the support threshold s; otherwise the bit is 0. A bucket, occupying 32 bits (4 bytes) is replaced by a single bit, so the bitmap occupies roughly 1/32 of main memory on the second pass. There is thus almost as much space available for counts on the second pass of the PCY Algorithm as there is for the A-Priori Algorithm. Figure 22.6 illustrates memory use during the first two passes of PCY.

On the second pass, $\{i, j\}$ is a candidate pair if and only if the following conditions are satisfied:

1. Both i and j are frequent items.

2. $\{i, j\}$ hashes to a bucket that the bitmap tells us is a frequent bucket.

Then, on the second pass, we can count only this set of candidate pairs, rather than all the pairs that meet the first condition, as in the A-Priori Algorithm.

22.2.6   When to Use the PCY Algorithm

In the PCY Algorithm, the set of candidate pairs is sufficiently irregular that we cannot use the triangular-matrix method for organizing counts; we must use a table of counts. Thus, it does not make sense to use PCY unless the number of candidate pairs is reduced to at most 1/3 of all possible pairs. Passes of the PCY Algorithm after the second can proceed just as in the A-Priori Algorithm, if they are needed.

Further, in order for PCY to be an improvement over A-Priori, a good fraction of the buckets on the first pass must not be frequent. For if most buckets are frequent, condition (3) above does not eliminate many pairs. Any bucket to which even one frequent pair hashes will itself be frequent. However, buckets to which no frequent pair hashes could still be frequent if the sum of the counts of the pairs that do hash there exceeds the threshold s. To a first approximation, if the average count of a bucket is less then s, we can expect at least half the buckets not to be frequent, which suggests some benefit from the PCY approach. However, if the average bucket has a count above s, then most buckets will be frequent.

Suppose the total number of occurrences of pairs of items among all the baskets in the dataset is P. Since most of the main memory M can be devoted to buckets, the number of buckets will be approximately $M/4$. The average count of a bucket will then be $4P/M$. In order that there be many buckets that are not frequent, we need $4P/M < s$, or $M > 4P/s$. The exercises allow you to explore some more concrete examples.

22.2.7   The Multistage Algorithm

Instead of counting pairs on the second pass, as we do in A-Priori or PCY, we could use the same bucketing technique (with a different hash function) on the second pass. To make the average counts even smaller on the second pass, we do not even have to consider a pair on the second pass unless it would be counted on the second pass of PCY; that is, the pair consists of two frequent items and also hashed to a frequent bucket on the first pass.

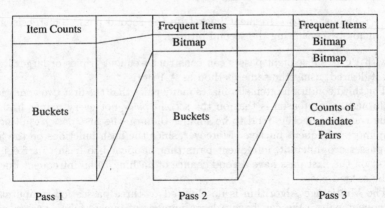

Figure 22.7: Main-memory use in the three-pass version of the multistage algorithm

This idea leads to the three-pass version of the *Multistage Algorithm* for finding frequent pairs. The algorithm is sketched in Fig. 22.7. Pass 1 is just like Pass 2 of PCY, and between Passes 1 and 2 we collapse the buckets to bits and select the frequent items, also as in PCY.

However, on Pass 2, we again use all available memory to hash pairs into as many buckets as will fit. Because there is a bitmap to store in main memory on the second pass, and this bitmap compresses a 4-byte (32-bit) integer into one bit, there will be approximately 31/32 as many buckets on the second pass as on the first. On the second pass, we use a different hash function from that used on Pass 2. We hash a pair $\{i, j\}$ to a bucket and add one to the count there if and only if:

1. Both i and j are frequent items.

2. $\{i, j\}$ hashed to a frequent bucket on the first pass. This decision is made by consulting the bitmap.

That is, we hash only those pairs we would count on the second pass of the PCY Algorithm.

Between the second and third passes, we condense the buckets of the second pass into another bitmap, which must be stored in main memory along with the first bitmap and the set of frequent items. On the third pass, we finally count the candidate pairs. In order to be a candidate, the pair $\{i, j\}$ must satisfy all of:

1. Both i and j are frequent items.

2. $\{i, j\}$ hashed to a frequent bucket on the first pass. This decision is made by consulting the first bitmap.

3. $\{i, j\}$ hashed to a frequent bucket on the second pass. This decision is made by consulting the second bitmap.

As with PCY, subsequent passes can construct frequent triples or larger itemsets, if desired, using the same method as A-Priori.

The third condition often eliminates many pairs that the first two conditions let through. One reason is that on the second pass, not every pair is hashed, so the counts of buckets tend to be smaller than on the first pass, resulting in many more infrequent buckets. Moreover, since the hash functions on the first two passes are different, infrequent pairs that happened to hash to a frequent bucket on the first pass have a good chance of hashing to an infrequent bucket on the second pass.

The Multistage Algorithm is not limited to three passes for computation of frequent pairs. We can have a large number of bucket-filling passes, each using a different hash function. As long as the first pass eliminates some of the pairs because they belong to a nonfrequent bucket, then subsequent passes will eliminate a rapidly growing fraction of the pairs, until it is very unlikely that any candidate pair will turn out not to be frequent. However, there is a point of diminishing returns, since each bitmap requires about 1/32 of the memory.

If we use too many passes, not only will the algorithm take more time, but we can find ourselves with available main memory that is too small to count all the frequent pairs.

22.2.8 Exercises for Section 22.2

Exercise 22.2.1: Simulate the A-Priori Algorithm on the data of Fig. 22.3, with $s = 4$.

Exercise 22.2.2: Imagine that there are 2100 items, of which 100 are "big" and 2000 are "little." A basket is formed by adding each big item with probability 1/10, and each little item with probability 1/200. Assume the number of baskets is large enough that each itemset appears in a fraction of the baskets that equals its probability of being in any given basket. For example, every pair consisting of a big item and a little item appears in 1/2000 of the baskets. Let s be the support threshold, but expressed as a fraction of the total number of baskets rather than as an absolute number. Give, as a function of s ranging from 0 to 1, the number of frequent items on Pass 1 of the A-Priori Algorithm. Also, give the number of candidate pairs on the second pass.

! **Exercise 22.2.3:** Suppose we want to count all itemsets of size n using one pass through the data.

a) What is the generalization of the triangular-matrix method for $n > 2$? Give the formula for locating the array element that counts a given set of n elements $\{i_1, i_2, \ldots, i_n\}$.

b) How much main memory does the generalized triangular-matrix method take if there are k items?

c) What is the generalization of the table-of-counts method for $n > 2$?

d) How much main memory does the generalized table-of-counts method take if there are p itemsets of size n that appear in the data?

! **Exercise 22.2.4:** Consider running the PCY Algorithm on the data of Exercise 22.2.2, with 200,000 buckets on the first pass. Assume that the hash function used distributes the pairs to buckets in a conveniently random fashion. Specifically, the 1,999,000 little-little pairs are divided as evenly as possible (approximately 10 to a bucket). One of the 200,000 big-little pairs is in each bucket, and the 4950 big-big pairs each go into a different bucket.

a) As a function of s, the ratio of the support threshold to the total number of baskets (as in Exercise 22.2.2), how many frequent buckets are there on the first pass?

b) As a function of s, how many pairs must be counted on the second pass?

! **Exercise 22.2.5:** Using the assumptions of Exercise 22.2.4, suppose we run a three-pass Multistage Algorithm on the dataset. Assuming that on the second pass there are again 200,000 buckets, and the hash function distributes pairs randomly among the buckets, answer the following questions, all in terms of s the ratio of the support threshold to the number of baskets.

a) Approximately how many frequent buckets will there be on the second pass?

b) Approximately how many pairs are counted on the third pass?

Exercise 22.2.6: Suppose baskets are in a file that is distributed over many processors. Show how you would use the map-reduce framework of Section 20.2 to:

a) Find the counts of all items.

! b) Find the counts of all pairs of items.

22.3 Finding Similar Items

We now turn to the version of the frequent-itemsets problem that supports marketing activities for on-line merchants and a number of other interesting applications such as finding similar documents on the Web. We may start with the market-basket model of data, but now we search for pairs of items that appear together a large fraction of the times that either appears, even if neither item appears in very many baskets. Such items are said to be *similar*. The key technique is to create a short "signature" for each item, such that the difference between signatures tells us the difference between the items themselves.

22.3.1 The Jaccard Measure of Similarity

Our starting point is to define exactly what we mean by "similar" items. Since we are interested in finding items that tend to appear together in the same baskets, the natural viewpoint is that each item is a set: the set of baskets in which it appears. Thus, we need a definition for how similar two sets are.

The *Jaccard similarity* (or just *similarity*, if this similarity measure is understood) of sets S and T is $|S \cap T|/|S \cup T|$, that is, the ratio of the sizes of their intersection and union. Thus, disjoint sets have a similarity of 0, and the similarity of a set with itself is 1. As another example, the similarity of sets $\{1, 2, 3\}$ and $\{1, 3, 4, 5\}$ is 2/5, since there are two elements in the intersection and five elements in the union.

22.3.2 Applications of Jaccard Similarity

A number of important data-mining problems can be expressed as finding sets with high Jaccard similarity. We shall discuss two of them in detail here.

Collaborative Filtering

Suppose we are given data about customers' on-line purchases. One way to tell what items to pitch to a customer is to find pairs of customers that bought similar sets of items. When a customer logs in, they can be pitched an item that a similar customer bought, but that they did not buy. To compare customers, represent a customer by the set of items they bought, and compute the Jaccard similarity for each pair of customers.

There is a dual view of the same data. We might want to know which pairs of items are similar, based on their having been bought by similar sets of customers. We can frame this problem in the same terms as finding similar customers. Now, the items are represented by the set of customers that bought them, and we need to find pairs of items that have similar sets of customers.

Notice, incidentally, that the same data can be viewed as market-basket data in two different ways. The products can be the "items" and the customers the "baskets," or vice-versa. You should not be surprised. Any many-many relationship can be seen as market-basket data in two ways. In Section 22.1 we viewed the data in only one way, because when the "baskets" are really shopping carts at a store's checkout stand, there is no real interest in finding similar shopping carts or carts that contain many items in common.

Similar Documents

There are many reasons we would like to find pairs of textually similar documents. If we are crawling the Web, documents that are very similar might be mirrors of one another, perhaps differing only in links to other documents at the local site. A search engine would not want to offer both sites in response to a search query. Other similar pairs might represent an instance of plagiarism. Note that one document d_1 might contain an excerpt from another document d_2, yet d_1 and d_2 are identical in only 10% of each; that could still be an instance of plagiarism.

Telling whether documents are character-for-character identical is easy; just compare characters until you find a mismatch or reach the ends of the documents. Finding whether a sentence or short piece of text appears character-for-character in a document is not much harder. Then you have to consider all places in the document where the sentence of fragment might start, but most of those places will have a mismatch very quickly. What is harder is to find documents that are similar, but are not exact copies in long stretches. For instance, a draft document and its edited version might have small changes in almost every sentence.

A technique that is almost invulnerable to large numbers of small changes is to represent a document by its set of *k-grams*, that is, by the set of substrings of length k. *k-Shingle* is another word for k-gram. For example, the set of 3-grams that we find in the first sentence of Section 22.3.2 ("A number of···") contains "A n", " nu", "num", and so on. If we pick k large enough so that the probability of a randomly chosen k-gram appearing in a document is small,

---

Compressed Shingles

In order that a document be characterized by its set of k-shingles, we have to pick k sufficiently large that it is rare for a given shingle to appear in a document. $k = 5$ is about the smallest we can choose, and it is not unusual to have k around 10. However, then there are so many possible shingles, and the shingles are so long, that certain algorithms take more time than necessary. Therefore, it is common to hash the shingles to integers of 32 bits or less. These hash-values are still numerous enough that they differentiate between documents, but they can be compared and processed quickly.

---

then a high Jaccard similarity of the sets of k-grams representing a pair of documents is a strong indication that the documents themselves are similar.

22.3.3 Minhashing

Computing the Jaccard similarity of two large sets is time consuming. Moreover, even if we can compute similarities efficiently, a large dataset has far too many pairs of sets for us to compute the similarity of every pair. Thus, there are two "tricks" we need to learn to extract only the similar pairs from a large dataset. Both are a form of "hashing," although the techniques are completely different uses of hashing.

1. *Minhashing* is a technique that lets us form a short signature for each set. We can compute the Jaccard similarity of the sets by measuring the similarity of the signatures. As we shall see, the "similarity" for signatures is simple to compute, but it is not the Jaccard similarity. We take up minhashing in this section.

2. *Locality-Sensitive Hashing* is a technique that lets us focus on pairs of signatures whose underlying sets are likely to be similar, without examining all pairs of signatures. We take up locality-sensitive hashing in Section 22.4.

To introduce minhashing, suppose that the elements of each set are chosen from a "universal" set of n elements $e_0, e_1, \ldots, e_{n-1}$. Pick a random permutation of the n elements. Then the *minhash value* of a set S is the first element, in the permuted order, that is a member of S.

Example 22.6 : Suppose the universal set of elements is $\{1, 2, 3, 4, 5\}$ and the permuted order we choose is $(3, 5, 4, 2, 1)$. Then the hash value of any set that contains 3, such as $\{2, 3, 5\}$ is 3. A set that contains 5 but not 3, such as $\{1, 2, 5\}$, hashes to 5. For another example, $\{1, 2\}$ hashes to 2, because 2 appears before 1 in the permuted order. □

Suppose we have a collection of sets. For example, we might be given a collection of documents and think of each document as represented by its set of 10-grams. We compute *signatures* for the sets by picking a list of m permutations of all the possible elements (e.g., all possible character strings of length 10, if the elements are 10-grams). Typically, m would be about 100. The signature of a set S is the list of the minhash values of S, for each of the m permutations, in order.

Example 22.7: Suppose the universal set of elements is again $\{1, 2, 3, 4, 5\}$, and choose $m = 3$, that is, signatures of three minhash values. Let the permutations be $\pi_1 = (1, 2, 3, 4, 5)$, $\pi_2 = (5, 4, 3, 2, 1)$, and $\pi_3 = (3, 5, 1, 4, 2)$. The signature of $S = \{2, 3, 4\}$ is $(2, 4, 3)$. To see why, first notice that in the order π_1, 2 appears before 3 and 4, so 2 is the first minhash value. In π_2, 4 appears before 2 and 3, so 4 is the second minhash value. In π_3, 3 appears before 2 and 4, so 3 is the third minhash value. □

22.3.4 Minhashing and Jaccard Distance

There is a surprising relationship between the minhash values and the Jaccard similarity:

- If we choose a permutation at random, the probability that it will produce the same minhash values for two sets is the same as the Jaccard similarity of those sets.

Thus, if we have the signatures of two sets S and T, we can estimate the Jaccard similarity of S and T by the fraction of corresponding minhash values for the two sets that agree.

Example 22.8: Let the permutations be as in Example 22.7, and consider another set, $T = \{1, 2, 3\}$. The signature for T is $(1, 3, 3)$. If we compare this signature with $(2, 4, 3)$, the signature of the set $S = \{2, 3, 4\}$, we see that the signatures agree in only the last of the three components. We therefore estimate the Jaccard similarity of S and T to be $1/3$. Notice that the true Jaccard similarity of S and T is $1/2$. □

In order that the signatures are very likely to estimate the similarity closely, we need to pick considerably more than three permutations. We suggest that 100 permutations may be enough for the "law of large numbers" to hold. However, the exact number of signatures needed depends on how closely we need to estimate the similarity.

22.3.5 Why Minhashing Works

To see why the Jaccard similarity is the probability that two sets have the same minhash value according to a randomly chosen permutation of elements, let S

and T be two sets. Imagine going down the list of elements in the permuted order, until you find an element e that appears in at least one of S and T. There are two cases:

1. If e appears in both S and T, then both sets have the same minhash value, namely e.

2. But if e appears in one of S and T but not the other, then one set gets minhash value e and the other definitely gets some other minhash value.

We do not meet e until the first time we find, in the permuted order, an element that is in $S \cup T$. The probability of Case 1 occuring is the fraction of members of $S \cup T$ that are in $S \cap T$. That fraction is exactly the Jaccard similarity of S and T. But Case 1 is also exactly when S and T have the same minhash value, which proves the relationship.

22.3.6 Implementing Minhashing

While we have spoken of choosing a random permutation of all possible elements, it is not feasible to do so. It would take far too long, and we might have to deal with elements that appeared in none of our sets. Rather, we simulate the choice of a random permutation by instead picking a random hash function h from elements to some large sequence of integers $0, 1, \ldots, B - 1$ (i.e., bucket numbers). We pretend that the permutation that h represents places element e in the position $h(e)$. Of course, several elements might thus wind up in the same position, but as long as B is large, we can break ties as we like, and the simulated permutations will be sufficiently random that the relationship between signatures and similarity still holds.

Suppose our dataset is presented one set at a time. To compute the minhash value for a set $S = \{a_1, a_2, \ldots, a_n\}$ using a hash function h, we can execute:

```
V := ∞;
FOR i := 1 TO n DO
    IF h(a_i) < V THEN V := h(a_i);
```

As a result, V will be set to the hash value of the element of S that has the smallest hash value. This hash value may not identify a unique element, because several elements in the universe of possible elements may hash to this value, but as long as h hashes to a large number of possible values, the chances of a coincidence is small, and we may continue to assume that a common minhash value suggests two sets have an element in common.

If we want to compute not just one minhash value but the minhash values for set S according to m hash functions $h_1, h_2, \ldots, h_m$, then we can compute m minhash values in parallel, as we process each member of S. The code is suggested in Fig. 22.8.

```
FOR j := 1 TO m DO
    V_j := ∞;
FOR i := 1 TO n DO
    FOR j := 1 TO m DO
        IF h_j(a_i) < V_j THEN V_j := h_j(a_i);
```

Figure 22.8: Computing m minhash values at once

It is somewhat harder to compute signatures if the data is presented basket-by-basket as in Section 22.1. That is, suppose we want to compute the signatures of "items," but our data is in a file consisting of baskets. Similarity of items is the Jaccard similarity of the sets of baskets in which these items appear.

Suppose there are k items, and we want to construct their minhash signatures using m different hash functions $h_1, h_2, \ldots, h_m$. Then we need to maintain km values, each of which will wind up being the minhash value for one of the items according to one of the hash functions. Let V_{ij} be the value for item i and hash function h_j. Initially, set all V_{ij}'s to infinity. When we read a basket b, we compute $h_j(b)$ for all $j = 1, 2, \ldots, m$. However, we adjust values only for those items i that are in b. The algorithm is sketched in Fig. 22.9. At the end, V_{ij} holds the jth minhash value for item i.

```
FOR i := 1 TO k DO
    FOR j := 1 TO m DO
        V_{ij} := ∞;
FOR EACH basket b DO BEGIN
    FOR j := 1 TO m DO
        compute h_j(b);
    FOR EACH item i in b DO
        FOR j := 1 TO m DO
            IF h_j(b) < V_{ij} THEN V_{ij} := h_j(b);
END
```

Figure 22.9: Computing minhash values for all items and hash functions

22.3.7 Exercises for Section 22.3

Exercise 22.3.1: Compute the Jaccard similarity of each pair of the following sets: $\{1, 2, 3, 4, 5\}$, $\{1, 2, 6, 7\}$, $\{2, 3, 4, 7\}$.

Exercise 22.3.2: What are all the 4-grams of the following string:

```
"abcd ef ghij"
```

Do not count the quotation marks as part of the string, but remember that blanks do count.

Exercise 22.3.3: Suppose that the universal set is $\{1, 2, \ldots, 10\}$, and signatures for sets are constructed using the following list of permutations:

1. $(1, 2, 3, 4, 5, 6, 7, 8, 9, 10)$

2. $(10, 9, 8, 7, 6, 5, 4, 3, 2, 1)$

3. $(4, 7, 2, 9, 1, 5, 3, 10, 6, 8)$

Construct minhash signatures for the following sets:

a) $\{2, 4, 6\}$.

b) $\{1, 3, 5, 7\}$

c) $\{8, 9, 10\}$

How does the estimate of the Jaccard similarity for each pair, derived from the signatures, compare with the true Jaccard similarity?

Exercise 22.3.4: Suppose that instead of using particular permutations to construct signatures for the three sets of Exercise 22.3.3, we use hash functions to construct the signatures. The three hash functions we use are:

$$f(x) = x \mod 10$$
$$g(x) = (3x + 1) \mod 10$$
$$h(x) = (5x + 2) \mod 10$$

Compute the signatures for the three sets, and compare the resulting estimate of the Jaccard similarity of each pair with the true Jaccard similarity.

! **Exercise 22.3.5:** Suppose data is in a file that is distributed over many processors. Show how you would use the map-reduce framework of Section 20.2 to compute a minhash value, using a single hash function, assuming:

a) The file must be partitioned by columns.

b) The file must be partitioned by rows.

22.4   Locality-Sensitive Hashing

Now, we take up the problem that was not really solved by taking minhash signatures. It is true that these signatures may make it much faster to estimate the similarity of any pair of sets, but there may still be far too many pairs of sets to find all pairs that meet a given similarity threshold. The technique called "locality-sensitive hashing," or LSH, may appear to be magic; it allows us, in a sense, to hash sets or other elements to buckets so that "similar" elements are assigned to the same bucket. There are tradeoffs, of course. There is a (typically small) probability that we shall miss a pair of similar elements, and the lower we want that probability to be, the more work we must do. After some examples, we shall take up the general theory.

22.4.1 Entity Resolution as an Example of LSH

Recall our discussion of entity resolution in Section 21.7. There, we had a large collection of records, and we needed to find similar pairs. The notion of "similarity" was not Jaccard similarity, and in fact we left open what "similarity" meant. Whatever definition we use for similarity of records, there may be far too many pairs to measure them all. For example, if there are a million records — not a very large number — then there are about 500 billion pairs of records. An algorithm like R-Swoosh may allow merging with fewer than that number of comparisons, provided there are many large sets of similar records, but if no records are similar to other records, then there is no way we can discover that fact without doing all possible comparisons.

It would be wonderful to have a way to "hash" records so that similar records fell into the same bucket, and nonsimilar pairs never did, or rarely did. Then, we could restrict our examination of pairs to those that were in the same bucket. If, say, there were 1000 buckets, and records distributed evenly, then we would only have to compare 1/1000 of the pairs. We cannot do exactly what is described above, but we can come surprisingly close.

Example 22.9 : Suppose for concreteness that records are as in the running example of Section 21.7: name-address-phone triples, where each of the three fields is a character string. Suppose also that we define records to be similar if the sum of the edit distances of their three corresponding pairs of fields is no greater than 5. Let us use a hash function h that hashes the name field of a record to one of a million buckets. How h works is unimportant, except that it must be a good hash function — one that distributes names roughly uniformly among the buckets.

But we do not stop here. We also hash the records to another set of a million buckets, this time using the address, and a suitable hash function on addresses. If h operates on any strings, we can even use h. Then, we hash records a third time to a million buckets, using the phone number.

Finally, we examine each bucket in each of the three hash tables, a total of 3,000,000 buckets. For each bucket, we compare each pair of records in each bucket, and we report any pair that has total edit distance 5 or less. Suppose there are n records. Assuming even distribution of records in each hash table, there are $n/10^6$ records in each bucket. The number of pairs of records in each bucket is approximately $n^2/(2 \times 10^{12})$. Since there are 3×10^6 buckets, the total number of comparisons is about $1.5n^2/10^6$. And since there are about $n^2/2$ pairs of records, we have managed to look at only fraction 3×10^{-6} of the records, a big improvement.

In fact, since the number of buckets was chosen arbitrarily, it seems we can reduce the number of comparisons to whatever degree we wish. There are limitations, of course. If we choose too large a number of buckets, we run out of main-memory space, and regardless of how many buckets we use, we cannot avoid the pairs of records that are really similar.

Have we given up anything? Yes, we have; we shall miss some similar pairs of records that meet the similarity threshold, because they differ by a few characters in each of the three fields, yet no more than five characters in total. What fraction of the truly similar pairs we lose depends on the distribution of discrepancies among the fields of records that truly represent the same entity. However, if the threshold for total edit distance is 5, we do not expect to miss too many truly similar pairs.   □

But what if the threshold on edit distance in Example 22.9 were not 5, but 20? There might be many pairs of similar records that had no one field identical. To deal with this problem, we need to:

1. Increase the number of hash functions and hash tables.

2. Base each hash function on a small part of a field.

Example 22.10: We could break the name into first, middle, and last names, and hash each to buckets. We could break the address into house number, street name, city name, state, and zip code. The phone number could be broken into area code, exchange, and the last four digits. Since phones are numbers, we could even choose any subset of the ten digits in a phone number, and hash on those. Unfortunately, since we are now hashing short subfields, we are limited in the number of buckets that we can use. If we pick too many buckets, most will be empty.

After hashing records many times, we again look in each bucket of each of the hash tables, and we compare each pair of records that fall into the same bucket at least once. However, the total running time is much higher than for our first example, for two reasons. First, the number of record occurrences among all the buckets is proportional to the number of hash functions we use. Second, hash functions based on small pieces of data cannot divide the records into as many buckets as in Example 22.9.   □

22.4.2   Locality-Sensitive Hashing of Signatures

The use of locality-sensitive hashing in Example 22.10 is relatively straightforward. For a more subtle application of the general idea, let us return to the problem introduced in Section 22.3, where we saw the advantage of replacing sets by their signatures. When we need to find similar pairs of sets that are represented by signatures, there is a way to build hash functions for a locality-sensitive hashing, for any desired similarity threshold. Think of the signatures of the various sets as a matrix, with a column for each set's signature and a row for each hash function. Divide the matrix into b bands of r rows each, where br is the length of a signature. The arrangement is suggested by Fig. 22.10.

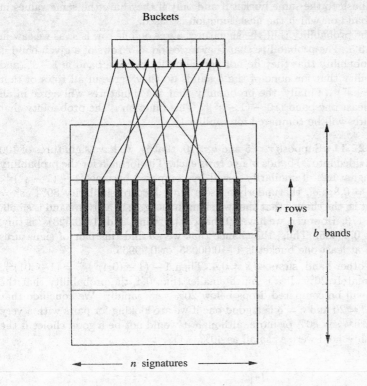

Figure 22.10: Dividing signatures into bands and hashing based on the values in a band

For each band we choose a hash function that maps the portion of a signature in that band to some large number of buckets, B. That is, the hash function applies to sequences of r integers and produces one integer in the range 0 to $B-1$. In Fig. 22.10, $B = 4$. If two signatures agree in all rows of any one band, then they surely will wind up in the same bucket. There is a small chance that they will be in the same bucket even if they do not agree, but by using a very large number of buckets B, we can make sure there are very few "false positives." Every bucket of each hash function has its members compared for similarity, so a pair of signatures that agree in even one band will be compared. Signatures that do not agree in any band probably will not be compared, although as we mentioned, there is a small probability they will hash to the same bucket anyway, and would therefore be compared.

Let us compute the probability that a pair of minhash signatures will be compared, as a function of the Jaccard similarity s of their underlying sets, the number of bands b, and the number of rows r in a band. For simplicity, we shall assume that the number of buckets is so large that there are no coincidences; signatures hash to the same bucket if and only if they have the same values in the entire band on which the hash function is based.

First, the probability that the signatures agree on one row is s, as we saw in Section 22.3.5. The probability that they agree on all r rows of a given band is s^r. The probability that they do not agree on all rows of a band is $1 - s^r$, and the probability that for none of the b bands do they agree in all rows of that band is $(1 - s^r)^b$. Finally, the probability that the signatures will agree in all rows of at least one band is $1 - (1 - s^r)^b$. This function is the probability that the signatures will be compared for similiarity.

Example 22.11 : Suppose $r = 5$ and $b = 20$; that is, we have signatures of 100 integers, divided into 20 bands of five rows each. The formula for the probability that two signatures of similarity s will be compared becomes $1 - (1 - s^5)^{20}$. Suppose $s = 0.8$; i.e., the underlying sets have Jaccard similarity 80%. $s^5 = 0.328$. That is, the chance that the two signatures agree in a given band is small, only about 1/3. However, we have 20 chances to "win," and $(1 - 0.328)^{20}$ is tiny, only about 0.00035. Thus, the chance that we *do* find this pair of signatures together in at least one bucket is $1 - 0.00035$, or 0.99965.

On the other hand, suppose $s = 0.4$. Then $1 - \left(1 - (0.4)^5\right)^{20} = (1 - .01)^{20}$, or approximately 20%. If s is much smaller than 0.4, the probability that the signatures will be compared drops below 20% very rapidly. We conclude that the choice $b = 20$ and $r = 5$ is a good one if we are looking for pairs with a very high similarity, say 80% or more, although it would not be a good choice if the similarity threshold were as small as 40%.   □

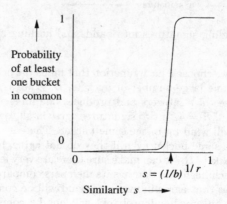

Figure 22.11: The probability that a pair of signatures will appear together in at least one bucket

The function $1 - (1 - s^r)^b$ always looks like Fig. 22.11, but the point of rapid transition from a very small value to a value close to 1 varies, depending on b and r. Roughly, the breakpoint is at similarity $s = (1/b)^{1/r}$.

22.4.3 Combining Minhashing and Locality-Sensitive Hashing

The two ideas, minhashing and LSH, must be combined properly to solve the sort of problems we discussed in Section 22.3.2. Suppose, for example, that we have a large repository of documents, which we have already represented by their sets of shingles of some length. We want to find those documents whose shingle sets have a Jaccard similarity of at least s.

1. Start by computing a minhash signature for each document; how many hash functions to use depends on the desired accuracy, but several hundred should be enough for most purposes.

2. Perform a locality-sensitive hashing to get *candidate* pairs of signatures that hash to the same bucket for at least one band. How many bands and how many rows per band depend on the similarity threshold s, as discussed in Section 22.4.2.

3. For each candidate pair, compute the estimate of their Jaccard similarity by counting the number of components in which their signatures agree.

4. Optionally, for each pair whose signatures are sufficiently similar, compute their true Jaccard similarity by examining the sets themselves.

Of course, this method introduces false positives — candidate pairs that get eliminated in step (2), (3), or (4). However, the second and third steps also allow some false negatives — pairs with a sufficiently high Jaccard similarity that are not candidates or are eliminated from the candidate pool.

a) At step (2), a pair could have very similar signatures, yet there happens to be no band in which the signatures agree in all rows of the band.

b) In step (3), a pair could have Jaccard similarity at least s, but their signatures do not agree in fraction s of the components.

One way to reduce the number of false negatives is to lower the similarity threshold at the initial stages. At step (2), choose a smaller number of rows r or a larger number of bands b than would be indicated by the target similarity s. At step (3) choose a smaller fraction than s of corresponding signature components that allows a pair to move on to step (4). Unfortunately, these changes each increase the number of false positives, so you must consider carefully how small you can afford to make your thresholds.

Another possible way to avoid false negatives is to skip step (3) and go directly to step (4) for each candidate pair. That is, we compute the true

Jaccard similarity of every candidate pair. The disadvantage of doing so is that the minhash signatures were devised to make it easier to compare the underlying sets. For example, if the objects being compared are actually large documents, comparing complete sets of k-shingles is far more time consuming than matching several hundred components of signatures.

In some applications, false negatives are not a problem, so we can tune our LSH to allow a significant fraction of false negatives, in order to reduce false positives and thus to speed up the entire process. For instance, if an on-line retailer is looking for pairs of similar customers, in order to select an item to pitch to each customer, it is not necessary to find every single pair of similar customers. It is sufficient to find a few very similar customers for each customer.

22.4.4 Exercises for Section 22.4

Exercise 22.4.1: The function $p = 1 - (1 - s^r)^b$ gives the probability p that two minhash signatures that come from sets with Jaccard similarity s will hash to the same bucket at least once, if we use an LSH scheme with b bands of r rows each. For a given similarity threshold s, we want to choose b and r so that $p = 1/2$ at s. we suggested that approximately $s = (1/b)^{1/r}$ is where $p = 1/2$, but that is only an approximation. Suppose signatures have length 30. We can pick any integers b and r whose product is 30. That is, the choices for r are 1, 2, 3, 5, 6, 10, 15, or 30, and b must then be $30/r$.

  a) If $s = 1/2$, determine the value of p for each choice of b and r. Which would you choose, if $1/2$ were the similarity threshold?

 ! b) For each choice of b and r, determine the value of s that makes $p = 1/2$.

! **Exercise 22.4.2:** This exercise is based on the entity-resolution problem of Example 22.9. For concreteness, suppose that the only pairs records that could possibly be total edit distance 5 or less from each other consist of a true copy of a record and another *corrupted* version of the record. In the corrupted version, each of the three fields is changed independently. 60% of the time, a field has no change. 20% of the time, there is a change resulting in edit distance 1 for that field. There is a 10% chance of edit distance 2 and 10% chance of edit distance 10. Suppose there are two million pairs of this kind in the dataset.

  a) How many of the two million pairs are within total edit distance 5 of each other?

  b) If we hash each field to a large number of buckets, as suggested by Example 22.9, how many of these two million pairs will hash to the same bucket for at least one of the three hashings?

  c) How many false negatives will there be; that is, how many of the two million pairs are within total edit distance 5, but will not hash to the same bucket for any of the three hashings?

22.5 Clustering of Large-Scale Data

Clustering is the problem of taking a dataset consisting of "points" and grouping the points into some number of *clusters*. Points within a cluster must be "near" to each other in some sense, while points in different clusters are "far" from each other. We begin with a study of distance measures, since only if we have a notion of distance can we talk about whether points are near or far. An important kind of distance is "Euclidean," a distance based on the location of points within a space. Curiously, not all distances are Euclidean, and an important problem in clustering is dealing with sets of points that do not "live" anywhere in a space, yet have a notion of distance.

We next consider the two major approaches to clustering. One, called "agglomerative," is to start with points each in their own cluster, and repeatedly merge "nearby" clusters. The second, "point assignment," initializes the clusters in some way and then assigns each point to its "best" cluster.

22.5.1 Applications of Clustering

Many discussions of clustering begin with a small example, in which a small number of points are given in a two-dimensional space, such as Fig, 22.12. Algorithms to cluster such data are relatively simple, and we shall mention the techniques only in passing. The problem becomes hard when the dataset is large. It becomes even harder when the number of dimensions of the data is large, or when the data doesn't even belong to a space that has "dimensions." Let us begin by examining some examples of interesting uses of clustering algorithms on large-scale data.

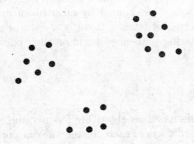

Figure 22.12: Data that can be clustered easily

Collaborative Filtering

In Section 22.3.2 we discussed the problem of finding similar products or similar customers by looking at the set of items each customer bought. The output of analysis using minhashing and locality-sensitive hashing could be a set of pairs of similar products (those bought by many of the same customers. Alternatively, we could look for pairs of similar customers (those buying many of the same products). It may be possible to get a better picture of relationships if we cluster products (points) into groups of similar products. These might represent a natural class of products, e.g., classical-music CD's. Likewise, we might find it useful to cluster customers with similar tastes; e.g., one cluster might be "people who like classical music." For clustering to make sense, we must view the distance between points representing customers or items as "low" if the similarity is high. For example, we shall see in Section 22.5.2 how one minus the Jaccard similarity can serve as a suitable notion of "distance."

Clustering Documents by Topic

We could use the technique described above for products and customers to cluster documents based on their Jaccard similarity. However, another application of document clustering is to group documents into clusters based on their "topics" (e.g., topics such as "sports" or "medicine"), even if documents on the same topic are not very similar character-by-character. A simple approach is to imagine a very high-dimensional space, where there is one dimension for each word that might appear in the document. Place the document at point $(x_1, x_2, \ldots)$, where $x_i = 1$ if the ith word appears in the document and $x_i = 0$ if not. Distance can be taken to be the ordinary Euclidean distance, although as we shall see, this distance measure is not as useful as it might appear at first.

Clustering DNA Sequences

DNA is a sequence of base-pairs, represented by the letters C, G, A, and T. Because these strands sometimes change by substitution of one letter for another or by insertion or deletion of letters, there is a natural edit-distance between DNA sequences. Clustering sequences based on their edit distance allows us to group similar sequences.

Entity Resolution

In Section 21.7.4, we discussed an algorithm for merging records that, in effect, created clusters of records, where each cluster was one connected component of the graph formed by connecting records that met the similarity condition.

SkyCat

In this project, approximately two billion "sky objects" such as stars and galaxies were plotted in a 7-dimensional space, where each dimension represented the radiation of the object in one of seven different bands of the electromagnetic spectrum. By clustering these objects into groups of similar radiation patterns, the project was able to identify approximately 20 different kinds of objects.

Euclidean Spaces

Without going into the theory, for our purposes we may think of a Euclidean space as one with some number of dimensions n. The points in the space are all n-tuples of real numbers $(x_1, x_2, \ldots, x_n)$. The common Euclidean distance is but one of many plausible distance measures in a Euclidean space.

22.5.2 Distance Measures

A *distance measure* on a set of points is a function $d(x, y)$ that satisfies:

1. $d(x, y) \geq 0$ for all points x and y.

2. $d(x, y) = 0$ if and only if $x = y$.

3. $d(x, y) = d(y, x)$ (*symmetry*).

4. $d(x, y) \leq d(x, z) + d(z, y)$ for any points x, y, and z (*triangle inequality*).

That is, the distance from a point to itself is 0, and the distance between any two different points is positive. The distance between points does not depend on which way you travel (symmetry), and it never reduces the distance if you force yourself to go through a particular third point (the triangle inequality).

The most common distance measure is the *Euclidean distance* between points in an n-dimensional Euclidean space. In such a space, points can be represented by n coordinates $x = (x_1, x_2, \ldots, x_n)$ and $y = (y_1, y_2, \ldots, y_n)$. The distance $d(x, y)$ is $\sqrt{\sum_{i=1}^{n}(x_i - y_i)^2}$, that is, the square root of the sum of the squares of the differences in each dimension. However, there are many other ways to define distance; we shall examine some below.

Distances Based on Norms

In a Euclidean space, the conventional distance mentioned above is only one possible choice. More generally, we can define the distance

$$d(x, y) = \left(\sum_{i=1}^{n} |x_i - y_i|^r\right)^{1/r}$$

for any r. This distance is said to be derived from the L_r-*norm*. The conventional Euclidean distance is the case $r = 2$, and is often called the L_2-norm.

Another common choice is the L_1-norm, that is, the sum of the distances along the coordinates of the space. This distance is often called the *Manhattan distance*, because it is the distance one has to travel along a rectangular grid of streets found in many cities such as Manhattan.

Yet another interesting choice is the L_∞-norm, which is the maximum of the distances in any one coordinate. That is, as r approaches infinity, the value of $\sum_{i=1}^n |x_i - y_i|^r)^{1/r}$ approaches the maximum over all i of $|x_i - y_i|$.

Example 22.12: Let $x = (1, 2, 3)$ and $y = (2, 4, 1)$. Then the L_2 distance $d(x, y)$ is $\sqrt{|1 - 2|^2 + |2 - 4|^2 + |3 - 1|^2} = \sqrt{(1 + 4 + 4)} = 3$. Note that this distance is the conventional Euclidean distance. The Manhattan distance between x and y is $|1 - 2| + |2 - 4| + |3 - 1| = 5$. The L_∞-norm gives distance between x and y of $\max(|1 - 2|, |2 - 4|, |3 - 1|) = 2$. $\square$

Jaccard Distance

The *Jaccard distance* between points that are sets is one minus the Jaccard similarity of those sets. That is, if x and y are sets, then

$$d(x, y) = 1 - (|x \cap y|/|x \cup y|)$$

For example, if the two points represent sets $\{1, 2, 3\}$ and $\{2, 3, 4, 5\}$, then the Jaccard similarity is $2/5$, so the Jaccard distance is $3/5$.

One might naturally ask whether the Jaccard distance satisfies the axioms of a distance measure. It is easy to see that $d(x, x) = 0$, because

$$1 - (|x \cap x|/|x \cup x|) = 1 - (1/1) = 0$$

It is also easy to see that the Jaccard distance cannot be negative, since the intersection of sets cannot be bigger than their union. Symmetry of the Jaccard distance is likewise straightforward, since both union and intersection are commutative.

The hard part is showing the triangle inequality. Coming to our rescue is the theorem from Section 22.3.4 that says the Jaccard similarity of two sets is the probability that a random permutation will result in the same minhash value for those sets. Thus, the Jaccard *distance* is the probability that the sets will *not* have the same minhash value. Suppose x and y have different minhash values according to a permutation π. Then at least one of the pairs $\{x, z\}$ and $\{z, y\}$ must have different minhash values; possibly both do. Thus, the probability that x and y have different minhash values is no greater than the sum of the probability that x and z have different minhash values plus the probability that z and y have different minhash values. These probabilities are the Jaccard distances mentioned in the triangle inequality. That is, we have shown that the Jaccard distance from x to y is no greater than the sum of the Jaccard distances from x to z and from z to y.

Cosine Distance

Suppose our points are in a Euclidean space. We can think of these points as vectors from the origin of the space. The *cosine distance* between two points is the angle between the vectors.

The Curse of Dimensionality

Our intuition is pretty good when clustering points in one or two dimensions. However, when the points are in a high-dimensional space, our intuition goes awry in several ways. For example, suppose our points are in an n-dimensional hypercube of side 1. If $n = 2$ (i.e., a square), there are many points near the center, and many near the edges. However, for large n, the volume of a hypercube of side just slightly less than 1 is tiny compared with the hypercube of side 1. That means almost every point in the hypercube is very near the surface. There is no "center" and no points to form clusters other than on the surface.

Example 22.13: Suppose documents are characterized by the presence or absence of five words, so points (documents) are vectors of five 0's or 1's. Let $(0, 0, 1, 1, 1)$ and $(1, 0, 0, 1, 1)$ be the two points. The cosine of the angle between them is computed by taking the dot product of the vectors, and dividing by the product of the lengths of the vectors. In this case, the dot product is $0 \times 1 + 0 \times 0 + 1 \times 0 + 1 \times 1 + 1 \times 1 = 0 + 0 + 0 + 1 + 1 = 2$. Both vectors have length $\sqrt{3}$. Thus, the cosine of the angle between the vectors is $2/(\sqrt{3} \times \sqrt{3}) = 2/3$. The angle is about 48 degrees. $\square$

Cosine distance satisfies the axioms of a distance measure, as long as points are treated as directions, so two vectors, one of which is a multiple of the other are treated as the same. Angles can only be positive, and if the angle is 0 then the vectors must be in the same direction. Symmetry holds because the angle between x and y is the same as the angle between y and x. The triangle inequality holds because the angle between two vectors is never greater than the sum of the angles between those vectors and a third vector.

Edit Distance

Various forms of edit distance satisfy the axioms of a distance measure. Let us focus on the edit distance that allows only insertions and deletions. If strings x and y are at distance 0 (i.e., no edits are needed) then they surely must be the same. Symmetry follows because insertions and deletions can be reversed. The triangle inequality follows because one way to turn x into y is to first turn x into z and then turn z into y. Thus, the sum of the edit distances from x to z and from z to y is the number of edits needed for one possible way to turn x into y. This number of edits cannot be less than the edit distance from x to y, which is the minimum over all possible ways to get from x to y.

22.5.3   Agglomerative Clustering

We shall now begin our study of algorithms for computing clusters. The first approach is, at the highest level, straightforward. Start with every point in its own cluster. Until some stopping condition is met, repeatedly find the "closest" pair of clusters to merge, and merge them. This methodology is called *agglomerative* or *hierarchical* clustering. The term "hierarchical" comes from the fact that we not only produce clusters, but a cluster itself has a hierarchical substructure that reflects the sequence of mergers that formed the cluster. The devil, as always, is in the details, so we need to answer two questions:

1. How do we measure the "closeness" of clusters?

2. How do we decide when to stop merging?

Defining "Closeness"

There are many ways we could define the closeness of two clusters C and D. Here are two popular ones:

a) Find the minimum distance between any pair of points, one from C and one from D.

b) Average the distance between any pair of points, one from C and one from D.

These measures of closeness work for any distance measure. If the points are in a Euclidean space, then we have additional options. Since real numbers can be averaged, any set of points in a Euclidean space has a *centroid*, the point that is the average, in each coordinate, of the points in the set. For example, the centroid of the set $\{(1, 2, 3),\ (4, 5, 6),\ (2, 2, 2)\}$ is $(2.33,\ 3,\ 3.67)$ to two decimal places. For Euclidean spaces, another good choice of closeness measure is:

c) The distance between the centroids of clusters C and D.

Stopping the Merger

One common stopping criterion is to pick a number of clusters k, and keep merging until you are down to k clusters. This approach is good if you have an intuition about how many clusters there should be. For instance, if you have a set of documents that cover three different topics, you could merge until you have three clusters, and hope that these clusters correspond closely to the three topics.

Other stopping criteria involve a notion of *cohesion*, the degree to which the merged cluster consists of points that are all close. Using a cohesion-based stopping policy, we decline to merge two clusters whose combination fails to meet the cohesion condition that we have chosen. At each merger round, we may merge two clusters that are not closest of all pairs of clusters, but are closer than any other pair that meet the cohesion condition. We even could define "closeness" to be the cohesion score, thus combining the merger selection with the stopping criterion. Here are some ways that we could define a cohesion score for a cluster:

i. Let the cohesion of a cluster be the average distance of each point to the centroid. Note that this definition only makes sense in a Euclidean space.

ii. Let the cohesion be the *diameter*, the largest distance between any pair of points in the cluster.

iii. Let the cohesion be the average distance between pairs of points in the cluster.

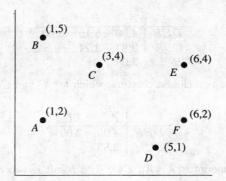

Figure 22.13: Data for Example 22.14

Example 22.14: Consider the six points in Fig. 22.13. Assume the normal Euclidean distance as our distance measure. We shall choose as the distance between clusters the minimum distance between any pair of points, one from each cluster. Initially, each point is in a cluster by itself, so the distances between clusters are just the distances between the points. These distances, to two decimal places, are given in Fig. 22.14

	A	B	C	D	E
F	4.00	5.83	3.61	1.41	2.00
E	5.39	5.10	3.00	3.16	
D	4.12	5.66	3.61		
C	2.83	2.24			
B	3.00				

Figure 22.14: Distances between points in Fig. 22.13

The closest two points are D and F, so these get merged into one cluster. We must compute the distance between the cluster DF and each of the other points. By the "closeness" rule we chose, this distance is the minimum of the distances from a node to D or F. The table of distances becomes:

	A	B	C	DF
E	5.39	5.10	3.00	2.00
DF	4.00	5.66	3.61	
C	2.83	2.24		
B	3.00			

The shortest distance above is between E and DF, so we merge these two clusters into a single cluster DEF. The distance to this cluster from each of the other points is the minimum of the distance to any of D, E, and F. This table of distances is:

	A	B	C
DEF	4.00	5.10	3.00
C	2.83	2.24	
B	3.00		

Next, we merge the two closest clusters, which are B and C. The new table of distances is:

	A	BC
DEF	4.00	3.00
BC	2.83	

The last possible merge is A with BC. The result is two clusters, ABC and DEF.

However, we may wish to stop the merging earlier. As an example stopping criterion, let us reject any merger that results in a cluster with an average distance between points over 2.5. Then we can merge D, E, and F; the cohesion (average of the three distances between pairs of these points) is 2.19 (see Fig. 22.14 to check).

At the point where the clusters are A, BC, and DEF, we cannot merge A with BC, even though these are the closest clusters. The reason is that the average distance among the points in ABC is 2.69, which is too high. We might consider merging DEF with BC, which is the second-closest pair of clusters at that time, but the cohesion for the cluster $BCDEF$ is 3.56, also too high. The third option would be to merge A with DEF, but the cohesion of $ADEF$ is 3.35, again too high. □

22.5.4 k-Means Algorithms

The second broad approach to clustering is called point-assignment. A popular version, which is typical of the approach is called k-*means*. This approach is really a family of algorithms, just as agglomerative clustering is. The outline of a k-means algorithm is:

1. Start by choosing k initial clusters in some way. These clusters might be single points, or small sets of points.

2. For each unassigned point, place it in the "nearest" cluster.

3. Optionally, after all points are assigned to clusters, fix the centroid of each cluster (assuming the points are in a Euclidean space, since non-Euclidean spaces do not have a notion of "centroid"). Then reassign all points to these k clusters. Occasionally, some of the earliest points to be assigned will thus wind up in another cluster.

One way to initialize a k-means clustering is to pick the first point at random. Then pick a second point as far from the first point as possible. Pick a third point whose minimum distance to either of the other two points is as great as possible. Proceed in this manner, until k points are selected, each with the maximum possible minimum distance to the previously selected points. These points become the initial k clusters.

Example 22.15: Suppose our points are those in Fig. 22.13, $k = 3$, and we choose A as the seed of the first cluster. The point furthest from A is E, so E becomes the seed of the second cluster. For the third point, the minimum distances to A or E are as follows.

$$B: 3.00, \ C: 2.83, \ D: 3.16, \ F: 2.00$$

The winner is D, with the largest minimum distance of 3.16. Thus, D becomes the third seed. □

Having picked the seeds for the k clusters, we visit each of the remaining points and assign it to a cluster. A simple way is to assign each point to the closest seed. However, if we are in a Euclidean space, we may wish to maintain the centroid for each cluster, and as we assign each point, put it in the cluster with the nearest centroid.

Example 22.16: Let us continue with Example 22.15. We have initialized each of the three clusters A, D, and E, so their centroids are the points themselves. Suppose we assign B to a cluster. The nearest centroid is A, at distance 3.00. Thus, the first cluster becomes AB, and its centroid is $(1, 3.5)$. Suppose we assign C next. Clearly C is closer to the centroid of AB than it is to either D or E, so C is assigned to AB, which becomes ABC with centroid $(1.67, 3.67)$. Last, we assign F; it is closer to D than to E or to the centroid of ABC. Thus, the three clusters are ABC, DF, and E, with centroids $(1.67, 3.67)$, $(5.5, 1.5)$, and $(6, 4)$, respectively. We could reassign all points to the nearest of these three centroids, but the resulting clusters would not change. □

22.5.5 k-Means for Large-Scale Data

We shall now examine an extension of k-means that is designed to deal with sets of points that are so large they cannot fit in main memory. The goal is not to assign every point to a cluster, but to determine where the centroids of the clusters are. If we really wanted to know the cluster of every point, we would have to make another pass through the data, assigning each point to its nearest centroid and writing out the cluster number with the point.

This algorithm, called the BFR Algorithm,[4] assumes an n-dimensional Euclidean space. It may therefore represent clusters, as they are forming, by their centroids. The BFR Algorithm also assumes that the cohesion of a cluster can be measured by the variance of the points within a cluster; the variance of a cluster is the average square of the distance of a point in the cluster from the centroid of the cluster. However, for convenience, it does not record the centroid and variance, but rather the following $2n + 1$ *summary statistics*:

1. N, the number of points in the cluster.

2. For each dimension i, the sum of the ith coordinates of the points in the cluster, denoted SUM_i.

3. For each dimension i, the sum of the squares of the ith coordinates of the points in the cluster, denoted SUMSQ_i.

The reason to use these parameters is that they are easy to compute when we merge clusters. Just add the corresponding values from the two clusters. However, we can compute the centroid and variance from these values. The rules are:

- The ith coordinate of the centroid is SUM_i/N.

- The variance in the ith dimension is $\text{SUMSQ}_i/N - (\text{SUM}_i/N)^2$.

Also remember that σ_i, the standard deviation in the ith dimension is the square root of the variance in that dimension.

The BFR Algorithm reads the data one main-memory-full at a time, leaving space in memory for the summary statistics for the clusters and some other data that we shall discuss shortly. It can initialize by picking k points from the first memory-load, using the approach of Example 22.15. It could also do any sort of clustering on the first memory load to obtain k clusters from that data. During the running of the algorithm, points are divided into three classes:

1. The *discard set*: points that have been assigned to a cluster. These points do not appear in main memory. They are represented only by the summary statistics for their cluster.

---

[4]For the authors, P. S. Bradley, U. M. Fayyad, and C. Reina.

2. The *compressed set*: There can be many groups of points that are sufficiently close to each other that we believe they belong in the same cluster, but they are not close to any cluster's current centroid, so we do not know to which cluster they belong. Each such group is represented by its summary statistics, just like the clusters are, and the points themselves do not appear in main memory.

3. The *retained set*: These points are not close to any other points; they are "outliers." They will eventually be assigned to the nearest cluster, but for the moment we retain each such point in main memory.

These sets change as we process successive memory-loads of the data. Figure 22.15 suggests the state of the data after some number of memory-loads have been processed by the BFR Algorithm.

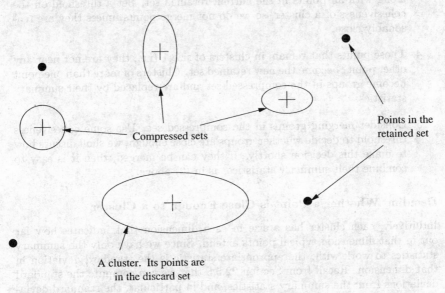

Figure 22.15: A cluster, several compressed sets and several points of the retained set

22.5.6 Processing a Memory Load of Points

We shall now describe how one memory load of points is processed. We assume that main memory current contains the summary statistics for the k clusters and also for zero or more groups of points that are in the compressed set. Main memory also holds the current set of points in the retained set. We do the following steps:

1. For all points $(x_1, x_2, \ldots, x_n)$ that are "sufficiently close" (a term we shall define shortly) to the centroid of a cluster, add the point to this cluster. The point itself goes into the discard set. We add 1 to N in the summary statistics for that cluster. We also add x_i to SUM_i and add x_i^2 to $SUMSQ_i$ for that cluster.

2. If this memory load is the last, then merge each group from the compressed set and each point of the retained set into its nearest cluster. Remember that it is easy to merge clusters and groups using their summary statistics. Just add the counts N, and add corresponding components of the SUM and SUMSQ vectors. The algorithm ends at this point.

3. Otherwise (the memory load is not the last), use any main-memory clustering algorithm to cluster the remaining points from this memory load, along with all points in the current retained set. Set a threshold on the cohesiveness of a cluster, so we do not merge points unless they are reasonably close.

4. Those points that remain in clusters of size 1 (i.e., they are not near any other point) become the new retained set. Clusters of more than one point become groups in the compressed set and are replaced by their summary statistics.

5. Consider merging groups in the compressed set. Use some cohesiveness threshold to decide whether groups are close enough; we shall discuss how to make this decision shortly. If they can be merged, then it is easy to combine their summary statistics, as in (2) above.

Deciding Whether a Point is Close Enough to a Cluster

Intuitively, each cluster has a size in each dimension that indicates how far out in that dimension typical points extend. Since we have only the summary statistics to work with, the appropriate statistic is the standard deviation in that dimension. Recall from Section 22.5.5 that we can compute the standard deviations from the summary statistics, and in particular, the standard deviation is the square root of the variance. However, clusters may be "cigar-shaped," so the standard deviations could vary widely. We want to include a point if its distance from the cluster centroid is not too many standard deviations in any dimension.

Thus, the first thing to do with a point $p = (x_1, x_2, \ldots, x_n)$ that we are considering for inclusion in a cluster is to normalize p relative to the centroid and the standard deviations of the cluster. That is, we transform the point into $p' = (y_1, y_2, \ldots, y_n)$, where $y_i = (x_i - c_i)/\sigma_i$; here c_i is the coordinate of the centroid in the ith dimension and σ_i is the standard deviation of the cluster in that dimension. The normalized distance of p from the centroid is the absolute distance of p' from the origin, that is, $\sqrt{\sum_{i=1}^{n} y_i^2}$. This distance is sometimes called the *Mahalanobis distance*, although it is actually a simplifed version of the concept.

Example 22.17: Suppose p is the point $(5, 10, 15)$, and we are considering whether to include p in a cluster with centroid $(10, 20, 5)$. Also, let the standard deviation of the cluster in the three dimensions be 1, 2, and 10, respectively. Then the Mahalanobis distance of p is

$$\sqrt{\big((5-10)/1\big)^2 + \big((10-20)/2\big)^2 + \big((15-5)/10\big)^2} = \sqrt{25 + 25 + 1} = 7.14$$

□

Having computed the Mahalanobis distance of point p, we can apply a threshold to decide whether or not to include p in the cluster. For instance, suppose we use 3 as the threshold; that is, we shall include the point if and only if its Mahalanobis distance from the centroid is not greater than 3. If values are normally distributed, then very few of these values will be more than 3 standard deviations from the mean (approximately one in a million will be that far from the mean). Thus, we would only reject one in a million points that belong in the cluster. There is a good chance that, at the end, the rejected points would wind up in the cluster anyway, since there may be no closer cluster.

Deciding Whether to Merge Groups of the Compressed Set

We discussed methods of computing the cohesion of a prospective cluster in Section 22.5.3. However, for the BFR algorithm, these ideas must be modified so we can make a decision using only the summary statistics for the two groups. Here are some options:

1. Choose an upper bound on the sum of the variances of the combined group in each dimension. Recall that we compute the summary statistics for the combined group by adding corresponding components, and compute the variance in each dimension using the formula in Section 22.5.5. This approach has the effect of limiting the region of space in which the points of a group exist. Groups in which the distances between typical pairs of points is too large will exceed the upper bound on variance, no matter how many points are in the group and how dense the points are within the region of space the group occupies.

2. Put an upper limit on the diameter in any dimension. Since we do not know the locations of the points exactly, we cannot compute the exact diameter. However, we could estimate the diameter in the ith dimension as the distance between the centroids of the two groups in dimension i plus the standard deviation of each group in dimension i. This approach also limits the size of the region of space occupied by a group.

3. Use one of the first two approaches, but divide the figure of merit (sum of variances or maximum diameter) by a quantity such as N or $\sqrt{N}$ that grows with the number of points in the group. That way, groups can occupy more space, as long as they remain dense within that space.

22.5.7   Exercises for Section 22.5

! **Exercise 22.5.1:** Show that for any $r \geq 1$, the distance based on the L_r norm satisfies the axioms of a distance measure. What happens if $r < 1$?

Exercise 22.5.2: In Example 22.14 we performed a hierarchical clustering of the points in Fig. 22.13, using minimum distance between points as the measure of closeness of clusters. Repeat the example using each of the following ways of measuring the distance between clusters.

  a) The maximum distance between points, one from each cluster.

  b) The average distance between points, one from each cluster.

  c) The distance between the centroids of the clusters.

Exercise 22.5.3: We could also modify Example 22.14 by using a different distance measure. Suppose we use the L_∞-norm as the distance measure. Note that this distance is the maximum of the distances along any axis, but when comparing distances you can break ties according to the next largest dimension. Show the sequence of mergers of the points in Fig. 22.13 that result from the use of this distance measure.

Exercise 22.5.4: Suppose we want to select three nodes in Fig. 22.13 to start three clusters, and we want them to be as far from each other as possible, as in Example 22.15. What points are selected if we start with (a) point D (b) point F?

Exercise 22.5.5: The BFR Algorithm represents clusters by summary statistics, as described in Section 22.5.5. Suppose the current members of a cluster are $\{(1,2),\ (3,4),\ (5,6),\ (0,4)\}$. What are the summary statistics for this cluster?

Exercise 22.5.6: For each pair of the points in Fig. 22.13:

  a) Compute the L_∞-norm.

  b) Compute the Manhattan distance (L_1-norm).

Exercise 22.5.7: For the cluster described in Example 22.17, compute the Mahalanobis distance of the points: (a) $(7,23,0)$ (b) $(10,15,20)$.

22.6 Summary of Chapter 22

✦ *Data Mining*: This term refers to the discovery of simple summaries of data.

✦ *The Market-Basket Model of Data*: A common way to represent a many-many relation is as a collection of baskets, each of which contains a set of items. Often, this data is presented not as a relation but as a file of baskets. Algorithms typically make passes through this file, and the cost of an algorithm is the number of passes it makes.

✦ *Frequent Itemsets*: An important summary of some market-basket data is the collection of frequent itemsets: sets of items that occur in at least some fixed number of baskets. The minimum number of baskets that make an itemset frequent is called the support threshold.

✦ *Association Rules*: These are statements of the form that say if a certain set of items appears in a basket, then there is at least some minimum probability that another particular item is also in that basket. The probability is called the confidence of the rule.

✦ *The A-Priori Algorithm*: This algorithm finds frequent itemsets by exploiting the fact that if a set of items occurs at least s times, then so does each of its subsets. For each size of itemset, we start with the candidate itemsets, which are all those whose every immediate subset (the set minus one element) is known to be frequent. We then count the occurrences of the candidates in a single pass, to determine which are truly frequent.

✦ *The PCY Algorithm*: This algorithm makes better use of main memory than A-priori does, while counting the singleton items. PCY additionally hashes all pairs to buckets and counts the total number of baskets that contain a pair hashing to each bucket. To be a candiate on the second pass, a pair has to consist of items that not only are frequent as singletons, but also hash to a bucket whose count exceeded the support threshold.

✦ *The Multistage Algorithm*: This algorithm improves on PCY by using several passes in which pairs are hashed to buckets using different hash functions. On the final pass, a pair can only be a candidate if it consists of frequent items and also hashed each time to a bucket that had a count at least equal to the support threshold.

✦ *Similar Sets and Jaccard Similarity*: Another important use of market-basket data is to find similar baskets, that is, pairs of baskets with many elements in common. A useful measure is Jaccard similarity, which is the ratio of the sizes of the intersection and union of the two sets.

✦ *Shingling Documents*: We can find similar documents if we convert each document into its set of k-shingles — all substrings of k consecutive characters in the document. In this manner, the problem of finding similar documents can be solved by any technique for finding similar sets.

✦ *Minhash Signatures*: We can represent sets by short signatures that enable us to estimate the Jaccard similarity of any two represented sets. The technique known as minhashing chooses a sequence of random permutations, implemented by hash functions. Each permutation maps a set to the first, in the permuted order, of the members of that set, and the signature of the set is the list of elements that results by applying each permutation in this way.

✦ *Minhash Signatures and Jaccard Similarity*: The reason minhash signatures serve to represent sets is that the Jaccard similarity of sets is also the probability that two sets will agree on their minhash values. Thus, we can estimate the Jaccard similarity of sets by counting the number of components on which their minhash signatures agree.

✦ *Locality-Sensitive Hashing*: To avoid having to compare all pairs of signatures, locality-sensitive hashing divides the signatures into bands, and compares two signatures only if they agree exactly in at least one band. By tuning the number of bands and the number of components per band, we can focus attention on only the pairs that are likely to meet a given similarity threshold.

✦ *Clustering*: The problem is to find groups (clusters) of similar items (points) in a space with a distance measure. One approach, called agglomerative, is to build bigger and bigger clusters by merging nearby clusters. A second approach is to estimate the clusters initially and assign points to the nearest cluster.

✦ *Distance Measures*: A distance on a set of points is a function that assigns a nonnegative number to any pair of points. The function is 0 only if the points are the same, and the function is commutative. It must also satisfy the triangle inequality.

✦ *Commonly Used Distance Measures*: If points occupy a Euclidean space, essentially a space with some number of dimensions and a coordinate system, we can use the ordinary Euclidean distance, or modifications such as the Manhattan distance (sum of the distances along the coordinates). In non-Euclidean spaces, we can use distance measures such as the Jaccard distance between sets (one minus Jaccard similiarity) or the edit distance between strings.

✦ *BFR Algorithm*: This algorithm is a variant of k-means, where points are assigned to k clusters. Since the BFR Algorithm is intended for data sets that are two large to fit in main memory, it compresses most points into sets that are represented only by their count and, for each dimension, the sum of their coordinates and the sum of the squares of their coordinates. each

22.7 References for Chapter 22

Two useful books on data mining are [7] and [10].

The A-Priori Algorithm comes from [1] and [2]. The PCY Algorithm is from [9] and the multistage algorithm is from [6].

The use of shingling and minhashing to discover similar documents is from [4] and the theory of minhashing is in [5]. Locality-sensitive hashing is from [8].

Clustering of non-main-memory data sets was first considered in [11]. The BFR Algorithm is from [3].

1. R. Agrawal, T. Imielinski, and A. Swami, "Mining associations between sets of items in massive databases," *Proc. ACM SIGMOD Intl. Conf. on Management of Data*, pp. 207–216, 1993.

2. R. Agrawal and R. Srikant, "Fast algorithms for mining association rules," *Intl. Conf. on Very Large Databases*, pp. 487–499, 1994.

3. P. S. Bradley, U. M. Fayyad, and C. Reina, "Scaling clustering algorithms to large databases," *Proc. Knowledge Discovery and Data Mining*, pp. 9–15, 1998.

4. A. Z. Broder, "On the resemblance and containment of documents," *Proc. Compression and Complexity of Sequences*, pp. 21–29, Positano Italy, 1997.

5. A. Z. Broder, M. Charikar, A. M. Frieze, and M. Mitzenmacher, "Minwise independent permutations," *J. Computer and System Sciences* **60**:3 (2000), pp. 630–659.

6. M. Fang, N. Shivakumar, H. Garcia-Molina, R. Motwani, and J. D. Ullman, "Computing iceberg queries efficiently," *Intl. Conf. on Very Large Databases*, pp. 299-310, 1998.

7. U. M. Fayyad, G. Piatetsky-Shapiro, P. Smyth, and R. Uthurusamy, *Advances in Knowledge Discovery and Data Mining*, MIT Press, 1996.

8. P. Indyk and R. Motwani, "Approximate nearest neighbors: toward removing the curse of dimensionality," *ACM Symp. on Theory of Computing*, pp. 604-613, 1998.

9. J. S. Park, M.-S. Chen, and P. S. Yu, "An effective hash-based algorithm for mining association rules," *Proc. ACM SIGMOD Intl. Conf. on Management of Data*, pp. 175–186, 1995.

10. P.-N. Tan, M. Steinbach, and V. Kumar, *Introduction to Data Mining*, Addison-Wesley, Boston MA, 2006.

11. T. Zhang, R. Ramakrishnan, and M. Livny, "BIRCH: an efficient data clustering method for very large databases," *Proc. ACM SIGMOD Intl. Conf. on Management of Data*, pp. 103–114, 1996.

Chapter 23

Database Systems and the Internet

The age of the World-Wide Web has had a profound effect on database technology. Conventional relational databases sit behind, and power, many of the most important Web applications, as we discussed in Section 9.1. But Web applications have also forced databases to assume new forms. Often, massive databases are not found inside a relational DBMS, but in complex, ad-hoc file structures. One of the most important examples of this phenomenon is the way search engines manage their data. Thus, in this chapter we shall examine algorithms for crawling the Web and for answering search-engine queries.

Other sources of data are dynamic in nature. Rather than existing in a database, the data is a stream of information that must either be processed and stored as it arrives, or thrown away. One example is the click streams (sequence of URL requests) received at major Web sites. Non-Web-related streams of data also exist, such as the "call-detail records" generated by all the telephone calls traveling through a network, and data generated by satellites and networks of sensors. Thus, the second part of this chapter addresses the stream data model and the technology needed to manage massive data in the form of streams.

23.1 The Architecture of a Search Engine

The search engine has become one of the most important tools of the 21st century. The repositories managed by the major search engines are among the largest databases on the planet, and surely no other database is accessed so frequently and by so many users. In this section, we shall examine the key components of a search engine, which are suggested schematically in Fig. 23.1.

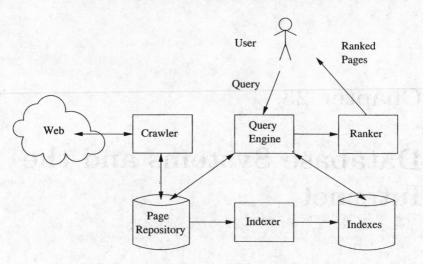

Figure 23.1: The components of a search engine

23.1.1   Components of a Search Engine

There are two main functions that a search engine must perform.

1. The Web must be *crawled*. That is, copies of many of the pages on the Web must be brought to the search engine and processed.

2. Queries must be answered, based on the material gathered from the Web. Usually, the query is in the form of a word or words that the desired Web pages should contain, and the answer to a query is a ranked list of the pages that contain all those words, or at least some of them.

Thus, in Fig. 23.1, we see the *crawler* interacting with the Web and with the *page repository*, a database of pages that the crawler has found. We shall discuss crawling in more detail in Section 23.1.2.

The pages in the page repository are indexed. Typically, these indexes are inverted indexes, of the type discussed in Section 14.1.8. That is, for each word, there is a list of the pages that contain that word. Additional information in the index for the word may include its location(s) within the page or its role, e.g., whether the word is in the header.

We also see in Fig. 23.1 a user issuing a query that consists of one or more words. A *query engine* takes those words and interacts with the indexes, to determine which pages satisfy the query. These pages are then ordered by a *ranker*, and presented to the user, typically 10 at a time, in ranked order. We shall have more to say about the query process in Section 23.1.3.

23.1.2 Web Crawlers

A crawler can be a single machine that is started with a set S, containing the URL's of one or more Web pages to crawl. There is a repository R of pages, with the URL's that have already been crawled; initially R is empty.

Algorithm 23.1: A Simple Web Crawler.

INPUT: An initial set of URL's S.

OUTPUT: A repository R of Web pages.

METHOD: Repeatedly, the crawler does the following steps.

1. If S is empty, end.

2. Select a page p from the set S to "crawl" and delete p from S.

3. Obtain a copy of p, using its URL. If p is already in repository R, return to step (1) to select another page.

4. If p is not already in R:

   (a) Add p to R.
   (b) Examine p for links to other pages. Insert into S the URL of each page q that p links to, but that is not already in R or S.

5. Go to step (1).

$\square$

Algorithm 23.1 raises several questions.

a) How do we terminate the search if we do not want to search the entire Web?

b) How do we check efficiently whether a page is already in repository R?

c) How do we select a page p from S to search next?

d) How do we speed up the search, e.g., by exploiting parallelism?

Terminating Search

Even if we wanted to search the "entire Web," we must limit the search somehow. The reason is that some pages are generated dynamically, so when the crawler asks a site for a URL, the site itself constructs the page. Worse, that page may have URL's that also refer to dynamically constructed pages, and this process could go on forever.

As a consequence, it is generally necessary to cut off the search at some point. For example, we could put a limit on the number of pages to crawl, and stop when that limit is reached. The limit could be either on each site or on the total number of pages. Alternatively, we could limit the *depth* of the crawl. That is, say that the pages initially in set S have depth 1. If the page p selected for crawling at step (2) of Algorithm 23.1 has depth i, then any page q that we add to S at step (4b) is given depth $i + 1$. However, if p has depth equal to the limit, then we do not examine links out of p at all. Rather we simply add p to R, if it is not already there.

Managing the Repository

There are two points where we must avoid duplication of effort. First, when we add a new URL for a page q to the set S, we should check that it is not already there or among the URL's of pages in R. There may be billions of URL's in R and/or S, so this job requires an efficient index structure, such as those in Chapter 14.

Second, when we decide to add a new page p to R at step (4a) of Algorithm 23.1, we should be sure the page is not already there. How could it be, since we make sure to search each URL only once? Unfortunately, the same page can have several different URL's, so our crawler may indeed encounter the same page via different routes. Moreover, the Web contains mirror sites, where large collection of pages are duplicated, or nearly duplicated (e.g., each may have different internal links within the site, and each may refer to the other mirror sites). Comparing a page p with all the pages in R can be much too time-consuming. However, we can make this comparison efficient as follows:

1. If we only want to detect exact duplicates, hash each Web page to a signature of, say, 64 bits. The signatures themselves are stored in a hash table T; i.e., they are further hashed into a smaller number of buckets, say one million buckets. If we are considering inserting p into R, compute the 64-bit signature $h(p)$, and see whether $h(p)$ is already in the hash table T. If so, do not store p; otherwise, store p in R. Note that we could get some false positives; it could be that $h(p)$ is in T, yet some page other than p produced the same signature. However, by making signatures sufficiently long, we can reduce the probability of a false positive essentially to zero.

2. If we want to detect near duplicates of p, then we can store minhash signatures (see Section 22.3) in place of the simple hash-signatures mentioned in (1). Further, we need to use locality-sensitive hashing (see Section 22.4) in place of the simple hash table T of option (1).

Selecting the Next Page

We could use a completely random choice of next page. A better strategy is to manage S as a queue, and thus do a breadth-first search of the Web from the starting point or points with which we initialized S. Since we presumably start the search from places in the Web that have "important" pages, we thus are assured of visiting preferentially those portions of the Web that the authors of these "important" pages thought were also important.

An alternative is to try to estimate the importance of pages in the set S, and to favor those pages we estimate to be most important. We shall take up in Section 23.2 the idea of PageRank as a measure of the importance that the Web attributes to certain pages. It is impossible to compute PageRank exactly while the crawl is in progress. However, a simple approximation is to count the number of known in-links for each page in set S. That is, each time we examine a link to a page q at step (4b) of Algorithm 23.1, we add one to the count of in-links for q. Then, when selecting the next page p to crawl at step (2), we always pick one of the pages with the highest number of in-links.

Speeding Up the Crawl

We do not need to limit ourselves to one crawling machine, and we do not need to limit ourselves to one process per machine. Each process that acts on the set of available URL's (what we called S in Algorithm 23.1) must lock the set, so we do not find two processes obtaining the same URL to crawl, or two processes writing the same URL into the set at the same time. If there are so many processes that the lock on S becomes a bottleneck, there are several options.

We can assign processes to entire hosts or sites to be crawled, rather than to individual URL's. If so, a process does not have to access the set of URL's S so often, since it knows no other process will be accessing the same site while it does.

There is a disadvantage to this approach. A crawler gathering pages at a site can issue page requests at a very rapid rate. This behavior is essentially a denial-of-service attack, where the site can do no useful work while it strives to answer all the crawler's requests. Thus, a responsible crawler does not issue frequent requests to a single site; it might limit itself to one every several seconds. If a crawling process is visiting a single site, then it must slow down its rate of requests to the point that it is often idle. That in itself is not a problem, since we can run many crawling processes at a single machine. However, operating-system software has limits on how many processes can be alive at any time.

An alternative way to avoid bottlenecks is to partition the set S, say by hashing URL's into several buckets. Each process is assigned to select new URL's to crawl from a particular one of the buckets. When a process follows a link to find a new URL, it hashes that URL to determine which bucket it belongs in. That bucket is the only one that needs to be examined to see if the new URL is already there, and if it is not, that is the bucket into which the new URL is placed.

The same bottleneck issues that arise for the set S of active URL's also come up in managing the page repository R and its set of URL's. The same two techniques — assigning processes to sites or partitioning the set of URL's by hashing — serve to avoid bottlenecks in the accessing of R as well.

23.1.3   Query Processing in Search Engines

Search engine queries are not like SQL queries. Rather they are typically a set of words, for which the search engine must find and rank all pages containing all, or perhaps a subset of, those words. In some cases, the query can be a boolean combination of words, e.g., all pages that contain the word "data" or the word "base." Possibly, the query may require that two words appear consecutively, or appear near each other, say within 5 words.

Answering queries such as these requires the use of inverted indexes. Recall from our discussion of Fig. 23.1 that once the crawl is complete, the indexer constructs an inverted index for all the words on the Web. Note that there will be hundreds of millions of words, since any sequence of letters and digits surrounded by punctuation or whitespace is an indexable word. Thus, "words" on the Web include not only the words in any of the world's natural languages, but all misspellings of these words, error codes for all sorts of systems, acronyms, names, and jargon of many kinds.

The first step of query processing is to use the inverted index to determine those pages that contain the words in the query. To offer the user acceptable response time, this step must involve few, if any, disk accesses. Search engines today give responses in fractions of a second, an amount of time so small that it amounts to only a few disk-access times.

On the other hand, the vectors that represent occurrences of a single word have components for each of the pages indexed by the search engine, perhaps tens of billions of pages. Very rare words might be represented by listing their occurrences, but for common, or even reasonably rare words, it is more efficient to represent by a bit vector the pages in which they occur. The AND of bit vectors gives the pages containing both words, and the OR of bit vectors gives the pages containing one or both. To speed up the selection of pages, it is essential to keep as many vectors as possible in main memory, since we cannot afford disk accesses. Teams of machines may partition the job, say each managing the portion of bit vectors corresponding to a subset of the Web pages.

23.1.4   Ranking Pages

Once the set of pages that match the query is determined, these pages are ranked, and only the highest-ranked pages are shown to the user. The exact way that pages are ranked is a secret formula, as closely guarded by search engines as the formula for Coca Cola. One important component is the "PageRank," a measure of how important the Web itself believes the page to be. This measure is based on links to the page in question, but is significantly more complex than that. We discuss PageRank in detail in Section 23.2.

Some of the other measures of how likely a page is to be a relevant response to the query are fairly easy to reason out. The following is a list of typical components of a relevance measure for pages.

  1. The presence of all the query words. While search engines will return

pages with only a proper subset of the query words, these pages are generally ranked lower than pages having all the words.

2. The presence of query words in important positions in the page. For example, we would expect that a query word appearing in a title of the page would indicate more strongly that the page was relevant to that word than its mere occurrence in the middle of a paragraph. Likewise, appearance of the word in a header cell of a table would be a more favorable indication than its appearance in a data cell of the same table.

3. Presence of several query words near each other would be a more favorable indication than if the words appeared in the page, but widely separated. For example, if the query consists of the words "sally" and "jones," we are probably looking for pages that mention a certain person. Many pages have lists of names in them. If "sally" and "jones" appear adjacent, or perhaps separated by a middle initial, then there is a better chance the page is about the person we want than if "sally" appeared, but nowhere near "jones." In that case, there are probably two different people, one with first name Sally, and the other with last name Jones.

4. Presence of the query words in or near the anchor text in links leading to the page in question. This insight was one of the two key ideas that made the Google search engine the standard for the field (the other is PageRank, to be discussed next). A page may lie about itself, by using words designed to make it appear to be a good answer to a query, but it is hard to make other people confirm your lie in their own pages.

23.2 PageRank for Identifying Important Pages

One of the key technological advances in search is the PageRank[1] algorithm for identifying the "importance" of Web pages. In this section, we shall explain how the algorithm works, and show how to compute PageRank for very large collections of Web pages.

23.2.1 The Intuition Behind PageRank

The insight that makes Google and other search engines able to return the "important" pages on a topic is that the Web itself points out the important pages. When you create a page, you tend to link that page to others that you think are important or valuable, rather than pages you think are useless. Of course others may differ in their opinions, but on balance, the more ways one can get to a page by following links, the more likely the page is to be important.

We can formalize this intuition by imagining a random walker on the Web. At each step, the random walker is at one particular page p and randomly

---

[1] After Larry Page, who first proposed the algorithm.

picks one of the pages that p links to. At the next step, the walker is at the chosen successor of p. The structure of the Web links determines the long-run probability that the walker is at each individual page. This probability is termed the *PageRank* of the page.

Intuitively, pages that a lot of other pages point to are more likely to be the location of the walker than pages with few in-links. But all in-links are not equal. It is better for a page to have a few links from pages that themselves are likely places for the walker to be than to have many links from pages that the walker visits infrequently or not at all. Thus, it is not sufficient to count the in-links to compute the PageRank. Rather, we must solve a recursive equation that formalizes the idea:

- A Web page is important if many important pages link to it.

23.2.2   Recursive Formulation of PageRank — First Try

To describe how the random walker moves, we can use the *transition matrix of the Web*. Number the pages $1, 2, \ldots, n$. The matrix $\mathbf{M}$, the transition matrix of the Web has element m_{ij} in row i and column j, where:

1. $m_{ij} = 1/r$ if page j has a link to page i, and there are a total of $r \geq 1$ pages that j links to.

2. $m_{ij} = 0$ otherwise.

If every page has at least one link out, then the transition matrix will be (*left*) *stochastic* — elements are nonnegative, and its columns each sum to exactly 1. If there are pages with no links out, then the column for that page will be all 0's, and the transition matrix is said to be *substochastic* (all columns sum to at most 1).

Example 23.2 : As we all know, the Web has been growing exponentially, so if you extrapolate back to 1839, you find that the Web consisted of only three pages. Figure 23.2 shows what the Web looked like in 1839.

We have numbered the pages 1, 2, and 3, so the transition matrix for this graph is:

$$\mathbf{M} = \begin{bmatrix} 1/2 & 1/2 & 0 \\ 1/2 & 0 & 1 \\ 0 & 1/2 & 0 \end{bmatrix}$$

For example, node 3, the page for Microsoft, links only to node 2, the page for Amazon. Thus, in column 3, only row 2 is nonzero, and its value is 1 divided by the number of out-links of node 3, which is 1. As another example, node 1, Yahoo!, links to itself and to Amazon (node 2). Thus, in column 1, row 3 is 0, and rows 1 and 2 are each 1 divided by the number of out-links from node 1, i.e., 1/2.   □

PageRank Combats Spam

Before Google and PageRank, search engines had a great deal of trouble recognizing important pages on the Web. It was common for unscrupulous Web sites ("spammers") to put bogus content on their pages, often in ways that could not be seen by users, but that search engines would see in the text of the page (e.g., by making the writing have the same color as the background). If Google had simply counted in-links to measure the importance of pages, then the spammers could have created massive numbers of other bogus pages that linked to the page they wanted the search engines to think was important. However, simply creating a page doesn't give it much PageRank, since truly important pages are unlikely to link to it. Thus, PageRank defeated the spammers of the day.

Interestingly, the war between spammers and search engines continues. The spammers eventually learned how to increase the PageRank of bogus pages, which led to techniques for combating new forms of spam, often called "link spam." We shall address link spam in Section 23.3.3.

Suppose y, a, and m represent the fractions of the time the random walker spends at the three pages of Fig. 23.2. Then multiplying the column-vector of these three values by $\mathbf{M}$ will not change their values. The reason is that, after a large number of moves, the walker's distribution of possible locations is the same at each step, regardless where the walker started. That is, the unknowns y, a, and m must satisfy:

$$\begin{bmatrix} y \\ a \\ m \end{bmatrix} = \begin{bmatrix} 1/2 & 1/2 & 0 \\ 1/2 & 0 & 1 \\ 0 & 1/2 & 0 \end{bmatrix} \begin{bmatrix} y \\ a \\ m \end{bmatrix}$$

Although there are three equations in three unknowns, you cannot solve these equations for more than the ratios of y, a, and m. That is, if $[y, a, m]$ is a solution to the equations, then $[cy, ca, cm]$ is also a solution, for any constant c. However, since y, a, and m form a probability distribution, we also know $y + a + m = 1$.

While we could solve the resulting equations without too much trouble, solving large numbers of simultaneous linear equations takes time $O(n^3)$, where n is the number of variables or equations. If n is in the billions, as it would be for the Web of today, it is utterly infeasible to solve for the distribution of the walker's location by Gaussian elimination or another direct solution method. However, we can get a good approximation by the method of *relaxation*, where we start with some estimate of the solution and repeatedly multiply the estimate by the matrix $\mathbf{M}$. As long as the columns of $\mathbf{M}$ each add up to 1, then the sum of the values of the variables will not change, and eventually they converge to

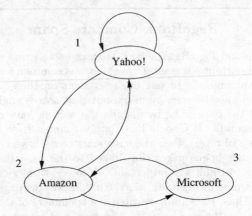

Figure 23.2: The Web in 1839

the distribution of the walker's location. In practice, 50 to 100 iterations of this process suffice to get very close to the exact solution.

Example 23.3: Suppose we start with $[y, a, m] = [1/3, 1/3, 1/3]$. Multiply this vector by **M** to get

$$\begin{bmatrix} 2/6 \\ 3/6 \\ 1/6 \end{bmatrix} = \begin{bmatrix} 1/2 & 1/2 & 0 \\ 1/2 & 0 & 1 \\ 0 & 1/2 & 0 \end{bmatrix} \begin{bmatrix} 1/3 \\ 1/3 \\ 1/3 \end{bmatrix}$$

At the next iteration, we multiply the new estimate $[2/6, 3/6, 1/6]$ by **M**, as:

$$\begin{bmatrix} 5/12 \\ 4/12 \\ 3/12 \end{bmatrix} = \begin{bmatrix} 1/2 & 1/2 & 0 \\ 1/2 & 0 & 1 \\ 0 & 1/2 & 0 \end{bmatrix} \begin{bmatrix} 2/6 \\ 3/6 \\ 1/6 \end{bmatrix}$$

If we repeat this process, we get the following sequence of vectors:

$$\begin{bmatrix} 9/24 \\ 11/24 \\ 4/24 \end{bmatrix}, \begin{bmatrix} 20/48 \\ 17/48 \\ 11/48 \end{bmatrix}, \dots, \begin{bmatrix} 2/5 \\ 2/5 \\ 1/5 \end{bmatrix}$$

That is, asymptotically, the walker is equally likely to be at Yahoo! or Amazon, and only half as likely to be at Microsoft as either one of the other pages. □

23.2.3 Spider Traps and Dead Ends

The graph of Fig. 23.2 is atypical of the Web, not only because of its size, but for two structural reasons:

1. Some Web pages (called *dead ends*) have no out-links. If the random walker arrives at such a page, there is no place to go next, and the walk ends.

2. There are sets of Web pages (called *spider traps*) with the property that if you enter that set of pages, you can never leave, because there are no links from any page in the set to any page outside the set.

Any dead end is, by itself, a spider trap. However, one also finds on the Web spider traps all of whose pages have out-links. For example, any page that links only to itself is a spider trap.

If a spider trap can be reached from outside, then the random walker may wind up there eventually, and never leave. Put another way, applying relaxation to the matrix of the Web with spider traps can result in a limiting distribution where all probabilities outside a spider trap are 0.

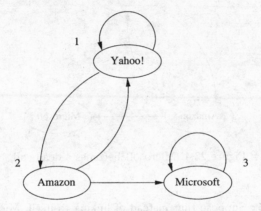

Figure 23.3: The Web, if Microsoft becomes a spider trap

Example 23.4: Suppose Microsoft decides to link only to itself, rather than Amazon, resulting in the Web of Fig. 23.3. Then the set of pages consisting of Microsoft alone is a spider trap, and that trap can be reached from either of the other pages. The matrix M for this Web graph is

$$M = \begin{bmatrix} 1/2 & 1/2 & 0 \\ 1/2 & 0 & 0 \\ 0 & 1/2 & 1 \end{bmatrix}$$

Here is the sequence of approximate distributions that is obtained if we start, as we did in Example 23.3, with $[y, a, m] = [1/3, 1/3, 1/3]$ and repeatedly multiply by the matrix M for Fig. 23.3:

$$\begin{bmatrix} 1/3 \\ 1/3 \\ 1/3 \end{bmatrix}, \begin{bmatrix} 2/6 \\ 1/6 \\ 3/6 \end{bmatrix}, \begin{bmatrix} 3/12 \\ 2/12 \\ 7/12 \end{bmatrix}, \begin{bmatrix} 5/24 \\ 3/24 \\ 16/24 \end{bmatrix}, \begin{bmatrix} 8/48 \\ 5/48 \\ 35/48 \end{bmatrix}, \dots, \begin{bmatrix} 0 \\ 0 \\ 1 \end{bmatrix}$$

That is, with probability 1, the walker will eventually wind up at the Microsoft page and stay there.   □

If we interpret these PageRank probabilities as "importance" of pages, then the Microsoft page has gathered all importance to itself simply by choosing not to link outside. That situation intuitively violates the principle that other pages, not you yourself, should determine your importance on the Web. The other problem we mentioned — dead ends — also cause the PageRank not to reflect importance of pages, as we shall see in the next example.

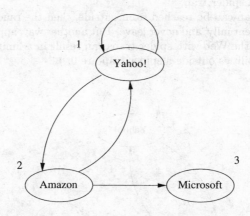

Figure 23.4: Microsoft becomes a dead end

Example 23.5: Suppose that instead of linking to itself, Microsoft links nowhere, as suggested in Fig. 23.4. The matrix $\mathbf{M}$ for this Web graph is

$$\mathbf{M} = \begin{bmatrix} 1/2 & 1/2 & 0 \\ 1/2 & 0 & 0 \\ 0 & 1/2 & 0 \end{bmatrix}$$

Notice that this matrix is not stochastic, because its columns do not all add up to 1. If we try to apply the method of relaxation to this matrix, with initial vector $[1/3, 1/3, 1/3]$, we get the sequence:

$$\begin{bmatrix} 1/3 \\ 1/3 \\ 1/3 \end{bmatrix}, \begin{bmatrix} 2/6 \\ 1/6 \\ 1/6 \end{bmatrix}, \begin{bmatrix} 3/12 \\ 2/12 \\ 1/12 \end{bmatrix}, \begin{bmatrix} 5/24 \\ 3/24 \\ 2/24 \end{bmatrix}, \begin{bmatrix} 8/48 \\ 5/48 \\ 3/48 \end{bmatrix}, \ldots, \begin{bmatrix} 0 \\ 0 \\ 0 \end{bmatrix}$$

That is, the walker will eventually arrive at Microsoft, and at the next step has nowhere to go. Eventually, the walker disappears.   □

23.2.4 PageRank Accounting for Spider Traps and Dead Ends

The solution to both spider traps and dead ends is to limit the time the random walker is allowed to wander at random. We pick a constant $\beta < 1$, typically in the range 0.8 to 0.9, and at each step, we let the walker follow a random out-link, if there is one, with probability β. With probability $1 - \beta$ (called the *taxation rate*), we remove that walker and deposit a new walker at a randomly chosen Web page. This modification solves both problems.

- If the walker gets stuck in a spider trap, it doesn't matter, because after a few time steps, that walker will disappear and be replaced by a new walker.

- If the walker reaches a dead end and disappears, a new walker will take over shortly.

Example 23.6: Let us use $\beta = 0.8$ and reformulate the calculation of Page-Rank for the Web of Fig. 23.3. If $\mathbf{p}_{new}$ and $\mathbf{p}_{old}$ are the new and old distributions of the location of the walker after one iteration, the relationship between these two can be expressed as:

$$\mathbf{p}_{new} = 0.8 \begin{bmatrix} 1/2 & 1/2 & 0 \\ 1/2 & 0 & 0 \\ 0 & 1/2 & 1 \end{bmatrix} \mathbf{p}_{old} + 0.2 \begin{bmatrix} 1/3 \\ 1/3 \\ 1/3 \end{bmatrix}$$

That is, with probability 0.8, we multiply $\mathbf{p}_{old}$ by the matrix of the Web to get the new location of the walker, and with probability 0.2 we start with a new walker at a random place. If we start with $\mathbf{p}_{old} = [1/3, 1/3, 1/3]$ and repeatedly compute $\mathbf{p}_{new}$ and then replace $\mathbf{p}_{old}$ by $\mathbf{p}_{new}$, we get the following sequence of approximations to the asymptotic distribution of the walker:

$$\begin{bmatrix} .333 \\ .333 \\ .333 \end{bmatrix}, \begin{bmatrix} .333 \\ .200 \\ .467 \end{bmatrix}, \begin{bmatrix} .280 \\ .200 \\ .520 \end{bmatrix}, \begin{bmatrix} .259 \\ .179 \\ .563 \end{bmatrix}, \ldots, \begin{bmatrix} 7/33 \\ 5/33 \\ 21/33 \end{bmatrix}$$

Notice that Microsoft, because it is a spider trap, gets a large share of the importance. However, the effect of the spider trap has been mitigated considerably by the policy of redistributing the walker with probability 0.2. □

The same idea fixes dead ends as well as spider traps. The resulting matrix that describes transitions is substochastic, since a column will sum to 0 if there are no out-links. Thus, there will be a small probability that the walker is "nowhere" at any given time. That is, the sums of the probabilities of the walker being at each of the pages will be less than one. However, the relative sizes of the probabilities will still be a good measure of the importance of the page.

Teleportation of Walkers

Another view of the random-walking process is that there are no "new" walkers, but rather the walker *teleports* to a random page with probability $1-\beta$. For this view to make sense, we have to assume that if the walker is at a dead end, then the probability of teleport is 100%. Equivalently, we can scale up the probabilities to sum to one at each step of the iteration. Doing so does not affect the ratios of the probabilities, and therefore the relative PageRank of pages remains the same. For instance, in Example 23.7, the final pageRank vector would be $[35/81, 25/81, 21/81]$.

Example 23.7: Let us reconsider Example 23.5, using $\beta = 0.8$. The formula for iteration is now:

$$\mathbf{p}_{new} = 0.8 \begin{bmatrix} 1/2 & 1/2 & 0 \\ 1/2 & 0 & 0 \\ 0 & 1/2 & 0 \end{bmatrix} \mathbf{p}_{old} + 0.2 \begin{bmatrix} 1/3 \\ 1/3 \\ 1/3 \end{bmatrix}$$

Starting with $\mathbf{p}_{old} = [1/3, 1/3, 1/3]$, we get the following sequence of approximations to the asymptotic distribution of the walker:

$$\begin{bmatrix} .333 \\ .333 \\ .333 \end{bmatrix}, \begin{bmatrix} .333 \\ .200 \\ .200 \end{bmatrix}, \begin{bmatrix} .280 \\ .200 \\ .147 \end{bmatrix}, \begin{bmatrix} .259 \\ .179 \\ .147 \end{bmatrix}, \dots, \begin{bmatrix} 35/165 \\ 25/165 \\ 21/165 \end{bmatrix}$$

Notice that these probabilities do not sum to one, and there is slightly more than 50% probability that the walker is "lost" at any given time. However, the ratio of the importances of Yahoo!, and Amazon are the same as in Example 23.6. That makes sense, because in neither Fig. 23.3 nor Fig. 23.4 are there links from the Microsoft page to influence the importance of Yahoo! or Amazon. □

23.2.5 Exercises for Section 23.2

Exercise 23.2.1: Compute the PageRank of the four nodes in Fig. 23.5, assuming no "taxation."

Exercise 23.2.2: Compute the PageRank of the four nodes in Fig. 23.5, assuming a taxation rate of: (a) 15% (b) 25%.

Exercise 23.2.3: Repeat Exercise 23.2.2 for the Web graph of

  i. Fig. 23.6.

  ii. Fig. 23.7.

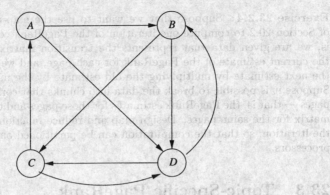

Figure 23.5: A Web graph with no dead-ends or spider traps

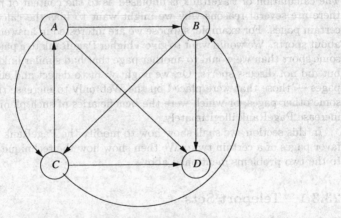

Figure 23.6: A Web graph with a dead end

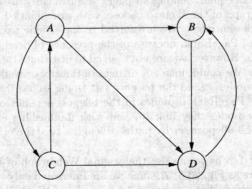

Figure 23.7: A Web graph with a spider trap

! Exercise 23.2.4: Suppose that we want to use the map-reduce framework of Section 20.2 to compute one iteration of the PageRank computation. That is, we are given data that represents the transition matrix of the Web and the current estimate of the PageRank for each page, and we want to compute the next estimate by multiplying the old estimate by the matrix of the Web. Suppose it is possible to break the data into chunks that correspond to sets of pages — that is, the PageRank estimates for those pages and the columns of the matrix for the same pages. Design map and reduce functions that implement the iteration, so that the computation can be partitioned onto any number of processors.

23.3 Topic-Specific PageRank

The calculation of PageRank is unbiased as to the content of pages. However, there are several reasons why we might want to bias the calculation to favor certain pages. For example, suppose we are interested in answering queries only about sports. We would want to give a higher PageRank to a page that discusses some sport than we would to another page that had similar links from the Web, but did not discuss sports. Or, we might want to detect and eliminate "spam" pages — those that were placed on the Web only to increase the PageRank of some other pages, or which were the beneficiaries of such planned attempts to increase PageRank illegitimately.

In this section, we shall show how to modify the PageRank computation to favor pages of a certain type. We then show how the technique yields solutions to the two problems mentioned above.

23.3.1 Teleport Sets

In Section 23.2.4, we "taxed" each page $1 - \beta$ of its estimated PageRank and distributed the tax equally among all pages. Equivalently, we allowed random walkers on the graph of the Web to choose, with probability $1 - \beta$, to teleport to a randomly chosen page. We are forced to have some taxation scheme in any calculation of PageRank, because of the presence of dead-ends and spider traps on the Web. However, we are not obliged to distribute the tax (or random walkers) equally. We could, instead, distribute the tax or walkers only among a selected set of nodes, called the *teleport set*. Doing so has the effect not only of increasing the PageRank of nodes in the teleport set, but of increasing the PageRank of the nodes they link to, and with diminishing effect, the nodes reachable from the teleport set by paths of lengths two, three, and so on.

Example 23.8: Let us reconsider the original Web graph of Fig. 23.2, which we reproduce here as Fig. 23.8. Assume we are interested only in retail sales, so we chose a teleport set that consists of Amazon alone. We shall use $\beta = 0.8$, i.e., a taxation rate of 20%. If y, a, and m are variables representing the PageRanks

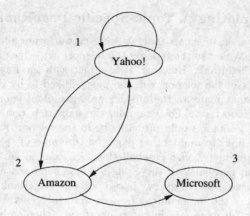

Figure 23.8: Web graph for Example 23.8

of Yahoo!, Amazon, and Microsoft, respectively, then the equations we need to solve are:

$$\begin{bmatrix} y \\ a \\ m \end{bmatrix} = 0.8 \begin{bmatrix} 1/2 & 1/2 & 0 \\ 1/2 & 0 & 1 \\ 0 & 1/2 & 0 \end{bmatrix} \begin{bmatrix} y \\ a \\ m \end{bmatrix} + 0.2 \begin{bmatrix} 0 \\ 1 \\ 0 \end{bmatrix}$$

The vector $[0, 1, 0]$ added at the end represents the fact that all the tax is distributed equally among the members of the teleport set. In this case, there is only one member of the teleport set, so the vector has 1 for that member (Amazon) and 0's elsewhere. We can solve the equations by relaxation, as we have done before. However, the example is small enough to apply Gaussian elimination and get the exact solution; it is $y = 10/31$, $a = 15/31$, and $m = 6/31$. The expected thing has happened; the PageRank of Amazon is elevated, because it is a member of the teleport set. $\square$

The general rule for setting up the equations in a topic-specific PageRank problem is as follows. Suppose there are k pages in the teleport set. Let t be a column-vector that has $1/k$ in the positions corresponding to members of the teleport set and 0 elsewhere. Let $1 - \beta$ be the taxation rate, and let M be the transition matrix of the Web. Then we must solve by relaxation the following iterative rule:

$$\mathbf{p}_{new} = \beta \mathbf{M} \mathbf{p}_{old} + (1 - \beta)\mathbf{t}$$

Example 23.8 was an illustration of this process, although we set both $\mathbf{p}_{new}$ and $\mathbf{p}_{old}$ to $[y, a, m]$ and solved for the fixedpoint of the equations, rather than iterating to converge to the solution.

23.3.2   Calculating A Topic-Specific PageRank

Suppose we had a set of pages that we were certain were about a particular topic, say sports. We make these pages the teleport set, which has the effect of increasing their PageRank. However, it also increases the PageRank of pages linked to by pages in the teleport set, the pages linked to by those pages, and so on. We hope that many of these pages are also about sports, even if they are not in the teleport set. For example, the page mlb.com, the home page for major-league baseball, would probably be in the teleport set for the sports topic. That page links to many other pages on the same site — pages that sell baseball-related products, offer baseball statistics, and so on. It also links to news stories about baseball. All these pages are, in some sense, about sports.

Suppose we issue a search query "batter." If the PageRank that the search engine uses to rank the importance of pages were the general PageRank (i.e., the version where all pages are in the teleport set), then we would expect to find pages about baseball batters, but also cupcake recipes. If we used the PageRank that is specific to sports, i.e., one where only sports pages are in the teleport set, then we would expect to find, among the top-ranked pages, nothing about cupcakes, but only pages about baseball or cricket.

It is not hard to reason that the home page for a major-league sport will be a good page to use in the teleport set for sports. However, we might want to be sure we got a good sample of pages that were about sports into our teleport set, including pages we might not think of, even if we were an expert on the subject. For example, starting at major-league baseball might not get us to pages for the Springfield Little League, even though parents in Springfield would want that page in response to a search involving the words "baseball" and "Springfield." To get a larger and wider selection of pages on sports to serve as our teleport set, some approaches are:

1. Start with a curated selection of pages. For example, the Open Directory (www.dmoz.org) has human-selected pages on sixteen topics, including sports, as well as many subtopics.

2. Learn the keywords that appear, with unusually high frequency, in a small set of pages on a topic. For instance if the topic were sports, we would expect words like "ball," "player," and "goal" to be among the selected keywords. Then, examine the entire Web, or a larger subset thereof, to identify other pages that also have unusually high concentrations of some of these keywords.

The next problem we have to solve, in order to use a topic-specific Page-Rank effectively, is determining which topic the user is interested in. Several possibilities exist.

a) The easiest way is to ask the user to select a topic.

b) If we have keywords associated with different topics, as described in (2) above, we can try to discover the likely topic on the user's mind. We can examine pages that we think are important to the user, and find, in these pages, the frequency of keywords that are associated with each of the topics. Topics whose keywords occur frequently in the pages of interest are assumed to be the preference(s) of the user. To find these "pages of interest," we might:

    i. Look at the pages the user has bookmarked.

    ii. Look at the pages the user has recently searched.

23.3.3 Link Spam

Another application of topic-specific PageRank is in combating "link spam." Because it is known that many search engines use PageRank as part of the formula to rank pages by importance, it has become financially advantageous to invest in mechanisms to increase the PageRank of your pages. This observation spawned an industry: *spam farming*. Unscrupulous individuals create networks of millions of Web pages, whose sole purpose is to accumulate and concentrate PageRank on a few pages.

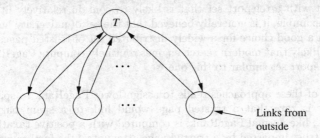

Figure 23.9: A spam farm concentrates PageRank in page T

A simple structure that accumulates PageRank in a target page T is shown in Fig. 23.9. Suppose that, in a PageRank calculation with taxation $1 - \beta$, the pages shown in the bottom row of Fig. 23.9 get, from the outside, a total PageRank of r, and let the total PageRank of these pages be x. Also, let the PageRank of page T be t. Then, in the limit, $t = \beta x$, because T gets all the PageRank of the other pages, except for the tax. Also, $x = r + \beta t$, because the other pages collectively get r from the outside and a total of βt from T. If we solve these equations for t, we get $t = \beta r/(1 - \beta^2)$. For instance, if $\beta = .85$, then we have amplified the external PageRank by factor $0.85/(1 - (0.85)^2) = 3.06$. Moreover, we have concentrated this PageRank in a single page, T.

Of course, if $r = 0$ then T still gets no PageRank at all. In fact, it is cut off from the rest of the Web and would be invisible to search engines. However, it is not hard for spam farmers to get a reasonable value for r. As one example, they create links to the spam farm from publicly accessible blogs, with messages like "I agree with you. See x123456.mySpamFarm.com." Moreover, if the number of pages in the bottom row is large, and the "tax" is distributed among all pages, then r will include the share of the tax that is given to these pages. That is why spam farmers use many pages in their structure, rather than just one or two.

23.3.4   Topic-Specific PageRank and Link Spam

A search engine needs to detect pages that are on the Web for the purpose of creating link spam. A useful tool is to compute the *TrustRank* of pages. Although the original definition is somewhat different, we may take the TrustRank to be the topic-specific PageRank computed with a teleport set consisting of only "trusted" pages. Two possible methods for selecting the set of trusted pages are:

1. Examine pages by hand and do an evaluation of their role on the Web. It is hard to automate this process, because spam farmers often copy the text of perfectly legitimate pages and populate their spam farm with pages containing that text plus the necessary links.

2. Start with a teleport set that is likely to contain relatively little spam. For example, it is generally believed that the set of university home pages form a good choice for a widely distributed set of trusted pages. In fact, it is likely that modern search engines routinely compute PageRank using a teleport set similar to this one.

Either of these approaches tends to assign lower PageRank to spam pages, because it is rare that a trusted page would link to a spam page. Since TrustRank, like normal PageRank, is computed with a positive taxation factor $1 - \beta$, the trust imparted by a trusted page attenuates, the further we get from that trusted page. The TrustRank of pages may substitute for PageRank, when the search engine chooses pages in response to a query. So doing reduces the likelihood that spam pages will be offered to the querier.

Another approach to detecting link-spam pages is to compute the *spam mass* of pages as follows:

a) Compute the ordinary PageRank, that is, using all pages as the teleport set.

b) Compute the TrustRank of all pages, using some reasonable set of trusted pages.

c) Compute the difference between the PageRank and TrustRank for each page. This difference is the *negative TrustRank*.

d) The spam mass of a page is the ratio of its negative TrustRank to its ordinary PageRank, that is, the fraction of its PageRank that appears to come from spam farms.

While TrustRank alone can bias the PageRank to minimize the effect of link spam, computing the spam mass also allows us to see where the link spam is coming from. Sites that have many pages with high spam mass may be owned by spam farmers, and a search engine can eliminate from its database all pages from such sites.

23.3.5 Exercises for Section 23.3

Exercise 23.3.1: Compute the topic-specific PageRank for Fig. 23.5, assuming

a) The teleport set is $\{A, C\}$.

b) The teleport set is $\{B, D\}$.

Assume a taxation rate of 25%.

Exercise 23.3.2: Repeat Exercise 23.3.1 for the graph of Fig. 23.6.

Exercise 23.3.3: Repeat Exercise 23.3.1 for the graph of Fig. 23.7.

!! **Exercise 23.3.4:** Suppose we fix the taxation rate and compute the topic-specific PageRank for a graph G, using only node a as the teleport set. We then do the same using only another node b as the teleport set. Prove that the average of these PageRanks is the same as what we get if we repeated the calculation with $\{a, b\}$ as the teleport set.

!! **Exercise 23.3.5:** What is the generalization of Exercise 23.3.4 to a situation where there are two disjoint teleport sets S_1 and S_2, perhaps with different numbers of elements? That is, suppose we compute the PageRanks with just S_1 and then just S_2 as the teleport sets. How could we use these results to compute the PageRank with $S_1 \cup S_2$ as the teleport set?

23.4 Data Streams

We now turn to an extension of the ideas contained in the traditional DBMS to deal with *data streams*. As the Internet has made communication among machines routine, a class of applications has developed that stress the traditional model of a database system. Recall that a typical database system is primarily a repository of data. Input of data is done as part of the query language or a special data-load utility, and is assumed to occur at a rate controlled by the DBMS.

However, in some applications, the inputs arrive at a rate the DBMS cannot control. For example, Yahoo! may wish to record every "click," that is, every page request made by any user anywhere. The sequence of URL's representing these requests arrive at a very high rate that is determined only by the desires of Yahoo!'s customers.

23.4.1   Data-Stream-Management Systems

If we are to allow queries on such streams of data, we need some new mechanisms. While we may be able to store the data on high-rate streams, we cannot do so in a way that allows instantaneous queries using a language like SQL. Further, it is not even clear what some queries mean; for instance, how can we take the join of two streams, when we never can see the completed streams? The rough structure of a data-stream-management system (*DSMS*) is shown in Fig. 23.10.

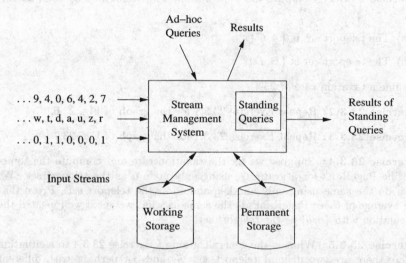

Figure 23.10: A data-stream-management system

The system accepts data streams as input, and also accepts queries. These queries may be of two kinds:

1. Conventional ad-hoc queries.

2. *Standing queries* that are stored by the system and run on the input stream(s) at all times.

Example 23.9: Whether ad-hoc or standing, queries in a DSMS need to be expressed so they can be answered using limited portions of the streams. As an example, suppose we are receiving streams of radiation levels from sensors around the world. While the DSMS cannot store and query streams from arbitrarily far back in time, it can store a *sliding window* of each input stream. It might be able to keep on disk, in the "working storage" referred to in Fig. 23.10, all readings from all sensors for the past 24 hours. Data from further back in time could be dropped, could be summarized (e.g., replaced by the daily average), or copied in its entirety to the permanent store (*archive*).

An ad-hoc query might ask for the average radiation level over the past hour for all locations in North Korea. We can answer this query, because we have all data from all streams over the past 24 hours in our working store. A standing query might ask for a notification if any reading on any stream exceeds a certain limit. As each data element of each stream enters the system, it is compared with the threshold, and an output is made if the entering value exceeds the threshold. This sort of query can be answered from the streams themselves, although we would need to examine the working store if, say, we asked to be alerted if the average over the past 5 minutes for any one stream exceeded the threshold. □

23.4.2 Stream Applications

Before addressing the mechanics of data-stream-management systems, let us look at some of the applications where the data is in the form of a stream or streams.

1. *Click Streams.* As we mentioned, a common source of streams is the clicks by users of a large Web site. A Web site might wish to analyze the clicks it receives for a number of reasons; an increase in clicks on a link may indicate that link is broken, or that it has become of much more interest recently. A search engine may want to analyze clicks on the links to ads that it shows, to determine which ads are most attractive.

2. *Packet Streams.* We may wish to analyze the sources and destinations of IP packets that pass through a switch. An unusual increase in packets for a destination may warn of a denial-of-service attack. Examination of the recent history of destinations may allow us to predict congestion in the network and to reroute packets accordingly.

3. *Sensor Data.* We also mentioned a hypothetical example of a network of radiation sensors. There are many kinds of sensors whose outputs need to be read and considered collectively, e.g., tsunami warning sensors that record ocean levels at subsecond frequencies or the signals that come from seismometers around the world, recording the shaking of the earth. Cities that have networks of security cameras can have the video from these cameras read and analyzed for threats.

4. *Satellite Data.* Satellites send back to earth incredible streams of data, often petabytes per day. Because scientists are reluctant to throw any of this data away, it is often stored in raw form in archival memory systems. These are half-jokingly referred to as "write-only memory." Useful products are extracted from the streams as they arrive and stored in more accessible storage places or distributed to scientists who have made standing requests for certain kinds of data.

5. *Financial Data.* Trades of stocks, commodities, and other financial instruments are reported as a stream of tuples, each representing one financial transaction. These streams are analyzed by software that looks for events or patterns that trigger actions by traders. The most successful traders have access to the largest amount of data and process it most quickly, because opportunities involving stock trades often last for only fractions of a second.

23.4.3   A Data-Stream Data Model

We shall now offer a data model useful for discussing algorithms on data streams. First, we shall assume the following about the streams themselves:

- Each stream consists of a sequence of tuples. The tuples have a fixed relation schema (list of attributes), just as the tuples of relations do. However, unlike relations, the sequence of tuples in a stream may be unbounded.

- Each tuple has an associated *arrival time*, at which time it becomes available to the data-stream-management system for processing. The DSMS has the option of placing it in the working storage or in the permanent storage, or of dropping the tuple from memory altogether. The tuple may also be processed in simple ways before storing it.

For any stream, we can define a *sliding window* (or just "window"), which is a set consisting of the most recent tuples to arrive. A window can be *time-based* with a constant τ, in which case it consists of the tuples whose arrival time is between the current time t and $t - \tau$. Or, a window can be *tuple-based*, in which case it consists of the most recent n tuples to arrive, for some fixed n.

We shall describe windows on a stream S by the notation $S\,[W]$, where W is the window description, either:

1. Rows n, meaning the most recent n tuples of the stream, or

2. Range τ, meaning all tuples that arrived within the previous amount of time τ.

Example 23.10 : Let Sensors(sensID, temp, time) be a stream, each of whose tuples represent a temperature reading of temp at a certain time by the sensor named sensID. It might be more common for each sensor to produce its own stream, but all readings could also be merged into one stream if the data were accumulated outside the data-stream-management system. The expression

    Sensors [Rows 1000]

describes a window on the Sensors stream consisting of the most recent 1000 tuples. The expression

```
Sensors [Range 10 Seconds]
```

describes a window on the same stream consisting of all tuples that arrived in the past 10 seconds. □

23.4.4 Converting Streams Into Relations

Windows allow us to convert streams into relations. That is, the window expressions as in Example 23.10 describe a relation at any time. The contents of the relation typically changes rapidly. For example, consider the expression Sensors [Rows 1000]. Each time a new tuple of Sensors arrives, it is inserted into the described relation, and the oldest of the tuples is deleted. For the expression Sensors [Range 10 Seconds], we must insert tuples of the stream when they arrive and delete tuples 10 seconds after they arrive.

Window expressions can be used like relations in an extended SQL for streams. The following example suggests what such an extended SQL looks like.

Example 23.11: Suppose we would like to know, for each sensor, the highest recorded temperature to arrive at the DSMS in the past hour. We form the appropriate time-based window and query it as if it were an ordinary relation. The query looks like:

```
SELECT sensID, MAX(temp)
FROM Sensors [Range 1 Hour]
GROUP BY sensID;
```

This query can be issued as an ad-hoc query, in which case it is executed once, based on the window that exists at the instant the query is issued. Of course the DSMS must have made available to the query processor a window on Sensors of at least one hour's length.[2] The same query could be a standing query, in which case the current result relation should be maintained as if it were a materialized view that changes from time to time. In Section 23.4.5 we shall consider an alternative way to represent the result of this query as a standing query. □

Window relations can be combined with other window relations, or with "ordinary" relations — those that do not come from streams. An example will suggest what is possible.

Example 23.12: Suppose that our DSMS has the stream Sensors as an input stream and also maintains in its working storage an ordinary relation

```
Calibrate(sensID, mult, add)
```

---

[2] Strictly speaking, the DSMS only needs to have retained enough information to answer the query. For example, it could still answer the query at any time if it threw away every tuple for which there was a later reading from the same sensor with a higher temperature.

which gives a multiplicative factor and additive term that are used to correct the reading from each sensor. The query

```
SELECT MAX(mult*temp + add)
FROM Sensors [Range 1 Hour], Calibrate
WHERE Sensors.sensID = Calibrate.sensID;
```

finds the highest, properly calibrated temperature reported by any sensor in the past hour. Here, we have joined a window relation from `Sensors` with the ordinary relation `Calibrate`. □

We can also compute joins of window-relations. The following query illustrates a self-join by means of a subquery, but all the SQL tools for expressing joins are available.

Example 23.13 : Suppose we wanted to give, for each sensor, its maximum temperature over the past hour (as in Example 23.11), but we also wanted the resulting tuples to give the most recent time at which that maximum temperature was recorded. Figure 23.11 is one way to write the query using window relations.

```
SELECT s.sensID, s.temp, s.time
FROM Sensors [Range 1 Hour] s
WHERE NOT EXISTS (
    SELECT * FROM Sensors [Range 1 Hour]
    WHERE sensID = s.sensID AND (
        temp > s.temp OR
            (temp = s.temp AND time > s.time)
    )
);
```

Figure 23.11: Including time with the maximum temperature readings of sensors

That is, the subquery checks if there is not another tuple in the window-relation `Sensors [Range 1 Hour]` that refers to the same sensor as the tuple *s*, and has either a higher temperature or has the same temperature but a more recent time. If no such tuple exists, then the tuple *s* is part of the result. □

23.4.5 Converting Relations Into Streams

When we issue queries such as that of Example 23.11 as standing queries, the resulting relations change frequently. Maintaining these relations as materialized views may result in a lot of effort making insertions and deletions that no one ever looks at. An alternative is to convert the relation that is the result of the query back into streams, which may be processed like any other streams.

For example, we can issue an ad-hoc query to construct the query result at a particular time when we are interested in its value.

If R is a relation, define Istream(R) to be the stream consisting of each tuple that is inserted into R. This tuple appears in the stream at the time the insertion occurs. Similarly, define Dstream(R) to be the stream of tuples deleted from R; each tuple appears in this stream at the moment it is deleted. An update to a tuple can be represented by an insertion and deletion at the same time.

Example 23.14: Let R be the relation constructed by the query of Example 23.13, that is, the relation that has, for each sensor, the maximum temperature it recorded in any tuple that arrived in the past hour, and the time at which that temperature was most recently recorded. Then Istream(R) has a tuple for every event in which a new tuple is added to R. Note that there are two events that add tuples to R:

1. A Sensors tuple arrives with a temperature that is at least as high as any tuple currently in R with the same sensor ID. This tuple is inserted into R and becomes an element of Istream(R) at that time.

2. The current maximum temperature for a sensor i was recorded an hour ago, and there has been at least one tuple for sensor i in the Sensors stream in the past hour. In that case, the new tuple for R and for Istream(R) is the Sensors tuple for sensor i that arrived in the past hour, but no other tuple for i that also arrived in the past hour has:

   (a) A higher temperature, or

   (b) The same temperature and a more recent time.

The same two events may generate tuples for the stream Dstream(R) as well. In (1) above, if there was any other tuple in R for the same sensor, then that tuple is deleted from R and becomes an element of Dstream(R). In (2), the hour-old tuple of R for sensor i is deleted from R and becomes an element of Dstream(R). □

If we compute the Istream and Dstream for a relation like that constructed by the query of Fig. 23.11, then we do not have to maintain that relation as a materialized view. Rather, we can query its Istream and Dstream to answer queries about the relation when we wish.

Example 23.15: Suppose we form the Istream I and the Dstream D for the relation R of Fig. 23.11. When we wish, we can issue an ad-hoc query to these streams. For instance, suppose we want to find the maximum temperature recorded by sensor 100 that arrived over the past hour. That will be the temperature in the tuple in I for sensor 100 that:

1. Has a time in the past hour.

2. Was not deleted from R (i.e., is not in D restricted to the past hour).

This query can be written as shown in Fig. 23.12. The keyword Now represents the current time.

Note that we must check that a tuple of I both arrived in the past hour and that it has a timestamp within the past hour. To see why these conditions are not the same, consider the case of a tuple of I that arrived in the past hour, because it became the maximum temperature t for sensor 100 thirty minutes ago. However, that temperature itself has an associated time that is eighty minutes ago. The reason is that a temperature higher than t was recorded by sensor 100 ninety minutes ago. It wasn't until 30 minutes ago that t became the highest temperature for sensor 100 in the sixty minutes preceding. □

```
(SELECT * FROM I [Range 1 Hour]
 WHERE sensID = 100 AND
       time >= [Now - 1 Hour])
     EXCEPT
(SELECT * FROM D [Range 1 Hour]
 WHERE sensID = 100);
```

Figure 23.12: Querying an Istream and a Dstream

23.4.6 Exercises for Section 23.4

Exercise 23.4.1: Using the Sensors stream from Example 23.11, write the following queries:

a) Find those sensors for which at least two readings have arrived in the past second.

b) Find the oldest tuple (lowest time) among the last 5000 tuples to arrive.

! c) Find those sensors for which more readings arrived in the past hour than arrived between one and two hours ago.

Exercise 23.4.2: Following the example of sensor data from this section, suppose that the following temperature-time readings are generated by sensor 100, and each arrives at the DSMS at the time generated: $(20,0)$, $(18,40)$, $(16,60)$, $(17,110)$. Times are in minutes. If R is the query of Fig. 23.11, What are the tuples of Istream(R) and Dstream(R), and at what time is each of these tuples generated?

! **Exercise 23.4.3:** Suppose our stream consists of baskets of items, as in the market-basket model of Section 22.1.1. Since we assume elements of streams are tuples, the contents of a basket must be represented by several consecutive tuples with the schema Baskets(basket, item). Write the following queries:

a) Find those items that have appeared in at least 5% of the baskets that arrived over the past hour.[3]

b) Find those pairs of items that have appeared in at least three times as many baskets in the previous half hour as in the half hour before that.

c) Find the most frequent pair(s) of items over the past day.

23.5 Data Mining of Streams

When processing streams, there are a number of problems that become quite hard, even though the analogous problems for relations are easy. In this section, we shall concentrate on representing the contents of windows more succinctly than by listing the current set of tuples in the window. Surely, we are not then able to answer all possible queries about the window, but if we know what kinds of queries we are expected to support, we might be able to compress the window and answer those queries. Another possibility is that we cannot compress the window and answer our selected queries exactly, but we can guarantee to be able to answer them within a fixed error bound.

We shall consider two fundamental problems of this type. First, we consider binary streams (streams of 0's and 1's), and ask whether we can answer queries about the number of 1's in any time range contained within the window. Obviously, if we keep the exact sequence of bits and their timestamps, we can manage to answer those questions exactly. However, it is possible to compress the data significantly and still answer this family of queries within a fixed error bound. Second, we address the problem of counting the number of different values within a sliding window. Here is another family of problems that cannot be answered exactly without keeping the data in the window exactly. However, we shall see that a good approximation is possible using much less space than the size of the window.

23.5.1 Motivation

Suppose we wish to have a stream with a window of a billion integers. Such a window could fit in a large main memory of four gigabytes, and it would have no trouble fitting on disk. Surely, if we are only interested in recent data from the stream, a billion tuples should suffice. But what if there are a million such streams?

For example, we might be trying to integrate the data from a million sensors placed around a city. Or we might be given a stream of market baskets, and try to compute the frequency, over any time range, of all sets of items contained in

---

[3]Technically, some but not all of a basket could arrive within the past hour. Ignore this "edge effect," and assume that either all or none of a basket's tuples appear in any given window.

those baskets. In that case, we need a window for each set, with bits indicating whether or not that set was contained in each of the baskets.

In situations such as these, the amount of space needed to store all the windows exceeds what is available using disk storage. Moreover, for efficient response, we might want to keep all windows in main memory. Then, a few windows of length a billion, or a few thousand windows of length a million exceed what even a large main memory can hold. We are thus led to consider compressing the data in windows. Unfortunately, even some very simple queries cannot be answered if we compress the window, as the next example suggests.

Example 23.16: Suppose we have a sliding window that stores stream elements that are integers, and we have a standing query that asks for an alert any time the sum of the integers in the window exceeds a certain threshold t. We thus only need to maintain the sum of the integers in the window in order to answer this query. When a new integer comes in, we can add it to the sum.

However, at certain times, integers leave the window and must be subtracted from the sum. If the window is tuple-based, then we must subtract the last integer from the sum each time a new integer arrives. If the window is time-based, then when the time of an integer in the window expires, it must be subtracted from the sum.

Unfortunately, if we don't know exactly what integers are in the window, or we don't know their order of arrival (for tuple-based windows) or their time of arrival (for time-based windows), then we cannot maintain the sum properly. To see why we cannot compress, observe the following. If there is any compression at all, then two different window-contents, W_1 and W_2, must have the same compressed value. Since $W_1 \neq W_2$, there is some time t at which the integers for time t are different in W_1 and W_2. Consider what happens when t is the oldest time in the window, and another integer arrives. We must have to do different subtractions from the sum, to maintain the sums for W_1 and W_2. But since the compressed representation does not tell us which of W_1 and W_2 is the true contents of the window, we cannot maintain the proper sum in both cases. □

Example 23.16 tells us that we cannot compress the sum of a sliding window if we are to get exact answers for the sum at all times. However, suppose we are willing to accept an approximate sum. Then there are many options, and we shall look at a very simple one here. We can group the stream elements into groups of 100; say the first hundred elements of the stream ever to arrive, then the next hundred, and so on. Each group is represented by the sum of elements in that group. Thus, we have a compression factor of 100; i.e., the window is represented by $1/100^{th}$ of the number of integers that are theoretically "in" in window.

Suppose for simplicity that we have a tuple-based window, and the number of tuples in the window is a multiple of 100. When the number of stream elements that have arrived is also a multiple of 100, then we can get the sum of the elements in the window exactly, just by summing the sums of the groups.

Suppose another integer arrives. That integer starts another group, so we keep it as the sum of that group. Now, we can only estimate the sum of all the integers in the window. The reason is that the last group has only 99 of its 100 members in the window, and we don't know the value of the integer, from the last group, that is no longer in the window.

The best estimate of the deleted integer is 1% of the sum of the last group. That is, we estimate the sum of all the integers in the window by taking 0.99 times the recorded sum of the last group, plus the recorded sums of all the other groups.

Forty-nine arrivals later, there are fifty integers in the group formed from the most recent arrivals, and the sum of the window includes exactly half of the last group. Our best estimate of the sum of the fifty integers of the last group that remain in the window is half the group's sum. After another fifty arrivals, the most recent group is complete, and the last group has left the window entirely. We therefore can drop the recorded sum of the last group and prepare to start another group with the next arrival.

Intuitively, this method gives a "good" approximation to the sum. If integers are nonnegative, and there is not too much variance in the values of the integers, then assuming that the missing integers are average for their group is a close estimate. Unfortunately, if the variance is high, or integers can be both positive and negative, there is no worst-case bound on how bad the estimate of the sum can be. Consider what happens if integers can range from minus infinity to plus infinity, and the last group consists of fifty large negative numbers followed by fifty large positive numbers, such that the sum for the group is 0. Then the estimate of the contribution of the last group, when only half of it is in the window is zero, but in fact the true sum is very large — perhaps much larger than the sum of all the integers that followed them in the stream.

One can modify this compression approach in various ways. For example, we can increase the size of the groups to reduce the amount of space taken by the representation. Doing so increases the error in the estimate, however. In the next section, we shall see how to get a bounded error rate, while getting significant compression, for the binary version of this problem, where stream elements are either 0 or 1. The same method extends to streams of positive integers with an upper bound, if we treat each position in the binary representation of the integers as a bit stream (see Exercise 23.5.4).

23.5.2 Counting Bits

In this section, we shall examine the following problem. Assume that the length of the sliding window is N, and the stream consists of bits, 0 or 1. We assume that the stream began at some time in the past, and we associate a *time* with each arriving bit that is its position in the stream; i.e., the first to arrive is at time 1, the next at time 2, and so on.

Our queries, which may be asked at any time, are of the form "how many 1's are there in the most recent k bits?" where k is any integer between 1 and

N. Obviously, if we stored the window with no compression, we could answer any such query exactly, although we would have to sum the last k bits to do so. Since k could be very large, the time needed to answer queries could itself be large. Suppose, however, that along with the bits themselves we stored the sums of certain groups of consecutive bits — groups of size 2, 4, 8,.... We could then decrease the time needed to answer the queries exactly to $O(\log N)$. However, if we also stored sums of these groups, then even more space would be needed than what we use to store the window elements themselves.

An attractive alternative is to keep an amount of information about the window that is logarithmic in N, and yet be able to answer any query of the type described above, with a fractional error that is as low as we like. Formally, for any $\epsilon > 0$, we can produce an estimate that is in the range of $1 - \epsilon$ to $1 + \epsilon$ times the true result. We shall give the method for $\epsilon = 1/2$, and we leave the generalization to any $\epsilon > 0$ as an exercise with hints (see Exercise 23.5.3).

Buckets

To describe the algorithm for approximate counting of 1's, we need to define a *bucket* of size m; it is a section of the window that contains exactly m 1's. The window will be partitioned completely into such buckets, except possibly for some 0's that are not part of any bucket. Thus, we can represent any such bucket by (m, t), where m is the size of the bucket, and t is the time of the most recent 1 belonging to that bucket. There are a number of rules that we shall follow in determining the buckets that represent the current window:

1. The size of every bucket is a power of 2.

2. As we look back in time, the sizes of the buckets never decrease.

3. For $m = 1, 2, 4, 8, \ldots$ up to some largest-size bucket, there are one or two buckets of each size, never zero and never more than two.

4. Each bucket begins somewhere within the current window, although the last (largest) bucket maybe partially outside the window.

Figure 23.13 suggests what a window partitioned into buckets might look like.

Representing Buckets

We shall see that under these assumptions, a bucket can be represented by $O(\log N)$ bits. Further, there are at most $O(\log N)$ buckets that must be represented. Thus, a window of length N can be represented in space $O(\log^2 N)$, rather than $O(N)$ bits. To see why only $O(\log^2 N)$ bits are needed, observe the following:

- A bucket (m, t) can be represented in $O(\log N)$ bits. First, m, the size of a bucket, can never get above N. Moreover, m is always a power of 2, so

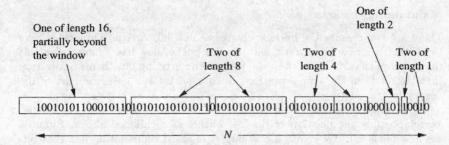

Figure 23.13: Bucketizing a sliding window

we don't have to represent m itself; rather we can represent $\log_2 m$. That requires $O(\log \log N)$ bits. However, we also need to represent t, the time of the most recent 1 in the bucket. In principle, t can be an arbitrarily large integer, but it is sufficient to represent t modulo N, since we know t has to be in the window of length N. Thus, $O(\log N)$ bits suffice to represent both m and t. So that we can know the time of newly arriving 1's, we maintain the current time, but also represent it modulo N, so $O(\log N)$ bits suffice for this count.

- There can be only $O(\log N)$ buckets. The sum of the sizes of the buckets is at most N, and there can be at most two of any size. If there are more than $2 + 2 \log_2 N$ buckets, then the largest one is of size at least $2 \times 2^{\log_2 N}$, which is $2N$. There must be a smaller bucket of half that size, so the supposed largest bucket is certainly completely outside the window.

Answering Queries Approximately, Using Buckets

Notice that we can answer a query to count the 1's in the most recent k bits approximately, as follows. Find the least recent bucket B whose most recent bit arrived within the last k time units. All later buckets are entirely within the range of k time units. We know exactly how many 1's are in each of these buckets; it is their size. The bucket B is partially in the query's range, and partially outside it. We cannot tell how much is in and how much is out, so we choose half its size as the best guess.

Example 23.17: Suppose $k = N$ and the window is represented by the buckets of Fig. 23.13. We see two buckets of size 1 and one of size 2, which implies four 1's. Then, there are two buckets of size 4, giving another eight 1's, and two buckets of size 4, implying another sixteen 1's. Finally, the last bucket, of size 16, is partially in the window, so we add another 8 to the estimate. The approximate answer is thus $2 \times 1 + 1 \times 2 + 2 \times 4 + 2 \times 8 + 8 = 36$. □

Maintaining Buckets

There are two reasons the buckets change as new bits arrive. The first is easy to handle: if a new bit arrives, and the last bucket now has a most recent bit that is more than N lower than the time of the arriving bit, then we can drop that bucket from the representation. Such a bucket can never be part of the answer to any query.

Now, suppose a new bit arrives. If the bit is a 0, there are no changes, except possibly the deletion of the last bucket as mentioned above. Suppose the new bit is a 1. We create a new bucket of size 1 representing just that bit. However, we may now have three buckets of size 1, which violates the rule that there can be only one or two buckets of each size. Thus, we enter a recursive combining-buckets phase.

Suppose we have three consecutive buckets of size m, say (m, t_1), (m, t_2), and (m, t_3), where $t_1 < t_2 < t_3$. We combine the two least recent of the buckets, (m, t_1) and (m, t_2), into one bucket of size $2m$. The time of the most recent bit for the combined bucket is that of the most recent bit for the more recent of the two combined buckets. That is, (m, t_1) and (m, t_2) are replaced by a bucket $(2m, t_2)$.

This combination may cause there to be three consecutive buckets of size $2m$, if there were two of that size previously. Thus, we apply the combination algorithm recursively, with the size now $2m$. It can take no more than $O(\log N)$ time to do all the necessary combinations.

Example 23.18 : Suppose we have the list of bucket sizes implied by Fig. 23.13, that is, $16, 8, 8, 4, 4, 2, 1, 1$. If a 1 arrives, we have three buckets of size 1, so we combine the two earlier 1's, to get the list $16, 8, 8, 4, 4, 2, 2, 1$. As this combination gives us only two buckets of size 2, no recursive combining is needed. If another 1 arrives, no combining at all is needed, and we get sequence of bucket sizes $16, 8, 8, 4, 4, 2, 2, 1, 1$. When the next 1 arrives, we must combine 1's, leaving $16, 8, 8, 4, 4, 2, 2, 2, 1$. Now we have three 2's, so we recursively combine the least recent of them, leaving $16, 8, 8, 4, 4, 4, 2, 1$. Now there are three 4's, and the least recent of them are combined to give $16, 8, 8, 8, 4, 2, 1$. Again, we must combine the least recent of the three 8's, giving us the final list of bucket sizes $16, 16, 8, 4, 2, 1$. □

A Bound on the Error

Suppose that in answer to a query the last bucket whose represented 1's are in the range of the query has size m. Since we estimate $m/2$ for its contribution to the count, we cannot be off by more than $m/2$. The correct answer is at least the sum of all the smaller buckets, and there is at least one bucket of each size $m/2, m/4, m/8, \ldots, 1$. This sum is $m - 1$. Thus, the fractional error is at most $(m/2)/(m-1)$, or approximately 50%. In fact, if we look more carefully, 50% is an exact upper bound. The reason is that when we underestimate (i.e., all m 1's from the last bucket are in the query range), the error is no more than $1/3$.

When we overestimate, we can really only overestimate by $(m/2) - 1$, not $m/2$, since we know that at least one 1 contributes to the query. Since $(m/2) - 1$ is less than half $m - 1$, the error is truly upper bounded by 50%.

23.5.3 Counting the Number of Distinct Elements

We now turn to another important problem: counting the distinct elements in a (window on) a stream. The problem has a number of applications, such as the following:

1. The popularity of a Web site is often measured by unique visitors per month or similar statistics. Think of the logins at a site like Yahoo! as a stream. Using a window of size one month, we want to know how many different logins there are.

2. Suppose a crawler is examining sites. We can think of the words encountered on the pages as forming a stream. If a site is legitimate, the number of distinct words will fall in a range that is neither too high (few repetitions of words) nor too low (excessive repetition of words). Falling outside that range suggests that the site could be artificial, e.g., a spam site.

To get an exact answer to the question, we must store the entire window and apply the δ operator to it, in order to find the distinct elements. However, we don't want to *see* the distinct elements; we just want to know how many there are. Even getting this count requires that we maintain the window in its entirety, but we can get an approximation to the count by several different methods. The following technique actually computes the number of distinct elements in the entire stream, rather than in a finite window. However, we can, if we like, restart the process periodically, e.g., once a month to count unique visitors or each time we visit a new site (to count distinct words).

The necessary tools are a number N that is certain to be at least as large as the number of distinct values in the stream, and a hash function h that maps values to $\log_2 N$ bits. We maintain a number R that is initially 0. As each stream value v arrives, do the following:

1. Compute $h(v)$.

2. Let r be the number of trailing 0's in $h(v)$.

3. If $r > R$, set R to be r.

Then, the estimate of the number of distinct values seen so far is 2^R. To see why this estimate makes sense, note the following.

a) The probability that $h(v)$ ends in at least i 0's is 2^{-i}.

b) If there are m distinct elements in the stream so far, the probability that $R > i$ is $(1 - 2^{-i})^m$.

c) If i is much less than $\log_2 m$, then this probability is close to 1, and if i is much greater than $\log_2 m$, then this probability is close to 0.

d) Thus, R will frequently be near $\log_2 m$, and 2^R, our estimate, will frequently be near m.

While the above reasoning is comforting, it is actually inaccurate, to say the least. The reason is that the expected value of 2^R is infinite, or at least it is as large as possible given that N is finite. The intuitive reason is that, for large R, when R increases by 1, the probability of R being that large halves, but the value of R doubles, so each possible value of R contributes the same to the expected value.

It is therefore necessary to get around the fact that there will occasionally be a value of R that is so large it biases the estimate of m upwards. While we shall not go into the exact justification, we can avoid this bias by:

1. Take many estimates of R, using different hash functions.

2. Group these estimates into small groups and take the median of each group. Doing so eliminates the effect of occasional large R's.

3. Take the average of the medians of the groups.

23.5.4 Exercises for Section 23.5

Exercise 23.5.1: Starting with the window of Fig. 23.13, suppose that the next sixteen bits to arrive are all 1's. What will be the sequence of buckets at that time?

Exercise 23.5.2: What buckets are used in Fig. 23.13 to answer queries of the form "how many 1's in the most recent k bits?" if k is (a) 12 (b) 20 (c) 30? What are the estimates for each of these queries? How close are the estimates?

! **Exercise 23.5.3:** We can modify the algorithm of Section 23.5.2 to use buckets whose sizes are powers of 2, but there are between p and $p + 1$ buckets of each size, for a chosen integer $p \geq 1$. As before, sizes do not decrease as we go further back in time.

a) Give the recursive rule for combining buckets when there are too many buckets of a given size.

b) Show that the fractional error of this scheme is at most $1/2p$.

! **Exercise 23.5.4:** Suppose that we have a stream of integers in the range 0 to $2^{16} - 1$. How can you adapt the method of Section 23.5.2 to estimate the sum of the integers in a window of size N, keeping the error to 50%? *Hint*: treat each of the sixteen bits that represent an integer as a separate stream.

Exercise 23.5.5: Suppose that we wish to estimate the number of distinct values in a stream of integers. The integers are in the range 0 to 1023. We'll use the following hash functions, each of which hashes to a 9-bit integer:

a) $h_1(v) = v + 59$ modulo 512.

b) $h_2(v) = v + 241$ modulo 512.

c) $h_3(v) = v + 457$ modulo 512.

Compute the estimate of the number of distinct values in the following stream, using each of these hash functions:

$$24, 45, 102, 24, 78, 222, 45, 24, 670, 78, 999, 576, 222, 24$$

Exercise 23.5.6: In Example 23.11 we observed that if all we wanted was the maximum of N temperature readings in a sliding window of time-temperature tuples, then when a reading of t arrives, we can delete immediately any earlier reading that is smaller than t.

! a) Does this rule always compress the data in the window?

!! b) Suppose temperatures are real numbers chosen uniformly and at random from some fixed range of values. On average, how many tuples will be retained, as a function of N?

23.6 Summary of Chapter 23

+ *Search Engines*: A search engine requires a crawler to gather information about pages and a query engine to answer search queries.

+ *Crawlers*: A crawler consists of one or more processes that visit Web pages and follow links found in those pages. The crawler must maintain a repository of pages already visited, so it does not revisit the same page too frequently. Shingling and minhashing can be used to detect duplicate pages with different URL's.

+ *Limiting the Crawl*: Crawlers normally limit the depth to which they will search, declining to follow links from pages that are too far from their root page or pages. They also can prioritize the search to visit preferentially pages that are estimated to be popular.

+ *Preparing Crawled Pages to Be Searched*: The search engine creates an inverted index on the words of the crawled pages. The index may also include information about the role of the word (e.g., is it part of a header?), and the index for each word may be represented by a bit-vector indicating on which pages the word appears.

✦ *Answering Search Queries*: A search query normally consists of a set of words. The query engine uses the inverted index to find the Web pages containing all these words. The pages are then ranked, using a formula that is determined by each search engine, but typically favors pages with close occurrences of the words, use of the words in important places (e.g., headers), and favors important pages using a measure such as PageRank.

✦ *The Transition Matrix of the Web*: This matrix is an important analytic tool for estimating the importance of Web pages. There is a row and column for each page, and the column for page j has $1/r$ in the ith row if page i is one of r pages with links from page j, and 0 otherwise.

✦ *PageRank*: The PageRank of Web pages is the principal eigenvector of the transition matrix of the Web. If there are n pages, we can compute the PageRank vector by starting with a vector of length n, and repeatedly multiplying the current vector by the transition matrix of the Web.

✦ *Taxation of PageRank*: Because of Web artifacts such as dead ends (pages without out-links) and spider traps (sections of the Web that cannot be exited), it is normal to introduce a small tax, say 15%, and redistribute that fraction of a page's PageRank equally among all pages, after each matrix-vector multiplication.

✦ *Teleport Sets*: Instead of redistributing the tax equally among all pages during an iteration of the PageRank computation, we can distribute the tax only among a subset of the pages, called the teleport set. Then, the computation of PageRank simulates a walker on the graph of the Web who normally follows a randomly chosen out-link from their current page, but with a small probability instead jumps to a random member of the teleport set.

✦ *Topic-Specific PageRank*: One application of the teleport-set idea is to pick a teleport set consisting of a set of pages known to be about a certain topic. Then, the PageRank will measure not only the importance of the page in general, but to what extent it is relevant to the selected topic.

✦ *Link Spam*: Spam farmers create large collections of Web pages whose sole purpose is to increase the PageRank of certain target pages, and thus make them more likely to be displayed by a search engine. One way to combat such spam farms is to compute PageRank using a teleport set consisting of known, trusted pages — those that are unlikely to be spam.

✦ *Data Streams*: A data stream is a sequence of tuples arriving at a fixed place, typically at a rate so fast as to make processing and storage in its entirety difficult. Examples include streams of data from satellites and click streams of requests at a Web site.

✦ *Data-Stream-Management Systems*: A DSMS accepts data in the form of streams. It maintains working storage and permanent (archival) storage. Working storage is limited, although it may involve disks. The DSMS accepts both ad-hoc and standing queries about the streams.

✦ *Sliding Windows*: To query a stream, it helps to be able to talk about portions of the stream as a relation. A sliding window is the most recent portion of the stream. A window can be time-based, in which case it consists of all tuples arriving over some fixed time interval, or tuple-based, in which case it is a fixed number of the most recently arrived tuples.

✦ *Compressing Windows*: If the DSMS must maintain large windows on many streams, it can run out of main memory, or even disk space. Depending on the family of queries that will be asked about the window, it may be possible to compress the window so it uses significantly less space. However, in many cases, we can compress a window only if we are willing to accept approximate answers to queries.

✦ *Counting Bits*: A fundamental problem that allows a space/accuracy trade-off is that of counting the number of 1's in a window of a bit-stream. We partition the window into buckets representing exponentially increasing numbers of 1's. The last bucket may be partially outside the window, leading to inaccuracy in the count of 1's, but the error is limited to a fixed fraction of the count and can be any $\epsilon > 0$.

✦ *Counting Distinct Elements*: Another important stream problem is counting the number of distinct elements in the stream without keeping a table of all the distinct elements ever seen. An unbiased estimate of this number can be made by picking a hash function, hashing elements to bit strings, and estimating the number of distinct elements to be 2 raised to the power that is the largest number of consecutive 0's ever seen at the end of the hash function of any stream element.

23.7 References for Chapter 23

References [3] and [8] summarize issues in crawling, based on the Stanford WebBase system. An analysis of the degree to which crawlers reach the entire Web was given in [15].

PageRank and the Google search engine are described in [6] and [16]. An alternative formulation of Web structure, often referred to as "hubs and authorities," is in [14].

Topic-specific PageRank, as described here, is from [12]. TrustRank and combating link spam are discussed in [11].

Two on-line histories of search engines are [17] and [18].

The study of data streams as a data model can be said to begin with the "chronicle data model" of [13]. References [7] and [2] describe the architecture of early data-stream management systems. Reference [5] surveys data-stream systems.

The algorithm described here for approximate counting of 1's in a sliding window is from [9].

The problem of estimating the number of distinct elements in a stream originated with [10] and [4]. The method described here is from [1], which also generalizes the technique to estimate higher moments of the data, e.g., the sum of the squares of the number of occurrences of each element.

1. N. Alon, Y. Matias, and M. Szegedy, "The space complexity of approximating frequency moments," *Twenty-Eighth ACM Symp. on Theory of Computing* (1996), pp. 20–29.

2. A. Arasu, S. Babu, and J. Widom, "The CQL continuous query language: semantic foundations and query execution,"

   http://dbpubs.stanford.edu/pub/2003-67

   Dept. of Computer Science, Stanford Univ., Stanford CA, 2003.

3. A. Arasu, J. Cho, H. Garcia-Molina, A. Paepcke, and S. Raghavan, "Searching the Web," *ACM Trans. on Internet Technologies* **1**:1 (2001), pp. 2–43.

4. M. M. Astrahan, M. Schkolnick, and K.-Y. Whang, "Approximating the number of unique values of an attribute without sorting," *Information Systems* **12**:1 (1987), pp. 11-15.

5. B. Babcock, S. Babu, M. Datar, R. Motwani, and J. Widom, "Models and issues in data stream systems," *Twenty-First ACM Symp. on Principles of Database Systems* (2002), pp. 261–272.

6. S. Brin and L. Page, "Anatomy of a large-scale hypertextual Web search engine," *Proc. Seventh Intl. World-Wide Web Conference*, 1998.

7. D. Carney, U. Cetintemel, M. Cherniack, C. Convey, S. Lee, G. Seidman, M. Stonebraker, N. Tatbul, and S. Zdonik, "Monitoring streams — a new class of data management applications," *Proc. Intl. Conf. on Very Large Database Systems* (2002), pp. 215–226.

8. J. Cho, H. Garcia-Molina, T. Haveliwala, W. Lam, A. Paepcke, S. Raghavan, and G. Wesley, "Stanford WebBase components and applications," *ACM Trans. on Internet Technologies* **6**:2 (2006), pp. 153–186.

9. M. Datar, A. Gionis, P. Indyk, and R. Motwani, "Maintaining stream statistics over sliding windows," *SIAM J. Computing* **31** (2002), pp. 1794–1813.

10. P. Flagolet and G. N. Martin, "Probabilistic counting for database applications," *J. Computer and System Sciences* **31**:2 (1985), pp. 182–209.

11. Z. Gyongyi, H. Garcia-Molina, and J. Pedersen, "Combating Web spam with TrustRank," *Proc. Intl. Conf. on Very Large Database Systems* (2004), pp. 576–587.

12. T. Haveliwala, "Topic-sensitive PageRank," *Proc. Eleventh Intl. World-Wide Web Conference* (2002).

13. H. V. Jagadish, I. S. Mumick, and A Silberschatz, "View maintenance issues for the chronicle data model," *Fourteenth ACM Symp. on Principles of Database Systems* (1995), pp. 113–124.

14. J. Kleinberg, "Authoritative sources in a hyperlinked environment," *J. ACM* **46**:5 (1999), pp. 604–632.

15. S. Lawrence and C. L. Giles, "Searching the World-Wide Web," *Science* **280**(5360):98, 1998.

16. L. Page, S. Brin, R. Motwani, and T. Winograd, "The PageRank citation ranking: bringing order to the Web," unpublished manuscript, Dept. of CS, Stanford Univ., Stanford CA, 1998.

17. L. Underwood, "A brief history of search engines," www.webreference.com/authoring/search_history

18. A. Wall, "Search engine history," www.searchenginehistory.com.

好书推荐

数据库系统概念（原书第5版）

作者：Abraham Silberschatz
　　　Henry F.Korth　S.Sudarshan 著
ISBN：978-7-111-19687-2
译者：杨冬青　马秀莉　唐世渭
定价：69.50元

本科教学版 978-7-111-23422-7 定价：45.00元

数据库系统导论（原书第8版）

作者：C. J. Date 著
ISBN：7-111-21333-8
译者：孟小峰　王珊　姜芳艽　等
定价：75.00元

数据库系统基础教程（英文版·第3版）

作者：Jeffrey D. Ullman;Jennifer Widom 著
ISBN 7-111-24733-3
定价：45.00元

	北京培生信息中心	Beijing Pearson Education
	中国北京海淀区中关村大街甲59号	Information Centre
	人大文化大厦1006室	Room1006,CultureSquare No.59 Jia,
		Zhongguancun Street
	邮政编码：100872	Haidian District, Beijing, China100872
	电话：(8610)82504008/9596/9586	TEL: (8610)82504008/9596/9586
	传真：(8610)82509915	FAX: (8610)82509915

尊敬的老师：

您好！

    为了确保您及时有效地申请教辅资源，请您务必完整填写如下教辅申请表，加盖学院的公章后传真给我们，我们将会为您开通属于您个人的唯一账号以供您下载与教材配套的教师资源。

请填写所需教辅的开课信息：

采用教材				□中文版　□英文版　□双语版
作　者			出版社	
版　次			ISBN	
课程时间	始于　　年　月　日		学生人数	
	止于　　年　月　日		学生年级	□专科　　　□本科1/2年级 □研究生　□本科3/4年级

请填写您的个人信息：

学　校		
院系/专业		
姓　名	职　称	□助教　□讲师　□副教授　□教授
通信地址/邮编		
手　机	电　话	
传　真		
official email(必填) (eg:XXX@ruc.edu.cn)	email (eg:XXX@163.com)	

是否愿意接受我们定期的新书讯息通知：　　　　□是　　□否

系 / 院主任：_____ （签字）

（系 / 院办公室章）

_____年_____月_____日

Please send this form to: Service.CN@pearson.com

Website: www.pearsonhighered.com/educator

教师服务登记表

尊敬的老师：

您好！感谢您购买我们出版的_____教材。

机械工业出版社华章公司为了进一步加强与高校教师的联系与沟通，更好地为高校教师服务，特制此表，请您填妥后发回给我们，我们将定期向您寄送华章公司最新的图书出版信息！感谢合作！

个人资料（请用正楷完整填写）

教师姓名		□先生 □女士	出生年月		职务		职称：□教授 □副教授 □讲师 □助教 □其他	
学校			学院			系别		

联系 电话	办公： 宅电： 移动：		联系地址 及邮编	
			E-mail	

学历		毕业院校		国外进修及讲学经历	
研究领域					

主讲课程	现用教材名	作者及 出版社	共同授 课教师	教材满意度
课程： □专 □本 □研 人数： 学期：□春□秋				□满意 □一般 □不满意 □希望更换
课程： □专 □本 □研 人数： 学期：□春□秋				□满意 □一般 □不满意 □希望更换

样书申请			
已出版著作		已出版译作	
是否愿意从事翻译/著作工作	□是 □否	方向	
意见和建议			

填妥后请选择以下任何一种方式将此表返回：（如方便请赐名片）
地　址：北京市西城区百万庄南街1号　华章公司营销中心　　邮编：100037
电　话：(010) 68353079 88378995　传真：(010)68995260
E-mail:hzedu@hzbook.com markerting@hzbook.com　　图书详情可登陆http://www.hzbook.com网站查询